Beginning Dreamweaver® MX 2004

Beginning Dreamweaver® MX 2004

Charles E. Brown
Imar Spaanjaars
Todd Marks

wrox
Programmer to Programmer™

Beginning Dreamweaver® MX 2004

Published by
Wiley Publishing, Inc.
10475 Crosspoint Boulevard
Indianapolis, IN 46256
www.wiley.com

For general information on our other products and services please contact our Customer Care Department within the United States at (800) 762-2974, outside the United States at (317) 572-3993 or fax (317) 572-4002.

Wiley also publishes its books in a variety of electronic formats. Some content that appears in print may not be available in electronic books.

Library of Congress Control Number is available from the publisher.

ISBN: 0-7645-5524-3

Printed in the United States of America

10 9 8 7 6 5 4 3 2 1

Trademarks Acknowledgments

About the Authors

Charles E. Brown

Charles E. Brown, Ph.D., is a noted author and teacher in the computer industry today. His first two books, *Beginning Dreamweaver MX* and *Fireworks MX: From Zero to Hero*, have received critical acclaim and are consistent best-sellers. He is also releasing books on VBA for Microsoft Access and on Microsoft FrontPage 2003. He is also a Fireworks MX contributor for the *MX Developer's Journal*.

In addition to his busy writing schedule, Charles conducts frequent seminars for Learning Tree International and the PC Learning Center. His topics include Java programming, using Dreamweaver, and the Microsoft Office environment.

Charles is also a noted classical organist, pianist, and guitarist who studied with such notables as Vladimir Horowitz, Virgil Fox, and Igor Stravinsky. It was because of his association with Stravinsky that he got to meet, and develop a friendship with, famed 20th-century artist Pablo Picasso.

Charles can be contacted through his Web site at `www.charlesebrown.net`.

I would like to thank Andy Nosalskiy at `www.dreamweaverdesk.com` for his invaluable assistance in designing great Dreamweaver templates.

Imar Spaanjaars

Imar Spaanjaars graduated in Leisure Management at the Leisure Management School in The Netherlands but accidentally ended up in Information Technology (IT). After working for a large corporation and doing some freelance work, he is now working in the software development department of a small IT company in The Netherlands that specializes in Internet, intranet, and wireless applications. As a software architect and lead developer, he's responsible for designing, building, and implementing medium- to large-scale intranets and wireless solutions. His current project involves the design and implementation of an application that allows employees to connect to enterprise data in real-time while on the road using a Pocket PC running the .NET Compact Framework.

When he is not busy writing software or teaching other people how to do so, Imar likes to read as much as possible about new developments in the software industry. He's a fanatic squash player and enjoys playing 3D shoot-'em-up games if he's got the time for it.

Imar lives in Utrecht, The Netherlands. You can contact him at `Imar.Spaanjaars@xs4all.nl`.

I would like to thank the people at Wrox for making this project possible. I would especially like to thank Brian MacDonald and Meryl K. Evans for their efforts during the editorial process.

I would also like to thank my parents, Jos and Bep, for the inspiration and motivation they have given me over the years.

Finally, I would like to thank my girlfriend, Fleur, for her love and her support during this project.

Todd Marks

Todd Marks is an avid developer, designer, instructor, and author of information display technologies. In 2000 Todd moved from teaching mathematics and computer science in the public sector to becoming VP of Research and Development at digitalorganism (www.digitalorganism.com). In 2002 Todd founded information technologies portal MindGrub Technologies (www.mindgrub.net). Todd currently works as a multimedia engineer for the MediaEdge division of Exceptional Software (www.media-edge.com). You can contact him at Todd.Marks@exceptionalsoftware.com.

Todd has worked extensively with ActionScript, ASP, PHP, Lingo, and numerous other development languages, placing cutting-edge code in several projects. Todd's efforts have earned three Flash Film Festival nominations, a Macromedia Site of the Day, two ADDY Awards, and several educational partnerships. Todd is a Macromedia Certified Developer, Designer, and Subject Matter Expert, and has written and contributed to several books, including *Flash MX Video*, *Foundation Dreamweaver MX*, *Beginning Dreamweaver MX*, *Advanced PHP for Flash MX*, *Flash MX Most Wanted Components*, and *Flash MX 2004 Magic*.

I would like to thank everyone at MediaEdge and Exceptional Software for their support. I would particularly like to express my love to my wife Betsy and daughters Sadie and Kara.

Credits

Authors
Charles E. Brown
Imar Spaanjaars
Todd Marks

Vice President and Executive Group Publisher
Richard Swadley

Vice President and Executive Publisher
Robert Ipsen

Vice President and Publisher
Joseph B. Wikert

Executive Editor
Chris Webb

Development Editor
Brian MacDonald

Editorial Manager
Mary Beth Wakefield

Executive Editorial Director
Mary Bednarek

Technical Editor
Meryl K. Evans

Production Editor
William A. Barton

Copy Editor
Stefan Gruenwedel

Project Coordinator
Regina Snyder

Graphics and Production Specialists
Carrie Foster
Lauren Goddard
Kristin McMullan

Quality Control Technician
Carl William Pierce

Text Design & Composition
Wiley Composition Services

Media Development Specialist
Kit Malone

Proofreading and Indexing
TECHBOOKS Production Services

Introduction

The rise of the Internet over recent years means that, for many of you, Web sites are now part of every-day life. You use them for research, news, purchases, tracking shipments, games, and information. There is a huge amount of information out there, and it is growing all the time.

In spite of the volume of information on the Web, and the sheer number of Web sites in existence these days, it's still possible to create a new Web site, get it out there on the Internet, and get it noticed. Of course, it's a good idea to have something interesting to say on your Web site, but that's not all—you can make your Web site attractive with a suitable page design and the appropriate use of features, and you can make it more functional and useful with the help of some back-end data storage and data manipulation.

That sounds great in principle, but how can you do it in practice? If you don't know the basics, then the amount you need to learn about each Web programming language (and how they work together) seems daunting. Even if you already know the basics of HTML, JavaScript, Active Server Pages, and so on, it's still more practical to use your knowledge to build attractive Web sites quickly and effectively, without the hassle of typing every last line of code.

For both types of Web developer, Macromedia Dreamweaver MX 2004 provides a solution. Dreamweaver is a powerful Web-development tool that helps you create attractive, dynamic, powerful Web sites. Its many tools and features not only enable you to create Web pages and Web sites quickly and painlessly, but they help you structure your Web sites in such a way that they are easy to maintain after you've built them.

If you're new to the various coding languages of the Web, fear not—Dreamweaver MX 2004 writes most of the code for you. If you're familiar with the basics, then Dreamweaver can help you create feature-rich Web sites with considerable ease. It generates the code for you *and* allows you to change the code it generates so that you have complete control over the final result.

What Does This Book Cover?

This book is a practical introduction to Dreamweaver MX 2004. In this book, we will quickly get you used to the features of Dreamweaver. We use step-by-step examples to show you the basics, and along the way you build three attractive, functional Web sites.

We also take a look at the code that Dreamweaver generates and explain how it works. This is impor-tant: You can achieve a lot just by using the point-and-click features of Dreamweaver, but you can achieve even more if you have an understanding of what is going on behind the scenes. Therefore, in this book, we examine both.

How Is This Book Structured?

In this book we create three complete Web sites. We use a step-by-step approach to build the sites and explain each step so that you know what's going on. We also provide the *complete* source code for all three sections at www.wrox.com so that you have the option of building as much as you like of each site for yourself, or simply placing the source code on a Web server and watching it work.

Each Web site is quite different in nature and achieves a different purpose. You can use each of the sites as a basis for your own ideas and, hence, develop them into sites that you will be proud to publish. Briefly, the three Web sites are as follows.

Section 1: The Cooking Place

In Section 1 of the book (Chapters 1–6), you create a hobbyist site called *The Cooking Place*. The purpose of this site is to be a resource for all things culinary: cooking techniques, recipes, equipment, news, and so on. As you build this site, you'll learn how to use Dreamweaver MX 2004 to do the following:

- ❑ Plan, create, and set up a Web site
- ❑ Add Web pages to the site and edit their content
- ❑ Use style sheets and templates to create a consistent style across the site
- ❑ Use tables and layers to control the layout of Web pages
- ❑ Add dynamic effects (like drop-down menus) to Web pages using JavaScript and DHTML
- ❑ Write a form to enable visitors to submit information and use dynamic ASP Web pages to capture submitted information and react to it

Section 2: The Soccer Site

As you progress through the book, the sites become increasingly ambitious. In Section 2 (Chapters 7–13), you build a soccer fan site that provides information on upcoming events for soccer fans around the world. As you build this site, you'll see how you can use Dreamweaver to do the following:

- ❑ Add logic to your ASP pages so that you can display different information to different users (depending on who they are or even what time of day it is)
- ❑ Keep track of users as they move around the site so that you can find out what parts of your site are the most popular
- ❑ Secure parts of the Web site so that only authorized users are allowed to see sensitive information
- ❑ Personalize the Web site for individual users so that the site appears in the colors of the user's favorite team or that they see only events occurring in their home country
- ❑ Store and extract information about users and upcoming events in a database and use this information to create Web pages dynamically

Section 3: MediaEdge and Building Blocks

In Section 3 (Chapters 14–18), you build a site that shows off many of the advanced features of Dreamweaver MX 2004. As you progress through these chapters, you'll see how to design a modular, extensible, and scalable Web site and create a set of dynamic Building Blocks that you can quickly modify and reuse in different sites.

As you build this site (which is used to display a set of images that users can view and purchase), you'll learn how to use Dreamweaver MX 2004 to accomplish the following:

❑ Create a set of Building Blocks whose look and content is determined dynamically by the settings in a database

❑ Create a content management page that you can use to mange the database that stores information about the images on the site, including their title, price, and how they should be laid out

❑ Put the Building Blocks you created earlier to a variety of uses, including a news blogger, a media display, and a product display

❑ Use Dreamweaver extensions to make your Building Blocks easy to reuse and to add e-commerce functionality to the site

The Appendixes

As you work through the book you learn enough about languages such as HTML, JavaScript, and Cascading Style Sheets (CSS) to have a good understanding of what Dreamweaver does for you behind the scenes. This is knowledge that will help you create better, more effective Web sites.

You also learn about server-side Web programming using Active Server Pages (ASP). This is a valuable skill in itself, but this will also prove useful if you plan eventually to build Web sites with JavaServer Pages (JSP), ASP.NET, PHP, or ColdFusion MX. Dreamweaver MX 2004 supports all of these server-side programming technologies; indeed, programming in any of these languages is very similar in Dreamweaver and the core concepts you learn in building Web sites with ASP are applicable and easily transferred to other languages. To help, this book includes four appendixes that provide fast-paced guides on getting started using JSP, ASP.NET, PHP, and ColdFusion MX with Dreamweaver MX 2004.

Why Not Try . . .

Each chapter concludes with a *Why Not Try . . .* section, which suggests tasks and exercises that you might try, using the concepts and techniques covered in that chapter. They're designed to help you reinforce the ideas for yourself, or to extend them — and to encourage you to experiment with new features of Dreamweaver and Web site development in general.

Some of the suggestions come with hints for how you should set about the task — but more detailed guides for each can be found at `http://p2p.wrox.com/exercises/`.

Who Is This Book For?

This book has two primary audiences. If you are new to the world of Web development and you have access to Dreamweaver MX 2004 (or you're thinking of buying Dreamweaver MX 2004) then you can use this book to learn about Web site development using Dreamweaver. We'll show you what to do and you'll learn enough about the important topics and about what happens behind the scenes to start creating attractive, functional Web sites very quickly.

If you've already done some Web site programming in the past but you're new to Dreamweaver (or just new to the latest version of Dreamweaver), then this book will show you how to achieve the tasks you've been working on, but in far less time and with far fewer bugs! Dreamweaver generates as much code as you want it to and it's a great tool for rapid application development and proof-of-concept development.

What You Need for This Book

To build and run the Web sites featured in this book you'll need the following:

❑ Microsoft Windows 2000 Professional or Server, Windows Server 2003, or Windows XP Professional Edition

❑ Microsoft Internet Information Services (IIS) 5.0, 5.1, or 6.0, which comes bundled with the operating systems listed above and which includes the necessary features to run server-side ASP coding

❑ Macromedia Dreamweaver MX 2004

If you don't already own a copy of Dreamweaver MX 2004, you can download a 30-day evaluation edition from Macromedia at www.macromedia.com/downloads/. The evaluation edition is full-featured and you'll be able to use it to work through the examples in the book.

If you have Microsoft Windows 98, Windows XP Home Edition, or Mac OS, you will need access to a remote server in order to run the ASP Web sites in the book. Appendix E and the Dreamweaver Help Documentation contain information about setting up a site to work with a remote server.

Conventions

We use a number of different styles of text and layout in the book to help differentiate between the various styles of information we provide. Here are examples of the styles we use along with explanations of what they mean.

Try It Out   Conventions

The *Try It Out* section is an exercise you should work through, following the text in the book.

1. They usually consist of a set of steps.

2.   Each step has a number.

3.   Follow the steps through.

4.   Then read *How It Works* to find out what's going on.

How It Works

After each *Try It Out*, the code you've typed in will be explained in detail.

> *Background information looks like this.*

Not-to-be-missed information looks like this.

Bulleted information is shown like this:

❑   *Important* words have a special italic font.

❑   Any `code fragments` or `file names` within normal text are highlighted in a `special font`.

❑   Menu items that require you to click on multiple submenus have a special symbol that looks like this: ⇨. For example: File ⇨ New ⇨ Folder.

Code shown for the first time, or other relevant code, is in the following format:

```
Dim intVariable
intVariable = 10
Response.Write(intVariable)
```

Less important code, or code that you have seen before, looks like this:

```
intVariable = 10
```

Customer Support

We offer source code for download, errata, and technical support from the Wrox Web site at www.wrox.com. In addition, you can join our mailing lists for author and peer discussions at http://p2p.wrox.com. (See the last section in this introduction for more info on the P2P site.)

Source Code and Updates

As you work through the examples in this book, you may choose either to type in all the code manually or use the source code files that accompany the book. All the source code referenced in this book is available for download at www.wrox.com. Once at the site, simply locate the book's title (either through the Search utility or by using one of the title lists) and double-click the Download Code link on the book's detail page to obtain the source code for the book.

Errata

We have made every effort to ensure that there are no errors in the text or in the code.

To find the errata page for this book, go to www.wrox.com and locate the title using the Search utility or one of the title lists. On the book's detail page, click the View Errata link. On this page you will be able to view all errata that have been submitted for this book and posted by Wrox editors. You can also click the Submit Errata link on this page to notify us of any errors you've found.

While we're on the subject of submitting errata, if you find an error in this book we definitely want to hear about it. In addition to the link on the book's detail page, you can also e-mail the information to techsupwrox@wrox.com. We'll check the information and, if appropriate, post a message to the book's errata page and fix the problem in subsequent editions of the book.

If you do e-mail us, your e-mail should include the following things:

❑   In the Subject field, include the book's title, the last six digits of the ISBN (555243 for this book), and the page number on which the error occurs.

❑   In the body of the message, include your name, contact information, and the problem.

We won't send you junk mail. We promise! We need these details to help you as quickly as possible.

E-mail Support

If you wish to query a problem in the book directly with an expert who knows the book in detail, then e-mail support@wrox.com, giving the title of the book and the last six numbers of the ISBN in the Subject field of the e-mail. A typical e-mail should include the following things:

❑   The title of the book, the last six digits of the ISBN, and the page number of the problem in the Subject field, for example: "Beginning Dreamweaver MX 2004, 555243, Page 42."

❑   Your name, contact information, and the problem in the body of the message.

When you send an e-mail message, it will go through the following chain of support:

1.   Your message is delivered to our **customer support staff**, who are the first people to read it. They have files on most frequently asked questions and will answer anything general about the book or the Web site immediately.

2.   Deeper queries are forwarded to the **technical editors** responsible for the book. They have experience with the programming language or particular product and are able to answer detailed technical questions on the subject.

3.   In the unlikely event that the editors cannot answer your problem, they will forward the request to the **authors**. The publisher does try to protect authors from distractions to their writing; however, the editors are quite happy to forward specific requests to them. All Wrox authors support their books. They will e-mail the editor with their responses so that all readers benefit.

The Wrox support process can support only issues that are directly pertinent to the content of your published title. Support for questions that fall outside the scope of normal book support is provided by the community lists at http://p2p.wrox.com.

p2p.wrox.com

For author and peer discussion, join the P2P forums at p2p.wrox.com. The forums are a Web-based system for you to post messages relating to Wrox books and related technologies and interact with other readers and technology users. The forums offer a subscription feature to e-mail you topics of interest of your choosing when new posts are made to the forums. Wrox authors, editors, other industry experts, and your fellow readers are present on these forums.

At http://p2p.wrox.com you will find a number of different forums that will help you not only as you read this book, but also as you develop your own applications. To join the forums, just follow these steps:

1. Go to p2p.wrox.com and click the Register link.

2. Read the terms of use and click Agree.

3. Complete the required information to join as well as any optional information you wish to provide and click Submit.

4. You will receive an e-mail with information describing how to verify your account and complete the joining process.

You can read messages in the forums without joining P2P, but in order to post your own messages, you must join.

Once you join, you can post new messages and respond to messages other users post. You can read messages at any time on the Web. If you would like to have new messages from a particular forum e-mailed to you, click the Subscribe to this Forum icon by the forum name in the forum listing.

For more information about how to use the Wrox P2P, be sure to read the P2P FAQs for answers to questions about how the forum software works as well as many common questions specific to P2P and Wrox books. To read the FAQs, click the FAQ link on any P2P page.

Contents

Contents

Contents

Contents

Contents

Contents

Contents

Contents

Contents

Contents

Contents

Contents

Part I: The Cooking Place

Chapter 1: Getting Started with Dreamweaver MX 2004

Chapter 2: Creating a Web Site

Chapter 3: Site Structure, Navigation, and Content

Chapter 4: Style Sheets and Templates

Chapter 5: Layers, Behaviors, and Dynamic Effects

Chapter 6: User Interaction with ASP and Forms

Getting Started with Dreamweaver MX 2004

Many years ago the famous concert pianist, and sometimes composer, Glenn Gould wrote a musical composition called "So You Want to Write a Fugue." In it he took the listener through the tools and steps necessary to write a composition in this musical form. This book attempts to achieve the same idea. Our form is going to be a Web site and our tool is going to be Dreamweaver MX 2004.

As you will see, Dreamweaver provides ease of use if you are a beginner who wants to build a simple site for a hobby, like The Cooking Place you will create in Section 1, and it provides sophistication if you are designing the Web site of a major company, like the MediaEdge site you will build in Section 3.

Dreamweaver achieves this diversity by presenting a simple, word-processor-like interface that allows you to type text and arrange graphics as you wish. While you do this, Dreamweaver generates the necessary programming code in the background. If you are somewhat experienced in Web coding, Dreamweaver allows you to edit and manipulate the code yourself.

As your needs get more demanding, Dreamweaver becomes an easy-to-use interface between higher programming languages and database programs. It enables you to drop database fields easily into your Web site and assists you in writing the code necessary to achieve dynamic effects.

There is no question that the technological demands of the Internet are growing. At one time Web designers simply used a descriptive language called HTML to build their pages. While HTML is just as important as it always was, you can also use a host of other technologies (such as scripting languages, Microsoft Active Server Pages, Macromedia ColdFusion, XML, and so on) to reach new levels of functionality.

The Dreamweaver IDE (integrated development environment) helps you harness these robust technologies quickly and easily. In many cases, a few simple menu selections is all Dreamweaver needs to write complex code. By eliminating the need to code by hand, Dreamweaver gives your projects quicker turnaround times so you can meet your deadlines better. In computer parlance, this is called rapid application development (RAD). As exciting as all this sounds, you must start at the beginning. Before you can do anything you must set up a few things. This chapter shows you how to do the following:

❑   Learn how Dreamweaver can assist you in creating Web sites.

❑   Install the tools you need to work through this book: the Dreamweaver MX 2004 Integrated Development Environment and Microsoft IIS (Internet Information Services) Web server.

❑   Set up the Dreamweaver workspace to suit your personal needs.

Over the course of Section 1, you build a Web site on the subject of food and cooking. You gain some familiarity with Dreamweaver and learn the fundamentals of Web development.

As you progress through the book, you'll learn a lot about HTML, scripting languages, and ASP, and see how Dreamweaver helps you create great Web sites using these important technologies.

A Brief Overview of Web Technology

You're probably quite familiar with using the Web. You open a browser, enter a Web site address (or click a button or link), and then, after a short time, see a page appear in the browser. It's simple!

Before you can request that Web page, however, somebody somewhere has to go through the trouble of creating and publishing it. They may even have used Dreamweaver to do that.

This section gives you a quick overview of creating a Web page and serving it to the browser. This procedure lies at the root of everything else you do in this book.

Static Web Pages

When the Web was first born (and even for a while after it started to become more widespread) all pages published on the Web were *static* pages. A static Web page is one that, like a piece of paper, is created once and never changes.

Even now, there are plenty of static pages out there on the Web, containing text, graphics, images, *hyperlinks* (links to other pages), and so on. The thing about a static Web page is that it always looks the same, regardless of who visits the page, when they visit it, or how they arrive at the page. The only time a static Web page changes is when the designer (Webmaster or Web author) physically locates the page file, opens it, and edits it.

HyperText Markup Language (HTML)

Static Web pages are composed using a language called *HyperText Markup Language* (HTML). This is a *markup language* whose purpose is to describe the *content, layout,* and *positioning* of all the elements on a page (text and graphics used). Later you'll learn about *programming languages*, which perform actions such as making decisions or repeating a block of code a certain number of times.

Here's a simple example of an HTML document:

```
<html>
  <head>
    <title>Welcome to Beginning Dreamweaver MX 2004</title>
  </head>
  <body>
    <h1>Welcome!</h1>
    <p>
      This is the first example in Wrox's <i>Beginning Dreamweaver MX</i>
      book. To learn more about Wrox books, go to
      <a href="http://www.wrox.com">www.wrox.com</a>.
    </p>
  </body>
</html>
```

HTML is composed of *tags* (the things enclosed in <...> characters) and text. Tags tell the browser how and where to display text:

❑   The phrase "Welcome to Beginning Dreamweaver MX 2004" sits between a `<title>` tag and a `</title>` tag. This tag tells the browser that this phrase should be displayed in the browser window's title bar.

❑   The phrase "This is the first example..." sits between a `<p>` tag and a `</p>` tag. These paragraph tags tell the browser that this phrase should be displayed as a paragraph.

This HTML example would usually be contained in an `.htm` or `.html` file. When this Web page is displayed in a browser, it looks something like Figure 1-1.

Figure 1-1

As Figure 1-1 shows, the HTML in this example also describes the following:

- ❏ The placement and format of the header "Welcome!" (in a larger font)

- ❏ Some italicized text (between <i> and </i> tags)

- ❏ A hyperlink to www.wrox.com (also known as an *anchor*, which is why HTML uses <a> and </a> tags to describe it)

There are different ways that authors of Web pages can generate HTML:

- ❏ They can type the HTML into a text editor such as Notepad.

- ❏ More likely they can design and compose Web pages using a product like Dreamweaver, which generates the HTML for them.

Don't worry too much about the finer details of HTML for now. You will learn as much as you need about HTML tags as you progress through the book. The main question for now is how HTML gets to the browser.

How a Web Page Gets to the Browser

The page, its content, and layout are *completely* determined by the HTML. No matter who visits the page, or when they visit it, it always looks the same—unless the author of the page rewrites it.

How does a static Web page appear on a browser? It's about clients and servers, and requests and responses. Figure 1-2 illustrates the entire process.

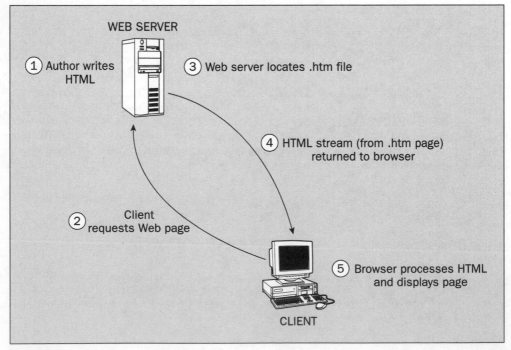

Figure 1-2

There are two machines in this diagram—a server and a client:

- The *client* is the machine on which users run their Web browser, which they use to request a Web page

- The *server* is a machine that runs the Web server software—the software that manages Web pages and makes them available to client machines (over the Internet or a local network)

In Step 1, an author composes the HTML file, saves it, and publishes it on a Web server. Any time after that, a user (using a browser on a client machine) types a Web address into the browser, or clicks the button, to make a *request* for the page (Step 2).

This request travels across the Internet (or the local network) and arrives at the Web server, which locates the .htm file that was requested (Step 3) and sends it back to the client machine (Step 4) as a *response*. If the HTML refers to any other files (such as images), then they are also sent as part of the response.

Finally, when the browser receives the response, it interprets the HTML tags and text and displays them on the screen as instructed by the HTML (Step 5). It surprises many people to learn they aren't looking at a Web page directly on the Web server but, instead, are viewing code that was downloaded to their own machine and interpreted by their browser.

Dynamic Web Content

As the Internet evolved, the limitations of static HTML pages became apparent:

- Designers couldn't write a page that would display the name of whoever was looking at it.

- Designers couldn't write a page that would reflect reality at any given moment, such as the current time or the latest weather conditions.

- Designers couldn't write a page whose content depended on choices users had made on the page they just came from.

Because Web authors needed something more flexible, *dynamic Web content* evolved. A *dynamic Web page* is a page that can contain both prewritten HTML and instructions for generating customized HTML. For example, have you ever gone to a Web page that identifies you by name or gives you the weather for your town? When a user requests a dynamic Web page, the response they get is still HTML; however, some (or all) of that HTML is generated by software on the server after the user requests the page. Therefore, it can react to the user's actions, the current situation, or the latest information that is available.

Server-Side Processing

Suppose you want to see list of all books written by Ernest Hemingway that Amazon.com carries. To do this, you type **www.amazon.com** in the Address box of your browser (this is called the Uniform Resource Locator or URL). You then type **Hemingway** into a text box (this is called a *Web form*, which you'll learn about in Chapter 6) and click a button to submit this request.

Amazon.com has information on millions of titles; how does its Web server know what information to show you? The answer is that the Web server analyzes the information your browser sends when you request the page and detects that you typed "Hemingway" into the text box. The Web server then sends the necessary information to a *database server*, which finds all the books whose author is Hemingway. Once the database server completes its task, it sends the list back to the Web server, where one of the dynamic technologies writes the necessary HTML code to display the list properly in your Web browser. Once that code is generated, it is sent back to your browser, which interprets the HTML and displays the page, just as it would a static page. Although this is a slight simplification, it helps you understand the fundamental concepts of the process.

This Web page is generated dynamically by the Web server at the time it's requested. You can compare the request/response process in Figure 1-3 with the process for a static page (in Figure 1-2). As you can see, there's only one extra step (Step 4).

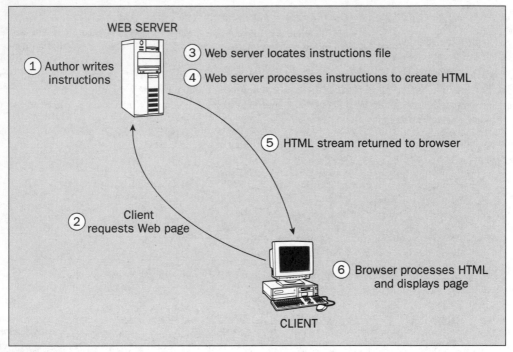

WEB SERVER

① Author writes instructions

③ Web server locates instructions file

④ Web server processes instructions to create HTML

⑤ HTML stream returned to browser

② Client requests Web page

⑥ Browser processes HTML and displays page

CLIENT

Figure 1-3

This example introduces another layer of technology called a database server. It allows the Web server to interface with the database. This type of server, which has a specific job, is sometimes called an *application server*.

In general, the capability of generating customized HTML is not automatically built into a Web server. You need to add this dynamic technology to your server. There are several technologies available that do the job more or less well:

- ❑ **Active Server Pages (ASP):** Developed by Microsoft, this technology comes as part of its IIS Web browser.

- ❑ **ColdFusion:** This technology was developed by Macromedia (the same people who created Dreamweaver). It requires installing the ColdFusion application server.

- ❑ **JavaServer Pages (JSP):** An offshoot of the Java programming language, it requires the installation of a Java application server.

- ❑ **PHP:** This growing dynamic technology is supported by many of today's most popular Web browsers.

- ❑ **ASP.NET:** This is the newest of the dynamic technologies and was developed by Microsoft as part of its .NET development environment. It requires installing the .NET Framework Server to function.

There are pros and cons to all of these technologies, which are discussed in other books. For the purposes of this book, the dynamic examples will use IIS as the Web server and ASP as the dynamic technology. IIS comes bundled with Windows 2000 Professional or Windows XP Professional. ASP is part of IIS and does not require any additional software to be installed.

Simple HTML isn't enough to support these dynamic technologies; you need a more mature language. *Scripting languages* offer a lot more capability than HTML but are not as complex as full-fledged programming languages such as Visual Basic or Java. We will be speaking a bit more about these languages further on in the book.

Client-Side Processing

Dynamic technology operates on the Web server. You can also write code that executes on the *client*. The effect is quite different.

Client-side code is not executed by the Web server. Instead, it is sent to the browser (along with HTML, as part of the response) and is processed by the browser; the browser then displays the results on the user's screen.

You can use client-side code to bring a page to life by making it react to the user's button clicks and mouse movements. For example, you could have rollover effects make a button change colors when the mouse pointer is over it, or you could create a way to verify that information in a form is correct before the browser sends it to the server.

Figure 1-4 extends the picture a little further by adding one more step (Step 6) to take care of client-side processing:

For your client-side code to work, the client machine (or browser) must support the language in which the code is written. JavaScript is probably the most commonly used language for writing client-side code. It's supported by all the major browsers (Internet Explorer, Netscape, Opera, and so on). As Chapter 2 explains, when you use Dreamweaver to create dynamic client-side effects, it generates JavaScript client-side code to power those effects.

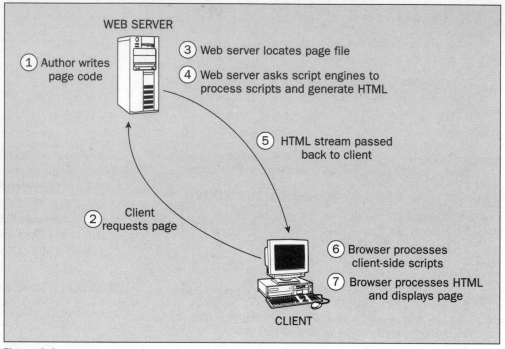

Figure 1-4

The Macromedia Suite

In 2003 Macromedia released its Studio MX 2004 development environment. The MX 2004 environment was developed to better encompass newer Web technologies, such as the Microsoft .NET environment, and to help streamline the work process.

Studio MX 2004 is an integrated suite of development tools that consists of the following products:

❑ **Flash MX 2004** delivers professional animation Web sites that lend themselves to being viewed with mobile technologies by needing fewer resources to run.

❑ **Fireworks MX 2004** develops exciting, attractive graphics.

❑ **ColdFusion MX 6.1** provides server technology for delivering dynamic Web content.

❑ **Dreamweaver MX 2004** is the principal development tool for bringing all the other components together.

Installing Dreamweaver MX 2004

There are several ways to obtain Dreamweaver MX 2004. You can download a 30-day evaluation copy from www.macromedia.com. You can purchase it by itself or buy it bundled with the Macromedia Studio MX 2004 suite. The installation process for all these versions is similar, with just a few minor differences.

The following section steps you through installing Dreamweaver MX 2004. The screenshots were taken from the Macromedia Dreamweaver MX 2004 installation disk, running Windows XP Professional. If you install it on a different operating system, or from a different source, you might see some differences. The overall process should not vary much, however.

Try It Out　　**Installing Dreamweaver MX 2004**

1. Run the installation program. If you're installing Dreamweaver from a CD, the installation program probably runs automatically when you insert the disc. If not, select Start⇨Run, click the Browse button, and browse to the Dreamweaver MX 2004 installer (called Dreamweaver MX 2004), as shown in Figure 1-5.

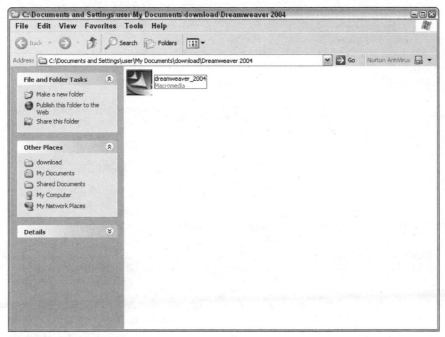

Figure 1-5

2. Double-click the installer icon to extract the necessary files. After that is completed, you are invited to install Dreamweaver MX 2004, as shown in Figure 1-6.

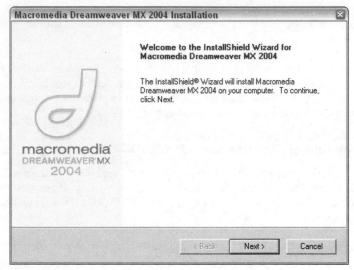

Figure 1-6

3. Read and accept the License Agreement, as shown in Figure 1-7, by clicking Yes.

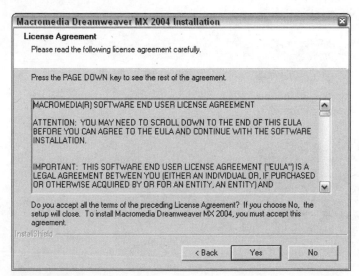

Figure 1-7

4. Dreamweaver allows you to decide what directory to install it in, as shown in Figure 1-8. In most instances, the default setting is fine.

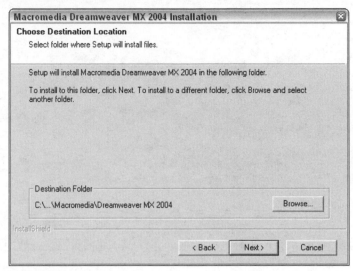

Figure 1-8

5. The next screen (see Figure 1-9) is an interesting one. It shows you all the technologies that Dreamweaver MX 2004 can handle, and asks you if you want the files associated with these technologies to use Dreamweaver as their default editor. You can simply check which files you want to associate automatically with Dreamweaver MX 2004.

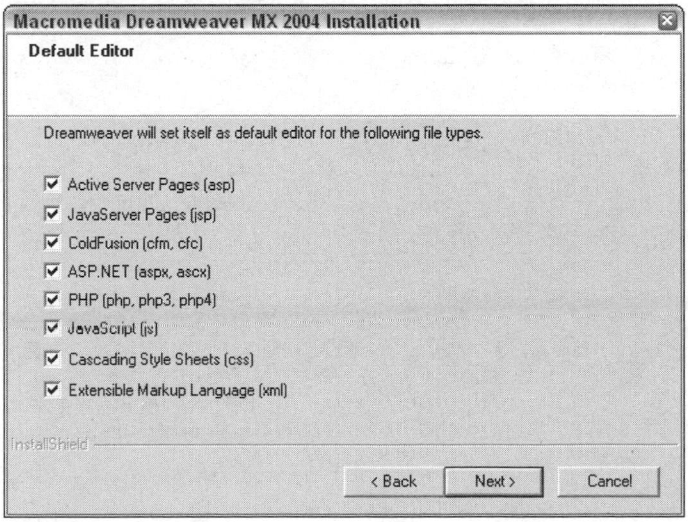

Figure 1-9

6. Double-check your installation settings before the process begins, as shown in Figure 1-10.

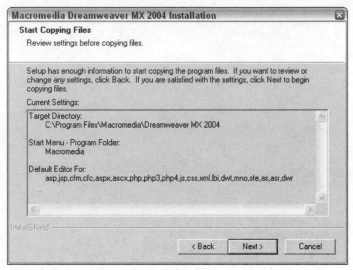

Figure 1-10

7. Click Next to begin the installation process. When completed, you will be prompted to click Finish. Depending on your configuration, you may be taken to the Dreamweaver MX 2004 icon and a page on the Macromedia Web site that contains some introductory text.

How It Works

This process installs all the necessary files and performs the configuration required to get Dreamweaver working. When it's complete, the Dreamweaver development environment will be ready to use. If you want, you can load Dreamweaver from the Start menu, using Programs⇨Macromedia⇨Macromedia Dreamweaver MX 2004.

By installing Dreamweaver MX 2004, you have access to a powerful code editor. If all you want to do is write static Web pages, your job is done. However, that would be using only a small part of Dreamweaver's capability. A major feature of this program is its ability to integrate with the server technologies we described above.

Installing a Web Server

As you've probably guessed from the discussion earlier in this chapter, you need a Web server in order to build the Web sites in this book. The choice of Web servers available to you depends on which operating system you're using:

❑   If you're using Windows 2000 (Professional, Server, or Advanced Server editions) or Windows XP (Professional Edition), the easiest thing to do is install Microsoft IIS Web server software.

❑ If you're using any other operating system, you need to consult Appendix E (or the Dreamweaver documentation) to find out more about how to use a remote Web server. Discussing the various possible combinations is beyond the scope of this chapter.

The exercises in this book use IIS Web server software, which is bundled with the versions of Windows 2000 and Windows XP listed previously.

IIS version 5.0 is supplied as part of Windows 2000, while Windows XP Professional ships with IIS version 5.1. For your purposes, there is not much difference between the two, so whichever version is supplied with your operating system will do. Please note that, as of this writing, Microsoft is releasing IIS version 6.0. Based on initial information, it should not present any differences when using Dreamweaver.

For the purposes of this book, we use the default installation. Your installation parameters may vary depending on your circumstances.

Try It Out Installing and Testing IIS 5.x

There are several ways to install IIS. If you are using Windows 2000 or XP Professional, just follow this simple procedure:

1. Launch your Windows 2000 or XP installation CD. The screen shown in Figure 1-11 appears. Select the Install Optional Windows Components option.

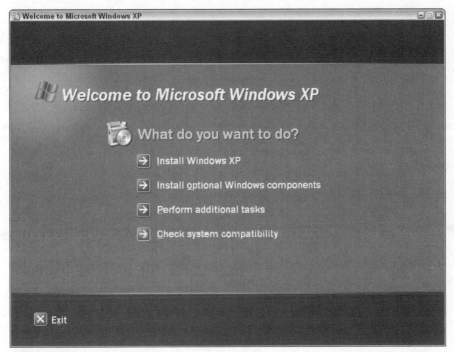

Figure 1-11

2. If the Internet Information Services (IIS) option is already checked (see the dialog box shown in Figure 1-12), IIS is already installed. Click Cancel and skip to Step 4 to test it. Otherwise, click this check box and then click Next.

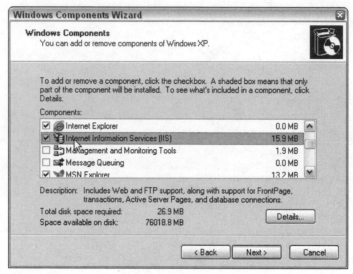

Figure 1-12

3. Click Next. The Wizard installs and configures the IIS components. As it does, it displays a status bar to inform you of the progress of the installation. After it finishes, you see a message that tells you that you have "successfully completed the Windows Components Wizard." Click Finish to close the Wizard.

You don't have to start the IIS installation from the operating system CD. Instead, you can get to the dialog box in Step 2 by selecting Start⇨Control Panel in Windows XP (or Start⇨Settings⇨Control Panel in Windows 2000), clicking Add or Remove Programs, and then Add/Remove Windows Components. From there, follow Steps 2 and 3. When you reach Step 3 you'll be asked to insert the operating system CD or specify the place on your network where the installation files exist.

4. It's a good idea to test the IIS installation now to ensure that ASP is running. Do this using the same machine onto which you've just installed IIS. Open your Web browser, type **http://localhost/localstart.asp** in the Address box and click Go. It should display the page shown in Figure 1-13, which states that your Web service is now running.

How It Works

Once you install IIS, it starts running automatically and continues to run in the background, listening for Web page requests.

In Step 4, you used a Web browser to make a request for a Web page at an address of `http://localhost/localstart.asp`. There are three important elements to this address:

❏ Starting at the end, `localstart.asp` is the name of the Web page you requested. It doesn't have an `.htm` extension. Because it has an `.asp` extension, it in fact uses the ASP server-side technology mentioned earlier. ASP is installed as part of IIS, so the page should work just fine.

❏ Before that, the bit just after the `//` indicates the location of the Web server on which you expect this page to be hosted. Here you specify "localhost" to indicate that you're trying to contact the Web server that's on the same machine as the browser.

❏ Before that, the address begins with `http://`. This causes the Web page request to be transported from the browser to the Web server using something called *HyperText Transfer Protocol*, or HTTP. HTTP is the protocol used by the Web to describe both requests and responses. Think of it as a standard format for Web requests and Web responses. Because HTTP is a standard, all Web servers and browsers and other machines on the Internet can understand the request or response message being sent.

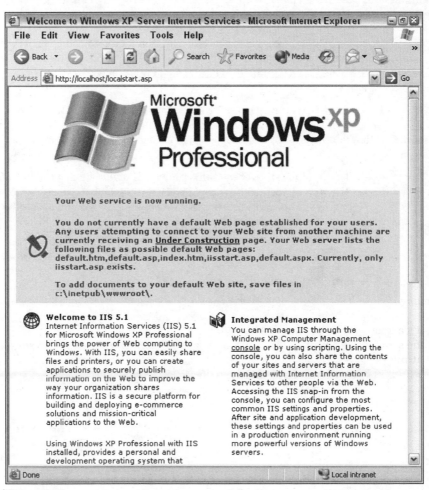

Figure 1-13

In this case, the browser and the Web server are on the same machine. But that isn't always the case. If you have a network set up, you should be able to browse to the `localstart.asp` page on your IIS Web server from other machines on your network (using an address like `http://<iis-machine-name>/localstart.asp`).

> **Be particularly sensitive to security risks if your Web server is exposed to the public Internet. There are plenty of precautions you can take. For example, download the necessary security patches as they become available, using Windows Update (`http://windowsupdate.microsoft.com`), or use some sort of Firewall configuration.**

If everything works properly, your browser should display a test page like the one shown in Figure 1-13. If you don't get this page, don't panic; it could be that something very simple is wrong. Here are a few suggestions to rectify the situation:

❑ If your browser displays the message "The page cannot be found" or "HTTP 404 File Not Found," it means that your page request reaches the Web server all right but the Web server can't find the page you're looking for. Perhaps you misspelled the name of the page. Check it and try again.

❑ If your browser displays the message "The page cannot be displayed," "Cannot find server," or "DNS error," it means that your page request does not reach the Web server. In this case, it could be that you misspelled the name of the Web server in the page address. Check it and try again.

❑ If you confirm the address still get the same problem, it could be that the installation process failed to start the Web server. To check this, select Start➪Control Panel➪Administrative Tools➪Services in Windows XP (or Start➪Settings➪Control Panel➪Administrative Tools➪Services in Windows 2000). In the window (see Figure 1-14), look for the World Wide Web Publishing item.

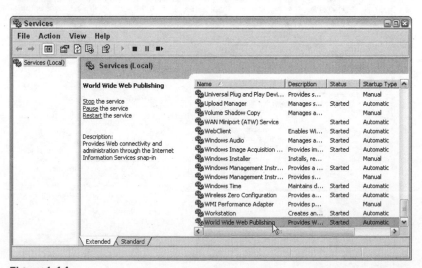

Figure 1-14

In the Status column, you should see the word "Started," which indicates that the Web server is running in the background and listening for page requests. If you do not see "Started," right-click World Wide Web Publishing and select Start to start the service.

If you continue to have problems with your IIS installation, or any other aspect of this book, contact Wrox Support at techsupport@wrox.com.

Exploring Dreamweaver MX 2004

Provided that everything installs properly, you should be ready to start putting it to work. In this section we show you how to use Dreamweaver to build a simple static Web page and then test it by viewing it in a Web browser. We also take a short tour of the Dreamweaver workspace and introduce you to the different features that appear when the program launches. Once you complete the example and this little tour, you'll know enough to get started on the Web site in Chapter 2.

Try It Out   **Building Your First Web Page**

1.   If you haven't done so already, launch Dreamweaver MX from your Start menu (this should be Start⇨(All) Programs⇨Macromedia⇨Macromedia Dreamweaver MX 2004). If this is the first time you are running it, you will be prompted to decide how you want Dreamweaver to open, as shown in Figure 1-15.

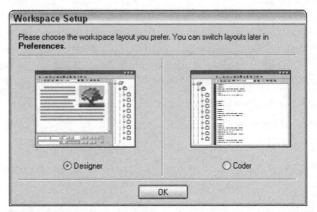

Figure 1-15

If you primarily want to work in a design mode, select Designer; if you like to jump into the code right away, select Code. Whatever you select here can be easily changed later on. If you are new to Web design, you will probably find Designer a bit easier to work with initially.

Also, if you are using Dreamweaver MX 2004 for the first time, you will be prompted to enter your serial number information, as shown in Figure 1-16

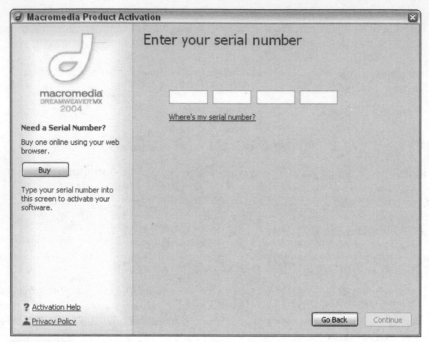

Figure 1-16

2. You should see an introductory page similar to Figure 1-17. The first column shows the Web sites you have been working on recently. The second column lists the types of Web pages you can create. The third column lists sample pages you can use as guides for your work. This is convenient if you are new to Web design.

    If you do not want to see this screen in the future, select Don't Show Again.

3. From the second column, Create New, select HTML.

4. You should see the Dreamweaver MX screen, as shown in Figure 1-18.

    If you open in Code view, click the Design button located in the upper-left corner of the work area, just below the tabs.

    This is the place where you do most of the development in this book. As you can see, there's quite a lot in this window. The next section describes the Dreamweaver workspace.

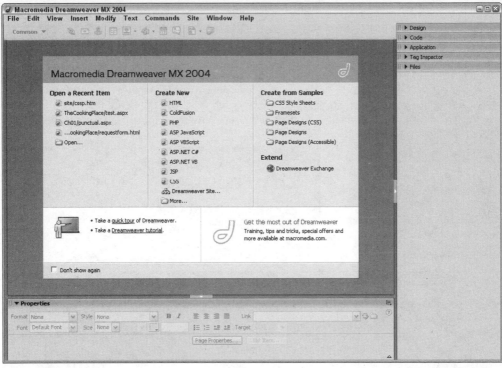

Figure 1-17

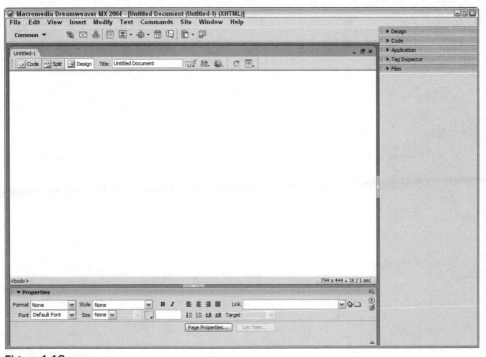

Figure 1-18

5. Now you're ready to create your first Web page. You could build this page using Dreamweaver's powerful features for designing and building Web pages, but to keep things brief in this first chapter, just type the necessary code instead. (You'll see plenty of those page design features in the rest of the book.)

Near the top left of the window, under the Document Name tab and just to the right of the word "View," you will see three buttons arranged as shown in Figure 1-19. If you float your mouse pointer over the three buttons, Dreamweaver tells you what they are for. If you select Code view, you should see a screen similar to the one shown in Figure 1-20. This is the HTML code.

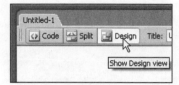

Figure 1-19

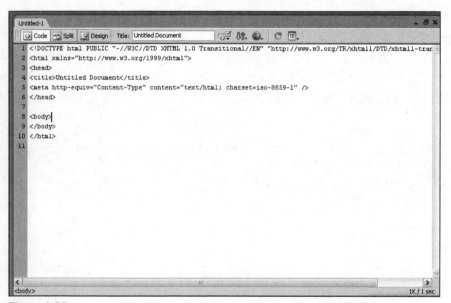

Figure 1-20

6. Change the existing code in this pane so that it reads as follows:

```
<!DOCTYPE HTML PUBLIC "-//W3C//DTD HTML 4.01 Transitional//EN">
<html>
  <head>
    <title>Welcome to Beginning Dreamweaver MX 2004</title>
  </head>
  <body>
```

```
<h1>Welcome!</h1>
<p>
   This is the first example in Wrox's <i>Beginning Dreamweaver MX</i>
   book. To learn more about Wrox books, go to
   <a href="http://www.wrox.com">www.wrox.com</a>.
</p>
</body>
</html>
```

Change only the lines highlighted here in gray. Alternatively, you can copy and paste the code from the file called welcome.htm *in the downloadable source code package for this book, available from* www.wrox.com.

7. Click the Show Design View button. In Design view, shown in Figure 1-21, Dreamweaver allows you to preview your work. More importantly, you can use this view to design pages, which means that most of the time you don't have to deal with code at all.

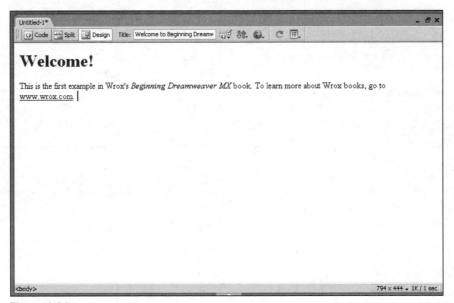

Figure 1-21

8. Save the file. Because you have not set up a Web site yet, keep this simple and just save it in the default My Documents folder. From the menu bar at the top of the window, choose File⇨Save As and then use the Save As dialog box to navigate to the My Documents folder (see Figure 1-22). Save the file with the name welcome.htm.

After you select Save, the tab located in the upper-left corner of the document window identifies this work as the welcome.htm *document.*

9. Test the page by viewing it in a Web browser. Dreamweaver has an easy way to do this. Pressing F12 causes a browser window to appear, with your page loaded in it, as shown in Figure 1-23.

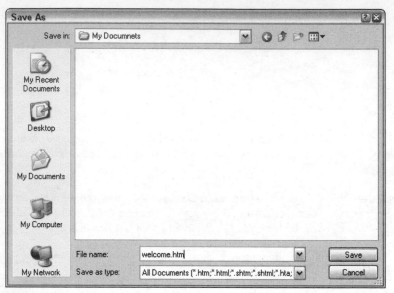

Figure 1-22

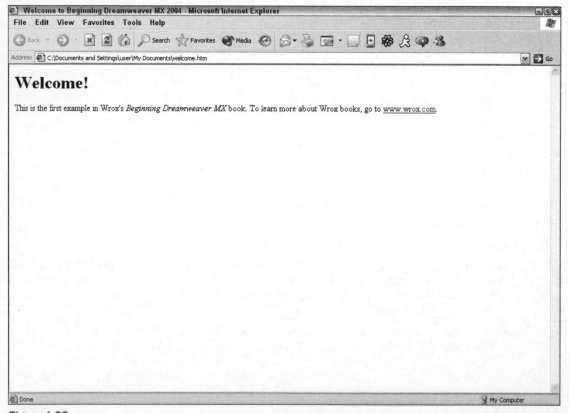

Figure 1-23

10. Doesn't it look great? However, there is one small issue here. Look at the address displayed in the Address box in the browser: It doesn't begin with http://. This means that Dreamweaver isn't making the page request through the HTTP protocol; the operating system, rather than the IIS Web server, is displaying the page in the browser instead.

This happens only because you have not yet configured Dreamweaver to set up a test Web site from which it can request pages through HTTP. You'll do that in Chapter 2.

How It Works

You examined the HTML code for this page earlier in the chapter, so we won't go over it again. It is worth noting the two views that you used in the exercise, however:

❑ Code view allows you to view and edit the code that makes up your Web page.

❑ Design view allows you to view and edit the design of your page.

By switching from Design view to Code view, adding some code, and switching back again, you can see the relationship between these two views. If you make a change in one view, the change affects whatever is in the other. In many ways, Design view is similar to working in a word processor.

From Chapter 2 onwards, you will begin to make much more use of Design view, and Dreamweaver's design tools, to build your pages.

If you want, you can see the HTML that the Web server sends to the browser. To do this, right-click the browser window and select View Source (or View Page Source or similar, depending on your browser), as shown in Figure 1-24.

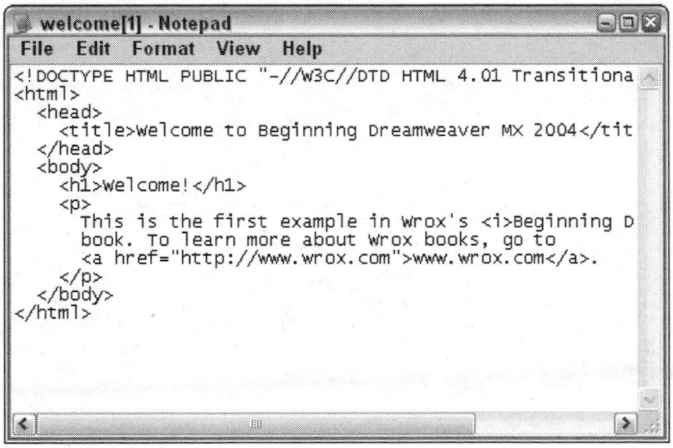

```
welcome[1] - Notepad                                           _ □ ✕
File   Edit   Format   View   Help
<!DOCTYPE HTML PUBLIC "-//W3C//DTD HTML 4.01 Transitiona
<html>
   <head>
     <title>Welcome to Beginning Dreamweaver MX 2004</tit
   </head>
   <body>
     <h1>Welcome!</h1>
     <p>
        This is the first example in Wrox's <i>Beginning D
        book. To learn more about Wrox books, go to
        <a href="http://www.wrox.com">www.wrox.com</a>.
     </p>
   </body>
</html>
```

Figure 1-24

This shows the code that the Web server sends to the browser and which the browser uses to build the page you see.

The Dreamweaver Workspace

Dreamweaver's *workspace* is standardized with the entire Macromedia MX 2004 environment. Many of the features here work the same way as their counterparts in the other Studio MX 2004 programs—Flash MX 2004, Fireworks MX 2004, and so on. This reduces the overall learning curve for the MX 2004 environment.

Beginning with the previous version, Dreamweaver MX, Macromedia dramatically redesigned the environment to emphasize organization and ease of use. The standard workspace is shown in Figure 1-25.

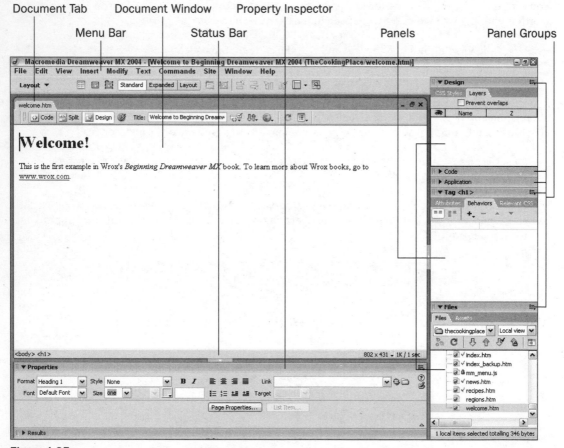

Figure 1-25

Panel Groups and Panels

One of the most important concepts about the work environment is the use of panels and panel groups, as shown in Figure 1-26.

Figure 1-26

A *panel* is a group of related tools. They are usually located along the right side of the workspace. For example, the Behaviors panel groups tools for client and server-side behaviors using dynamic technologies. Instead of describing all of the many panels available now, we discuss them as you need them through the book.

If you are using Dreamweaver for the first time, you'll see a few panels open on the right. More panels are available from the Window menu. For example, to open the History panel, select Window⇨History (or press Shift+F10). The panel should appear on the right.

The MX 2004 environment helps you to stay organized further by grouping related panels into *panel groups*. For instance, the Selection panel group contains the Properties, Behaviors, and CSS panels.

Hiding and Revealing Panel Groups

You can close, regroup, or rename panel groups to suit your demands. As you become more familiar with Dreamweaver, you may decide to customize your panel groups by selecting the control box to the right of the name in the panel group title bar (see Figure 1-27).

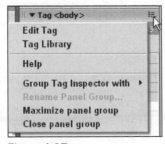

Figure 1-27

You can also collapse a panel group by clicking on the arrow to the left of the name in the group's title bar (see Figure 1-28).

Figure 1-28

27

Moving and Docking Panel Groups

To move a panel group around the workspace, you must pick it up by its *gripper*—the pattern of dots in the top-left corner of the panel group—as shown in Figure 1-29, and move it to its new location. This allows you to do the following:

❑ **Undock** a panel group so that it is not displayed with the other panel groups but floats in a separate "window."

❑ **Dock** an undocked panel group to move it back into the main Dreamweaver workspace window.

❑ **Change the order** of the docked panel groups by dragging the panel group by its gripper and dropping it in its new location.

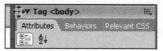

Figure 1-29

The Property Inspector

Holding a special place of honor, at the bottom of the workspace, is a very important panel called the *Property inspector*. The Property inspector is where you view and change the properties of whatever element or item you've selected in your document. The Property inspector is context-sensitive: If your cursor is inside an HTML paragraph, the Property inspector shows the properties of that paragraph (see Figure 1-30); if you select a JavaScript behavior, the Property inspector shows the properties of that behavior.

Figure 1-30

Figure 1-30 shows the properties of an HTML paragraph (`<p>`) element: The font selected for this paragraph is the default font, there is no set font size, and so on. The buttons on the right enable you to apply bold or italic, adjust the alignment (left, center, right, or justified), add bullets, and do various other things. You'll make good use of these options over the coming chapters.

The Insert Panel Group

Along the top of the screen is the Insert panel group (see Figure 1-31). This panel group contains many of the tools commonly used for controlling layout and text, creating and controlling tables, and creating frames, forms, and so on.

Figure 1-31

Many of the tools in this panel group are hidden until needed. To access the other panels, click the Common button located at the beginning of this panel, as shown in Figure 1-32.

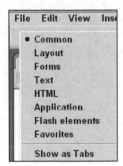

Figure 1-32

New to this version of Dreamweaver is the ability to create a customized panel in this group called Favorites, shown in Figure 1-33. Use this to group tools that you use a lot but either aren't on other panels or are spread over different panels.

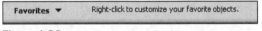

Figure 1-33

Right-click the mouse and select Customize Favorites. The Customize Favorite Objects dialog box shown in Figure 1-34 opens to allow you to select the icons you use most.

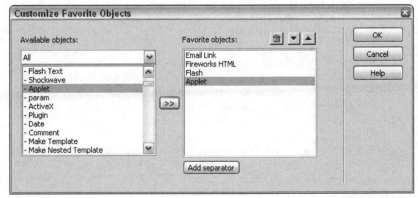

Figure 1-34

Click on the Common menu selection to see a feature that users of past versions of Dreamweaver will appreciate—the Show as Tabs feature, as shown in Figure 1-35.

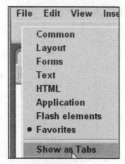

Figure 1-35

This changes the Insert panel to the older style used in previous versions of Dreamweaver, as shown in Figure 1-36.

Figure 1-36

Setting up the Preview Browsers

The purpose of this book is to build Web sites. Therefore you're going to need a browser to test the fruits of your work. As you've already seen, Dreamweaver allows you to view a Web page by pressing F12 (Preview in Browser). Dreamweaver is probably already configured to allow you to use Microsoft Internet Explorer to view Web pages. However, it's a good idea to install the latest versions of both Internet Explorer and Netscape and to configure Dreamweaver so that it gives you an F12-type Preview in Browser shortcut for each browser, not just one. That way you can check what you've done easily by using whichever browser you're interested in.

Many Web developers retain earlier versions of the major browsers for testing purposes. When you publish your Web site, there is no guarantee that everyone who visits it will be using the latest and greatest browser. For that reason, it's a good idea to test your work under as many conditions as possible, and with as many different browsers as possible. As you progress through this book, you will learn about some of Dreamweaver's additional tools that aid browser compatibility.

Before you begin this final exercise, find out which browsers you have installed already on your machine, and consider installing additional ones. For example, get the latest version of Internet Explorer from www.microsoft.com, get the most recent version of Netscape from www.netscape.com, and download Opera, a popular alternate browser, from www.opera.com.

Try It Out   **Configuring Dreamweaver for Browser-Based Page Previews**

1. In Dreamweaver, select Edit⇨Preferences to open the Dreamweaver Preferences dialog box, as shown in Figure 1-37. Click the Preview in Browser category.

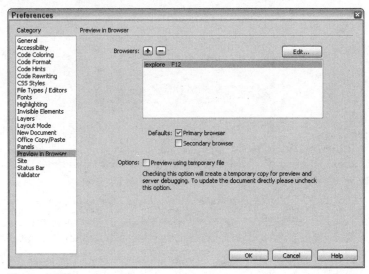

Figure 1-37

2. Check the browser for which Dreamweaver has already been configured. If your Browsers box contains an entry, click on it and then click the Edit button. The Edit Browser dialog box shown in Figure 1-38 appears.

Figure 1-38

This dialog box tells you the name of the browser. It also specifies the file that runs whenever you use this option. (Figure 1-38 shows Dreamweaver configured to preview Web pages with Internet Explorer.) Don't change the settings here; just click OK to close the dialog box.

3. Add a second browser. Click the plus button to bring up the Add Browser dialog box.

If your Dreamweaver installation is already configured to use Internet Explorer (as in Step 2), and you've already installed Netscape, then configure Dreamweaver to allow previews in Netscape as well:

31

❑ For the Application field, browse to the executable file for Netscape (it is probably in a folder such as `C:\Program Files\Netscape\Netscape\Netscp7.exe`) so that the dialog box looks like the one in Figure 1-39.

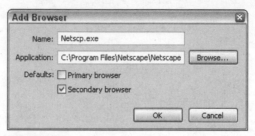

Figure 1-39

Alternatively, if Dreamweaver is not already configured for Internet Explorer and you want to configure it here, do so:

❑ For the Name field, type **Internet Explorer 7** (or something similar).

❑ For the Application field, browse to the executable file for Internet Explorer (it is probably somewhere like C:\Program Files\Internet Explorer\iexplore.exe).

Click the Primary Browser or Secondary Browser check box. (This is simply for convenience's sake. Press F12 to preview in the primary browser and press Ctrl+F12 to preview in the secondary browser.) Click OK to exit the Add Browser dialog box.

4. In the Preferences dialog box you should now see the browsers listed in the Browsers box, as shown in Figure 1-40.

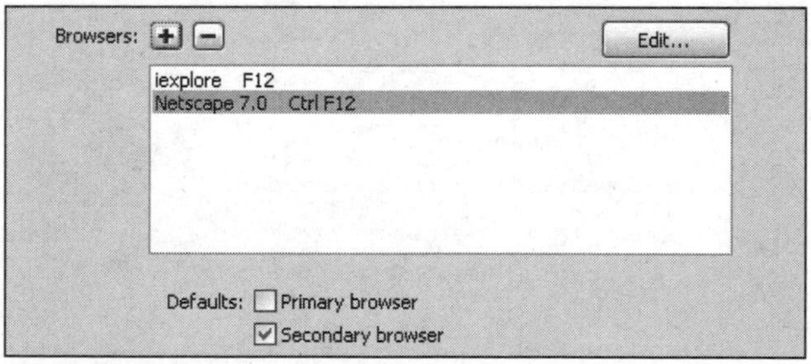

Figure 1-40

If you make Netscape your secondary browser, you should find that Internet Explorer has been configured automatically as the primary browser.

5. You have one other thing to decide regarding how Dreamweaver uses browsers, and that is the Preview Using Temporary File option (which is also in the Preferences dialog box). Uncheck this option and click OK to exit the Preferences dialog box.

6. Test the configuration. Press F12 to view `welcome.htm` in your primary browser; press Ctrl+F12 to view it in your secondary browser, as shown in Figure 1-41.

Figure 1-41

How It Works

You can add as many browsers as you like to the list. Make one of them your primary browser and another one your secondary browser. This enables you to preview pages in those browsers using the F12 or Ctrl+F12 keyboard shortcuts. Once you add other previewing browsers, use them by right-clicking the page in the Files panel of the Files panel group and selecting the Preview in Browser option.

If you are unsure how to get there, open the panel by either selecting the Files Panel group or pressing F8. (You could also select Window⇨File.)

If you keep the Preview Using Temporary File option checked, Dreamweaver doesn't preview the actual file you're working on. Instead, it creates a temporary file. The problem with this arrangement is that each time you edit the file, you must start a new browser session to preview it; refreshing the current browser view doesn't work. Temporary files also create clutter. (Dreamweaver is supposed to delete these temporary files when it shuts down but our experience has shown that this does not always happen.)

If you uncheck the Preview Using Temporary File option, you must save the file before previewing it. This is not really a hassle, however. It's good practice anyway to save your work frequently. Going this route also prevents temporary files from cluttering your folders or uploading them accidentally to the server.

Summary

Dreamweaver is a powerful tool for building Web sites. As you saw in this chapter, Dreamweaver gives you easy access to code in Code view. Perhaps more importantly, it also gives you a Design view and a wealth of powerful tools that you can use to generate code quickly and accurately. This means that you can quickly get down to the task of building attractive Web sites with minimal effort.

It's helpful to know what happens behind the scenes and to picture the request/response process that occurs whenever someone wants to see a Web page. The user's browser formulates an HTTP request message (describing the request) and sends that request across the Internet (or other network) to the Web server. When the Web server receives the request, it processes it and returns an HTTP response, containing the requested page, to the browser. The browser finally displays the page on the screen.

This is the request/response in its simplest form, of course. We touched on the notion of client-side and server-side processing, and how they bring dynamic effects and dynamic content to Web pages. You'll learn more about client-side processing in Chapter 2 and server-side processing in Section 2.

You're now ready to create a Web site—The Cooking Place—and build the pages that comprise the site, along with graphics and client-side effects.

Why Not Try . . .

1. Take a moment to explore the various panels of the Insert panel group. You'll find that the Insert panel group is a versatile and powerful tool, enabling you to add many different elements and features to your Web pages. You'll learn more about them in the coming chapters. For now, however, use the buttons in the Common panel to add more elements to `welcome.htm`.

2. Add and remove buttons from the Favorites panel located in the Insert panel group.

3. Look at the different panel groups and panels in Dreamweaver. The best way to access all the different panels is by using the Window menu (which lists the relevant keyboard shortcut for each panel). You have already seen a little of the Insert panel group and the Properties panel (the Property inspector). You'll meet many more over the course of the upcoming chapters. For now, just look around and see what's available.

Creating a Web Site

In Chapter 1 you got a small taste of using Dreamweaver MX 2004 and some of its capabilities. You built a simple Web page and viewed it in a browser. You also discussed some of the technology behind building a Web site.

In this chapter, you build on this foundation. You use Dreamweaver MX 2004 to create a Web site, called The Cooking Place, and also create a page design for your site. Although the site consists mostly of static pages, you can include a number of effects that use client-side processing. Chapter 3 very briefly introduces you more to the world of server-side processing within The Cooking Place.

> *You'll study server-side processing with ASP in much more detail in Section 2 of this book, when you look at a soccer-related Web site.*

This chapter shows you how to do the following:

- ❑ Use Dreamweaver MX 2004 to create a Web site
- ❑ Set up the development options for building the Web site
- ❑ Configure Dreamweaver MX 2004 in tandem with your Web server so that you can test the pages you build
- ❑ Create your first Web page
- ❑ Build a simple but attractive page design that you'll subsequently use for a number of pages in your site

Creating Your First Web Site

In Chapter 1 you created a single Web page and viewed it in a browser. Now suppose you decided to quit your present job and develop the true passion in your life: cooking. You plan to start a small business offering recipes, wines, cooking classes, cooking news, and so on. You call it The Cooking Place. Of course, your business needs a Web site.

The term *Web site* is a fairly generic one. In general when you talk about a "Web site," you mean a collection of related, interconnected Web pages:

❑ They're *related* in the sense that they (often, although not always) have some common theme. For example, all the pages at www.wrox.com contain information about books, products, opinions, and articles published by Wrox Press. Similarly, all the pages in your Cooking Place Web site will be about food and cooking techniques.

❑ They're *interconnected* in the sense that the site is designed to enable users to click between related pages of the same site in a natural way.

Of course, the relatedness and interconnectedness of a Web site's pages depend on what you want to publish in your Web site, and how you design it! In principle, however, you should be able to choose any Web site and browse through a few of its pages to see how the pages are related and interconnected.

In Dreamweaver MX 2004, start creating the Web site itself. To begin, it will not contain any Web pages at all. It will be the repository into which you start adding pages. This is a good way for you to set various configuration settings and to tell Dreamweaver about the type of site you want to create.

Physical Directories and Virtual Directories

Consider the physical directories and virtual directories in your site. You may recall from Chapter 1 that when you created the welcome.htm Web page, you saved it to a folder on your computer. For instance, you may have saved it here:

```
C:\Documents and Settings\user\My Documents\welcome.htm
```

This is the physical location of the file on the Web server machine's hard disk. By contrast, when you request a Web page through HTTP using a browser you do so using a "virtual" address like this:

```
http://localhost/welcome.htm
```

If you try this out now, it will not work. We are just using this for illustrative purposes. Later in the chapter you will be using virtual addresses.

Obviously these two addresses are equivalent in some way because when you request http://local host/welcome.htm in a Web browser you get the file that is stored at C:\Documents and Settings\ user\My Documents\welcome.htm on the Web server. How is this?

The *Web server* manages this. When the Web server receives a request for a file in the form of a "virtual" address like http://localhost/welcome.htm, it needs to work out the physical location of the Web page file that the user is requesting so that it can send that page to the browser. To do this, it maps each *virtual directory* to a *physical directory* on the Web server machine:

❑ The virtual directory structure is the structure that the end user sees when they browse the pages of the Web site though a browser.

❑ The physical directory structure is the actual folder structure that is used on the Web server's hard disk for organizing and storing the pages and resources of the Web site.

Each virtual directory is just the "alias" of a physical directory. Use this mapping of virtual directories to physical ones to place the Web site's source files in the most convenient place on your Web server, and to hide your Web server's physical organization from end users.

For the examples in this book, you are using the built-in Web server that comes with either Windows 2000 Professional or Windows XP Professional, called Microsoft IIS or Internet Information Services. If you set it up as directed in Chapter 1, you have a directory called C:\inetpub\wwwroot. This directory is the Web server's root directory, and Windows handles the mapping from the physical to the virtual directory automatically. For example, say the page `welcome.htm` is stored in the physical directory `C:\inetpub\wwwroot\cookingplace`. Users visit the page by browsing to it using its virtual directory `http://localhost/`. If you are a beginner to this technology, this is the simplest and most straightforward way to handle things.

In the following exercise, your machine takes on three roles at once:

❑ **Local:** This is where you create and edit the Web site's files.

❑ **Testing Server:** This is the server that allows you to test server-side behaviors (discussed later in the book) and to see your Web site as the visitors will.

❑ **Remote Server:** This is where the files eventually end up so that your intended audience can access the Web site.

For the purposes of this book you are mainly concerned with the first two of these functions. But you can instruct Dreamweaver to update the testing and remote servers automatically whenever you edit files locally.

With this in mind, you can go ahead and use Dreamweaver MX 2004 to create your Cooking Place Web site. You need to specify both the physical location for the Web page files (on the Web server) and the virtual location by which you'll test them in a Web browser.

The Site Definition Feature

To help you create a Web site, Dreamweaver MX 2004 provides the Site Definition dialog boxes. This feature has two modes, Basic and Advanced:

❑ Basic mode comes in the form of a wizard that walks you through the process of creating a site.

❑ If you want a little more exposure to the terminology, use the Advanced mode, which gives you a little more control and flexibility over creating your site.

Use the Advanced mode; it's not that difficult and it gives you a chance to get a good feel for what it is you're actually creating. It's easy to relate the features of the Advanced mode to the Basic mode, too.

Try It Out   Creating a New Web Site

1. Start Dreamweaver MX 2004, if you haven't already. Choose Site⇨Manage Sites from the menu. This brings up the Manage Sites dialog box, as shown in Figure 2-1.

Figure 2-1

2. Click New. You are given the choice between setting up a new site or an FTP (File Transfer Protocol) or RDS (Remote Development Service) connection. For our purposes, just select Site. The Site Definition Wizard appears, as shown in Figure 2-2.

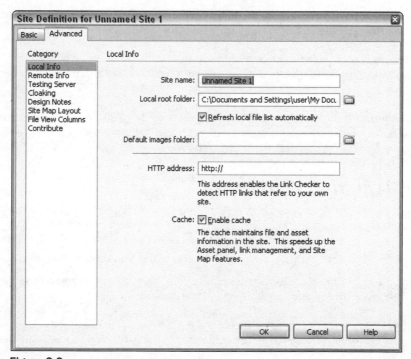

Figure 2-2

3. There are two tabs in this dialog box, representing the two different ways you can define a site. You can either use the Basic tab (which starts a Wizard that walks you through it) or you can use the Advanced tab and enter your own specifications. Make sure the Advanced tab is selected.

4. Make sure the Local Info category is selected on the left of the dialog box. Set the Site Name as **TheCookingPlace**. (Do not use any spaces; they could cause problems under certain circumstances.)

To set the local root folder, click on the Browse button to the right of the Local Root Folder field and navigate back to the root of your disk drive—say, C:\. (The field may have a default location, such as www\inetpub\wwwroot. Ignore this for now.) Click the Create New Folder button and call the new folder **TheCookingPlace** too. Select that folder and click Select.

To set the default images folder, click on the Browse button to the right of the Default Images Folder text box and navigate to the C:\TheCookingPlace folder you just created. Click the Create New Folder button and call the new folder **images**. Select that folder and click Select.

Set the HTTP Address field to **http://<your-test-server>/TheCookingPlace**, where *<your-test-server>* is the Web address of the Web server you're using to test the Web site. (For example, if you used the Web address http://localhost/welcome.htm for the example in Chapter 1, type **http://localhost/TheCookingPlace** here.)

Leave the Refresh Local File List Automatically and the Cache options checked, so the dialog box looks like the one in Figure 2-3. Don't click OK yet.

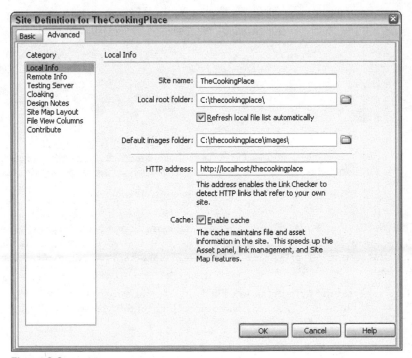

Figure 2-3

5. Click the Remote Info category on the left. You'll see a drop-down list called Access. Change its value from None to Local/Network; some extra fields will appear. To set the Remote Folder field, use the Browse button to navigate to the folder on your Web server's hard disk that is the root of the Web server (if you're using IIS, this will be C:\inetpub\wwwroot unless you've changed it elsewhere). Use the Create New Folder button to add a folder called **TheCookingPlace** and select that folder.

Make sure the Refresh Remote File List Automatically option is checked and that the Automatically Upload Files to Server on Save option is also checked. The dialog box looks like the one shown in Figure 2-4. Don't click OK yet.

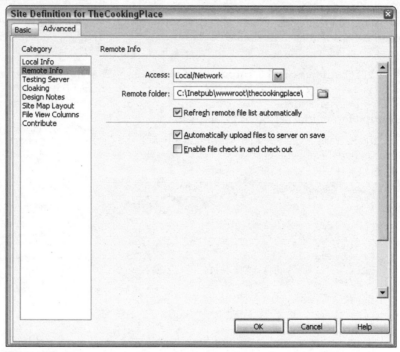

Figure 2-4

6. Click the Testing Server category on the left. Set the Server Model to None. Again, change the Access drop-down list's value from None to Local/Network; some extra fields will appear. This time, the Testing Server Folder and URL Prefix values should automatically be filled in for you, as shown in Figure 2-5.

7. Make sure that the Refresh Remote File List Automatically option is selected and then click OK. This creates the site in Dreamweaver. Select Done on the Manage Sites dialog box.

8. To see the site you just created, select the Site panel from the Files panel group. (If you can't see this panel, press F8 to make it appear.) If you do not see something similar to Figure 2-6, select Local View in the right drop-down box.

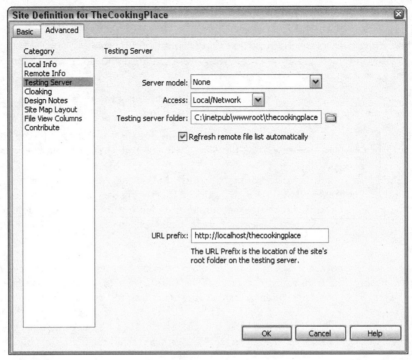

Figure 2-5

Figure 2-6

How It Works

You just configured your Cooking Place Web site. The first thing you need to understand is the significance of all the folders you created.

Some of the folders you created are used for building the Web site and some are used for testing it:

❑ The *local machine* is the machine that you use for building the Web site. This is usually the machine on which Dreamweaver is running. Configure your local machine in Step 4, using the settings in the Local Info category.

❑ The *remote server* is the Web server you use to publishing the Web site (so that users can see it). Configure your remote machine in Step 5, using the settings in the Remote Info category.

❑ The *testing server* is a Web server you can use specifically for testing the Web site as you build it. Configure your testing server in Step 6, using the settings in the Testing Server category.

Here's the usual way how this works: You create and edit the pages of your Web site on the local machine and then Dreamweaver uploads the work to the testing server so you can test it. When you're happy with it, you upload it to the remote server, after which it is live (and accessible to viewers worldwide). In this case, you set the remote server to be a local Web server and, by default, the testing server configuration adopts the same settings.

> It's okay to run Dreamweaver MX 2004 and IIS Web server on the same machine; it simply means that your local machine and testing server are one and the same. To keep them distinct, use different physical folders to keep the "local" (site-building) and "testing" (site-testing) elements distinct.

Look at your local machine settings first. In Step 4, you set the Local Root Folder to `C:\TheCookingPlace`. This is simply a physical folder in which you store a local copy of all the Web site's files.

Build a subfolder structure beneath that. (For Web sites that have more than a few files, this is a good idea.) In fact, Dreamweaver MX 2004 starts off by allowing you to create a folder especially for your Web site's images files. You chose the folder `C:\TheCookingPlace\images` for this purpose. You can see this folder structure in the Site panel, as shown in Figure 2-6.

Now look at the "remote" and "testing" server settings.

As we stated earlier, you are going to ask your machine to do triple duty here. In most cases, the "real world" scenario would have the local files and testing server on the same machine and the remote, or working, server located in a different location. When you define a site, as you did in this exercise, you define the physical location where the files end up locally and on each of the servers. In most cases, you want the folder structure on each of the servers to mirror the folder structure of the local site files. If you don't do this, you could encounter path problems with your links. Dreamweaver handles this mirroring process for you.

By setting the testing (and, in your example, the remote) folder to `C:\inetpub\wwwroot\TheCooking Place`, you're saying that this is the physical directory for the root folder of the Web site. In other words, this is the physical location where you want the server to store all the Web site's files and subfolders.

When you create your first Web page (later in this section), Dreamweaver saves a local copy of the page at `C:\TheCookingPlace` and also uploads a remote copy of the page to `C:\inetpub\wwwroot\TheCookingPlace` (so that you can see it in a Web browser). In addition, to preserve the mirroring, it creates the image subfolder on the remote server and transfers any images you saved in it. That way, the integrity of the links is maintained.

As an exercise, change the view in the Files panel from local view to either remote or testing views. You should see that the folder structure has been copied automatically, as shown in Figure 2-7.

Figure 2-7

If you do not see it in the Files panel, you may need to return to the local view and select the Put icon. This forces Dreamweaver to copy the site structure and files to a remote server.

We've talked about the root physical directory being `C:\inetpub\wwwroot\TheCookingPlace`. The root virtual directory is `http://localhost/TheCookingPlace`. In other words . . .

❑   The physical path of every file in your Web site begins with `C:\inetpub\wwwroot\TheCookingPlace`.

❑   The virtual path of every file in your Web site will begin `http://localhost/TheCookingPlace`.

Now return to the Basic mode of the Site Definition tool again. You can do this by returning to the Manage Sites dialog box (which you can get to through the Site menu selection), selecting thecooking-place, and then selecting Edit. The Test URL feature of this wizard allows you to test your testing server connection and URL parameters.

Even if you used the Advanced mode to create the site definition, you can switch back to the Basic mode at any time to check the settings. You simply click on the Basic tab and step though the wizard, accepting all the steps (which will assume the values you set in the Advanced tab). After a few steps of the wizard, you get to the Site Definition screen shown in Figure 2-8.

Click the Test URL button to test the connection to the testing server. It should return a message indicating that the URL prefix connected and tested successfully.

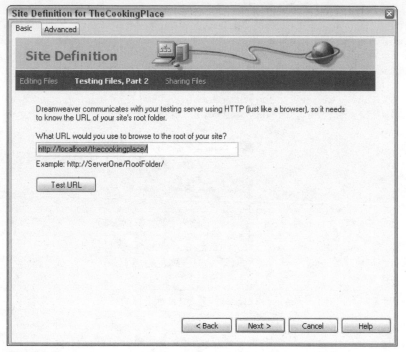

Figure 2-8

Creating a Web Page

Now you have defined a Web site. In fact, Dreamweaver MX 2004 has created a local version (for building) and a remote version (for testing). For the "remote" version, it has configured both physical and virtual directories.

Now create your first Web page. Because The Cooking Place contains a number of Web pages, which share the same design, what you'll do is spend the rest of this chapter creating one page, and then use it to create the other pages. We discuss the design shortly; first, create a page, save it, and make sure you can see it on your test server.

Try It Out	Creating Your First Web Page

1. Select File⇨New to bring up the New Document dialog box, as shown in Figure 2-9. You want to create a simple HTML page, so select Basic Page in the left-hand column, and then select HTML in the right-hand column. Also click the Make Document XHTML Compliant option. Click Create to create the page.

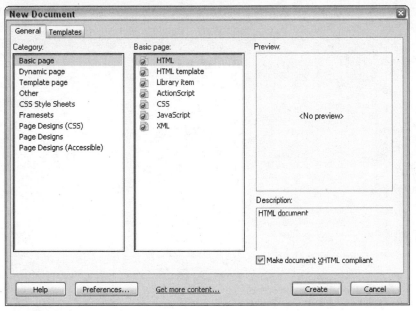

Figure 2-9

2. An untitled page document appears in the Dreamweaver workspace. Click on the Design View button and then select Modify⇨Page Properties from the menu (or Page Properties in the Property inspector) to bring up the Page Properties dialog box shown in Figure 2-10.

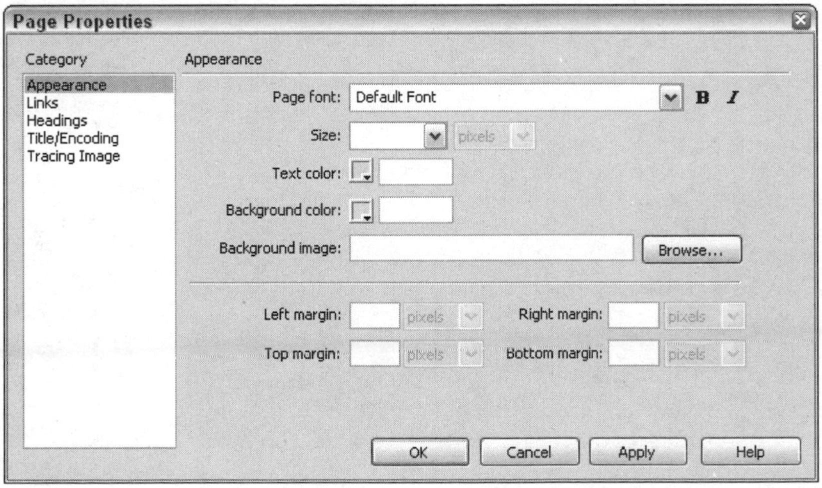

Figure 2-10

3. Click the Appearance category and change the settings to reflect Figure 2-11.

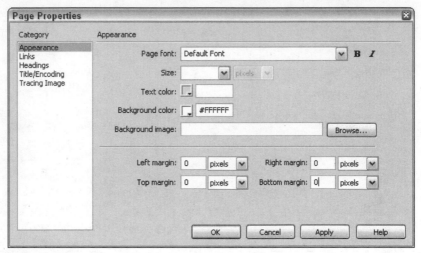

Figure 2-11

4. Click the Title/Encoding category and type **The Cooking Place – Home Page** in the title field.

5. Click OK to save your changes.

6. Select File⇨Save As to save the file. Select the folder C:\TheCookingPlace and name the file index.htm, as shown in Figure 2-12.

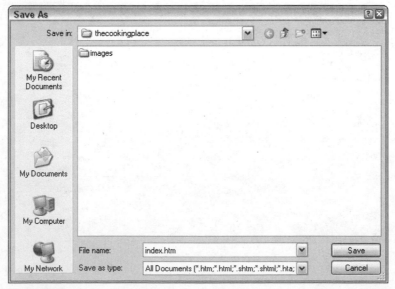

Figure 2-12

After you click Save, the tab located on the upper left of your document reflects the name you used.

7. Click on the page (say, `This is our home page`), as shown in Figure 2-13, to test the page. Then select File⇨Save to save the changes.

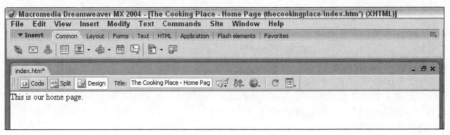

Figure 2-13

8. To test the file in your primary browser, press F12; to test it in a secondary browser, press Ctrl+F12. You may see the Dependent Files dialog box shown in Figure 2-14. (If you don't, do not worry about it.)

Figure 2-14

The Dependent Files dialog box informs you that the version of `index.htm` saved on the local machine is about to be uploaded to the testing server. (If the testing server is on the same physical machine as the local version, Dreamweaver will upload a copy from `C:\TheCookingPlace` to the Web server's physical directory at `C:\inetpub\wwwroot\TheCookingPlace`). You should be the only person working on this page at the moment, so click Yes to proceed. (You can click the Don't Show Me option before clicking Yes to avoid seeing the same warning in the future.)

If you see a dialog box asking you whether to include dependent files, click Yes again. Dreamweaver uploads a copy of `index.htm` to the testing server. Then it opens a browser window, shown in Figure 2-15, and requests the page from the testing server.

Figure 2-15

How It Works

Here you created a simple HTML Web page and saved it within the C:\TheCookingPlace folder on the local machine. When you made the request to preview the page in the Web browser, Dreamweaver did some work in the background:

1. It uploaded the file from the local machine to the testing server.

2. It opened a browser and requested the page from the Web server on the testing server.

You can see the location of index.htm by using the Site panel in the Files panel group. With TheCookingPlace Web site selected in the left drop-down list, and Local View selected in the right-hand list, you can see the page index.htm displayed under the root of the Web site (next to the Images folder), as shown in Figure 2-16.

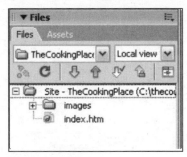

Figure 2-16

If you select Testing Server in the right-hand list, as shown in Figure 2-17, you see the index.htm copy that Dreamweaver MX 2004 uploaded to the testing server.

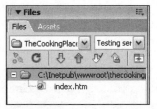

Figure 2-17

It's worth mentioning the Page Properties dialog box again. If you have used past versions of Dreamweaver, you will notice that this dialog box has been completely redesigned from the one-screen format to show categories. In this dialog box, you can set the values of certain properties of the page, including background colors, link colors, and so on. You make use of this dialog box again in subsequent chapters. Here you just use it to set the title of the page (this is the value that appears in the browser's title bar); you also set the page's margins.

Setting these values to 0 is not the same as leaving these values empty. If you were to leave these values blank, the browser would use its own default values for the settings. You can't be certain that all browser types use the same default values, so it's better to specify values explicitly here, thereby exerting some control over these values and the overall look of the page.

You may notice that, when you edit in the document window, an asterisk appears in the title bar and in the name tab of the window. This indicates that changes have been made since the last time you saved the page.

In this exercise, you used Design view to enter the test text for the page. If you switch from Design view to Code view in Dreamweaver MX 2004 (using the Show Code View button, as you did in Chapter 1), you'll be able to see the HTML that was generated in this page:

```
<?xml version="1.0" encoding="iso-8859-1"?>
<!DOCTYPE html PUBLIC "-//W3C//DTD XHTML 1.0 Transitional//EN"
"http://www.w3.org/TR/xhtml1/DTD/xhtml1-transitional.dtd">
<html xmlns="http://www.w3.org/1999/xhtml">
<head>
<title>The Cooking Place - Home Page</title>
<meta http-equiv="Content-Type" content="text/html; charset=iso-8859-1" />
<style type="text/css">
<!-
body {
    background-color: #FFFFFF;
    margin-left: 0px;
    margin-top: 0px;
    margin-right: 0px;
    margin-bottom: 0px;
}
-->
</style></head>

<body>
This is our home page.
</body>
</html>
```

Dreamweaver placed the page's title between the <title> and </title> tags that are embedded within the <header> and </head> tags. Within the same <head> tags you will see one of Dreamweaver's new features: *styles*. We will be discussing styles much more in Chapter 4. However, a short discussion is in order here.

In the early days of Web design, the structural and stylistic elements of a page were loosely intermingled with the use of attributes within the structural tags. For example, the margin and background color attributes were part of the <body> tag. However, newer technological demands call for the separation of stylistic elements from structural ones. Beginning with Dreamweaver MX 2004, that need is accommodated in the code it produces.

The power of Dreamweaver MX 2004 is that you can produce sophisticated Web applications with very little coding. If you don't feel confident with XHTML or other languages, don't worry! Dreamweaver handles most of the details for you. You will, however, gain more and more knowledge as you proceed.

> **A brief word about the XHTML setting. Think of XHTML as a very precise version of HTML.**

Fortunately, Web browsers are generally very forgiving about strong rules of syntax. However, the Web is moving, in general, toward more structured data, XML, and XHTML. In addition, many of the newer "appliances" that can access the Internet (cell phones, PDAs, and so on) require very precise syntax in their coding. By clicking the Make Document XHTML Compliant option, you are simply asking Dreamweaver to create HTML that adheres to the syntax rules of XHTML, which means being more attentive to matching start- and end-tags, and to nesting elements properly.

Extensive discussion of XHTML and XML is beyond the scope of this book, but for more information go to www.w3schools.com/xhtml.

Adding Metadata and Header Information

You want potential visitors to be able to find your Web site when you release it. One way that visitors can find your site is through a search engine such as Google (www.google.com). For that to work, it's a good idea to help the search engines find your site so that they can collect information about what your site is about.

The simplest way to maximize the likelihood that your Web page will be listed by search engines is to include special descriptive data in the header of each page. This type of descriptive information is broadly referred to as *metadata*, or "data about data." You can provide keywords, titles, and descriptions, which help search engine users evaluate whether your page is the one they're looking for.

Try It Out   **Adding Metadata to a Web Page**

1. To have Dreamweaver MX 2004 assist you in entering keywords select Insert⇨HTML⇨Head Tags⇨Keywords.

As with many of the commands you learn, you can add this command to the Favorites panel of the Insert panel group, as discussed in Chapter 1.

2. In the resulting Keywords dialog box, shown in Figure 2-18, enter the keywords you want to use for the site.

Figure 2-18

Separate consecutive keywords (or phrases) with a comma. When you have finished, click OK.

The main search engines provide guidelines about what keywords are good ones to choose and how many to include. When you create your own Web site, visit the search engines you're interested in and check out their FAQs. We will not discuss keyword selection theory here; the keywords above will do for your purposes. For more information about getting your pages indexed by search engines, check out the guidelines provided by the search engines themselves. For example, for information about how Google works, visit `www.google.com/intl/mt/Webmasters/faq.html`.

3. Many search engines use a description of the site. You can have Dreamweaver assist you in this by selecting Insert⇨HTML⇨Head Tags⇨Description. This opens the Description dialog box, shown in Figure 2-19, into which you can type a description of the Web site.

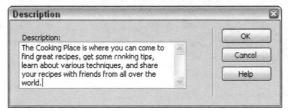

Figure 2-19

Click OK when you've finished.

How It Works

You just added keywords and a description to your Web page document. If you switch to Code view, you can see what Dreamweaver has done behind the scenes. Dreamweaver took all the information you entered in the Keywords and Description dialog boxes and placed it inside `meta` tags nested between the `<head>` and `</head>` tags (usually after the style sheet information), as follows:

```
<meta name="Keywords" content="cooking, food, ... , cooking equipment" />
<meta name="Description" content="The Cooking Place is where ... all over the
world. " />
```

There is one `meta` tag for the `Keywords` information and another for the `Description` text (as indicated by the `name` attributes of the two tags). Search engines employ *spiders* to index Web sites. These are programs that catalog sites and follow links from one site to the next. When a spider examines your page, it does not look at the whole page. It looks only at these `meta` tags and it uses the `content` that it finds in these tags to index your page. Thus, when a user types the phrase **cooking equipment** into a search engine, it might return a link to your site, along with the site description that you've supplied.

Building the Page Design

The remainder of this chapter covers building a design for your Web pages. Our aim is to build a very flexible page design. In particular:

❑ You want to use the same design for a number of different pages. Each of those pages may contain different types or amounts of content. But if your design is sufficiently flexible, you can use it for all these pages and achieve a consistent look and feel across the entire site.

❑ Because you don't know what size the visitor's browser window is, you have no control over their screen resolution. You need your page to look attractive regardless of the window size and resolution they choose (within reason, of course).

To create your graphical design, use images and build it using a *table structure*. Tables allow you to position images precisely in relation to one another so that the overall graphical effect of the page is always the same. Figure 2-20 shows a preview of the page design you will build by the end of this chapter.

Figure 2-20

Use tables within tables to give your design as much flexibility as possible. That way, if you need to expand the contents of a page, the table expands right along with it. In the process, it may seem like you are doing some odd things. However, if you follow these steps through to the end, it will all come together and make sense.

The Table Structure

This design looks complex and ambitious but it's actually not that difficult. The trick is to break it down into portions that are manageable and easy to control. Use a table structure to achieve this. Start out with three tables, stacked on top of each other, so that the page resembles Figure 2-21.

Most of this is fairly simple to do. There is one complex cell—the left side of the middle table—whose positioning you control using a nested table technique.

Figure 2-21

Browser Compatibility

The Cooking Place project was tested using Internet Explorer 6 and Netscape 7. There are some compatibility problems between the code used here and earlier versions of Netscape. Unfortunately, it is beyond the scope of this book to discuss all of the compatibility issues with HTML code and earlier browsers.

Dreamweaver helps you out a bit with the Browser Target Check located on the Document toolbar. If something is not compatible with a particular browser, you will see the icon shown in Figure 2-22.

Figure 2-22

Set this toolbar to flag code that may not be compatible with certain target browsers. For example, click the Browser Target Check button (shown in Figure 2-22) and select Settings to see the Target Browsers dialog box shown in Figure 2-23.

Figure 2-23

53

Select the minimum versions of Internet Explorer, Netscape, or Opera for which you want to test. For example, if you test for Netscape Navigator 4.0, Dreamweaver MX 2004 checks compatibility with Navigator 4.0 and all later versions of Netscape.

If you select OK and then click Browser Target Check again, make sure that Auto-Check on Open is selected (shown in Figure 2-24). This scans the code each time the document is open. If you want to check compatibility at any other time, you need to manually select the icon. Dreamweaver does not check code continually.

Figure 2-24

Select Check Browser Support to scan your code. Then open the menu again and select Show All Errors. This returns the panel shown in Figure 2-25, which shows you the document, line number, and error.

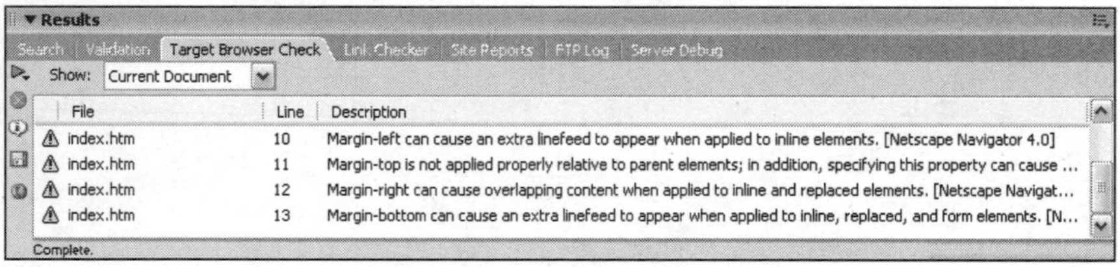

Figure 2-25

Double-clicking one of the error messages takes you to the code and displays the problem area with a red wavy line underneath. Rolling your mouse over the wavy line brings up a tooltip that tells you what the problem is.

In real life you should test against as many browser versions as possible because you want to accommodate as wide an audience as is feasible. Dreamweaver can help you out a great deal and, as you progress through the book, you will learn about other aids as well.

Preparing the Workspace

There are a couple of things you need to do before you start building a page. First, make sure you have the image files you need in the page design. Second, set up the page window so that it is representative of a user's browser.

Preparing the Workspace

1. Make sure you have the image files at hand. If you have not done so already, go to the Wrox Press Web site (www.wrox.com) and download the source files that accompany this book. They come in a .zip file; unpack them to a location on the hard drive of your local machine (the machine on which you're running Dreamweaver MX 2004).

2. In Dreamweaver, look at the Files panel in the Files panel group (press F8 to bring it up if it's not available in the panels area). In the left drop-down list, select Local Disk (C:). You should see the contents of your local drive in much the same way as in Windows Explorer, as shown in Figure 2-26. Expand the folder you unloaded the .zip file and maneuver to the images subfolder for Chapter 2.

Figure 2-26

    Select all of the image files in this folder. Drag the files to the images subfolder of your Web site. Dreamweaver displays a little + symbol to indicate you are copying these files from one place to another. If for some reason you find it inconvenient to work in the Files panel, you can just as easily transfer these files using Windows Explorer.

3. Change the Files panel back to The Cooking Place using the left drop-down list. You should see all the files that were copied to the images folder.

4. Set the Design view to emulate Web page dimensions. In order to use this feature, do *not* maximize your Design view. If it is maximized, click the Restore Down button in the middle (see Figure 2-27) to take it out of that mode.

Figure 2-27

5. The bottom section of the Design window is called the status bar. On the right side, you should see the present dimensions with a small downward arrow just to the right. Click that arrow and you'll see the Web Page Dimensions drop-down list, shown in Figure 2-28. Select 760 × 420 (800 × 600, Maximized).

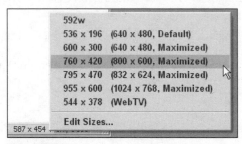

Figure 2-28

This adjusts the size of the pane to reflect a maximized window on an 800 × 600 pixel screen. (If the sizes are grayed out, the document window is still in maximized mode.)

How It Works

As far as the image files are concerned, there is little to explain here; you're simply placing image files within the structure of your site so that you can begin to build Web pages that contain these images. This isn't particularly interesting by itself but it's essential for what you do in the remainder of this chapter and section.

The reason for changing the size of the Web page pane is a little more interesting. As you design your Web page, it is important to take into account the equipment that will be used by your site's audience. In particular, keep in mind certain restrictions about what screen resolution a visitor is likely to use. The most common combination you'll encounter is an 800 × 600 pixel screen resolution (which means that the screen display consists of 800 pixels horizontally and 600 pixels vertically). If the browser is maximized to a screen of this resolution, the border takes up some of this area and the remaining area is estimated to be around 760 × 420 pixels.

You can't gain any control over the user's screen resolution but you can use this setting to simulate the size of the window and thus gauge your design against a reasonably-sized window on the user's screen.

You don't have to keep the pane at this size. As you proceed, it's quite possible you'll want to adjust the size of the pane in order to see other panes, or just to make the workspace more manageable. Simply remember that whenever you want to compare your design against an expected browser window size, use the Window Size drop-down list to try it out in various sizes.

You can also create customized sizes for highly precise needs. When you click on the Dimensions drop-down list, the last selection is Edit Sizes, which brings you the Status Bar category of the Preferences dialog box, shown in Figure 2-29.

Click on any of the sizes it to accommodate special sizes, should the need arise.

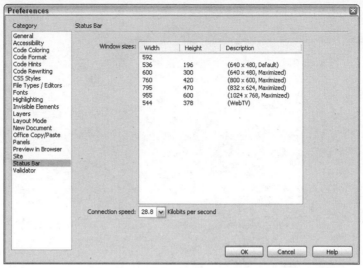

Figure 2-29

Building the Top Table

As you have seen, there are three tables in your page design. Start building the first of these tables.

Try It Out   **Creating an HTML Table**

1. Make sure you look at the document window in Design view. Delete the text
This is our home page that you placed in the page to test it earlier in the chapter.

2. Select the Common panel in the Insert panel group. Select the Table button, as shown in
Figure 2-30.

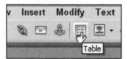

Figure 2-30

This brings up the Table dialog box. Specify that you want to add a table containing one row
and two columns, as shown in Figure 2-31.

Set the other fields in this dialog box to the values shown here and click OK.

3. The dialog box disappears, leaving you with the full-width table in the Design view of the
index.htm page, as shown in Figure 2-32.

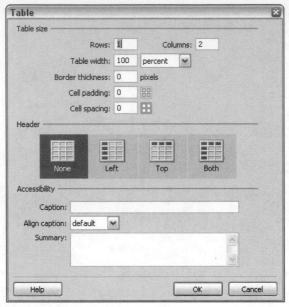

Figure 2-31

Figure 2-32

The Property inspector also changes to reflect the fact that the table is the thing that's currently selected. Note the Table ID caption in the top left of the Property inspector, shown in Figure 2-33, which tells you that these are the properties of a table.

If you see only the top half of the Property inspector, you can expand it by clicking on the small arrow, pointing downward on the lower right-hand side of the panel.

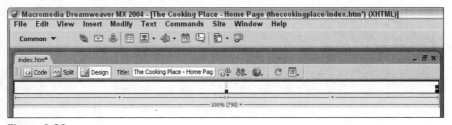

Figure 2-33

Use the Property inspector to adjust the properties of whatever item on the page is currently selected. Right now it displays properties of the table; anytime you check or edit the table's properties, select the table and use the Property inspector.

4. The width of the table is shown underneath it in the document window. You may find this a little confusing in this exercise. You can shut it off by selecting View➪Visual Aids➪Table Widths.

5. Don't adjust the table's properties further; just check the properties of the two cells of this table.

Select the left cell by clicking inside the cell (so that the cursor flashes at the left end of the left cell). The Property inspector now shows the properties for that cell. Use the Property inspector to set the cell's width to 50 percent, as shown in Figure 2-34.

Figure 2-34

If you left the Table Width Visual Aid turned on, you should see 50 percent under the left cell as well as the pixel width.

Select the right cell by clicking inside the cell (so that the cursor is flashing at the left end of the right cell). Use the Property inspector to set this cell's width to 50 percent.

How It Works

This doesn't look like much so far but it's a good time to take a break and see what you've done. Switch to the Code view and you'll see that Dreamweaver has added some new HTML to the body of the page within the `<body>`...`</body>` tags:

```
<table width="100%" border="0" cellspacing="0" cellpadding="0">
  <tr>
    <td width="50%"> </td>
    <td width="50%"> </td>
  </tr>
</table>
```

What you've added is an *HTML table*. You can see an opening `<table>` tag and a closing `</table>` tag; the table is completely described by the elements and tags contained between these two tags. In the opening `<table>` tag, see the table's `width`, `border`, `cellspacing`, and `cellpadding` settings that you specified in the Table dialog box:

❑ When you set the table's `width`, you have two choices:

❑ You can use an absolute value (in pixels). Do this when you want the table to be the same size, regardless of the size of the user's browser.

❑ You can specify a percentage (as you've done here). This is a percentage of the width of the element in which the table is contained. In this case, the table is contained just inside the body of the page and has a width of 100 percent, so this table will always adopt a width of 100 percent of the page's width.

❑ The border setting controls the thickness of the line used to separate neighboring cells in the table. By setting the border to 0, you ensure that these borderlines are invisible (Remember from earlier that 0 and blank are not the same thing. Blank means the Web browser is free to make its own choices).

❑ The cellpadding defines the amount of room there is between the border of a cell and its contents, and cellspacing defines the distance between neighboring cells. You want zero spacing and padding here because you intend to place images into all these cells and you want them to be placed flush to one another to create the overall effect of the graphic.

What about the rows and columns of the table? In HTML, the structure of a table is described in terms of rows and cells (not rows and columns) and this detail is embedded within the <table>...</table> tags:

❑ Each <tr>...</tr> pair represents one row of the table.

❑ Inside each row that, each <td>...</td> pair represents one cell of the row.

Rows and cells are specified from top to bottom, and from left to right, as you would expect. You can see that there is just one row and that it contains two cells. You can also see where you explicitly set the width of each cell to 50 percent of the total width of the row; this is represented in the HTML by the attribute width="50%".

Finally, notice that each cell contains the expression . This is the HTML code for a nonbreaking space. Dreamweaver places a space character into each cell by default to maintain the integrity of the table structure. As soon as you add content to the cell, this placeholder is replaced.

Adding Content to the Top Table

Place the necessary images and text into this table. Form here on, you'll really see the page design come to life.

Adding Content to a Table

1. Ensure that the Files panel (within the Files panel group) is visible. Click on the images folder for TheCookingPlace Web site, shown in Figure 2-35, to reveal the image files that you placed there earlier in this chapter. You'll make use of this in a moment.

Figure 2-35

2. Make sure you view the `index.htm` page in Design view. Select the table. The easiest way to do this is to click inside the left cell of the table and then select the `<table>` tag on the tag selector (in the bottom-left corner of the Design view pane, as shown in Figure 2-36).

Figure 2-36

3. The Property inspector has fields for handling the table's background image, color, and border. To the right of the background image (Bg Image) field there are two icons: a yellow file folder and a circle (see Figure 2-37).

Figure 2-37

The circle is called the Point to File tool. Use it to point to the file you want to use as the table's background. Click on the Point to File icon and, *holding down the mouse button,* move the mouse across to the Site panel and hold it over the image file called `topbkg.gif`. Release the mouse button. In Design view, the table should go black.

4. Insert an image in the left cell. Click inside the left cell; you should see the cursor flashing at the left end of the left cell.

5. To place an image in the cell, click on the Images icon on the Common panel of the Insert panel group, as shown in Figure 2-38.

Figure 2-38

6. Use the resulting Select Image Source dialog box, shown in Figure 2-39, to browse to the images folder and select the file `topleft.gif`. If you wish, you can preview it within the dialog box by clicking the Preview Images option.

This dialog box also gives you the dimensions, size, and download time of the image. Select OK when you're done. Now your Design view should look like Figure 2-40.

You can also drag-and-drop the file name from the Files panel. For consistency in this book, we use the technique just described. However, the other is just as correct and can be used at any time.

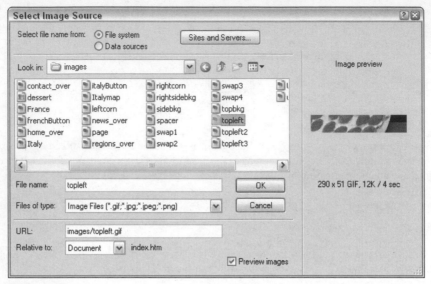

Figure 2-39

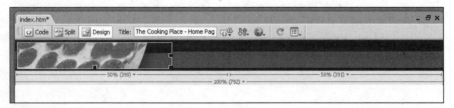

Figure 2-40

7. Add some content to the right cell. Click inside the right cell (you should see the cursor flashing at the left end of the right cell) and type the words **The Cooking Place**. This text doesn't look very special yet but you can fix it in the Property inspector.

8. With the mouse highlight the text you just typed. Using the Property inspector, change the font from "Default Font" to "Arial, Helvetica, Sans-Serif" and change the size from None to 36 pixels.

Make your text white so it stands out better against the red and black background. To do this, click the square Text Color icon (just to the right of the Size drop-down list) and select the white color from the color selector dialog box that appears, as shown in Figure 2-41.

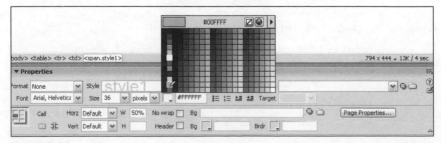

Figure 2-41

With the text still selected, click the B button to make the text bold and click the center alignment button. The result should look like what you see in Figure 2-42.

Figure 2-42

9. Save your file (by choosing File⇨Save or pressing Ctrl+S) and then preview it in a browser by pressing F12 or Ctrl+F12. What you see should look like what appears in Figure 2-43.

Figure 2-43

You face two potential problems here:

If your images do not appear in the Web browser, click on the Put button in the Files panel. This forces your image files to upload to the test server.

If you have trouble rendering this in Netscape, it may be related to an XHTML instruction that Dreamweaver inserts in the document. To resolve this situation, switch to the Code view and delete the following line of code (which you'll find it near the top of the file):

```
<!DOCTYPE html PUBLIC "-//W3C//DTD XHTML 1.0 Transitional//EN"
         "http://www.w3.org/TR/xhtml1/DTD/xhtml1-transitional.dtd">
```

How It Works

You first inserted a background image (in this case, a simple black image) for the table. This image acts as a background for every cell in the table. When you insert a background image like this, the browser uses the image as if it were a *tile*, repeating it horizontally and vertically so that the entire specified area is covered. That way, if the table needs to expand or contract, the image adjusts with it. This is good for flexibility. (Since it is a solid image, you won't see any actual tiling effect.)

Adding an image to a cell works differently; no tiling effect is used. The image placed into the left cell, containing the pizza and the red stripe, is displayed over the background image. In the right cell the text you've inserted also appears over the table's background.

If you switch to the Code view, you can see the code that has been added:

```
body {
  background-color: #FFFFFF;
  margin-left: 0px;
```

```
      margin-top: 0px;
      margin-right: 0px;
      margin-bottom: 0px;
   }
   .style2 {
      color: #FFFFFF;
      font-family: Arial, Helvetica, sans-serif;
      font-size: 36px;
   }
   -->
   </style></head>

   <body>
   <table width="100%"  border="0" background="images/topbkg.gif">
     <tr>
       <td width="50%"><img src="images/topleft.gif" width="290" height="44" /></td>
       <td width="50%"><span class="style2">The Cooking Place</span> </td>
     </tr>
   </table>
```

If you have used previous versions of Dreamweaver, you will see a lot of new code here. You can see the style sheet, `.style1`, which was set up to accommodate the text formatting in the table. You have a more extensive discussion of styles in Chapter 4. However, a brief discussion of styles is in order here. Styles are a way of formatting outside of HTML. As you will see, a style gives you a lot of design flexibility. In this case, the style sheet applies the settings of the style to a specific group of words.

As you learn in Chapter 4, the style is called a *class*, and Dreamweaver is giving it the default name of `style1`. It is attached to the `<span>` element as follows:

```
<span class="style2">
```

See the `<img>` tag in the first (left) cell for the pizza image. The source file for the image is specified by the src attribute (`src="images/topleft.gif"`).

It's worth mentioning the tag selector again because it is a particularly handy tool. We've talked about HTML tags being nested within other tags. The tag selector shows you the nesting hierarchy at the position currently occupied by the cursor. For example, when the cursor is in the left cell of the table shown in the preceding code, the tag selector looks like what you see in Figure 2-44.

Figure 2-44

Perhaps the best way to read this display is from right to left: The cursor is currently inside the `<img>` tag, which is embedded inside a `<td>` tag, which is embedded within a `<tr>` tag, which is inside the `<table>` tag, which is embedded within the `<body>` tag. One useful feature of this tool is that it allows you to change the focus. For example, to select the entire table in which this cell lives, simply click `<table>` on the tag selector.

When you build a table design like this, it's generally recommended that you first build your table structure and add your background images before adding any foreground content to the table cells. If you add foreground content too soon, Dreamweaver may add extra spacing that causes the page to render improperly in the browser.

Building the Middle Table

You've completed the top table of your three-table page design. Now you can move on to the most complex one, the middle table. This table has one row of three cells, and some of those cells contain smaller, nested tables. There are quite a few steps here, but this exercise serves as a good way to practice the techniques you've already seen in this chapter. We strongly suggest you do this exercise slowly and pay attention to all the steps. If you make a mistake, the rest of the exercise may not function correctly.

Try It Out   **Building the Middle Table**

1. Switch your `index.htm` pane back to Design view and click underneath the table that you've put there. The tag selector will show just a `<body>` tag to show that the cursor is placed inside the page body but outside the table.

2. Click the Table button (in the Common panel of the Insert panel group) or select Insert⇨Table from the menu. In the resulting Table dialog box, shown in Figure 2-45, set the table to have one row, three columns, and 100 percent width. Leave the other attributes set to 0.

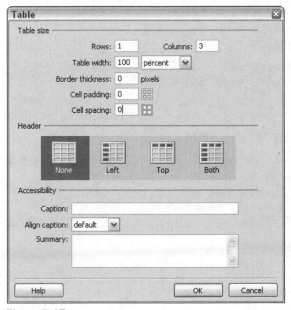

Figure 2-45

When you click OK, the new table should appear in Design view, right under the existing table.

3. Now use the Property inspector to set "temporary" widths of the three cells in the table. Click inside the left-hand cell. Using the Property inspector, change the cell's width (the W field) to 20 percent, as shown in Figure 2-46.

Figure 2-46

In the same way, click inside the middle cell and set its width to 60 percent. Click inside the right-hand cell and set its width to 20 percent.

You are doing this in order for the table to retain its structure while you work on it. If you do not do this, the cells may collapse, making them difficult to work with when you add graphics.

4. Handle each of the three cells one at a time. Start by completing the content of the right-hand cell. You have only four things to do:

    1. Set its background image to `rightsidebkg.gif`. To do this, place your cursor in the cell to select it, find the Bg property in the Property inspector, and click on the Point to File icon next to it. Hold the mouse button down and move the mouse so that it is over the file `rightsidebkg.gif` (in the `images` folder in the Site panel). Release the mouse button. The cell turns red.

    2. Insert the same file as the "foreground" image. To do this, make sure the cursor is inside the cell and click the Image button in the Common panel (in the Insert panel group). In the resulting dialog box, select `rightsidebkg.gif` from the `images` folder and click OK.

    3. Click on the image. (It should be selected after you insert it. If it isn't, you might find it easy to select the <img> tag using the tag selector.) Using the Property inspector, change the image's width to 24 pixels, as shown in Figure 2-47.

Figure 2-47

    4. Use the tag selector to select the <td> tag for this cell and change its width from 20 percent to 1 percent.

If it seems strange to add the same image as both background and content, there is a good reason for it. By putting the background image in the cell, you ensure that the entire cell is colored red. By also putting the image in the "foreground," you force the cell to have a nonzero width. This is important because you will not always be sure of the width of the content that goes in the middle cell. If the middle cell gets too wide, then the right-hand cell will narrow itself to compensate. By placing an image as content into the cell, you can stop the browser from squeezing the cell to zero width, just to make room for a greedy middle cell.

5. Turn now to the left-hand cell; there's much more to do here. First, set the background image to `sidebkg.gif` (using the same technique you used a moment ago). The cell turns red. Set the vertical alignment field to Top. You may see a slight gap in the cell's right margin. Don't worry about this now; it will rectify itself as you progress.

Change the width of this cell from 20% to 257 pixels. This ensures that the cell's width remains at 257 pixels (and does not adjust itself the way a percentage-width cell does).

The Property inspector for the left-hand cell should look like it does in Figure 2-48.

Figure 2-48

6. Insert a small table within this cell. With your cursor inside the left-hand cell, click the Insert Table button and specify the following values to create a one-row, one-column table, as shown in Figure 2-49.

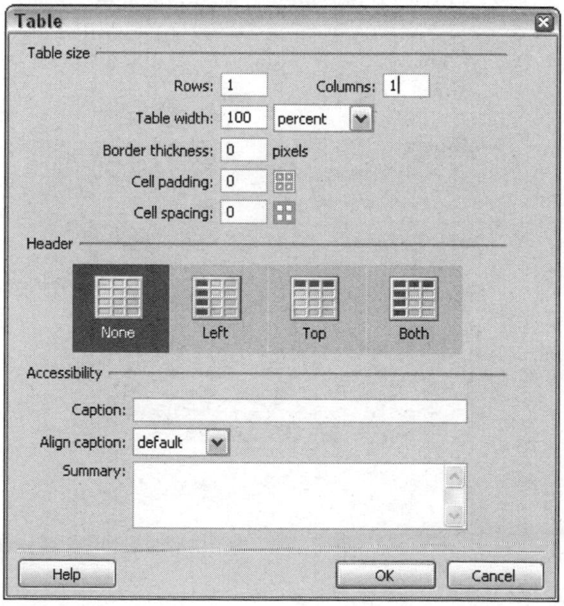

Figure 2-49

The left-hand cell should look like what appears in Figure 2-50, with the smaller one-cell table highlighted inside it.

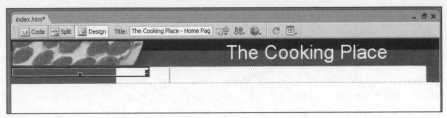

Figure 2-50

7. Place your cursor inside the single cell of this small table. To check that the cursor is in the right place, the tag selector should resemble Figure 2-51.

Figure 2-51

Click the Images button (in the Common panel of the Insert panel group) and select the image file `topleft2.gif`. This places another segment of pizza into the single cell of this small table.

8. To complete the pizza, you need one more table in the left-hand cell, just below the one you created. The tricky bit is placing the cursor in the right position to add the second table. To do it right, click the image you just inserted and then use the tag selector to select the small nested table, as shown in Figure 2-52.

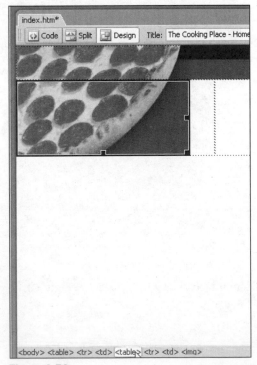

Figure 2-52

Click the Insert Table button and add a one-row, two-column table, as shown in Figure 2-53.

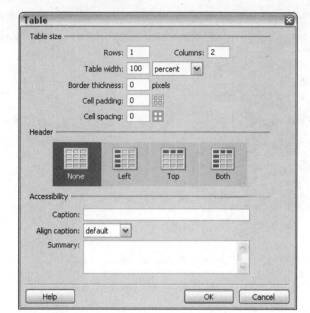

Figure 2-53

Dreamweaver automatically inserts this table beneath the selected one, which is exactly what you want.

9. Set the Width of each of these two cells to 50 percent and set their vertical alignment to Top.

Set the background image of the first of the two cells to `rightsidebkg.gif` (using the Point to File icon). Then use the Image button to insert the image `topleft3.gif` to complete the pizza image.

Select the second of these two cells and use the Image button to insert `page.gif`. This file is deliberately elongated in order to force the table to expand. Hence, you use the size of the graphics to force the table layout, as shown in Figure 2-54.

10. You are now ready to insert four navigation buttons. Eventually, these four buttons will be used as links to take the user to different pages within the site. For now, just insert four images as placeholders.

Start by getting the cursor into the right place. Click on the `topleft3.gif` image (that's the bottom bit of pizza) and press the down arrow key on the keyboard. There's nothing below this image, so Dreamweaver places the cursor immediately to the right of the image; you should see it flashing there.

This technique is used often when a graphic occupies an entire cell.

11. Press Shift+Enter to insert a line break inside the cell so that the cursor is just below the pizza image. Click the Images button (in the Common panel of the Insert panel group) and insert the image `buttonblank.gif`.

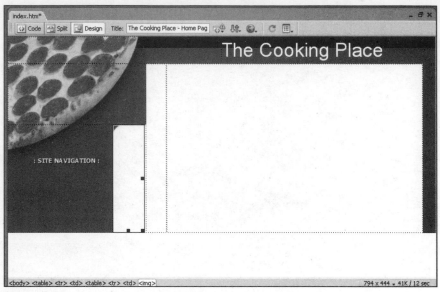

Figure 2-54

12. Repeat Step 11 three times. You should have four images in total, as shown in Figure 2-55.

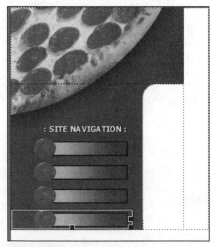

Figure 2-55

Notice that your table expanded as you added more buttons. You get this flexibility from the nature of your table design. This completes the left-hand cell of the table.

13. Now you can deal with the middle cell—that's the big white one in the middle of your page. This time, you embed just one smaller table within it. Before you do so, however, ensure that the embedded table is flush against the top of this cell. To do that, click inside the middle cell and go to the Property inspector to set the vertical alignment to Top.

Set the final width of this cell. Use the Property inspector to change it from 60 percent to 99 percent.

14. With the cursor still inside the middle cell, use the Insert Table dialog box to insert a table that has one row, three columns, width equal to 100 percent, and all other settings equal to 0. Apply the following settings for the three cells of this new table:

❑ Set the width of the left-hand cell to 1 percent and set its vertical (Vert) alignment to Top.

❑ Set the width of the right-hand cell to 1 percent and set its vertical (Vert) alignment to Top. Also set its horizontal (Horiz) alignment to Right.

❑ Set the width of the middle cell to 98 percent.

Figure 2-56 shows you what it should look like at this stage.

Figure 2-56

15. Place the cursor in the first of these three small cells (it's perhaps easiest to place the cursor in the middle small cell and then press the left arrow button on the keyboard) and use the Image button to insert the image `leftcorn.gif`.

Place the cursor in the last of these three small cells (again, place the cursor in the middle small cell and press the right arrow button on the keyboard) and use the Images button to insert the image `rightcorn.gif`, as shown in Figure 2-57.

Figure 2-57

That's it! The second table of your three-table structure is complete.

How It Works

There is very little new to describe here. As well as putting together the second table in the three-table structure, you got familiar with the idea of placing the cursor in the right place (using the Design view of the page) and then adding new elements or adjusting properties. The one new thing you've seen is the notion of nested tables—one table inside another. If you look at Code view you can see how this works.

The following code shows the big three-cell table that you just created. The overall code is abridged in places because what's most interesting here is the overall structure and the nesting:

```
<table width="100%" border="0" cellspacing="0" cellpadding="0">
  <tr>
    <td width="33%" valign="top" background="images/sidebkg.gif">
      <table width="100%" border="0" cellspacing="0" cellpadding="0">
        row and cell structure for table nested within left-hand cell

      </table>
      <table width="100%" border="0" cellspacing="0" cellpadding="0">
        row and cell structure for table nested within left-hand cell

      </table>
    </td>
    <td width="99%" valign="top">
      <table width="100%" border="0" cellspacing="0" cellpadding="0">
        row and cell structure for table nested within middle cell

      </tr>
      </table>
    </td>
    <td width="2%" background="images/rightsidebkg.gif">
      img tag for image contained in right-hand cell

    </td>
  </tr>
</table>
```

Nesting tables is clear. The smaller, nested table is entirely contained within the <td>...</td> tags of a cell in a larger table. You can even nest two tables in the same cell, one after the other.

Building the Bottom Table

After the tricky exercise of building the middle table, the bottom one should be very easy.

Try It Out   **Building the Bottom Table**

1.   Switch the index.htm pane back to Design view and click underneath the existing structure. There's nothing in the page below the second table, so Dreamweaver places the cursor immediately to the right of the second table. Again, you see the cursor flashing at the right of the table and the tag selector shows just <body> to show that the cursor is placed inside the page body but outside the table.

2.   Click the Insert Table button to create a one-row, two-column table with width 100 percent. Set the border, cellpadding, and cellspacing to 0.

3.   With this new table selected, use the Property inspector to set its background image to bot-bkg.gif (use the Point to File icon again). You will not see a change in the Design view from this step, but that's OK.

4.   Click inside the left cell. Using the Property inspector, set its width to 50 percent. Click the Image button (in the Common panel of the Insert panel group) and insert the image botleft.gif.

5. Click inside the right cell and use the Property inspector to set its width to 50 percent; also click on the Align Right button, as shown in Figure 2-58.

Figure 2-58

Now use the Image button to insert the image botright.gif in this cell. The design is now complete.

6. Save your work and preview it in the Web browser. It should look like what you see in Figure 2-59.

Figure 2-59

How It Works

That's it. Notice that as you resize the browser window to make it wider, the page design automatically adjusts itself to fill the width of the page. That's because you set the width of the three big tables in your design to 100 percent. This means they fill 100 percent of the width of the element in which they are contained. The immediate container of each of these tables is the page body itself:

```
<body leftmargin="0" topmargin="0" marginwidth="0" marginheight="0">
    <table width="100%" border="0" cellpadding="0" cellspacing="0"
        background="images/topbkg.gif">
    ...tags to describe top table...
```

```
    </table>
    <table width="100%" border="0" cellspacing="0" cellpadding="0">
      ...tags to describe middle table...

    </table>
    <table width="100%" border="0" cellpadding="0" cellspacing="0"
          background="images/botbkg.gif">
      ...tags to describe bottom table...

    </table>
  </body>
```

Hence, these tables take 100 percent width of the page body.

Summary

In this chapter, you created your first Web site and began to build a Web page within it. You went through a number of important configuration steps in setting up Dreamweaver to build your site. In all, Dreamweaver managed three copies of the site on your behalf:

❏   One on the local machine, which is the one you use for building pages

❏   One on a remote server, which can, eventually, be the "live" server—the one exposed to the Internet that responds to page requests from visitors

❏   One on a test server, which you use for testing pages using the Preview in Browser option or pressing F12 or Ctrl+F12

With that in place, you were in a position to begin building. You used HTML <table> tags to structure your page. As you saw, HTML tables appear to have rows and columns, but the reality is subtly different. In fact, each table is composed of rows and each row is composed of cells; the columns result from this structure in a natural way.

You used three tables to break the page down into three layers (top, middle, and bottom). This allowed you to split the top and bottom "layers" into two sections, and the middle "layer" into three sections. In the middle table, which was the most complex, you used table nesting (nesting a smaller table within a cell of a larger table) to achieve a high level of control over positioning elements within sections of the page.

Dreamweaver's workspace features help you to create pages and tables. This means you can create attractive, complex designs very quickly, without the need to type many lines of code. You built the whole page simply by putting the cursor in the right place, adding the elements, and setting the properties as you needed them. You didn't need to type a single line of code.

The images for this page were created in Fireworks MX, which is the graphic editor of the Macromedia Studio MX suite. They were then sliced into smaller images for easy handling and faster loading. It is beyond the scope of this book to discuss how these images were created.

In Chapter 3, you're going to take this basic page design and apply it to a number of different pages. You'll create some simple client-side effects and do some more work on the navigational buttons of the pages.

Why Not Try . . .

Take a copy of index.htm (right-click the file in the Site panel and select Duplicate; then right-click the new duplicate file and rename it from "Copy of index.htm" to temporary.htm). Experiment with this file. Use Design view to add some text to the large white space in the middle of the page. Use the Property inspector to add some styles—change the font and font size, use bold or italic, and so on. Don't worry about making mistakes. You don't use temporary.htm elsewhere in the book.

Site Structure, Navigation, and Content

In Chapter 2, you got off to a rousing good start by creating your Web site and building up a single document that contains the fundamental design of your pages. In this chapter, you build on that foundation by creating a number of pages, each of which uses this basic design. Once you create a few pages, you'll see that it becomes necessary to create some sort of mechanism to help users to find their way around your site. Such a navigational tool closely reflects the overall purpose of your site.

It's important for developers to find their way around the site structure, so you'll learn about Dreamweaver's site map facility. Finally, you'll add some text and images to your pages, as well as hyperlinks to enrich the user experience.

In this chapter, you do the following:

❑ Create some pages for your Web site.

❑ Build a simple navigation system for your Web site to allow visitors to find their way around it.

❑ Employ some simple client-side effects within the navigation buttons.

❑ See how Dreamweaver allows you to keep track of the site's structure.

❑ Add some content to the pages in your site.

Along the way, you will come across a concept that is very important in Web development—specifically in terms of creating features using client-side functionality. That concept is known as *behaviors*, and you'll put it to good use as you build your navigation bar.

Site Structure and Navigation

Right now your Web site contains just a single page—the index.htm page you built in Chapter 2. During the course of this chapter and the next few chapters, you're going to add more pages to your site. Many of these pages contain hyperlinks to other pages within the site, links that allow visitors to jump from one part of the site to another.

As you add more pages and hyperlinks to the site, the overall structure of the site is likely to get more complex. There is a danger of it getting too complex, so that . . .

❑ You (as the Web developer) find it increasingly difficult to maintain the site.

❑ Your visitors find it difficult to understand the structure of the site and find their way around it.

You want to avoid these situations, of course! The following section sets up a simple navigation system that reflects the structure and content of your site so that visitors can find their way around easily. Dreamweaver also helps you visualize the network of pages and hyperlinks in the site.

Expanding the Site

Before we immerse you in a discussion of site structure and navigation, create a few more pages to work with. The index.htm page you created in Chapter 2 has a page structure you want to use in the other pages on your site. This exercise takes advantage of the work you've done so far to create a couple more pages.

Try It Out   **Duplicating Files in Dreamweaver**

1. Open Dreamweaver MX 2004. By default, it always opens to the last site you worked on. If you have not done anything else since the last chapter, you should be in The Cooking Place site. If not, select your local copy of The Cooking Place site, by using the drop-down lists in the Site panel of the Files panel group (see Figure 3-1).

Figure 3-1

Make a copy of index.htm to keep as a backup. To do this, right-click the file in the File panel and select Edit⇨Duplicate. Then right-click the new file, select Edit⇨Rename, and change its name from Copy of index.htm to index_backup.htm. (You can also duplicate the file by selecting the file and pressing Ctrl+D. Rename the file by selecting the file and pressing F2.) You don't need the file here but you will need it in Chapter 4 when you study templates.

2. You need a total of three pages that use the page design you built in `index.htm`. For now, the easiest way to copy that page design is to make duplicates of `index.htm` and rename those copies.

3. Repeat Step 2 twice to create two additional files: `regions.htm` and `news.htm`. Now you should see four `.htm` files in the Files panel, as shown in Figure 3-2.

Figure 3-2

How It Works

You simply used the Duplicate mechanism to create two copies of `index.htm`. You now have four Web page files in your site: `index.htm`, `index_backup.htm`, `news.htm`, and `regions.htm`. At the moment they all contain identical page structures. If you like, you can preview any of them in the browser or open them in Dreamweaver to view them in Design view or Code view.

Building a Navigation System

Your Web site consists of a set of related Web pages. In order to help visitors to find their way around these pages, you need to build a *navigation system*. A good navigation system fulfills at least three distinct responsibilities. It helps the visitor in the following ways:

❑ Establish what is available within the Web site

❑ Know where they are within the structure of the Web site

❑ Navigate to other parts of the Web site

A fundamental concept here is the notion of a *link* or *hyperlink*—an image or fragment of text that visitors click so the browser requests a different page. This is the usual means by which visitors find their way around any Web site. You should arrange hyperlinks in your pages to make the structure and navigation as clear and easy as possible.

Many Web sites employ *drill-down navigation* techniques to organize their content. For example, a visitor searching your Web site for information on, say, recipes of northern Italy would first arrive at your home page. From that page, they would "drill down" to a page that lists the different cuisines that you cover. From there, they might go to a page devoted to generic Italian recipes; and from there, you might provide specific pages for different regions of Italy, which would allow the visitor to drill down even further.

Some Web sites have a fairly "flat" structure, where most pages are accessible directly from the home page and very little drilling down is required. Other Web sites have a narrower, deeper structure, with the potential for very deep drilling down.

For some Web sites, a few well-placed buttons are enough to allow users to find their way around the site.

There are many other things you can do. For instance, your site will display a map of Italy, with the map divided into (invisible) regions that, when clicked, bring visitors to a page on your site devoted to recipes from that region. This is called *image mapping* and you look at this technique in Chapter 5.

Your navigation system should give readers a visual indication of where the currently displayed page sits within the context of the site. Often, you can do that simply by repeating the navigation buttons on every page of the site and changing the color of the button that represents the page currently on display. This gives visitors a visual cue as to which page they are on.

Some sites use *breadcrumbs*. This is where a page shows the path that the visitor traces to get where they are, rather like leaving a trail of breadcrumbs. This establishes a set of links, so that visitors can retrace their steps. Go to www.yahoo.com and click a Web Site Directory category to see the breadcrumb at the top of the page (for example, `Directory > Computers and Internet > Internet > World Wide Web`).

> *It is beyond the scope of this book to discuss the coding necessary to create breadcrumbs. However, it is possible to build breadcrumbs with relative ease using the appropriate Dreamweaver extension. Extensions provide additional functionality over and above what Dreamweaver does out of the box. There are many extensions available from a number of sources, including Macromedia (see www.macromedia.com/exchange/). We cover extensions more thoroughly in Chapter 18.*

Implementing Navigation Buttons

The basis of your site navigation mechanism in The Cooking Place are the four buttons you added to your page design in Chapter 2. Each button represents a different section of the site. The labels on these buttons are Home, News, Regions, and Contact Us. Each Web page will shows these four buttons so that whichever page visitors land on, they can navigate to other areas of the site quickly and easily.

As we've said, a good navigation system should also help visitors know where they are within a site, so you also need a way to distinguish the "current page" button from the others. Take this opportunity to use a simple client-side *rollover effect* animation, which makes each button light up as the mouse rolls over it (while keeping the button relating to the current page lit). For example, on the News page the News button is permanently lit while the other buttons light up when the mouse moves over them, as shown in Figure 3-3.

This neat effect uses a programming language in the background called *JavaScript* to create this "behavior." Don't get scared! All you do is learn a few simple menu selections and Dreamweaver handles the complexity of inserting the code. You will learn more about behaviors in Chapter 5.

Figure 3-3

Try It Out   Creating a Navigation System

1.   Open `index.htm` in Dreamweaver and switch to Design view. The `index.htm` file is the home page of The Cooking Place site. When this page is displayed, you want the Home button to be permanently lit to indicate that this is the home page. To achieve this effect, select the first `buttonBlank.gif` image so that `<img>` is selected in the tag selector. In the Property inspector, change the Src setting from `images/buttonBlank.gif` to `images/home_over.gif` (you can use either the Point to File or the folder icon to change the image). The buttons in Design view should look like Figure 3-4.

Figure 3-4

2.   You want the other three buttons to behave differently on this page because they link to pages on your Web site. Each of these three buttons should have a rollover effect and a hyperlink. There are several ways to do this, and you'll employ one of those techniques here.

Select the second `buttonBlank.gif` image (the one just below the `home_over.gif` image) and delete it (just press the Delete key).

3.   From the menu bar, select Insert⇨Image Objects⇨Rollover Image. This brings up the Insert Rollover Image dialog box. Enter the values shown in Figure 3-5 into the fields in this dialog box. Use the Browse buttons provided to enter the values of the Original Image, Rollover Image, and When Clicked fields.

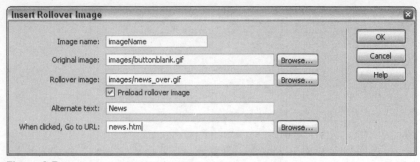

Figure 3-5

The Image Name field should use the exact capitalization indicated in Figure 3-5 because you will refer to this image by its image name in JavaScript code later in this chapter, and JavaScript is a case-sensitive language. It has become a programming standard to use all lowercase names and, in the event of multiple words, use midword capitalization. Notice that the file names of all your image files do not contain spaces. Image names become important if you need to reference them in your code (as you will do later) and file names with spaces can cause problems.

When you've done all that, click OK.

4. Save the file and view it in the browser (by pressing F12 or Ctrl+F12). When you roll your mouse over the second button, you should see it change from the plain button to one with the word "News" on it, as shown in Figure 3-6.

Figure 3-6

Notice that the graphic's alternate text appears when you mouse over the News button in Internet Explorer. (However, as of this printing, this does not happen in Netscape.)

5. Repeat Step 2 for the remaining two buttons. The third button is the Regions button, so you should set the values shown in Figure 3-7 in the Insert Rollover Image dialog box.

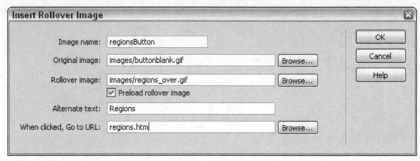

Figure 3-7

The final button is the Contact button. You'll do something a little different with this one. For the link, type in the string that points to your own personal e-mail address. Here we use `mailto: charles@thecookingplace.com`, as shown in Figure 3-8.

Figure 3-8

6. Save the file and try it in the browser again. This time when you click on Contact Us, it launches your e-mail software and addresses a new outgoing message to the specified e-mail address.

If for some reason you cannot see any of this in your browser, use the Put button located in the Files panel to copy the files to the server you're browsing.

How It Works

As far as the Home button on this page is concerned, there is nothing fancy happening at all. You simply placed the file `home_over.gif` in that location; `index.htm` displays `home_over.gif` at the top of the column of buttons all the time.

When the user clicks on this image, nothing happens because there's no hyperlink associated with it. That's because it usually doesn't make sense for a Web page to contain a link to itself. If you did so, clicking the button would simply load the same page already in the browser, which would be a pointless exercise.

What happens with the other three buttons is interesting. Look at the second one (the News button); the other two work the same way. For this button, there are two things to consider—the rollover effect and the hyperlink:

❑   When you first view this page in the browser, you see the `buttonblank.gif` image in this posi-
    tion. When you roll the mouse over that button, the browser swaps out `buttonblank.gif` and
    replaces it with `news_over.gif` (the two files are identical except that the latter includes the
    word "News" superimposed on the graphic).

❑   When you click on the image, you cause the browser to load `news.htm` from the Web server.

You can see the code for the News button yourself by switching to the Code view of `index.htm`. Notice that the News button is actually defined by an HTML `<img>` tag contained within an HTML `<a>...</a>` element, as follows:

```
<a href="news.htm" onmouseout="MM_swapImgRestore()"
    onmouseover="MM_swapImage('newsButton','','images/news_over.gif',1)">
   <img src="images/buttonblank.gif" alt="News" name="newsButton"
        width="181" height="31" border="0" id="newsButton" />
</a>
```

The `<a>...</a>` tags are HTML *anchor tags*; they create hyperlinks. If the user clicks on anything between the opening and closing `<a>` tags, the browser requests the Web page specified in the `<a>` tag's `href` attribute. If you click on the image here, the browser tries to request `news.htm` from the Web server.

That explains the hyperlink, but what about the rollover effect? You can't create a rollover effect simply using a markup language like HTML on its own. Rather, you need to make use of a procedural program-ming language. The language of choice for most browser effects (and other client-side processing) is JavaScript.

We cannot include an exhaustive discussion of JavaScript here. One of the best books on the subject is
Beginning JavaScript by Paul Wilton (Wrox Press). But we will show you the essence of the JavaScript
code that Dreamweaver generated when you followed the steps above.

The anchor tags in the preceding code contain two other attributes: `onmouseover` and `onmouseout`:

❑   The `onmouseover` attribute allows you to specify what should happen when the user's mouse
    pointer passes into the area containing the hyperlink.

❑   The `onmouseout` attribute allows you to specify what should happen when the user's mouse
    pointer passes outside the area containing the hyperlink.

As you can see, this code indicates that when the mouse pointer passes over the hyperlink area, the function `MM_swapImage(...)` should be executed. `MM_swapImage()` is a JavaScript function; if you like, you can see it for yourself in the Code view of `index.htm`. However, we will not show it here; Dreamweaver generates this code, arranges for the browser to replace one image with another.

Similarly, when the mouse passes outside the hyperlink area, the function `MM_swapImgRestore()` should be executed. This is another JavaScript function, which simply arranges for the browser to swap the two images back again.

Note that the `swapImage()` function makes use of the Image Name that you gave the button when you created this rollover effect. The button's name, `newsButton`, is the `MM_swapImage()` function's way of identifying which element of the page should be affected. It is for this reason that every such element in a page must have its own unique identity.

Finally, note that when you created each of these rollover effects, you opted to check the Preload Rollover Image option. There is a good reason for this. This option controls the point at which the `news_over.gif` image is downloaded from the Web server to the browser:

❑   By preloading the image, the browser has it ready and available whenever the user rolls the mouse pointer over the button.

❑   If you don't preload the image, the browser needs to load the image when it needs it—exactly when the visitor first rolls the mouse pointer over the button. The time it takes to load the image at that moment could delay the animation—possibly long enough to make it ineffective.

If the visitor has a slow connection, or if the image is very large, you might opt to uncheck this option and reduce the initial download time for the page. Most of the time, however, you will want this feature on.

We will discuss JavaScript behaviors much more in Chapter 5.

Try It Out   Configuring the Navigation Buttons on news.htm and regions.htm

You've learned how to replace one image with another, and how to set the rollover effect for buttons that link to other pages. Here you adjust the buttons in `news.htm` and `regions.htm` so they behave in a similar way to the buttons in `index.htm`:

1.   Repeat the process creating the rollover buttons you did in the previous Try It Out—this time, for `news.htm` and `regions.htm`. As you did with the home button on `index.htm`, make the button for that page just an image insertion and not a rollover. This shows your visitors what page they're on. This is the second button in `news.htm` and the third button in `regions.htm`.

2.   As we discussed in Chapter 1, and earlier in this chapter, the HTML should automatically be copied to the IIS Web server root directory, provided you selected the option in the site setup. However, should it not happen for some reason, you can easily remedy that by selecting the Put File(s) button located in the Files panel, as shown in Figure 3-9.

Figure 3-9

You get a confirmation dialog box asking if you want to include dependent files. You usually answer yes.

3. View `index.htm` in the browser. As you click on the different buttons, you'll be taken to the different pages you created.

How It Works

The technique you used here is exactly the same as the technique in `index.htm`. Now that you've employed it over a few pages, the overall effect that this has (in terms of allowing visitors to find their way around your Web site using these buttons) becomes clear.

Pop-up Menus

Earlier in the chapter, we mentioned the notion of drill-down navigation. This is one way to allow users to find their way to the information they seek on your site. It involves starting at a very general page and systematically narrowing in on the level of detail they desire by choosing successively more focused pages. In many cases you want your navigation buttons to allow that.

One way to achieve this is by using a *pop-up menu*. You can use a pop-up to show a hierarchy of successive levels of pages. The top-level menu appears when the visitor rolls the mouse pointer over some image; as the visitor rolls the mouse to select an item from that menu, a submenu appears to allow the user to drill down even further. In Figure 3-10, the Show Pop-Up Menu dialog box shows what options the visitor sees in the pop-up menu for the Italian top-level menu.

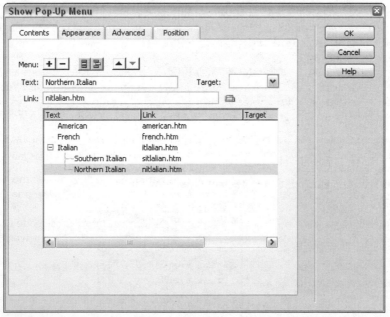

Figure 3-10

Macromedia Fireworks MX 2004 offers additional flexibility for creating dynamic pop-up menus. However, Dreamweaver MX 2004 does the job quite nicely!

Behaviors

If you build pop-up menus, you need to learn about *behaviors*. This term describes the idea that when something happens, you can react to it. In other words, when an event occurs, you can perform an action.

Behaviors come in two basic flavors: client-side and server-side. These names are pretty self-explanatory; they indicate where the JavaScript runs to cause these behaviors to happen.

You already saw some client-side behaviors in this chapter when you created the rollover effect for the Home, News, Regions, and Contact Us buttons on index.htm, news.htm, and regions.htm. For each button, you actually applied two behaviors to each <a> tag.

To see the code behind these behaviors, open index.htm in Dreamweaver, click inside the second button image, and use the tag selector to select the <a> tag. Switch to the Behaviors panel of the Tag panel group, as shown in Figure 3-11. (If you can't see this panel, press Shift+F3 to make it appear.)

Figure 3-11

You can see two client-side behaviors here. Each is the combination of an event and an action:

❑ When the onMouseOver event occurs (that is, when the user moves the mouse pointer into the area covered by the <a> tag), the browser reacts by running the Swap Image action.

❑ When the onMouseOut event occurs (that is, when the user moves the mouse pointer out of the area covered by the <a> tag), the browser reacts by running the Swap Image Restore action.

As you've already seen, each of these actions is a JavaScript function, whose code is contained within the page's HTML. You can see it by looking at the Code view of the page in Dreamweaver.

In the next exercise, you create a pop-up menu for the Regions button on the regions.htm page. As you see, this generates some more behaviors.

Try It Out — Creating a Pop-up Menu

1. Open the regions.htm file and switch to Design view.

2. Each component, or object, associated with a JavaScript program must have a unique name in order for JavaScript to refer to it properly. These names are case-sensitive and you will use the naming convention discussed earlier. To do this, click on the Regions button (the third of the four navigation buttons) and take a look at its properties in the Property inspector.

Here in the Property inspector, use the field shown in Figure 3-12 to assign the name **regionsButton** to the button.

Figure 3-12

3. Make sure the Regions image is still selected in Design view. Now attach a new behavior to the selected element. To do this, open the Behaviors panel (in the Tag panel group; press Shift+F3 if you like) and click the + button to add a behavior.

In the resulting menu, select Show Pop-Up Menu to open the Show Pop-Up Menu dialog box, as shown in Figure 3-13.

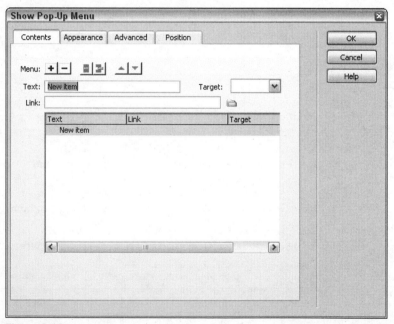

Figure 3-13

4. The Show Pop-Up Menu dialog box inserts the first pop-up menu entry for you. Change it so that the Text field contains the word **American** (this is the wording you want to appear in the menu) and the Link field contains **american.htm** (this is the Web page associated with that menu item—that is, the page you want visitors to go to as a result of selecting that menu item). You have not created this page yet, but you will later on. For the time being, just set up the link.

Click the + button to create a new menu item and insert the text and link (**French** and **french.htm**) for that item. Do the same for the third item (**Italian** and **italian.htm**).

For the fourth item, click the + button to create the new menu item and then click the Indent Item button, shown in Figure 3-14, to indent it. This makes it part of a submenu that appears under the Italian menu item, as you'll see shortly.

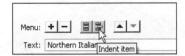

Figure 3-14

Insert the text (**Southern Italian**) and link (**sitalian.htm**) as you've done for the others.

If you didn't do so when you added the Italian link, click the + button and add the final item; set its text to **Northern Italian** and the link to **nitalian.htm**. This entry is created at the same level as Southern Italian, which is what you want. The whole dialog box now should look like what's shown in Figure 3-15.

Show Pop-Up Menu

| Contents | Appearance | Advanced | Position |

Menu:

Text: Northern Italian   Target:

Link: nitlalian.htm

Text	Link	Target
American	american.htm	
French	french.htm	
⊟ Italian	itlalian.htm	
Southern Italian	sitlalian.htm	
Northern Italian	nitlalian.htm	

OK

Cancel

Help

Figure 3-15

You don't need to insert anything into the Target field for any of these; we'll discuss that later. After you've added all five menu items, click OK to close the dialog box.

5. Save your `regions.htm` file and preview it in the browser. Watch what happens when your mouse rolls over the Regions button (see Figure 3-16).

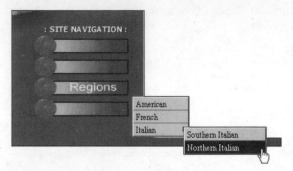

Figure 3-16

How It Works

You have created two behaviors here, an onMouseOver behavior and an onMouseOut behavior. This makes sense: The pop-up menu appears when the user rolls the mouse pointer over the Regions image and it disappears when the user rolls the mouse pointer away.

Because you added the pop-up menu, new behaviors were added. Click on the Regions button and look at the Behaviors panel, shown in Figure 3-17.

Figure 3-17

As you can see, the actions corresponding to these two events are different. This time when the onMouseOver event occurs, the browser is asked to respond by running the Show Pop-Up Menu action; when the onMouseOut event occurs, the browser is asked to respond by running the Hide Pop-Up Menu action.

As before, these two actions correspond to JavaScript functions in the page. This time they have the names MM_showMenu() and (slightly more obscurely) MM_start_Timeout(); if you're curious, you can see those functions if you go to the Code view of regions.htm. The great thing is that, once again, you don't have to write a single line of JavaScript code, nor a single HTML tag—Dreamweaver generates the whole thing for you.

You can easily edit the pop-up menu by simply double-clicking Show Pop-Up Menu in the Behaviors panel, as shown in Figure 3-18.

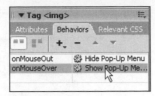

Figure 3-18

Discussion of these JavaScript functions is beyond the scope of this chapter; if you want to know more about JavaScript, try Beginning JavaScript by Paul Wilton (Wrox, 2003).

One final note: Notice that your pop-up menu does not match the colors or style of the rest of the Web page. At the end of this chapter, a little exercise will help you fix that.

Organizing the Site with the Files Panel

Up to this point, you have used the Files panel to do some file management of your site—moving, duplicating, and renaming files. Now that you have some additional files and navigation in your little Web site, this is a good time to take a closer look. You will learn the tremendous power that Dreamweaver gives you for managing sites.

Begin by taking a quick look at the buttons available in the panel's own toolbar (see Figure 3-19).

Figure 3-19

- ❏ The first button, Connects to Remote Host, allows you to connect to and disconnect from the remote server. This can be handy if you want to prevent accidental uploading of files to the server.

- ❏ The second button, Refresh, allows you to see the latest list of files in the view you have chosen. Occasionally things can get a little buggy when moving a lot of files between servers and the remote computer. It's a good idea to click Refresh from time to time to ensure that you are seeing correct results.

- ❏ The third button, Get File(s), retrieves files from the remote server and downloads them to the local site. If you have no files selected, it downloads the entire site.

- ❏ The fourth button is the counterpart of the previous button. The Put File(s) button uploads files from the local computer to the remote server. The mechanics of using this button is identical to the Get File(s) button.

- ❏ The fifth and sixth buttons pertain to file check out and check in. We will be talking about this a bit more later on. In short, they help the project manager find out who is working on what files and prevents simultaneous changes from happening.

With the View set to Local View, click the last button, Expand/Collapse, as shown in Figure 3-20.

Figure 3-20

This opens the panel to a full screen, as shown in Figure 3-21.

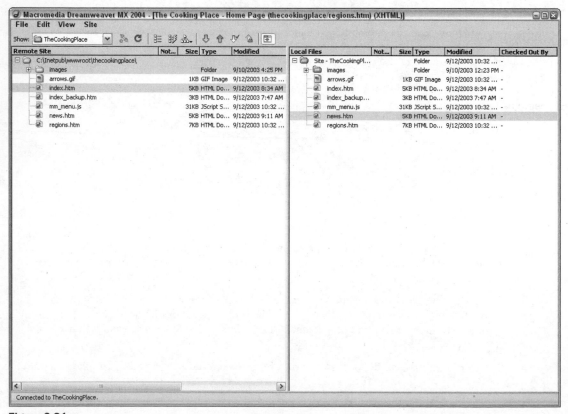

Figure 3-21

The screen is divided into two panes: The left pane gives you a view of the files located on the remote server, while the right pane shows the local view.

This is a great way to control the movement of files between the servers as well as comparing their structures. For example, you can select a file or folder on the remote side then drag it to the server side while seeing any resulting structural changes, if any.

You can also compare the local files with the testing server by clicking the Testing Server button, shown in Figure 3-22.

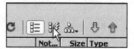

Figure 3-22

Notice that each pane is divided into columns. We will discuss the meaning of those columns in a bit. Although you will rarely need to do this, you can change the order, add, or delete columns. To do this, select Site⇨Manage Sites⇨The Cooking Place⇨Edit⇨Advanced⇨File View Columns, as shown in Figure 3-23.

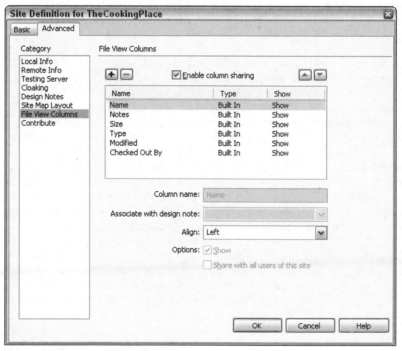

Figure 3-23

Site Synchronizing

Sometimes coordinating a site can be confusing, especially if it is a large site with many files. For example, you may forget to upload files to the necessary servers or, with very large projects, there may be teams of developers working in different locations. In all these cases, site synchronization helps you out.

You already did a bit of it when you set up the site and selected the option to automatically update the servers on save. There are some additional options too.

Select Site⇨Synchronize to see the Synchronize Files dialog box shown in Figure 3-24.

Figure 3-24

Here you fine-tune your synchronization. The first box gives you the option of synchronizing the entire site (which is what you would choose in most cases) or only certain selected files you would choose in the Files panel.

The second box allows you to decide the direction of the synchronization. This is especially handy if you have teams of developers uploading files from different locations.

You can put newer files onto the server, download newer files from the server to the local computer, or perform both operations in one shot. As we mentioned, if you have teams of developers in different locations, these options can coordinate an awful lot.

There is a check box that allows you to delete remote files that are not on the local drive. I would recommend that you use this option with caution. If you are a single developer who works with one computer, this is a great way to clean up garbage files that may be on the remote server. However, if there are teams of people working in different locations on your site, this could present a problem. Just because a file is not on your local computer does not mean it is not on another person's.

Start the process of synchronization by clicking the Preview button. This compares the files between the two servers and gives you a report as to which files will be moved. If no files need to be transferred, it reports that no synchronization is necessary. In most cases, you should get the No synchronization is necessary message, shown in Figure 3-25. This is because you have set your site for automatic synchronization.

Figure 3-25

If you do need to synchronize, however, the dialog box advises you of this and proceeds after you click OK.

The Site Map

The navigation buttons you've built so far in this chapter are specifically designed to help site visitors find their way around your site. Visitors tend not to think in terms of individual files, and links between files; rather, they think in terms of the different types of information that they require. Consequently, you must design your Web site's navigation system to address that point of view.

What about a navigational aid for developers? While you're building your Web site, it's often useful to have a visual representation of the files in the Web site and how they relate to one another. In the development process, you tend to think more in terms of individual files, so you need a rather different representation of the site's structure. To this end, Dreamweaver provides the *site map*.

Since your File panel should still be expanded, click the Site Map button, located in the toolbar (see Figure 3-26), and then select Map and Files. (You can actually select either Map or Map and Files. The second one is a little handier to work with.)

Figure 3-26

The result should resemble the screen shown in Figure 3-27.

Here you see the structure of your site. Unless you specify otherwise, Dreamweaver assumes that the home page for the Web site is index.htm and, therefore, it automatically puts index.htm at the top of the hierarchy. Dreamweaver then examines all the links contained in index.htm and represents those on the site map too. Thus, from the screenshot above, you can see that index.htm contains links to news.htm, regions.htm, and the mailto: link).

Notice that the direction of a hyperlink is represented by the arrowhead (so the preceding links are links from index.htm to news.htm, regions.htm, and mailto:).

To see what links are contained in the regions.htm page, simply click the + symbol on the left of the regions.htm icon in the site map. Figure 3-28 shows what you should see if you do that.

This confirms that regions.htm contains links to index.htm and news.htm Web pages, and a mailto: link.

> *You may also see a node named javascript:;. If you do, that's because Dreamweaver built the pop-up menu in regions.htm by wrapping the image in <a>...</a> tags, like this:*
>
> ```
> <a href="javascript:;" ... ><img src="..." /></a>
> ```
>
> *If you don't see this node in the site map, don't worry; it simply means that Dreamweaver has built the pop-up menu using a different (but equally valid) HTML technique.*

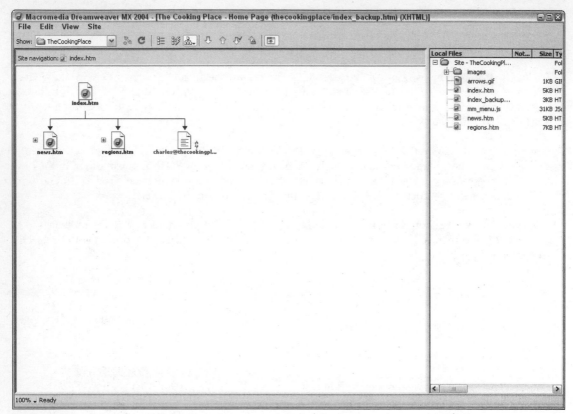

Figure 3-27

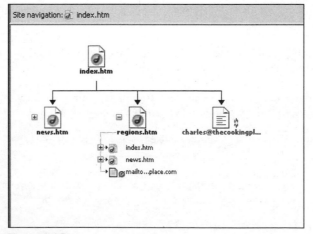

Figure 3-28

Although the site map is not the best way of creating links, it works well if you need to get the job done quickly.

Even though there is a link between `index.htm` and `regions.htm`, you can quickly create a secondary one using the site map. Simply click on `index.htm`, select the point-to-file icon to the right of `index.htm`, and drag a line to `regions.htm`, as shown in Figure 3-29.

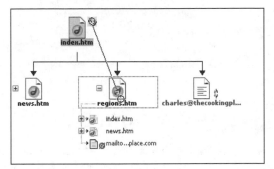

Figure 3-29

If you now open `index.htm`, shown in Figure 3-30, you see the link automatically created in the lower left corner.

Figure 3-30

As we stated earlier, this is not terribly sophisticated but it gets the job done if needed.

To delete this link, just highlight it in Design view and delete it as you would any other element.

When you are finished with your expanded Files panel/site map, return it back to the panel where it originally came from. Do *not* close this as you would close any other window, or else you'll exit Dreamweaver. Instead, click on the Expand/Collapse button again, as shown in Figure 3-31.

Figure 3-31

You should now be back to a normal Files panel.

Tools to Assist the Team

With the advent of increasingly complex technology, most Web sites are the result of a team effort. A good integrated development environment (IDE) has tools that not only help developers write the program but assist in the management and organization of the team. You have already seen some of Dreamweaver's tools, such as file synchronization, that assist the team. There are four other powerful tools that you have yet to look at: Check In/Out, Notes, Link Manager, and Site Reports.

Check In/Out

Imagine Jack Developer working on the `index.htm` file in New York. While he is working, Sally Designer decides to work on the same file in London. Sally does not know that Jack is working on the file. Jack may move a modified version of the file to the live site when he's finished. Sally is now working on an older version of the same file, so her work is wasted. Worse, she may upload a different version of the file to the site when she's finished, wiping out all of Jack's work. You can easily see where this could lead to a lot of confusion. Dreamweaver has a tool so that Sally can easily see that Jack is working on the file. That tool is called Check In/Out.

Before you can use the tool, however, it must be specifically activated for this Web site in the site definition panel you use to set up the site. Select Site➪Manage Sites➪The Cooking Place➪Edit.

Once you are there, go to the Advanced option and select the Remote Info Category, as shown in Figure 3-32.

Click the Enable File Check In and Check Out option.

When you check in or out, you are doing so from the remote server and are editing the file on the local machine. In order to identify yourself, you must give the local structure an identifier of some sort so that others can easily see who checked the files out. Dreamweaver asks you to enter your name and e-mail address.

There is also one option that you should use most of the time: Check Out Files When Opening. Normally, if Jack was opening `index.htm` on the remote server, there would be no indication that he'd opened the file until he physically indicated that he was working on the file. Jack may just be looking at the file and not actually doing any editing. With the Check Out Files When Opening option selected, however, the moment Jack opens that file, Dreamweaver will indicate that he has checked it out.

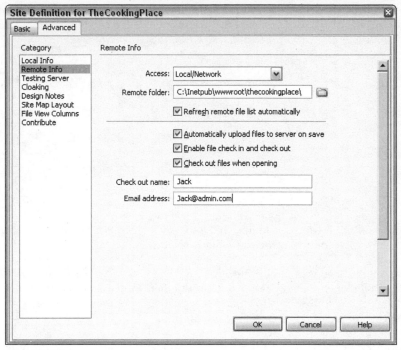

Figure 3-32

When you're done with this dialog box, click OK.

Assuming the automatic option was not selected, let's suppose you want to check out `index.htm`. Go to the Files panel, select the `index.htm` file, and click the Check Out button located on the panel's toolbar, as shown in Figure 3-33.

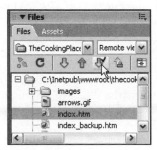

Figure 3-33

Dreamweaver asks if you want to check out any dependent files too, if any. As soon as you check the file out, a check mark appears next to the file in the Remote Server view. That file is now set to read-only mode for the other people who can access it. That way, there can be no scenarios as we discussed at the beginning of this section.

If you expand the panel, as you did earlier, you see the information shown in Figure 3-34.

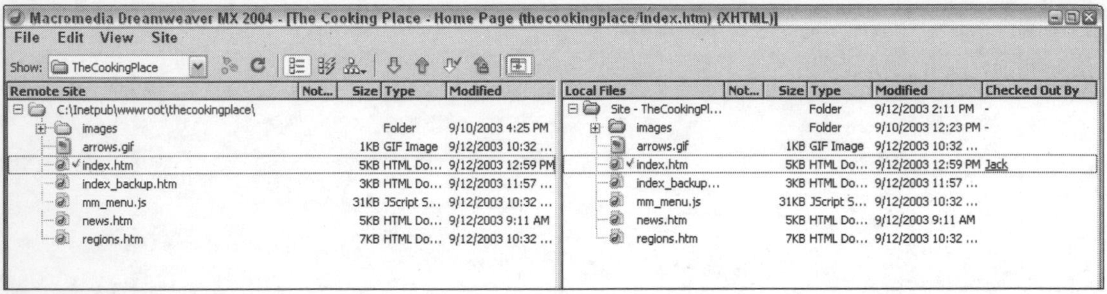

Figure 3-34

The file is checked out on both the remote and local sides. However, the local panel on the other developers' machines will also display the check mark, indicating that Jack checked the file out.

A word of caution: When you check a file out from the remote server, Dreamweaver locks the copy of the checked-out file on the remote server to prevent others from simultaneously editing the file. However, this lockout applies only to Dreamweaver. It does not prevent people with other HTML editors from getting to the file. Why is this important?

When you talk about checking out a file, you must familiarize yourself with the term *version control*. For the checkout process to be effective, everyone *must* edit *only* from the files on the remote server. Failing that, as we stated earlier, Jack could upload a file to the server and completely wipe out the work Sally had done to it earlier. To prevent that from happening, all members of the development team must play by the same rules. Unfortunately, while Dreamweaver has the ability to show that a file has been checked out, it does not effectively enforce the rules by preventing someone using different software from uploading a different version to the same remote server.

Here's another little quirk: If you work on a local version of the file, it prevents the remote server's version of the same file from checking out automatically when opening (even though that feature is selected). However, we strongly advise you *not* to use this as a version checking tool. It tends to be inconsistent.

While Check In/Out is an effective tool, do not use it as a replacement for good and enforceable project-management rules and guidelines. If you are going to use this as a project-management tool, you may want to turn off, in the site's definition, the ability to automatically upload a file upon saving. We strongly suggest you study the quirks of these features effectively before incorporating them into the workflow of your project.

Design Notes

For anyone who has done Web design, either with a team or as a single designer, notes play an important part in the process. If you are a member of a team, you may want to see what work was done previously to your own work. The needs for notes are numerous.

Dreamweaver helps you out with the Design Notes feature. It uploads the notes to the remote server so that other members of the team can access them. As you will see in a bit, Dreamweaver also has a tool to help you clean up those notes.

Before you get started with Design Notes, as with Check In/Out, you must activate the feature by using the Advanced tab in the Manage Site dialogue box. You can see in Figure 3-35 a category for Design Notes.

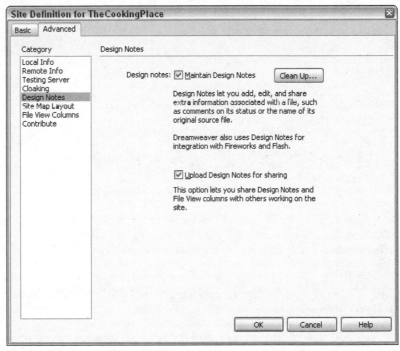

Figure 3-35

You need to click Maintain Design Notes to activate the feature. It is also a good idea, if you are working with a team, to select the option Uploading Design Notes for Sharing. That way, other members of the team can easily see them. If you are a sole designer, this option is not as important.

Since Dreamweaver uploads the notes as separate files, it is possible to have notes on files that no longer exist on the server. The Clean Up feature helps clean this problem up and eliminate unnecessary clutter on the server.

Once you click the feature on, using it is very easy. Open a note by selecting the file in the Files panel and either right-clicking and selecting Design Notes (you *must* be in Local view for this technique to work; design notes are unavailable in Remote view) or selecting File⇨Design Notes in the Files panel's menu bar. Either way, you get the Design Notes dialog box, shown in Figure 3-36.

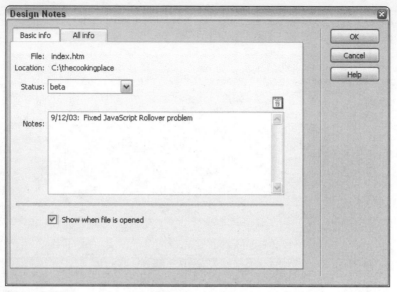

Figure 3-36

The Status field allows you to select a category for your notes, and the Date icon allows you to add a date automatically. In addition, you can force any other designers on your team to read the notes by selecting the Show When File Is Opened option. This automatically opens the notes when a designer accesses the file.

Many designers like to use the All Info tab, shown in Figure 3-37. This allows you to insert additional notes by using the + button and to add additional categories.

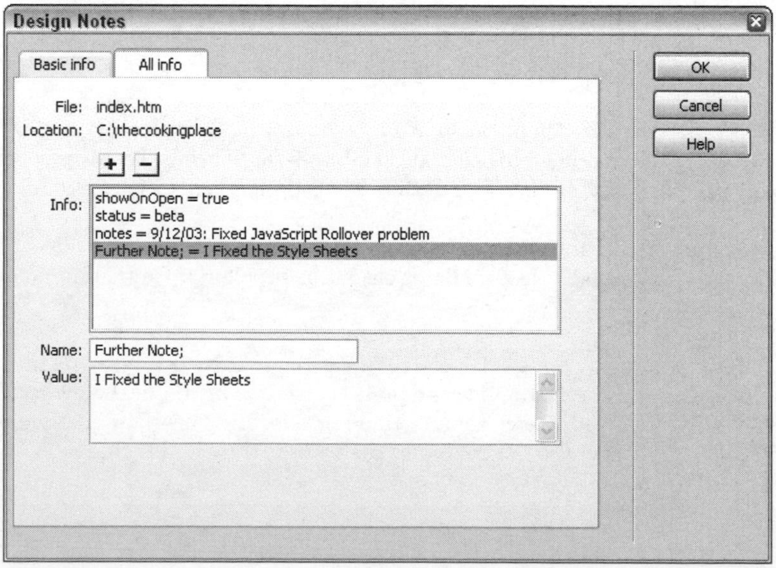

Figure 3-37

If you expand the Files panel and look at the site's files, you see the indicator that a note is attached to the file, as shown in Figure 3-38.

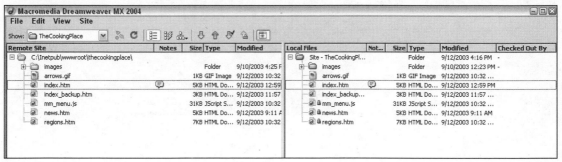

Figure 3-38

If you want to delete a note, open it, go to the All Info tab, and click the – button to delete all content from it. When you select OK, the empty note will be deleted.

Managing Links

As sites grow in complexity, you could end up using multiple folders to contain files of different categories. This could result in your moving pages to new locations. If you have links to those pages, they could become invalid because the page is no longer where the link is looking for it. If you have a small Web site, this is easily fixed. However, if your site has a lot of pages, it is easy to lose track of links or, at best, make changing all those links a long and tedious job. Again, Dreamweaver helps you out by managing the links for you.

The General category in the Edit↩Preferences dialog box, shown in Figure 3-39, allows you to decide how Dreamweaver should manage those links:

❑ **Always:** This automatically updates all links in the background without further prompting.

❑ **Never:** This disables the automatic update feature.

❑ **Prompt:** This lets you know what links it is changing.

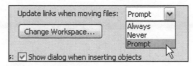

Figure 3-39

If you select Prompt and then use the Files panel to move a file to a different folder, you should see something like the prompt shown in Figure 3-40.

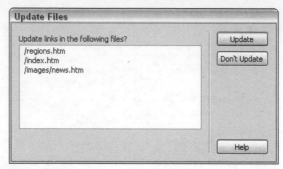

Figure 3-40

You can then decide if you want the links updated or not.

You can also change all links that are directed to one Web page to another. For instance, let's assume you want to change all links that go to news.htm to point to another page. Select the news.htm file in the Files panel, choose Site⇨Change Link Sitewide in the menu bar to open the Change Link Sitewide dialog box shown in Figure 3-41, and enter the link's new page name.

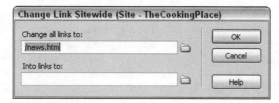

Figure 3-41

Site Reports

Periodically you should run reports about various aspects of the Web site. Let's assume you want to check whether all of your links are still valid, or who checked files out, or validate your HTML code. You would do all of this in the Results panel, shown in Figure 3-42. Open the panel by either selecting Windows⇨Results or by pressing F7.

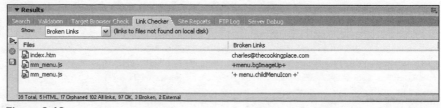

Figure 3-42

As of this writing, many of the site reports have bugs that result in them showing problems where none exists. For example, HTML validation shows errors in Dreamweaver's own code. Check with the Macromedia site periodically for possible fixes or patches.

This is a great aid to the project manager because you can generate a number of reports. For example, to check all the links on your site to verify that they are still valid, select Link Checker. Then select the right-pointing triangle located in the left side bar.

The Validation tab checks the syntax of your Web pages for validity against the W3C standard. The W3C is an international organization begun in 1994 whose purpose is to set standards for many Web technologies, such as HTML, accessibility for people with special challenges, and graphic standards. You can read more about this organization at www.w3c.org. Studying their site is a wonderful way to improve your Web design skills.

The Site Reports and Search tabs open separate dialog boxes. For example, if you select Site Reports and click on the Run button you get the dialog box shown in Figure 3-43.

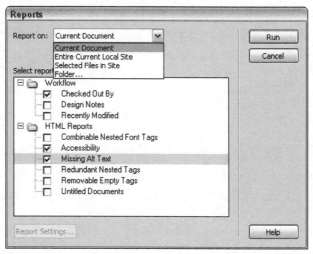

Figure 3-43

Here you can decide which reports you want. In addition, you can use the Report On drop-down list to select the scope of the report. The search produces the Find and Replace dialog box shown in Figure 3-44.

Here you can do a search or replace for a word or phrase in one document or the whole site. What is interesting here is that you can save the Find and Replace parameters as a separate file if it's one you use frequently. The search allows you to search text, tags, or advanced text. The Advanced Text option allows you to set up Where clauses for the search. For instance, you can search for tags with particular attributes, as shown in Figure 3-45. In addition, you can use the + button to add Where clauses.

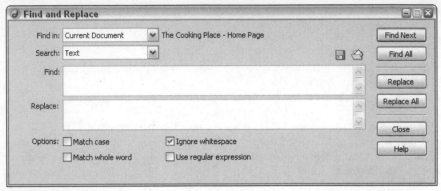

Figure 3-44

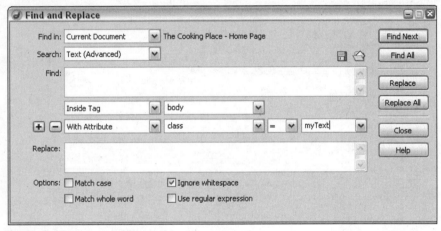

Figure 3-45

From this overview, you can see that Dreamweaver features some very powerful site and team management tools. We could devote an entire book to just exploring the finer points of these tools. As you work with these tools you will find that they greatly speed up the development process.

Adding Content to Pages

So far, you have some pretty looking pages and a nice little navigation system, but you don't have any content to attract people to your Web site. You need to add text, images, hyperlinks, and other things that will enrich the user experience. In this exercise, you start to add some content to your pages.

Inserting and Formatting Tables

Begin by adding some simple static content to your pages. As we described in Chapter 1, "static" content means that you insert it once in the HTML file and it becomes visible to anyone who reads the page in their browser.

In Section 2, you'll develop a site that contains a good deal of dynamic content—using server-side processing (specifically ASP) to take content from files and databases and insert it into the page immediately after the visitor requests it.

It's easy to add static content to your pages.

Try It Out   **Adding Content to news.htm**

1. If you have not done so, return from the site map to the workspace and click the Expand/Collapse button. In the Site panel, you may need to change the view from Map view back to Local view in the right-hand drop-down list.

2. Open the news.htm file and switch to Design view if necessary.

3. You're going to add content to the large white area in the middle of the page (the middle cell of the middle table of your three-table page structure). If you're careful to put the cursor in the right place each time you add or change something, it should be fairly straightforward.

First, click inside the center cell of the table that is nested inside the big white cell (the hierarchy shown in the tag selector should be `<body><table><tr><td><table><tr><td>`). Then type the phrase **Cooking World News**. Highlight the text and, using the Property inspector, center the text (using the Align Center button) and make it bold by clicking the Bold (B) button. What you see should look like Figure 3-46.

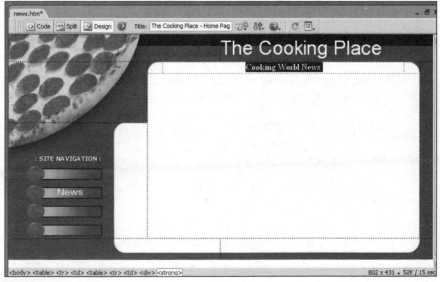

Figure 3-46

Don't change the font size of this text because it could throw the rest of the table out of alignment with the graphics.

4. Click inside the main cell (but below the table nested inside it). There's nothing inside this cell after the nested table so the cursor will flash at the right-hand end of the nested table and the tag selector will show the hierarchy <body><table><tr><td>.

Insert another table here. To do that, select Insert⇨Table. In the resulting dialog box, set the new table to have three rows and three columns, a width of 75 percent, border thickness and cell padding both equal to 2, and cell spacing equal to 0, as shown in Figure 3-47.

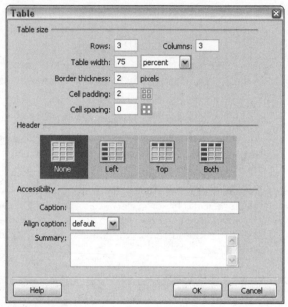

Figure 3-47

5. Notice that the Property inspector has now changed. In the Align drop-down list, change the alignment of the table to Center, as shown in Figure 3-48.

Figure 3-48

Now your Design view should look like what you see in Figure 3-49.

Figure 3-49

6. Merge the three cells in the top row of this new table so that you can add a headline to the table. Click inside any cell in the first row and use the tag selector to select the table row (`<tr>`) tag. Then select Modify⇨Table⇨Merge Cells from the menu bar to merge all the cells in this row. The result should look like what Figure 3-50 shows.

Figure 3-50

7. In the merged cell, type the phrase **November Cooking News**. Highlight the text and use the Property inspector (as you've done before) to make it center-aligned and bold.

8. Click in the first cell of the second row and start typing the text shown in Figure 3-51 into the cells. You'll add three news items here. To move from one cell to the next, press the Tab key. When you complete the right-hand cell on the third row (the one about the annual chili contest), press Tab again. This creates another row of cells for the New York City news item. Don't worry about the column widths now. You will fix those in the next step.

Figure 3-51

Notice the acute accent on the letter *e* in the word *soufflé*. Dreamweaver allows you to insert this character. To do so, first click on the position where you want the character to appear. Select Insert⇨HTML⇨Special Characters⇨Other to open the Insert Other Character dialog box, shown in Figure 3-52.

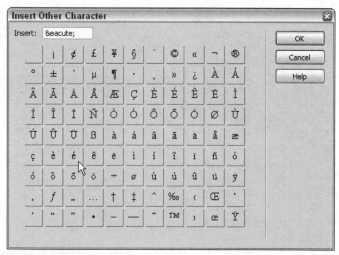

Figure 3-52

Select the desired character, as shown, and click OK to insert it.

9. Experiment a bit with the rows in this table. You can tab past the last cell in the table to create a new row at the bottom, or select a row and use Modify⇨Table⇨Insert Row to insert a row immediately above it. You can easily delete an unwanted row by selecting it and either pressing the Delete key or choosing Modify⇨Table⇨Delete Row.

10. If you think the table looks a little too cramped, you can adjust its size. There are a number of ways to do this. You can click any inner cell-border and drag it to the position you want it. You can also do this with the right-hand outer border of the table.

You can also enlarge the whole table. To do this, first select the table by clicking inside the table and then selecting <table> in the tag selector. When you do this, you'll see three graphic handles on the outer border: one on the right-hand border, one on the lower border, and one in the lower right-hand corner. Click any of these handles and drag it to the appropriate position to resize the table. Keep doing so until you feel that the table looks good to you.

11. While you're in the mood to experiment, this is a good time to see how cell padding and border settings work. Select the entire table and, using the Property inspector, set the CellPad field to 10 and press Enter. Notice that the distance between the text and cell borders increases.

Experiment with the Border size setting and Brdr Color setting too, using the Property inspector.

12. Your table still looks a little ordinary. Dreamweaver can help you out with its built-in formats. Click anywhere inside the table and select Modify⇨Table⇨Select Table.

13. Choose Commands⇨Format Table. You'll see the Format Table dialog box, shown in Figure 3-53.

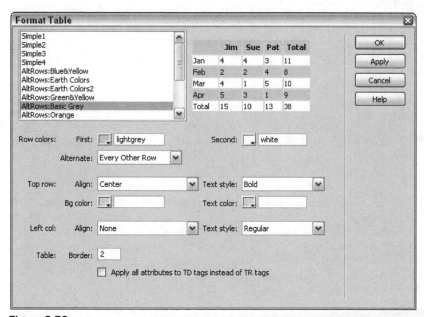

Figure 3-53

Here you can select a predefined format for your table, or even design your own formatting. Select colors and select which rows you want those colors to appear in. In addition, you can adjust the Align attribute and the Border size here.

Go for something understated: choose AltRows:Basic Grey from the drop-down list. This feature overrides your previous table settings. For that reason, set the Border to 2 and click OK to apply the setting and exit the dialog box.

14. Save your work and preview news.htm in the browser. It should look like Figure 3-54.

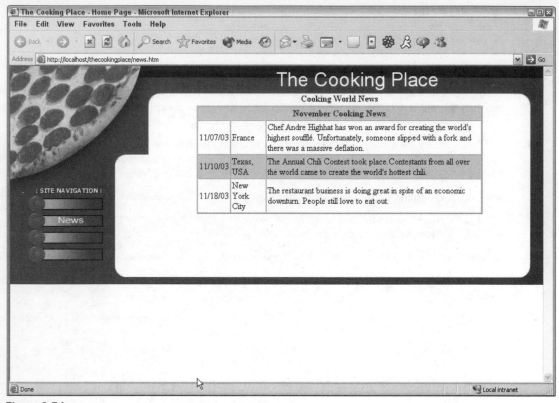

Figure 3-54

How It Works

Initially, the new table you created contains three rows of three cells each. In the first row, when you merge the three cells into one, Dreamweaver replaces the three `<td>...</td>` cell elements with a single `<td>...</td>` element. This new element has an attribute `colspan="3"`, to indicate that this single cell should span three columns:

```
<table width="75%" border="0" cellspacing="0" cellpadding="2" >
<tr>
  <td> </td>
  <td> </td>
  <td> </td>
</tr>
<tr>
  <td> </td>
  <td> </td>
  <td> </td>
</tr>
<tr>
  <td> </td>
  <td> </td>
```

```
        <td> </td>
    </tr>
    </table>
```

When you type text into the Design view, Dreamweaver automatically converts it into HTML and places it in Code view. In particular, it's worth looking at the first news item:

```
<tr bgcolor="white">
    <td width="17%">11/07/02</td>
    <td width="29%">France</td>
    <td width="54%">Chef Andre Highhat has won an award for creating the
    world's largest souffl&eacute;. Unfortunately, someone slipped with
    a fork and there was a massive deflation.</td>
</tr>
```

The permitted character set for writing HTML is limited to alphanumeric characters plus a number of special characters, but it is limited. In particular, it does not include characters such as *é*. Therefore, Dreamweaver encodes the *é* character as é. When the browser receives the page, it decodes é and displays the character *é* at the correct place in the page. If you do use any special characters, be sure to test them in as many browsers as possible. Many older browser technologies do not always display them as expected.

When you apply the table formatting at the end of the exercise, Dreamweaver simply converts these settings to HTML attributes and adjusts the HTML accordingly. In this case, you've elected to color alternate rows light gray and white, so Dreamweaver has added bgcolor attributes to the <tr> tags:

```
<table width="75%" border="0" align="center"
        cellpadding="2" cellspacing="0">
    <tr align="center" bgcolor="lightgrey">
      ...
    </tr>
    <tr bgcolor="white">
      ...
    </tr>
    <tr bgcolor="lightgrey">
      ...
    </tr>
    <tr bgcolor="white">
      ...
    </tr>
    </table>
```

Inserting Text

If you want to create an arrangement of text and graphics on the page, with the text wrapping around images, Dreamweaver can do that for you too. In the next example, you create some suitably seductive welcoming text for the home page and decorate it with some images of fine foods. You do this in two stages. First you add the text; later you add the images.

Try It Out   **Inserting and Styling Text**

1. If you have not done so already, close the `news.htm` file you edited in the last exercise and, using the Site panel, open the `index.htm` file in Design view.

2. Click inside the large white cell and enter the text shown in Figure 3-55.

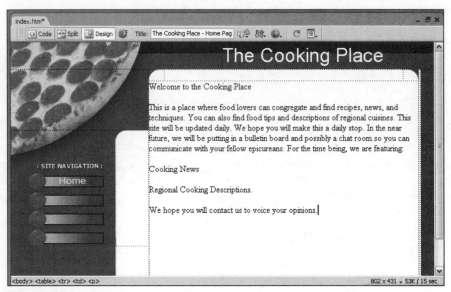

Figure 3-55

Hit Enter at the end of each paragraph to move on to the next one. Alternatively, you can copy-and-paste this text from the file `Cookingtext.doc` supplied with the source code for this chapter.

3. Format this text. You will do most of the work using the Property inspector.

    Click inside the first line of text and change it to a level-1 heading. To do this, choose Heading 1 from the Format drop-down list in the Property inspector. Also click the Align Center button (in the Property inspector) to center the heading.

4. Format the two lines containing the phrases "Cooking News" and "Regional Cooking Descriptions" into a list. In HTML there are two types of lists:

    ❑ An *ordered list* is one whose entries are enumerated: 1, 2, 3, etc.; (i), (ii), (iii), etc.

    ❑ An *unordered list* is one whose entries are denoted by bullet points

    There are buttons for both of these list formats in the Property inspector. (The Unordered List button is selected in Figure 3-56 and the Ordered List button is to its right.)

Figure 3-56

Select the two lines of text and click the Unordered List button. This formats them as a list with a bullet preceding each item, as shown in Figure 3-57.

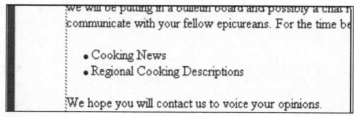

Figure 3-57

Notice that this changes the line spacing also. As an experiment, switch to Ordered List and notice that this preserves the bulleted formatting but uses numbers instead of black discs to label the bullets. Switch back to Unordered List.

5. Click at the end of the text (after the word *opinions*) and press the Enter key twice. Notice that your table area expands automatically. This is a consequence of the well-designed layout. It expands with your needs, allowing you to insert as much content as you like into this cell.

6. Insert a copyright notice, which reads © **2003 The Cooking Place**. The copyright symbol is another special character. As you did before, select Insert⇨HTML⇨Special Characters⇨ Copyright. (This time you don't need to go all the way to the table as you did before.) Press the right arrow on your keyboard to move the cursor past the copyright character, then type a space, and then type **2003 The Cooking Place**.

Finally, change the size of the copyright line. Highlight the text in the copyright line and change the Size setting, on the Property inspector, to x-small.

How It Works

Take a look at the HTML you created here:

```
<h1 align="center">Welcome to the Cooking Place</h1>
<p>This is a place where food lovers can congregate and find recipes, news,
and techniques. You can also find food tips and descriptions of regional
   cuisines. This site will be updated daily. We hope you will make this a
   daily stop. In the near future, we will be putting in a bulletin board
      and possibly a chat room so you can communicate with your fellow
epicureans. For the time being, we are featuring:</p>
   <ul>
    <li>Cooking News</li>
    <li>Regional Cooking Descriptions</li>
   </ul>        <p>We hope you will contact us to voice your opinions</p>
<p> </p>
<p><span class="style2">&copy; 2003 The Cooking Place</span></p></td>
```

There are a number of things to pick out here. First, Dreamweaver uses <h1>...</h1> tags to set the top line as a level-1 heading. In fact, there are six levels of header tags allowable in HTML: <h1> through <h6>. By default, the browser sets this range in size from about 24 points to about 10 points (1 point is $\frac{1}{72}$ of an inch).

The <p>...</p> tags divide the content into paragraphs in much the same fashion that the Enter key does in a word processor.

The ordered list contains two sets of tags. The list itself is defined by the <ul>...</ul> tags (*ul* stands for *unordered list*). Embedded within that, each item in the list is defined by using the <li>...</li> tags (where *li* stands for *list item*).

> *If you'd opted for an ordered list instead of an unordered list, Dreamweaver would have employed* <ol>...</ol> *tags instead of* <ul>...</ul> *tags.*

If you are familiar with previous versions of Dreamweaver, you will notice that Dreamweaver MX 2004 handles font sizes a bit differently than before. While it is beyond the scope of this book for an extensive discussion of this topic, let's take a brief overview.

There are three ways of defining font sizes: *absolute, relative*, and *pixel*, as shown in Figure 3-58.

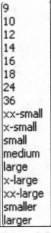

Figure 3-58

The first set of numbers is the specific font size. You can set the unit of measurement. In most cases, when designing for a Web site, you want to use pixels. While the points feature is available, many planners tend to avoid sizing text in point units because it could lead to some problems with Web site accessibility.

The next range, xx-small to xx-large, are the absolute sizes (*absolute* meaning that they do not change even if the size of the browser is adjusted). Absolute sizes employ the use of these keywords. Each unit is roughly 1.2 times the size of the next. Many designers limit the use of absolute values unless they know the size of the output. If the user resizes the browser, it could result in the absolute values being out of proportion to the rest of the page.

Smaller and Larger are the relative keywords. But smaller or larger than what? In design terms, it is relative to the size of a parent element. So if you have an <h1> element embedded within a <body> element, "larger" in the <h1> element would be larger compared to the size set in the <body> element. This is the preferred technique used by most designers today.

Most font sizing is controlled by styles, which we discuss in Chapter 4.

Inserting Graphics in Text

Now you're in a position to add those food pictures to the page. You can position the images relative to the text to make the overall layout attractive and have the text wrap around them.

We will discuss *assets*. These are outside files, such as pictures, Macromedia Flash animations, Java applets, etc. that are used as part of the page.

Try It Out   **Inserting Graphics**

1.   You should still have index.htm open from the previous exercise. Switch back to Design view if necessary. Now open the Assets panel (in the Files panel group) and make sure that the images icon is selected, as shown in Figure 3-59.

Figure 3-59

2.   Select the image dessert.jpg (from the Assets panel), drag it onto the Design view of the index.htm file, and drop it approximately onto the word *techniques* (at the end of the first sentence), as shown in Figure 3-60. Precise placement is not critical here.

Figure 3-60

3. The way it's been done in Figure 3-60, there's an unsightly gap between the first two lines. Using the Property inspector, change the Align drop-down list to Left so the image appears as in Figure 3-61.

Figure 3-61

Don't worry if the words seem to break in odd locations. This will rectify itself when it is rendered in the browser.

4. Adjust the size of this image in much the same way as you adjusted the size of a table earlier in the chapter. That is, if you select the image you'll see three handles:

   ❑ One on the right-hand edge of the image

   ❑ One on the lower edge of the image

   ❑ One in the lower-right corner of the image

   The handle in the corner will resize the image proportionately (that is, resize the height in the same proportion to the width). The other two will stretch the image (for example, the first one stretches its width while preserving its height). Here, use the corner handle to reduce the image to the height of about four lines of text.

   If you ever use this technique to increase the size of an image, remember there are practical limitations with regards to maximum resolution. A low-resolution image—such as 72 dpi (dots per inch)—can't be magnified much before it starts looking grainy. This changes the size of the image file too. Dreamweaver will prompt you about that fact.

5. An alternative way to adjust the image is using the Tag Editor dialog box, shown in Figure 3-62. Select the image and then choose Modify⇨Edit Tag.

   You can use this feature to edit the attributes of any HTML tag, but it is particularly useful for graphics. You can manually adjust the Width and Height attributes to the precise values you desire, which is useful because it is often to difficult to set the image size accurately using the handles. There are a few other features that are worth mentioning here. The Border attribute allows you to place a border around the graphic and the Horizontal Space and Vertical Space attributes allow you to decide how much distance you want between the image and the text.

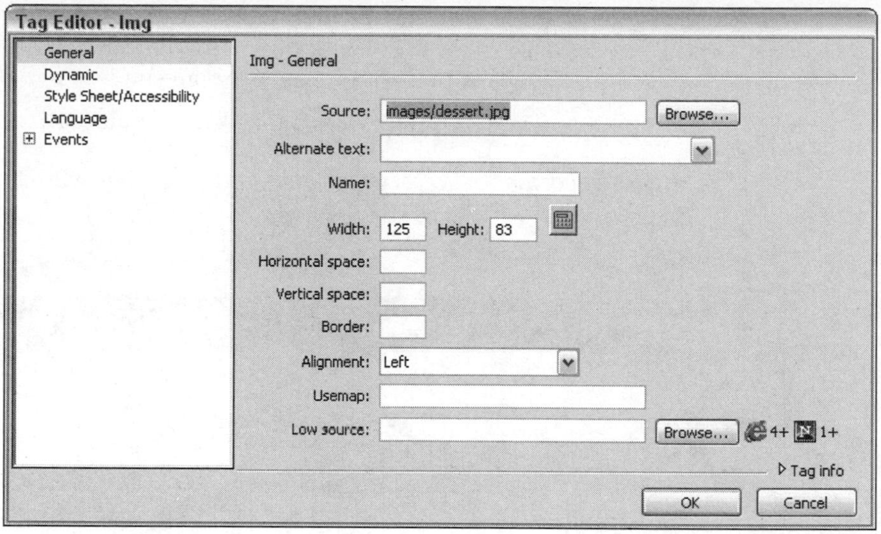

Figure 3-62

The Tag Editor also advises you as to browser compatibility. For example, look at the Low Source field. If you expect some of your site's visitors to use low connection speeds to the Internet, you should consider this field. You can use it to plug in a smaller, quicker-loading graphic, which the visitor will see while the larger graphic is still downloading. This feature helps you to eliminate the empty spaces that low-connection speed users sometimes see when downloading highly graphical pages.

To the right of this field, you can see two icons (one for Microsoft Internet Explorer and one for Netscape) and some digits. Here the Tag Editor advises you that this feature is compatible with IE version 4 or later, and also with Netscape Navigator version 1 or later.

If you want to learn more about the tag being used (in this case the `<img>` tag), click on Tag Info in the lower-right corner. This expands the dialog box to present documentation about the tag in question, as shown in Figure 3-63.

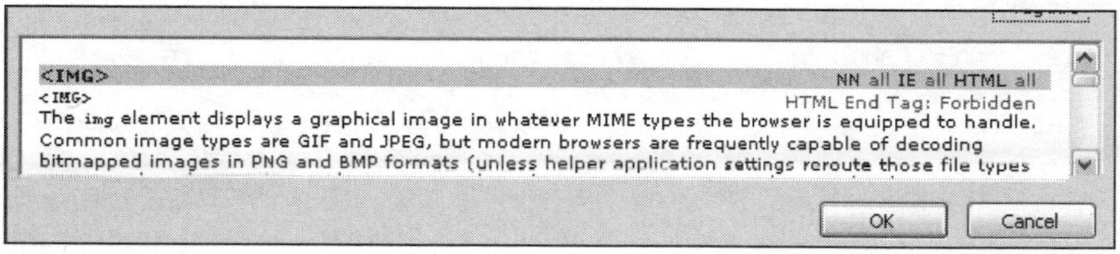

Figure 3-63

In the top-right corner, this tells you that the `<img>` tag works in all versions of Netscape and Internet Explorer, that it is supported in all versions of HTML, and that an `<img>` element does not require an end (`</img>`) tag.

Select Cancel for now.

6. Follow the process in Steps 2 through 4 to insert the image `coffee.jpg` file into the page. Drag it from the Assets panel and drop it near the word *featuring*. This time, use the Property inspector to align the image to the right, and then resize the image until you're happy with it.

7. Save your work and preview it in the browser. It should look like Figure 3-64.

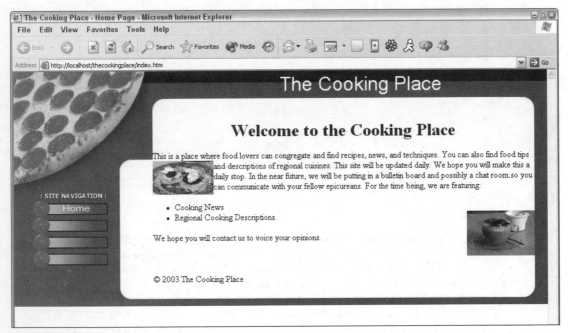

Figure 3-64

How It Works

HTML uses the `<img>` tag to place image files into the page. When you use the drag-and-drop feature to insert images into the page, Dreamweaver generates an `<img>` tag in the page's HTML code to represent the image, its size, and its position with respect to other elements of the page:

```
<p align="left">This is a place where food lovers can congregate and find
    recipes, news, and techniques.<img src="images/dessert.jpg" width="105"
    height="63" align="left" /> You can also find food tips and descriptions
    of regional cuisines. This site will be updated daily. We hope you will make
    this a daily stop. In the near future, we will be putting in a bulletin board
    and possibly a chat room so you can communicate with your fellow epicureans.
    For the time being, we are featuring:</p>
<ul>
<li>Cooking News<img src="images/coffee.jpg" width="125" height="83"
align="right" /></li>
```

Here, the `src` (or source) attribute provides the necessary information about the location of the image file. If the image file specified in the `src` attribute does not exist, you'll see a placeholder at the position where the image should be located, as in Figure 3-65.

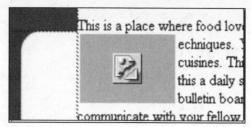

Figure 3-65

The width, height, and align attributes in the <img> tags above are self-explanatory. Sometimes in an <img> tag you may see an alt attribute, which is used to specify *alternative text*. This essentially acts as a substitute for the image. This has three distinct uses:

❑　In some browsers, when you roll your mouse pointer over the position of the image, the alternative text is displayed in a text label. This is particularly useful when users wait for images to download; they can read the text label to find out what the image is about.

❑　It provides audio cues for visually impaired users who have access to specialized equipment, such as a speech synthesizer.

❑　In certain older browsers that cannot handle graphics, and for users on slow connections who disable image loading to improve their download times, the alternative text is a replacement for the image entirely.

Use the Tag Editor dialog box to insert alternative text for an image or for any other tag that accepts it. In fact, with site accessibility such a major issue today, Dreamweaver has an *accessibility feature* to assist you in this process. To enable it, select Edit➪Preferences and then choose the Accessibility category, as shown in Figure 3-66. Check the tag types for which you want to add alt tags.

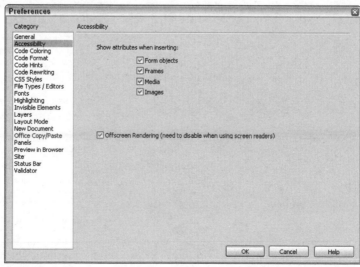

Figure 3-66

Click OK. In future, whenever you create a tag of the specified type, you'll be prompted for alternative text.

Adding Links to the Text

You've already got your navigation mechanism (in the form of the Home, News, Regions, and Contact Us buttons) but that doesn't stop you from adding hyperlinks to the page content itself. You can make an image or a line of text "hot" (that is, you can turn it into a hyperlink) very easily. Round out this page now by picking out a couple of the phrases used in your text and turning them into hyperlinks. In addition, add an e-mail link to the words *contact you*.

Try It Out   **Adding Links**

1. Switch to the Design view of the `index.htm` file.

2. Open the Files panel so that you can see the `news.htm` file. In the `index.htm` file in the main part of your workspace, highlight the words *Cooking News*. Use the Point to File feature (next to the Link field in the Property inspector) to drag a line to `news.htm` in the Site panel, as shown in Figure 3-67.

Figure 3-67

3. Highlight the words *Regional Cooking Descriptions* and, using the same technique, link it to `regions.htm`.

4. Highlight the words *contact you* (in the final sentence). In the Link field of the Property inspector, type in the string that will point to your own personal mailbox: something like **mailto:charles@thecookingplace.com?Subject=Suggestions**. This automatically plugs the word *Suggestions* into the subject line of the e-mail message going to `charles@thecookingplace.com`.

How It Works

You've met anchor tags earlier in this chapter. To create a hyperlink, Dreamweaver creates an `<a href="...">...</a>` element in the HTML. The value of the `href` attribute is the page or resource to which the hyperlink links.

There are three types of `href` paths: absolute, document-relative, and root-relative:

❑   An *absolute* path is a fully qualified path which starts with `http://` and specifies the full address of the page. Use an absolute path to address a page outside your Web site's own structure (although you can also use them to create links to pages within the same Web site).

❑   A *document-relative* path is one in which the address of the destination page is specified starting from the folder in which the linking page is stored. To link to another page in the same folder, simply use the file name of the destination page, as here:

```
<a href="news.htm">Cooking News</a>
```

This type of path is useful if the relative locations of the two files are likely to remain unchanged.

❏ A *root-relative* path is one in which the address of the destination page is specified starting from the root folder of the Web site. To distinguish it as a root-relative path and not a document-relative path, it begins with a leading forward-slash, like this:

```
<a href="/news/recent/februarynews.htm">February's News</a>
```

This type of path is useful if the relative locations of the two files may change, but the location of the destination page is likely to remain unchanged.

Use document-relative and root-relative paths only to create links to other files in the same Web site. There are no hard and fast rules as to when to use a root-relative path instead of a document-relative path. However, if you are doing a lot of rearranging of your Web site, or you move files around a lot, a root-relative path could probably save you a lot of broken links.

By default, the text of a text-based hyperlink is styled differently from nonlinked text. It is usually displayed underlined and in a blue font to indicate that it is a hyperlink. In fact, you can control these style attributes by using the Page Properties dialog box (choose Modify⇨Page Properties⇨Links Category), shown in Figure 3-68.

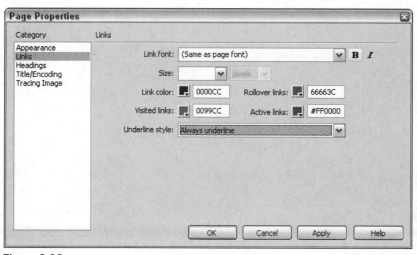

Figure 3-68

Here you have four potential color attributes for a link that you can set. The Links field controls the color of the hyperlink text in its normal state. The Visited Links field controls the color that the hyperlink text assumes when the visitor has already clicked it once before. The Rollover Links field controls the color the link changes into when the mouse rolls over it. As you will see in the code that follows, the Rollover link field here shows up as the a:hover rule in the style sheet.

The fourth one is the Active Links field. The purpose of this field is based on the fact that when a visitor clicks on a link, the link does not go into action till the visitor releases the mouse button. With this fact in mind, the Active Links field controls the color that the hyperlink text takes after the visitor clicks the mouse button on the link, but before releasing it. (Here is a little experiment. Change the Active Links attribute to red and submit the change by clicking OK in this dialog box. View the page in the browser; left-click a link but don't release the mouse button. You should see the text change to red and it won't go to the linked page until you release the button.)

Each link has a color palette associated with it (as does any place where you need to select a color in Dreamweaver). After selecting a color, however, you see a hexadecimal code that begins with the # symbol. On the Web, colors are created by blending intensities of red, green, and blue (known as RGB color). The intensity of each color is represented by a number between 0 through 255, which, in hexadecimal notation, are the numbers 00 through FF. 00 means 0 intensity, and FF means an intensity of 255. In colors, the first two digits are the intensity of red, the next two are the intensity of green, and the final two are the intensity of blue.

Since these attributes are set for all text links on the page, they are not set in the text attributes. Instead, they are set in the style definition of the `<body>` tag as a series of styles:

```
body {
    background-color: #FFFFFF;
    margin-left: 0px;
    margin-top: 0px;
    margin-right: 0px;
    margin-bottom: 0px;
}
.style1 {
    font-family: Arial, Helvetica, sans-serif;
    font-size: 36px;
    color: #FFFFFF;
}
.style2 {font-size: x-small}
a:link {
    color: #0000CC;
}
a:visited {
    color: #0099CC;
}
a:hover {
    color: #6633CC;
}
a:active {
    color: #FF0000;
}       ...
```

Summary

You covered a lot of ground in this chapter. Once you created the basic page design in Chapter 2, it was easy to duplicate that file and generate a number of pages with a similar look and feel.

With a number of Web pages in your Web site, it was clear that you needed to create some kind of navigation mechanism to help users recognize which page they're looking at and to get to the other pages in the site. Fortunately, you thought of that and built it into your page design, employing the four image-based buttons to do the job. By creating simple rollover behaviors and pop-up menu behaviors, powered by JavaScript and executed by the browser, you made it easy for users to find their way around.

As the number of pages in a Web site grows, it's easy even for the Web developers to get lost! Dreamweaver helps you out here, too, by providing the site map feature. This feature tells you what hyperlinks exist in any given page in the site and also tells you about any image files (and other assets and dependent files) that are used by a page.

You looked at the features to help a design team, such as Design Notes, Check In/Out, and Site Reports.

When it comes to creating content, Dreamweaver helps you there too. You can easily add static content to a page. Dreamweaver helps you style and format the text, insert and position images, and create hyperlinks. There's even an accessibility feature to encourage you to insert alt text for the elements in your page.

Overall, your site is beginning to shape up nicely. In the next chapter, you will automate your styling work with Cascading Style Sheets and templates. This helps things go a lot quicker and smoother.

Why Not Try . . .

1.   If you haven't already done so, complete the configuration of the navigation buttons on news.htm and regions.htm. We outlined the steps briefly earlier in the chapter. Now is a good time to do it if you haven't already.

2.   There's plenty of scope for adding different content to the middle cell in index.htm. Try styling the text or inserting more images. Create links to other areas of the site or to other culinary Web sites.

3.   Alternatively, remove the existing images and insert a centered 3 × 3 table with nine food images—one in each cell—to give you a really appetizing centerpiece on the page. Add a text label to each image so that the user can see what each image is.

   You could even turn these images into hyperlinks and have each image link to a Web page containing the recipe. You'll start creating recipe pages in Chapter 5.

4.   Open up the Pop-up Menu editor and use the Attributes tag to change the colors and style of the menu to match the navigation bar better.

Style Sheets and Templates

In Chapters 2 and 3 you learned some basic concepts of Web page design and how Dreamweaver MX 2004 can play a powerful role in that process. Your page design so far has made extensive use of HTML tables to control layout. In Chapter 3 you began building upon your single-page design to produce the beginnings of your Web site—which will eventually consist of many pages. You examined the structure of your site and added navigation to allow your users to move within the site.

In this chapter we show you two very powerful tools: Cascading Style Sheets (CSS) and Dreamweaver templates. These tools give you great flexibility and control not only during the design and development of your site but, most importantly, while maintaining the site once it is "live."

You want to create a similar look and feel across all the pages in your site, and with only three Web pages (as you have now) it has not been too difficult to do that. But if you want to add more pages you have to create each page by copying an existing page and laboriously changing the relevant parts. Even worse, if you ever decide to change the design across the site, then achieving even a simple change—like adding an extra navigation button—involves editing every single page and (hopefully) making the same change consistently on all pages. In a site with more than a few pages, this is a big job!

It doesn't have to be this way. The problem with your site at the moment is that each Web page is completely self-contained. Each contains its own styles and structure information. What you need is to define this style and structure in a central location and have all the pages make use of that single central definition. That way you can add pages simply by building them from these central definitions. And you can make a sitewide change to a page's style or structure by making just a single change—to the definition itself. The result is a much more maintainable Web site.

With this important consideration in mind, let's take a closer look at how CSS and templates help. Cascading Style Sheets give you excellent control over the visual styling of your pages and templates allow you to reuse a page design easily. Together these tools aid you in the development of Web sites—particularly when you are working within the realm of a rapid application development (RAD) cycle.

In this chapter you will do the following:

- ❑ Construct a Cascading Style Sheet to control some style attributes in your pages
- ❑ See how to use CSS styles within a page or within a single tag
- ❑ Create a Dreamweaver MX 2004 template and use it to reproduce the page design consistently over multiple pages
- ❑ Construct a Dreamweaver MX 2004 library item and employ it as a reusable element to be placed into many Web pages

Begin by taking a look at what we mean by "style" in Web pages, and at Cascading Style Sheets.

Cascading Style Sheets

If you have used previous editions of Dreamweaver, you are going to see some significant changes in its use of styles. You already got a taste of them in the first three chapters of this book when you formatted text or changed page properties. As we pointed out, rather than place these formatting changes as attributes within an HTML tag, Dreamweaver writes styles. Why is that so significant? Before we can talk about that, we need to examine the correct role of HTML.

HTML and Structure

If you pick up a newspaper or book you should see two distinct components: the structure and the presentation. Some of the newspaper's or book's structural aspects include paragraphs, headers, and body of the text. Among the presentation qualities are the fonts, text size, text color, and the background color of the page.

Without getting into a long history of HTML, which you have probably read many times before, suffice it to say that the original intent was to define just the structure. Along the way, Web browsers came along with their own built-in style sheets, which stated that an `<h1>` tag should look like this, or a `<block quote>` tag should look like that. This posed a serious problem to designers: The `<h1>` and `<block quote>` tags might look one way in Internet Explorer and a different way in Netscape Navigator. While there has been some standardization between the browsers, some significant differences still remain.

Designers were given some control with the use of *tag attributes*. These are instructions that the designer can build into a tag to tell the browser how to display that tag. For example, you might see a `<body>` tag that looks something like this:

```
<body bgcolor=#000000 text="yellow">
```

While the attributes helped the designer, they presented some additional problems. Say that the `<h1>` tag used a certain set of attributes and the designer wanted that set of attributes to be consistent throughout the site. If that site used 50 `<h1>` tags, the designer would need to set that attribute 50 times. In addition, if the designer changed his or her mind, it would need to be changed in 50 different places.

To solve this problem, along came *Cascading Style Sheets* (CSS) or, as they are more commonly known, *styles*.

How Styles Works

When you use styles, you return HTML to its original purpose, as follows:

❑   In your HTML you indicate the purpose of each element of your page (`<h1>` for a level-1 heading, `<h2>` for a level-2 heading, `<p>` for a paragraph, `<table>` for a table, and so on).

❑   In your CSS you specify rules for how each element is to be displayed by the browser.

The syntax of CSS is rather different from the syntax of HTML. However, like HTML, you can create styles using Dreamweaver and then view the code in Code view. If you are feeling more confident, you can type CSS styles straight into Code view, just as you type HTML into Code view.

Whether you like to write code or not, it's worth taking a look at how CSS works. Then you can have a go at creating your own CSS styles using Dreamweaver MX 2004.

CSS Rules

A CSS style consists of one or more rules. These rules can be located within the HTML document or located in a separate file called a *style sheet*. Each rule is applied to certain parts of a page by way of a *selector*, which (as the name suggests) selects the element(s) it applies to. Each rule consists of one or more attributes—which control the many possible display characteristics such as underlining, font family, color, etc.—and appropriate attribute values for each style setting. If you were writing the code for this rule in style syntax, you would need to arrange it like this:

```
selector { property : value; }
```

The parenthesis is the declaration and, within that declaration, you define the attribute in the paired set of property and value, separated by a colon.

Here's an example. Suppose you want to set up a style that ensures that all `<h1>` tags are colored green. To achieve this, you need to write a line of CSS code with the selector h1; the property you want to affect is the color and you want the value of this property to be green. So the CSS style rule that achieves this is as follows:

```
h1 {color : green }
```

Suppose that you want to change multiple properties in the `<h1>` tag. Each property value combination is separated by a semicolon:

```
h1 {color : green; text-align : center;}
```

Please notice that white space (inserted with the spacebar, tabs, line breaks, and so on) does not affect the declaration. Some designers prefer to put each property on a separate line within the declaration:

```
h1 {color : green;
    text-align : center;}
```

You can write lots of rules like this one and store them in a file that is separate from your Web pages. This file is called a CSS style sheet. By convention, an external CSS style sheet is stored in a file with the extension `.css`.

129

Creating and Implementing a CSS Style Sheet

Now it's time for you to put some of this knowledge into practice by creating a style that forces any text contained in <h1>...</h1> tags to appear red and centered and then applying it to all your pages so that the style appears consistently throughout the Web site.

Try It Out   Creating an External Cascading Style Sheet

1. Open the index.htm document. Locate the <h1> tag for Welcome to the Cooking Place, located roughly around line 90 in the code, and take out the text-align attribute.

2. Switch to Design view.

3. Select the CSS Styles panel, shown in Figure 4-1, in the Design panel or by pressing Shift+F11.

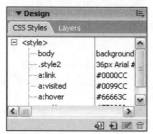

Figure 4-1

4. Your site currently contains several styles that were created earlier by Dreamweaver when you did some formatting in previous chapters. When you manually create your own styles, Dreamweaver helps by offering dialog boxes showing the options available.

5. Click on the New CSS Style button (the plus sign) in the lower right corner of the CSS Styles panel (as shown in Figure 4-1). This brings up the New CSS Style dialog box, shown in Figure 4-2.

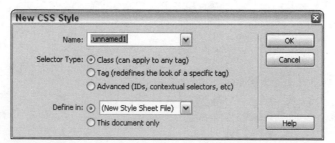

Figure 4-2

6. You want your new style to apply to HTML <h1> tags, so change Selector Type to Tag (which redefines the look of a specific tag). In the Tag drop-down list, select h1.

7. Dreamweaver wants to know how you're going to store this style rule. You want to store it in a new style sheet file, so make sure to select (New Style Sheet File) in the Define In drop-down list

and click the radio button next to it. The dialog box should look like the one shown in Figure 4-3. When you've done that, click OK.

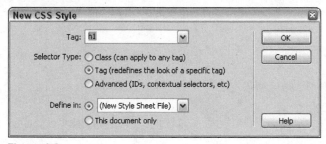

Figure 4-3

8.	As you've probably guessed, there are actually a number of different ways to store a CSS style. For now we'll concentrate on storing styles in an external style sheet file; we'll discuss the other techniques later in the chapter.

9.	Dreamweaver asks you to put aside the style creation for a moment while it deals with the administrative task of naming the new style sheet file. Figure 4-4 shows that dialog box.

Figure 4-4

10.	Click the Create New Folder button (near the top of the dialog box) to create a new folder called **stylesheets** (inside the root folder of the site); then navigate to your new stylesheets folder and save the style sheet file by giving it the file name **cookingPlaceStyles.css**. Click the Save button.

11.	With that simple admin job done, you can return to the task of creating your styles. You should now see a dialog box with formatting categories on the left side. Use this dialog box to specify the details of the style you're creating.

131

12. The effect you want to create for the `<h1>` tags is red center-aligned text. The first of these two style characteristics relates to the text itself. To set it, select the Type category on the left of the dialog box, as shown in Figure 4-5. Then change the Color property on the right either by clicking on the box and selecting from the color palette (as shown) or by typing the color code **#FF0000** into the box next to it.

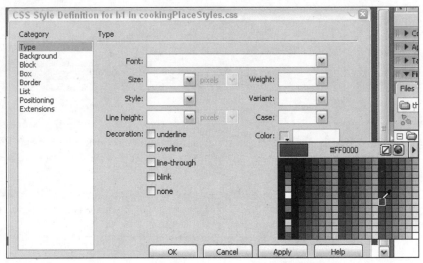

Figure 4-5

To set the second of the style characteristics (the center-alignment), first switch to the Block category. Then set the Text Align setting to center, as shown in Figure 4-6.

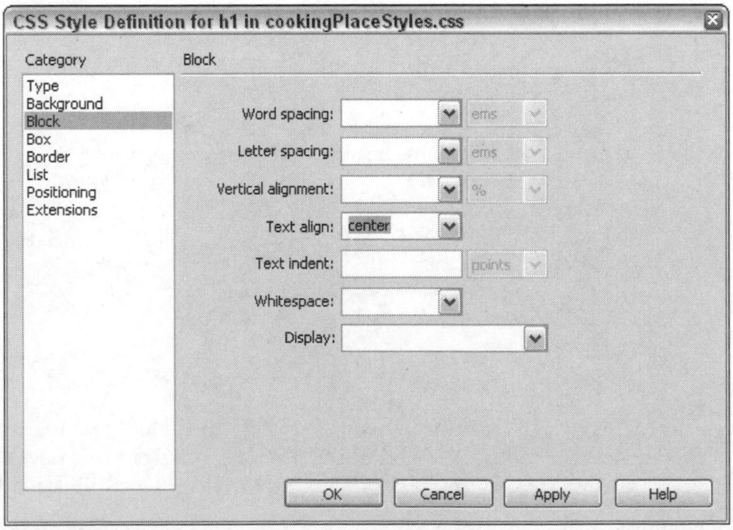

Figure 4-6

13. Now you've done everything to describe the style, so click OK. In the Design view of `index.htm`, you should see the effect immediately. Welcome to the Cooking Place should now appear in red and center-aligned, as shown in Figure 4-7.

Figure 4-7

14. Notice that Dreamweaver has made a change to `index.htm` during this process (as indicated by the * symbol in the title bar); we'll explain that shortly. Right now, before you preview the page in a Web browser, remember to save `index.htm`, and, if necessary, upload the new version of this file and the new style sheet file to the testing server (for example, by using the Put button in the Site panel).

How It Works

The first thing to look at is the style sheet file that Dreamweaver creates. To look at this, go to the Files panel—you'll see the newly created `cookingPlaceStyles.css` file there in the style sheets folder (see Figure 4-8).

Figure 4-8

Notice that the style sheet has a "+" to the left of it, indicating that it is expandable. If you click on the plus sign you will see a list of styles available on the sheet.

Double-click the file to open it. It opens in Code view and shows you this code:

```
h1 {
  color: #FF0000;
  text-align: center;
}
```

This should look familiar. It contains a selector, declaration, and property/value pairs just as you described at the start of the chapter. This says that if a page using this style sheet has any `<h1>` elements, then the text color of those elements should be red (#FF0000) and that text should be center-aligned.

Since this sheet is external to the index.htm file, thus making it an asset, there must be a link between them. This link is in the form of an import URL, which is placed within the .htm file.

To see this, switch to the index.htm page and then switch to its Code view. In the last line between the <head> and </head> tags, you'll see this tag:

<link href="stylesheets/cookingPlaceStyles.css" rel="stylesheet" type="text/css" />

The <link/> tag sets the link between the index.htm document and the cookingPlaceStyles.css style sheet.

Adding More Styles to a Style Sheet

Your style sheet contains just one style instruction, for the <h1> tag. What if you want to add more styles to this style sheet? You can apply the same attribute/value settings to many different tags at the same time, and you can also add more instructions so that other tags are styled in different ways. In addition, you can link your style sheet to the other pages in your Web site so that all your Web pages adopt the same styles.

In the following example, you'll add some more styles to cookingPlaceStyles.css and also make sure the other pages are using it.

Try It Out   **Adding More Styles to the Style Sheet and Linking It to Other Pages**

1. Make the necessary change to news.htm and regions.htm so that they are both using the cookingPlaceStyles.css style sheet. Close all the open files in your Dreamweaver workspace and open news.htm. Go to the CSS Styles panel shown in Figure 4-9 (in the Design panel group) and click the Attach Style Sheet button.

Figure 4-9

2. Use the Browse button of the resulting dialog box (see Figure 4-10) to select the cooking PlaceStyles.css file. For consistency, set the Add As setting to Link. (Most of the time, you will use Link. You use Import in certain programming situations such as Java or C#.) Click OK.

You can now see that the style sheet is in the CSS panel for news.htm. Since this page is not using the <h1> tags, you will not see any difference at this point.

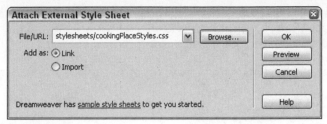

Figure 4-10

3. Save the `news.htm` file and close it.

4. Repeat Steps 1 and 2 for `regions.htm`; save the file when you finish but don't close it.

5. Add some more styles to the style sheet. To illustrate, add a style for all the other "heading" tags (h2, h3, h4, h5, h6) and make them all red, italic, and left-aligned. (You'll use them by adding some content to `regions.htm`.)

6. With `regions.htm` still open, go to the CSS Styles panel and click the New CSS Style button (see Figure 4-11).

Figure 4-11

7. In the New CSS Style dialog box, ensure the Type is set to Tag and then select h2 in the Tag drop-down list. Because you're adding this style rule to `cookingPlaceStyles.css`, make sure that file is selected in the bottom drop-down list, as shown in Figure 4-12. Then click OK.

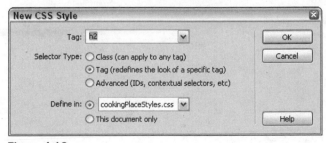

Figure 4-12

8. This time, the rule for the h2 heading will specify red, italic, left-aligned text. To achieve the first two characteristics, go to the Type category, set Style to italic, and (as before) set the color to red (#FF0000), as shown in Figure 4-13.

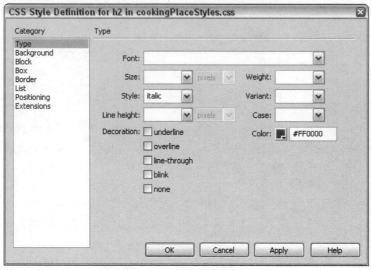

Figure 4-13

9. To achieve the third style characteristic, go to the Block category and set Text Align to left (see Figure 4-14).

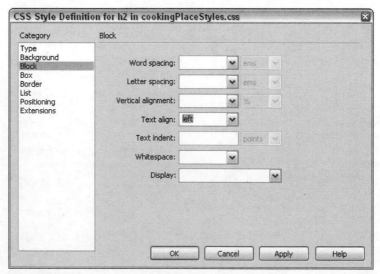

Figure 4-14

10. Click OK to save that rule to the style sheet. You should see the h2 rules under cookingPlaceStyles in the CSS panel.

11. There are two ways to create the rules for h3, h4, h5, and h6. If you wish, you can repeat Steps 5–7 four more times—once for each rule. But here's a quicker way. Go to the Site panel and double-click cookingPlaceStyles.css to open it. You should see the following code:

```
h1 {
 color: #FF0000;
 text-align: center;
}

h2 {
 font-style: italic;
 color: #FF0000;
 text-align: left;
}
```

12. The h2 rule here is identical to the rules you want for h3, h4, h5, and h6, so just add in these remaining selectors, as shown in the highlighted line of code, like this:

```
h1 {
 color: #FF0000;
 text-align: center;
}
h2, h3, h4, h5, h6 {
 font-style: italic;
 color: #FF0000;
 text-align: left;
}
```

13. It's that easy! Now save the cookingPlaceStyles.css file and close it. If you look at the CSS panel, you should see all the new styles under the style sheet.

14. Let's add some content to regions.htm so that you can see these styles being used. Your regions.htm file should still be open; if not, open it. Switch to Design view.

15. Click inside the large white area in the middle of the window and press Enter. Type the words **The Regions** and highlight this text and use the Property inspector to change the format to Heading 1. The text should now conform to the h1 rules.

16. Place the cursor after the word *Regions* and press Enter. Type in a short paragraph of text—make something up or take the text from the regionstext.doc file that is available with the source code for this book. At the end of the text, press Enter again.

17. Enter text for the France, America, and Italy headings (and format these headings as Heading 3). You should see the headings adopt the styles that you created in the cookingPlaceStyles.css style sheet, as shown in Figure 4-15.

18. Save the file and preview it in the browser. You'll see that the <h1> style rule you originally created for index.htm is also being used in here along with the <h3> style rule you just created.

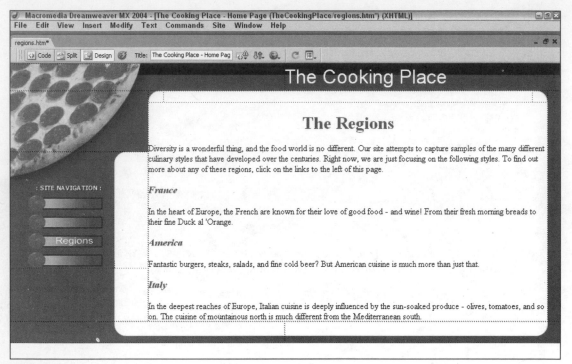

Figure 4-15

How It Works

The first thing you do is link the style sheet to the news.htm and regions.htm files so that they too can use whatever styles are defined in the style sheet This is exactly what you did with the index.htm document earlier. If you look in the code, you will see the same link command you saw earlier.

Then you add another style rule—one with five selectors. Adding this rule to the style sheet file makes the rule apply to all the .htm files that link to it:

```
h2, h3, h4, h5, h6 {
  font-style: italic;
  color: #FF0000;
  text-align: left;
}
```

Specifying a CSS rule with a comma-separated list of selectors is merely a compact way of repeating the same rule for more than one selector. It is a simple form of code reuse, in that you're using the same rule to apply to a number of different tags.

As we mentioned earlier, if you change the rules in the external style sheet, any documents attached to it will reflect those changes.

Techniques for Inserting CSS

So far, we've talked about defining your CSS rules within an external style sheet file and then linking the style sheet to each of your Web pages. In fact, that's not the only way to apply a CSS style to a Web page—there are two other techniques you can use also. The following list explains all three techniques:

❑ As you've seen, you can place style rules into an external style sheet. This is a collection of style instructions stored separately from the Web pages of the site in a file of its own. External CSS files are typically given a .css extension. The pages of the site then link to the external style sheet when they are loaded by the browser. Any changes made to the external style sheet will be reflected in all pages that link to it. This is where the power of CSS can really be seen. Imagine being able to alter radically the appearance of a large Web site by simply editing one CSS file!

In this case, there's another advantage. Once the browser has received the external style sheet, it can store (or cache) the file locally so that it doesn't need to be downloaded again. This helps reduce the download times of subsequent pages that use the same external style sheet.

❑ You can place embedded styles into an individual Web page. Place a group of embedded styles inside `<style>...</style>` elements and then place them all in the `<head>...</head>` elements of the page, like this:

```
<style type="text/css">
<!--
 body { font-family: verdana, sans-serif; font-size: 10pt; }
 h1 { text-align: right; }
-->
</style>
```

In the example above, the `<!--` and `-->` tags simply serve the purpose of hiding these CSS rules from older browsers that do not support CSS.

Styles applied to a page in this way affect only that page. This technique still allows you to achieve the goal of separating the content from your CSS settings. But you can now make alterations to one page without inadvertently breaking something else. You saw Dreamweaver use this technique in Chapters 2 and 3 when you changed some formatting.

❑ You can place inline styles into an individual HTML tag in a page. Place these directly into the tag, using the `style` attribute, like this:

```
<p style="text-align:right;">
 The quick brown fox jumped over the lazy dog.
</p>
```

Or do it like this:

```
<p>
 If you ever wondered how to use CSS to underline a single word, you'll find
 that <span style="text-decoration:underline;">this</span> is one way
 to do it.
</p>
```

While this technique allows you to utilize many CSS settings, it hinders your goal of producing an easily maintainable site—because a CSS style in a style attribute affects only that one tag and must still be individually edited.

If you want to apply a style consistently across many HTML tags of the same type, in many different files, you should write style rules into an external style sheet. If you want to write some style rules that apply only to the tags in a single page, however, the embedded styles technique is just fine. And if you want to make a very local adjustment to a single tag, then the inline styles technique is the one to use.

Editing Styles

You have already discovered how easy it is to create styles in Dreamweaver. As you are about to see, editing styles is just as easy. In this example, you are going to make a couple of simple adjustments to the body selector embedded in the news.htm document.

There are several ways you can do it. The Edit Style button brings you to the same dialog box you used to create them. However, there is another interesting technique you can use.

Try It Out   **Creating Embedded CSS**

1.   Close any documents you have open and open news.htm.

2.   Start by editing the body selector. There are several ways you can edit it. The easiest is to simply select the Edit Style button. However, let's take a look at an alternative technique.

In the CSS panel, double-click body. Several things should happen: The document window should split between Code view and Design view. The Code view should show the body selector embedded in the code. Right below the CSS panel, the CSS Properties panel should open and show the properties of the body selector (see Figure 4-16).

Figure 4-16

3.   If necessary, click the plus sign to expand the Font property and then click the right column next to font-family.

4.   From the drop-down list, select the "Arial, Helvetica, sans-serif" option. After you select it, you should see a corresponding change for the body selector in Code view:

```
body {
  background-color: #FFFFFF;
  margin-left: 0px;
  margin-top: 0px;
  margin-right: 0px;
  margin-bottom: 0px;
  font-family: Arial, Helvetica, sans-serif;
}
```

How It Works

This exercise is pretty self-explanatory. What is good here is that you can see the direct and quick inter-action between Dreamweaver's tools and the HTML code. This facilitates rapid application development by producing bug-free code quickly and easily.

CSS Classes

It is often convenient to use the HTML tags as selectors because you need only to create the individual rules, and they are employed automatically by the browser. However, there is one main drawback to this approach—it doesn't easily allow you to apply different rules to different types of information that happen to be rendered using the same HTML tag (or no tag at all).

For example, what if you wanted to display two paragraphs using different margins for each, or if you wanted to highlight one using italicized text? This is where CSS classes come to the rescue. Instead of only having control over all paragraphs at any one time, you can specify subgroups of elements and apply different CSS rules to each group.

The simplest explanation of CSS classes is that they allow you to create as many selectors as you need, without being restricted to the standard HTML tag names. In other words, you can give the rule any name you like. Once you've created a class in CSS, you can apply it to an HTML tag by using the `class` attribute of the tag you're applying it to. For example:

```
<h3 class="countryheading">France</h3>
```

This HTML code applies the rule for the class selector `countryheading` to the contents of this `<h3>` tag.

Here's another example. In the paragraph below, the words "stewed red cabbage" are part of a bigger paragraph—but they are the only words within the paragraph to which the rule for the recipe class selector is applied:

```
<p>
  In March, you're planning to publish a recipe
  for <span class="recipe">stewed red cabbage</span>; your team of
  food technologists is currently working to perfect it.
</p>
```

In this example, the `<span>...</span>` *tags are used (span meaning a span of words) to specify exactly where the style rule should be applied. The* `<span>...</span>` *tags specify an inline element.*

The process of creating a class is virtually identical to the process you've followed up to now. However, instead of specifying an HTML tag as the selector for a rule, you can make up your own and precede it by a period. For example, you could apply the following `class` selector to any element that is to be highlighted, regardless of the particular HTML tag used to specify that element:

```
.highlight { background-color: silver; }
```

Try this out right now.

Using a CSS Class

1. Close any open documents and open `index.htm`. Click the New CSS Style button in the CSS Styles panel.

2. In the resulting dialog box, choose Class (Can Apply to Any Tag). Type **highlight** in the Name field. Define the new style in your `cookingPlaceStyles.css` file. The dialog box should look like Figure 4-17. Click OK when you're done.

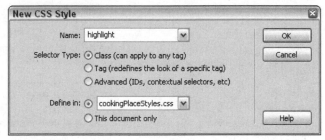

Figure 4-17

3. In the CSS Style Definition dialog box that comes next, select the Background category and choose silver (#CCCCCC) as the background color, as shown in Figure 4-18. Then click OK.

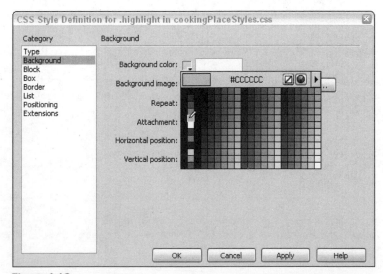

Figure 4-18

4. Now you should see your new class in the CSS Styles panel attached to the style sheet. Notice that there is a period before the name.

5. Switch to the Design view of `index.htm`. Highlight the text "This site will be updated daily" in the middle of the main paragraph.

6. This version of Dreamweaver handles it a little differently than previous versions. In the Property inspector, there is a field called Style. Open the drop-down list, as shown in Figure 4-19.

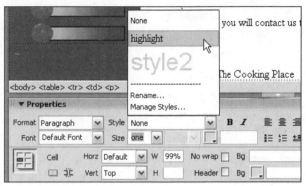

Figure 4-19

7. After selecting Highlight, you should see the change in the text background (see Figure 4-20).

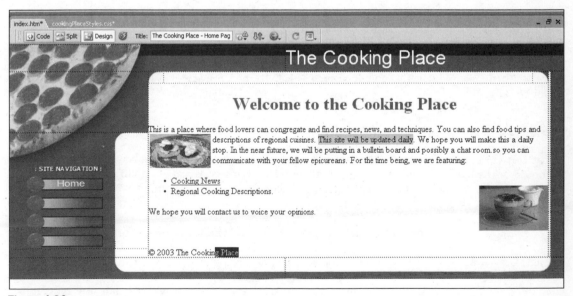

Figure 4-20

8. Preview the page in your browser to check that it worked.

How It Works

You already know that the index.htm file will be presented using the styles in the cookingPlace Styles.css file because it contains a <link> tag that points at the .css file. If you look at the Code view of this page, you'll find the following HTML ... tags enclosing the text you just formatted using the class:

```
<p>
...
You can also find tips and descriptions of regional cuisines.
<span class="highlight">This site will be updated daily.</span> We
hope you will make this a daily stop. In the near ...
...
</p>
```

Because this text is a part of a sentence—we refer to it as *inline text*—Dreamweaver has used ... tags to mark the text that you selected for styling. Then it added a class attribute and specified the .highlight class you created.

It's worth taking a quick look at the cookingPlaceStyles.css style sheet file to see how CSS defines class rules differently from rules for HTML tags. As you can see, it does this by preceding the class name with a period:

```
.highlight {
background-color: #CCCCCC;
}
```

You can also see here that the CSS attribute background-color has been used to apply the silver background highlight.

For a list of the available CSS attributes and some tutorials, see the excellent resources provided by the W3C (the people who design things such as HTML and CSS) at www.w3schools.com/css/css_ intro.asp.

Classes and Logical Markup

The concept of logical markup describes what each element is or what it means rather than how it should be displayed. Given the freedom that you can use any class names you like, you can create selectors and rules specifically for each distinct type of content in your pages and have as many of them as you need.

For example, consider the content that you put in your news.htm page (see Figure 4-21).

There are a number of distinct types of content here, the styling of which you can control using CSS. What can you say about this content? Well, it consists of one news item per row (with the background color of alternate rows white and light gray). The information itself consists of a date, the geographical source of news, and the news item itself.

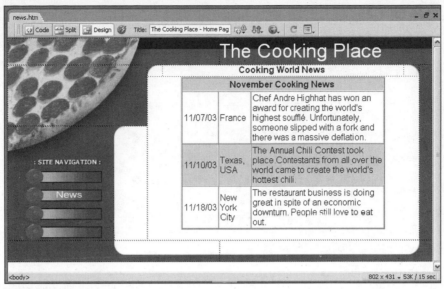

Figure 4-21

In fact, with the page as it is now, you can identify six distinct types of elements:

- ❏ Site-wide title (The Cooking Place)
- ❏ News page title (Cooking World News)
- ❏ News month title (November Cooking News)
- ❏ Date of the news item
- ❏ Location (or geographical source) of the news item
- ❏ The news item itself

For this example you'll focus on the items with relevance to the news page. You create some CSS classes to reflect this logical breakdown of information and then apply them to the corresponding items in the page.

Try It Out   Logical Markup Using CSS Classes

1. After identifying the distinct page elements in news.htm, the first thing to do is decide on a suitable name for a class corresponding to each. For the five news-relevant types above, use the following:

- ❏ newsPageTitle
- ❏ newsMonthTitle
- ❏ newsItemDate
- ❏ newsItemLocation
- ❏ newsItemStory

2. Create the embedded style rules. Because these are all news-relevant items, it should be fine to store these styles on the news.htm page because it's unlikely they'll be needed elsewhere. If you haven't done so already, open up news.htm and click New CSS Style in the CSS Styles panel.

3. Set Type to Class and set Name to **newsPageTitle**. Also define it as in This Document Only. The dialog box should look like Figure 4-22, after which you can click OK.

Figure 4-22

4. To keep things simple at this stage, simply select the Type category, change Color to something distinctive (lime green will do), change Size to Large, and click OK. You should now be able to see your new class in the CSS Styles panel, as shown in Figure 4-23.

Figure 4-23

5. Apply this new class to the corresponding page element. Highlight the heading text "Cooking World News." If necessary, click the bold format off. Use the Property inspector to format the text as h2.

6. Open the style field list in the Property inspector. You should see the class you created. Click it and your text should format to the properties you set. Moreover, the class name should now be shown in the <h2> tag in the tag selector, as shown in Figure 4-24.

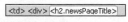

Figure 4-24

7. It's your turn now to get some practice at this process! Repeat Steps 2–4 another four times to create the remaining four classes (newsMonthTitle, newsItemDate, newsItemLocation, newsItemStory). For the sake of experimentation, simply give each of these classes a distinctive color for now. When you are ready to apply each class to its corresponding page element, simply highlight the text you want the class applied to and use the Property inspector to select it.

By the end, you should see the correct color applied to each of the five logical elements. In Figure 4-25 imagine that all dates are rendered in dark blue, locations are orange, and news stories are a darkish gray.

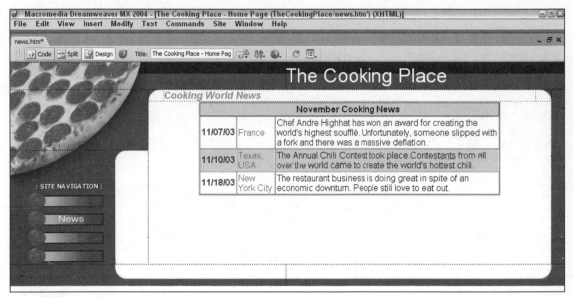

Figure 4-25

How It Works

Take a look at Code view to see what Dreamweaver has generated for you. Here's an example:

```
<tr bgcolor="lightgrey">
 <td class="new-item-date">11/10/02</td>
 <td class="news-item-location">Texas, USA</td>
 <td class="news-item-story">
  The Annual Chili Contest took place. Contestants
  from all over the world came to create the world's
  hottest chili.
 </td>
</tr>
```

Thinking in terms of logical elements is an important first step in structuring your pages to allow good use of CSS style rules. It is all about naming your style rules to reflect the nature and purpose of the data in the page.

Once you have created your logical class names and CSS rules (in this example you simply used text color) you attach each class to the corresponding page elements—in most cases this involves selecting the element and then clicking the style you wish to apply. In slightly more complex cases you may need to select the entire element in the tag inspector. This is particularly true with table cells and rows.

What remains for your news.htm page is to fine-tune the rules for your logical classes. You might like to go back to the classes you just created and try specifying some additional attributes to see how they affect the news items.

Pseudo-Classes and Pseudo-Elements

Up to this point, styles have been controlling and augmenting elements found in your HTML documents. However, styles have the ability to add elements and classes unique only to them. These unique components are called *pseudo-classes* and *pseudo-elements*.

For example, the `:hover` pseudo-class applies to an `<a>` element only when the user moves the mouse over the hyperlink. You will define the characteristics of the mouse hover effect.

Similarly, the `:first-letter` pseudo-element is based on a block element (such as a paragraph of text) and allows you to apply rules to the first character of the paragraph (to achieve, for example, a raised capital effect).

The raised capital is a good example, actually, so look at it now. Figure 4-26 shows the type of effect we're talking about.

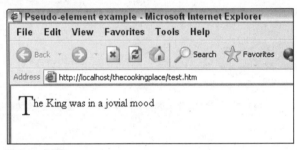

Figure 4-26

To achieve an effect like this, you use the `:first-letter` pseudo-element, defined like this:

```
<style type="text/css">
<!--
p.capital:first-letter {font-size:250%; float : left}
-->
</style>
</head>
<body>
<p class="capital">The King was in a jovial mood</p>
</body>
```

Pseudo-classes are commonly applied to hyperlinks. You can use pseudo-classes to create simple rollover effects with links. These are a very popular and useful dynamic effect. In Chapter 3 you already used some rollover effects in hyperlinks when designing your navigation buttons. When using images for the hyperlink, though, there is a drawback—the browser needs to download two images for each link.

Developers sometimes avoid this extra download overhead by using text-based links instead of image-based links. To achieve the same rollover effect, they use pseudo-classes in the hyperlinks.

One commonly used effect involves removing the underlining from the hyperlinked text and then using a `:hover` pseudo-class rule to display the underlining again when the mouse hovers over the link. Let's look at the use of the `:hover` pseudo-class now to achieve this interesting effect.

Try It Out   **Using a Pseudo-Class to Create a Rollover in a Text Hyperlink**

1. Remove the underlining from the text hyperlink. If it isn't open already, open `news.htm` in Design view. Click the New CSS Style button at the bottom of the CSS Style Sheet panel. Select Redefine HTML Tag (the second Selector Type), choose the "a" tag from the Tag drop-down list, and indicate that you want to create this style in your external CSS file `cookingPlaceStyles.css`, as shown in Figure 4-27. Click OK.

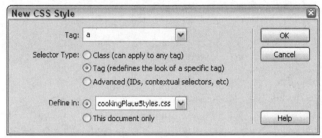

Figure 4-27

2. In the CSS Style definition dialog box, choose the Type category and then set the Decoration attribute to None (as shown in Figure 4-28). Click OK.

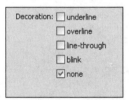

Figure 4-28

3. Click the New CSS Style button again in the CSS Style Sheet panel. This time set the Type option to Advanced (IDs, Contextual Selectors, Etc.) and from the Selector list select a:hover, as shown in Figure 4-29. You will save this new rule in the external file as well. Click OK.

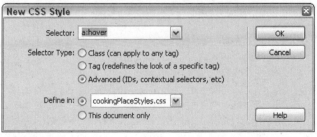

Figure 4-29

4. Specify the style for the a:hover pseudo-class. To do this, just change the Decoration attribute to Underline (as shown in Figure 4-30). If you would like, you can change the color also. Click OK.

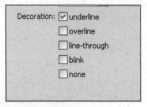

Figure 4-30

5. Insert a hyperlink into news.htm so that you can see this effect in action. While still in Design view of news.htm, click the text "Annual Chili Contest" in the third column of the table of news items. In the Property inspector, enter the address **http://www.annualchilicontest.com** in the Link field (as shown in Figure 4-31). Press Enter.

Figure 4-31

6. Press F12 to preview the page in your browser. You should be able to move the mouse pointer over and off the Annual Chili Contest text link and observe the rollover effect. Figure 4-32 illustrates the rollover effect by showing what you should see when the mouse pointer is away from the hyperlink, and when it hovers over the hyperlink.

Figure 4-32

How It Works

Because you've used the basic HTML anchor tag and one of its pseudo-classes, you don't need any special code in the HTML document itself. All the changes occur in the style sheet file, and the browser applies them automatically for you.

If you look at the code in the `.css` file, you'll see that two new rules appear:

```
a {
 text-decoration: none;
}
a:hover {
 text-decoration: underline;
}
```

These rules simply indicate that the hyperlink should have no decoration (and therefore no underline) under normal conditions but should be underlined when the mouse hovers over the hyperlink.

You've seen only the `:hover` pseudo-class here. In fact, the `<a>` element has a couple of other pseudo-classes. You can use the `:visited` pseudo-class to specify what a hyperlink should look like to a user who has recently viewed that linked page. You can use the `:active` pseudo-class to specify what a hyperlink should look like when the user has depressed the mouse button on the hyperlink but not yet released the button. As an exercise, you could try extending this example to add styles for the `:visited` and `:active` pseudo-classes. Simply repeat Steps 3 and 4 above, selecting the appropriate pseudo-class from the drop-down list in each case.

If you want to learn more about pseudo-classes, go to `www.w3schools.com/css/css_pseudo_elements.asp`. *There are also a number of excellent books available on the subject.*

Templates

As you've seen, CSS—particularly in the form of external style sheets—allows you to define a style in a single location and easily reuse that style definition throughout your site. But how can you easily reuse a page design? The answer comes in the form of Dreamweaver templates.

You certainly want all of your pages to have a consistent and identifiable look. But you already have three pages and you may well add more to your site as you build it up. Can you imagine the work involved if you wanted to make a little change to your page design? You would need to edit every single page that was affected by the design change—and that could take a long time. It's also a process that is prone to errors.

Instead, here is a more sensible solution. Design a template and then apply the template to each of your pages. When you want to make a change to your page design, apply it to the template. Dreamweaver will ensure that the change is implemented in every page that uses the template.

Creating a Template

From the point of view of your Cooking Place application, it would be a good idea to create a template for your three pages: `index.htm`, `news.htm`, and `regions.htm`. You built all three pages from copies of a version of `index.htm` that you completed in Chapter 2. It would be good to use that version of `index.htm` as the basis of your template.

You should have made a backup of that version of `index.htm` right at the beginning of Chapter 3—you called it `index_backup.htm`. If you didn't do that, don't worry; grab a copy from the Chapter04 files of the source code that accompanies this book (downloadable from www.wrox.com). The index_backup.htm file should be in the C:\TheCookingPlace folder of your local machine. (If you just added it to that folder now, select View⇨Refresh in the Site panel to refresh the panel and see the file.)

Now use this file to create a template.

Try It Out   Creating a Dreamweaver Page Template from an HTML File

1. In Dreamweaver, close any open files and open index_backup.htm.

2. Select File⇨Save As Template from the Dreamweaver menu bar. In the Save As Template dialog box, type **cookingplace_template** in the Save As text box, as shown in Figure 4-33, and then click Save. You may be prompted to update links. If so, click Yes. This ensures that all the links on the page are handled properly.

Figure 4-33

3. Look at the Files panel (see Figure 4-34). You should see that Dreamweaver has created a new folder called Templates. Double-click the folder to reveal its contents. It contains a new file called cookingplace_template.dwt. This is the template file that Dreamweaver has created for you.

Figure 4-34

4. As an exercise, activate the rollover images for the buttons, as you did in Chapter 3. By doing this, the behavior will automatically appear on every new page you create from this template.

5. Close the newly created template for now. You may be prompted that the template has no editable regions. If you are, just select OK. You will fix that problem in a bit.

How It Works

Dreamweaver does all the work for you here. It takes the basic page structure contained in your `index_backup.htm` file and stores it in a special form in the `cookingplace_template.dwt` file. The file extension, `.dwt`, stands for "Dreamweaver template."

Creating New Pages from a Template

Having created a template, it is now very easy to create additional pages for your Web site. You can either open a new page with the template attached or attach the template at some future point. If you are new to Dreamweaver and Web design, we strongly suggest that you use the former technique. Attaching a template to an existing page can be tricky.

Let's step through an example in which you create a page that contains a list of recipes, called `recipes.htm`. It will feature the same page design as your existing pages.

Try It Out   Creating Pages from a Template

1.   Choose File⇨New to open the New Document dialog box. Click on the Templates tab at the top.

2.   In the list of sites in the Templates For column, click `thecookingplace` site. This reveals (on the right) a list of the templates defined for this site. Click once on `cookingplace_template`. This previews the template in the Preview pane, as shown in Figure 4-35. When you've done that, click the Create button.

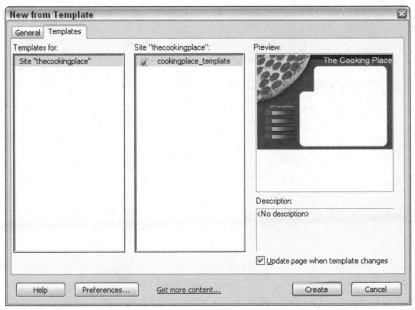

Figure 4-35

3.   You should now have a new untitled Web page, which contains the familiar Cooking Place page design. Save it immediately to a file. To do this, select File⇨Save As and save it as `recipes.htm`.

How It Works

Instead of creating a new, empty XHTML file with only the basic tags but no content, you asked Dreamweaver MX 2004 to copy the code from the cookingplace_template template instead.

With the page open in Design view, try to type in the main cell area (just click the cursor anywhere on the page and try typing something). You should find that you're not allowed to do this. An error message should appear, indicating that you are unable to make changes to the page (see Figure 4-36).

Figure 4-36

If you look at the document in Code view, you will see that the code is grayed out; it's code that's noneditable.

If you look near the top of the Code view, you will see where this page links to the template:

```
<!- InstanceBegin template="/Templates/cookingplace-template.dwt"
    codeOutsideHTMLIsLocked="false" ->
```

The reason you see the error message is that all regions of this template-based Web page file are, as yet, noneditable. That means you can't change them in the Web page.

Editable and Noneditable Regions

While your template, as it stands, ensures that all the pages based on it look the same, there is little value in having a lot of pages that look exactly identical! In this site, you want your pages to have the same page design but different content. In order to achieve this, you need to make your template a bit more useful—you must make sure it has some editable regions.

When you consider the nature of editable regions, the potential of templates becomes clear:

❑   Certain parts of the template remain noneditable. Those parts are the same within every single page that is built on the template. To control the content of the noneditable regions, you edit the template itself.

❑   All other parts of the template are editable. You can alter them as necessary within the page.

❑   When the template is altered in any way, all noneditable areas of the pages based on the template can be updated automatically without altering the content in the editable regions. As you'll see in a moment, introducing editable regions to a template is easy.

Editing Template-Based Documents

The overall process of creating and using Dreamweaver MX 2004 templates is quite straightforward:

1. Create a template containing one or more editable regions. These editable regions allow you to place distinct content onto different pages created from the template.

2. Create the pages themselves using the template.

3. Add content to the pages (quite separately from the design of the template).

Any changes you make to the template will be reflected in all the Web pages based on that template. Conversely, you can make changes to the content in the editable regions on a template-based page without affecting any other pages in the site.

You can demonstrate this by defining two editable regions in your template. One displays the title for a recipe and the other displays some comments relevant to the recipe, while also demonstrating the concept known as *repeating tables*. You need to open and edit your template to achieve this.

Try It Out   **Editing Template-Based Documents**

1. There are two ways to open your template for editing: You can double-click the template file `cookingplace_template.dwt` in the templates folder in the Files panel or select File⇨Open and maneuver to the Templates folder for the site. Either way, you should see the text `<<Template>>` displayed in the title bar of the Dreamweaver window, as shown in Figure 4-37.

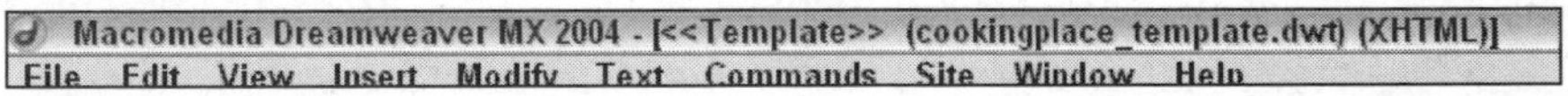

Figure 4-37

2. In Design view, click inside the main cell (the large white area) and press Enter three times to insert three paragraphs. You'll put your editable regions inside these paragraphs.

3. Now leave your cursor where it is and switch to Code view. Notice the three `<p>...</p>` elements for the three paragraphs, each with a nonbreakable space inside:

```
<p> </p>
<p> </p>
<p> </p>
```

4. Either place the cursor somewhere between the first pair of `<p>` and `</p>` tags and then switch back to Design view, or just go to Design view and select the first line you just created.

5. From the menu bar select Insert⇨Template Objects⇨Editable Region.

6. In the New Editable Region dialog box (see Figure 4-38), you must give the editable region a name. Call it **recipe_heading**.

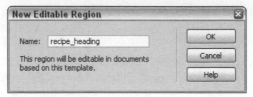

Figure 4-38

7. Click OK. The name of the editable region appears in the Design view of the template, as shown in Figure 4-39.

Figure 4-39

8. Put a repeating table below your first editable region in the second paragraph. Either switch back to Code view and place the cursor between the third pair of paragraph tags and then return to Design view, or click on the third line you created in Design view.

9. In the menu bar, once again select Insert⇨Template Objects. This time select Repeating Table.

10. In the Insert Repeating Table dialog box, opt for a two-row, two-column table. In the Region Name field, name the editable region **recipe_details**. Leave the other fields on their default settings (see Figure 4-40) and click OK.

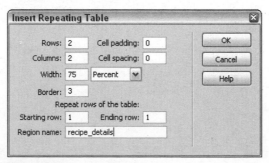

Figure 4-40

11. Save the file. When you do this, you will be presented with the Update Template Files dialog box (see Figure 4-41), which gives you the option of updating any pages linked to the template. You want to update these pages, so click on Update.

Figure 4-41

12. The Update Pages dialog box reports how everything went with the update, as shown in Figure 4-42. Take a moment to look at it. When you're ready, click Close.

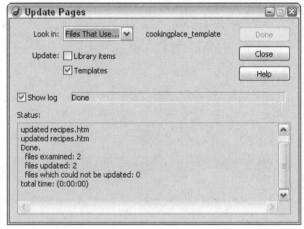

Figure 4-42

13. Now switch to the Design view of `recipes.htm`. You should see the editable regions marked off in the file, as shown in Figure 4-43.

If you had `recipes.htm` open in your Dreamweaver workspace while you were updating the template, you'd need to save it again now. Any pages that depend on a template, and which are open at the time the template is updated, will have those changes made to them while they are open, but will not be saved. The asterisk change flag appears to let you know that Dreamweaver has changed the page, and you must save the change manually.

14. In the recipe_heading area, type **Here is a list of recipes sent to you by some of your visitors**. You may also have to delete the temporary text that Dreamweaver inserts into the editable region (it uses the name of the region).

15. Change the formatting to bold and italic by using the Property inspector.

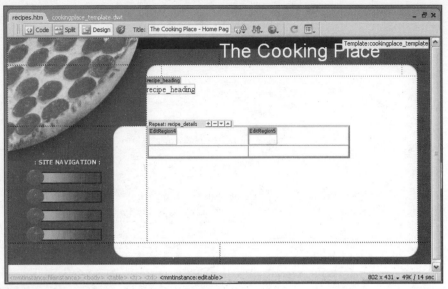

Figure 4-43

16. Here comes the nice part about repeating tables. You can add and subtract rows as you need them, clicking using the plus (+) and minus (–) buttons above the table. Also, each cell has an editable region within it. In the left cell of the first row, type **Pasta**. In the right cell type **A great low fat alternative to Fettuccine Alfredo**.

17. Click the plus button. In the first cell of the next row, type **Curry**. In the second cell type **A fast way to prepare a tasty curry base for use in many of your favorite recipes**.

18. If you like, do a little formatting to make it look nicer. Then save the file and preview it in the browser, as shown in Figure 4-44.

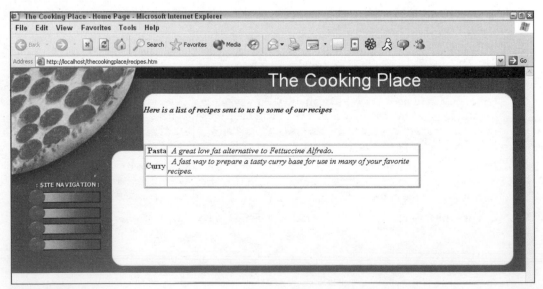

Figure 4-44

How It Works

You can now create as many pages as you want based upon the template. You'll benefit from templates even if you're building a relatively simple Web site because they'll help you to gain a consistent design across all the pages in the site.

As you've seen here, when you edit a template, Dreamweaver takes care of updating all pages that are based on the template. Make whatever changes you like to the page design in a template. As soon as you save those changes, Dreamweaver searches the site for all pages that are based on that template—pages that contain the following code:

```
<!— InstanceBegin template="/Templates/cookingplace-template.dwt"
     codeOutsideHTMLIsLocked="false" —>
```

Dreamweaver then makes the necessary changes to all Web page files that contain this code.

Adding a Template After the Fact

Of course, it's sensible to create your template first and then create all the pages (index.htm, news.htm, regions.htm, and recipes.htm) from that template. The first three of these pages don't contain a repeating table, though the last one does, so this template isn't quite perfect for index.htm, news.htm, and regions.htm. However, let's assume circumstances forced you to reverse the process.

| Try It Out | Applying a Template to an Existing Document |

1. Close any documents you may have open right now and start a new HTML document.

2. Type the text, as you did before: **Here is a list of recipes sent to you by some of your visitors**.

3. In the Files panel group, switch to the Assets panel. Select the Templates category from the left side, as shown in Figure 4-45.

Figure 4-45

4. Click the template name, cookingplace_template, and drag it anywhere inside the document. The Inconsistent Region Names dialog box shown in Figure 4-46 appears.

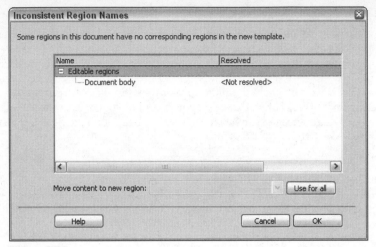

Figure 4-46

5. Dreamweaver is asking you to assign the text in the document's body to an editable region. To do this, click Document Body in the tree structure.

6. Open the drop-down menu on the bottom of the dialog box, as shown in Figure 4-47, and select recipe_heading.

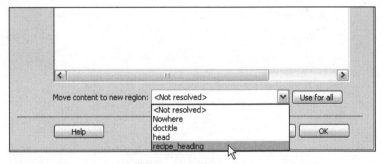

Figure 4-47

7. After clicking OK, your template is applied and the text is assigned to the proper editable regions. That is all there is too it.

How It Works

As we said from the outset, this is not always the best way to design a page. It is far easier, and preferable, to start with the template in place. However, should you be forced to reverse the workflow, or even apply a different template, you can do it easily.

Breaking the Template Link

One handy technique that is sometimes used is to apply a template and, after all the graphics and looks are in place, detach the template from the page. This leaves the look in place without the editable region restrictions of the template. The downside to this, however, is that if you update the original template for any reason, the detached page will not automatically update itself. To detach the template, select Modify⇨ Templates⇨Detach from Template.

Libraries

Library items are closely related to CSS and templates. A library item consists of HTML and is basically a minitemplate that you can place in any Web page in a particular site. Library items work like templates in that any changes to a library item will propagate throughout the site. You might use a library item to represent a company logo, copyright notice, block of disclaimer text, and so on. Each item is saved in a library file with the file extension .lbi.

Dreamweaver MX 2004 handles library items a little differently than previous versions. Let's set up a simple library item now. Click on the New Library Item button located on the Asset panel or create the item in a document and insert it into the library. You may find the latter technique a little easier to work with. However, both techniques ultimately bring you to the same place. In the following exercise, you are going to use the latter technique.

Try It Out   **Working with Library Items**

1. Create a new HTML document. You will not be saving the document but just using it to create a library object.

2. Type the words **We are not responsible for anyone dying from our recipes.** into the document.

3. Highlight all the text and, using the Property inspector, change Size from None to X-Small.

4. Make sure the Assets panel is open in the Files panel group (see Figure 4-48). If not, you can open it with the Window menu or by pressing F11. Select the Library category.

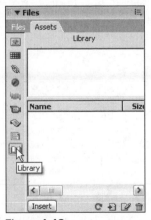

Figure 4-48

5. With the text still highlighted, click the New Library Item button in the Asset panel. You should see the text in the top preview window and the word *Untitled* in the bottom name window.

6. Name your object **disclaimer** by typing over the word *Untitled* in the bottom window and pressing Enter.

7. Close the open document without saving the changes because you used it to just create the library item. If you look in the Files panel, you should see that there has now been a `Library` folder created that contains all of your library entries for the site.

8. Use this new library item in your page. Open the `index.htm` file and make sure the Assets panel is visible. Click at the end of the copyright notice and press the spacebar a couple of times. Click and drag the library item from the Assets panel to the document, dropping it next to the copyright notice, as shown in Figure 4-49.

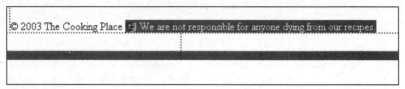

Figure 4-49

9. Notice that the disclaimer isn't editable. You may also notice that the inserted area is shaded. This indicates that it is a library entry; the browser should display it just fine.

10. Save the file.

How It Works

The library file is simply a file containing HTML. If you open the `.lbi` file in Code view, you'll see this. When you add the completed library item to a Web page, Dreamweaver simply copies the HTML code from the library item file and inserts it (as noneditable code) at the chosen point.

If you like, you can open the library item and alter it in some way; as soon as you save the changes to the library file, you'll prompt Dreamweaver to update all pages in the site that contain that library item.

Summary

You have expanded your set of Web development tools with three very powerful tools:

❑ Styles are powerful tools that enable you to style your Web pages. As you've seen, you can use styles to style an individual tag and define styles to be used in a particular page. Perhaps most significantly, you can write a style sheet file and link many Web pages to that file, enabling you to gain consistency of style across all pages in your site.

❑ Dreamweaver templates enable you to place all your page design into a single template file and then build lots of Web pages based on that template.

❑ Dreamweaver library items enable you to create nuggets of content that appear consistently and easily on many Web pages (such as a copyright notice or company logo).

Style sheet files, templates, and library items all help you, as the Web developer, to build your sites with a high level of consistency and control. They also make site maintenance easy. They are based on the notion of creating reusable code that you can use over and over again. A sensible designer builds a large array of these tools over a period of time and reuses them each time they create a new site. Remember, the emphasis today is on getting the job done rapidly. By using the tools you have seen in this chapter you will be turning out your sites quickly and flawlessly.

We covered several different ways of making your designs consistent from page to page. In the next chapter, you are going to study some additional techniques you can use for your design work.

Why Not Try . . .

1. Add a style rule to `cookingPlaceStyles.css` for the HTML `<body>` tag to specify that the preferred fonts for these pages should be Arial, Helvetica, sans-serif (in order of preference).

2. Add pseudo-class rules to `cookingPlaceStyles.css` for the `a:visited` and `a:active` pseudo-classes. Use the link in `news.htm` you created earlier to see them in action.

3. You may have assigned some quite garish colors to the five content-related classes in `cookingPlaceStyles.css` (newsPageTitle, newsMonthTitle, newsItemDate, newsItemLocation, and newsItemStory). Use the CSS Styles panel to edit them so that they all adopt the default color (which is black—for each one, simply clear the Color field in the Type category) and then apply some more tasteful italicizing, underlining, and bold instead. You might also like to experiment with margins and border attributes.

Layers, Behaviors, and Dynamic Effects

Up to this point we've concerned ourselves primarily with page- and site-design techniques, focusing on the task of positioning page elements and improving maintainability of your Web site. However, we have also made brief excursions into other areas. For example, we took time out in Chapter 3 to create rollover buttons and a pop-up menu with the purpose of creating an effective and attractive navigation tool.

In this chapter we'll focus your attention on the user interface and how you can make it more engaging for your users.

In Web site development circles, hardly a day goes by without the release of some new technology or gadget designed to make the Web more useful or exciting. The first Web browser that was capable of displaying images came as a revolution at the time (although we're used to it today) and led to a new level of Web design creativity, taking advantage of the fact that your pages could now be adorned with graphics and images as well as simple text and hyperlinks.

It wasn't long before Web designers started demanding greater interactivity with the user. This led to dynamic pages (instead of simply static HTML documents). Developers were able to make the pages dynamic through the use of behaviors. Examples of these include pop-up menus, changing page properties, swapping one image for another, etc. You can even create a behavior to check which browser the visitor uses, which lets you create alternative versions of your pages that will always ensure compatibility.

As we will be discussing, these behaviors are controlled most of the time with a programming language called JavaScript. While knowledge of JavaScript is useful, Dreamweaver MX 2004 handles most of the more commonly used behaviors with just a couple of simple menu selections. This allows you to turn out exciting looking Web pages rapidly.

It's also possible to design different elements of a page so that they overlap. When elements overlap, there must be a sense of one element being "above" the other. This is the concept of layers. You will be using layers, combined with JavaScript, to create some clever dynamic effects.

In this chapter you will look at how Dreamweaver MX 2004 writes events and behaviors for you. You will do the following:

- Create and use some Dreamweaver MX 2004 behaviors and event handlers
- Build some dynamic layers
- Create image rollovers
- Use an image map to display a page in a pop-up window

An Overview of Browser Scripting

The introduction of JavaScript has made it possible to take the dynamic user interface effects we're accustomed to in desktop programs and employ them on Web pages. This means that the browser is no longer restricted to displaying static HTML pages; it allows users to carry out more sophisticated tasks on the Web page. For example, in Chapter 3 you used JavaScript to power a rollover effect and a pop-up menu. You can also use JavaScript to do things like checking the contents of a form before it's submitted to a Web server.

HTML by itself cannot provide this dynamic behavior. As we discussed in earlier chapters, HTML is used only to describe the parts of the document. Developers needed the flow controls of a full programming language: `if` statements to make decisions and loops to repeat a sequence of code a determined number of times. However, early dynamic Web pages could not use the programming languages of the time easily. As an alternative, scripting languages were developed.

JavaScript is an example of a *scripting language*. Scripting languages are often simpler and quicker for creating useful functions than the traditional languages used for software development. VBScript and Perl are examples of other scripting languages used widely today.

The name JavaScript derives from its relationship with the Java programming language at the time it was developed. The developers of the JavaScript language intended its syntax to be familiar to Java developers while also being simpler to use and quicker for writing small snippets of code. Hence the name JavaScript. This is suggestive of its "lite" nature relative to the sophistication of Java.

You've probably noticed that HTML has a simple text format, which means that it is compatible with any computer suitably equipped to access the Internet. JavaScript is also a text-based language, partly for the same reason. The JavaScript contained in a Web page is in human-readable form, and is not compiled into the binary (1s and 0s) form that computers understand until the browser requires it. Then the browser takes care of interpreting the human-readable code, translating it into instructions the computer can run.

Dynamic HTML

The discussion brings you now to Dynamic HTML, or DHTML. Think of DHTML as essentially a combination of HTML, JavaScript, and CSS. Dreamweaver MX 2004 allows you to take advantage of a number of excellent dynamic features called behaviors, which you can connect easily to elements on your Web pages.

Before we go any further, let's create a very simple example to demonstrate a behavior in action.

Try It Out   **A JavaScript Demonstration**

1. Select File⇨New and create a new Basic HTML page. Save it with the file name **behaviortest.htm**.

2. In Design view, type the words shown in Figure 5-1.

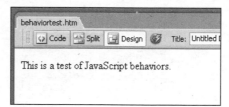

Figure 5-1

Before attaching a behavior to part of this text, you must add a suitable element. You'll use a hyperlink with a slight difference. Highlight the word *JavaScript* and enter a hash character (#) into the Link box of the Property inspector. This is a common technique for creating a dummy hyperlink. You can use this to trigger an event without requesting a page.

3. Attach the behavior to this <a> element. Click somewhere on the word *JavaScript* (so that you see <body><a> in the tag selector). Open the Tag panel group and select the Behaviors panel (or press Shift+F3). Notice the <a> in the Behaviors panel's title caption, which indicates that Dreamweaver MX 2004 is ready to attach an action to the <a> tag you selected, as shown in Figure 5-2.

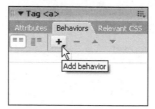

Figure 5-2

4. Click the plus (+) button and select Popup Message from the list of available behaviors. The Popup Message dialog box appears, as shown in Figure 5-3. Enter the text shown and click OK.

Figure 5-3

167

5. Check that the correct event triggers your pop-up message behavior. Look at the Behaviors panel (see Figure 5-4). On the left side, it should say onClick. On the right side, it should say Popup Message. The left side is the triggering event and the right side is the resulting action. If something other than onClick is shown here, you must change it now.

You can change it by clicking on the event and selecting the drop-down list. Then simply select the event you want (in this case, onClick). The panel should look like Figure 5-4.

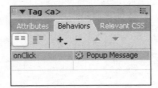

Figure 5-4

6. Save the file and press F12 to preview it in the Web browser.

7. Point to the JavaScript link in the page and click the mouse button. You should a message appear, like the one shown in Figure 5-5.

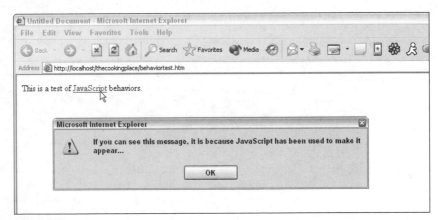

Figure 5-5

How It Works

This simple example demonstrates how Dreamweaver MX 2004 makes it easy for you to make use of the power of JavaScript and DHTML. As we mentioned from the outset, you don't need to understand JavaScript at all or even write a single line of code!

When you made the word *JavaScript* a hyperlink, Dreamweaver MX 2004 wrapped it in <a> and </a> tags. Behaviors don't only apply to <a>...</a> tags but this choice is convenient for this simple example. Then you simply attached the onClick behavior to the <a>...</a> tags and instructed Dreamweaver MX 2004 to create JavaScript code that triggers a pop-up message whenever the user clicks on the hyperlink. Here's how Dreamweaver MX 2004 made that change:

```
<a href=# onClick=MMpopupMsg(If you can see ...etc. )>JavaScript</a>
```

The onClick event is added as an attribute, indicating that if the user clicks on the <a> element, this event should be triggered.

The value of the onClick attribute describes *exactly* how that event should be handled. This is the *event handler*. In this example, the value for this attribute (the portion surrounded in double-quotes) is a JavaScript command that runs some prewritten code to display your pop-up message. You can see the text of the message as well.

The series of events here can be summarized as follows:

1. The page is displayed in the browser. The page includes an element that invites the user to interact with it in some way. In this case, it is a hyperlink, which the vast majority of users recognize as an invitation to click the element.

2. The user may place the mouse cursor over the hyperlinked text. The browser changes the cursor icon to the hand icon, which indicates that the cursor has been placed over a hyperlink of some sort. This is also a example of an event and a behavior.

3. The user may then press and release the appropriate mouse button. The browser examines the element the user clicked on to see if an event handler for the onClick event has been specified. In this case, there is an onClick event specified.

4. The browser executes the JavaScript code it finds in the event handler. Voilà! The pop-up message appears.

Targeting a Browser

Each generation of Web browser increases the number of available behaviors. Dreamweaver MX 2004 helps you address the problem of browser compatibility. As an example, the onClick behavior you created in the last exercise is not available for Internet Explorer version 3.0 and earlier.

Now to look at a small demonstration. In the Behaviors Panel, click on the plus (+) and select the Show Events For menu option. Then click to see the events that are available for IE 3.0 (see Figure 5-6).

Notice that the onClick event disappears from the Behaviors panel. Don't worry, it is just hidden; you have not lost it.

Select the Show All Events button on the panel, shown in Figure 5-7.

Only two events are available. Now repeat this and select IE 6.0 as your target browser. You should see a much larger list.

It is a good idea to know your target audience and what software they use. However, when in doubt, most designers select something between the oldest and newest browsers.

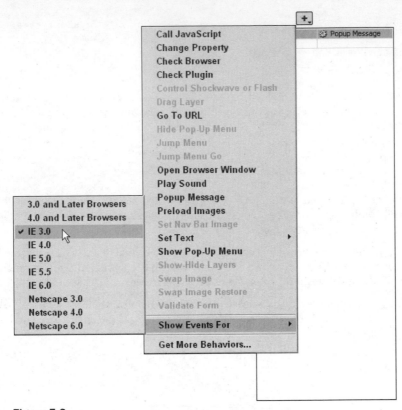

Figure 5-6

Figure 5-7

Here's a list of some available event handlers:

Event	Description
onKeyDown	A keyboard key is pressed down (but not including the release)
onKeyPress	A keyboard key is pressed and released
onKeyUp	A keyboard key is released
onLoad	The page is finished loading

Event	Description
onMouseDown	The user presses a mouse button
onMouseOver	The cursor moves over a page element
onMouseOut	The cursor moves off a page element
onMouseUp	The user releases a mouse button
onSubmit	The user submits a form

The most commonly used event handlers are onMouseOver and onMouseOut for creating image rollovers and layer effects, onClick for a wide range of functions, and onSubmit for useful tasks such as form validation. Note that not all of these events are triggered by the user. Some, such as onLoad, are caused by a change in the document's state.

Attaching Multiple Behaviors to an Element

It's possible to add more than one behavior to a single element. You can easily extend the previous example to demonstrate that. If you run behaviortest.htm in your browser again and run your mouse over the hyperlink, you may notice that the target address of the hyperlink appears in the status bar of your browser (see Figure 5-8).

> http://localhost/thecookingplace/behaviortest.htm#

Figure 5-8

As you can see, it displayed http://localhost/thecookingplace/behaviortest.htm#, which isn't particularly useful or informative. In fact, you aren't using this hyperlink to request a new document, you're using it to trigger your behavior. So remove this potentially confusing link information from the status bar and replace it with a more informative message. To do this, add another behavior to the <a> element.

Try It Out   **Attaching Multiple Behaviors to a Single Element**

1. With behaviortest.htm still open, switch back to Design view and click on the hyperlink again (so that you can see <body><a> in the tag selector).

2. Click the plus (+) button in the Behaviors panel and choose Set Text⇨Set Text of Status Bar. Enter the text shown in Figure 5-9 into the dialog box and then click OK.

Set Text of Status Bar

Message: Click to see a JavaScript demonstration...

OK

Cancel

Help

Figure 5-9

171

3. Check the Behaviors panel, which should now show a second behavior (see Figure 5-10).

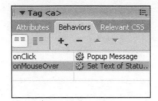

Figure 5-10

By default, Dreamweaver MX 2004 should have created it as an onMouseOver event; if not, change it to onMouseOver using the drop-down Events list.

4. Save behaviortest.htm and preview it in your browser. When you roll the mouse over the hyperlinked word *JavaScript*, you will see the text appear in the status bar, as shown in Figure 5-11.

Figure 5-11

How It Works

Once again, you simply attach a behavior to the <a> anchor tag. To view the code for the behavior, click on the hyperlink now in Design view and switch to Code view. You'll see that Dreamweaver MX 2004 has added the onMouseOver event handler to the <a> tag, like this:

```
<a href=#
 onClick=MMpopupMsg( This is a test\r...)
 onMouseOver=MMdisplayStatusMsg(Click to see a JavaScript demonstration...);
    return document.MMreturnValue>
 JavaScript
</a>
```

This event handler uses another built-in command (the MMdisplayStatusMsg() command created automatically by Dreamweaver MX 2004) to display the message.

In general, you need to be a little cautious when changing the status bar text in this manner. Some experts (notably Jakob Nielsen on his usability Web site www.useit.com, but also others) urge Web designers never to change the status bar text. The logic behind this opinion is that the status bar is an important source of information for users, particularly when they are considering which link to follow next. As a general rule, it's usually best to leave the status bar as it is when dealing with normal hyperlinks that link to other pages.

However, if you use a hyperlink in the manner we have here—as a trigger for an event—then it may be useful and tidier to hide messy details of JavaScript commands and confusing dummy hyperlinks from the user. In these cases, instead of displaying a definite message, simply set the status bar text to an empty string by leaving the Set Text of Status Bar dialog box empty.

Layers

You've seen several different ways of positioning content within your pages. Each of these techniques presents some limitations with regard to positioning. You are now going to learn another technique, called *layers*. This tool gives you greater flexibility in positioning elements on the page. However, as you will shortly see, you must make sure that your target audience is using only newer versions of Internet Explorer or Netscape.

Not only can CSS style the various elements of your page, but CSS also contains attributes that allow you to specify the position of an element. This concept is generally referred to as *CSS positioning*. Often the easiest way to position a set of elements is to place them all inside HTML's general-purpose `<div>...</div>` element and assign inline CSS positioning attributes to this `<div>...</div>` element. (If that all sounds complicated, don't worry—you'll see an example in a minute.)

Dreamweaver MX 2004's layers are constructed using CSS positioning and the `<div>` element. You can use layers to construct animations, pop-up messages, navigation menus, and image-swapping, and you can even overlap layers to produce visual effects using text.

See the Microsoft Typography Gallery (`www.microsoft.com/typography/css/gallery/entrance.htm`) for some interesting possibilities using CSS and layers.

Try constructing some layers now.

Try It Out   Constructing Layers

1. Open the file `regions.htm` and delete any text content that you added to the main cell of the page in Chapter 4. You're going to replace it with something a little more attractive.

2. Click the white main area in the page to place the cursor there. Open the Layout panel from the drop-down list in the Insert panel group, as shown in Figure 5-12.

Figure 5-12

3. Select the Draw Layer icon.

4. Your mouse will take the form of a little "+". Use it to draw an approximately square shape. Size and position are not critical.

5. Fine-tune the position and size of the layer. To do this, click one of the borders of the layer. The `<div#Layer1>` tag should be selected in the tag selector. The Property inspector changes to display the properties for the layer. Set the left (L) position to 300px and the top (T) position to 150px. Set both the width (W) and height (H) to 200px (see Figure 5-13). You could also use the graphic handles to resize the layer and drag it to the desired position.

Figure 5-13

6. Open the Files panel of the Files panel group and expand the Images folder. Click the file USA.gif and drag it onto the layer, as shown in Figure 5-14.

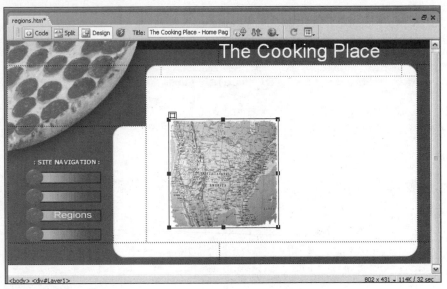

Figure 5-14

7. Notice a small rectangular icon at the top left of the selection in Design view: This marks the position of the actual <div> element in the code.

8. If you work with many layers, things can sometimes get a little confusing. Even though you have a relatively simple scenario here, this is a good time to look at the Layers panel, shown in Figure 5-15. Either select the Design panel group and select Layers, or press F2.

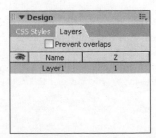

Figure 5-15

9. This panel allows you to select a layer. There are two features on this panel worth noting. First, the eye icon allows you to turn the visibility of the layer on and off. Second, the z (or z-index) column allows you to decide the stacking order of layers. Each layer has a different number; if two layers overlap one another, the one with the lower z-index appears to be behind the other.

10. Click Layer1 in the Layers panel and take a look at the Property inspector, as shown in Figure 5-16. Change its name from Layer1 to **usaMap**. We used proper naming conventions for JavaScript discussed earlier in the book. The reason for this is that you are going to add some JavaScript behaviors to these layers in the next chapter.

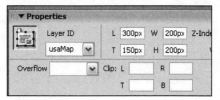

Figure 5-16

New to Dreamweaver MX 2004 are fields for Overflow and Clip. Overflow determines what happens if the image overflows the dimensions of the layer. The options are shown in Figure 5-17.

Figure 5-17

Clip allows you to set a visible area smaller than the dimensions of the Layer. You can set these by hand. For purposes of this exercise, you will leave both of these fields empty.

11. Using the eye icon in the Layer panel, hide this layer.

12. Repeat Steps 2 to 8 to create a second layer with the same dimensions. Insert the image `france.gif` into this layer and name it **franceMap**.

13. Repeat Steps 2 to 8 to create a third layer with the same dimensions. Insert the image `italy.gif` into this layer and name it **italyMap**. The Layers panel should now look like Figure 5-18.

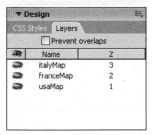

Figure 5-18

How It Works

Use the Layers panel to click one of the layers. You should see a `<div#...>` tag in the tag inspector. Switch to Code view. You'll be able to see all three layers together. We've changed the indenting here a little to make it easier to read:

```
<div id=usaMap
  style=position:absolute; left:300px; top:150px; width:200px; height:200px;
    z-index:1; visibility: hidden;>
<img src=images/USA.gif width=200 height=200 />
</div>
<div id=franceMap
  style=position:absolute; left:300px; top:150px; width:200px; height:200px;
    z-index:2; visibility: hidden;>
<img src=images/France.gif width=200 height=200 />
</div>
<div id=italyMap
  style=position:absolute; left:300px; top:150px; width:200px; height:200px;
    z-index:3; visibility: hidden;>
<img src=images/Italy.gif width=200 height=200 /> </div>
```

Each layer consists of a `<div>...</div>` element that contains an `<img>` tag. The ID of the `<div>` tag identifies the layer. Dreamweaver MX 2004 has also used an inline style sheet to describe the position of the layer. It does this using CSS positioning attributes. You used the Property inspector to set the position and size of each layer (and, in fact, you gave them all the same position and size so that they lie one above the other). As a result of the settings you specified, Dreamweaver MX 2004 generates the following CSS attribute values:

```
position:absolute; left:300px; top:150px; width:200px;
height:200px;
```

Giving each `<div>` tag an absolute position means that the browser positions it with respect to the top-left corner of the browser. By necessity, each layer is a rectangle. As you can see, you have positioned the top-left corner of each layer at a position of 300 pixels from the left edge of the browser window and 150 pixels from the top. Each layer is 200 pixels in both height and width.

Each layer has a different z-index. That is the stacking order of the layers.

Layers are a genuinely flexible positioning technique. But if layers are so great, why don't we use them exclusively? There is one significant caveat to consider when using layers: namely, many older browsers do not support them. Support begins with Internet Explorer 4 and Netscape Navigator 4. Netscape Navigator 4 is not fully compliant either because it cannot read layers within the `<div>` tags. Instead, it uses either the `<layer>` tag for absolute positioning or the `<ilayer>` tag for relative positioning. If this is a concern to you, you will need to code that by hand in Dreamweaver MX 2004.

If you use an older browser to look at a site that employs layers, what you see is, at best, unformatted text and, at worst, an incomprehensible mess. This is why you should test your pages using a suitably broad range of popular browsers. You may want to have alternate pages and use something called *browser sniffing*, which we will discuss shortly.

Hidden Layers

As you've probably worked out by now, it's possible to place more content into a Web page than the visitor sees at any one time. You are now going to apply JavaScript behaviors to your layers.

Controlling Layer Visibility

1.   If you closed it, reopen `regions.htm` in Design view.

2.   Toward the top of the page, draw a new layer. After it is drawn, click the border of the layer and use the Property inspector to set the L, T, W, H, and Layer ID properties as shown in Figure 5-19.

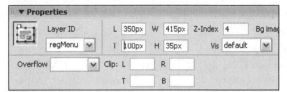

Figure 5-19

In Design view, the layer may appear to go past the right side of the red border area (depending on your resolution and browser-side settings). Don't worry about this. It should work fine in the browser.

You're going to turn this layer into a navigation bar. By placing the navigation bar into a layer, you have a bit more flexibility over its exact placement within the page. Also, as you see during the course of this exercise, you get some additional programming capabilities that you can use to good effect.

3.   Click inside the regMenu layer. Click the Image button in the Common panel and insert the image `italyButton.gif` into the layer. Repeat the process twice more to insert the image `usaButton.gif` and the image `frenchButton.gif`. Save the file and check it in the browser. It should look like Figure 5-20.

Figure 5-20

4. Close the browser and return to Design view.

5. Go to the Layers panel. You should find something like Figure 5-21.

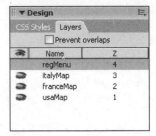

Figure 5-21

There are four layers altogether. Three of them (italyMap, franceMap, and usaMap) were created in the last exercise; the other one (regMenu) is the one you created above. You're going to add some behaviors that cause these maps to appear when the user clicks on the button. To do that, use the `onClick` event to display the corresponding layer and also hide the other two layers. In this way, the three country links (contained in the regionMenu layer) appear to load the corresponding map instantaneously.

6. In Design view, click once on the Italy button (in the regMenu layer) so that the tag hierarchy <body><div#regMenu><img> appears in the tag selector. Then go to the Behaviors panel, click the plus (+) button, and select Show-Hide Layers to open the Show-Hide Layers dialog box (see Figure 5-22).

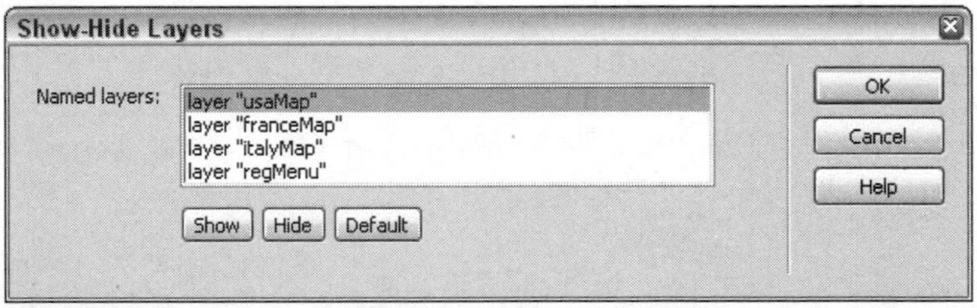

Figure 5-22

As you can see, it shows the four layers on the page. With the USA layer selected, click the Hide button. Select the France layer and click the Hide button. Select the Italy layer and, this time, click the Show button. Finally, make sure the regMenu layer shows. The dialog box should now look like Figure 5-23.

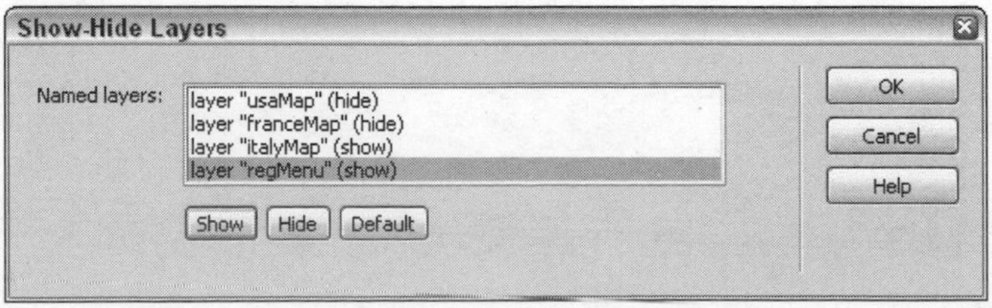

Figure 5-23

7. Click OK. Go to the Behaviors panel to see what Dreamweaver MX 2004 has created (see Figure 5-24). There is just a single behavior that's capable of hiding and revealing multiple layers.

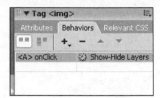

Figure 5-24

The behavior *should* be triggered by the onClick event. If Dreamweaver MX 2004 has created the behavior for a different event, change it to onClick using the Event drop-down list.

8. Click the United States button (in the regMenu layer) and repeat Steps 5 and 6. This time, make sure the usaMap layer appears and the France and Italy layers are hidden (see Figure 5-25).

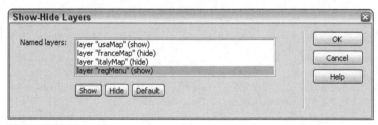

Figure 5-25

9. In the Behaviors panel, make sure the behavior is set to the onClick event.

    Click the France button (in the regMenu layer) and repeat Steps 5 and 6 once more. This time, make sure the franceMap layer appears and the usaMap and italyMap layers are hidden (see Figure 5-26).

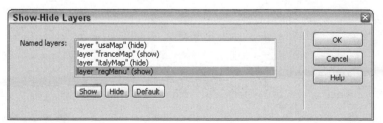

Figure 5-26

In the Behaviors panel, once again make sure that the behavior is set to the onClick event.

10. Save the file and preview it in the browser. Click the Italy, United States, and France buttons. As you do so, you should see the image change to show the relevant country map. Each time you click, you're asking the browser to reveal one of the map layers and hide the other two, as shown in Figure 5-27.

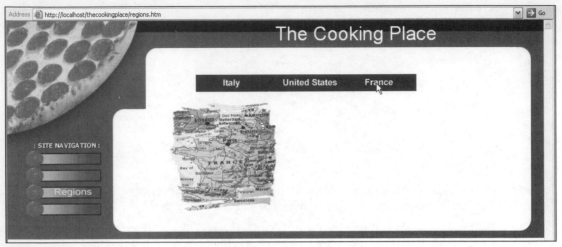

Figure 5-27

How It Works

This is a very handy technique to use when you want to pack a lot of content into a single screen-sized page design. All you're doing is allowing the user to decide what appears in the available space. If they want to see a map of France, they click the France button; if they want to see a map of the United States, they click the United States button. It's careful use of real estate!

Using Layers to Provide Extra Information

When you're browsing the Web, it's always frustrating when you come across navigation links that are confusing, ambiguous, or wrong. Links that deposit the user in a completely unexpected destination are sometimes referred to as *mystery meat* (or *click and pray*) *navigation*. Usability and good navigation design are important if you want to help your users to find their way round your Web site easily:

❑ If you create a link to a downloadable file, it's a good idea to provide additional information such as the size of the file.

❑ If you create a link to a different site, you could tell the user that it goes offsite, and perhaps suggest they right-click to open the link in a new window.

❑ Even for a link to another page within your own site, a little extra information about the nature of the target page can radically improve the user's experience of your site.

Dreamweaver MX 2004's behaviors and layers can be invaluable tools for this purpose. Let's construct a feature in your Cooking Place site that tells users a little more about your navigation buttons by explaining where the link will take them.

We'll show you how to apply the change to index.htm, and then you can apply it to the other pages. Alternatively, you could use the technique on the template you created in Chapter 4 and then rebuild index.htm, news.htm, and so on so that they all use the template.

Try It Out   **Attaching a Pop-up Layer to a Hyperlink**

1. In Dreamweaver MX 2004, close all open files and open `index.htm` in Design view.

2. Before you add these new effects, remove the old rollover effects from the navigation buttons. First, click on the second button (the News button) and, in the Property inspector, change the Src property from images/buttonblank.gif to **images/newsover.gif**.

3. In the Behaviors panel, delete the `onMouseOver` and `onMouseOut` behaviors by selecting them and clicking the minus (–) button.

4. Repeat Steps 2 and 3 for the third button (the Regions button), setting the Src property to **images/regionsover.gif**.

5. Repeat Steps 2 and 3 for the fourth button (the Contact Us button), setting the Src property to **images/contactover.gif**. Now your navigation buttons should look like Figure 5-28.

Figure 5-28

6. Construct the layer to display your link information for the News link. Start by drawing the layer anywhere on the page. As you did before, select the Draw Layer option on the Layout Tools button (which is in the Layout panel), click and hold the mouse button at the position where you want the top-left corner of the layer, and drag the mouse to the position of the bottom-right corner before releasing the mouse button.

7. Click the border of the layer to select it and set its properties in the Property inspector as shown in Figure 5-29.

Figure 5-29

Here you've made the layer 250 pixels wide and 50 pixels high, and placed it approximately adjacent to the News link (which is 200 pixels from the left edge and 280 pixels from the top).

We've also set the background color to #999999 (a dark shade of gray) and set the name of the layer to **newslinkinfo**. Figure 5-30 shows what the Design view should look like now.

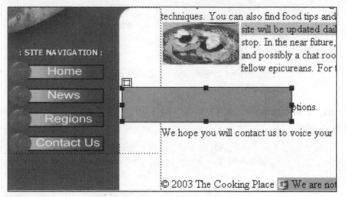

Figure 5-30

8. Click inside the layer and enter some descriptive text, like what's shown in Figure 5-31.

Figure 5-31

If you test this now in your browser, you may or may not see the layer in the position you placed it. Also, the size may not be as planned. As a remedy to this, a style sheet allows you the most control.

9. Create a CSS style and attach it to your paragraph layer. Open the CSS Styles panel and click the New CSS Style button, the one with the plus (+) at the bottom of the panel. Set the Type to Class (Can Apply to Any Tag), set Name to link_info, and define the new rule as This Document Only. The dialog box should look like Figure 5-32.

10. When you click OK, you need to specify the styles for the layer. In the Type category, set the Font, Size, Color, and Weight properties as shown in Figure 5-33.

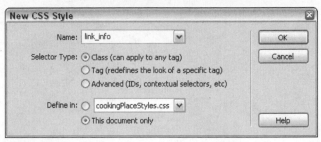

Figure 5-32

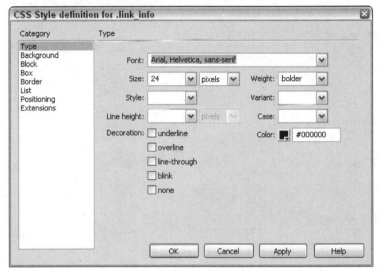

Figure 5-33

11. In the Background category, set the background image to **images/layerImage.jpg**. Also, set the Repeat field to No-Repeat and make the Horizontal and Vertical positions Center.

12. In the Block category, set Text Align to Center.

13. Use the Positioning category to ensure that your browser sizes and positions your layer properly. Set the Width field to 260 pixels and the Height field to 60 pixels. Also, set the Top field to 285 pixels and the Left field to 205 pixels. The settings should look like Figure 5-34.

14. Click OK. You'll see the new link_info style appear in the CSS Styles panel. Now apply the new style to the layer. To do this, click somewhere inside the layer. New to Dreamweaver MX 2004 is the ability to attach a style using the Property inspector. When you open the Style drop-down list, you should see the style you just created (see Figure 5-35).

15. Select link_info and your layer's formatting should look like Figure 5-36.

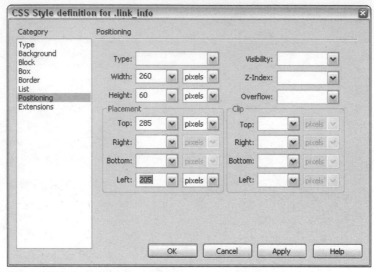

Figure 5-34

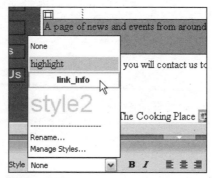

Figure 5-35

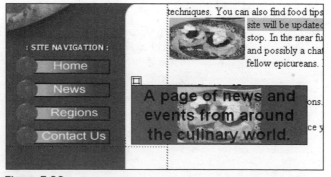

Figure 5-36

16. If you save the document and preview it in a Web browser, you will see that your layer is currently visible by default. The next thing to do is make sure it is hidden by default (so that you can show it when users mouse over the News link). In the Layers panel under the Design panel group, click once on your layer and click once or twice in the left column (on the eye icon), until you see a closed eye next to the newsLlink layer. The layer should disappear in Design view.

17. Attach the behavior that makes your informative layer appear and disappear. Still in Design view, click once on the News button. Click the plus (+) button in the Behaviors panel and select Show-Hide Layers to open the Show-Hide Layers dialog box shown in Figure 5-37.

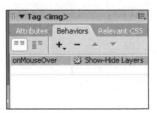

Figure 5-37

Because your page currently has only one layer defined, Dreamweaver MX 2004 has selected this layer by default. Click the Show button (the word *show* should appear in parentheses after the layer's name) and click OK.

18. Still looking at the Behaviors panel in Figure 5-38, check that the behavior you just added is set to use the onMouseOver event. If it isn't, change it to onMouseOver by selecting it from the Events list.

Figure 5-38

19. Save the page and preview it in the browser. Check that initially the layer is not visible and that it appears when you place the cursor over the News link.

20. Unfortunately, the layer remains visible now when you move the mouse off the News link. You have yet to add in a behavior that *hides* the layer again when the mouse rolls off the News button. Repeat Step 17 but, this time, click the Hide button (instead of Show) and ensure the onMouseOut event is selected instead of onMouseOver (see Figure 5-39).

21. Save the page and preview it again. The layer should now appear and disappear.

22. Repeat these steps for the remaining two links (Regions and Contact Us) to create two additional layers. Name the two new layers **regionslinkinfo** and **contactlinkinfo**, respectively. When you position these layers, you might like to keep them all at the same coordinates or place them closer to the link to which they refer.

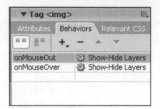

Figure 5-39

How It Works

You attached two behaviors to the News button. One reacts to the mouse entering the area of the News button by running the onMouseOver event handler, which causes the layer to be revealed. The other reacts to the mouse leaving the area by running the onMouseOut event handler, which hides it again. Once again, Dreamweaver MX 2004 writes the required JavaScript code without you needing any knowledge of or interaction with it.

You revisited, and revised, some techniques from Chapter 4 by using some CSS settings to make the text and layer stand out a little from the information in the background. Experiment with different styles.

Swapping Images

You encountered probably the most widely used dynamic effect on the Internet, the image rollover, when you first built the navigation buttons back in Chapter 3. These rollover buttons use the simple exchange of one image for another in reaction to the onMouseOver event, and a return to the original image in reaction to the onMouseOut event.

There is one other type of image-swapping effect that can be very effective: A *disjointed rollover effect* is when the image exchange occurs at a different location in the page. Like most JavaScript behaviors, this can be handled easily in Dreamweaver MX 2004.

Try It Out   Creating Disjointed Images

1. With index.htm open in Design view, click the Contact Us button and use the right arrow on your keyboard to move the cursor just past the button. Press Enter to add some space under the Contact Us button.

2. Select Insert⇨Image. (Alternatively, click the Image button on the Common panel of the Insert panel group.) In the Select Image Source dialog box, select the image swap1.gif, as shown in Figure 5-40. Click OK.

3. With the image still selected, click the Center Align button in the Property inspector to center it. Assign the name **swapHome** to the image, as shown in Figure 5-41.

   This is important because when you create the image-swapping functionality, Dreamweaver MX 2004 needs to be able to identify the image as the base image for swapping and use that name in the JavaScript code it generates. The page should now look like Figure 5-42.

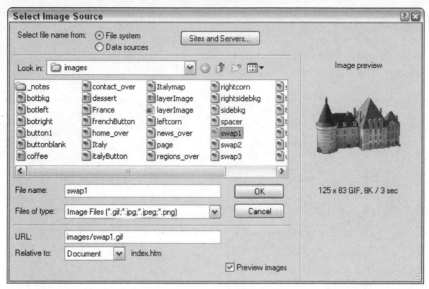

Figure 5-40

Figure 5-41

Figure 5-42

4. Select the News button. Click the plus (+) button in the Behaviors panel and select Swap Image. In the Swap Image dialog box (see Figure 5-43), select the image that you just added—image "swapHome." (Note that you're identifying this image by the unique name you gave it in Step 3.) Using the Browse button next to the Set Source To field, select the image swap2.jpg; this is the image that will be shown in place of the swapHome image.

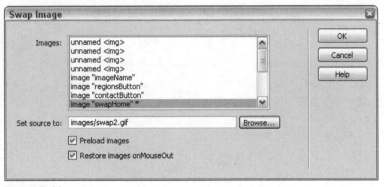

Figure 5-43

Leave Preload Images and Restore Images onMouseOut checked (as shown in Figure 5-43) and click OK.

You've seen the preload option before. It refers to the technique of loading all images (including the swapped image) that aren't visible initially when the page loads. Thus the image swap can happen immediately when the user activates it. Without this, the browser firsts send a request for the swap image to the Web server and the rollover effect suffers a short delay while the server responds (probably ruining the effect and confusing the user).

You used the onMouseOut *option in the previous exercise. With this set, Dreamweaver MX 2004 generates code that restores the original image when the mouse leaves the button.*

5. Repeat Step 4 for the next two buttons (Regions and Contact Us). Each time, the image to be swapped out is image swapHome. Use the following swap images:

   ❑ For the Regions button, the image to be swapped in is swap3.jpg

   ❑ For the Contact Us button, the image to be swapped in is swap4.jpg

6. Save your Web page document and preview it in the browser.

How It Works

Notice that each button has double-duty now and quite a few behaviors attached to it. Each button serves as a link to another page and, at the same time, triggers a behavior to swap a picture. As you roll the mouse over the different buttons in the browser, you'll see the image change and the layer appear (see Figure 5-44).

You can see a list of the individual behaviors for each button in the Behaviors panel. For example, select the News button and look at the Behaviors panel shown in Figure 5-45.

Figure 5-44

Figure 5-45

There are two onMouseOver behaviors and two onMouseOut behaviors. Each time the user's mouse pointer rolls over the image, both onMouseOver behaviors run, revealing the helpful text layer that you created earlier and swapping the disjointed image from a "home" to a satellite dish. Each time the user's mouse pointer rolls back out of that image, both onMouseOut behaviors run, hiding the layer and swapping the disjointed image back.

It is very simple to remove any unwanted behavior by clicking on it (in the Behaviors panel) and clicking the minus (–) button. When you eliminate a behavior, the corresponding JavaScript code is automatically deleted as well. Once again, all this was accomplished without you touching a line of code.

Using Image Maps with Behaviors

In the next example, we'll use an image map to display alternative blocks of descriptive text for regions in the maps. By using *image maps* or *hotspots* (both terms are used), you can create more than one hyperlink for a single image by attaching different links to different areas of the image. Image maps divide an image into sections, to which you apply a hyperlink or a JavaScript behavior.

In the Cooking Place Web site, you're treating northern Italy and southern Italy separately, so you can create an image map to demonstrate this technique. You already have your map of Italy, so you can use this technique to highlight the two regions of Italy.

What region shapes can you use? Well, Dreamweaver MX 2004 gives you a few options, as you'll see if you click an image and view the Property inspector (see Figure 5-46).

Figure 5-46

You can create rectangular or circular regions; they are perhaps the easiest. You can also use the polygon tool, which allows you to create irregular straight-sided shapes. Use this tool to draw around the area using a series of clicks around the outside of the area.

Try It Out   Image Mapping

1. Open the regions.htm file in Design view. Draw a new layer, click the border, and use the Property inspector to set the L, T, W, H, and Name properties, as shown in Figure 5-47.

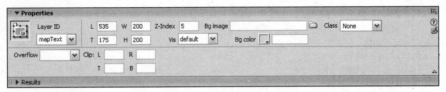

Figure 5-47

2. Using the Layers panel, show the ItalyMapLayer layer (by changing the eye icon to an open eye) and hide the other two map layers (by ensuring their eye icons are closed eyes).

3. In Design view, click the image of Italy so that you see <body><div#Italy><img> in the tag selector. Enter the name **italyMap** in the Map text box in the Property inspector (as shown in Figure 5-48). Using the Property inspector, click the Rectangular Hotspot Tool button.

Figure 5-48

4. Draw a rectangle capturing Milan and Rome (see Figure 5-49).

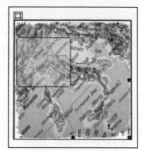

Figure 5-49

5. With the hotspot (that is, the rectangular area you've just created) selected, click the plus (+) in the Behaviors panel and select Set Text⇨Set Text of Layer. In the resulting Set Text of Layer dialog box, shown in Figure 5-50, select the mapText layer and type the text, including the HTML tags, as shown. Click OK.

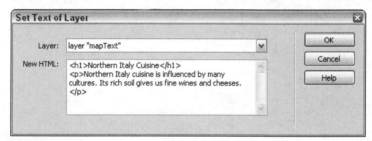

Figure 5-50

6. Check the Behaviors panel to ensure that Dreamweaver MX 2004 has created this as an onMouseOver behavior. If not, use the drop-down list to change it. This is enough to render the HTML in the mapText layer whenever the user's mouse passes over the hotspot.

7. Set it so that the text disappears when the mouse moves out of the hotspot. To do this, select the hotspot, click the plus (+) in the Behaviors panel again, and select Set Text⇨Set Text of Layer again. In the resulting dialog box, select the mapText layer again but this time leave the text box blank. Click OK and use the Behaviors panel to check that the new behavior is set to the onMouseOver event, as shown in Figure 5-51.

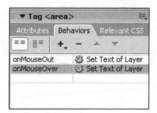

Figure 5-51

191

8. Draw a second hotspot on the map that encompasses the southern part of Italy (see Figure 5-52). Do not overlap the hotspots.

Figure 5-52

9. Repeat Steps 5–7, setting the descriptive text for southern Italy as shown in Figure 5-53.

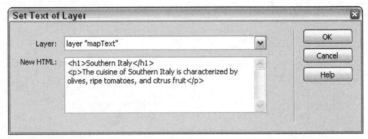

Figure 5-53

Make sure you have one behavior for the `onMouseOver` event and one for the `onMouseOut` event.

10. Save and test your page in the browser. You should see the text pop up as you roll over the hotspots, as shown in Figure 5-54.

Figure 5-54

11. To practice this technique more, set up some hotspots for the other maps and put in some more suitable text.

How It Works

The image map or hotspot is actually a basic HTML technique. However, when used in this way with Dreamweaver MX 2004 behaviors, you can construct an interactive and informative interface.

Each hotspot in the image map can be thought of as a simple hyperlink to which you attach behaviors as you've done previously. In this case, the behavior is a little more sophisticated. Instead of simply showing and hiding separate layers, as you did in the previous map example, you reuse the same layer by actually inserting HTML code into it.

Summary

We just covered a lot of ground and created some really cool dynamic behaviors for your Web site. There is only one real limit to using these behaviors—your imagination. There is enough material on behaviors and JavaScript to fill an entire textbook. We suggest you spend some time deciding which types of dynamic effects you find really effective and experiment with those as much as possible using different images and types of content.

In the next chapter, you start your transition toward dynamic database-driven Web sites. We will be discussing forms in the XHTML environment.

Why Not Try . . .

1. Apply the navigation behaviors to the Home, News, Regions, and Contact Us buttons in the template. Make those areas of the template editable so that the individual pages can opt out of the behavior contained in the template. Try rebuilding `index.htm`, `news.htm`, and `regions.htm` from the template. (It's a good idea to make backups of the existing files, in case you want to go back to them.)

2. Use the Change Property behavior with the hotspots you've created to alter the background color of the mapText layer. Specify `div` as the object type and choose `style.backgroundcolor` as the property you wish to change. Try creating some different hotspots and setting a different background color for each one you create. Remember to keep the text readable. Include the behavior using `onMouseOver` and remember to set the background color back to white using `onMouseOut`.

User Interaction with ASP and Forms

In the last chapter, we discussed how you could use JavaScript to enhance your Web pages. Despite these dynamic features, however, your users are still viewing static content. For your Web sites to be truly dynamic you must be able to provide content that adapts to a number of different situations.

Dynamic sites are an example of the important concept we've mentioned a couple of times previously: separating content from presentation. Content is *what* data your page displays, whereas presentation is *how* it's presented. Up to this point, you have been concentrating mainly on presentation.

When you examined Dreamweaver MX 2004 templates in Chapter 4, you saw how they can disentangle your site design from your content. You can design and modify your Web page designs while leaving your content unchanged by editing a template and automatically updating any pages linked to that template. In a similar fashion, CSS allows you to control the visual presentation of your content quite separately from your content—once you've used your logical markup to describe the structure of your content. (Remember how you used classes to do this?)

Simply clicking hyperlinks doesn't really take advantage of the potential of the Web. For starters, this method of interaction (hypertext documents) was designed in the 1960s with only the very basic, text-only computers of the time in mind, rather than the powerful, media-rich computers used by most people today. Imagine a phone conversation where only one party could talk and the other had no choice but to listen—this is how the Web started. While the Internet was obviously capable of carrying data in both directions, the design of HTML didn't take into account the need for information (other than mouse clicks) to flow from the user. As HTML evolved, the capability to carry information from the user to a different location came into being.

In this chapter we will look at this critical aspect of interactive Web sites—obtaining user input using forms as well as an introduction to the technology behind dynamic pages.

Forms are, as the name suggests, forms! They are based on their paper counterparts. When you are handed a form to fill in at the bank or when you apply for a new credit card, you provide the necessary information by filling it in and mailing it or handing it back to the teller or cashier. Generally the form as a whole has a single purpose—identifying you to the bank, obtaining credit references, supplying name and address details, and so on, and the information the form asks for is relevant to this purpose.

Web forms are no different. When your browser presents you with a form, you fill it in using the mouse and keyboard. You type your answers into text boxes and make choices from a list of options, just like it's a multiple-choice questionnaire.

Forms are so widely used today that it would be hard to find a Web site that doesn't use at least one somewhere. Whether to provide a simple search facility or a long-winded questionnaire or customer registration, forms have become the primary mechanism by which Web users interact with Web sites, e-commerce sites, and, most importantly, search engines. Forms are even more critical today following the massive growth of the use of dynamic Web site technologies over the past five years.

As you progress through this chapter, you will do the following:

❑   Learn to construct forms using Dreamweaver MX 2004

❑   Look at ways to construct user-friendly forms

❑   Use JavaScript to check or validate the information entered into a form

❑   Look at how data from a form is processed

❑   Construct some simple server-based pages using ASP and VBScript

HTML Forms

The capability of filling in a form is built into HTML. Web pages can be constructed that allow you to do one or more of the following:

❑   Enter text into a text field (a name, a sentence, or a few words) or a text area (a message or paragraph), as shown in Figure 6-1.

Figure 6-1

❑   Mark one or more choices from a list of options using check boxes, as shown in Figure 6-2.

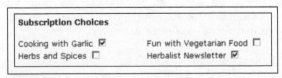

Figure 6-2

❑   Mark one or more choices from a menu or drop-down list, as shown in Figure 6-3.

Figure 6-3

❑ Make only one choice from a range of options (a radio button group), as shown in Figure 6-4.

Figure 6-4

HTML forms are designed usually with their paper equivalent in mind—with labels and instructions indicating which pieces of information should be entered where and how. Users then provide the requested information. Once the form is complete, clicking the Submit button serves the equivalent function as handing a paper form back to the clerk or teller. This initiates a process in the browser that collects the items of information from the form and transmits them to a server of some sort. Typically the information is processed in the context of a database.

Individual text fields, check boxes, radio buttons, and so on are referred to as *form controls.* Each control is typically accompanied by a piece of descriptive text called a *label,* which appears in the browser next to the control. In the first example above, the text box has the label "Book Title."

As you'd expect by now, all this functionality is accomplished using tags. The tags corresponding to the examples above are as follows:

❑ A text box is created using the `<input type="text">` tag

❑ A check box is created using the `<input type="checkbox">` tag

❑ A list is slightly more complicated, requiring a `<select>` tag and one `<option>` tag for each list item

❑ A radio button group is created using the `<input type="radio">` tag

We'll look at these tags in more detail soon.

As we mentioned previously, when users finish filling in a form and wish to send the information off for processing, they generally click the Submit button.

HTML requires you to indicate which form controls are related together as one form by using the `<form>...</form>` tags so the browser knows which pieces of information are to be sent together as a unit. By wrapping your form controls in a form, the browser is able to collect the right information before sending it off. The `<form>` tag includes important details such as where the information is to be sent.

197

Before you look at forms in any more detail, we want to get you building your own form using Dreamweaver MX 2004. The process you follow here is one you'll no doubt use many times to construct your own forms:

1. Construct a table with at least two columns—one for your labels and one for your form controls—and as many rows as you have form controls, including a Submit button.

2. Wrap the table in a pair of <form> tags and tell the form where the data should be sent when the user clicks Submit.

3. Place the form controls and the corresponding text labels.

This example is based upon a user providing information to register for a newsgroup or e-mail contact list. The form you construct will include a text box, radio button group, Submit button, and select list.

If you've got the Accessibility options turned on (Edit⇨Preferences) you will see an extra dialog box when you add each form control. We'll discuss this at the end of the example. For now, simply click OK or turn the setting off in the Preferences dialog box.

Try It Out   Creating a Simple Form

1. Open a new HTML document and name it **requestForm.htm**.

2. Select the Forms panel on the Insert panel group (see Figure 6-5). This panel contains buttons for easily placing form controls into the form. Place your mouse pointer over each one in turn so you can see what is available.

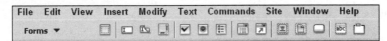

Figure 6-5

3. Select the first button, which is the Form button. This inserts a new form into the page.

4. See the red dotted line drawn in the Design view of the page, showing the area of the form within the page? Don't worry if this looks a little small; it expands as you add your table and form controls. Click the form area, switch to Code view, and you'll see that you simply added a pair of <form> tags and nothing else. Your table and form will go between these two tags. Switch back to Design view. If it isn't already highlighted, click the form area in the tag inspector and name the form **cust_form** in the Property inspector.

5. As we mentioned, you will be using a table to control the layout of your form controls. Click inside the form area and select Insert⇨Table. The Table dialog box appears, as shown in Figure 6-6. Use it to set the new table to contain six rows, three columns, a cell spacing of 5, a width of 75 percent, and a border thickness of 0. Click OK.

6. Select the table and, using the Property inspector, set the align field to center. This centers the table within the form border, as shown in Figure 6-7.

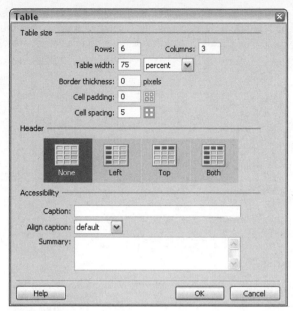

Figure 6-6

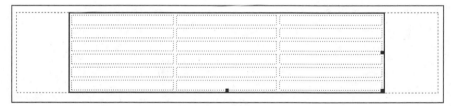

Figure 6-7

7. To ensure that you have a small gap between the labels and the form controls, set the middle column to be 10 pixels wide. Place your mouse pointer slightly above the top row of the middle table. You should get an arrow pointing downward. The entire middle column should be selected.

8. Press the Merge Selected Cells Using Spans button on the Property inspector (see Figure 6-8). It should look like a large box in the middle of the table.

Figure 6-8

9. Your middle column is now one big cell. Using the Property inspector, change the width to 10 pixels.

10. Put captions in the left column and the corresponding form controls on the right. Enter the following captions into the first five cells of the left column, so that the Design view looks like Figure 6-9. (Notice that the right column of the table may shrink a bit. This is because there is no content in the cells. If this happens, don't be too concerned with it. You will fix that in a bit.)

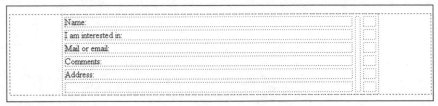

Name:
I am interested in:
Mail or email:
Comments:
Address:

Figure 6-9

11. Align these text labels to the right of the column. Select these five cells. You can use the Property inspector to set the properties of all five cells at once. Click the Right Align button to right-align the content of these cells

12. Click the B (bold) button so that the text in these cells will be styled bold.

13. If it isn't already checked, click the No Wrap check box. This forces the browser to attempt to display the text in these cells on a single line with no forced line breaks.

14. The first form control you insert is a text box for the visitor's name. Click inside the right cell of the top row and click the Text Field button on the Forms panel of the Insert panel group (see Figure 6-10). This inserts a text box form control onto the page.

Text Field

Figure 6-10

15. Now turn your attention to the Property inspector, as shown in Figure 6-11.

▼ Properties

TextField   Char width 40   Type ⊙ Single line   ○ Multi line   ○ Password   Class None
cust_name   Max Chars 40   Init val
Wrap

Figure 6-11

The first rule of forms is that each form control must be named, so that the server can distinguish between the pieces of data.

16. Call this form control **cust_name** (to indicate that it contains the name of the visitor). Set both Char Width and Max Chars to 40. These specify the maximum number of characters displayed by the browser and the maximum number of characters that the field will accept, respectively.

17. In Dreamweaver MX 2004 the Text Field button is used for both this type of simple text field and also the multiline Textarea control. The `cust_name` text box is going to be a Single Line text field. Leave Init Val blank.

18. In the right cell of the second row, use a control that allows visitors to select from a number of features you're offering. To achieve this, click inside the cell and select the List/Menu control from the Forms panel (see Figure 6-12).

Figure 6-12

19. Look at the Property inspector for this element. Call this control **cust_interest** and set it as a menu rather than a list. (Selecting Menu creates a drop-down menu, while selecting List creates a scrollable list box.) Some of the options are not available to you if you set it to Menu. For instance, users won't be able to mark multiple selections. If you specify List, however, you can also decide how many options you want to display in the scroll window.

20. The list will not be much use if you don't put some menu items or options into it. To populate your list, click on the List Values button in the Property inspector and then use the plus (+) button to add the four items shown in Figure 6-13. You'll need to click the plus (+) button four times; each time, enter the item label followed by the appropriate value. (You can also tab between Label and Value.)

Figure 6-13

21. For each menu item, enter two things. The Item Label is the text the visitor sees in the menu. When a user selects one of the available options, the value is sent to the Web server along with the rest of the form data. The server uses this to record which option the visitor selected. You'll be making extensive use of this mechanism in Sections 2 and 3 of this book.

22. When you enter these four items, click OK. The Property panel should look like Figure 6-14.

Figure 6-14

23. In the third row, you want the visitor to select one of the two options: Email or Mail. For this you can use a pair of radio buttons to limit the user to one selection only. Click inside the right cell and click Radio Button (see Figure 6-15). Click after the button and type **Mail**. You will notice that Dreamweaver MX 2004 automatically inserts a space for you (as a mater of fact, the spacebar is disabled).

Figure 6-15

24. Enter a space and click on Radio Button again. Type **Email** after the button.

25. You must set two important properties for these two radio buttons. Radio buttons are named after the push-button tuning system in old car radios. Each time you pressed one of the five or six buttons in, the previously pressed-in button popped out. In other words, the selections were mutually exclusive. The mechanism for achieving this using HTML radio buttons relies on the naming of the buttons—radio buttons with the same name are referred to as a *radio button group*. The browser ensures that only one of the group is selected at a time.

Use the Property inspector to give them both the name **cust_contact_type** (see Figure 6-16).

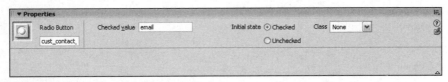

Figure 6-16

26. For the radio button labeled Email, set the Checked Value to be **email**.

27. For the other radio button, set the Checked Value to be **mail**. These values will be sent to the server when the user selects either one.

28. It is good practice to make one of the radio buttons the default setting to ensure that the form returns a definite answer even when the user overlooks this particular control. Make the E-mail button the default. To do that, select the corresponding radio button and set its Initial State to Checked, as shown in Figure 6-16. (When the page is displayed, the browser ensures that all other radio buttons in the group have their initial state set to Unchecked, adhering to the requirement that only one can be checked.)

29. In the fourth row, the users are invited to submit any comments they might wish to pass on. Like the text box in the first row, this is a text-based field. But unlike the text box, you want it to allow the user to type a few sentences if necessary, possibly spanning several lines. A Text Area control is designed for this purpose. Click inside the right cell of the fourth row and then click on the Textarea icon in the Form panel (see Figure 6-17).

Figure 6-17

30. The Text Area control opens a text box and activates the scroll bars if the text overflows the box's dimensions. Take a look at its properties in Figure 6-18.

Figure 6-18

31. Name the textbox **cust_comments**. Set Char Width to 40 and Num Lines to 5. Leave Wrap set to Default and ensure that Type is set to Multi line (it should be, by default). Notice that as soon as you selected the Multi line option, the text box changed its size and added scroll bars.

32. In the fifth line, you're inviting users to enter their e-mail address. Simply copy and paste the cust_name text box and rename it for simplicity's sake. Click cust_name and select Edit⇨Copy or press Ctrl+C, and then move to the fifth line and select Edit⇨Paste or press Ctrl+V.

33. Now that you've created a duplicate text box, what has Dreamweaver MX 2004 done for you? If you consult the Property inspector for this new text box you'll see that the name has been changed to cust_name2. Rename this to **cust_email**.

34. You've done everything for a visitor to enter information on the form. Now you need a way for them to submit the information when they have finished filling in the form. For this, you need a Submit button.

35. Click in the left cell of the last row of the table and then click the Button icon in the Form panel (see Figure 6-19).

Figure 6-19

36. Look at the Property inspector, as shown in Figure 6-20.

Figure 6-20

37. Delete the button name and change Label from Submit to **Send My Information**. Notice that the size of the button automatically adjusts to accommodate the lengthier text.

38. The one thing you haven't done yet is specify *where* the browser should send the information in the form when users submit it. Turn your attention to the form tag to take care of this. Click anywhere on the form and you'll see <form#cust_form> displayed in the tag inspector. Click it and look at the Property inspector. The most important attribute is Action. Set this to **register.asp**. This is an ASP file you haven't constructed yet. We'll review what you've done so far before taking care of that.

39. A second important attribute is Method, which determines how the form data is sent to the server. Set this to GET, as shown in Figure 6-21.

Figure 6-21

40. Save the page and preview it in your browser. Clicking the Submit button at this stage produces an error because you have yet to construct register.asp. You will, however, be able to see the various form controls you've used and look at the code behind them.

How It Works

You've been through a process of using a table to position your form controls with your form tags placed around the table. Layout is particularly important when it comes to Web forms and careful use of alignment and clear labeling are critical. You copied one of your text boxes as an easy way to reuse the same sized box—a technique for ensuring a uniform appearance. You aligned all your labels to the same (right) margin and all form controls to the left. A ten-pixel column was used to provide some space between each control and its corresponding label.

Where possible, it is good visual practice to use similarly sized text boxes and text areas to improve the alignment and uniformity of your forms—copying an existing text box helps with this.

The Submit button has a close cousin, the Reset button. Although it may seem like a good idea, this is a case of "just because you can do it doesn't mean you have to use it." The Reset button is very unpopular among experts who conduct Web site usability and user-friendliness tests. It turns out that the Reset button is more often clicked accidentally than it is used to intentionally clear a form (for instance, if users decide they don't want to complete the registration process). It is also one more item of clutter on the screen for the user to deal with when they're trying to make sense of the form. For these reasons we recommend you not insert a Reset button unless you absolutely have to. Simply instruct users to click their browser's Back button, enter a new Web site address, or perform a hard refresh (in IE, press Ctrl+F5) of the form to throw away the unwanted form data.

You also used the GET action. We will discuss this in greater detail shortly.

The form controls you used include a text box, a text area, radio buttons, and a Submit button. Let's examine these and some additional options in a little more detail.

The <input> tag

As you might have noticed, most of the form controls you use are part of the <input> tag. The only thing that changes is the type attributes of the tag. This attribute is used to specify text boxes, radio buttons, check boxes, Submit and Reset buttons, hidden fields, image fields, and password boxes. Dreamweaver MX 2004 sets the type attribute of the <input> tag to specify which of these controls appears in the browser.

> *A password box is identical to a standard text box, except that the browser doesn't display the actual characters that the user enters. Instead, the browser uses an asterisk or similar placeholder. This prevents someone from reading the user's password over their shoulder while they're typing it. Click one of the two text boxes you just used and switch to Code view. Notice the* type *attribute for the* <input> *tag and see if you can find the other input tags in the code as well.*

If you switch back to Design view and look at the Property inspector for this tag, you can examine the options, some of which we mentioned during the example:

❑   **Char Width** determines the maximum number of characters displayed in the field.

❑   **Max Chars** determines the maximum number of characters that users can enter into the field.

❑   **Init Val** allows you to set a default value when the page is loaded.

❑   **Type** specifies a Single line (textbox), Multiline (textarea), or Password control.

The name you assigned to the control also appears as two separate attributes: name and id. This is a transitional issue in the ever-changing world of Web design standards. In XHTML, the name attribute is being phased out (the technical term is *deprecated*) in favor of the id attribute.

The <select> tag

The menu or select list is a slightly more complicated animal. Click on the menu in Design view and switch to Code view.

The <select> tag is actually a wrapper for a group of <option> tags:

```
<select name="interest" id="interest">
 <option value="Recipes" selected>New Recipes</option>
 <option value="Technique">Cooking Technique</option>
 <option value="Sharing">Sharing Recipes</option>
 <option value="Gourmet">Finding Gourmet Food</option>
</select>
```

The value of each item in the list is contained within an <option> tag with a value attribute. The text that you want the user to see is inserted between the opening and closing tags.

Inserting form controls with Dreamweaver MX 2004 is quick and easy. In general, once you learn a few of the controls, as you did here, the rest are pretty similar.

Sending Form Data to the Server

One last important aspect to discuss here is what happens when you submit the form. Although you'll currently receive an "HTTP 404 Page Not Found" error message, as we pointed out earlier, you can still examine the mechanism used to collect the form data and send it off to the address specified in the action attribute.

If you have not already done so, bring your form up in the Web browser. Enter some data into the text boxes and text area, choose some values from the menu and radio buttons, and then click Submit. Now turn your attention to the address bar of your browser once the 404 error page has finished appearing. You should see something similar to Figure 6-22.

Figure 6-22

If you click the Address bar and scroll all the way to the left, you'll find the URL constructed something like this:

```
http://localhost/thecookingplace/register.asp?cust_name=John+Smith&cust_interest=
Techniques...
```

This is a fairly typical HTTP URL up to the question mark. Then some new stuff starts happening.

First, the question mark. It follows immediately after the file name `register.asp` and tells the Web server that the URL also includes URL encoded data or querystring data (you may come across other terms). Immediately after the question mark, you find pairs of names separated by equal signs and ampersands like this:

```
name=value&name1=value2&name3=value3...
```

Take a closer look and you'll see that the URL data consists of the names you gave the form controls and the actual data you entered or selected before submitting the form. What's going on here?

Recall from the last exercise that you instructed the form to post using the GET method. The GET method is the most common technique used to submit forms. GET appends the name/value pairs onto the URL. This technique offers the advantage of being easy to cache with a busy server. However, as popular as the GET method is, it has a couple of distinct disadvantages. First, because the form's information is right in the URL, it is not very secure and can be seen by anyone. Second, some browsers limit the size of a URL. This could be hard to overcome if you have a very large form.

The alternative to the GET method is the POST method. This encodes the form's information so that it cannot be seen. In addition to being more secure, it will not encounter any size limitations imposed by the browser. These methods are discussed in greater detail in Chapter 7.

Go back to the previous exercise and change the method to POST. When you submit the form in the browser, look at the much different URL (as shown in Figure 6-23).

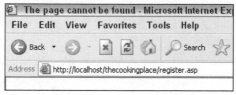

Figure 6-23

We will discuss when to use each technique more in Chapter 7.

Form Validation

Obtaining valid information from a user is a major and critical aspect of any piece of software, especially over the Web. Incorrectly completed forms can be a source of frustration for the visitor and a drain on server resources.

Busy Web sites may be adversely affected if their processing resources are occupied by hundreds of incorrect form submissions. Ideally, a form will be well constructed, easy to follow, and will be submitted only once. In practice, however, forms tend to be difficult to use and users end up relying on submitting a form multiple times using a trial-and-error approach. How many times have you tried to submit a form only to receive a message that information was missing? Worse still, how many times were you unsure what information was missing because the message was unclear? It can be pretty frustrating and time-consuming.

The best approach is to take advantage of good form design and what can be called *client-side form validation*. The browser uses a client scripting language such as JavaScript to check the form data against a set of rules before it sends the form to the server. While the details of writing JavaScript code to carry out these types of checks are beyond the scope of this book, we will examine Dreamweaver MX 2004's built-in support for client-side form validation.

Let's add some checks to the form you created in the previous example.

Try It Out   Setting Up Validation Rules

1. Open the Tag panel group and select the Behaviors panel (or press Shift+F3).

2. You are going to attach the validation behavior directly to the form. Using the tag selector, in Design view, select the `<form#cust_form>` tag.

3. Click on the plus (+) and select Validate Form. The dialog box shown in Figure 6-24 appears.

4. Select text "cust_name" in form "cust_form" and click the Required box. You'll see the expression (R) appear next to the field name. This forces the user to enter something in this control before submission to the server will be successful.

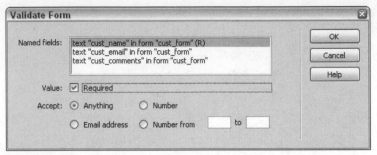

Figure 6-24

5. Save your work and test your form in the Web browser.

6. Select an Interest and type in a comment. Leave the Name and Email fields blank. Then click the Submit button. You'll see a dialog box similar to Figure 6-25.

Figure 6-25

7. The dialog box informs you that you must complete the missing fields.

How It Works

Dreamweaver MX 2004 allows you to use prebuilt form-validation code, which is able to check only the simplest of requirements—in this case, that text fields aren't empty. To carry out more sophisticated client-side form validation requires a moderate level of JavaScript and browser scripting knowledge. However, without touching a line of code, you are able easily to perform some practical and useful checks.

A well designed form with a generous amount of helpful text puts users at ease and minimizes data-entry errors. However, when errors do occur, explanations of what users must do to fix the problem must be clear and not complicate matters. While we limit our discussion of client-side form validation to Dreamweaver MX 2004's built-in support, we recommend that you spend some time researching the many excellent tutorials and free-to-download scripts that allow you to include more sophisticated professional validation in your pages.

One question that often comes up is "What is a valid e-mail address?" The answer is simple: It is an address that has an @ in it.

Improving Forms with CSS

You've just finished designing your best page yet. You are extremely pleased with your efforts and are busy using the design to create a Dreamweaver MX 2004 template for the site you are working on. Your content looks great with the CSS you've applied. It's all going well. Then you come to the customer registration form—and no matter what you do you can't make up for the sad fact that form controls just look, well, less than amazing.

For many years this was a daily frustration for Web designers. With the introduction of CSS and gradual improvement in browser support, the problem of integrating form controls into visual page designs has largely been solved.

Let's take a quick look at some simple CSS rules that can transform your forms from glaringly out-of-date to crisp and modern in a second.

Try It Out   **Applying CSS Rules to Forms**

1.   If it is not already open, open `requestform.htm`.

2.   You need to create some new CSS styles. Earlier in the book you created an external style sheet called `cookingplacestyles.css`. Append your new styles to that style sheet. First, however, attach that style sheet to this page. If you are an experienced Dreamweaver user, the procedure has changed slightly in Dreamweaver MX 2004.

3.   Using the tag selector, select the `<body>` tag for the page.

4.   Select the Style drop-down list in the Property inspector (see Figure 6-26) and select Manage Styles.

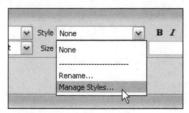

Figure 6-26

5.   This brings up the Edit Style Sheet dialog box shown in Figure 6-27.

6.   Click Attach and then select `stylesheets/cookingPlaceStyles.css`. You should now see the attached style in the CSS panel. Click Done to exit the dialog box.

7.   Click the plus (+) in the CSS panel and create a new class, in `cookingPlacesStyles.css`, called **input_text** (see Figure 6-28).

Figure 6-27

Figure 6-28

8.   Under the Type category, specify the following:

❑   Font: Verdana, Arial, Helvetica, Sans-serif

❑   Weight: Bold

❑   Color: #333333 (approximately almost black)

Under the Background category specify:

❑   Background Color: #FFFF99 (or some light color you prefer)

Under the Border category set:

❑   Style: Solid

❑   Width: 1 px

❑   Color: #000000 (black)

9.   Specify Same for All for all three.

10.   Click OK.

11. In Design view, select the `form` tag and, using the Class list in the Property inspector, attach the style to the form. Depending on your settings, you should see something like Figure 6-29.

Figure 6-29

How It Works

After many years of gradual improvement, support for CSS today means you can easily and quickly take care of essential presentation details. In this case you're improving your form's visual appeal as a part of the important task of making your forms easy to understand and pleasant to use.

We suggest you research some other good form designs and color schemes and spend some time experimenting with CSS to find what works.

Introduction to Dynamic Content

If you buy the same newspaper two days in a row, you can guarantee that the second copy you bought will be completely different from the first. The news stories, advertising, articles, and so on will be different but the design of the paper will be the same. If newspapers didn't publish the latest news, they wouldn't be useful for keeping up to date with events.

The world, in general, is dynamic. For this reason, newspapers are relatively out of date as soon as they are published. When events are unfolding rapidly, televised news shows or Internet news sites are where most people go for up-to-date coverage. The idea of live coverage is the ultimate—it grabs the viewer's attention with the promise of enabling viewers to watch history unfold in front of their eyes.

It is to this critical aspect of the Web that we now turn your attention.

Dynamic Web Pages

The most basic mechanism of the Web is when your browser sends a request for a page to a Web server and the server responds by sending the page to the browser. Assuming the page is found somewhere on the server, it is transmitted to your browser as a stream of characters—one at a time.

The browser receives this stream of characters and looks for the HTML tags, which tell it how to display the data it contains—as well as telling it which other resources should also be requested (such as images) to complete the display. This process is shown in Figure 6-30.

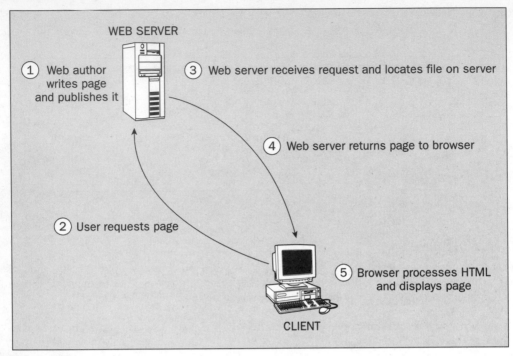

WEB SERVER

1. Web author writes page and publishes it

3. Web server receives request and locates file on server

4. Web server returns page to browser

2. User requests page

5. Browser processes HTML and displays page

CLIENT

Figure 6-30

A Web server that provides *dynamic content* simply follows instructions that tell it where to obtain the appropriate content—maybe from a database—and then how to assemble the content into a Web page. The Web page design, content, and instructions have all been produced by someone and can all be changed separately. The Web page itself—the page displayed by the browser—doesn't actually exist on the server at all. It is created on demand using a number of sources of information before being sent to the user's browser. This process is shown in Figure 6-31.

The browser has no idea how the Web page was created. It simply receives the data and displays the result. From this point of view, the page could have been created by a Web designer or a journalist, or it could be the output from a dynamic Web server—the browser would be none the wiser, and the reader, too, wouldn't necessarily know the difference.

There is more going on here, though, than simply this ideal separation of content from the page itself. We've also discussed the importance of interaction. How is the user allowed to interact with this dynamic process?

This makes the Web a demand-publishing medium. Why not show each user exactly what they want to see? Because everyone thinks and acts in unique ways, why not put the power of the Web at their disposal and allow them to search and navigate sites in a personalized manner?

The ability to remember site visitors and their preferences is a huge industry today. Probably the largest example of this at work is the Microsoft Passport system, which allows many thousands of Web sites to use a central database of nearly 200 million registered passport users. These Web sites can find out the preferences of their clients without the client having to reenter information each time.

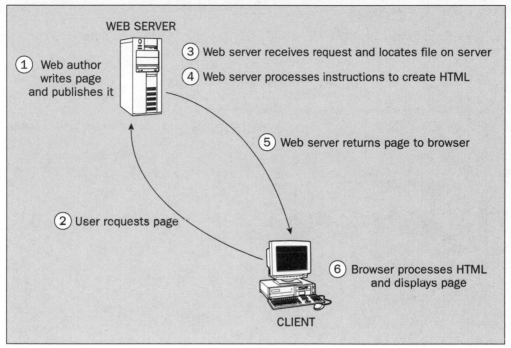

WEB SERVER

① Web author writes page and publishes it

③ Web server receives request and locates file on server

④ Web server processes instructions to create HTML

⑤ Web server returns page to browser

② User requests page

⑥ Browser processes HTML and displays page

CLIENT

Figure 6-31

With all this in mind, how does one set about producing dynamic content? There are a number of dynamic Web server technologies in use today:

❑ **Active Server Pages** (ASP) is Microsoft's highly successful system attached to its Internet Information Server (IIS) Web server. We will examine this technology in detail for the remainder of this book. IIS currently serves approximately 30 percent of the world's Web sites.

❑ **ChiliASP**, released by ChiliSoft and now maintained by Sun Microsystems, allows non-Windows Web servers to offer ASP support.

❑ **Apache** is by far the most widely used Web server. It is open source and closely allied to the world of Linux and Unix. PHP is the predominant dynamic Web technology in the Apache world. Approximately 60 percent of Web sites worldwide use Apache.

❑ **ColdFusion** is Macromedia's entry into the dynamic technology market. It employs a proprietary server (ColdFusion Server) and HTML-like tags. Dreamweaver MX 2004 is the main development platform for doing ColdFusion development.

❑ **JavaServer Pages** uses the Java programming language as its code. Many servers support JSP technology, including Macromedia JRun.

❑ **ASP.NET** is a part of Microsoft's newest technology platform, called .NET. It uses a variety of compiled codes, including Visual Basic, C#, and C++, as its languages.

❑ The **Common Gateway Interface** (CGI) is probably the oldest dynamic technology, steadily diminishing in popularity. It is often used in conjunction with the Perl language.

Active Server Pages

Microsoft ASP includes the IIS Web server and a scripting engine, which executes instructions written in a programming language such as JavaScript.

ASP pages are given the `.asp` file suffix to distinguish them from simple HTML pages, as they are obviously treated differently. Where a Web server would normally simply fetch an HTML page from disk and send it back to the server, an ASP page must be processed before the output can be sent back to the browser. After the Web server receives the request for an ASP page, the server fetches the file and hands it over to the scripting engine.

Look at a simple ASP example:

```
<html>
 <head>
  <title>And ASP Example</title>
 </head>
 <body>
  <h1>Welcome</h1>
  The present time is <% = Time %> and the present date is <% = Date%>
 </body>
<html>
```

This example does not run in Dreamweaver MX 2004 yet.

Notice that his page has three distinct types of items on it:

❑ **HTML tags:** Used just as you have used them before to create a Web page

❑ **Plain text:** Used just as you used it before to create a Web page

❑ **ASP script:** The special instructions we spoke of earlier, surrounded by `<%` and `%>` brackets

When you save an ASP page, you use the file extension `.asp` rather than `.htm`. This tells IIS to send this page along to the ASP processor. ASP ignores the HTML tags and plain text and searches for the ASP script. Once it finds it, it processes the instructions and converts the results into HTML. Finally, it incorporates the results into the HTML tags and text, sends it back to IIS, and IIS returns it to the browser.

Admittedly, this is a very simple explanation. It is beyond the scope of this book to give an extensive discussion of ASP and its finer points. For that, we recommend *Beginning Active Server Pages 3.0* by David Buser, *et al*. (Wrox, 2000). However, we will be discussing the most important points of ASP in this and subsequent chapters.

In our previous discussion, we indicated that there were servers involved. This implies two computers: the local computer, where visitors make their requests, and the remote computer, which contains the server that processes the ASP code and returns the completed HTML document.

ASP cannot function without a server. Because you will be testing your work with this server, Dreamweaver MX 2004 calls it the *testing server*. It may or may not be the actual server that visitors use. In most instances, it is not. You test on one server and, when everything is functioning properly, you upload your files to the working server.

You may have noticed that when you installed IIS in Chapter 1 it created a folder structure on your computer called `c:\inetpub\wwwroot`. When you develop an ASP dynamic site, you usually create it in a folder structure under the `wwwroot` folder. This serves as the folder for the remote computer and the testing server.

If you were setting up the actual working server, you would need to set up a virtual directory. This is a mapping construct to shield the actual working directory. Without it, your visitors would need to go here to see your site:

```
http://www.thecookingplace.com/intepub/wwwroot/thecookingplace
```

Not a very convenient or secure way of doing things, is it? It is far easier for users to go to the domain name (`www.thecookingplace.com`). Once they're there, the virtual directory knows where to look in the server structure. It serves as an alias and hides the actual directory structure of your site from visitors.

When using a test server in Dreamweaver MX 2004, it is not necessary to set up a virtual directory; Dreamweaver handles the mappings for you. Again, just to make it clear, this is only for the testing server.

Assuming you completed the steps in Chapter 1 to set up IIS, your computer can serve in both capacities, as the local and the remote computer.

Creating an ASP Page

As we pointed out earlier, an ASP page is a document containing HTML tags, plain text, and ASP scripting language instructions—in this case, VBScript. Later on you'll use Dreamweaver MX 2004 to build this code for you. Initially, however, you're going to dig into the code a bit. Let's take a first look at it by building the very simple ASP page you saw previously.

Try It Out   **Building Your First ASP Page**

1. Close all open files and choose File⇨New to open the New Document dialog box. Under the General tab, click Dynamic Page in the left column (under Category). In the right column (under Dynamic Page) click ASP VBScript. Click the Create button.

2. Select File⇨Save As and save this document as **my_first.asp** in the local site folder.

3. When you open the drop-down list in the Insert panel, you will see that there something new there. Dreamweaver MX 2004 makes the ASP panel available, as shown in Figure 6-32.

Figure 6-32

4. Switch to Code view (see Figure 6-33).

5. You should see `Untitled Document` in the title text box and also between the `<title>` and `</title>` tags in the code. Type **Testing** into the title box and press Enter. You should be able to spot the change in Code view.

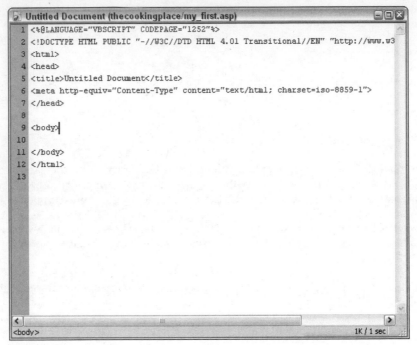

Figure 6-33

6. You've used Dreamweaver MX 2004 to set most of the document properties up to now. Let's have a go at modifying it in the code itself. Highlight Testing between the `<title>` and `</title>` tags and change it so it reads:

```
<title>My First ASP Document </title>
```

7. Click between the `<body>` and `</body>` tags and add the following line:

```
<body>
Today's date is Date and the present time is Time.
</body>
```

8. Highlight Date and select the Output tag on the ASP panel (see Figure 6-34).

Figure 6-34

9. Repeat this with Time. Figure 6-35 shows what you should see in Code view now.

```
 9  <body>
10      Today's date is <%= Date %> and the present time is <%= Time %>.
11  </body>
```

Figure 6-35

10. Save the document and preview it in the browser. It should display the current date and time, as shown in Figure 6-36.

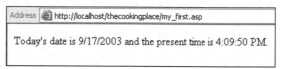

Figure 6-36

11. Choose View⇨Source (in IE). There is no ASP code to be found. It's all HTML now.

12. Just to emphasize the basic concept behind this, you can also view this file the wrong way. Select File⇨Open in your browser and browse to `my_first.asp` in the site root folder on your hard drive. Once you browse to the site folder, you will see the Files of Type list set to HTML Files. (Choose All Files to see `my_first.asp`). Right-click `my_first.asp` and choose Open With⇨Internet Explorer. You should see something like Figure 6-37.

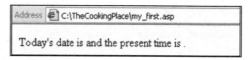

Figure 6-37

13. Select View⇨Source. Notice that the ASP hasn't been processed and can still be seen in the code for the page.

How It Works

We discussed the basics of this simple ASP page earlier on. The ASP code is processed by IIS during processing of your request for the page. What you see in the browser is the output from the two small pieces of ASP code.

In Step 12 you opened the file directly from the disk without it being processed first by the server. If you compare the URLs in these two cases, you'll notice that it worked correctly when you requested the page from the server using `http://localhost/...` and that the file wasn't processed by the server when you used the local path.

If you switch Dreamweaver MX 2004 over to Design view, you will not be able to see the ASP results directly. Instead, you just see ASP place markers, as in Figure 6-38.

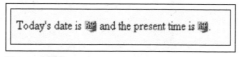

Figure 6-38

The reason for this is that the ASP needs to be processed through the ASP server before you can view the output.

Using Forms with ASP

With a little ASP under your belt, let's get back to the main issue we mentioned earlier: using forms and ASP to interact with users.

Earlier in the chapter, you created a form. You are now going to make a few minor alterations to it and use it in an ASP setting. In order to do this, you are going to need to create some variables to assist in getting the information from point A to point B. Before you begin, make sure you are back to the Local view in the Site panel.

Try It Out   **Using Forms with ASP**

1. Close any open documents.

2. Open the `requestForm.htm` document you created earlier in the chapter.

3. With the page open in Design view, take a few moments to refresh your memory of the Form Control names you used. You're going to need them in the next steps. You can see them by clicking on each form control and looking in the Property inspector:

- ❑ `cust_name`: Text box for the user's name
- ❑ `cust_interest`: Menu for the user's interests
- ❑ `cust_contact`: Radio button group for the user's preferred contact method
- ❑ `cust_comments`: Text area for the user's comments
- ❑ `cust_e-mail`: Text box for the user's e-mail address

4. Leave this document open and select File⇨New.

5. As you did previously, select Dynamic from the category list and choose ASP VBScript. Even though you set the site to work with JavaScript, you are not locked into it. That just specifies a default. VBScript has slightly easier syntax if you are a beginner.

6. Switch to Code view.

7. Save the page as **register.asp**.

8. Change the code in the document so it reads as follows (changes are highlighted):

```
<%@LANGUAGE="VBSCRIPT" CODEPAGE="1252"%>
<html>
 <head>

   <title>Thank you</title>
   <meta http-equiv="Content-Type" content="text/html;
    charset=iso-8859-1">
 </head>

 <body>

   <%
   Dim strName, strInterest, strContact, strComments, strEmail
   strName = Request.Querystring("cust_name")
   strInterest = Request.Querystring("cust_interest")
   strContact = Request.Querystring("cust_contact_type")
```

```
      strComments = Request.Querystring("cust_comments")
      strEmail = Request.Querystring("cust_email")
   %>
   Thank you <em><%= strName %></em> for your interest in <em><%= strInterest
 %></em>.
  </body>
 </html>
```

9. Switch back to requestForm.asp and make sure the form submit method is set to GET.

10. Save both files and preview requestForm.htm in the browser. Fill in the fields. (Remember, you added validation earlier in this chapter, so you must fill in the fields accurately!) Click the Send My Information button. You should see the returned document with the date and time. If all works well, what you see in the browser should look like Figure 6-39.

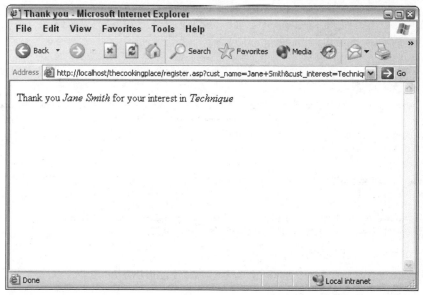

Figure 6-39

11. Notice that you placed italic tags around the two ASP commands. Also note that the data you entered in the form can be seen as URL-encoded data in the Address bar.

How It Works

The form data is attached to the URL for the form action you specified. The ASP code you write retrieves the data and displays it on the page.

When you click the Submit button on the form, the name of each control is set up as a variable in memory. The information that the user of the form types in are the values of those variables. Then the form's action instructs to server to get the register.asp file.

The crucial parts of this simple ASP script take over and do the following:

❑ Retrieve the form data using `strName = Request.QueryString("cust_name")`. The server examines the incoming URL and detects the form data—it extracts it for you and makes it available in `Request.QueryString`. You simply use the name of each form control to retrieve the data sent from the form.

❑ Display this data in the page using `<%= strName %>`.

This could also be written like this:

```
<% Response.Write strName %>
```

Use `Response.Write`, or its more compact shorthand version `<%=`, to send output to the browser. You are simply sending back the data sent from the form—in this case, from the `cust_name` text box.

The process consists of first retrieving the data and then processing it. In this case, the processing simply shows users what they sent with a thank-you message.

Conditional Output

Now you write some ASP commands that decide between two or more actions based on a test of some of the form data. In programming-speak these are called *conditional statements*—they specify what happens under what circumstances. It's very similar to us saying, "If it's raining, I'll go to a movie but if it's sunny, I'll go for a walk."

If your visitors choose e-mail as the desired method of contact, you display different output than if they select regular (postal) mail.

Try It Out   Having Your Form Make a Decision

1. If it is not open, open up `register.asp`.

2. Go to Code view and add the following code (highlighted).

```
<%@LANGUAGE="VBSCRIPT" CODEPAGE="1252"%>
<html>
 <head>
  <title>Thank you</title>
  <meta http-equiv="Content-Type" content="text/html;
   charset=iso-8859-1">
 </head>

 <body>
  <%
  Dim strName, strInterest, strContact, strComments, strEmail
  strName = Request.Querystring("cust_name")
  strInterest = Request.Querystring("cust_interest")
  strContact = Request.Querystring("cust_contact_type")
  strComments = Request.Querystring("cust_comments")
  strEmail = Request.Querystring("cust_email")
  %>
  Thank you <em><%= strName %></em> for your interest in <em><%= strInterest
%></em>
```

```
<br><br>
  <%
   if strContact = "email" then
    Response.Write("You will email the information to you at <strong>" & strEmail &
"</strong>.")
   Else
    Response.Write("You will post the requested information to you at home.")
   End if
  %>
 </body>
</html>
```

3. Save the file.

4. Switch back to the form and preview it in the browser. If your visitor selects e-mail as their contact preference, the response going out is shown in Figure 6-40.

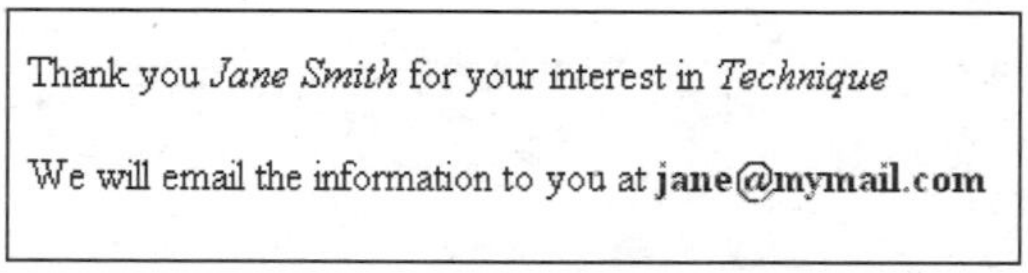

Thank you *Jane Smith* for your interest in *Technique*

We will email the information to you at **jane@mymail.com**

Figure 6-40

5. However, if the response is postal mail, ASP should respond with Figure 6-41.

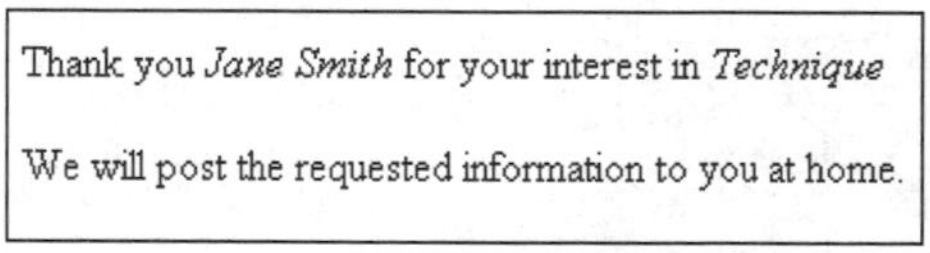

Thank you *Jane Smith* for your interest in *Technique*

We will post the requested information to you at home.

Figure 6-41

How It Works

As we mentioned, the use of `<% If...Then...Else...End If %>` is very similar to the everyday decisions you make. In this case, *if* the visitor has e-mail, *then* show the message in Figure 6-40; *else* show the message in Figure 6-41.

As you can see, the behavior of `register.asp` is determined by what the user chooses on `requestForm.htm`. Voilà! Dynamic content, albeit simple but nonetheless based on user interaction. Once you get into Chapter 7, or onward, you will be delving into this in a lot more detail.

Bringing It All Together

The last thing we need to do is put your dynamic efforts into the same context as the rest of our examples using the page design for The Cooking Place. Most of what you do here is a review of several topics covered already. However, it will bring together many diverse issues and wrap the site up nicely for you.

Try It Out   **Finishing Up the Cooking Place**

1. Open the template file `cookingplace_template.dwt`. You're going to edit this to produce a new general purpose template. Choose File⇔Save As Template and enter **main** as the template name. Click Save.

2. Because you used this template initially to examine editable regions, you should see two editable regions in the main table of the page. Click recipe_heading and press the Delete key. Now click somewhere in the second editable region (the repeating table). Click <table> next to the <mmtemplate:repeat> tag in the tag inspector. Press the Delete key. Both editable regions should now be gone.

3. With the main cell of the page layout empty, insert a new general-purpose editable region. Right-click inside this cell and choose Templates⇔New Editable Region. Call it **main** and click OK.

4. Click the Contact Button graphic (see Figure 6-42) and, using the Property inspector, change the link to **requestForm.htm**.

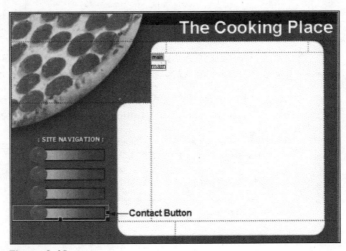

Figure 6-42

5. Save the template. Decline the offer to check the site for pages that need to be updated. Close the file.

6. Now open the `requestForm.htm` document.

7. Make sure you are in Design view. Using the Assets panel, drag the main template onto the document.

8. Because you aren't simply creating a new empty page from your template, Dreamweaver MX 2004 needs to put the existing HTML and ASP code into one of the template's editable regions. It presents you with a list of existing content (see Figure 6-43) and asks you to choose where it should be put in the template structure. Click each item in turn and choose the name of an editable region in the Move Content to New Region list. In your case, this is simple because you have only one region: main.

Figure 6-43

9. Click Document Body and, using the Move Content to New Region list, assign it to the main editable region you defined earlier.

10. Earlier, when Dreamweaver MX 2004 created the form verification JavaScript, it embedded a lot of the code in the `<head>` tags. The head also possibly contains some CSS.

11. Select Document Head and assign that to the head region.

12. The Inconsistent Region Names dialog box should now be resolved, as shown in Figure 6-44.

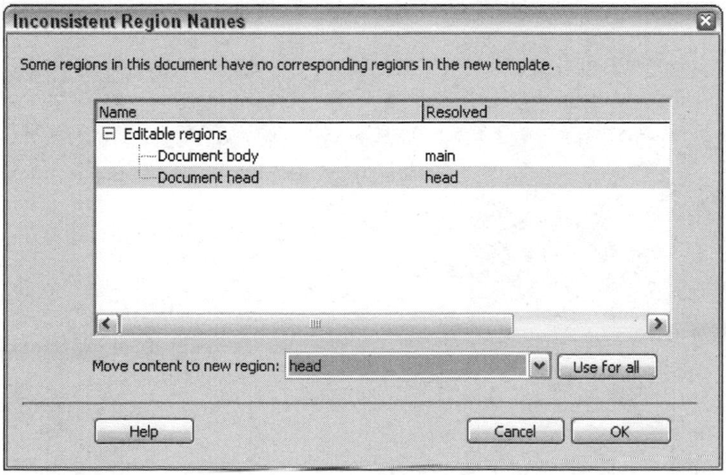

Figure 6-44

13. Click OK and save the document. The file should look like Figure 6-45.

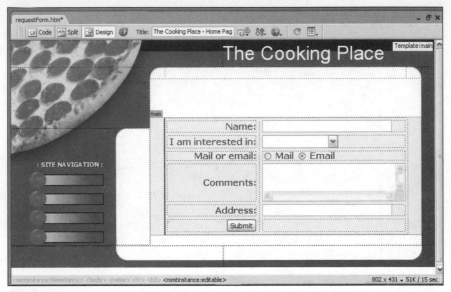

Figure 6-45

14. Leave `requestForm.htm` open and open `register.asp`.

15. Drag the main template from the Assets panel.

16. Resolve the Document Body name to the main editable region.

17. Add some line breaks to the start of the main region so that the response text appears clearly on the page (see Figure 6-46).

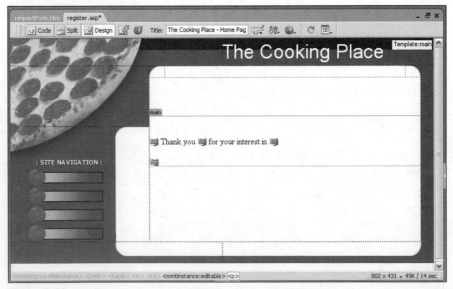

Figure 6-46

18.   Save the file.

19.   Preview requestForm.htm in the browser, fill in the form, and submit it. You should see something like Figure 6-47.

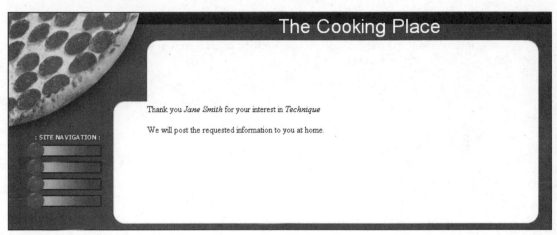

Figure 6-47

How It Works

You simply apply techniques you learned in Chapter 4 to give your Web site a consistent look and feel. As we stated in Chapter 4, it is not always the best idea to apply a template after the fact. In most cases, the existing information maps easily to the editable regions of the template. However, do not take that as a guarantee. Situations in which there are complex levels of data, database fields, and so forth could end up being misplaced or deleted.

Summary

We've come a long way in this chapter. We've taken a good look at how to build forms and have introduced you to the concepts of dynamic content and constructed a simple ASP page.

Although this chapter has only touched on the subject of ASP, you should now have a foundation on which to build in the rest of this book.

In the real world, data you submit from a form would be used to examine or update a database, rather than simply showing the user what they entered. However, allowing users to check what they enter is an important part of good form design.

Although we'll be focusing on ASP and VBScript in the rest of this book, we do examine some alternative dynamic server technologies supported by Dreamweaver MX 2004 in the book's appendixes. Examining these as well as ASP will help cement your understanding of these concepts and techniques.

Why Not Try . . .

1. Go back to the style sheet you used in the form and try different settings to see how they affect the outcome.

2. Using the techniques you learned, as well as following the coding, design your own form and build an ASP page to receive the information. This would be a nice preparatory for the chapters that follow. Examine the coding you used in the exercises and, if you feel adventurous, add an `If...Then...Else` statement.

Part II: The Soccer Site

Adding Logic to Your ASP Pages

In Section 1 of this book, the first six chapters, you have been using Dreamweaver MX 2004's tools and features to create a relatively static site. Although The Cooking Place introduced interactivity, such as image rollovers, most of this interactivity took place on the client side. You can greatly enhance your Web site by implementing *server-side logic* with a technology like Microsoft Active Server Pages (ASP). You can add user tracking, page protection and customization, use databases to store and display information on your Web site, and much more.

In this and the next six chapters you are going to build a soccer fan site that introduces a range of server-side techniques. You'll be using VBScript in ASP pages to get information from a user and save it to either the server or the client. You'll use this information to allow visitors of the site to log in and customize the appearance of the site. You'll connect to a database to retrieve information about soccer events which you will display in the browser. You'll also create a section where an administrator of the site can create, modify, and delete soccer events in the database. Using these techniques, you'll be able to create a truly dynamic Web site that adapts its appearance to the users who visit it.

One of the biggest problems that dynamic sites face is the stateless nature of the Web. By *stateless* we mean that there is no continuous connection between a Web browser and a Web server. The connection only exists during a page request and the period that the page is served. After that period, the connection is closed and the Web server forgets about the client. This isn't a problem when ordinary static pages are requested. You browse to a page, read it, and then click on a link to request the next page. But when you want to add server-side logic to your site to enhance the browsing experience of your user, things become completely different.

A dynamic Web site somehow needs to maintain information about the user that has requested a page. You can see how critical this is if you think about a restricted Web site that can only be accessed once you have supplied a valid username and password. If the connection between the Web server and yourself were completely stateless, you would need to log in every time you requested a page. That's not very user-friendly!

To overcome these problems, you need to find a way to *save state*; that is, you need a mechanism that enables you to store information about a specific request by a visitor and relate that stored information back again on subsequent requests from the same visitor.

In this chapter we will look at various ways to save state in one ASP page and across multiple Web requests. You learn how to do the following:

- ❑ Pass information from one page to the next
- ❑ Store and retrieve information for use in one page
- ❑ Use sessions to store and use information that can be used throughout the complete site for a unique visitor
- ❑ Store and use information in the application so it can be shared by all users visiting your site

The Sample Site: GlobalSoccerEvents.com

Before you try out samples that submit data from the client to the server, let's first explain a little bit about the sample site you will build in this and the next six chapters. You'll create a Web site for a fictitious soccer fan club, called GlobalSoccerEvents.com. The site brings information to fans about upcoming events in the soccer world. You start by creating a very simple site and expand its features in the following chapters.

Your completed site will host the following features:

- ❑ Anyone visiting the site can view information about soccer events around the globe
- ❑ Members of your site can personalize the site to fit their preferences
- ❑ Administrators of the site can track the users of the site and see statistics about page hits and user behavior
- ❑ Administrators can add, change, and delete events from the database that you use to store the events displayed on the site

The page where your visitors can view the events you have listed on your site looks like Figure 7-1.

The administrator's section of your site, where authorized users can maintain the event list, will end up looking like Figure 7-2.

If you want to see the finished site, download the complete code and installation instructions from www.wrox.com.

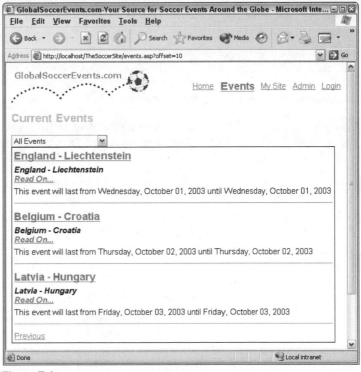

Figure 7-1

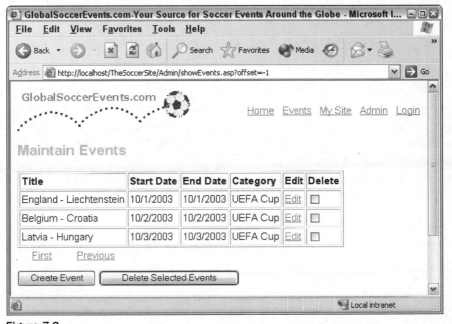

Figure 7-2

Creating the Basics of Your Site

In previous chapters you have seen how the powerful features of Dreamweaver MX 2004 help you build professional-looking and easily maintainable sites. To ensure a consistent look and feel throughout your site, you should begin now by creating a site template and a library item with a navigation menu that you can use on almost all your pages. Once you have the template and menu ready, you can add pages to your site that are based on this template with the menu.

Since you have already seen how to set up a site in the first chapters of this book, we won't be covering the complete process here. We will, however, show a few screenshots of the site settings so you can see what values to enter for the examples to work flawlessly.

Try It Out   **Creating the Site**

1. Create the folders to store your local site and images. Open Windows Explorer and create the folders C:\TheSoccerSite\ and C:\TheSoccerSite\Images.

2. Start Dreamweaver and, if it's not visible, open the Files panel on the Files panel group by pressing F8 (see Figure 7-3).

Figure 7-3

3. Click Manage Sites at the top of the panel to open the Manage Sites dialog box. Click the New button and choose Site from the menu that appears.

4. If necessary, switch to the Advanced tab and fill in the fields for the Local Info tab so your dialog box looks like Figure 7-4. Browse to the folders you created in Step 1 by clicking the folder icons to the right of Local Root Folder and Default Images Folder fields.

You could have a different folder for Local Root Folder and Default Images Folder. This depends on where you prefer to store your local documents. Make sure, however, that HTTP Address shows http://localhost/TheSoccerSite/. *If you are not using your local machine as a test Web server, refer to Appendix E for details about working with remote hosts.*

5. Click the Remote Info category and fill in the details as shown in Figure 7-5. (Again, first create the folder TheSoccerSite under the folder C:\Inetpub\wwwroot\ and then browse to it, just as you did for the Local Info tab.) If you have stored your wwwroot folder in another location or on another drive, make sure you adjust the path accordingly.

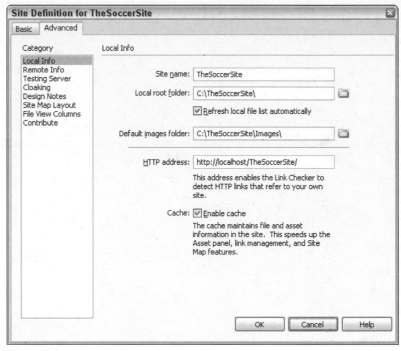

Figure 7-4

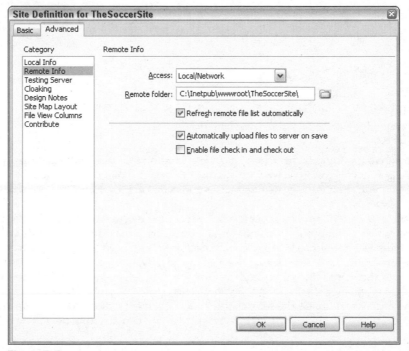

Figure 7-5

6. Fill in the Testing Server category (see Figure 7-6). You're using ASP VBScript for server-side scripting in this and the next six chapters, so verify that you have chosen the correct Server model.

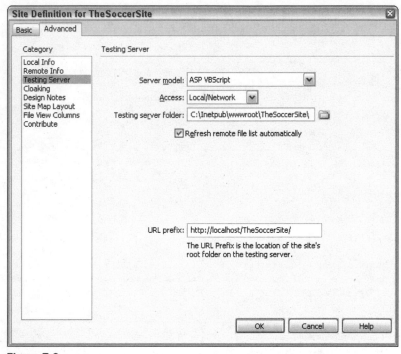

Figure 7-6

7. Click OK to close the Site Definition dialog box and click Done to close the Manage Sites window.

The new site now appears in the Sites drop-down list in the Files panel.

How It Works

You saw in Chapters 1 and 2 how to set up a site, including providing information on the Remote Info and Testing Server categories, so we won't go over that again. What's important about the site you just defined is that you should be aware of certain settings that are used for The Soccer Site.

The Web site is placed in a subfolder called `TheSoccerSite` below the root folder of the Web server. This means that you can't refer to images or include files using a leading / to indicate the root of your Web server. Instead, you have to insert images *relative* to the current document in your sample site. You'll get this option the first time you insert an image in Dreamweaver MX 2004 using Insert⇨Image. If your images turn up as broken images in your Web browser, make sure you haven't inserted them relative to the root, using the leading /. If you do encounter this problem, simply insert another image in a page using Insert⇨Image and set Relative To to Document at the bottom of the dialog box. From now on, Dreamweaver will use this setting as the default when inserting new images to your pages.

Creating the Site Structure

Before you can create the first page for this site, you need to think about the site's design. Decide how to create a navigation system, what menu items you need, and how to present your pages to your visitors. For this sample site, we'll keep the site's structure simple so we can focus on the server-side techniques that are used instead of the site's navigational structure. Therefore, you will use a simple frameless page.

In the next Try It Out exercise, you'll create a navigation system using a *library item* so the menu can be used on each page in your Web site. When you change the menu in subsequent chapters, it'll be very easy to update all the pages that make use of it. You can put the library item inside a *template* together with some other layout restrictions, and then use that template as the basis for each Web page.

At the start of the Web application the navigational menu consists of the following three items:

❑ **Home:** The home page of your site where you can welcome your users

❑ **Events:** The list of upcoming soccer events (static at first but you'll upgrade it to a database-driven page in Chapter 12)

❑ **My Site:** The main entrance to the section where your users can customize the look and feel of the site

In later chapters you will expand the menu by adding new items and create the functionality behind these menu items.

Try It Out   Creating a Template

1. Add a new page to your site that serves as the basis for the template. Make sure to select Local view in the drop-down list on the right of the Files panel. Select File⇨New and make sure the General tab is selected in the New Document dialog box. In the Category list, choose Dynamic Page and then choose ASP VBScript from the Dynamic Page list (see Figure 7-7).

2. Click the Create button and the new page will be displayed in Dreamweaver. You'll add some basic formatting to this page and then convert it to a template.

3. If necessary, switch to Design view (press Ctrl+~) and choose Insert⇨Table. Fill in the Table dialog box as shown in Figure 7-8 and click OK.

4. Click inside the first row of the table in Design view and then select Text⇨Paragraph Format⇨ Heading 2. You can also press Ctrl+2 or choose Heading 2 from the Format drop-down list on the Property inspector to format text in the Heading 2 style.

5. Type **-Page Title Here-** in the first table cell and **-Page Content Here-** in the second. In the third cell, add five line breaks (press Shift+Enter) and then type **-Footer Here-**. Adding the line breaks makes sure that the footer is separated from the rest of the page by some white space. Center the contents of the third cell by choosing Center from the Horz drop-down list on the Property inspector.

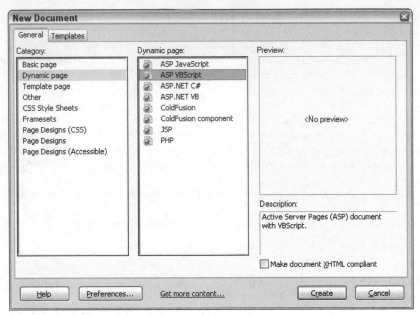

Figure 7-7

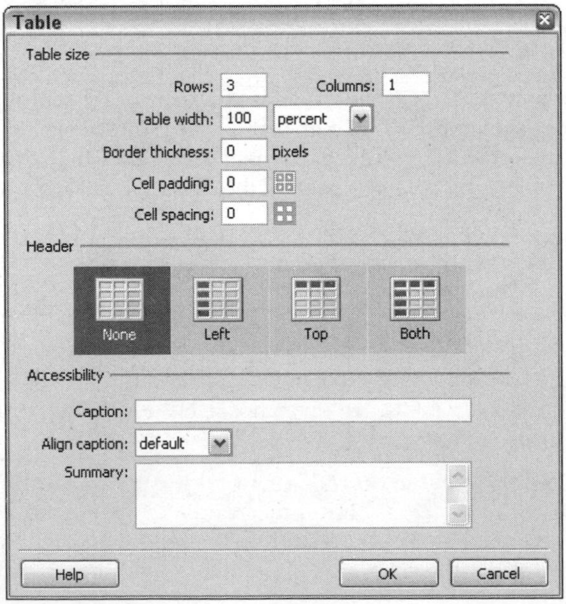

Figure 7-8

6. Select the text -Page Title Here- in the first cell of the table in Design view and then choose Insert⇨Template Objects⇨Editable Region (or press Ctrl+Alt+V). Dreamweaver prompts you that it will convert your page to a template (see Figure 7-9).

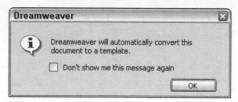

Figure 7-9

If you don't see this dialog box you may have checked Don't Show Me This Message Again in a previous Dreamweaver session.

Once you click OK, you'll see the New Editable Region dialog box shown in Figure 7-10.

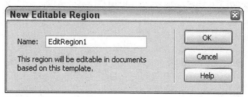

Figure 7-10

Type **Title** in the Name text box and click OK. Repeat this step for the second cell of your table, but select the text `-Page Content Here-` and name the region **Content**. For the last cell containing the footer, only select the text `-Footer Here-` and make sure you don't select the `<br>` tags. You don't want the users of your template to remove the white space before the footer. Name this region **Footer**.

7. Before you can save the page as a template, change the name that appears on the title bar of your page when you view it in a Web browser. That way, should you ever forget to give a new page based on this template a title, you won't look like an amateur with "Untitled Document" as the default document title. Instead, name it **GlobalSoccerEvents.com - Your Source for Soccer Events Around the Globe** in the template so that each new page starts with that title. You can type the title directly in Code view between the `<title>` and `</title>` tags or you can enter it in the Title text box on the Document tool bar. You'll find the Document tool bar right above your document in Code view or Design view. If the Document tool bar is hidden, choose View⇨Toolbars⇨Document to display it.

8. If you prefer nicely formatted HTML, take some time to indent the code to your liking. Remember, almost every page in your Web site will be based on this template, so this code will get used quite a lot.

9. Save the page (press Ctrl+S). This presents you with the Save As Template dialog box shown in Figure 7-11.

10. Type **maintemplate** in the Save As text box and click Save. The template will now be saved as `maintemplate.dwt.asp` in the `Templates` folder of your site.

Figure 7-11

How It Works

The methods you used to set up the template should be familiar, as you used them in Chapter 4. The template is very simple: You created three editable regions, one for the page title that is placed inside a <h2> element, one where the main content should be placed, and one to hold your page footer. The three regions were put in an HTML table so you can influence the way they appear on-screen. Later on, you will add a logo and style sheet definitions to improve the design of the site. Because the logo and styles are added in the template, you only have to make these changes once.

Try It Out   **Adding a Menu to Your Template**

1. It's time to create a menu for the site. While still in the template page, switch to Code view and make some room directly after the <body> tag, but before the <table> tag by pressing Enter once. Choose Insert⇨Table (or click the Table button on the Common category of the Insert bar) and enter the details shown in Figure 7-12.

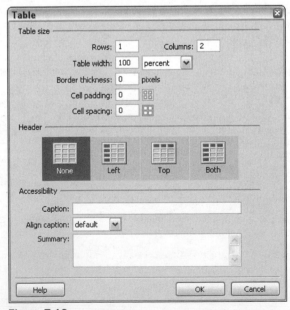

Figure 7-12

Click OK to add the table to your page.

2. This new table is going to contain a *nested table,* which means that one of the cells of the table you just inserted will hold another table. In Code view, click inside the right cell (the second pair of <td> tags) of the table you just created and remove the nonbreaking space ( ). Choose Insert⇨Table again and enter the details shown in Figure 7-13.

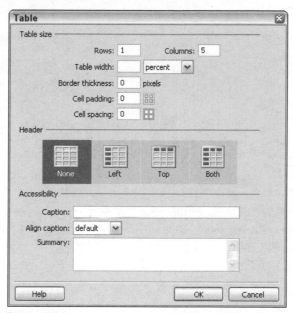

Figure 7-13

The browser will handle the size of the table, so there is no need to set an explicit width for the <table> tag. Click OK.

3. Enter Home in the first cell, **Events** in the third cell, and **My Site** in the fifth cell of the nested table. Remove the extraneous   code in these cells. Use the Code view window for this because the table is now too small to distinguish the individual cells adequately in Design view. Enter two extra nonbreaking spaces ( ) in cells 2 and 4 so that they contain three non-breaking spaces each. This creates some room between the menu items. To create a nonbreaking space quickly, press Ctrl+Shift+spacebar.

4. Set the Align attribute of the nested table to Right using the Property inspector so that it aligns against the right side of the browser window. Add an extra <br> after the closing tag of the outer table so you can be sure that any content that follows will be placed on the next line. Your code will now look similar to the following (notice that we changed the indention a bit to make the code easier to read):

```
</head>
<body>
<table width="100%" border="0" cellspacing="0" cellpadding="0">
 <tr>
  <td> </td>
  <td>
   <table border="0" align="right" cellpadding="0" cellspacing="0">
    <tr>
     <td>Home</td>
```

```
     <td>   </td>
     <td>Events</td>
     <td>   </td>
     <td>My Site</td>
   </tr>
   </table>
  </td>
 </tr>
</table>
<br>
<table width="100%" border="0" cellspacing="0" cellpadding="0">
<br>
```

5. Select the word Home in Code view and make it a hyperlink by choosing Insert➪Hyperlink. The text Home is automatically placed in the Text field. Enter ../home.asp in the Link field. You can leave all the other fields empty. Click OK to dismiss the Hyperlink dialog box.

Another way to turn text into a hyperlink is to type the address (../home.asp in this case) in the Link text box on the Property inspector for the selected text.

6. Add an ID attribute to the hyperlink that Dreamweaver inserted. To do this, select the <a> tag using the tag selector and then press Ctrl+F5 to bring up the Tag Editor dialog box. Click the Style Sheet/Accessibility page, set the ID value to **home**, and click OK. The tag will now look like this:

```
<a href="../home.asp" id="home">Home</a>
```

7. Repeat Steps 5 and 6 for the Events and My Site cells. Link them to ../events.asp and ../mySite.asp, respectively, and give them the IDs **events** and **mysite**. The code for the inner navigation table now looks like this:

```
<table border="0" align="right" cellpadding="0" cellspacing="0">
 <tr>
  <td><a href="../home.asp" id="home">Home</a></td>
  <td>   </td>
  <td><a href="../events.asp" id="events">Events</a></td>
  <td>   </td>
  <td><a href="../mySite.asp" id="mysite">My Site</a></td>
 </tr>
</table>
```

8. To finish the menu, type the following JavaScript code in Code view right after the <br> tag you added after the outer table in Step 4:

```
</table>
<br>

<script language="JavaScript" type="text/javascript">
  var sPageName = '<%=Request.ServerVariables("SCRIPT_NAME")%>';
  sPageName = sPageName.substr(sPageName.lastIndexOf('/')
                          + 1).toLowerCase();
  sPageName = sPageName.substr(0, sPageName.lastIndexOf('.'));
  if (document.getElementById(sPageName))
  {
    document.getElementById(sPageName).style.fontWeight = 'Bold';
```

```
        document.getElementById(sPageName).style.fontSize = '14pt';
    }
</script>
<table width="100%" border="0" cellspacing="0" cellpadding="0">
```

This code changes the layout of a selected menu item so that it appears as bold and with a larger font size. This only works in modern browsers such Internet Explorer 5 or above, Netscape 6 or above, Mozilla, and recent versions of Opera. Older browsers such as Netscape Navigator 4 won't generate an error but each menu item will stay the same, whether it is selected or not.

9. Save the page. Dreamweaver now displays the message box shown in Figure 7-14.

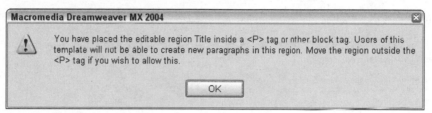

Macromedia Dreamweaver MX 2004

You have placed the editable region Title inside a <P> tag or other block tag. Users of this template will not be able to create new paragraphs in this region. Move the region outside the <P> tag if you wish to allow this.

OK

Figure 7-14

Although this message looks confusing at first, Dreamweaver is telling you that users of your template can't create new paragraphs inside the Title section because you are using an <h2> element. Because the title section should just contain the <h2> tag, this is exactly what you want so you can click OK to dismiss the message box. Unfortunately, there is no way to turn off this message, so you'll see it every time you save your template.

Because you haven't created any pages based on this template yet, you can't really test the menu code. You can, however, preview the template in your browser by pressing F12. After you have created a few pages based on this template in a later Try It Out exercise of this chapter, you'll see the menu code at work.

How It Works

The way the menu is set up is probably new to you. The menu uses some DHTML techniques to make a menu item appear as selected. It works by retrieving the actual file name of the current page without its extension. The code then looks inside the menu to see if it can find a menu item that has the same ID as the file name of the page you are viewing. If the item can be found, the font size and weight of the menu item are changed. Notice that you can't test the menu yet because the pages that the menu links to have not been created. In subsequent Try It Out exercises, you'll add those pages so the menu becomes fully functional.

Take a look at the code to see how it works:

```
<script language="JavaScript" type="text/javascript">
  var sPageName = '<%=Request.ServerVariables("SCRIPT_NAME")%>';
```

First a script block is opened and its language and type are set to JavaScript. Then a variable called sPageName is created and as a value it gets the name of the current page. Request.ServerVariables ("SCRIPT_NAME") is an ASP-specific way to retrieve the full virtual location of the current document.

For example, for a document called `events.asp` this returns `/TheSoccerSite/events.asp`. For the same document inside a folder called `Admin`, it returns `/TheSoccerSite/Admin/events.asp`. Don't worry about how this works too much; you'll see more about `Request` in a later section of this chapter. The code block is placed between `<%=` and `%>` tags, which means it runs at the server but its results are sent to the browser. You'll see more about how the `<%= ...%>` statement works later when we discuss outputting information to the browser.

If you open a page that is based on this template in your browser and look at the source code, you'll see something similar to this:

```
var sPageName = '/TheSoccerSite/events.asp';
```

Now that you have the page name in your JavaScript code, it's time to do something useful with it. First you need to remove the path from the file name. If you have a page with the path of `/TheSoccerSite/events.asp`, all you are interested in is `events.asp`. So you need to find the last `/` in the code and then get any text from there to the end:

```
sPageName = sPageName.substr(sPageName.lastIndexOf('/')
                     + 1).toLowerCase();
```

This line of code performs multiple actions in one line. First it executes a *method* called `lastIndexOf`. Think of a method as a block of code that performs some kind of action. This JavaScript method is part of the browser, so you can't look at its source, but when it is called, it searches a string (`sPageName` in this case) for a specific character or characters (the `/` in this example) and then returns the zero-based location of the last occurrence of that character in the string.

In the example above where the page is placed in the folder `TheSoccerSite` (`/TheSoccerSite/events.asp`) this returns 14. (Go ahead and count them. You'll find the `/` on the 15th location, which means an index of 14.) In the second example, where the file is placed in the `Admin` folder, this returns 20. Next 1 is added to this return value to skip the `/` itself. When this number (15) is passed to the `substr` method it returns the contents of the string starting at this position. When applied to the page `/TheSoccerSite/events.asp`, it would look like this:

```
sPageName = sPageName.substr(15).toLowerCase();
```

The variable `sPageName` now contains `events.asp`.

The `toLowerCase` function (another built-in JavaScript method) is called to lowercase the entire contents of the string. Finally, the return value of `substr` is assigned back to the `sPageName` variable.

After this line of code, the complete file name without the full path is stored in `sPageName`. The following line removes the extension from the name as well:

```
sPageName = sPageName.substr(0, sPageName.lastIndexOf('.'));
```

This code uses a different variation, also called an *overloaded* version, of the `substr` method which allows you to pass a start and an end position. You want the function to start at 0 and return anything up to the last dot. You can retrieve the value of the last dot by using `lastIndexOf` again.

At this point, no matter where the file is located and what extension it has, sPageName contains events for a page originally named /TheSoccerSite/events.asp, for example.

The following code is responsible for actually locating and changing the appearance of the menu item:

```
if (document.getElementById (sPageName))
{
  document.getElementById(sPageName).style.fontWeight = 'Bold';
  document.getElementById(sPageName).style.fontSize = '14pt';
}
</script>
```

First, you use getElementById(sPageName) to see if there is a menu item that has an ID equal to the page name. The getElementById method searches the entire document to see if it can find an HTML element with the same ID attribute as the one that is passed to this method. So if sPageName contained events it will find this <a> tag of the menu:

```
<a href="../events.asp" id="events">Events</a>
```

If the menu item is found, the code in the if block will execute. In that block, style.fontWeight and style.fontSize are used to change the appearance of the selected menu item.

> If you get an error when you click a menu item, make sure that all ID attributes of menu items are in lowercase. JavaScript is case-sensitive, so *Home* is a different menu item from *home*.

Try It Out   Spicing Up the Template

1. With the navigational links in place, it's now time to spice up your template a little by adding a logo and some style sheet definitions. You will add the logo to the left cell of the outer table you created in Step 1 of the previous Try It Out exercise.

Copy the file logo.gif from the code download to the Images folder of your local Dreamweaver site (C:\TheSoccerSite\Images). Once you return to Dreamweaver, the new image will appear in the Images folder in the Files panel. You can also create a logo yourself using your favorite graphics editor, such as Macromedia Fireworks MX 2004.

The easiest way to insert logo.gif in your page is to place the cursor in the left cell of the outer menu table in Code view and then select Insert⇨Image. Browse to the image in the Images folder, select it, and make sure that Relative To is set to Document. Click OK to insert it in the page. To have Dreamweaver insert the width and height properties for the image, you may need to click the Refresh button (the one with the blue rounded arrow on it) next to the W and H fields on the Property inspector for the image. Your final code should look like this:

```
</head>
<body>
<table width="100%" border="0" cellspacing="0" cellpadding="0">
 <tr>
   <td><img src="../Images/logo.gif" width="257" height="58"></td>
   <td><table border="0" align="right" cellpadding="0" cellspacing="0">
```

Don't forget to copy the image from your local site folder to the Images folder on the testing server. To do so, right-click the image in the Files panel and choose Put.

2. Next it's time to add a few CSS definitions. To keep things simple at this point, you will override only the `<td>` and `<a>` tags with a new style definition for the font and color. Open the CSS Styles panel (press Shift+F11), right-click somewhere in the panel, and choose New from the context menu. Fill in the New CSS Style dialog box as shown in Figure 7-15

New CSS Style

Tag: td

Selector Type: ○ Class (can apply to any tag)
⦿ Tag (redefines the look of a specific tag)
○ Advanced (IDs, contextual selectors, etc)

Define in: ○ (New Style Sheet File)
⦿ This document only

OK Cancel Help

Figure 7-15

After you click OK you'll see the CSS Style definition dialog box for the `<td>` tag. Select Arial, Helvetica, Sans-Serif as the Font and set its Color to black (**#000000**). You can change the color by clicking the little square right after the word Color and then choosing a color from the color picker. Alternatively, you can type **#000000** in the Color text box directly. Click OK to close the dialog box and apply the style.

3. Repeat the previous step for the `<a>` tag (type **a** in the Tag text field) except, this time, set the color to a green that matches the color of the logo (**#669933**). If you want, change the indention of the content of the newly inserted `<style>` tag so it aligns better with the other tags in the `<head>` section of the page. In Design view, your page should look like Figure 7-16.

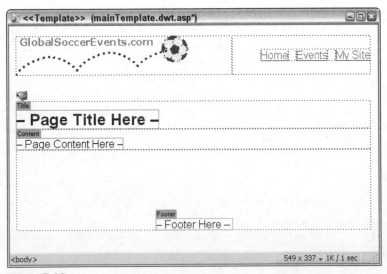

Figure 7-16

How It Works

You haven't done anything here that you shouldn't already be familiar with; you used the same techniques here that you learned in Chapter 4. Your site is beginning to look more professional now, with a logo and some style sheet definitions. By using style sheets to lay out your site, you make it easier to change its overall appearance. Instead of manually changing each `<td>` tag in the site, you can now simply change the CSS definition for that tag once to change the look of the entire page. In Chapter 9 you'll improve the site's maintainability even further by moving the CSS definitions to an external style sheet that can be reused in multiple pages of your site.

Try It Out   **Implementing the Menu as a Library Item**

1.   Before you can save the template again, you first need to change the menu into a *library item*. Select the entire menu in Code view (make sure you select the complete code from the opening `<table>` tag of the outer table, right after the opening `<body>` tag, to the closing `</script>` tag) and then go to the Assets panel (press F11). Click the Library icon at the bottom of the side panel and then, with the code block still selected, click the New Library Item button on the bottom part of the panel—the third button from the right. Dreamweaver presents you with the following warning dialog box, as shown in Figure 7-17.

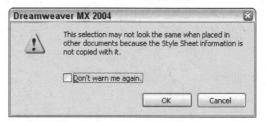

Figure 7-17

Dreamweaver gives you this warning because you added style sheet information to the page to change the way table cells and links look. There is no guarantee that you will reuse this code on a page with the exact same CSS definition, so it may end up looking different. Understanding the implications of this, you can safely check the Don't Warn Me Again option and click OK.

2.   Rename the library item from Untitled to **mainMenu** (see Figure 7-18).

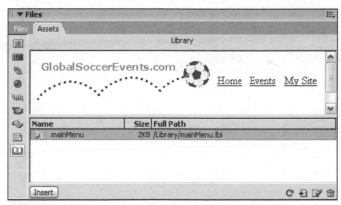

Figure 7-18

245

Now when you save the page by pressing Ctrl+S, Dreamweaver not only saves the template but also changes the background color of the code to yellow to indicate that the menu is a library item.

How It Works

You might think that saving the menu in the template makes it reusable enough because when you change the template, all pages that are based on this template are automatically updated. This is true but what if you don't use this template for your entire site? You may want to create pages that are not based on this template but that still need the menu. Now that you have turned your menu into a library item, you can create multiple templates for the site that all use the same menu.

In the next Try It Out exercise you'll create a few pages that use the new template. You create an events page that displays upcoming soccer events. You also create a home page on which you welcome users. These two new pages allow you to test the site menu you have created.

Try It Out   **Applying the Template**

1. Create a new file in the root of your site. To do this, open the New Document dialog box by selecting File⇨New (or press Ctrl+N). Switch to the Templates tab, select TheSoccerSite from the Templates For list, and then select maintemplate in the right-hand list (see Figure 7-19).

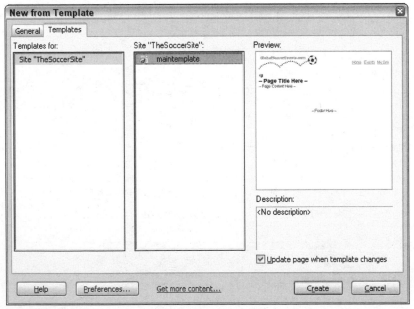

Figure 7-19

Click Create to create a new file based on the template. Press Ctrl+S to save the page. Give it the name **events.asp** and make sure it's saved in the root of your site.

2. Enter **Current Events** in the editable region called "Title." The page should look like Figure 7-20 in Design view.

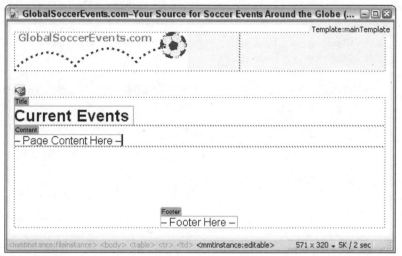

Figure 7-20

You can see from Figure 7-20 that Dreamweaver is unable to display your menu in the library item correctly. Don't worry about that too much; the menu will be visible in the browser when you request the page. If you need to see the contents of the menu in Design view, here's a little trick to make the menu visible: Open the library item `mainMenu.lbi` and locate the first `<table>` tag in the document. Change the `border` attribute of the tag from 0 to 1:

```
<meta http-equiv="Content-Type" content="text/html; charset=utf-8">
<table width="100%" border="1" cellspacing="0" cellpadding="0">
```

Save the library item so that all pages that use it are updated as well. When you switch back to the page that is using the menu, you'll see that it is visible now and has a small border around it. Don't forget to turn off the border again when you copy your files to your production server.

3. Repeat the previous two steps but create a page called `home.asp` instead. Enter the following details in the page:

Region	Text
Title	Welcome to GlobalSoccerEvents.com
Content	Your Source for Soccer Events Around the Globe.
Footer	Having difficulties? Contact the Webmaster.

4. Save the page and open it in your browser by pressing F12. Your site should now look like Figure 7-21. Notice that the Home menu item appears selected because it's bold and a little bigger than the other menu items. As soon as the page is opened in the browser, the JavaScript code that you added for the menu executes, retrieves the name of the requested page (home.asp), and makes the correct menu item appear as selected.

    If the logo shows up as a broken image (a small rectangle with a red cross on it) you need to upload it to your server. To do this, right-click the image in the Files panel and choose Put.

Figure 7-21

5. Click the Events menu item to bring up the page events.asp. Notice that it has a design identical to the home page. All that changes is the content of the page and the menu item.

How It Works

You added two new pages to your site, which are used to list upcoming soccer events around the world and welcome your visitors. Because you spent some time creating a template for your site early on, it was easy to ensure that your new pages maintain a consistent style.

Now that you've set up the basic structure for the site, we turn your attention to an important topic: maintaining state between page calls. One of the most common methods to maintain state is passing values from page to page. In the next section, we'll discuss the methods you have available to pass information around and how you can retrieve that information again.

Passing Values from Page to Page

The act of passing values from page to page is one of the most common ways to get information from the user to the server and back again. For example, if you perform a query in a search engine, you pass information from the search page you are viewing to the server. The server then performs a query based on the information you entered and sends back a page with the results. There are two methods available to implement this: GET and POST.

When you use GET, the information you send is appended to the URL of the Web address in the form of a *name-value pair*. All name-value pairs together are generally referred to as the *QueryString*. For example, when you search for *Soccer* and *Results* on www.google.com, this is how the address looks:

```
http://www.google.com/search?hl=en&ie=UTF-8&oe=UTF-8&q=Soccer+Results
```

As you can see, the terms `Soccer` and `Results` are appended to some other information that www. google.com needs for the search and sent to the server. In the example above, `q` is the *name* for the information you want to pass and `Soccer+Results` is the *value*. Everything after the question mark is the QueryString. The first name-value pair is separated from the address with a question mark. Each subsequent name-value pair is separated by an ampersand (&).

The other method you have available is POST. With POST, the information is not appended to the address but is sent in the body of the HTTP request that is sent to the server.

Both methods have their advantages and disadvantages. The GET method is useful when you want your visitors to bookmark your pages. If you bookmark the Google example above, you can always go directly to the page with the search results by opening the bookmark instead of retyping the query. Another advantage of the GET method is that you can send information from one page to another through a hyperlink; simply add the values you want to send to the address you are linking to and they are ready to be retrieved by the linked page. You'll see how to put this into action in the following chapters.

One disadvantage of the GET method is that the size of the message you can send is limited. The actual size may vary with the browser that is used but usually you'll get into trouble when you try to pass more than 1,024 characters.

The POST method does not have this limitation. You can send virtually unlimited amounts of data through this method, which is why it is used to upload files to a server, for example. A minor drawback of the POST method is that you can't see what you are submitting as easily as you can with the GET method. The contents of the POST body are base64 encoded, which means they are not sent as plain text. It's worth noting that base64 isn't the greatest encryption mechanism around and it can be decoded easily, so be careful when you send sensitive data such as usernames and passwords.

In the next sections we will explain how you can retrieve information submitted with either GET or POST and how you can display that information on another page.

Creating a Form That Uses GET

In the next Try It Out exercise you create a simple HTML form with a single text input box and a Submit button. Once you enter some text in the text box and click the button, the contents of the form will be submitted to another page where you can retrieve the value that you typed in the text box.

To retrieve the value in the second page, you need to use one of the built-in objects that ASP supports. *ASP objects* are objects that are available throughout your entire ASP application. Think of an object as a block of code in computer memory that has a bunch of properties to store information about itself and methods to perform useful actions. Recall from the section where you created the menu system for the site that you used a method called `getElementById`. This method belongs to the *document object* and is able to search the object it belongs to (the document) for specific HTML elements. Another example is the fontWeight property of the *style object*. This property changes the font of the style object it belongs to so it appears as bold in the browser. You'll see a lot more objects and their properties and methods at work in the remainder of this book.

In ASP 3.0, which Dreamweaver fully supports, you have access to the following ASP objects:

❑ The **Application** object is used to store information that is available to all users on all pages in your site.

❑ The **Session** object stores information for individual users and makes it available in all pages of your site.

❑ The **Response** object deals with sending information from the server to the client.

❑ The **Request** object retrieves information for the current request, such as the QueryString, and the name of the page being requested.

❑ The **Server** object deals with actions that take place at the server, such as executing another ASP page or retrieving the physical location of an ASP page.

❑ The **ObjectContext** object is used in advanced operations on databases and transactions, and its use is beyond the scope of this book.

These objects are often called *intrinsic objects*, which means they are available in your entire Web application without the need to write any code to create, or *instantiate*, them. We'll introduce most of the objects in this chapter as you need them.

In addition, there is another object, called the ASPError object. This object isn't accessible directly but can be retrieved by executing the GetLastError method of the Server object. The ASPError object can retrieve information about the last error that occurred in your ASP scripts. You could use this object to create a custom error page that logs the error to a database or notifies the Webmaster of the error by sending an e-mail.

> We won't get into this here but if you're interested, search the Web for "custom error page" and "asperror"; you'll find plenty of examples.

The Request Object

The Request object contains all kinds of information related to the request that the client has made to your site. Use it to retrieve information about the following:

❑ Cookies (which we will discuss in Chapter 8)

❑ Information sent to the page by either GET or POST

❑ The user's browser

❑ The currently requested page, which is available at the server

The Request object has one property (Request.TotalBytes), one method (Request.BinaryRead), and five collections. A *collection* is an object that represents a set of other objects. This provides easy access to multiple properties, for example QueryString values, through the use of one single property name.

In this and the next couple of chapters using ASP you will use the following four collections of the Request object:

Collection Name	Description
Cookies	This collection reads values from Cookies that are sent by the browser with each request to the page. We cover Cookies in Chapter 8.
Form	The Form collection retrieves values from an HTML form that is submitted using POST.
QueryString	The QueryString collection retrieves values from an HTML form that is submitted using GET. This chapter covers both Form and QueryString.
ServerVariables	This collection gets information about many different values from both the client and the server, such as browser type, IP addresses, and page names. You saw the ServerVariables collection at work in the menu code when you used Request.ServerVariables("SCRIPT_NAME") to retrieve the name of the current page.

We won't be discussing the method, the property, and the fifth collection (ClientCertificate) of the Request object because their usage is beyond the scope of this book.

As the Request object handles information regarding the request from the user to the server for a specific page, it shouldn't come as a surprise that it has a counterpart that takes care of the response from the server to the user.

The Response Object

The Response object is mainly used to send output to the browser. All of the collections, properties, and methods it supports are related to displaying information in the client browser. In this chapter we will look at the Write method. In later chapters we will discuss the End and Redirect methods. We discuss its only collection, Cookies, in the next chapter.

Method Name	Description
End	This method stops the processing of the current ASP page and sends all output created so far to the browser.
Redirect	The Redirect method sends a redirect instruction to the browser, telling it to request another page.
Write	This method outputs data to the browser.

Sending Values with GET

The Request and Response objects are the only two you need to create a few simple pages that allow a user to send information to a Web site, so next you will build an example that demonstrates these objects.

Try It Out   **Sending Values with GET**

1.   Add a new page based on your template to the site. Use the New from Template dialog box for this, which you can open by pressing Ctrl+N and then switching to the Templates tab if necessary. Save the page as `submitUsingGet.asp` in the root of your site. Delete the `-Page Content Here-` and `-Footer Here-` placeholders, and change the title of the page to **Submit Using GET**.

2.   Insert an HTML form by first clicking inside the content region in Code view. If you have trouble finding the exact location of the content region in the HTML code, click inside the content region of Design view and then press Ctrl+~ to switch back and forth between Design and Code view.

   Choose Forms from the category drop-down list on the Insert bar and then click the Form button. It's the first button on the Forms toolbar. Fill in the Tag Editor - Form dialog box so it looks like Figure 7-22

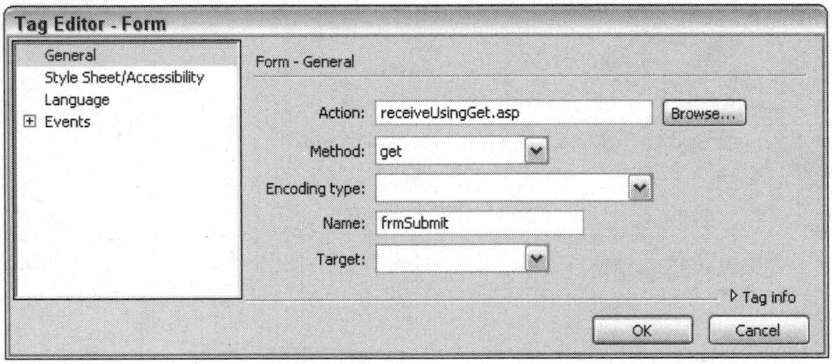

Figure 7-22

Because the Code view has the focus, Dreamweaver presents you with the Tag Editor dialog box for the form. With the focus in Design view, Dreamweaver inserts a default form that you can't use in this example.

3.   Click OK to insert the form in the page.

4.   Make sure your cursor is inside the form in Code view and click the Text Field button on the Insert tool bar. In the Tag Editor - Input dialog box, make sure that Type is set to Text and give the text field a name of **txtValue**. Click OK.

5.   Add a button by clicking the Button button on the Insert bar. Change its Type to submit, set its Name to **btnSubmit**, and enter Click to Submit in the Value field. Click OK to finish.

   The code for the form should now look like this (notice that we indented the code to improve its readability):

```
<form action="receiveUsingGet.asp" method="get" name="frmSubmit">
 <input name="txtValue" type="text">
 <input name="btnSubmit" type="submit" value="Click to Submit">
</form>
```

6. Save and run the page in your browser. It should look like Figure 7-23.

Figure 7-23

7. Type some text in the textbox and click the Click to Submit button. You'll receive an error message that the page cannot be found. You can ignore that for now; you'll create that page next. Notice how the address in your browser has changed:

```
http://localhost/TheSoccerSite/receiveUsingGet.asp?txtValue=your_string&btnSubmit=
Click+to+Submit
```

How It Works

The value you type in the text field is appended to the address for the page you are submitting to because the GET method was used to submit the page. The page where the information is submitted to is determined by the `action` attribute of the form element.

The *value* of the button, the text that appears on the button in the browser, is submitted as well. This can be useful if you have multiple submit buttons on your page and you want to find out which button was used to submit the form. Only the button that was clicked will be submitted.

If you don't see the name-value pair for the Submit button, you may have pressed Enter instead of clicking the Submit button. When you press Enter on a form with just a single text box and a button, the button is not submitted. Keep this in mind when you design a form that checks whether a certain button has been clicked or not.

You can also see that the spaces in the value of the button have been replaced with the plus (+) symbol. The value of the button was Click to Submit, but it has been submitted as Click+to+Submit. This is called *encoding* and is used to make sure you can submit special characters as well.

You may have noticed that we prefix all our form elements with three letters describing their type. For example we use `txt` to indicate a text field and `btn` to indicate a button. This is not a requirement but it's a naming convention that helps us understand what kind of elements we are working with.

Retrieving Submitted Values

Now that you know how to submit information to another page, it's time to create a page that retrieves the values from the QueryString and displays them on your page.

Try It Out   Retrieving Values

1. Add a new page based on the main template (once again, use the New from Template dialog box for this) and save the page as `receiveUsingGet.asp`. Remove the default content and footer placeholders from the template and enter **The QueryString Value is:** in the content region. Change the title to **Receive QueryString**.

2. Switch to Code view, place the cursor in the content block right after `The QueryString is:`, and select Insert⇨ASP Objects⇨Output. The following should appear:

```
<%= %>
```

3. Leave the cursor in the same place and choose Insert⇨ASP Objects⇨Trimmed QueryString Element. Type **txtValue** between the double quotes so the code in Code view looks like this:

```
The QueryString Value is: <%= Trim(Request.QueryString("txtValue")) %>
```

4. Save the page and then open `submitUsingGet.asp`. Press F12 to open it in your browser, type **Charles Shoots!** in the text box, and click the Submit button. The text you entered will appear on the screen, as shown in Figure 7-24.

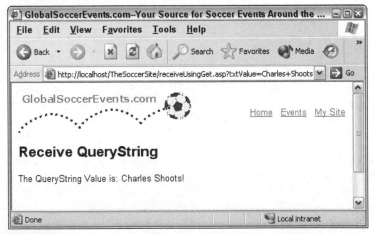

Figure 7-24

How It Works

There are three important parts in the previous code that retrieves the value from the QueryString and outputs it to the browser. First, `Request.QueryString("txtValue")` is used to retrieve a specific value from the QueryString (`txtValue` in this case). Then the `Trim` method is used to remove any leading or trailing spaces from the value. This isn't strictly necessary but it may be convenient at times, so

Dreamweaver inserts it for you automatically. Finally, this code block is placed between the `<%=` and `%>` delimiters so it will be output to the browser.

Another way to output content to the browser is to use the `Write` method from the `Response` object so the code looks like this:

```
<% Response.Write(Trim(Request.QueryString("txtValue"))) %>
```

As you can see, `<%= ...%>` is shorthand for the complete ASP statement. Usually, you use `Response.Write` to output HTML to the browser from within a server-side ASP code block. You'll see the `<%= ...%>` notation in places where plain HTML is mixed with ASP values.

Sending and Receiving Values Using POST

Using POST is rather similar to using the GET method. To use POST instead of GET, you need to make two adjustments. First, change the method attribute of the form to POST. Second, in the receiving page, use the `Form` collection instead of the `QueryString` collection to retrieve the values that were submitted to your page.

Try It Out   **Using POST**

1.   Create a copy of `submitUsingGet.asp` and rename it as **submitUsingPost.asp**. The fastest way to do this is to click the file on the Files panel once and then press Ctrl+D to duplicate the file. Press F2 to rename it.

2.   Change the title to **Submit Using POST** and then change the `<form>` tag so the method is POST and it points to `receiveUsingPost.asp`. The code for the form now reads:

```
<form action="receiveUsingPost.asp" method="post" name="frmSubmit">
```

You can now save the page.

3.   Duplicate the page `receiveUsingGet.asp` and call it **receiveUsingPost.asp**. Change the three occurrences of `QueryString` to **Form**. You'll find one in the title and two others in the ASP code block. The line that outputs the form value now looks like this:

```
The Form Value is: <%= Trim(Request.Form("txtValue")) %>
```

4.   Save and run the page `submitUsingPost.asp` in your browser, type **What a save by Todd!**, and click the Submit button. You'll see that the text you typed is still displayed on the screen. This time, however, the text is not visible in the address bar and neither is the value for the Submit button.

How It Works

The POST example is almost identical to GET (see Figure 7-25). It's just the method by which you send information to the server and display it again that is different.

In the page with the form, you changed the method attribute from GET to POST. The only thing that changed in the receiving page is the collection you used to retrieve your values. Instead of `Request.QueryString` you now use `Request.Form`.

Figure 7-25

Using Postback to Post Back to the Current Page

Instead of posting to a new page as you did in the previous two examples, it is also possible to submit to the same page that contains the form. This is known as a *postback*. Although the term may make you suspect that this only works for the POST method, you can use it with the GET method as well. A great advantage of postback is that you can maintain the values in the form. That is, when a user types some text and clicks a button, you can show the same text in the text box again when the page is reloaded.

In the next example, you create a very simple calculator that demonstrates the postback mechanism. You enter two numbers, select an operator, and then click a button to perform a calculation on those two numbers. You only create one page that posts back to itself. The numbers are retained in their text boxes, so it is easy to select just a different operator and perform a new calculation.

Try It Out   Creating a Calculator Using Postback

1. Create a new page based on the main template and save it as **calculator.asp** in the root of the site. Set the title to **Calculator** and remove the other two template placeholders.

2. Add a POST form to the content region of the page. To bring up the Tag Editor for the Form tag, click inside the content region in Code view and click the Form button from the Forms category of the Insert bar. Set its Action to **calculator.asp**, its Method to **post**, and Name to **frmCalculator** (see Figure 7-26).

   When you leave out the Action attribute altogether, the page posts back to itself by default. However, stating the Action attribute explicitly makes your intentions clearer to other developers who might need to change your code one day.

3. Insert a table of two rows and four columns between the form tags. Leave the width of the table unspecified. Add a text field to both columns 1 and 3 of the first row and call them **txtNumber1** and **txtNumber2**, respectively. Set their value attribute to `<%=dblNumber1%>` and `<%=dblNumber2%>`, respectively.

4. Add a button to the fourth cell and set its Type to **submit**, its Name to **btnCalculate**, and its Value to **Calculate**.

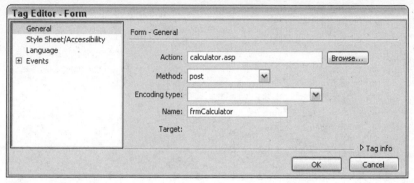

Figure 7-26

5. Merge all cells from the second row to one. To do this, select all four cells in Design view, right-click the selection, and choose Merge Cells from the Table menu item. In the merged cell, type the text **The outcome is:**, as shown:

```
<tr>
 <td colspan="4">The outcome is: </td>
</tr>
```

6. Add a drop-down list so the user can select a type of operation they want to perform on the numbers. Click in the second cell of the top row in Design view and choose Insert➪Form➪List/Menu from the menu bar. Dreamweaver inserts a default `<select>` tag. On the Property inspector, rename the list from `select` to **lstOperator**.

7. While still in the Property inspector, click the List Values button so a dialog box appears where you can add options for the drop-down list. Add four items for addition, subtraction, multiplication, and division, as shown in Figure 7-27. Click OK to add the items to the list on the form.

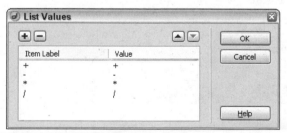

Figure 7-27

8. Next, you'll need to set up a way to do the calculation. The calculation will be performed on the server, so you'll need some ASP code to accomplish this.

Locate the line that starts with `<!DOCTYPE HTML PUBLIC` at the top of your page in Code view and press Enter once before it to create some room between the line starting with `<!DOCTYPE HTML PUBLIC` and the line that starts with `<%@LANGUAGE`. Enter the following ASP code, which performs the calculation:

```
<%@LANGUAGE="VBSCRIPT" CODEPAGE="1252"%>

<%
  Dim dblResult
  Dim dblNumber1
  Dim dblNumber2
  If Request.Form("btnCalculate") <> "" Then
    dblNumber1 = CDbl(Request.Form("txtNumber1"))
    dblNumber2 = CDbl(Request.Form("txtNumber2"))
    Select Case Request.Form("lstOperator")
      Case "+"
        dblResult = dblNumber1 + dblNumber2
      Case "-"
        dblResult = dblNumber1 - dblNumber2
      Case "*"
        dblResult = dblNumber1 * dblNumber2
      Case "/"
        dblResult = dblNumber1 / dblNumber2
    End Select
  End If
%>
<!DOCTYPE HTML PUBLIC "-//W3C//DTD HTML 4.01 Transitional//EN"
  "http://www.w3.org/TR/html4/loose.dtd">
```

9. Before you can run the page, create a space where you can show the outcome of the calculation. Place the cursor right after The outcome is: but still before the </td> tag and then choose Insert⇨ASP Objects⇨Output from the menu bar. Type **dblResult** between <%= and %>. Your code should look like the following:

```
<td colspan="4">The outcome is: <%= dblResult %></td>
```

10. When you save and run the page, you can test your calculator. Type two numbers in the two text boxes, select an operator, and click Calculate. The outcome of your calculation appears onscreen (see Figure 7-28).

Figure 7-28

Notice that the code assumes you type in valid numbers. It will crash if you try to divide *Soccer* by *Wrox* for example. You'll see in Chapter 9 how you can validate user input on the server.

How It Works

There are a few new techniques used in this example that we should explain. Let's first take a look at the drop-down list from which you can select an operator. The options in the list are mutually exclusive by default. That means that only one item can be selected at one time, which is perfect for this situation.

The rest of the HTML form looks pretty standard by now: two text boxes and a Submit button. It's the ASP code that's more interesting to look at. First three variables are declared: two for the values retrieved from the form and one for the result. You need to use the keyword Dim to indicate that you want to *dimension* a variable. This reserves space for the value of the variable in memory:

```
<%
   Dim dblResult
   Dim dblNumber1
   Dim dblNumber2
```

We prefixed the variables with dbl to indicate that we expect them to hold a *double*, a numeric data type that can hold large positive and negative numbers, with a fractional part as well. Next, the code checks whether the form has been submitted, or this is the first time the page is requested:

```
If Request.Form("btnCalculate") <> "" Then
   dblNumber1 = CDbl(Request.Form("txtNumber1"))
   dblNumber2 = CDbl(Request.Form("txtNumber2"))
```

When the form is submitted with the Calculate button, Request.Form("btnCalculate") has a value so the code in the If block will run. Inside that block, the values for dblNumber1 and dblNumber2 are retrieved from their text boxes on the form. These values are converted to doubles using the CDbl function. This is necessary to avoid problems with the + operator. If you don't convert the values to doubles (or another numeric type) ASP gets a bit confused and concatenates the two values instead of adding them together. In that case 2 + 2 ends up as 22 instead of 4—not a very reliable answer for a calculator!

Next a Select Case statement is used to find out which value was selected in the drop-down list:

```
Select Case Request.Form("lstOperator")
   Case "+"
      dblResult = dblNumber1 + dblNumber2
   Case "-"
      dblResult = dblNumber1 - dblNumber2
   Case "*"
      dblResult = dblNumber1 * dblNumber2
   Case "/"
      dblResult = dblNumber1 / dblNumber2
```

Instead of using a few nested If Then Else statements, ASP provides a clean way to test for a certain value. The principle of the Select Case is quite simple: First the value for Request.Form ("lstOperator") is retrieved. You know in advance that you have only four possibilities, so you can test for one of those. If Request.Form("lstOperator") contains a +, for example, the code in the + block will run. After that code has finished, the code will exit the Select statement so any code in the other Case blocks will not be executed. Inside each block a simple math calculation is performed based on the operator the user has chosen.

259

Finally the `Select` statement, the `If` block, and the entire ASP code block are closed:

```
    End Select
  End If
%>
```

In the HTML part of the page the outcome of the calculation is displayed, using the now-familiar output method:

```
The outcome is: <%= dblResult %>
```

Again, `<%=` and `%>` are used to display the value of `dblResult`, which holds the result of the calculation, on-screen.

You may have noticed that the text boxes for the numbers retain their values after you have submitted the page. This is not the default behavior for a text box, however. You need to add some extra code to make sure that the value gets written back to the text box again. In this example you do that by setting the `value` attribute of the text box to `<%=dblNumber1%>`. The first time the page loads, the variable `dblNumber1` does not have a value so the text box is empty. After you click the Calculate button the contents of txtNumber1 are assigned to `dblNumber1`, so when the page is displayed onscreen again, this number is placed inside the text box.

The drop-down list doesn't remember its state yet. You'll see in the next chapter how you can change the code for a drop-down list so it's able to remember which item a user selects.

The examples we have created so far are rather trivial and aren't the greatest help in the real world. Don't worry, though; you'll see plenty of other examples in this and the next chapters that demonstrate the power and usefulness of the GET and POST methods.

Using Information on Multiple Pages

Creating pages that collect information from a client and send it back to a server is a day-to-day task for most Web developers. Submitting data with GET or POST is one way to accomplish this but it has a major drawback: You can't use the information on all pages in your Web site. The information you submit from page A to page B is only available on page B. If you need the information on page C as well, the only way to get it there is to submit it from page B to page C. If there is information you need on all pages of your Web site, you will soon lose track of which page submits what value to another page. This is where the *Session* object becomes useful.

The Session Object

The `Session` object allows you to store information for a specific user on the server and use that information in all pages throughout the entire site. Each unique visitor is tied to a unique `Session` object through the `SessionID`, which is saved as a cookie on the user's computer. A *cookie* is a small text value that can be saved either in memory or on the user's local hard disk. You'll learn more about cookies in the next chapter.

With each request that is made, this cookie is sent to the server, where it is used to connect the current page to the Session object again. All this happens behind the scenes and does not require any coding from your side. All you need to do is assign a value to a session variable when you want to save information and retrieve the information again when you need it in your pages.

Although sessions are a great way to store information, there are a few drawbacks that you need to be aware of:

❑   The SessionID is stored as a cookie on the user's computer. If for some reason a visitor of your site does not have cookies enabled in the browser, you can't use sessions for that visitor. Microsoft has released a workaround for this, called the *cookie munger*, but its implementation is far from ideal. It's beyond the scope of this book to get into the cookie munger, but you can find it in the Microsoft Internet Information Server Resource Kit.

❑   Sessions consume valuable resources on the server, so you should store as little as possible in the session state. Because each unique visitor gets a unique Session object, you could soon degrade the performance of your server. It's usually better to store information in a database and just use the SessionID as an identifier to store and retrieve data. Alternatively, you could store a unique user ID in the Session object and use that to track the user. Although using a database may be a little slower, it enables you to scale your site so it can handle more users concurrently.

❑   Do not store large objects in session state. People often try to save objects like Recordsets and Connections (which you will learn about in Chapters 11, 12, and 13) in a session, but we strongly recommend against doing this. This makes it near impossible to scale your site for more than a handful of users. As a rule of thumb, try to save as little as possible in session state.

❑   Sessions do not end when users close their browsers; they expire after a set amount of time (20 minutes is the default). This means that long after a user has left your site, their Session object may still be consuming resources.

❑   The SessionID that is assigned to a user is not guaranteed to be unique over a long period of time. This means you cannot use this ID reliably to track unique individual visitors to your site.

Now that we have looked at some disadvantages of sessions, let's find out why and how they can be great for you as well.

Enabling Session State

Before you see sessions at work, you need to make sure your current Web site supports their use. With IIS, you can control the use of session state through the MMC console. Each Web site or *virtual directory* can control whether sessions are enabled or not, so even if you already have some sites using sessions, make sure that you enable them as well for your application.

Try It Out   Enabling Session State

1.   To check whether sessions are enabled, open Internet Information Services (IIS) from the Administrative Tools category in the Control Panel (see Figure 7-29).

2.   Locate the folder where you stored your Web site, called TheSoccerSite, under Default Web Site, right-click it, and choose Properties.

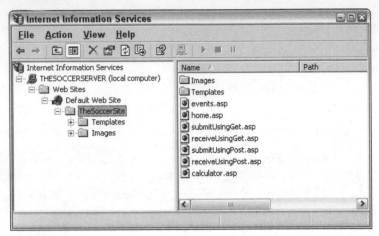

Figure 7-29

3. On the Directory tab, click Create. The details for your site should appear in the Application Settings area of the TheSoccerSite Properties dialog box shown in Figure 7-30.

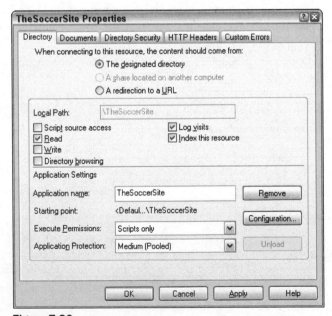

Figure 7-30

4. Click Configuration and open the Options tab in the Application Configuration dialog box (see Figure 7-31).

5. Make sure Enable Session State is checked and that Session Timeout is set to a reasonable time. The default of 20 minutes is usually fine.

6. Click OK twice to apply the settings.

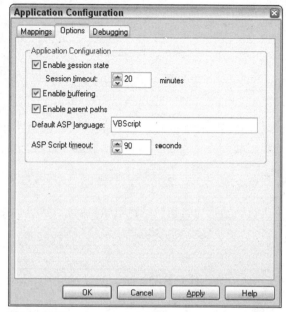

Figure 7-31

How It Works

IIS allows you to determine whether you want session state enabled on a site-to-site basis. This may be useful if you want to reduce the amount of memory used by a site if that site does not use session state at all. In the case of TheSoccerSite, it's advisable to take the performance hit in return for the added value given by Sessions, so make sure your Web site supports sessions.

The timeout that you have set is what we call a *sliding timeout*. This means that the session does not expire exactly 20 minutes after the first page is requested, but the timeout restarts counting down from 20 minutes each time a new page is requested. Theoretically, a session could be kept alive indefinitely by requesting a new page every 19 minutes and 59 seconds.

Exploring Session State

With the theoretical and administrative issues behind you, you can now use session state to save the name of your current visitor in a session. In the next Try It Out exercise, you'll create a form where users can type their name and then submit it to the server. On other pages, you can use this name to personalize the site.

Try It Out   **Exploring Session State**

1. Open the home.asp page you created earlier in this chapter. Switch to Code view and position your cursor right after the text in the content region. Add two `<br>` tags by pressing Shift+Enter twice.

2. Insert a new form right after the breaks in the content section. To do this, keep your cursor in the same position (after the two breaks) in Code view and choose Insert⇨Form⇨Form. Set the Action to **home.asp**, the Method to **POST**, and the Name to **frmUserName**.

3. Add a text field to the page inside the form. Set its Name to **txtUserName** and leave its value empty.

4. Add a button to the form right after the text field. Name the button **btnSubmit**, set its Type to **Submit** and its Value (the label that will be displayed on the button) to **Tell Us Your Name** (see Figure 7-32).

Figure 7-32

5. Type some text above the form to inform users that they should type their name and then click the Tell Us Your Name button. In Code view the complete form should end up looking like this (after indenting it a bit):

```
Your Source for Soccer Events Around the Globe.
<br><br>
Please enter your name and hit the "Tell Us Your Name" button.<br>
<form action="home.asp" method="post" name="frmUserName">
  <input name="txtUserName" type="text">
  <input name="btnSubmit" type="submit" value="Tell Us Your Name">
</form>
<!— InstanceEndEditable —>
```

6. Next you'll need to write some code that retrieves the username from the form and saves it in a session variable. At the very top of your page, place the cursor right before the line that starts with `<!DOCTYPE HTML PUBLIC` and press Enter once. Choose Insert⇨ASP Objects⇨Code Block.

Type the following code block with the `If` statement between the ASP code tags to save the username from the form in a session variable:

```
<%@LANGUAGE="VBSCRIPT" CODEPAGE="1252"%>
<%
 If Trim(Request.Form("txtUserName")) <> "" Then
  Session("UserName") = Trim(Request.Form("txtUserName"))
 End If
%>
<!DOCTYPE HTML PUBLIC "-//W3C//DTD HTML 4.01 Transitional//EN"
  "http://www.w3.org/TR/html4/loose.dtd">
<html>
```

To save some typing, remember that you can use Dreamweaver to insert the two `Trim(Request.Form(""))` blocks (select Insert⇨ASP Objects⇨Trimmed Form Element).

7. To hide the input form once users have entered their name, wrap the entire form inside an `If` block that checks whether the `UserName` session variable has already been set. If the variable does not exist, you show the form; otherwise you display the visitor's name.

   Place the cursor before the descriptive text you added in Step 5. Choose If from the Insert⇨ASP Objects menu and type **Session("UserName") = ""** between the `If` and `Then` that Dreamweaver inserts:

```
Your Source for Soccer Events Around the Globe.
<br><br>
<% If Session("UserName") = "" Then %>
Please enter your name and hit the "Tell Us Your Name" button.<br>
```

8. Place the cursor after the `</form>` tag and choose Else from the same menu. After the `Else` statement, type the following:

```
<% Else %>
   Welcome, <%= Session("UserName") %>.
<!- InstanceEndEditable ->
```

9. Close the `If` statement by choosing End from the ASP Objects menu:

```
   Welcome, <%= Session("UserName") %>.
   <% End If %>
<!- InstanceEndEditable ->
```

10. Save and run the page in your browser. Type your name and click the Tell Us Your Name button. Your name appears and the form disappears. Refresh your browser and notice that your username is still visible. Click a link to another page in the menu and then return to the home page by selecting Home again. You will see that your username is still there, as shown in Figure 7-33. Pure magic!

11. Close your browser (make sure that all browser windows are closed) and browse to `home.asp`. This time the form reappears and asks you to enter your name again.

Figure 7-33

How It Works

You can assign values to session variables and use them again at any location in your site where you might need them. You assign a value to a session variable with the following general syntax:

```
Session(SessionVariableName) = Value
```

This mechanism was used at the top of the page:

```
If Trim(Request.Form("txtUserName")) <> "" Then
   Session("UserName") = Trim(Request.Form("txtUserName"))
End If
```

First a check is made to see whether users have typed a value in the text box. If they have, its value will not equal "" (a zero-length string) so the username from the form is stored in a session variable called `UserName`. From this point onwards, you can retrieve this value again in all pages of your site.

In the HTML section of the page, the form is shown if the session variable hasn't yet been set:

```
<% If Session("UserName") = "" Then %>
```

If it has, the welcome message and the username from the session are shown:

```
Welcome, <%= Session("UserName") %>.
```

In the last step of this exercise, when you close and reopen the browser, the session variable is gone. This is because the `SessionID` that is stored as a cookie is not stored on disk but in memory.

As soon as you close the browser this cookie is lost; you get a new `SessionID` and `Session` object once you request a new page. There is no way to get access to the old object again. If you find that your session variables are maintained, you may not have closed all your browser windows. If that's the case, use the Windows Task Manager to check whether there are any `iexplore.exe` processes still running. Use the End Process button to kill any processes that remain.

Until the timeout of the session, the old session continues to consume resources on the server, after which it is destroyed and the memory is freed. If you want to explicitly destroy the `Session` object using code, use the `Session.Abandon()` method. You can place that instruction anywhere you want in an ASP page to destroy the `Session` object, but you usually place it on a logout page where users can decide to explicitly end their session.

The Global.asa File

Whenever a new user requests the first page from your site, ASP automatically creates a new `Session` object. When this happens, ASP fires an *event* called `Session_OnStart`. Think of an event as a method that can be called by other code whenever something interesting happens. ASP knows two different types of methods: *Subs* and *Functions*. Both can be used to group logically related code together, so it can be called with just one statement. The difference between a `Sub` and a `Function` is that a `Function` can return a value, whereas a `Sub` can't.

At the start of a new session a `Sub` called `Session_OnStart` is executed by the ASP runtime. For example, you can use this method to record the date and time a user first hits your Web site, or count the number of active users on your site. This `Sub` should be placed in a special file called `global.asa` in the root of your site. Note that the extension is slightly different from normal `.asp` pages. Besides the `Session_OnStart` event, three other events can be placed on that page: `Session_OnEnd`, `Application_OnStart`, and `Application_OnEnd`. We will discuss the latter two in the next section when we discuss the `Application` object.

`Session_OnEnd` fires whenever a session expires or whenever you explicitly destroy the session by using `Session.Abandon()`. A little warning is in place though: `Session_OnEnd` is not guaranteed to run for each and every session. If the Web server shuts down unexpectedly, all sessions will be destroyed without the event firing. This means you should never place any code in this event that *must* be run for every user.

In the next exercise, you create the `global.asa` file and add some code to both the `Session_OnStart` and the `Session_OnEnd` events. In the start event you add some code that records the current date and time and saves that in a session variable. On your home page you can then display the time that has elapsed since the user started browsing your site. You'll see the `Session_OnEnd` event at work in a later section when we discuss the `Application` object.

Try It Out   Adding Code to the global.asa File

1. Create a file called `global.asa` in the root of your site. Unfortunately, Dreamweaver does not have a default template for this so you should add a normal `.asp` page (choose Dynamic Page and then ASP VBScript on the General tab of the New Document dialog box) and then save it as `global.asa` in the root of your site.

2. Clear the entire contents of the file and enter the following code in the page:

```
<script language="vbscript" runat="server">
Sub Session_OnStart

End Sub

Sub Session_OnEnd

End Sub
</script>
```

These two code blocks are the skeletons for the events. To indicate to ASP that you want to define a Sub you need to use a Sub SubName End Sub block. The same principle is used to declare a Function, but the keyword Function is used instead of Sub.

3. Add the following line of code to the Session_OnStart sub:

```
Sub Session_OnStart
    Session("StartTime") = Now()
End Sub
```

This is all you need to do with global.asa for now, so save and close the file.

4. Open the home.asp page again and locate the <% End If %> block in the Content section of your page. Enter the following:

```
Welcome, <%= Session("UserName") %>.
    You have been browsing this site since <%= Session("StartTime") %>
    which was <%= DateDiff("S", Session("StartTime"), Now()) %>
    seconds ago.
<% End If %>
```

5. Save the page and open it in a new browser window. After you type in your name and click the Tell Us Your Name button, you'll see a message that indicates the number of seconds you have been browsing this site (see Figure 7-34). If you refresh the page a couple of times by clicking the Home menu item, you'll see the number of seconds increase.

How It Works

To calculate the time spent on the Web site, the code in the Session_OnStart event first retrieved the current date and time:

```
Session("StartTime") = Now()
```

The Now() method is used to get the date and time at the server and its return value is stored in a session variable called StartTime:

```
You have been browsing this site since <%= Session("StartTime") %>
which was <%= DateDiff("S", Session("StartTime"), Now()) %> seconds ago.
```

Figure 7-34

The DateDiff function is used to calculate the difference between two datetime values (a data type that holds both the date and the time). The DateDiff function takes three arguments: the interval you want to calculate, S for seconds, and two datetime values you want to subtract from each other. The smallest datetime should be passed first; otherwise you'll get a negative number. The output, in seconds, is displayed on the page through the <%=... %> construct.

In the next section we discuss methods that enable you to store information that can be accessed by all users. In that section we also show an example of how to use the Session_OnEnd event.

The Application Object

By now you can probably think of some useful examples where you can use session variables to store information about a specific user, but how useful is the Session object if you want to store information that applies to all your users? For example, you may want to display the Webmaster's e-mail address so that people can send feedback about the site. If you store the address in a session variable in the Session_OnStart event, the e-mail address will be duplicated for each user browsing your site. Fortunately, the developers of ASP thought about this and created the *Application object* that works more or less like the Session object, but applies to all users.

The Application object is used to share information between all users on all pages throughout your site. It has the same two events that the Session object has but they are called Application_OnStart and Application_OnEnd. Application_OnStart fires once when the application is started (for example, after a reboot when the first page is requested). Application_OnEnd only runs if the Web server is shut down as intended by its designers; it doesn't run when the server crashes. To see how you can use these events, Try It Out.

Try It Out   **Using Application_OnStart**

1. Add the following `Sub` skeletons to the `global.asa` file. Make sure they fall within the `<script>` tags you added in the previous Try It Out exercise:

```
Sub Application_OnStart

End Sub

Sub Application_OnEnd

End Sub
```

2. Type the following line of code in the body of the `Application_OnStart` event and then save the file:

```
Sub Application_OnStart
    Application("EMailAddress") = "Webmaster@GlobalSoccerEvents.com"
End Sub
```

Next, open `home.asp` again and locate the text "Having difficulties? Contact the Webmaster." in the footer region in Code view. Double-click `Webmaster` to select it and then turn it into an e-mail link by choosing Insert⇨Email Link. Enter **<%=Application("EmailAddress")%>** as the e-mail address. The code in the footer should now look like this:

```
Having difficulties? Contact the
<a href="mailto:<%=Application("EmailAddress")%>">Webmaster</a>.
```

3. Save the page and open it in your browser. You can see in Figure 7-35 that the word *Webmaster* is linked to the Webmaster's e-mail address.

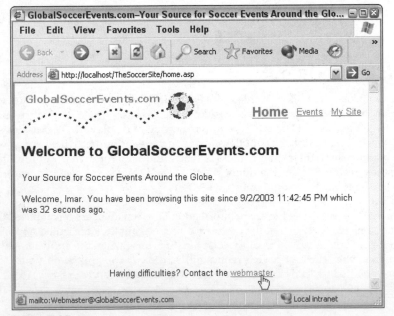

Figure 7-35

How It Works

Just as with the `Session_OnStart` event, you are able to add values to the `Application` object in its `Application_OnStart` event. In this exercise, you stored the e-mail address of the Webmaster from your site in an application variable called `EmailAddress`:

```
<a href="mailto:<%=Application("EmailAddress")%>">Webmaster</a>
```

In your home page, you then retrieved that value again using the now familiar `Application(ApplicationVariableName)` syntax.

The ASP engine is smart enough to notice a change in the `global.asa` file. Whenever you make a change to this file and save it, the ASP application silently restarts. This means that any changes in the code become available immediately.

> Avoid making too many changes to the `global.asa` file on a production server. When the application is restarted all `Session` objects are destroyed, so your visitors might lose any information that was stored in a session for them. It's generally a good idea to make all modifications to this file on the testing server, and when you're satisfied about the results, upload it to your production server. This way you minimize the number of times the application on the production server has to be restarted.

Creating a Hit Counter

Storing the e-mail address of the Webmaster in application state is useful but there are other ways to accomplish the same thing. You could easily store the address in a library item or in your main template as well. In the next example, we'll show you some usage for the application that cannot be done with Dreamweaver-specific features: a hit counter. In the `global.asa` file you will increase the counter for any user that starts a new session on the server and store that number in two variables in the `Application` object: one to track the total number of visitors to your site and another to track the current number of users. When a session ends, only the current number of users is decreased.

Try It Out   **Creating a Hit Counter**

1.   Open the `global.asa` file and add the following code to the `Session_OnStart` event:

```
Sub Session_OnStart
    Session("StartTime") = Now()
    Application.Lock
    Application("TotalNumberOfUsers") = _
      Application("TotalNumberOfUsers") + 1
    Application("CurrentNumberOfUsers") = _
      Application("CurrentNumberOfUsers") + 1
    Application.Unlock
End Sub
```

2. Add the next lines of code to the `Session_OnEnd` event:

```
Sub Session_OnEnd
   Application.Lock
   Application("CurrentNumberOfUsers") = _
      Application("CurrentNumberOfUsers") - 1
   Application.Unlock
End Sub
```

3. Create a new page called `hitCounter.asp` based on your main template, set its title to **Hit Counter**, clear the contents of the content and footer regions, and add the following block of code to the main content area in Code view:

```
Currently, <%=Application("CurrentNumberOfUsers")%> user(s) are
browsing your site.
<br><br>
You've received <%=Application("TotalNumberOfUsers")%> visit(s) since the start
of the application.
```

4. Save and run the page. Notice that currently you are the only user browsing the site. Open a new browser and browse to the hit counter page. Don't just open a new browser window by pressing Ctrl+N but start a fresh instance of the browser or use a whole different brand of browser, like Mozilla or Netscape, as in Figure 7-36. If you press Ctrl+N to open a new browser window, both browsers will share the same `Session` object on the server and you won't get the right information.

Now you can see that there are two users browsing the Web site (see Figure 7-36).

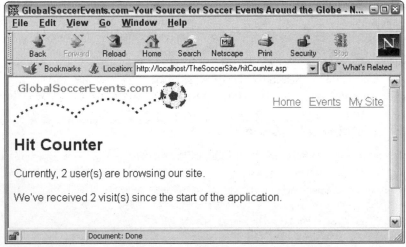

Figure 7-36

If you have the patience, you can close both browsers and wait for at least 20 minutes. Then start the hit counter page again. You'll find that the current number of users has been reset to 1, while the total number has been increased by one.

How It Works

In Session_OnStart you have added some code that increases two counters that are stored in application state:

```
Application.Lock
Application("TotalNumberOfUsers") = _
  Application("TotalNumberOfUsers") + 1
Application("CurrentNumberOfUsers") = _
  Application("CurrentNumberOfUsers") + 1
Application.Unlock
```

This code retrieves the current number of users from the application state, increases it by one, and then saves it back to the application variable. This step is repeated for CurrentNumberOfUsers as well.

Notice how the underscore character indicates that the code continues on the next line. You can use this character in VBScript code to break a long line of code over multiple lines. If you omit the underscore character, the ASP engine interprets the next line as a new instruction, which will most likely result in an error. The underscore is not required, however. It's perfectly legal to create really long lines of VBScript code but by breaking them up, your code will be easier to read and understand.

Before the variables are changed in the Application object, the application is *locked* by using Application.Lock. This prevents two users from changing the value at the same time. When the application is locked, only one user has write access to the values and all other requests are queued up. After the variables have been changed, the Application object must be *unlocked* again so it becomes available for other users:

```
Application.Lock
Application("CurrentNumberOfUsers") = _
  Application("CurrentNumberOfUsers") - 1
Application.Unlock
```

In the Session_OnEnd event only the counter for the current number of users is decreased. This way, you can keep track of the number of users that currently browse your site and the total number of visitors since the start of your application. Here, Lock and Unlock are used again for the same reasons.

```
<%=Application("CurrentNumberOfUsers")%>
```

Finally, <%= ...%> is used to retrieve the values and show them on the page. There is no need to lock the application first because all the code does is read the values without changing them.

Summary

Because the Web is stateless by design, you need to find a way to send information from the client to the server where you can store and use that information. In this chapter you have seen two ways to send that data from the client to the server: with GET and POST. The amount of data you can send with the GET method is limited but it's easier to bookmark a page and, at times, it requires less work to pass data between pages. POST, on the other hand, enables you to send large quantities of data. This can be useful when you want to allow users to send a lot of text or upload a file.

Once the information is at the server you can use it in your page for display purposes or decision-making. Normally, the information is only available for the page that the data was sent to. If you need to save the data so you can use it in multiple pages, you need to store it at a safe location, either at the client or at the server.

To store information at the server, you have the Session and the Application objects available. A Session object is unique for a visitor and can be used for information that only applies to an individual user of your site. The Application object is used to store information for all users of your site.

Both the Session and the Application object come with two events that run when they start and end. You can use these events to record information, like the current date and time, or the number of hits to a page, so it becomes globally available in your entire Web site.

In the next chapter you will use the techniques that you have learned in this chapter to track users as they progress through your site.

Why Not Try . . .

1. On your calculator page, the label The Outcome Is is always visible even when you haven't performed a calculation yet. Try to hide the label until the form has been submitted and the user has typed in values for number 1 and number 2.

   Hint: Use Request.Form("btnCalculate") *again to determine whether the form has been submitted by clicking the button.*

2. In this chapter you saw how to use Session.Abandon() to destroy a session explicitly at the server. Create a page called logout.asp that calls this method in an ASP code block. You can also add a menu item in the menu inside the library item to provide easy access to it for your users. The logout.asp page will come in handy in Chapter 9 when we discuss how to secure your Web site.

3. Right now, home.asp is the only page that has a footer with a link to the e-mail address of the Webmaster. Why not try to move this footer to the main template of your site so that all pages in your site can benefit from it? When you do so, you have two choices:

   ❑ Leave the editable region in place. This way, you can provide a default footer for each page that can be changed on a page-to-page basis. This lets you have a different footer on some pages, while the majority of your pages use the default footer.

   ❑ Remove the editable region. By removing the editable region, you create a locked footer that cannot be changed on individual pages.

   In both cases, you need to change the template and then save it to change all the pages based on your template as well.

Keeping Track of Users

When your Web site starts to grow and you are not the only visitor anymore, it's likely you'll want to find out how people are using your site. For example, you may want to know which page users go to first after the home page or you may be interested in the type of information users request on a dynamic page. You can then use this information to enhance your visitors' browsing experience by changing some parts of your site's design. If, for example, you find out that the events page is the most popular page of your site, you may decide to shuffle your menu around so the events menu item is easier to reach. You could also use this information to change the content in real time, while users are browsing your site. Showing the most popular categories first increases the chance that visitors will get what they are looking for on your site.

To get this user information, you could of course analyze the Web server's log files and see what pages are requested, but this has a few drawbacks. First of all, it only shows *which* pages users have requested, not *how*, and, more importantly, the information from the log files is only available *after* people have visited your site, not during their visit. This makes it nearly impossible to use this data to change the presentation of your site during a visit.

To collect user information in such a way that it's actually useful, it is important that you *know your visitors*. In this chapter we will demonstrate how you can track the users of your site so you can distinguish returning visitors from new ones and find out how they use the site.

We will be looking at how to do the following:

- ❑ Use cookies to count the number of times a user has visited a page
- ❑ Save information about surfing behavior in a cookie so you can improve the way the site works for a user
- ❑ Find out which pages your visitors go to first after they have seen your home page
- ❑ Use `Subs`, `Functions`, and `Include` files to created better structured code

Saving Information About a Page

When you want to save information about a Web page on a user-by-user basis, you have two options for where to store this information:

- ❏ On the server
- ❏ On the client

In Chapter 7, you saw how to use the `Session` and `Application` objects to store information on the server. In this chapter you use a combination of these two methods to track user behavior through your site.

If you want to store information on the client, you need to make use of *cookies,* which are simple text values that a server sends to a client. These text values are either stored in memory or on your local hard disk in either a single file or multiple files (depending on the browser). They are used to save small amounts of data on the client that can be passed back and forth to the server. Cookies can greatly enhance the user's browsing experience. For example, at a secured site where you need to log in before you can gain access, it's often a good idea to let the server remember that the user has already logged in.

On many other sites, however, security is not the biggest issue; it's *personalization* that counts. Personalization can be applied to many parts of the Web site: Changing background colors and fonts, deciding where you want to place your navigation menu, and showing content about only those topics that interest you are all great examples of personalization that cookies make possible. Because this information is not secret, there really is no need to hide these personalization settings behind a password; instead, this information can be saved on the client in a cookie. Quite often on a Web site you get an option to "Remember Me" without the need to type in a username or password. In that case, it's likely that your preferences or other settings have been stored in a cookie.

> **Although some people are afraid that cookies can harm their privacy, it's generally agreed that most cookies are harmless and enhance the user's browsing experience. Unfortunately, it is possible to misuse this technology to track the surfing behavior of individuals across multiple Web sites. Some advertising agencies use a unique cookie ID to track your trails on the Web. To verify that visitors to your site understand what information you are retrieving about them, it's usually a good idea to add a privacy statement to your site describing the intent and usage of the cookies, and any personal data being stored.**

Before we start an exercise showing the use of cookies, let's step back and explain in some detail how they work and what it takes to use them.

Cookies in Detail

In Chapter 7 you used the `Request` object to get information about requests to a site and used the `Response` object to output responses to the client. Both the `Request` and `Response` objects also have a cookie collection. The `Request` object's cookie collection is used to read cookies from the client and the `Response` object's cookie collection is used to write to them. Storing a cookie can be as simple as assigning a value to a variable, just as you did with session variables, for example.

Whenever you output a cookie to the client, by default it remains there only for the current session. As soon as the user closes the browser, the cookie is gone. This is often referred to as a *session cookie* (not to be confused with the SessionID from the previous chapter, although the SessionID is stored as a type of session cookie).

To make a cookie last between browser sessions, you need to set its *expiry date*. As soon as the expiry date has passed, the browser no longer sends the cookie to the requesting server and deletes it from the local hard drive.

You can limit the scope of the cookie by setting a *path* that applies to the cookie. If you don't supply a path, the cookie is visible throughout the entire site. If you set the path to /TheSoccerSite/ for example, the cookie can only be read from within the /TheSoccerSite/ folder. This is useful when you and other people share the same server at your ISP, for example. This means that any cookie you set for the path www.your ISP.com/You/ cannot be read by other Web sites, such as www.yourISP.com/SomeOtherSite/.

You can also store a cookie as a collection of values, or *keys*. For example, you could create a cookie called User, with keys FirstName and LastName, both of which contain data about the user. This way you can logically group related information together, which can be a great help whenever you need to store a lot of information. Depending on the browser, you can only store around 20 cookies per Web site on the user's computer, but by using keys to store multiple values per cookie, you can greatly increase the amount of data you can store on the client.

All the information that you store in a cookie is sent back to the server for every request a user makes. This may cause your site to slow down if you try to pass too much data.

To clarify things, take a look at how to create cookies:

```
<%
  ' Single Cookie
  Response.Cookies("FavoriteClub") = "Ajax, Amsterdam"
  Response.Cookies("FavoriteClub").Expires = Date() + 10
  Response.Cookies("FavoriteClub").Path = "/"
  ' Cookie with keys
  Response.Cookies("User")("FirstName") = "David"
  Response.Cookies("User")("LastName") = "Beckham"
  Response.Cookies("User").Expires = "October 30, 2003"
  Response.Cookies("User").Path = "/TheSoccerSite/Admin/"
%>
```

The first example, a single cookie, saves a user's favorite soccer club in a cookie called FavoriteClub. It expires 10 days after it's created. Since the path is set to /, the cookie is available in the entire domain or Web server and not just in the /TheSoccerSite virtual directory.

The second example shows how to use keys with cookies. A cookie called User is created that contains two keys: FirstName and LastName. Both the Expires and the Path properties apply to the entire cookie, not to just one of the keys. The Expires property in this example demonstrates how to expire the cookie on a particular date. Because the path is set to /TheSoccerSite/Admin/, the cookie can only be retrieved from this folder and cannot be read by other folders or applications.

To learn more about cookies in ASP 3.0, search Google or the MSDN site at http://msdn.microsoft.com for Response.Cookies.

Now that you know you can use cookies to store information on the client, create a simple page that counts the number of times a user visits that page.

Saving the Number of Hits to a Page

1. Add a new page to your site and make sure it is based on your main template. To do this, press Ctrl+N to open the New Document dialog box and then switch to the Templates tab. Select your site from the Template For list and double-click the mainTemplate template in the Site "TheSoccerSite" list. Save the page as cookieCounter.asp in the root of your site. Name the page **Cookie Counter** in the Title region of the page. Clear the placeholders for the Content and Footer sections of your template.

2. Insert some ASP code at the top of the page that sets and retrieves a cookie. Although Dreamweaver MX 2004's built-in support for working with cookies is rather limited, you can save yourself some typing by creating a request variable on the Bindings panel. This way, you can drag the variable in your code at places where you need to retrieve the value of a cookie; the variable is then also available as a dynamic value. (You'll see more about this in Chapter 12.)

    Open the Bindings panel (see Figure 8-1) on the Application panel group by pressing Ctrl+F10, and then click the plus (+) button. Choose Request Variable from the menu. Select Request.Cookie from the Type list and type **HitCounter** in the Name box. Click OK to add the variable to your Dreamweaver site.

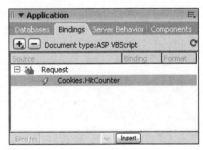

Figure 8-1

If you wonder where Dreamweaver MX 2004 stores the request variable, take a look at your local _notes folder (C:\TheSoccerSite_notes). Inside that folder Dreamweaver creates an XML file with the name of your page but with an additional .mno extension that holds the request variable.

3. With the request variable in place, it's time to add the ASP code. At the top of the page, right after the line that starts with <%@LANGUAGE, insert an ASP code block by choosing Code Block from the ASP Objects menu item on the Insert menu. Inside the block enter the following code:

```
<%@LANGUAGE="VBSCRIPT" CODEPAGE="1252"%>
<%
   Dim iNumberOfHits
   iNumberOfHits =
%>
<!DOCTYPE HTML PUBLIC "-//W3C//DTD HTML 4.01 Transitional//EN"
   "http://www.w3.org/TR/html4/loose.dtd">
<html>
```

From the Bindings panel, drag the request variable Cookies.HitCounter you created in Step 2 and drop it at the end of the line that says `iNumberOfHits =`, as shown in Figure 8-2.

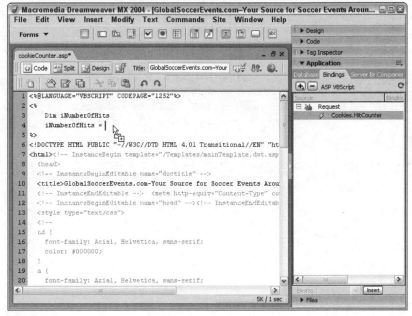

Figure 8-2

Once you drop the variable, Dreamweaver inserts the code `Request.Cookies("HitCounter")` for you.

4. Complete the code block by adding the following ASP code:

```
<%
  Dim iNumberOfHits
  iNumberOfHits = Request.Cookies("HitCounter")

  If Len(iNumberOfHits) > 0 Then
    iNumberOfHits = iNumberOfHits + 1
  Else
    iNumberOfHits = 1
  End If
  Response.Cookies("HitCounter") = iNumberOfHits
  Response.Cookies("HitCounter").Expires = Date() + 10
%>
<html>
```

5. Add the following ASP code block to the Content region of your page in Code view:

```
<%
If iNumberOfHits > 10 Then
  Response.Write("Aren't you tired of this page yet?")
Else
  If iNumberOfHits > 1 Then
```

```
      Response.Write("You must really like this page!")
    Else
      Response.Write("Since this is your first visit here, " & _
            "I'd personally like to welcome you.")
    End If
  End If
%>
```

6. Save (press Ctrl+S) and open the page in your browser (press F12). You'll see that this is the first time you have viewed the page. Refresh the browser window to see the message change. If you have viewed the page more than 10 times, you'll see the message change again (see Figure 8-3). Even when you close your browser and open it again, you'll see that the value of the counter has been preserved.

Figure 8-3

How It Works

To see how this cookies example works, let's go over the code line by line. First, a variable is declared that will hold the number of hits to this page. Just as in the previous chapter, Dim is used to dimension the variable. It then gets the value from the cookie HitCounter with the Request.Cookies("HitCounter") statement:

```
<%
Dim iNumberOfHits
iNumberOfHits = Request.Cookies("HitCounter")
```

The code then checks if the cookie contains a value. If the page has never been visited before, the cookie doesn't exist, so no value is returned and the length of iNumberOfHits is zero.

```
If Len(iNumberOfHits) > 0 Then
 iNumberOfHits = iNumberOfHits + 1
Else
 iNumberOfHits = 1
End If
```

The Len function tests the length of a string. If it is larger than zero, it means the cookie contains a value so it can be increased by one. If the cookie doesn't exist, the hit counter is initialized to 1.

The following two statements ensure the cookie is created and that it will last for some time:

```
Response.Cookies("HitCounter") = iNumberOfHits
Response.Cookies("HitCounter").Expires = Date() + 10
```

The first line creates the actual cookie, HitCounter, and assigns the value of iNumberOfHits to it. If the cookie doesn't exist, it's created; otherwise, it's overwritten with the new value.

The second line sets the Expires property of the cookie so that it survives browser sessions. The Date() function gets the current date. By adding 10 to this date, you make sure that the cookie remains valid for the next 10 days.

Finally, a message to the user appears depending on the number of hits on the page:

```
<%
If iNumberOfHits > 10 Then
  Response.Write("Aren't you tired of this page yet?")
Else
  If iNumberOfHits > 1 Then
    Response.Write("You must really like this page!")
  Else
   Response.Write("Since this is your first visit here, " & _
          "I'd personally like to welcome you.")
  End If
End If
%>
```

The If statements are used to determine the number of times the user has requested this page and an appropriate response is displayed using the Response.Write method.

Notice that we used the underscore character again to denote a line break. Because the code needs to be split in the middle of a string, you can't simply add the underscore somewhere in the middle of the text. If you want to break up a string, you have to close it first using double-quotes and then use the ampersand (&) to concatenate the rest of the text. Using the underscore after the ampersand allows you to place the rest of the code on the next line.

Forewarned Is Forearmed

If you are working with cookies in ASP, you are sure one day to run into the following error:

```
Response object error 'ASP 0156 : 80004005'
Header Error
/cookieCounter.asp, line 53
The HTTP headers are already written to the client browser. Any HTTP header
modifications must be made before writing page content.
```

Although this message looks rather cryptic at first, it describes the problem very accurately. To send cookies to a client browser, cookies are sent in the *header* of the response. The HTML and all other output are placed in the *body* of the response. For various technical reasons, the header must be sent before the body.

This means that if you have already started to output content to the browser with `Response.Write` or with plain HTML, and then try to write a cookie with `Response.Cookies`, you will encounter this error. Because you are outputting content to the body, the header must have already been sent, so the cookies statement can't modify it anymore. This only applies to *writing* a cookie with the `Response` object. You can read from the cookie using the `Request` object from anywhere within the code.

You also should be aware that even a single space, a tab character, the `<html>` tag, or many other things in your code can cause this error to appear. To clarify this, look at an example:

```
<!DOCTYPE HTML PUBLIC "-//W3C//DTD HTML 4.01 Transitional//EN"
  "http://www.w3.org/TR/html4/loose.dtd">
<html>
 <head>
  <%
  Response.Cookies("FavoriteClub") = "Manchester United"
  Response.Cookies("FavoriteClub").Expires = Date() + 10
  %>
  <title>GlobalSoccerEvents.com</title>
 </head>
 <body>
  <h2>Welcome to GlobalSoccerEvents.com</h2>
 </body>
</html>
```

As you can see, before the cookie is created, the `DOCTYPE` and the `<html>` and `<head>` tags have already been sent to the browser. This will result in the error message shown earlier.

There are two ways to avoid this problem: buffer the output or change your coding logic (moving the code that writes the cookies to the beginning of your page).

Buffering the Output

When you buffer the output, ASP stores all the information it is going to output in memory. When the complete page is stored, it sends the entire contents of the buffer to the client all at once. During the buffering, you can still write to the header as well as to the body of the response, thus avoiding the error you saw in the previous section.

Turning on buffering for a specific page is very simple. Add the following statement to each ASP page that requires buffering:

```
<% Response.Buffer = True%>
```

Make sure you place it after the `<%@language` statement but before any other ASP or HTML code.

As an added benefit, the performance of your page increases slightly when buffering is enabled because communication between the client and the server takes place in fewer blocks of data, but each block is larger. This reduces the amount of overhead involved in sending the data.

In IIS, you can turn on buffering for all the pages in your site through the IIS management console. To change the setting, open up Internet Information Services, which you can find in the Administrative Tools item of the Windows Control Panel. Locate the virtual directory called `TheSoccerSite` that you created in Chapter 7, right-click it and choose Properties. On the Directory tab, click the Configuration button and then the Options tab (see Figure 8-4). Make sure that Enable Buffering is checked.

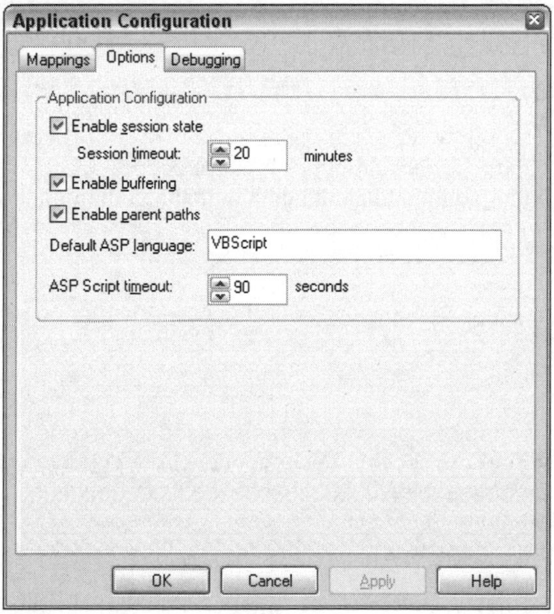

Figure 8-4

Changing Your Coding Logic

The other way to avoid this error is by changing the coding logic. Instead of adding the Response.Cookies statement in the middle of the page, move it all the way up to the top of the page, before the <html> tag. Look at a revised version of the example you saw earlier:

```
<%
 Response.Cookies("FavoriteClub") = "Manchester United"
 Response.Cookies("FavoriteClub").Expires = Date() + 10
%>
<!DOCTYPE HTML PUBLIC "-//W3C//DTD HTML 4.01 Transitional//EN"
  "http://www.w3.org/TR/html4/loose.dtd">
<html>
 <head>
  <title>GlobalSoccerEvents.com</title>
 </head>
 <body>
  <h2>Welcome to GlobalSoccerEvents.com</h2>
 </body>
</html>
```

By writing the code like this, the cookie is appended to the *header* of the response before any content of the page gets written to the *body* of the response.

It's best to use a combination of these two methods. Use buffering to increase the performance of your site and try to make the most of your business logic decisions, including writing to and reading from cookies, before outputting any content to the browser. This way, all your coding logic is nicely packed together so that it can be easily viewed and, more important, easily understood by others.

Improving the User's Browsing Experience

The previous example was rather trivial; it's not too useful to simply count page hits and then display a message on the screen. In the next example you build something more useful for TheSoccerSite. You'll expand the events page that you built in Chapter 7 so that it contains a drop-down list with different categories for the soccer events you can show on your site, such as the Champions League, UEFA Cup, National League, U.S. Major League Soccer, World Cup, Women's World Cup, and so on.

When a user selects a category from the list, the list of events is filtered so it shows just the events from that category. For the time being, hard-coded text for the events is used but you'll get a chance to upgrade the page in Chapter 12 when you make the page data-driven.

Once the drop-down list on the events page is in place, add some code logic to ensure that when a user chooses a new category from the list, this item remains selected on the page. In the next chapter, we'll show you how to use Dreamweaver MX 2004 to create a drop-down list that remembers its selected item. Since it is sometimes necessary to create an entire drop-down list through ASP code, in this chapter we show you how to apply this behavior to a drop-down list yourself.

This Try It Out exercise also shows you how to add even more intelligence to the drop-down list so it can remember which category was chosen the last time the user visited your site. This way, the drop-down lists remembers the selection even between browser visits.

Try It Out   Creating Intelligent Drop-Down Lists

1. Open the events.asp page and remove the placeholders for the Content and the Footer regions of the template. Click inside the content region in Design view and then switch to Code view by pressing Ctrl+~. With the cursor still in the content region, insert a form by clicking the Form button on the Forms category of the Insert bar. Fill in the Tag Editor dialog box as shown in Figure 8-5 and then click OK to create the form.

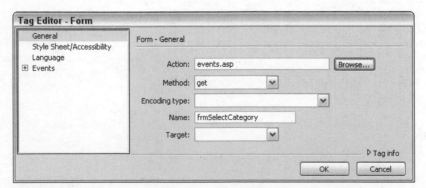

Figure 8-5

2. Add a drop-down list to the form by selecting Insert⇨Form⇨List/Menu or by clicking the List/Menu button on the Forms category of the Insert bar. Name the drop-down list **lstCategory** and then click OK. Save the page and then switch back to Design view. Make sure the drop-down list is selected by clicking it once (you'll see a dashed border around it).

3. On the Property inspector for the drop-down list, click the List Values button and add the following five items:

Item Label	Value
Select a Category	
Champions League	1
UEFA Cup	2
National League	3
US Major League Soccer	4

Use the plus (+) button to add items or just press Tab after each item to insert a new one. Click OK when you're finished. Dreamweaver didn't insert a `value` attribute for the first `<option>` element because you left the value field empty. However, for the sample site you need to add an empty `value` attribute. If you don't do this, the browser will submit the contents of the `<option>` element ("Select a Category") as the value for the drop-down list instead of an empty string. To fix this, locate the first `<option>` element in Code view and change it to this (note the change in bold):

```
<select name="lstCategory" onChange="document.frmSelectCategory.submit();">
<option value="">Select a Category</option>
<% If iLastCategory = 1 Then sSelected = " selected=""selected""" _
```

If you wonder where the values for the categories come from, they are the IDs from the categories in the database for TheSoccerSite. You'll see more of this when you make the events page database-driven in Chapter 12.

4. Next, you need to find a way to reload the page as soon as your visitor requests a new category from the list. You can do this by adding some JavaScript code to the `onChange` event of the drop-down list. The `onChange` event fires whenever a user makes a new selection in the list. The idea behind this event is the same, as with the `Application_OnStart` event that fires when the application is started; you can write custom code that executes whenever something interesting happens. In this case, the form should be submitted to the server automatically when a new category is chosen so the user doesn't have to click a button. You can submit a form through code using `document.formName.submit()`, where `formName` is the name of the form as you have defined it in its `name` attribute.

Dreamweaver supplies an easy way to add client code for events to various HTML elements. With the drop-down list still selected in Design view, press Ctrl+F5 to open the Tag Editor dialog box (see Figure 8-6). Alternatively, right-click the drop-down list and choose Edit Tag <select> from the menu.

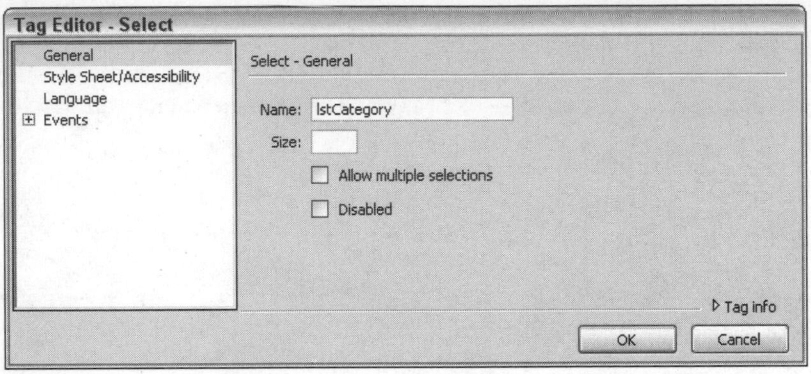

Figure 8-6

Expand Events, select the onChange item, type the following code in the text field to the right, and then click OK:

```
document.frmSelectCategory.submit();
```

After indenting the code to improve readability, the form looks like this:

```
<td>
<!- InstanceBeginEditable name="Content" ->

<form action="events.asp" method="get" name="frmSelectCategory">
 <select name="lstCategory" onChange="document.frmSelectCategory.submit();">
  <option value="">Select a Category</option>
  <option value="1">Champions League</option>
  <option value="2">UEFA Cup</option>
  <option value="3">National League</option>
  <option value="4">US Major League Soccer</option>
 </select>
</form>
<!- InstanceEndEditable ->
</td>
```

5. Make some room right before the line that starts with `<!DOCTYPE HTML PUBLIC` at the top of the page and insert the following ASP code block:

```
<%@LANGUAGE="VBSCRIPT" CODEPAGE="1252"%>

<%
 Dim iLastCategory
 If Request.QueryString("lstCategory") <> "" Then
  ' Category has been chosen, so let's save it in a cookie
  iLastCategory = Request.QueryString("lstCategory")
  Response.Cookies("LastCategory") = iLastCategory
  Response.Cookies("LastCategory").Expires = Date() + 10
 End If
%>
<!DOCTYPE HTML PUBLIC "-//W3C//DTD HTML 4.01 Transitional//EN"
   "http://www.w3.org/TR/html4/loose.dtd">
<html>
```

Remember that you can create a request variable for lstCategory using the Behaviors panel just as you did earlier with the cookie variable. This enables you to drag the variable in your code instead of typing it in each time.

6. With the drop-down list and the code to track the list in place, write the code that hides or displays the events. After the `</form>` tag in the Content region, type the following block of code that writes out the HTML content for the category chosen. Currently, just a content placeholder is used but in your site you can replace the placeholders with real information about events:

```
</form>
    <%  Select Case iLastCategory
    Case 1 ' Champions League
    Response.Write("<h3>Champions League</h3>") %>
    — HTML Content for Champions League Events here —
    <%  Case 2 ' UEFA Cup
    Response.Write("<h3>UEFA Cup</h3>")  %>
    — HTML Content for UEFA Cup Events here —
    <%  Case 3 ' National League
    Response.Write("<h3>National League</h3>") %>
    — HTML Content for National League Events here —
    <%  Case 4 ' US Major League Soccer
    Response.Write("<h3>US Major League Soccer</h3>") %>
    — HTML Content for US Major League Soccer Events here —
    <%  Case Else ' No category chosen  %>
    Please select a category from the drop-down list.
    <%  End Select  %>
    <!— InstanceEndEditable —></td>
```

7. Save (press Ctrl+S) and run the page in the browser (press F12). The first time you open it, you'll be asked to select a category from the drop-down list (see Figure 8-7). When you select one, the content for that category will be shown.

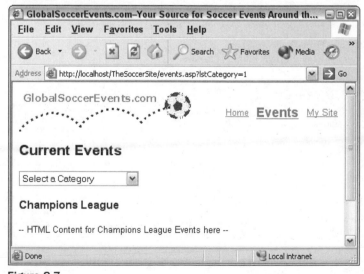

Figure 8-7

8. You may have noticed a problem with the drop-down list. As soon as you select a category, it forgets which item was selected and defaults back to Select a Category. To modify the drop-down list so it remembers its state, change the `<option>` elements for the drop-down list so they look as in the following code. To save you from some typing, you could create just a single `<option>` element plus the two lines of ASP code preceding it and then use Copy and Paste to create the three additional items:

```
<select name="lstCategory" onChange="document.frmSelectCategory.submit();">
<option value="">Select a Category</option>
  <% If iLastCategory = 1 Then sSelected = " selected=""selected""" _
     Else sSelected = ""%>
   <option value="1"<%=sSelected%>>Champions League</option>
  <% If iLastCategory = 2 Then sSelected = " selected=""selected""" _
     Else sSelected = ""%>
   <option value="2"<%=sSelected%>>UEFA Cup</option>
  <% If iLastCategory = 3 Then sSelected = " selected=""selected""" _
     Else sSelected = ""%>
   <option value="3"<%=sSelected%>>National League</option>
  <% If iLastCategory = 4 Then sSelected = " selected=""selected""" _
     Else sSelected = ""%>
   <option value="4"<%=sSelected%>>US Major League Soccer</option>
</select>
```

9. Save and run the page again. After you choose a category, the drop-down list remembers the selection you made. The number of the category you have chosen is visible in the address bar of the browser. In Figure 8-8, you can see in the address bar that `lstCategory` has a value of 3.

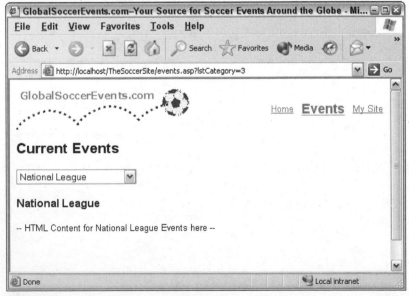

Figure 8-8

10. There is still one improvement to make. When the page first loads, the last category that a user chose during a previous visit should be preselected. But if no selection has been made before, the default option of Select a Category should be shown. Because most of the logic is already in place, making this modification is easy. In the ASP code block you inserted earlier at the top of the ASP page, in Step 5, add an `Else` clause for the `If` statement. The `Else` clause fires when there is no category in the `QueryString`, which means the page must have been requested directly. Add an `Else` clause to the code block so it now looks like this:

```
<%
Dim iLastCategory
If Request.QueryString("lstCategory") <> "" Then
 ' Category has been chosen, so let's save it in a cookie
 iLastCategory = Request.QueryString("lstCategory")
 Response.Cookies("LastCategory") = iLastCategory
 Response.Cookies("LastCategory").Expires = Date() + 10
Else
  ' Page is requested directly, so get the cookie
  If Len(Request.Cookies("LastCategory")) > 0 Then
   iLastCategory = CInt(Request.Cookies("LastCategory"))
  End If
End If
%>
```

11. Save the page and refresh it in your browser. The category you chose last is preselected. Select a new category, close your browser, and open the events page again. The drop-down list remembers its state even between browser sessions. This time, the category is not visible in the address bar of the browser because the form hasn't been submitted yet. The value for the category was retrieved from the cookie instead.

How It Works

There are three main code areas that are responsible for displaying the events and the drop-down list. The part that shows only the content for a specific category is nothing new; you saw how to use the `Select Case` statement in Chapter 7, so we won't cover that again.

Notice the comments after each `Case` statement to indicate what category you are testing for. In ASP you can add comments in your code using a single apostrophe. Any text that is preceded by the apostrophe is considered a comment. As you can see from this example, it's possible to add descriptive text at the end of each line of code:

```
<%  Select Case iLastCategory
    Case 1 ' Champions League
    Response.Write("<h3>Champions League</h3>") %>
```

Right now, with only four categories, it's easy to see what category is referred to with the number 1 or 2, but if you had 50 items in a `Select Case` statement, the comments might help you or others remember or understand the code better. Commenting code helps avoiding "magic numbers," a programmer's term referring to numbers that appear to be randomly chosen and from which you cannot extract any meaning.

The next section of code that is worth looking at is the ASP block at the top of the page. Let's break it down and see what it does:

```
<%
Dim sSelected
Dim iLastCategory
If Request.QueryString("lstCategory") <> "" Then
```

First, two variables are declared. One determines which item needs to be preselected, and the other holds the category that was selected. The code then checks whether this page was loaded because a new category was chosen in the drop-down list or because the page was requested directly. If a category was chosen, `Request.QueryString("lstCategory")` does not equal an empty string, and the code in the `If` block runs.

The value of the selected category is saved in a cookie called `LastCategory` and then the `Expires` property is set to `Date() + 10` to ensure it lasts for the next 10 days:

```
' Category has been chosen, so let's save it in a cookie
iLastCategory = Request.QueryString("lstCategory")
Response.Cookies("LastCategory") = iLastCategory
Response.Cookies("LastCategory").Expires = Date() + 10
```

If the page was requested directly, the code in the `Else` block runs:

```
Else
  ' Page is requested directly, so get the cookie
  If Len(Request.Cookies("LastCategory")) > 0 Then
   iLastCategory = CInt(Request.Cookies("LastCategory"))
  End If
End If
%>
```

If the `LastCategory` cookie has been set before (that is, its length is greater than zero), its value is assigned to the `iLastCategory` variable. The `CInt` function converts the value between the parentheses to a number.

At this point, `iLastCategory` only contains a value if the page was reloaded because either a new category was chosen or the `LastCategory` cookie existed and had a value.

In the HTML section of the page, `iLastCategory` is then used to determine which `<option>` element should be preselected:

```
<% If iLastCategory = 1 Then sSelected = " selected=""selected""" _
   Else sSelected = ""%>
```

For each option in the drop-down list, this code construct is used. First, the code checks whether the chosen category (`iLastCategory`) matches the value of the list option that needs to be displayed. If they match, the value `selected=""selected""` is assigned to the variable `sSelected`; otherwise, the value of this variable is cleared.

Notice the use of two double-quotes in the code, instead of one. This is because a double-quote denotes the end of a string. Since you don't want to end the string, but just use the literal value of a quote, you need to *escape* it with an extra double-quote. In the browser, this ends up as `selected="selected"`.

Using `selected="selected"` is an XHTML-compatible way to select a list option. In HTML, using an empty attribute called `selected` would be enough; however, XHTML does not allow empty attributes so it needs to be changed to `selected="selected"`. Older browsers will still understand this.

```
<option value="1"<%=sSelected%>>Champions League</option>
```

Finally, within the `<option>` element, `sSelected` is used to determine whether the element should be selected or not. If the user chooses the Champions League category, for example, `iLastCategory` equals 1, so `selected="selected"` is assigned to `sSelected`. When the option for this category is sent to the browser, it eventually looks like this:

```
<option value="1" selected="selected">Champions League</option>
```

This is what makes the item appear to be preselected in the list.

Site Tracking

Now that you have seen how you can track the surfing behavior of an individual user, it's time to find out how you can track visitors on specific areas of your site. For example, it could be interesting to find out whether new users behave differently from existing users. To accomplish this, you need to add some coding logic that determines whether a user is new to your site or not. Then you can follow up to observe what page they request after they make the initial connection.

The code you create can be used in multiple pages on your site. This means you have to structure your code in such a way that it can be easily reused in all the pages that require it. To create reusable code, you can use `Functions`, `Subs`, and `Include` files in ASP to group logically related code together. You have already learned a little bit about `Functions` and `Subs`, but in the next section we'll discuss them in more detail. Once you know how `Functions` and `Subs` work, we'll show you how you can use `Include` files to make your code even easier to reuse and maintain.

Grouping Code Together

In Chapter 7 you saw that a `Function` or a `Sub` groups related code so it can be called with only one statement. You also looked at the general declaration for a `Function` or `Sub`. The difference between the two is that a `Function` can return a value, whereas a `Sub` can't. Take a look at an example of how to actually create a `Function` and a `Sub` that can be reused multiple times.

Suppose you use `Response.Write` repeatedly to output content from the server to the browser. To make the output readable on-screen, you may use a `<br>` tag to create a line break on the screen and you may also use `vbCrLf` to insert a line break in the source code of the page.

The `vbCrLf` is a built-in constant that defines a carriage-return/line-break combination. This is not visible in the browser, but it can help to lay out the source of your page. If you don't use the `vbCrLf` constant, you'll end up with really long lines of HTML in the source of your page, which may be difficult to debug.

Look at some sample code that writes some text and line breaks:

```
Response.Write("<br>" & vbCrLf)
Response.Write("Something interesting")
Response.Write("<br>" & vbCrLf)
Response.Write("Some more interesting things")
Response.Write("<br>" & vbCrLf)
```

As you can see, a line break is written to the browser three times, which requires a lot of coding. In this example, a Sub that outputs a line break would be very convenient if you'd like to minimize the code written. Because a Sub cannot return a value, you need to use Response.Write to send the output to the browser directly.

Creating a Sub is easy. Within an ASP block on the page, add the following code block:

```
<%
  Sub LineBreak()
    Response.Write("<br>" & vbCrLf)
  End Sub
%>
```

Now you can change the code that originally wrote the line breaks to this:

```
LineBreak()
Response.Write("Something interesting")
LineBreak()
Response.Write("Some more interesting things")
LineBreak()
```

You are not saving yourself that much typing, but we wanted to use this simplified example to explain how it works. You'll see the real power of Subs when you change the code to write multiple line breaks:

```
Sub LineBreak(ByVal iNumberOfBreaks)
  Dim i
  For i = 1 To iNumberOfBreaks
    Response.Write("<br>" & vbCrLf)
  Next
End Sub
```

To write three line breaks to the browser, you can now call this Sub like this:

```
LineBreak(3)
```

The code in the Sub simply loops for iNumberOfBreaks number of times, outputting a <br> and a vbCrLf on each iteration. As you can see, this might save you from a lot of typing if you need to write lots of line breaks in your pages.

With the Sub, the output of the Response.Write statement is added directly to the response of the current page. There is no way you can do anything with the output it creates. If you need to perform an action on the output of a Sub, you'll need to use a Function instead because a Function can return a value.

Returning a value from a `Function` is easy: just set the name of the `Function` equal to the value you want to return. If you rewrite the `Sub` from the example above, this is how it will look:

```
Function LineBreak(ByVal iNumberOfBreaks)
 Dim i
 Dim sTempResult
 For i = 1 To iNumberOfBreaks
  sTempResult = sTempResult & "<br>" & vbCrLf
 Next
 LineBreak = sTempResult
End Function
```

First a temporary string is created to hold the return value for the function. On each iteration of the loop the return value string is extended by adding `<br>` and `vbCrLf`. In the end, the complete string is returned by setting the `Function` name (`LineBreak`) to equal the return value (`sTempResult`).

The `Function` does not use `Response.Write` to send the output to the browser, so you need another way to call this `Function`, for example:

```
Response.Write("Something interesting" & LineBreak(3))
```

The *calling* code uses `Response.Write` to output content to the browser. `LineBreak(3)` simply returns a string that contains the required number of line breaks.

As you can see, `Function`s and `Sub`s are a very easy and powerful way to group code. Not only do they save you from a lot of typing, but they also make your site a lot easier to maintain. Suppose you decided to insert a `<p>` element instead of a `<br>` to start a new line or you decided to add a / to the `<br>` tag to make it XHTML-compatible (`<br />`). With a `Function` or a `Sub`, you would need to make only one change to one line of code instead of replacing every `<br>` in the file. This leaves less room for errors.

`Function`s and `Sub`s are great for use on one page to encapsulate code logic but they become even more powerful when they are used in `Include` files.

Using Include Files

An `Include` file allows you to create code that can be reused on all pages that require it. Instead of defining your `LineBreak` `Function` on every page in the site, you can put it in an `Include` file. You can then include the contents of this page in other pages in your site. At runtime, before the entire page is processed, the contents of the `Include` file are injected in the main page. This means that as far as the ASP engine is concerned, there is no real difference between a page that uses an `Include` file and one that contains all the code itself without an include file. The code that gets passed to the ASP processing engine will be identical in both cases.

The biggest advantage of an `Include` file is that you only need to write the code once in one file. Not only does this save you from a lot of typing but it helps you debug and stabilize your code as well. If you find a bug and fix it in the `Include` file, all pages using that code will automatically benefit from that change.

You may think that you can easily use Dreamweaver MX 2004's templates or library items to simulate the Include file behavior. This is true, but an Include file has one big advantage over a template or a library item: You can make a change on the production server without the need to upload each and every page that has been affected by the change.

Take the menu of your site, for example. Suppose that your site has grown really big and now contains over 100 pages. If you want to add an extra menu item to the menu, you could make the change in the library item. Dreamweaver would then change each page in your local site that uses the menu. Once the update is done, you would have to upload all those pages to your production server as well to have the new menu item available to your users.

If you move your menu to an Include file, however, all you need to upload is the Include file itself to have all those pages start using the new menu. Because TheSoccerSite is a relatively small site, we'll stick to using a library item for the menu, but if your site grows really big you should definitely consider using Include files for elements that repeat, like a menu.

Dreamweaver MX 2004 makes it easy to include a file—you simply select Insert⇨ASP Objects⇨Include to insert the following code into a page:

```
<!--#include virtual=""-->
```

Between the "" pair, you enter the path to the file you want to include. ASP uses two different notations for Include files, depending on the way you want to refer to them. When you use the word virtual as in the example above, ASP expects a file path beginning with a *virtual directory*. In our sample site, you would need to type /TheSoccerSite/myFile.asp, for example.

If you want, you can also use a *relative location*. For that to work, you need to change the word virtual to file. Say that in Admin/admin.asp you want to include the file Tools/functions.asp. The complete Include statement will then look like this:

```
<!--#include file="../Tools/functions.asp"-->
```

Include files are added to the page before the page gets executed, so it is not possible to dynamically include a file. The following code will fail because when the Include file is inserted, aFileName does not yet have a value:

```
Dim aFileName
aFileName = Request.QueryString("FileName")
<!--#include virtual=" & aFileName & "-->
```

In IIS 5 and above, you can use Server.Execute *to dynamically execute certain pages so you can simulate dynamic inclusion, but coverage of that is beyond this book. Refer to* http://msdn.microsoft.com *and search for* Server.Execute *for more information.*

Now that you have seen why and how to use Subs, Functions, and Include files, let's take a look at an example that uses these concepts to create code that you can easily reuse in other pages of your Web site.

Page Monitoring

In the following example you create an `Include` file that tracks which page users visit first after they land on your home page. You can distinguish between new and returning visitors by setting a cookie the first time they visit your site. If the cookie exists, you have a returning visitor; otherwise the user is considered new. Once you know what page the user visits first, you can save that information to the `Application` object so you have access to this information from other pages in your site.

A second cookie indicates that you have already checked the first page that gets requested during the current browsing session; this way you avoid counting a requested page more than once during a single browser session of a user. The code that sets the cookie is placed inside a `Sub`. You also create a management page where you can view usage statistics. The code that displays the page counters is placed in a `Function` inside the `Include` file as well.

Try It Out   **Tracking User Behavior**

1. Open the Files panel (press F8), right-click your site in Local view (Site—TheSoccerSite), choose New Folder, and name the folder **Tools** (see Figure 8-9).

Figure 8-9

Repeat this step, but this time create a folder called **Admin**. This folder will contain ASP pages that an administrator of your site can request to see site statistics.

2. Add a new page to the `Tools` folder. To do this, don't use the template but choose ASP VBScript from the Dynamic page category in the New Document dialog box (press Ctrl+N). Save the page as **functions.asp** in your `Tools` folder.

3. Clear the entire contents of the page by pressing Ctrl+A (Select All) and then pressing Delete.

4. Add an ASP code block to the page by choosing Insert⇨ASP Objects⇨Code Block from the menu.

5. To enable a page to record its usage, create a `Sub` that can be called from other pages. Inside the ASP code block in the file `functions.asp`, add the following `Sub` definition:

```
<%
Sub SetFirstVisitedPage ()
 Dim sPageName
 sPageName = Request.ServerVariables("URL")
 If Len(Request.Cookies("CheckFirstPage")) = 0 Then
  If Len(Request.Cookies("RevisitingUser")) = 0 Then
   ' New user
   Application("Page_New_" & sPageName) = _
    Application("Page_New_" & sPageName) + 1
  Else
   ' Revisiting user
   Application("Page_Revisit_" & sPageName) = _
    Application("Page_Revisit_" & sPageName) + 1
  End If
  Response.Cookies("CheckFirstPage") = "Done"
  Response.Cookies("RevisitingUser") = "Yes"
  Response.Cookies("RevisitingUser").Expires = Date() + 30
 End If
End Sub
%>
```

6. To create a report that shows you which page is visited first, you have to create a `Function` that displays this information. You can pass an argument to that function to determine whether you want to see the information for new users or for returning users. There can be a big difference between the two because, for example, new users might open an FAQ page first, while returning users may open the events page immediately. The following `Function` displays this usage information, and because this function is called from various pages, it's a good idea to add it to your `functions.asp` file, right after the `Sub` you created in the previous step:

```
   Response.Cookies("RevisitingUser").Expires = Date() + 30
  End If
 End Sub
```

```
Function GetFirstVisitedPage(ByVal bNewUsers)
  Dim iMaxHits
  Dim sAppVar
  Dim sFirstVisitedPage
  iMaxhits = 0
  For Each sAppVar in Application.Contents()
   If Left(sAppVar, 5) = "Page_" Then
    If bNewUsers = True Then
     If Left(sAppVar, 9) = "Page_New_" Then
      If CInt(Application(sAppVar)) > iMaxHits Then
       iMaxHits = Application(sAppVar)
       sFirstVisitedPage = Right(sAppVar, Len(sAppVar) - 9)
      End If
     End If
    Else
     If Left(sAppVar, 13) = "Page_Revisit_" Then
```

```
        If CInt(Application(sAppVar)) > iMaxHits Then
          iMaxHits = Application(sAppVar)
          sFirstVisitedPage = Right(sAppVar, Len(sAppVar) - 13)
        End If
      End If
    End If
  End If
Next
GetFirstVisitedPage = sFirstVisitedPage & " with " & iMaxHits & " hits."
End Function
%>
```

Save the functions.asp page.

7. Create a new page based on the main template for your site and save it as **popularFirstPage.asp** in the Admin folder you created in Step 1. This page displays the usage statistics. Remove all the placeholders and give it the title **Most Popular First Page** in the Title region of the template.

8. Create another templated page in the Admin folder and call this one **admin.asp**. Once again, remove all placeholders and then give the page a title of **Admin Menu** in the Title region of the template. This page contains your administrator's menu with links to other pages.

9. On admin.asp, create the first menu item inside the content region of the template. To do this, make sure you are in Design view and position your cursor in the Content region. Type **Most Popular First Page** and then select that text. On the Property inspector, click the Point to File icon (the image with the crosshair on it) and then, with the mouse button still held down, drag the pointer to popularFirstPage.asp inside the Admin folder on the Files panel and release the mouse button (see Figure 8-10).

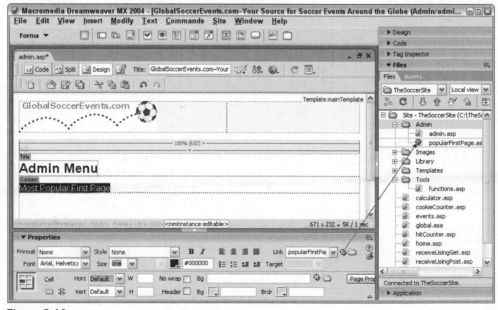

Figure 8-10

This way, the text Most Popular First Page now links to the file popularFirstPage.asp. The contents of the Content section of the template should look like this:

```
<a href="popularFirstPage.asp">Most Popular First Page</a>
```

You can now save and close the page.

10. Open popularFirstPage.asp, place your cursor right before the line starting with <!DOCTYPE HTML PUBLIC, and press Enter. This creates some room to insert your Include statement. Position your cursor on the empty line and then on the Insert menu choose ASP Objects and then Include. Change the word virtual to file and type **../Tools/functions.asp** between the two double-quotes. The Include statement now looks like this:

```
<%@LANGUAGE="VBSCRIPT" CODEPAGE="1252"%>
```

```
<!--#include file="../Tools/functions.asp"-->
<!DOCTYPE HTML PUBLIC "-//W3C//DTD HTML 4.01 Transitional//EN"
    "http://www.w3.org/TR/html4/loose.dtd">
```

11. Add the following code to the content section of the page:

```
The most popular first page for new users is:
<%= GetFirstVisitedPage (True)%>
<br>
The most popular first page for returning visitors is:
<%= GetFirstVisitedPage (False)%>
```

You can save the page because it's ready now.

12. With the code to track your users and display the results in place, it's time to create a page that you want to track. Add a page called **mySite.asp** to the root of your site. Make sure it's based on your main template. Remove the default placeholders and give the page the title **My Site** in the Title region of the template.

13. Add the following block of code between the line starting with the <%@LANGUAGE statement and the line starting with <!DOCTYPE HTML PUBLIC at the top of the page:

```
<%@LANGUAGE="VBSCRIPT" CODEPAGE="1252"%>
```

```
<!--#include file="Tools/functions.asp"-->
<% SetFirstVisitedPage() %>
<!DOCTYPE HTML PUBLIC "-//W3C//DTD HTML 4.01 Transitional//EN"
    "http://www.w3.org/TR/html4/loose.dtd">
```

14. Repeat Step 13 for the page events.asp. You just need to add the two lines with the Include statement and the call to the SetFirstVisitedPage function right after the first line in the page and before the code block that requests the category:

```
<%@LANGUAGE="VBSCRIPT" CODEPAGE="1252"%>
```

```
<!--#include file="Tools/functions.asp"-->
<% SetFirstVisitedPage() %>
<%
Dim iLastCategory
```

15. Save any page you may have open (you can choose File⇨Save All to do this) and then open home.asp in Dreamweaver. Press F12 to open the page in your browser and then click the My Site menu item.

16. Close your browser, switch to Dreamweaver again, and open the page admin.asp from the Admin folder. Press F12 again to open the page in your browser and click the Most Popular First Page link. You should see something like Figure 8-11.

Figure 8-11

Next, close and reopen your browser and request the page events.asp. Repeat this step three times.

17. Open the admin.asp in your browser again and click the Most Popular First Page link. You can see that the most popular page for returning visitors is now events.asp (see Figure 8-12).

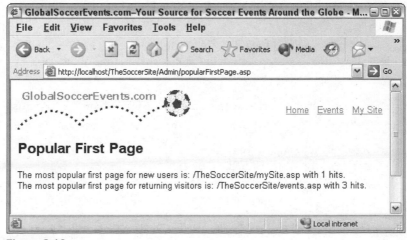

Figure 8-12

If you find that the counter for returning visitors hasn't changed, make sure you close *all* open browser windows, including windows you didn't open using Dreamweaver. As long as there is at least one browser open, the session cookie CheckFirstPage will not be destroyed.

How It Works

This example introduced quite a lot of code, so let's break it down to demonstrate how it works. First, take a look at the Sub in `functions.asp` that counts page hits and sets the cookie, `SetFirstVisitedPage`:

```
Sub SetFirstVisitedPage()
 Dim sPageName
 sPageName = Request.ServerVariables("URL")
```

The code starts off with the Sub declaration. Next, a variable is declared to hold the name of the current page, sPageName, which is assigned a value with the `Request.ServerVariables("URL")` statement. Earlier we said the contents of the Include file are added to the page that includes them, and this statement illustrates our point. When you run the page that has `functions.asp` included, `Request.Server Variables("URL")` returns the name of the page that uses the include file, and not `/TheSoccerSite/Tools/functions.asp`.

The code then checks if the first page has already been determined during this browser session by checking the length of the CheckFirstPage cookie:

```
    If Len(Request.Cookies("CheckFirstPage")) = 0 Then
```

The next code determines whether the user is visiting for the first time or is a returning visitor:

```
If Len(Request.Cookies("RevisitingUser")) = 0 Then
 ' New user
 Application("Page_New_" & sPageName) = _
    Application("Page_New_" & sPageName) + 1
Else
 ' Revisiting user
 Application("Page_Revisit_" & sPageName) = _
    Application("Page_Revisit_" & sPageName) + 1
End If
```

If the user is new to the site, the length of the cookie RevisitingUser is zero so the code in the If block runs. In that block, the value of an application variable with the name of the page increases by 1. This variable is prefixed with Page_New_ to indicate that this is a counter for pages requested by new users.

These steps are repeated in the Else clause, this time increasing the counter for returning visitors. Finally, two cookies are set:

```
    Response.Cookies("CheckFirstPage") = "Done"
    Response.Cookies("RevisitingUser") = "Yes"
    Response.Cookies("RevisitingUser").Expires = Date() + 30
   End If
End Sub
```

The first cookie indicates that during this session you have already tracked the first requested page. Because the Expires property is not set for this cookie, it is created as a session cookie. This means that as soon as the user closes the browser, the cookie is destroyed and you can be sure that the next time the user visits you, you can once again check which page is visited first.

The second cookie indicates that the user is considered a returning user. The cookie lasts for 30 days; as long as the site is revisited in that period, the user counts as a returning visitor.

By using an `Include` file, other pages are able to see the `Sub SetFirstVisitedPage` defined in `functions.asp`. By calling this `Sub`, each page can set the first page visited. In `events.asp` and `mySite.asp` you added the following statement:

```
<!--#include file="Tools/functions.asp"-->
```

This adds all the code in the `Include` file to the current page at runtime, so you can call any `Function` or `Sub` that is defined in it.

To call the actual `Sub`, an ASP code block is used that contains the `Sub` name followed by a pair of parentheses:

```
<% SetFirstVisitedPage() %>
```

Now when the page loads, the `SetFirstVisitedPage` method is called and the code in the `Sub` is executed.

The page-tracking mechanism is now in place. The next step is to create a page that reports the results to an administrator of the site. This data is displayed in the browser with a function called `GetFirstVisitedPage`.

To display site tracking statistics in the browser, you can use the `GetFirstVisitedPage` function. You'll need to pass a *Boolean* value to this function. A Boolean is a data type that holds either `True` or `False`. If you pass `True` to `GetFirstVisitedPage`, the results for new users are displayed. `False`, or any other value, results in the statistics for revisiting users. This is because the code in the `Else` block runs if the incoming value is not equal to `True`.

This is how the code looks in the report page:

```
The most popular first page for new users is:
<%= GetFirstVisitedPage (True)%>
<br>
The most popular first page for returning visitors is:
<%= GetFirstVisitedPage (False)%>
```

Because a `Function` in a separate file is used, you can keep the report page nice and clean. The page is not cluttered with lots of ASP code; all you have is two simple `Function` calls. The `Function` itself looks rather complicated at first, so let's walk through it:

```
Function GetFirstVisitedPage(ByVal bNewUsers)
 Dim iMaxHits
 Dim sAppVar
 Dim sFirstVisitedPage
 iMaxhits = 0
```

First, the function header is declared. As a parameter, it expects a Boolean, bNewUsers, to determine whether to show information for new users (bNewUsers will be `True`) or for your loyal visitors (bNewUsers will be `False`).

```
For Each sAppVar in Application.Contents()
 If Left(sAppVar, 5) = "Page_" Then
```

Then a For Each statement is used to loop through all the variables that are stored in the Application object. The Left function is used to retrieve the first five characters of the Application variable. When this variable starts with Page_, you know that it is a page-tracking variable because you have prefixed each page counter variable with these five characters. Although it's unlikely you will have any other application variables that use page names as the variable name, using the prefix makes your intentions clearer to other readers of your code and minimizes the chances of errors.

```
If bNewUsers = True Then
   If Left(sAppVar, 9) = "Page_New_" Then
```

Next the code checks whether to display information for returning or for new visitors. If bNewUsers is True, the code in the If block runs. Inside that code block, each application variable is examined to see if it starts with Page_New_ by using the Left function. If it does, it means that this variable is used to track the behavior for a new user and the code in the next If block runs:

```
If CInt(Application(sAppVar)) > iMaxHits Then
   iMaxHits = Application(sAppVar)
   sFirstVisitedPage = Right(sAppVar, Len(sAppVar) - 9)
 End If
End If
```

Inside the If block the counter in the application variable is compared with a local counter (iMaxHits) that is used in the function. The CInt function is used again to convert both sides of the comparison to numbers. This ensures that you are not comparing apples with pears, or strings and numbers in this case. iMaxHits holds the number of hits for your most popular page so far, so it only gets updated with a new value if the hit count for a page is greater than any page that has already been checked.

The variable sFirstVisitedPage gets the value of the original page name from the application variable. The prefix Page_New_ is removed by using the Right function in combination with the Len function. Right takes a substring from another string, starting at the right end of that string. By subtracting 9 from the length of the string, you are effectively removing the Page_New_ prefix from the variable value. After this operation, sFirstVisitedPage holds the name for the most popular page retrieved from the Application variables so far.

As the code loops, iMaxHits contains the number of hits to the most popular page, while sFirstVisitedPage contains the name of that page. These two variables are updated only when another page is found that is more popular than the previous most popular page:

```
Else
  If Left(sAppVar, 13) = "Page_Revisit_" Then
   If CInt(Application(sAppVar)) > iMaxHits Then
    iMaxHits = Application(sAppVar)
    sFirstVisitedPage = Right(sAppVar, Len(sAppVar) - 13)
   End If
  End If
End If
```

The exact same principle is used in the Else clause, but this time only application variables that hold information about returning visitors are checked. The Right method is used again to remove the Page_Revisit_ prefix from the file name, just as with the Page_New_ prefix.

```
      End If
    Next
    GetFirstVisitedPage = sFirstVisitedPage & " with " & iMaxHits & " hits."
  End Function
```

Finally, the `If` block and the `For Each` loop are closed, and the function returns a string that contains the number of hits and the page name by setting the function name `GetFirstVisitedPage` equal to the value you want to return.

Summary

Keeping track of users as they visit your site provides two benefits:

❑   You can learn more about how people navigate your Web site. This can be useful if, for instance, you want to modify the menu so that popular pages are easier to reach. Also, by knowing which pages are popular, you can focus your marketing efforts (like banner ads) on these pages.

❑   You can provide visitors with a personalized experience as they use the Web site.

In this chapter you saw how to use cookies to store information about a user between visits to the site, allowing you to keep track of them. You used cookies to do the following:

❑   Count the number of requests made for a specific page by a client.

❑   Improve the quality of the choices visitors make on a page by remembering their choice from a previous visit. This allowed users to continue browsing from where they left off previously.

There is a common pitfall that Web developers run into when using cookies—trying to write cookies after the headers of a response have been sent to the client. We looked at two ways around this problem: using buffering and placing your ASP code at the start of your pages before any HTML.

To increase the maintainability and reusability of your code you added structure to your pages using `Functions`, `Subs`, and `Include` files. You used `Functions` and `Subs` to group related logic, which you can then easily call with just a single line of code. `Include` files make it possible to reuse code you have written once in multiple pages. This makes it easier to reuse your code and minimizes the chances of errors, as you only have to write the code once.

Finally, you worked through an advanced example that tracks site usage. Using all the concepts you learned in this chapter—cookies, `Subs` and `Functions`, `Include` files, and some ASP coding logic—you built a utility that determines which page a user visits first after landing on the home page. The results of this can be used to understand better how visitors use your site. This enables you to rearrange links in the menu accordingly, for example.

In the next chapter we take the concept of personalization one step further. You'll create a protection mechanism that prohibits unauthorized users from accessing protected parts of your site. Then in Chapter 10 you will spend even more time on personalization when we discuss various methods to change the look and content of your site.

Why Not Try . . .

1. Currently, the message that shows the number of hits on the popularFirstPage.asp page looks a little odd when no page has been visited before. Since you are using an Include file, this can easily be fixed by just the Function in functions.asp. Change the Function so that it displays a message like "There is no information available for new users" or "There is no information available for returning users."

   Hint: Use iMaxHits *in your code to check the number of hits.*

2. Gaining knowledge about the category of events that users prefer is another interesting thing to track on your site. Knowing which categories are popular allows you to focus on these categories when it comes to providing new event information. Why not see if you can create a tracking mechanism for the Events category drop-down list as well. Here are the steps you need to follow to make this possible:

   ❑ Add a Sub called SetPopularCategory to your functions.asp page. Have it accept the ID of the category as a parameter. Inside the Sub set an application variable that updates the number of hits for the requested category. Prefix your Application variable with something like Category_. There is no need to set a cookie this time because you should log any category a user might select, even when they change the category multiple times during a visit.

   ❑ Add a function called GetPopularCategory to the functions.asp page that returns the number of hits that all categories have received as a string. You'll need to loop through all Application variables again and extract the values for the variables that start with Category_. Unlike the GetFirstVisitedPage function, however, there is no need for a parameter distinguishing between new and revisiting users.

   ❑ Create an additional admin page that displays the favorite categories. All this page needs to do is make a call to GetPopularCategory.

   ❑ The last action you need to accomplish is call SetPopularCategory from within your events.asp page. After the last If code block at the top of that page, make a call to SetPopularCategory and pass it the ID of the requested category (iLastCategory).

9

Securing Web Sites

Until now your Web site has been freely accessible to any user visiting you. Every individual visitor can do the same as any other—browse your home page and request information about events. Also, the functionality that remembers the events category a visitor has chosen is available to everyone. And if your visitors could guess the name of your admin pages, like `popularFirstPage.asp`, they could even access your admin pages.

It's often useful to restrict certain sections of a Web site to trusted users only—for example, allow only administrators to access administration pages where they can view site statistics, or change the events list. You may also want to provide different services to returning members and new visitors.

To restrict access to those certain pages, you need to implement a security mechanism. When you deal with security, you often come across two terms: *authentication* and *authorization*. Authentication refers to supplying the correct user *credentials*, such as a username and password. Once you are authenticated, you gain access to the site. Authorization, on the other hand, is all about the *rights* you have to perform specific actions within the application, based on your username and password.

For example, you can supply a valid username and password and then be authenticated to access a site. Within that site, you may be authorized to view the member pages, but you may not be authorized to view pages in the admin section.

This chapter is mostly concerned with creating an authentication mechanism. The pages you create will use a very simple form of authorization to allow or block access to specific pages depending on whether the user is logged in or not.

We will discuss the authorization techniques of Dreamweaver MX 2004 in greater detail in Chapter 11, where we will show you how to use access levels.

In this chapter, you will learn how to do the following:

- ❑ Create a login form so users can log in to your site
- ❑ Protect specific pages on your site

❑   Use JavaScript to perform client-side validation of the information a user tries to submit to your site

❑   Use Cascading Style Sheets to improve the look of your login form

❑   Work with the `FileSystemObject` to retrieve usernames and passwords from a file

Creating a Login Form

The features that Dreamweaver MX 2004 provides to restrict access to a page are powerful and, at the same time, very easy to use. Most of the code you need to protect a page is automatically generated by Dreamweaver using *server behaviors*. This generated code uses *session variables* to store information about the user, so you need to make sure that sessions are enabled at your server for the examples in this chapter to work. Find out more about enabling session state in Chapter 7.

When you restrict access to a specific page, Dreamweaver inserts ASP code that checks the presence of an ASP session variable at runtime. If this variable is not set, the user is redirected to the login page where they need to supply a username and password. Once the user logs in correctly, the session variable is set and the user gains access to the protected pages.

To protect a page effectively, you need to perform two actions:

❑   Create a login form where a user can log in by supplying a username and password

❑   Block access to the page for unauthenticated users using a server behavior

Because you cannot fully test the protection mechanism without a way to log in, we'll start off by creating the login form in the next exercise. Later on, we will use a server behavior to restrict access to specific pages.

In the next Try It Out exercise, you create the login form for the soccer site. This is the page users are redirected to when they try to request a protected page without having logged in first. On this page, the user types a username and password and then sends that information to the server by clicking the Login button. On the server the username and password are checked to see if the login attempt is valid. If the username and password are correct, a session variable is set and the user is redirected to another page; otherwise the login form is displayed again and the user is presented with a message saying that the username and password combination is invalid.

This example uses hard-coded values for the username and password so you can concentrate on how the authentication mechanism works. In a later Try It Out exercise in this chapter you'll upgrade the login page to use a text file containing the usernames and passwords. Because storing data like passwords in a text file isn't very secure and is not a suitable solution for a large site, we'll show you in Chapter 11 how to create a third version of the login form that uses a database to store this information. The example with the text file in this chapter creates a nice foundation on which you can easily build a database-driven login mechanism.

After you complete the next three Try It Out exercises, your login form for the soccer site will look like Figure 9-1.

Figure 9-1

Try It Out   **Creating a Login Form**

1. Before you create the login form, it's a good idea to create a new menu item that links to your login page. This way a user can log in before requesting any of the protected pages. Open the `mainMenu.lbi` library item by double-clicking it in the `Library` folder.

2. Add an extra menu item with the title of **Login** under the `My Site` item and let it link to `../login.asp`. Don't forget to create an empty table cell before the new menu item:

```
<td><a href="../mySite.asp" id="mysite">My Site</a></td>
<td>   </td>
<td><a href="../login.asp" id="login">Login</a></td>
</tr>
```

Once you save the page, the main template and all pages that use that template will be updated. You can close the library item again because it is finished.

3. Create a new file from your main template and save it as **login.asp** in the root of your site. Name the page **Login to GlobalSoccerEvents.com** in the Title region of the template. Remove the two placeholders for the Content and Footer sections of the template.

4. Open the Snippets panel on the Code panel group by pressing Shift+F9. Expand the Content Tables folder and then the one-pixel-border folder. Drag the item called `Form: 2 Fields` to the content region of your page in Design view. Dreamweaver will insert a ready-made form in the page (see Figure 9-2).

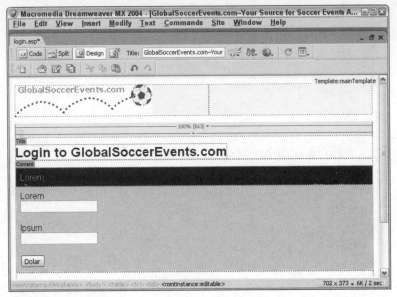

Figure 9-2

5. Using the Property inspector, rename the first text field as **txtUserName**. To accomplish this, select the text field in Design view and change `textfield` on the Property inspector to **txtUserName**. Repeat this for the second text box, but name it **txtPassword**. While still in the Property inspector, change the Type of the password text box from Single Line to **Password**. In the browser, a text box with its Type attribute set to Password displays an asterisk for any character you type. This way, someone peeking over your shoulder can't see what password you enter.

6. Rename the button as **btnLogin**. Just as with the text boxes, you should select it and then change `Submit` to **btnLogin** in the Property inspector.

Switch to Code view and change the `name` of the form to **frmLogin**, set its action to **login.asp**, and its method to **post**. By using POST instead of GET, the username and password won't show up in the address bar of the browser. This reduces the chance that someone can steal your password. The code for your `<form>` tag should look like this:

```
<tr>
    <form name="frmLogin" action="login.asp" method="post">
    <td width="100%" bgcolor="#CCCCCC" colspan="2">
```

Change the text above the text fields and on the button so they describe their purpose better (**Username**, **Password**, and **Login**). You can also add an instructive message to the user of the login form so they know how to use it. When you have finished, your login form should look like Figure 9-3 in Design view.

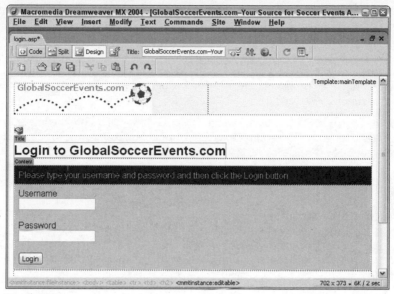

Figure 9-3

If you want to get a better picture of how your login form will eventually look in the browser, make sure that the Design view has the focus and then press Ctrl+Shift+I or select View⇨Visual Aids⇨Hide All. This hides all visual aids, including table borders and the template labels like Title and Content. This way, it's much easier to see how the final page will look in the browser, and you can still change the design of the page using all the familiar Dreamweaver features. Press the same key combination again to turn the visual aids back on.

7. The code in the snippet is not completely XHTML-compliant because the `<form>` tags surround the `<td>` tag instead of the other way around. Fortunately, the fix for this is easy; in Code view simply move the opening `<form>` tag below the next line containing the `<td>`, and move the closing tag of the form one line up. In the end, the code for the login form should look similar to the following:

```
<td width="100%" bgcolor="#CCCCCC" colspan="2">
 <form action="login.asp" method="post" name="frmLogin">
  <p>Username<br>
   <input name="txtUserName" type="text" id="txtUserName">
  </p>
  <p>Password<br>
   <input name="txtPassword" type="password" id="txtPassword">
  </p>
  <p>
   <input name="btnLogin" type="submit" id="btnLogin" value="Login">
  </p>

 </form>
</td>
```

8. Next it's time to put in some ASP code that handles the validation of the username and password that are submitted to the server. In Chapter 11 you'll learn how to create validation code using a server behavior, but this behavior needs a database connection, so right now the username and password are compared against hard-coded values in your page. Obviously, this isn't something you'd want in a live site, as this is very hard to maintain. But using hard-coded values now allows us to concentrate on how the login mechanism works rather than where the user information is stored.

    Place the cursor at the top of your page in Code view, just before the line starting with <!DOC-TYPE HTML PUBLIC. Press Enter to create some room, place your cursor on the empty line, and then select Insert⇨ASP Objects⇨Code Block. Enter the following code:

```
<%@LANGUAGE="VBSCRIPT" CODEPAGE="1252"%>
<%
  Dim sErrorMessage
  If Request.Form("txtUserName") <> "" And _
        Request.Form("txtPassword") <> "" Then
   If Request.Form("txtUserName") = "UserName" And _
         Request.Form("txtPassword") = "Password" Then
    Session("MM_Username") = Request.Form("txtUserName")
    Response.Redirect("Admin/admin.asp")
   Else
    sErrorMessage = "<br>" & _
        "Login failed. Please type a valid username and password"
   End If
  End If
%>
<!DOCTYPE HTML PUBLIC "-//W3C//DTD HTML 4.01 Transitional//EN"
  "http://www.w3.org/TR/html4/loose.dtd">
```

9. When the user tries to log in with an incorrect username and password combination, you'll need to present them with an error message. A good place for this message is right after the instruction telling people to enter their username and password. So go ahead and change the content of the <td> tag to this:

```
<td>
  <font color="#CCCCCC">Please type your username and password and
  then click the Login button
  <%= sErrorMessage %></font>
</td>
```

10. Save the page (press Ctrl+S) and then open it in your browser (press F12). Log in with an invalid username and password, like **Ronaldo** and **Brazil**, for example. The login page will show an error message in the black title bar with the text Login failed. Please type a valid username and password (see Figure 9-4). The error message doesn't stand out much yet, but you will fix that in a later Try It Out exercise.

11. Log in correctly by typing **UserName** and **Password** and clicking the Login button. You'll see the admin menu appear. Notice that although the VBScript that is used to write ASP pages is not case-sensitive, string comparison *is* case-sensitive. This means you need to type **UserName** with a capital *U* and *N*, or otherwise you can't log in.

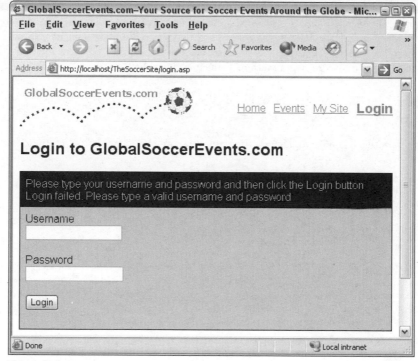

Figure 9-4

How It Works

Most of the steps in this Try It Out should be familiar by now. You changed the mainMenu library item by adding an additional menu item and then inserted a standard form on your page. You then changed some of the form's properties so it POSTs to itself. When the user fills in a username and password and clicks the Login button, code is executed at the server to check whether you want to grant the user access to your site.

Take a look at the validation code to see how it works:

```
Dim sErrorMessage
If Request.Form("txtUserName") <> "" And _
        Request.Form("txtPassword") <> "" Then
```

First, a variable is declared that will hold an error message when the login attempt fails. The code then checks whether the user typed in a username and a password. If the user left any field empty, there is no use trying to validate them because you already know those values are not going to match.

```
If Request.Form("txtUserName") = "UserName" And _
        Request.Form("txtPassword") = "Password" Then
```

Next the username and password are checked against the hard-coded values `UserName` and `Password`. In this example, the username and password are case-sensitive because string comparison in VBScript is case-sensitive. If you want to make it easier for your users to remember their username and password, you could make the login procedure case-insensitive. You can do this by changing the values of the username and password to lowercase using the `LCase` function, like this:

```
If LCase(Request.Form("txtUserName")) = "username" And _
    LCase(Request.Form("txtPassword")) = "password" Then
```

If you use this method, be sure to change the value you are checking against to lowercase as well, or else you will never be able to log in.

If the username and password match, a session variable called `MM_Username` is filled with the user's name to indicate that the user has successfully logged in:

```
Session("MM_Username") = Request.Form("txtUserName")
```

MM_Username is the name of a built-in variable that Dreamweaver MX 2004 inserts when you use a server behavior for user authentication. To stay forward-compatible with the changes you are going to make to the login form in Chapter 11, and to ease the upgrade process later, you are using this variable name here.

Then the user is redirected to the admin page:

```
Response.Redirect("Admin/admin.asp")
```

The `Response.Redirect` call sends an instruction to the browser to request a new page, `Admin/admin.asp` in this case. This ensures that after a successful login users will see the admin menu instead of the login page again.

If login failed, a variable called `sErrorMessage` is filled with a message informing the user that they could not be logged on:

```
    Else
     sErrorMessage = "<br>" & _
        "Login failed. Please type a valid username and password"
    End If
End If
```

You shouldn't tell the user whether the username or password was incorrect, but just that login has failed. This helps to make the site a little more secure. The less useful information about usernames and passwords you provide, the less chance you have of malicious users getting access to your site by guessing a username and password.

The current implementation of the login form looks a bit plain at this point. You can hardly see the error message and you don't get a message when you click on the Login button without providing a username and a password. In the next section, we look at some ways to spice up the login form a bit.

Enhancing the Login Form

In the current login page, the login form is shown again when the user did not type a username and a password. You can improve the login page by providing immediate feedback when the user clicks the Login button. By adding some client-side field validation you can present the user with an error message when one of the fields has not been filled in. Because this error message is presented on the client, you can save yourself a round trip to the server, which minimizes the response time.

Of course, the authentication check for the username and password should still be done on the server, not on the client.

In the next Try It Out exercise you will let Dreamweaver add some JavaScript to check the username and password before the form is submitted. If one or both of the fields are still empty when the user clicks the Login button, an error message is displayed and the form is not submitted.

Try It Out   **Adding Client-Side Validation to the Login Form**

1. Open login.asp and select the entire <form> element using the tag selector at the bottom of your screen. Open the Behaviors panel on the Tag <form> panel group by pressing Shift+F3, and select Validate Form from the plus (+) menu on the panel's toolbar (see Figure 9-5).

Figure 9-5

2. In the Validate Form dialog box select txtUserName and make sure to click the Required and Anything options. Repeat this for the txtPassword field as well. The dialog box should look like Figure 9-6.

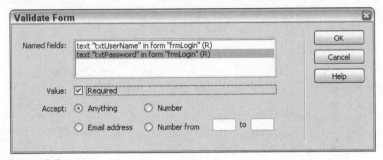

Figure 9-6

The (R) indicates that this is a required field. Once you click OK, Dreamweaver modifies your <form> tag and adds some JavaScript code to the top of the page.

3. Save the page by pressing Ctrl+S and open it in your browser. Leave both the username and password fields empty and click the Login button. You'll be presented with the error message in Figure 9-7.

Figure 9-7

4. Log in again by typing **UserName** and **Password** and clicking the Login button. This time instead of the error message you are redirected to the Admin menu.

How It Works

When you add the Validate Form behavior to your login form, Dreamweaver adds two blocks of code to the page. The first is added to the onsubmit attribute of the form. The second is placed inside a JavaScript block at the top of your page.

Let's look at both to find out how the validation works:

```
<form action="login.asp" method="post" name="frmLogin"
  onsubmit="MM_validateForm('txtUserName','','R','txtPassword','','R');
  return document.MM_returnValue">
```

The `onsubmit` event fires before the form gets submitted. In the event the JavaScript function `MM_validateForm` is called. The name of each field that needs to be validated and some options are passed to this function. In this example, `txtUserName` and `txtPassword` are passed as the fields that need to be checked. Notice how `R` is passed as well to denote that the fields are required. If you had chosen an optional e-mail address, Dreamweaver would have inserted `NisEmail` (where `N` stands for *not required* and `isEmail` indicates that the field should contain an e-mail address).

The validation code that Dreamweaver generates is rather limited, though, and wouldn't be too good in most real-world applications. For example, an e-mail address is considered valid when it contains at least one `@` character. Of course you need to check other rules as well, like the presence of a username, a domain name, a dot and a top-level domain extension. In Chapter 13 we take a look at *regular expressions* that can be used to do some powerful data validation. The code that Dreamweaver MX 2004 inserts, however, can be used for some simple validation, like checking a required field, as we showed in this example.

The code that performs the actual validation consists of two functions: `MM_findObj` and `MM_validateForm`. `MM_findObj` is a helper function and is used to retrieve a reference to the form object on the page whose value you are validating.

`MM_validateForm` performs the actual validation. We won't go over the complete code but we'll explain the principle. Let's assume you want to test for a required e-mail address. In this case, you are passing the name of the text field, `txtEmailAddress`, and the string `'RisEmail'` to the function. Inside the function, Dreamweaver splits up this latter parameter to see if it is required and to find out its type. The validation routine supports four different types: `Anything`, `Email Address`, `Number`, and `Number in range`. The code performs a validation to see if the data in the text box you have passed in is of the required type. With an e-mail address, it will check if the text box contains at least an `@`. With a number, it checks if the value of the text box can be converted to a valid number; and with the range type, it also checks to see if the value is within the given range.

If the validation routine has discovered an error in any of the fields, an error message will be displayed to the user using the alert method. Finally, the function sets a variable called `MM_returnValue` to `true` if there were no errors found, or to `false` when any of the fields contains invalid data.

Now, take a look again at the `onsubmit` event of your form to see how it all fits together:

```
onsubmit="MM_validateForm('txtUserName','','R','txtPassword','','R');
return document.MM_returnValue"
```

As we said earlier, the `onsubmit` event fires right before the form gets submitted to the server. So the best place to cancel the form from being submitted when the validation function finds an error is inside this event. If you return `false` from this event, the browser knows that it should not send the form to the server.

As you can see in the code for the `onsubmit` event, after the validation function has been called, the code returns the value of the variable, `document.MM_returnValue`. This variable has been set at the end of the validation function and contains either `false` (an error) or `true` (no errors). In case of an error, the `onsubmit` event of the form will return `false`, which stops the form from being submitted. If there were no errors found, the event returns `true` and the form's contents will be sent to the server.

As you may have noticed, the error message displays the names of the offending text boxes in the error message. Unfortunately, there is no way in Dreamweaver MX 2004 to customize the error message that appears when one or both of the required fields are empty. The names of the text boxes will always be used in the message. If you want to stick to a strict naming scheme by prefixing your text boxes with txt, for instance, like we have done in this example, but still want to present a friendly message to the user, you'll need to modify the code that Dreamweaver creates or create your own validation code. In Chapter 13 you will look at ways to create a validation mechanism where you can have complete control over the error messages that users see.

With the validation code you added, you improved the usability of the form so that when the user forgets to fill in any of the required fields, they get immediate feedback. Without the client-side code, a roundtrip to the server would be needed to validate the fields and return an error message informing users about the errors they made. By using JavaScript at the client, the user gets a quicker response and you save valuable bandwidth and server processing time.

In the next Try It Out exercise, you improve the login form even further by adding Cascading Style Sheets (CSS) information to your main template so it becomes available in all the pages you base on this template. Inside your login form you can use a CSS class defined in the style sheet to make the error message stand out more. Another CSS class is used to change the looks of your text fields from the default 3D border style to a more professional looking flat style with a small black border.

Try It Out   Adding Style Sheets to Your Login Form

1. It is good practice to store related pages together in their own folder, so you should create a new folder called Styles in the root of your site to hold the style sheets you are going to create for the soccer site. Right-click the site in the Files panel and choose New Folder. Name the folder **Styles**.

2. Add a new, empty style sheet to the site. To do this, choose File⇨New and choose CSS from the Basic Page category on the General tab. Click on Create and save the page as **mainStyles.css** in the Styles folder.

3. Open the file mainTemplate.dwt.asp from the Templates folder. In Chapter 7 you added some simple inline style sheet information that is used throughout your pages. Because a separate CSS file is used from now on, move the inline styles to your new style sheet. Select the following block of code between the <style> tags and press Ctrl+X to cut it from the template page:

```
td {
  font-family: Arial, Helvetica, sans-serif;
  color: #000000;
}
a {
  font-family: Arial, Helvetica, sans-serif;
  color: #669933;
}
```

Switch to the style sheet page and paste the text you just removed from the template in this file, right after the first line that starts with /* CSS Document /*.

4. Switch back to the template document and remove the empty style tags and comment tags from the template as they are no longer useful:

```
<!- TemplateEndEditable ->
```

```
<style type="text/css">
<!-
->
</style>
</head>
```

Don't save the template yet; there are still some other changes to make.

5. Go back to the mainStyles.css page again and add the following style information to the end of the sheet, right after the code you pasted in Step 3:

```
a {
  font-family: Arial, Helvetica, sans-serif;
  color: #669933;
}
```

```
.clsErrorMessage {
  font-weight: bold;
  color: red;
}
.clsTextInput {
  font-size: 10pt;
  background-color: #ffffff;
  border: 1px solid #000000;
}
```

You can either type in this code directly or you can use the CSS Styles panel to create the classes. If you want to use the panel, right-click mainStyles.css in the panel and choose Edit to see the Edit Style Sheet dialog box in Figure 9-8.

Figure 9-8

Click the New button to go to the screen where you can define your new style. Type **clsErrorMessage** in the Name box and make sure that Type is set to Class (Can Apply To Any Tag) and that Define In is set to This Document Only. The New CSS Style dialog box should now look like Figure 9-9.

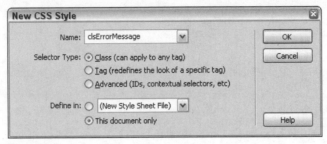

Figure 9-9

Click OK and you'll get the style sheet editor. On the Type panel, set the Weight for the font to **bold** and the Color to **red** (**#ff0000**). Click OK to insert the style sheet class in the document.

Click the New button again and create a class called **clsTextInput**. Set its font size to **10** points and on the Background page change the Background Color to **white** (**#ffffff**). Click Border to open the Border page. Fill in the dialog box as shown in Figure 9-10.

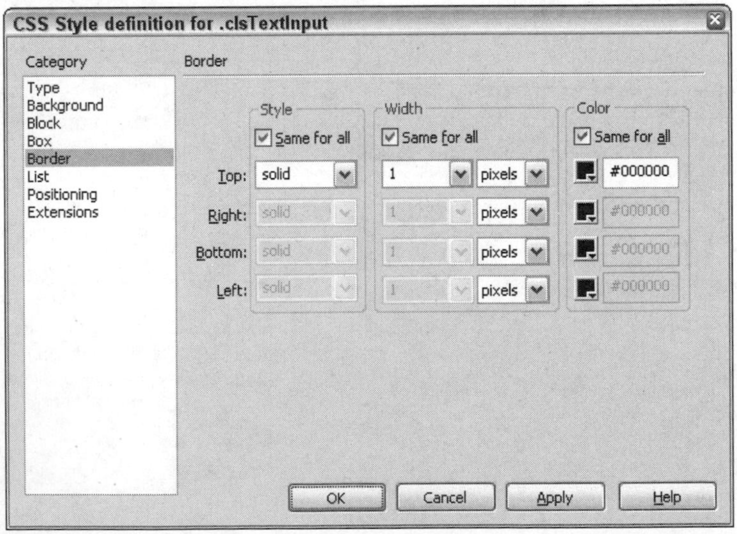

Figure 9-10

Click OK and then click Done so the styles will be added to the style sheet. Press Ctrl+S to save the style sheet and then close the document.

6. With the style sheet file done, it is time to create a link between the main template and this style sheet. Switch to your template `mainTemplate.dwt.asp` again and open the CSS Styles panel (Shift+F11).

7. Right-click the CSS Styles panel and choose Attach Style Sheet (see Figure 9-11).

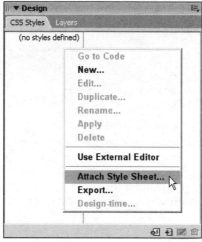

Figure 9-11

8. Click the Browse button and select the `mainStyles.css` file you created in Step 2 from the `Styles` folder. Make sure that Relative To is set to Document, as shown in Figure 9-12.

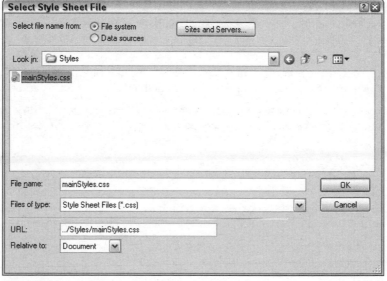

Figure 9-12

9. Click OK to select the style sheet, and then in the Attach External Style Sheet dialog box make sure Add As is set to Link, as shown in Figure 9-13. This adds a reference to the style sheet that guarantees backwards compatibility with older browsers.

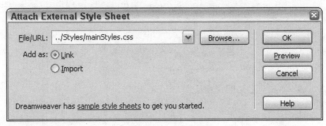

Figure 9-13

Using Link to add a style sheet to a page has been around for a long time, so many pages on the Web are using it. This means it's likely that new browsers will support it for some time. But if you are only targeting relatively modern browsers like Internet Explorer 4 or later and Netscape 6 or later you can choose Import instead of Link. Import is the preferred way to reference a style sheet according to the latest W3C specifications, so this guarantees that your pages will continue to work in future browsers as well.

If you want to see how your page ends up with the style sheet applied, click the Preview button. Dreamweaver displays the current page and applies the selected style sheet to it.

10. Click OK again to insert the style sheet in the document. Save the template (press Ctrl+S) so all pages that depend on it are changed as well, and then close the template.

11. Open `login.asp` again and locate the error message you assigned to `sErrorMessage` in the top ASP code block. The error message will be wrapped inside a `<span>` tag, so you can apply a CSS class to the error message. You can't apply CSS classes to text directly in HTML, so you need to wrap the text in an HTML element and then apply the class to that element. The `<span>` tag is ideal for this purpose, as it renders no visible output to the browser. It just serves as a container for your message.

To put the error message inside a `<span>` tag, you can type **** and **** before and after the message, inside the double-quotes that mark the beginning and the end of the string.

Alternatively, you can use Dreamweaver to insert the tag for you. To do so, in Code view select the whole error message from the first double-quote ("`<br>`") to the last double-quote (`pass-word`"):

```
sErrorMessage = "<br>" & _
        "Login failed. Please type a valid username and password"
```

Right-click the selection and choose Insert Tag from the context menu. The Tag Chooser appears. At the left-hand side of the dialog box select HTML Tags from the Markup Language Tags item. In the right-hand pane, scroll down the list until you find the span tag and click it. If you want information about this tag, click the Tag Info button at the bottom of the dialog box. The dialog box expands and shows information about the tag, as you can see in Figure 9-14.

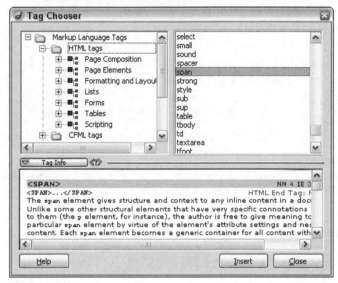

Figure 9-14

Click the Insert button and you'll see the Tag Editor dialog box for the `<span>` tag. Type **clsErrorMessage** in the Class text box, click OK, and then click Close to close the Tag Chooser. Dreamweaver changes the error message to this:

```
Response.Redirect("Admin/admin.asp")
Else
```

```
sErrorMessage = <span class="clsErrorMessage">"<br>" & _
    "Login failed. Please type a valid username and password"</span>
End If
```

You may have noticed that Dreamweaver doesn't recognize the selected text as an ASP string, so it messed up your quotes a bit: the `<span>` tag should be inside the double-quotes and the double-quotes around the `clsErrorMessage` class should be escaped. Fix the code so it looks like this:

```
sErrorMessage = "<span class=""clsErrorMessage""><br>" & _
    "Login failed. Please type a valid username and password</span>"
```

As you can see, using the Dreamweaver IDE to wrap the error message inside a `<span>` tag is quite a lot of work, so it's usually much quicker to type the code directly. However, when you need to add a lot of attributes, like Class, ID, and code for various events, using the Tag Editor may be easier.

12. The next step is to apply style sheet information to the text boxes for the username and password. Most browsers render text boxes with a rather old-fashioned looking 3D border style, so you can apply a CSS class to the text boxes that overrides this border property and changes it to a nice black thin border. Select the text field for the username in Design view and then on the Property inspector choose clsTextInput from the Class drop-down list. Repeat this step for the password box.

Dreamweaver doesn't apply the new class information to the text box in Design view but it does change the code. Here's how it should look after you change both text boxes:

```
<p>Username<br>
  <input name="txtUserName" type="text" class="clsTextInput"
  id="txtUserName">
</p>
<p>Password<br>
  <input name="txtPassword" type="password" class="clsTextInput"
  id="txtPassword">
</p>
```

If you are working with Internet Explorer on Windows XP, you might notice a small width difference between a default text box and a password text box in the browser. You can easily fix this by applying a style with a specified width to the text box. You may be tempted to do this in your clsTextInput *style definition but since you may be reusing this class for other text boxes as well, you don't want to force the width through the* class *attribute. Instead, add the following style attribute to both of your text boxes:*

```
style="width: 150px;"
```

This is what the final text box for the username should look like:

```
<input name="txtUserName" type="text" class="clsTextInput"
    id="txtUserName" style="width: 150px;">
```

13. Save and run the page in your browser by pressing F12. The text boxes now have a thin black border around them and they are both the same size. Try to log in by using an invalid username and password. You'll see that the error message stands out a lot more than in the previous example. It's hard to see on a black and white screenshot (Figure 9-15), but the message is now displayed in a red and bold font.

How It Works

The information in the style sheet should be to be available throughout your site, so the best place to add a reference to this style sheet is in your main template. This way, all pages based on this template will be able to use the styles that you defined in your style sheet. You may wonder why you added a reference to the style sheet rather than use an Include file to insert the contents of the style sheet into the template page. If you use an Include file for the style sheet, its contents will be sent with every page the user is going to request on your site. Because your style sheet isn't likely to change very often, this would mean you are wasting a lot of bandwidth for no reason. By adding the style sheet as a reference, the browser will only request it once and then save a local copy of it in its cache, saving you from some unnecessary network traffic.

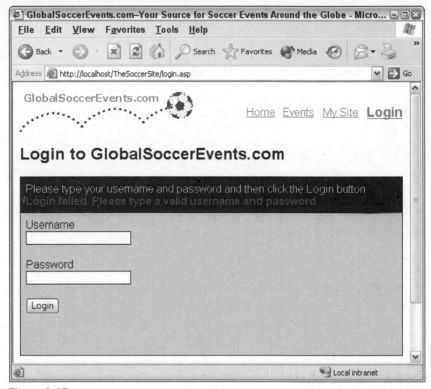

Figure 9-15

By inserting the style sheet relative to the template document, you can be sure that your style sheet works in all the pages you create for the soccer site. Here you can see some of the real power of the Dreamweaver MX 2004 templates feature. You may notice that Dreamweaver adds the link to the style sheet like this: ../Styles/mainStyles.css. This means one level up from the current folder (Templates) and then one level down again into the Styles folder. However, a path like this only works from within a subfolder that's only one level deep from the root of your site. What about pages in the top directory of your site, or for files in a folder that's inside the Admin folder? To see how Dreamweaver handles this, open the page home.asp in the root of your site. Locate the <link> tag, which you find right before the closing </head> tag:

```
<!- InstanceBeginEditable name="head" -><!- InstanceEndEditable ->
<link href="Styles/mainStyles.css" rel="stylesheet" type="text/css">
</head>
```

When you save the template, Dreamweaver updates all the pages that use the template as well. But when it inserts the <link> tag, it also recalculates the relative path to the style sheet. For home.asp it removes the leading two dots and the forward slash so the link refers correctly to your style sheet. If you created a new file called Admin/NewFolder/newPage.asp and applied your template to it, you'd find that Dreamweaver adds the <link> tag as follows:

```
<link href="../../Styles/mainStyles.css" rel="stylesheet" type="text/css">
```

This feature definitely saves you from a lot of trouble when you start moving pages around in your site or when you add new pages in folders a few levels deep.

The server-side code hasn't changed much but you have added a `<span>` element around your error message and given it a CSS class:

```
sErrorMessage = "<span class=""clsErrorMessage""><br>" & _
    "Login failed. Please type a valid username and password</span>"
```

Because you also hooked up the style sheet that defines `clsErrorMessage` to the template that `login.asp` is based on, the error message now appears in red. Notice how the double-quotes around the class name are escaped by adding a second double-quote. In the browser the two double-quotes end up as only one double-quote.

The same principle applies to the way you change the looks of the text boxes. You add the style `clsTextInput` to both of the text boxes:

```
<input name="txtUserName" type="text" class="clsTextInput" id="txtUserName">
```

At the client, the browser looks up the layout definition for the class `clsTextInput` in the linked style sheet and applies it to the text box.

Now that you have seen how to create a form that enables a user to log in to your site, let's take a look at how to protect pages from unauthenticated users. In the next Try It Out exercises you will protect the admin menu of your site so only authenticated users can access it. When users request the admin menu without having logged in first, they are redirected to your login form where they can supply their username and password. You'll make the login page as user-friendly as possible by redirecting the user back to the page that was initially requested.

Protecting Your Pages

Because of the way the login mechanism was set up in the previous section, restricting access to specific pages is now very easy. You may recall from our first discussion about the login form that upon successful login a session variable called `MM_Username` was set. This variable stores the username. All you need to do in pages that you want to protect is see if this session variable is set or not. If you think that this is easy, you may be surprised by the fact that Dreamweaver makes this even easier for you by providing a server behavior called Restrict Access to Page. In the next Try It Out exercise you will modify your `admin.asp` page so it is only accessible for logged-in users.

Try It Out **Protecting Your Admin Menu**

1. Open the `admin.asp` page from the `Admin` folder.

2. Open the Server Behaviors panel (press Ctrl+F9). Click the plus (+) button and select User Authentication➪Restrict Access to Page to open the Restrict Access to Page dialog box in Figure 9-16.

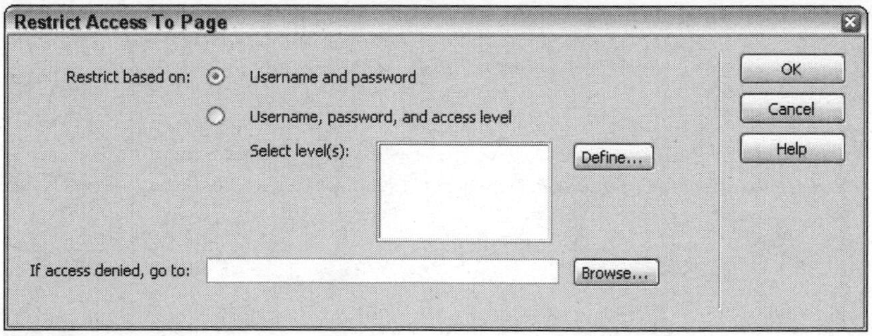

Figure 9-16

Click the Browse button next to the If Access Denied Go To text box and browse to `login.asp` in the Select File dialog box. This is the page the code redirects users to when they try to request the admin page without having logged in first. Click the Username and Password option. (You'll see how to use the other option—Username, Password, and Access Level—in Chapter 11.)

Once you click OK, Dreamweaver inserts an ASP code block at the top of your page. Save the page.

3. If you have any browser windows open, close them all before requesting the `admin.asp` page by pressing F12. This ensures that you get a new session so you'll be forced to log in first. Instead of the `admin.asp` page, you'll be presented with the login form. Type **UserName** and **Password** and then click the Login button. The admin page you requested will load in your browser.

How It Works

Although the steps you need to perform to protect a page are very easy, the code generated by Dreamweaver MX 2004 isn't. Finding out whether a user is logged in and, if necessary, redirecting them to the login form page while maintaining the initially requested page requires some complex ASP code. Don't worry if you don't understand the next section completely; in most scenarios there isn't any need to modify the code yourself. If you do want to follow along, put your thinking hat on!

As soon as you request the `admin.asp` page, the block of ASP code that has been inserted at the top of the page gets executed. Let's look at that code now to find out how the page is protected against unauthenticated users:

```
<%
' *** Restrict Access To Page: Grant or deny access to this page
MM_authorizedUsers=""
MM_authFailedURL="../login.asp"
MM_grantAccess=false
```

First, a few variables are declared. `MM_authorizedUsers` is used in combination with access levels, so it's redundant until Chapter 11, when you implement access levels. Apparently the designers of Dreamweaver decided to generate the same block of code, whether or not access levels are used.

The variable `MM_authFailedURL` defines the page that the user is redirected to if they haven't logged in yet. `MM_grantAccess` determines whether the user is allowed to view this page. It is initialized as `false` but if they have logged in it will be set to `true` by the next code block:

```
If Session("MM_Username") <> "" Then
 If (true Or CStr(Session("MM_UserAuthorization"))="") Or _
  (InStr(1,MM_authorizedUsers,Session("MM_UserAuthorization"))>=1) Then
  MM_grantAccess = true
 End If
End If
```

This block of code first checks whether the session variable `MM_Username` has been set, which it should be if a valid user is logging in. In that case, the code in the `If` block performs an additional check to find out if the user has the correct access level permissions to request this page. This does not apply to this example, so you could remove the additional code block; however, we will leave it here ready to use in Chapter 11.

Without the redundant code block, the code that checks whether a user is logged in or not can be simplified to this:

```
If Session("MM_Username") <> "" Then
   MM_grantAccess = true
End If
```

The code only checks one session variable. If it's set, the user has logged in and access can be granted. If access is denied, the code determines the page the browser is redirected to:

```
If Not MM_grantAccess Then
 MM_qsChar = "?"
 If (InStr(1,MM_authFailedURL,"?") >= 1) Then
  MM_qsChar = "&"
```

Next, you need to preserve the value of the QueryString from the page the user initially requested. If the user requested a page like `Admin/admin.asp?id=12` you need to remember the QueryString `id=12` as well, so after a successful login, you can redirect to the correct page. You have seen in previous chapters that only the first item in the QueryString is separated by a `?` character and that all other name-value pairs should be separated with an `&` character. The code checks if the page you want to redirect to already contains a question mark. If it does, the `&` is used to add subsequent name-value pairs to the QueryString of `MM_authFailedURL` instead of the question mark:

```
MM_referrer = Request.ServerVariables("URL")
if (Len(Request.QueryString()) > 0) Then _
    MM_referrer = MM_referrer & "?" & Request.QueryString()
```

The name of the current page is retrieved by using `Request.ServerVariables("URL")` and assigned to `MM_referrer`. If the page also contains a QueryString, it also gets appended to the value of `MM_referrer`.

```
MM_authFailedURL = MM_authFailedURL & MM_qsChar & _
          "accessdenied=" & Server.URLEncode(MM_referrer)
```

MM_authFailedURL is extended with the separation character and then an additional QueryString variable, called accessdenied, is appended. Notice that we have added an extra underscore and a line break in the previous code block to split the code over two lines. This improves readability but the code works fine without it.

Finally, the code appends the URLEncoded value of MM_referrer, which holds the complete file name of the page you need to redirect to after a successful login. The call to Server.URLEncode is necessary to escape illegal characters in the URL that you want to redirect to. For example, a slash in a URL is used to denote a directory and a dot usually indicates the start of a file extension. Passing these values directly would certainly confuse the Web server, so to be able to transfer them directly you need to translate them using the URLEncode method.

This may look a bit confusing, so let's take a look at an example. Imagine that you haven't logged in yet and that you request the admin page by entering the following URL in the browser: http://localhost/TheSoccerSite/Admin/admin.asp?id=12.

To calculate the page you need to redirect to, start by assigning Request.ServerVariables("URL") to MM_referrer, which will then hold /TheSoccerSite/Admin/admin.asp. Because the page also has a QueryString (id=12), MM_referrer is extended with this QueryString so now it contains:

```
/TheSoccerSite/Admin/admin.asp?id=12
```

This value is URLEncoded and then appended to MM_authFailedURL, together with the separator character and the accessdenied variable. The complete URL of the page you are going to redirect to now looks like this:

```
/TheSoccerSite/login.asp?accessdenied=%2FTheSoccerSite%2FAdmin%2Fadmin%2Easp%3Fid%3
D12
```

As you can see, the forward slash, the dot, the question mark, and the equal sign have been "translated" to %2F, %2E, %3F, and %3D, respectively, so they can be safely passed in the QueryString.

When the full URL you want to redirect to is known, the Response.Redirect statement will take the user to that page:

```
  Response.Redirect(MM_authFailedURL)
 End If
%>
```

This may seem like a lot of work for nothing if all you want to do is just redirect to the login.asp page, but the information you have appended to the QueryString turns out to be pretty useful if you want to improve the usability of the site. Instead of always redirecting to the admin page, you now have a mechanism to redirect the user to the page they initially requested. In the next example we'll show you how you can accomplish this.

Improving Usability: Using the Referrer

Whenever you log in to the site using the Login menu item, you are presented with the main admin menu. This is fine in a small site where you have only one or two pages that you want to protect;

however, when your site starts to grow, this may not be feasible. The main reason you may not want to redirect visitors is that not every visitor is an administrator. This means that you don't want to allow regular members to view the admin page, so you can no longer redirect to that page. You'll see in Chapter 11 how you can distinguish between different types of users and redirect them accordingly after they log in.

Another reason for not redirecting directly to the admin page is the usability of your site. Suppose you have made a bookmark to the page /TheSoccerSite/Admin/popularFirstPage.asp you created in the previous chapter. When you open the bookmark, you're redirected to the login page first. In the current implementation of your login form, after you log in successfully you are presented with the admin menu instead of the requested popularFirstPage.asp page. This is not very user-friendly.

In the next Try It Out exercise you'll modify the login.asp page so it can see what page the user initially requested. Upon successful login, the user is redirected to the page they requested, if possible; otherwise they are still redirected to the admin menu.

Try It Out   Redirecting to the Referring Page

1. Open login.asp and locate the frmLogin form you created in an earlier Try It Out exercise.

2. Place the cursor just before the </form> tag in Code view and select Insert⇨Form⇨Hidden Field. Fill in the resulting Tag Editor dialog box so it looks like Figure 9-17.

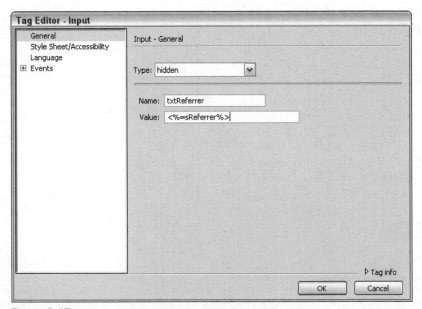

Figure 9-17

Name the hidden form control **txtReferrer** and set its value to an ASP variable called sReferrer, which is created next. Click OK. The form field that has been inserted should look like this:

```
<input name="txtReferrer" type="hidden" value="<%=sReferrer%>">
```

3. Locate the ASP code block at the top of the page and add the following code right after the `Dim sErrorMessage` line:

```
Dim sErrorMessage
```

```
Dim sReferrer
If Request.Form("txtReferrer") = "" Then
 sReferrer = Request.QueryString("accessdenied")
Else
 sReferrer = Request.Form("txtReferrer")
End If
If sReferrer = "" Then
 sReferrer = "Admin/admin.asp"
End If
If Request.Form("txtUserName") <> "" And _
```

4. In the block of code *below* the code you just added, change the line with the redirect so it reads:

```
Session("MM_Username") = Request.Form("txtUserName")
```

```
Response.Redirect(sReferrer)
Else
```

Save and close `login.asp`.

5. To block access to `popularFirstPage.asp` as well, open the file and then open the Server Behaviors panel by pressing Ctrl+F9. Click the plus (+) button and choose User Authentication⇨ Restrict Access To Page. Make sure you choose Username and Password as the restriction mechanism and let the page redirect to `../login.asp` in the If Access Denied Go To text box. Click OK to accept this action and then save the page.

6. Open `popularFirstPage.asp` in your browser (make sure you have closed any open browser first). You'll see the login page appear with the name of the initially requested page appended to the URL, as shown in Figure 9-18.

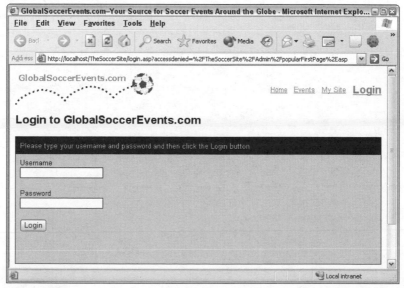

Figure 9-18

7. Take a good look at the Address bar of your browser—it should look like this:

    ```
    http://localhost/TheSoccerSite/login.asp?accessdenied=%2FTheSoccerSite%2F
    Admin%2FpopularFirstPage%2Easp
    ```

    Log in with an incorrect username and password. You'll see the red error message. The address bar has now changed to this:

    ```
    http://localhost/TheSoccerSite/login.asp
    ```

    Log in correctly using **UserName** and **Password**. If all has gone as planned, you'll now see `popularFirstPage.asp`. Finally, close your browser and request the admin page. Login in again and you'll now be presented with the admin page. Fantastic!

How It Works

As you have seen, the login page is able to remember which page the reader wants to be redirected to, even if they supply an incorrect username and password. The magic that makes this happen is a combination of the QueryString and the Form collection of the `Response` object. As you saw from the first image with the Address bar, `login.asp` is called with the `accessdenied` parameter. This parameter contains the page you need to redirect to after you have successfully logged in. To maintain this value between various calls to the same login page, this value is saved to a hidden form field. A hidden field behaves the same as a normal text field in that you can save text to it. However, it renders no visual output to the screen and is therefore invisible to the user.

To see this in action, close all your browser windows and request the `admin.asp` page again. You'll be redirected to the login page where you are asked for your username and password. On the login page, open the source of the page (in most browsers this can be done by right-clicking the page and then selecting View Source or View Page Source). You'll see something similar to Figure 9-19.

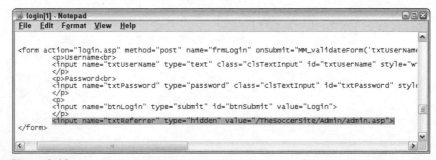

Figure 9-19

Notice how the value from the QueryString has now been saved to the hidden form field and that the ASP engine has silently decoded the value, returning all the escaped characters in their original format.

Take a look at the ASP code that makes this happen:

```
Dim sReferrer
If Request.Form("txtReferrer") = "" Then
 sReferrer = Request.QueryString("accessdenied")
```

```
  Else
   sReferrer = Request.Form("txtReferrer")
  End If
  If sReferrer = "" Then
   sReferrer = "Admin/admin.asp"
  End If
```

The code first checks if `Request.Form("txtReferrer")` has a value; if it does, it means the form has been submitted by clicking the Login button. This value is then assigned to `sReferrer`. If the form hasn't been submitted yet, the value of `sReferrer` is retrieved from `Request.QueryString("accessdenied")` instead.

There is also a mechanism to ensure that `sReferrer` always has a valid value. If `sReferrer` is still empty, it gets a value of `Admin/admin.asp`. This may be useful when the login page is requested directly because in this scenario neither `Request.Form("txtReferrer")` nor `Request.QueryString("accessdenied")` has a value, so the user is redirected to the `admin.asp` page by default.

```
  <input name="txtReferrer" type="hidden" value="<%=sReferrer%>">
```

The value of `sReferrer` is stored in a hidden form field so it will be available the next time the form is submitted. No matter how many times a user types in an incorrect username or password, the hidden form field keeps its value because it is submitted to the server every time the user tries to log in.

```
  Response.Redirect(sReferrer)
```

Finally, if the visitor logs in successfully, he or she is redirected to the page initially requested.

Preparing for Growth

The login mechanism you have built is nice for a site where you want to restrict access to pages where there are only one or two people that should access them. If you give them both the username and password they can log in and reach your admin section; however, if you need to provide access to 10, 100, or even more users, the solution we have presented here is not going to work. The way you check a hard-coded username and password is very hard to scale to a large number of users, so we'll have to look to a different solution.

In the next section, we discuss a method where a text file is used to store your usernames and passwords. The code you create can easily be upgraded so it uses a database instead of a text file. You'll see in Chapter 11 how to do this.

Because there is no built-in support for working with text files in Dreamweaver, you need to do some hand-coding to get things to work; however, in real-world applications, you'll often need to write to or read from a text file, so we think it's a useful addition to show you how to work with them.

Besides the built-in ASP objects that we introduced in the previous chapter, when you work with ASP you have access to a lot of other objects as well. They often come as freeware or commercial third-party objects that can be installed on your server, such as objects that can accept uploaded files, send e-mail, generate graphs, or execute programs on the server. In this example, we make use of the `FileSystemObject` provided by Windows. Although you can use it from within an ASP application, it's not part of ASP itself; it's part of the operating system (the Microsoft Scripting Runtime, to be exact); you can use the `FileSystemObject` from other programming languages as well.

As its name implies, the `FileSystemObject` allows you to work with files. You can copy, delete, and move files; create and remove directories; and read from and write to text files. Currently, there is no support to write binary files, which can be used to represent images, although you can use the `FileSystemObject` to copy, move, and delete those files.

> *There is not enough room in this chapter to discuss all the functionality that the `FileSystemObject` supports, but we encourage you to read the documentation at* `http://msdn.microsoft.com`. *Searching for the keyword **FileSystemObject** takes you to the documentation as well as to many technical articles with sample code.*

The `FileSystemObject` is your main entry point to other objects, methods, and properties that are contained in this object. In the next example, we will make use of one additional object, the `TextStream` object, which can be created by calling the `OpenTextFile` method on the `FileSystemObject`.

The `TextStream` object, in return, supports methods like `Read`, `ReadLine`, `WriteLine`, and `Close`. In the example, you'll be mostly interested in its `ReadLine` method because it allows you to read a file line by line.

In the next Try It Out exercise you'll modify the login page and change the code that validates the user. Instead of comparing the username against hard-coded values, the code opens a text file and reads it line by line until either the username and password are found, or until the end of the file is reached.

> **Working with a text file in a client-server environment can severely hinder the scalability of your site. Don't apply the login solution presented here to a Web site with thousands of users. For large-scale projects, a database that stores usernames and password is the preferred way to go because it can handle lots of concurrent users and is easier to maintain. We'll show you how to implement a database solution in Chapter 11.**

Try It Out   Using the FileSystemObject

1. Add a text file to the `Tools` folder of your site. To add the file, press Ctrl+N to open the New Document dialog box. On the General tab, click Other, select Text in the Other list and then click Create. Save the page in the `Tools` folder as **users.txt**. Saving the file in the `Tools` directory and giving it a very obscure name might help to stop people from guessing the filename, so they can't download it. However, *security by means of obfuscation* is generally considered a bad security practice, so on a production server you need to take extra measures to protect the file.

> **One of the ways to protect your file is to store it in a folder that is outside the Web root, like `C:\Webfiles`. Another solution is to use the NTFS security mechanism that Windows NT 4, Windows 2000, Windows XP, and Windows Server 2003 provide. In Chapter 11 we discuss both methods in detail when we explain how you can prevent a database from being downloaded. Refer to this chapter for information on protecting your text file with usernames and passwords.**

2. Inside the text file, type a number of usernames and passwords, separated by just a tab character. Make sure each entry is on its own line and that there are no spaces in the username or password. Your file should be in this format:

```
CharlesEBrown  VerySecret
ToddMarks  EvenMoreSecret
ImarSpaanjaars  TopSecret
```

Remember your username and password so you can log in when the details are requested. Save and close the file.

3. Open the `login.asp` page and remove the following shaded lines of code from the second half of the ASP code block at the top of the file:

```
If Request.Form("txtUserName") <> "" And _
    Request.Form("txtPassword") <> "" Then
```

```
  If Request.Form("txtUserName") = "UserName" And _
      Request.Form("txtPassword") = "Password" Then
    Session("MM_Username") = Request.Form("txtUserName")
    Response.Redirect(sReferrer)
  Else
    sErrorMessage = "<span class=""clsErrorMessage""><br>" & _
        "Login failed. Please type a valid username and password</span>"
  End If
End If
```

4. At the location where you removed these lines of code, add the following code block (and remember that you can use the downloaded source code for this chapter to save you from typing in this code yourself.):

```
Const ForReading = 1
Dim oFileSystemObject
Dim oTextStream
Dim sFileLocation
Dim sTempString
Dim arrTemp
Dim bUserFound
If Request.Form("btnLogin") <> "" Then
  sFileLocation = Server.MapPath("Tools/users.txt")
  ' Create an instance of the FileSystemObject
  Set oFileSystemObject = Server.CreateObject("Scripting.FileSystemObject")
  ' Create a reference to our text file so we can read from it
  Set oTextStream = oFileSystemObject.OpenTextFile(sFileLocation, ForReading)
  ' Read in each line until we reach the end of the file
  Do While (Not oTextStream.AtEndOfStream = True)
    ' Read a line
    sTempString = oTextStream.ReadLine()

    ' If the line contains text
    If Len(sTempString) > 0 Then
      ' The line should hold the username and password, separated by a tab
      ' Split the line based on a tab, so we get the username and password
      ' in two separate array elements
      arrTemp = Split(sTempString, vbTab)
```

```
    If IsArray(arrTemp) Then
    ' An UBound of 1 means two elements in the array, the username
    ' and the password. If we haven't found both, we do not continue

    If UBound(arrTemp) = 1 Then
      ' Compare array elements with username and password
      If arrTemp(0) = Request.Form("txtUserName") And _
            arrTemp(1) = Request.Form("txtPassword") Then
      bUserFound = True
      Exit Do
    End If
  End If
  End If
 End If
Loop

' Close our textstream and clean up our objects
oTextStream.Close
Set oTextStream = Nothing
Set oFileSystemObject = Nothing
If bUserFound = True Then
 Session("MM_Username") = Request.Form("txtUserName")
 Response.Redirect(sReferrer)
Else
 sErrorMessage = "<span class=""clsErrorMessage""><br>" & _
    "Login failed. Please type a valid username and password</span>"
End If
End If
```

5. Save and run the page. Notice that you can log in using the usernames and passwords you have defined in the file users.txt. Whenever you need to add or remove a user, there is no longer a need to modify the coding logic in the login page; all you need to do is change the contents of users.txt.

> Most anti-virus software programs have a feature called *script blocking*. This feature is supposed to block harmful script files that may contain viruses; however, they are sometimes too good and block your precious ASP scripts that use the File SystemObject. If you find that your server hangs for no particular reason when you run a page that uses the FileSystemObject, check the properties of your anti-virus program. If that appears to be the problem, it's up to you whether you want to sacrifice some security on your system for the added value of the FileSystemObject.

How It Works

Not much has changed in the login page except for the routine that does the validation of the username and password, so we'll go over that code. It's quite large, so we'll break it up again.

At the beginning of the code, a constant and a few variables are declared that are needed throughout the code:

```
Const ForReading = 1
Dim oFileSystemObject
Dim oTextStream
Dim sFileLocation
Dim sTempString
Dim arrTemp
Dim bUserFound
```

A *constant* behaves more or less like a variable, only you can't change its value in the script at runtime. Using this constant, you can avoid seeing magic numbers pop up in your code again. It's usually a good idea to move all the constants you use in your site to a separate file and then include this file in the main template so the constants are available in all pages in your site. This way they are easier to maintain and there is no need to declare them in each page that needs them. You'll see more about the `ForReading` constant when we discuss the code that opens the text file later in the code.

The `oFileSystemObject` and `oTextStream` variables are used to hold a reference to a `FileSystemObject` and a `TextStream`, respectively (we'll introduce the other variables as you progress through the code):

```
If Request.Form("btnLogin") <> "" Then
 sFileLocation - Server.MapPath("Tools/users.txt")
 ' Create an instance of the FileSystemObject
 Set oFileSystemObject = Server.CreateObject("Scripting.FileSystemObject")
 ' Create a reference to our text file so we can read from it
 Set oTextStream = oFileSystemObject.OpenTextFile(sFileLocation, ForReading)
```

First, it's necessary to check whether the form has been submitted by clicking the Login button or not. If it has, `Request.Form("btnLogin")` doesn't equal an empty string and the code in the `If` block runs.

The `OpenTextFile` method expects a full path to the file that must be opened, so `Server.MapPath` is used to get the physical location of the file `users.txt`. This returns a path like this: `C:\Inetpub\wwwroot\TheSoccerSite\Tools\users.txt`.

Then an instance of the `FileSystemObject` is created with the `Server.CreateObject` method. The name, or in technical terms, the *progID,* of the object you want to create is passed to this method and a reference to the object it has created is returned. This reference is stored in the variable `oFileSystemObject`. Once this object has been created, you can call its `OpenTextFile` method. This method uses two arguments in this example: First the complete path and file name (`sFileLocation`) of the file you want to open are passed. The second argument, `ForReading`, indicates that you only want to read from the file and not write to it. As you can see, passing the constant `ForReading` makes your code much easier to understand than if you just passed the obscure number 1.

The `OpenTextFile` method returns a reference to the text file you opened so you can read it. This reference is stored in `oTextStream`. There are various methods available to read from the file, like `ReadAll` and `Read`, but in this example just the `ReadLine` method is used to read the file line by line:

```
 ' Read in each line until we reach the end of the file
 Do While (Not oTextStream.AtEndOfStream = True)
  ' Read a line
  sTempString = oTextStream.ReadLine()
  ' If the line contains text
  If Len(sTempString) > 0 Then
```

```
' The line should hold the username and password, separated by a tab
' Split the line based on a tab, so we get the username and password
' in two separate array elements
arrTemp = Split(sTempString, vbTab)
```

The loop continues to read lines until the end of the file is reached. The `ReadLine` method returns a string, which in this example holds a username and a password separated by a tab. At the end of the file, the property `AtEndOfStream` is `True`, so the loop ends.

Before you can see if there is a username and password in the line, you first need to check the length using the `Len` function to avoid reading in blank lines that may appear in the file. The `Split` method breaks the line into an array, `arrTemp`. An *array* is a bit like a collection you saw in previous chapters, in that you can store multiple variables using only one variable name. You can access these variables by using an index on the array (the *index* is a number that goes from 0 to the number of items in the array minus 1) on the array. Take a look at the following short example to see how this works:

```
<%
Dim SoccerClubs(1)
SoccerClubs(0) = "Manchester United"
SoccerClubs(1) = "Ajax"

Response.Write(SoccerClubs(0) & "<br>")
Response.Write(SoccerClubs(1) & "<br>")
%>
```

In this example, an array `SoccerClubs` is created and is dimensioned to hold two elements. Since the index of an array is zero-based, the 1 between the parentheses actually indicates the array is large enough to hold two values, with indexes 0 and 1, respectively. The next two lines assign values to the two items in the array. The two `Response.Write` lines demonstrate that the values are really stored in the array by writing out their values again. The output in the browser will be `Manchester United` and `Ajax` on two different lines.

A built-in ASP constant, `vbTab`, which defines the tab character, is passed to the `Split` method as the delimiter. If all goes well, the array should now have two elements, the first holding the username and the second holding the password.

To avoid errors, the `IsArray` method is used to check whether the `Split` method returns an array:

```
If IsArray(arrTemp) Then
' An UBound of 1 means two elements in the array, the username
' and the password. If we haven't found both, we do not continue
If UBound(arrTemp) = 1 Then
```

Next, you need to find out how many elements the array contains. The `UBound` function returns the number of the last element in your array. Because arrays are zero-based, if `UBound` has a value of 1, the array contains two elements, which is exactly what you want: an element for the username and an element for the password.

You can check whether the username and password that the user submits match a pair in the text file:

```
' Compare array elements with username and password
If arrTemp(0) = Request.Form("txtUserName") And _
        arrTemp(1) = Request.Form("txtPassword") Then
 bUserFound = True
 Exit Do
End If
```

The first element in the array, arrTemp(0), is used to check for the username and the second element, arrTemp(1), for the password. If they match, the flag bUserFound is set to True and the loop ends. If they don't match, the loop continues with the next line in the file until the user is found or the file is completely read.

At the end of the code block, the If statements, the Loop, and finally the TextStream object are closed:

```
    End If
   End If
  End If
Loop
' Close our textstream and clean up our objects
oTextStream.Close
```

It's generally considered good programming practice to set your objects to Nothing once you have finished with them. ASP does this automatically for you once the page has finished loading, but by doing it yourself you make your intentions clearer to others:

```
Set oTextStream = Nothing
Set oFileSystemObject = Nothing
```

Finally, the code decides whether the user should be granted access:

```
If bUserFound = True Then
  Session("MM_Username") = Request.Form("txtUserName")
  Response.Redirect(sReferrer)
Else
  sErrorMessage = "<span class=""clsErrorMessage""><br>" & _
      "Login failed. Please type a valid username and password</span>"
End If
End If
```

If the flag bUserFound is True, the session variable MM_Username is set and the user is redirected to the initially requested page. Otherwise, the error message is shown again.

That concludes the login page that uses a text file to store usernames and passwords. You now have a complete and functional login mechanism that you can use throughout your site. To make use of the login mechanism, you can add a Restrict Access To Page behavior to all your pages in your site that need protection.

Summary

This has been a rather code-heavy chapter, partly because of the code that Dreamweaver MX 2004 generates for you. If you are using Dreamweaver to create dynamic and interactive Web sites, you are likely to encounter quite a lot of code in your Web pages. For this reason, we have looked at some common coding scenarios you might need in your projects.

First you saw ASP code at work when you created a login page. A very simple form of authentication is used to allow or block access to specific pages, depending on whether the user is logged in or not.

You extended your login form by adding some JavaScript that checks the fields the user has to fill in so they can't try to log in without filling in the required fields. You saw that adding client-side field validation saves a roundtrip to the server, which minimizes the response time, making the site quicker to use.

Next you looked at a way to protect specific pages in your site. Dreamweaver provides a useful server behavior called Restrict Access To Page, which you can apply to pages you want to protect. No one can access these pages without first logging in.

You then improved the login page even further by providing a redirect mechanism. This feature sends your visitor back to the page they initially requested, allowing them to navigate to a page on your site using a bookmark and gain access to it right after entering their username and password. This extra usability aims to make visits to the site as simple as possible.

At the end of the chapter you changed your login page once again so it reads usernames and passwords from a text file instead of using the hard-coded values you used in earlier examples. It's a lot easier to add or remove users that are allowed to access your site using a text file, and this method of authentication is an improvement over hard-coding the values in the code. Unfortunately, a text file is only useful in a small-scale site with a limited number of users. If a lot of users access the Web site at the same time, you should consider using a database instead, which we will discuss in Chapter 11.

In the next chapter, we will use this login mechanism to distinguish between authenticated and unauthenticated users. You will build a page where visitors can change their preferences, like site colors and the logo of the site. As an incentive to become a member of your site, this functionality is just available for authenticated users.

Why Not Try . . .

1. As you may have noticed, the calculator you created in Chapter 7 does not check the two numbers the user can enter; the page will happily accept anything typed in, causing an error at the server when you try to subtract *Soccer* from *Events*, for example. Why not try and see if you can add some input validation to both the text boxes in `calculator.asp`?

   Hint: Add a `Validate Form` *behavior from the Behaviors panel. Make sure you set both fields to* **Required** *and accept just a* **Number** *for the input.*

2. The login page currently uses colors that were defined in the form code snippet you added to the page. However, these default colors may not match your color scheme or personal preferences. Why not try and improve the looks of this page by adding some CSS information to the page? You can add your own custom classes to `styles.css` and then use these styles on the various HTML elements on the page.

3. Your protection mechanism just blocks the pages in the admin section from prying eyes. You could however, decide to block access to other pages as well. For example, you may decide that you don't want your visitors to know how many hits your site has already received. In that case, you'll need to add a Restrict Access To Page server behavior to the page `hitCounter.asp`. If you decide to protect `events.asp` as well, be sure to make a backup copy of this page first. You'll need an unprotected version for Chapters 11 and 12.

4. The "Why Not Try" section at the end of Chapter 7 suggests that you create a page called `logout.asp` that calls `Session.Abandon()`. Now that you have a working login mechanism, why not enhance the logout page so it really logs a user out? If you haven't already done so, add a new menu item that points to `logout.asp` in the library item. Upon `logout.asp` you should clear the entire contents of the page and just add an ASP code block. Inside that code block, make a call to `Session.Abandon()` to end the user's session. You can also add a `Response.Redirect` statement that sends users back to `home.asp` after they have successfully logged out.

Personalizing Web Sites

If you want to change casual visitors of your site into loyal members, you need to offer them something special that gives them a reason to come back. Besides good content (which should always be the number-one priority for your site), you could offer them a way to personalize the way the site looks and behaves. For example, in the soccer fan site, it would be a cool feature if users could change the site to the colors of their favorite team or even display their favorite club's badge (or logo). *Personalization* is the key to creating sites that behave and look the way the user wants.

In this chapter we look at a few ways to change the appearance of your site. In particular, you will learn how to do the following:

❑ Let a user choose from a set of predefined themes that can be applied to the site

❑ Build a custom color picker to change site elements that are not defined in the style sheet

❑ Change the images used in the site by letting a user choose their favorite team's badge as the logo for the site

Using Themes

Many popular sites allow you to change the theme of their site to match your preferences. An example of this is www.yahoo.com where you can change the appearance of popular applications, including the calendar, e-mail program, and address book. In the next three Try It Out exercises we will show you how simple it is to add different themes to your site and let your user change them on the fly.

After these exercises you can present your visitors with a list menu containing three theme names. They can see a preview image of the new theme by clicking one of the theme names in the list. If they find a theme they like, they can click a button so the theme is applied to all pages of the site. Cookies are used again to persist the choice the users make, so the site looks the same next time they return. Your final theme page will look like Figure 10-1.

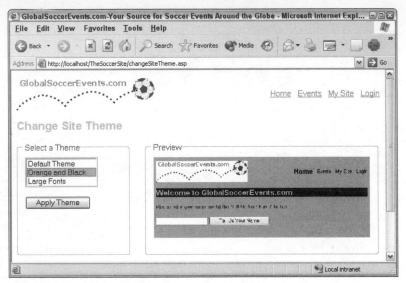

Figure 10-1

Start by adding two additional style sheet definitions and changing the ones you already had in your style sheet. These style definitions are used to determine site aspects like color and font.

Creating Themes

1. Open the `mainStyles.css` style sheet that you created in the previous chapter. At the bottom of the sheet, type **h2** followed by a pair of curly brackets (also known as *braces*), as in the example below:

```
.clsTextInput {
  background-color: #ffffff;
  font-size: 10pt;
  border: 1px solid;
}
```

```
h2 {
}
```

2. Open the CSS Styles panel (press Shift+F11). The tag definition you entered in Step 1 is added to the list under `mainStyles.css`. If the panel is already open, you need to click the panel first. This refreshes its contents so the h2 tag becomes visible, as shown in Figure 10-2.

3. Right-click the h2 tag in the CSS Styles panel and choose Edit. The CSS Style Definition for h2 dialog box appears, as shown in Figure 10-3.

    Select **Arial, Helvetica, Sans-Serif** from the Font list, set the Size to **16** points, Weight to **bold**, and the Color to **#99ccff**. Click on Background in the left part of the dialog box and set the Background Color to **white (#ffffff)**.

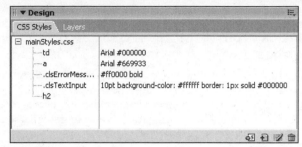

Figure 10-2

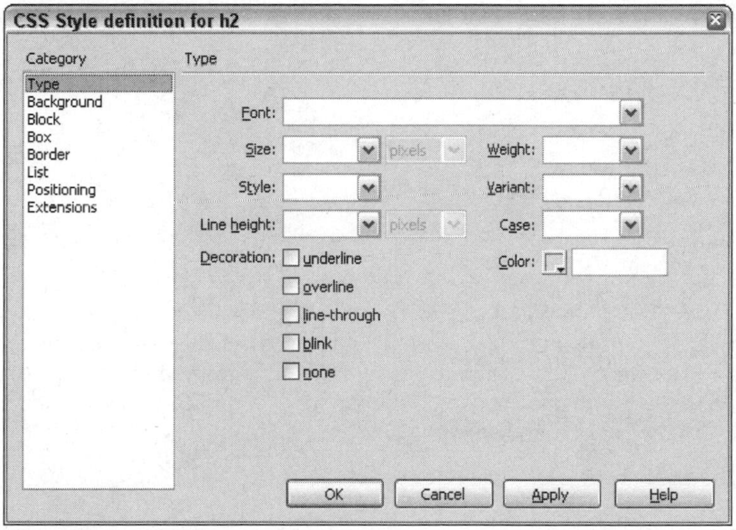

Figure 10-3

If you decide to change a color, here is a tip to ensure the color looks good on most computers. Click the square block right next to Color on the Type area of the CSS Style definition dialog box. This opens the color picker. Next click the right arrow in the upper right corner of the color picker and make sure that Snap to Web Safe is selected in the menu that appears (see Figure 10-4).

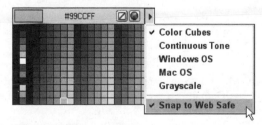

Figure 10-4

A *Web-safe color* is a color that can be viewed on computers capable of displaying at least 8-bit color (256 different colors). Most computers today can display this number of colors. Out of those 256 colors, only 216 colors will appear exactly the same on each different type of monitor; these are the colors in the Web-safe palette.

With the Web Safe option enabled, you can be sure that the colors you choose will look exactly the same on your visitor's computer because Dreamweaver MX 2004 will choose the nearest color from the Web safe palette whenever you choose an unsafe color. The Color Cubes and Continuous Tone palettes are both Web-safe, so you can get reliable results with these palettes, even with the Snap to Web Safe option turned off.

Click OK to insert the style information to your style sheet.

4. Type **body** at the bottom of the file, followed by a pair of braces. Repeat Steps 2 and 3 by opening the CSS Style definition dialog box again and applying the styles shown in the following code:

```
body {
  font-family: Arial, Helvetica, sans-serif;
  font-size: 11pt;
  color: #000066;
  background-color: #ffffff;
}
```

5. Apply a white background color to the `td` element and your custom class `.clsErrorMessage`, which was already in your style sheet. All your links are inside a `<td>` tag, so they inherit the background color from the `<td>` tag. That means there is no need to set an additional background color for the `<a>` element. Change the background by right-clicking each definition in the CSS Styles panel and choosing Edit. On the Background page of the panel, choose **white** (**#ffffff**) as the background color.

6. Save the style sheet. The CSS Styles panel should look like Figure 10-5.

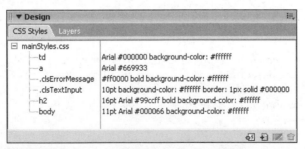

Figure 10-5

> When you define a color for a tag or class, be sure to supply a pleasant contrasting background color. If people are using their own default style sheet and you only override the color property of the font, you might end up with unreadable text. For example, white text on a light yellow background becomes almost invisible.

7. Before you can preview your new style sheet in the browser, you need to adjust the layout of the table in the login form. The form that Dreamweaver inserted when you added the form snippet in the previous chapter uses the `<font>` tag and the `bgcolor` attribute to change the colors in the page. In most Web browsers, CSS takes precedence over HTML, so the colors in the style sheet override those that are defined in the login page. You want to avoid this.

Open `login.asp` and in Code view locate the opening tag of the outer table that holds your login form. Remove the `bgcolor` attribute and its value, set `cellpadding` to **0**, and add a style attribute to the table tag:

```
<td><!- InstanceBeginEditable name="Content" ->
  <table width="100%" border="0" cellspacing="0" cellpadding="0"
    style="border: 1px solid black;">
   <tr>
```

Add the following style definition to the `<td>` tag that holds the message instructing users to type their name and password:

```
<td style="background-color: #000000">
```

Remove the `<font>` and `</font>` tags around the instructions and replace them with a different style in `<span>` tags:

```
<td style="background-color: #000000">
  <span style="color: #cccccc">
    Please type your username and password and then click the Login button
  </span>
    <%= sErrorMessage %>
```

Finally, replace the `bgcolor` attribute of the inner table cell that holds your form with a style definition:

```
  </td>
  </tr>
  <tr>
    <td width="100%" style="background-color: #cccccc" colspan="2">
```

8. Save the page and run it in your browser by pressing F12. The login page is a good example of how your styles will look in the browser because it uses all the different elements you have defined in the style sheet.

This is also a good moment to test your page in different browsers if you have them available. Although your form will look more or less the same in most modern browsers, there are a few minor differences. For example Figure 10-6 shows how the page looks in Netscape 7.

Testing your pages in various flavors of browsers is really important. Make sure that your important styles are consistent on as many browsers as possible and be careful when referring to screen elements in your text. If you instruct your users to click the blue button and they have a browser that doesn't support CSS, they won't be able to find the button. If you have trouble getting your page to look exactly the same in all browsers, one solution is to use images or Flash animations for elements like buttons and menus.

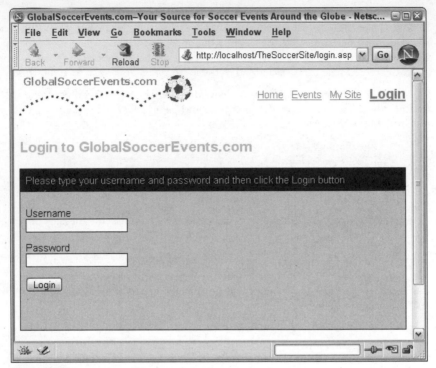

Figure 10-6

9.   Copy `mainStyles1.css`, `mainStyles2.css`, and `mainStyles3.css` from the code download for this chapter to the `Styles` folder of your site, located at `C:\TheSoccerSite`. Your Files panel should update and look like Figure 10-7.

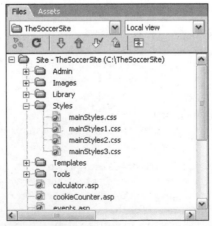

Figure 10-7

If the panel doesn't show the new style sheets, click the button with the round arrow on the toolbar to refresh the Files panel.

10. If you want, change the styles in the second and third style sheet so they look different from the first but still give a consistent look and feel between the different elements you defined in the style sheet. You could, for example, change the background color and text colors to match the colors of your favorite soccer team. When you're done, right-click the `Styles` folder and choose Put. This will upload the style sheets to your remote server.

11. Create a link to the page that allows a user to select a new theme. The best place to add this link (and other customization links) is on the page `mySite.asp`, so go ahead and open that page. Type the text **Change Site Theme** in the Content section. Select the text in Code view and choose Insert⇨Hyperlink to convert the text into a link. Set the page link to `changeSiteTheme.asp`, which you'll create in the next Try It Out exercise.

12. Save the page and preview it in your browser. You should see something similar to Figure 10-8, which shows the page in Opera 7.

Figure 10-8

How It Works

In this exercise you added a few style definitions that are used throughout the site. You also changed the tables that hold the login form so they are formatted with CSS styles instead of HTML markup. Just as with Web pages, Dreamweaver offers you a choice of how to create your code for the style sheet. You can use Dreamweaver's Integrated Development Environment (IDE) to create and modify style definitions, or you can type the code directly.

When you test the page in different browsers, notice the differences in the way browsers render the page on-screen. Although CSS has been around for a while, not every browser implements the specification correctly. If you preview your page in older browsers like Netscape Navigator 4, Internet Explorer 3, or Opera 5, you'll see that these browsers have great trouble rendering the page the way you intend. Fortunately, these browsers are becoming less common among Web surfers. Most of your visitors will use a relatively modern browser, like Internet Explorer 5 or later, Netscape 6 or later, Opera 6 or later, or Mozilla.

With three copies of the style sheet and a link on the `mySite.asp` page in place, it is time to create the page where users can choose among your three themes. On the theme page, you will add a *select list* with three different theme names. You'll also add an image that shows a preview of the theme. When the user selects a new theme from the list, the image is updated to reflect the new theme.

Creating changeSiteTheme.asp

1. Create a new file based on your main template and save it as **changeSiteTheme.asp** in the root of your site. Give the page a title of **Change Site Theme** in the Title section of the template, and remove the other two placeholders.

2. Add a table with one row and three columns to the Content section of the page. Set its width to 670 pixels and its border to 0. Once you insert the table, set the width of the first cell to 230, the second to 40, and the third to 400. Set the vertical alignment for all three cells to Top using the Property inspector. Select Top from the drop-down list next to the label with Vert on it. Make sure you set the alignment separately for each cell. If you select all three cells at once, Dreamweaver adds the `valign` property to the `<tr>` tag, which can cause some troubles in older browsers.

    Click inside the first cell in Code view, delete the ` ` that Dreamweaver inserted, and add a form by choosing Insert⇨Form⇨Form. Name the form **frmSelectTheme** and set its Method to POST. Set the Action to **changeSiteTheme.asp** so the form POSTs back to itself and then click OK.

3. With the cursor still between the `<form>` tags, select Insert⇨Form⇨List/Menu and type **lstTheme** as the Name. Before you close the dialog box, expand the Events list, click `onChange`, and type the following JavaScript in the text box at the right:

```
changeThemeImage();
```

The code for the `changeThemeImage()` function will be added later.

Click OK to insert the select list in the page.

Next, save the page and press F5 to update the page in Design view. After the update, the Property inspector changes as well, showing a List Values button. Click that button and then add the following options:

Item Label	Value
Default Theme	1
Orange and Black	2
Large Fonts	3

Once you click OK, Dreamweaver adds the following `<option>` elements to the select list:

```
<select name="lstTheme" onchange="changeThemeImage();">
  <option value="1">Default Theme</option>
  <option value="2">Orange and Black</option>
  <option value="3">Large Fonts</option>
</select>
```

4. Select the entire `<select>` tag using the tag selector and then change the Type of the list from Menu to List on the Property inspector, as shown in Figure 10-9. Change the Height of the list to 3.

Figure 10-9

5. To improve the looks of the page, create a *fieldset* around the select list. A fieldset is a container object in which you place other HTML elements. In the browser it draws a border around those elements and displays a caption at the top of the border. It's often used in desktop applications to group logically related controls together. Fieldsets are not used very much on Web pages, but we think they're great because they make your pages easier to understand for users since they clearly distinguish page sections from one another.

With the whole of the `<select>` statement still selected, choose Insert⇨Form⇨Fieldset. Type **Select a Theme** in the Label text box, as shown in Figure 10-10, and click OK.

Figure 10-10

6. Set an inline CSS style to the `<fieldset>` tag of `height: 200px;`. You can either type the style directly in Code view or right-click the `<fieldset>` tag, choose Edit Tag `<fieldset>`, and type in the style definition in the Style text box. Your `<fieldset>` tag now looks like this:

```
<form action="changeSiteTheme.asp" method="post" name="frmSelectTheme">
  <fieldset style="height: 200px;">
    <legend>Select a Theme</legend>
```

7. Next it's time to add images of your different style sheets in action. In the code download for this chapter you'll find three preview images that are used in this chapter (`theme1.gif`, `theme2.gif`, and `theme3.gif`). If you changed the second and third style sheets in Step 10 of the previous Try It Out exercise, you should make new preview images so they show the correct themes. Simply create a screenshot of the page `home.asp` using the new theme and then resize the file to 400 × 148 pixels. To have `home.asp` use the new theme, you can temporarily add a `<link>` tag to that page pointing to `mainStyles2.css` and `mainStyles3.css`, because that's currently the only way for `home.asp` to use these styles. You could also finish this and the next Try It Out exercise to finish the theme selector so you can apply the new themes to your site and then update the screenshots afterwards.

Add the theme images to the Images folder of your site. Make sure you copy the images to your remote server as well by right-clicking the Images folder on the Files panel and choosing Put. If you forget this step, the images won't be available in the browser.

8. Open the Assets panel on the Files panel group (press F11) and select the Images category, as shown in Figure 10-11. If the images don't appear in the list, click the small refresh button on the bottom bar of the panel.

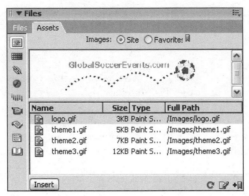

Figure 10-11

9. Drag `theme1.gif` to the Design view and drop it in the third cell of the table you created in Step 2. Because you need to be able to refer to your image by code, give it an ID attribute. To do this, select the image in Design view and type **imgSiteTheme** in the name/ID box on the Property inspector, right below Image, 5K, as shown in Figure 10-12.

Figure 10-12

10. With the image still selected in Design view, add another fieldset to the page by choosing Insert⇨Form⇨Fieldset again. Name this fieldset **Preview** and add the same inline style to it as you did with the first fieldset, so the height of the fieldset is now 200 pixels, too. If you view the page in your browser, you should see something similar to Figure 10-13.

As you can see, both the select list and the image are very close to the border of the fieldset. This is because the fieldset has very small padding. You may be tempted to add padding to the fieldset through an inline style but this causes some odd behavior in different browsers. For example, Internet Explorer creates padding to the left, right, and bottom borders of the fieldset, but not to the top. Instead, wrap the entire contents of the fieldset in a `<span>` tag and then set the style properties of the span, rather than the fieldset, to ensure the best cross-browser compatibility.

Right after the closing `</legend>` tag of the first fieldset, add a `<span>` tag with an inline style:

```
<span style="display: block; padding: 10px">
```

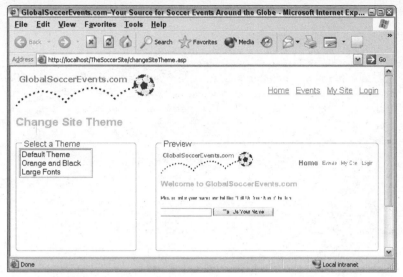

Figure 10-13

Add the closing `</span>` tag right before the closing `</fieldset>` tag. Repeat these two steps for the second fieldset.

Just to make sure you have followed the steps correctly, here's the full code for the table containing the select list and the image:

```html
<table width="670" border="0" cellspacing="0" cellpadding="0">
<tr>
 <td width="230" valign="top">
  <form action="changeSiteTheme.asp" method="post" name="frmSelectTheme">
   <fieldset style="height: 200px;"><legend>Select a Theme</legend>
    <span style="display: block; padding: 10px">
     <select name="lstTheme" size="3" onChange="changeThemeImage();">
      <option value="1">Default Theme</option>
      <option value="2">Orange and Black</option>
      <option value="3">Large Fonts</option>
     </select>
    </span>
   </fieldset>
  </form>
 </td>
 <td width="40" valign="top">
   
 </td>
 <td width="400" valign="top">
  <fieldset style="height: 200px;"><legend>Preview</legend>
   <span style="display: block; padding: 10px">
    <img src="Images/theme1.gif" name="imgSiteTheme"
        width="400" height="148" id="imgSiteTheme">
   </span>
  </fieldset>
```

```
    </td>
  </tr>
</table>
```

11. With the fieldsets and image in place, it's time to create a JavaScript function that shows a different preview image for each theme in the select list. Add the following JavaScript code block to the default `head` editable region that Dreamweaver has created when you turned your page into a template in Chapter 7 (you can find the `head` region just below the `<title>` tag at the top of the page):

```
<!- InstanceBeginEditable name="head" ->
```

```
<script language="JavaScript" type="text/javascript">
 function changeThemeImage()
 {
  var iSelectedIndex = document.frmSelectTheme.lstTheme.selectedIndex;
  var iSelectedValue =
     document.frmSelectTheme.lstTheme[iSelectedIndex].value;
  document.images["imgSiteTheme"].src =
     'Images/theme' + iSelectedValue + '.gif';
 }
</script>
```

```
<!- InstanceEndEditable ->
<link href="Styles/mainStyles.css" rel="stylesheet" type="text/css">
```

Although we have indented the code here so it fits on the page, the actual JavaScript code consists of just three lines. The two extra indented lines should be placed at the end of their preceding lines.

12. Save the page and open it up in your browser. Click a theme in the select list in the left part of the page. When you change to a new theme, the image on the right of the screen is updated, as shown in Figure 10-14. If the images appear broken, you may have forgotten to upload them to the remote server. To do this, right-click the images in the Files panel and choose Put from the context menu.

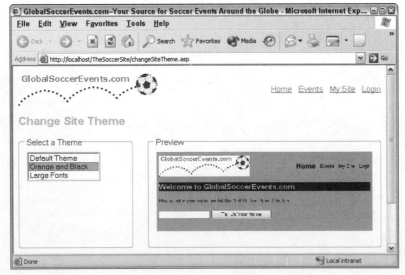

Figure 10-14

How It Works

You've already seen most of the techniques in this exercise in earlier chapters. You added a form with a select list and an image to your page. You used some inline styles to change the way the contents of your fieldset are rendered. In the theme list, you added a theme called Large Fonts. The style sheet for this theme uses a bigger font size for all the HTML elements. Because the font size is dictated through CSS, the user of your site can no longer change the font size themselves; but by providing a style sheet with large fonts, you can accommodate people who are visually impaired.

What may be new in this code is the way the JavaScript changes the images. Let's take a look at the JavaScript code to see how it works:

```
<script language="JavaScript" type="text/javascript">
function changeThemeImage()
{
  var iSelectedIndex = document.frmSelectTheme.lstTheme.selectedIndex;
```

The code starts with a JavaScript tag and a function header. Then a variable called `iSelectedIndex` is created and assigned a value. This variable holds the number of the currently selected item and is retrieved from the `<select>` list on the form. You can retrieve this number by using the general syntax of `document.FormName.SelectListName.selectedIndex`, where `FormName` and `SelectListName` refer to the name of your form and select list, respectively.

```
  var iSelectedValue =
        document.frmSelectTheme.lstTheme[iSelectedIndex].value;
```

Once you have the selected index, you can use it to retrieve the value of the selected item, which should be 1, 2, or 3. You can use `document.FormName.SelectListName` again to get at the value of the selected item. Pass in the value of `iSelectedIndex` to indicate from which item you want the value.

Next, the `src` property of the image in your page is changed:

```
  document.images["imgSiteTheme"].src =
        'Images/theme' + iSelectedValue + '.gif';
}
</script>
```

You can refer to any image in your document using `document.images[imageName]`, where `imageName` is either the `id` or the `name` of the image in your code. By appending the value of `iSelectedValue` to your image name, you can change the preview image to `theme1.gif`, `theme2.gif`, and `theme3.gif`.

The example we have presented here uses a strict naming convention for the preview images. Each image starts with `theme`, is followed by a sequential number, and ends with `.gif`. Don't worry if you want to name your images differently in your own site. The code can easily be changed to use different file names. Start by changing the value attribute of each `<option>` element in your select list to the name of your image, for example:

```
<select name="lstTheme" size="3" onchange="changeThemeImage();">
    <option value="defaultTheme">Default Theme</option>
    <option value="myCoolTheme">Cool Theme</option>
    <option value="blueWhite">Blue and White</option>
</select>
```

Next, change the line of JavaScript that changes the image to this:

```
document.images["imgSiteTheme"].src = 'Images/' + iSelectedValue + '.gif';
```

It's a good idea to change the name of the variable `iSelectedValue` to `sSelectedValue` to indicate you expect it to hold a string, not a number. If you have your images stored in a folder other than `Images`, don't forget to change the path in the code accordingly.

Remembering the User's Theme

As the page stands now, users can select a new theme from a select list and see a preview image of it. It is not really useful yet, however, because it doesn't apply the theme to your Web site. In the following exercise you'll change the sample page so it applies and remembers the theme the user chooses. Once the page is submitted to the server, you can retrieve the value from the select list and save it in a cookie. This cookie can be used in the template page to dynamically link the right style sheet to your pages.

Try It Out   Applying the Theme

1. In `changeSiteTheme.asp`, locate the closing `</select>` tag of the theme select list. Type two `<br>` tags right after it and then insert a new submit button. Name it **btnApply** and set its value to Apply Theme. Make sure its type is set to submit and not to button. The button should look as follows:

```
</select>
<br><br>
<input name="btnApply" type="submit" value="Apply Theme">
</span>
```

2. Add an ASP code block to the top of your page, right after the line that starts with `<%LANGUAGE`, and add the following code to it:

```
<%@LANGUAGE="VBSCRIPT" CODEPAGE="1252"%>
<%
If Request.Form("btnApply") <> "" Then
  Response.Cookies("SiteTheme") = Request.Form("lstTheme")
  Response.Cookies("SiteTheme").Expires = Date() + 30
End If
%>
```

    This code saves the theme the user selects in a cookie so you can use it on other pages as well. Save the page and close any file you may have open in Dreamweaver.

3. Now that you have a way to store the theme in a cookie, use that information to link to a different style sheet dynamically. Since all your pages should use the theme, the best place to add the code for this is in the main template. Open `mainTemplate.dwt.asp` and locate the line with the link to the style sheet. Add the following style sheet link *after* the one that's already declared in your template. Make sure you leave the old one in there as well:

```
<link href="../Styles/mainStyles.css" rel="stylesheet" type="text/css">
```

```
<link href="../Styles/mainStyles<%=iTheme%>.css" rel="stylesheet"
  type="text/css">
</head>
```

4. Right before the two style sheet links, insert an ASP block and add the following code to it:

```
<!- TemplateBeginEditable name="head" -><!- TemplateEndEditable ->
<%
```

```
Dim iTheme
If Len(Request.Cookies("SiteTheme")) > 0 Then
 iTheme = Request.Cookies("SiteTheme")
Else
 iTheme = 1 ' Our default theme
End If
```

```
%>
<link href="../Styles/mainStyles.css" rel="stylesheet" type="text/css">
```

Notice that this is the first time you don't add the ASP code directly after the first line that defines the language for the ASP page. If you try to add the code there, you'll notice that Dreamweaver warns you that this code will not be copied to other pages based on the template. Since the ASP code needs to be available in all the pages in your site, you need to add it to the `<head>` section of the page.

5. Save the template so all your pages are updated with the new code. If you have any files open, such as `changeSiteTheme.asp`, make sure you save those as well.

6. Right-click your site in the Files panel and choose Put. Dreamweaver asks if it's OK to Put the entire site. Since you need to upload the pages that have changed by modifying your template, this is exactly what you want, so go ahead and click OK.

7. Open `changeSiteTheme.asp` in your browser. Select a new theme from the list and click the Apply Theme button. The new theme is applied and the page now uses different colors and font sizes. Click the links in the navigation menu to see that all pages in your site use your new theme (see Figure 10-15). Pretty cool, don't you think?

Figure 10-15

How It Works

Whenever the user chooses a new theme from the select list, the preview image is updated at the client only. Once they click the Apply Theme button, however, the form is submitted to the server where the theme is remembered.

```
<%
  If Request.Form("btnApply") <> "" Then
    Response.Cookies("SiteTheme") = Request.Form("lstTheme")
    Response.Cookies("SiteTheme").Expires = Date() + 30
  End If
%>
```

The code first checks whether the form was submitted by clicking the Apply Theme button. If that's the case, the value from the form element is retrieved from the form element `lstTheme` and saved in a cookie. The cookie lasts for 30 days by calling the `Date()` function, which returns today's date, and adding 30 days to it. The cookie, in turn, is retrieved in every page that's based on your template:

```
<%
  Dim iTheme
  If Len(Request.Cookies("SiteTheme")) > 0 Then
    iTheme = Request.Cookies("SiteTheme")
  Else
    iTheme = 1 ' Our default theme
  End If
%>
```

Before you can use the cookie's value in your style sheet link, you need to make sure it has a value. If it doesn't have a value yet, most likely because you have a new user or your user hasn't used your personalization feature yet, `iTheme` gets a default value of 1. This means that `mainStyles1.css` will be used as the theme for the site. If you'd like another style sheet to be the default, simply change the default value for `iTheme`.

If the cookie does return a value, it is assigned to `iTheme`, which is then used to create the link to the style sheet:

```
<link href="../Styles/mainStyles<%=iTheme%>.css" rel="stylesheet"
  type="text/css">
```

At runtime, when the page is requested, `<%=iTheme%>` becomes 1, 2, or 3, so the link points to one of your three style sheets.

When you added the dynamic link, we advised you to leave the link to the old style sheets in there as well. Dreamweaver can't resolve the value for `Request.Cookies("SiteTheme")` at design-time, so the styles defined in your style sheet won't show up in the CSS Styles panel. This makes it very hard to apply styles to the various parts of your document during development. With a link to your default style sheet, Dreamweaver lists all your available styles and classes.

Once you have finished designing your site, you could remove the hard-coded style link from your template and update all the pages that are based on the template. This isn't strictly necessary, though. The dynamic style sheet is defined *after* the hard-coded one, so all classes defined in the first link are over-written by those defined in the second. Hence, when you run the page in your browser, it applies the design from the theme the user chose. However, removing the reference to the style sheet saves the browser from downloading a style sheet that is never used.

Because a dynamic value is used for the actual style sheet name, we have created a little problem for Dreamweaver. You may find that when you create a new page based on the template and save it, Dreamweaver is not able to recalculate the path for the style sheet. The `href` attribute of the `<link>` tag will point to `href="file:///C|/TheSoccerSite`, as you can see in the following code:

```
%>
<link href="Styles/mainStyles.css" rel="stylesheet" type="text/css">
<link href="file:///C|/TheSoccerSite/Styles/mainStyles<%=iTheme%>.css"
   rel="stylesheet" type="text/css">
</head>
```

Fortunately, you can fix this easily. Choose Modify⇨Templates⇨Update Current Page from the menu bar and Dreamweaver will correctly change the path to the style sheet. Your code now looks like this for a page in the root of your site:

```
%>
   <link href="Styles/mainStyles.css" rel="stylesheet" type="text/css">
   <link href="Styles/mainStyles<%=iTheme%>.css"
     rel="stylesheet" type="text/css">
</head>
```

Creating a Custom Color Picker

Before we continue discussing other ways of personalization, there is one feature we would like to show you: the *custom color picker*.

In many desktop applications, including Dreamweaver, you can use a color picker to select a color from a palette that contains a defined set of colors. These color pickers allow you to choose a color visually instead of knowing the value that is used in HTML (for example, `#ffffff` for white) or its RGB value (red, green, and blue components). These palettes are not available in ordinary Web browsers so you need to create your own if you want to allow your visitor to select their own colors.

In the next exercise you'll build a simple palette that holds 48 colors. Each color is linked to a JavaScript function that retrieves the selected color and saves it in a hidden form field. Once the form with the hidden field is submitted to the server, the value with the chosen color is saved in a cookie and used to influence the background of the `<body>` tag through a style definition.

At the end of this exercise, the page with the color picker will look like Figure 10-16.

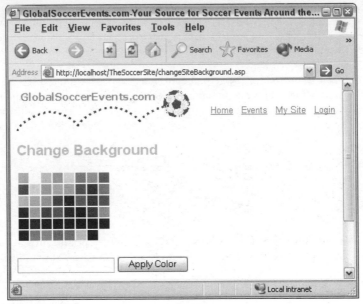

Figure 10-16

Try It Out   Building a Custom Color Picker

1. Because you are using a *spacer image* in this example, you need to add one to your site first. A spacer image is usually a small transparent .gif file of 1 × 1 or 2 × 2 pixels that can be used for layout purposes. You can place spacer images in your pages to help align your page elements properly. Because the image is transparent, it isn't visible in the browser but it creates room between HTML elements.

    Open Dreamweaver's Preferences dialog box by pressing Ctrl+U and then select the Layout Mode category. Click the Create button and create a spacer called spacer.gif in the Images directory of your local site. Once you close the Save Spacer Image File As dialog box, the Preferences dialog box should look like Figure 10-17.

    You'll need to upload the spacer image to the remote server as well, so that the image is available in the browser. If you don't see the spacer image appear under your Images folder in the Files panel, click the refresh button on the toolbar of the Files panel. Then right-click the spacer image and choose Put.

2. To give users access to the page where they can change the background color, you need to provide them with a menu item on the My Site page. Open the page mySite.asp from the root of your site and locate the link to the page changeSiteTheme.asp. After the closing </a> tag, type <br> and then type **Change Background**. Select the text in Code view and then choose Insert⇨Hyperlink to change the text into a link. Set the page link to **changeSiteBackground.asp**, which you'll create next. Save and close mySite.asp.

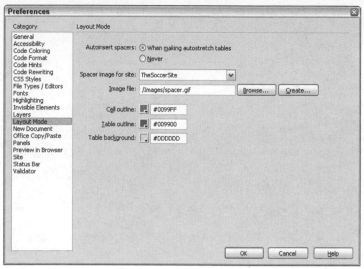

Figure 10-17

3. Create a new templated page and save it as **changeSiteBackground.asp** at the root of your site. Name the page **Change Background** in the Title region of the template. Remove the placeholders for the Content and Footer sections.

4. Type the following JavaScript block in the Content area of the page in Code view:

```
<script language="JavaScript" type="text/javascript">
arrColors = new Array();
arrColors = ([
'ff9999', 'ffffff', '66ff99', '00ff66', '99ffff', '3399ff',
'ff66cc', 'ff00ff', 'ff0000', 'ffff00', '33ff33', '66ff33',
'00ffff', '336699', '660099', 'ff33ff', 'cccc99', 'efbd00',
'33ff00', '006666', '0000aa', '6666cc', '990033', 'ff0099',
'660000', 'ff9933', '007700', '00aa00', '0000ff', '0000aa',
'990099', '33cccc', '220000', '660033', '002200', '001100',
'000077', '000055', '000033', '000099', '001100', '999900',
'999966', '777777', '339999', 'cccccc', '000000', 'ffffff',])
document.writeln('<table cellpadding="0" cellspacing="2"><tr>');
var q = 0;
for (p=0 ; p < 6 ; p++)
{
 for (i=0 ; i < 8 ; i++)
 {
  document.writeln('<td>');
  document.writeln('<a href="JavaScript:setColor(\'#');
  document.writeln(arrColors[q] + '\');">');
  document.writeln('<span style="background-color:' + arrColors[q] + '">');
```

```
    document.writeln('<img src="Images/spacer.gif" width="15" height="15"');
    document.writeln('alt="Click to change the background color to ');
    document.writeln(arrColors[q] + '" border="0"></span></a></td>');
    q++;
  }
  document.writeln('</tr><tr>');
}
document.writeln('</tr></table>');
function setColor(sColor)
{
  document.frmSetColor.txtColor.value = sColor;
}
</script>
```

The complete example is available in the code download for this chapter.

5. Add a form with a text box and a submit button to the page right after the script block you inserted in the previous step. Make sure it looks like this:

```
  document.frmSetColor.txtColor.value = sColor;
}
</script>
```
```
<form action="changeSiteBackground.asp" method="post" name="frmSetColor">
  <input name="txtColor" type="text" value="">
  <input name="btnSetColor" type="submit" value="Apply Color">
</form>
```

6. Insert an ASP code block at the top of the page, right after the line that starts with `<%@LAN-GUAGE="VBSCRIPT"`, and add the following code to it:

```
<%@LANGUAGE="VBSCRIPT" CODEPAGE="1252"%>
<%
```
```
  If Request.Form("btnSetColor") <> "" Then
    Response.Cookies("BackGroundColor") = Request.Form("txtColor")
    Response.Cookies("BackGroundColor").Expires = Date() + 30
  End If
```
```
%>
<!DOCTYPE HTML PUBLIC "-//W3C//DTD HTML 4.01 Transitional//EN"
  "http://www.w3.org/TR/html4/loose.dtd">
```

7. This example uses a few techniques (like writing tables and a `<span>` tag with a background color using JavaScript) that confuse most browsers (Internet Explorer, Mozilla, and Netscape) if you have defined a `<!DOCTYPE>` tag. To fix this issue, simply remove the entire DOCTYPE declaration for this page. Remove the code that is shown as the last two lines of the code block of the previous step. There is no need to remove this DOCTYPE for other pages in your site; it's just this color picker page that confuses browsers. If you don't remove the DOCTYPE, the color picker will be invisible in your site.

8. When you save and view the page you get a matrix with 48 colors defined in the JavaScript code, as shown in Figure 10-18. Once you click a color, its HTML color value is placed in the text box.

Save and close all the pages you may have open in Dreamweaver, because in the next step the template is once again updated.

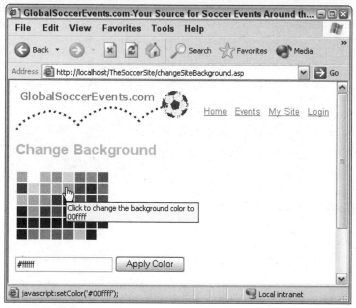

Figure 10-18

9. To apply the color that a user can select as the background of the page, you need to make two adjustments to your pages. You need to retrieve the cookie containing your background color and apply that color to the body tag. Open the template `mainTemplate.dwt.asp` and add this code in the ASP code block you created in the previous Try It Out exercise:

```
<!- TemplateBeginEditable name="head" -><!- TemplateEndEditable ->
<%
   Dim sBackgroundColor
   If Len(Request.Cookies("BackgroundColor")) > 0 Then
    sBackgroundColor = Request.Cookies("BackgroundColor")
   Else
    sBackgroundColor = "#ffffff" ' Our default background color
   End If
   Dim iTheme
   If Len(Request.Cookies("SiteTheme")) > 0 Then
```

10. Modify the `<body>` tag so it looks like this:

```
<body style="background-color: <%=sBackgroundColor%>">
```

11. Save your template so all pages using it are updated. You'll need to upload your pages as well so that the changes in the template are applied to the pages at the remote server. The easiest way to do this is to use the Put command for the entire site by right-clicking the site in the Files panel and choosing Put. Click OK when Dreamweaver asks for confirmation, and all the pages you have in your local site will be copied to the remote server.

12. Open `changeSiteBackground.asp` in your browser again, select a color, and click the Apply Color button. The page will refresh and the new background will be applied, as shown in Figure 10-19. If you browse to other pages in your site, they all show your new background color. You'll also see that just the outer border of the page has a changed background. Your menu and the content region still use the background color that you defined earlier in your style sheet (by providing a background color for the `<td>` tag). At the end of this chapter, we'll give you a clue as to how to solve this problem.

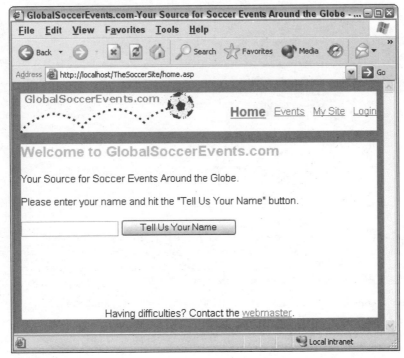

Figure 10-19

How It Works

The most interesting part of this exercise is the JavaScript function that creates the color matrix. By using an array populated with the color names and the `document.writeln` statements to create the actual table, you have designed a very easily maintainable solution. If you had used a client-side image map like you did with the map of Italy in Chapter 5, you would have had to create 48 regions that linked to the same JavaScript function. Also, if you wanted to change or add colors, or resize each color square, you would have had to redo the entire image map. With the JavaScript solution, it's easy to add or remove colors and change the appearance of each color square, as well as change the number of rows and columns in the table that holds the colors.

Now look at the code in more detail to see how it works:

```
<script language="JavaScript" type="text/javascript">
arrColors = new Array();
arrColors = ([
```

```
'ff9999', 'ffffff', '66ff99', '00ff66', '99ffff', '3399ff',
... // other colors here
'999966', '777777', '339999', 'cccccc', '000000', 'ffffff',])
```

First, a JavaScript array is declared that will hold all the color values. This array is then filled by assigning it a list of color values inside the square brackets, separated by commas.

```
document.writeln('<table cellpadding="0" cellspacing="2"><tr>');
```

You use the `document.writeln` function to write out the opening tag for the table that holds the color squares. If you used plain HTML instead, Dreamweaver would color half your page in yellow, indicating that you are missing some closing table tags. By writing the entire table using JavaScript, you can still generate valid markup.

```
var q = 0;
for (p-0 ; p < 6 ; p++)
{
 for (i=0 ; i < 8 ; i++)
 {
```

The variable `q` is a counter that goes from 0 to 47 to retrieve each of the 48 elements in the color array. Two loops are set up: The outer loop defines each row in the table and the inner loop is responsible for each column. Since there are 48 colors defined in the array, you create six rows with eight cells each. The outer `for` statement uses three blocks separated by semicolons to determine how long the loop should continue. For each iteration of the loop, a table row is created. It starts off by setting `p` to `0`. The loop continues as long as `p` is less than 6. At the end of each loop, the value of `p` is incremented by one. This causes the code to loop six times, from zero to five. The same principle is used with the `i` variable, only this time the code loops eight times to create each column of the matrix.

The `p++` and `i++` statements are a JavaScript coding shortcut to increase the value of a variable by one. `p++` is exactly the same as `p = p + 1`, where the value of `p` is increased by 1 and then assigned back to `p`.

If you add or remove colors, you should adjust the values for `p` and `i` as well. When you multiply `p` by `i`, the result must equal the number of colors defined in the array.

```
document.writeln('<td>');
document.writeln('<a href="JavaScript:setColor(\'#');
document.writeln(arrColors[q] + '\');">');
document.writeln('<span style="background-color:' + arrColors[q] + '">');
document.writeln('<img src="/Images/spacer.gif" width="15" height="15"');
document.writeln('alt="Click to change the background color to ');
document.writeln(arrColors[q] + '" border="0"></span></a></td>');
q++;
}
```

Inside the inner loop the opening `<td>` tag is created and then an `<a>` element is added that links to the `setColor` function. The color value that is retrieved from the array using `arrColors[q]` is passed to this function. The `<span>` element that is created next has a background color that matches the one from the array value. The transparent spacer image that is added to this `<span>` tag gets `width`, `height`, `alt`, and `border` properties. Because the spacer image is transparent, you can see the background that is defined for the `<span>` tag. The `alt` property of the image is used to display a tool tip that instructs the user to click a color to change the background. Finally, the `<span>`, `<a>`, and `<td>` tags are closed.

The `document.writeln` statement works more or less the same as the `Response.Write` statement of the ASP you used in earlier chapters, but in this case the code is executed at the client. This way you need to send only a couple of JavaScript lines to create a table with 48 cells instead of the complete HTML markup for all the `<td>` tags. By limiting the size of the page, the browser downloads it much faster:

```
  document.writeln('</tr><tr>');
}
```

In the outer loop, each table row is closed and a new one opened:

```
document.writeln('</tr></table>');
```

When all table cells have been written, the last row and the table are closed as well:

```
function setColor(sColor)
{
  document.frmSetColor.txtColor.value = sColor;
}
</script>
```

Finally, a simple JavaScript function is used to put the color in the text box, which should be familiar by now.

When you look at the source of the page in the browser, you'll see the original JavaScript and not the outcome of the `writeln` statements. To see what you end up with, look at the source as the browser creates it internally to render a single table cell:

```
<td>
<a href="JavaScript:setColor('ff9999');">
 <span style="background-color: # ff9999">
   <img src="Images/spacer.gif" width="15" height="15" alt="Click to
      change the background color to ff9999" border="0">
 </span>
</a>
</td>
```

As you can see, nothing fancy is going on—it's just a simple transparent image in a span with a background color that links to a JavaScript function.

The method used to retrieve the value from the cookie and place it inside the `<body>` tag is the same as the method used for the style sheet to change your theme earlier in this chapter, so we won't go over that again.

In this example, you used the color picker to change the background color of the `<body>` tag. However, you could expand this example so visitors can change other aspects of the site as well. You could, for example, change the color and background color of the `<h2>` tag used throughout the site, or define a custom CSS class in the template and change its color. If you are going to store multiple values in cookies, it's best to save them as a key collection in one cookie because this minimizes the number of cookies you need to create in your site.

As you saw in Chapter 8, storing keys in a cookie is very easy. All you need to do is provide a key name between parentheses after the name of the cookie. Here's a short example:

```
<%
  Response.Cookies("SiteSettings")("BackGroundColor") = "blue"
  Response.Cookies("SiteSettings")("TextColor") = "white"
  Response.Cookies("SiteSettings").Expires = Date() + 30
%>
```

The code above creates one cookie called SiteSettings with two keys: BackGroundColor and TextColor. The entire cookie with both keys lasts for 30 days. To retrieve this cookie again, use the same (CookieName)(KeyName) mechanism, but this time use the Request object:

```
<%
  Response.Write("<br>Background color is " & _
          Request.Cookies("SiteSettings")("BackgroundColor"))
  Response.Write("<br>Text color is " & _
          Request.Cookies("SiteSettings")("TextColor"))
%>
```

As a completely different solution for changing the appearance of your site, you can let users choose various style elements in a form, including colors and fonts, and then save those values in a dynamically generated style sheet. I once built a site for a client where complete control over all the visual parts of the site was very important. In that site, I used a form where users could select various CSS classes and then change the color, font, borders, and other CSS styles. Once they submitted their forms to the server, a new style sheet was generated on the fly using the FileSystemObject. The file was saved with the user's ID as its name, so it was easy to hook up that personal style sheet whenever the visitor returned to the site.

As you can see, there are many ways you can allow visitors to change the appearance of your site. However, changing the colors alone may not be enough. In the next Try It Out exercise you can let users choose the badge of their favorite club to match the colors they have selected. The badge replaces the logo that otherwise appears in the upper left corner of the site's pages.

Changing the Site Badge

This section describes a few different techniques you can use to create a page where users select a country and then choose the badge (or logo) from the soccer clubs that play in that country to replace the site's logo. First you will use a dynamically created drop-down list so that users can select a country. Then the badges of the clubs that play in that country are shown. Once your visitors select a badge, their preferences will be saved in a cookie and they'll be redirected to mySite.asp, which shows the new badge.

The page that allows you to change the site badge looks like Figure 10-20.

Figure 10-20

This example contains quite a bit of repetitive code. For example, the definition and behavior of an image with the badge is the same for each club. We won't list all of the code here but you can find the complete example in the chapter's code download, along with the necessary image files.

Try It Out   **Creating the Country Drop-Down List**

1. Add another page to the root of your site and call it **changeSiteBadge.asp**. Don't forget to base the page on your main template. You may need to choose Modify⇨Templates⇨Update Current Page to update the link to the dynamic style sheet. Name the page **Select Your Favorite Badge** in the Title region of the template. Remove the placeholders for the other two template regions.

2. Once again, create a menu item so the user can reach changeSiteBadge.asp from the My Site page. Open mySite.asp and locate the link to changeSiteBackground.asp in Code view. Type **
** right after it and press Enter, or just press Shift+Enter to create both the <br> tag and the new line in one stroke. Type **Change Site Badge**, highlight it, and choose Insert⇨Hyperlink to turn the text into a link. Choose changeSiteBadge.asp as the page you want to link to and click OK to close the Hyperlink dialog box. The code for the menu now looks like this:

```
<a href="changeSiteTheme.asp">Change Site Theme</a><br>
<a href="changeSiteBackground.asp">Change Background</a><br>

<a href="changeSiteBadge.asp">Change Site Badge</a>
```

Save the page and close it.

3. On the `changeSiteBadge.asp` page, click inside the content region of the template in Code view and choose Insert⇨Form⇨Form from the menu bar. Set the form's action to **changeSiteBadge.asp**, its method to **post**, name it **frmSelectBadge**.

4. Inside the form create a dynamic drop-down list that holds a list of countries. Before you can add the list, create a dynamic variable that preselects an item in the list. Open the Bindings panel on the Application panel group (press Ctrl+F10) and click the plus (+) button. Choose Request Variable from the list and fill in the resulting Request Variable dialog box so it looks like Figure 10-21.

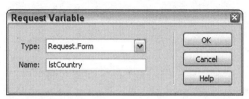

Figure 10-21

Click OK to insert the variable into your site.

5. Add a drop-down list to the form by selecting Insert⇨Form⇨List/Menu. Make sure you are still in Code view so you get the Tag Editor for the `<select>` tag. Name the list **lstCountry**, expand the Events list, and type **document.frmSelectBadge.submit();** in the text box for the `onChange` event. Click OK to close the Tag Editor. This bit of JavaScript causes the form to be automatically submitted to the server as soon as the user selects a new item from the list.

6. Behind the closing `</select>` tag, enter four `<br>` tags to create some room in the page after your drop-down list. Your form definition now looks like this (notice we indented the code to improve readability):

```
<!- InstanceBeginEditable name="Content" ->
```
```
<form action="changeSiteBadge.asp" method="post" name="frmSelectBadge">
<select name="lstCountry" onChange="document.frmSelectBadge.submit();">
</select>
<br><br><br><br>
</form>
```

7. Save the page, switch to Design view, select the drop-down list you just created, and then click the Dynamic button on the Property inspector. Add four items to the list by clicking the plus (+) button, and set Value and Label as shown:

Value	Label
	Select a Country
1	England
2	The Netherlands
3	USA

The Dynamic List/Menu dialog box should look like Figure 10-22.

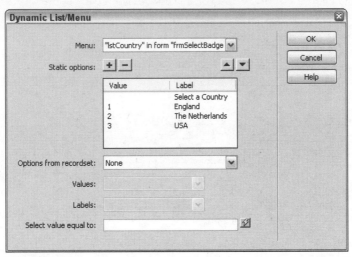

Figure 10-22

8. Click the button with the lightning bolt right after the Select Value Equal To text box. This allows you to select a variable that determines which country in the drop-down list appears selected in the browser. In the Dynamic Data dialog box that follows, expand Request and select Form.lstCountry, as shown in Figure 10-23.

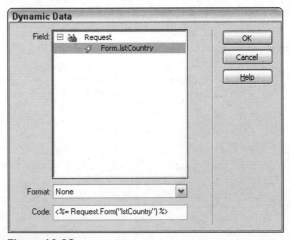

Figure 10-23

9. Once you select Form.lstCountry, Dreamweaver adds `<%= Request.Form("lstCountry") %>` to the Code box at the bottom of the dialog box. Click OK twice to close the Dynamic Data and the Dynamic List/Menu dialog boxes. Dreamweaver has inserted the following `<option>`- elements between your `<select>` tags:

```
<select name="lstCountry" onchange="document.frmSelectBadge.submit();">
<option value="" <%If (Not isNull(Request.Form("lstCountry"))) Then _
  If ("" = CStr(Request.Form("lstCountry"))) Then _
    Response.Write("SELECTED") : _
      Response.Write("")%>>Select a Country</option>
<option value="1" <%If (Not isNull(Request.Form("lstCountry"))) Then _
  If ("1" = CStr(Request.Form("lstCountry"))) Then _
    Response.Write("SELECTED") : _
      Response.Write("")%>>England</option>
<option value="2" <%If (Not isNull(Request.Form("lstCountry"))) Then _
  If ("2" = CStr(Request.Form("lstCountry"))) Then _
    Response.Write("SELECTED") : _
      Response.Write("")%>>The Netherlands</option>
<option value="3" <%If (Not isNull(Request.Form("lstCountry"))) Then _
  If ("3" = CStr(Request.Form("lstCountry"))) Then _
    Response.Write("SELECTED") : _
      Response.Write("")%>>USA</option>
</select>
```

Dreamweaver puts each statement on one line, but we added a few underscores to this code to improve readability as it wraps over multiple lines.

10. Save the page, view it in your browser by pressing F12 and select an item from the drop-down. The dynamic drop-down list remembers the selection you make (see Figure 10-24).

Figure 10-24

How It Works

After you created the initial page, you added a drop-down list containing a list of countries. You used a dynamic value to make the drop-down list remember its last selection. Take a look at the code that Dreamweaver created for you:

```
<option value="1" <%If (Not isNull(Request.Form("lstCountry"))) Then _
   If ("1" = CStr(Request.Form("lstCountry"))) Then _
     Response.Write("SELECTED") : _
       Response.Write("")%>>England</option>
```

`Request.Form("lstCountry")` has a value after the form has been submitted through the `onchange` handler you added to the `<select>` tag. Inside this block of HTML, a check is performed with some inline ASP script to see if the value from `Request.Form("lstCountry")` equals the value for the current option tag. If they are equal, the text SELECTED is written to the browser so the item appears selected in the browser. This check is repeated for each item in the drop-down list.

The way this code works is pretty much the same as in Chapter 8, where you built the select mechanism yourself. You now have two ways to create intelligent drop-down lists. You can use Dreamweaver if you need to create a quick drop-down that remembers its selection. But you can also create one by hand if you need finer control over the way the drop-down list appears in the browser.

With the drop-down list in place, you can now add the images with the badges for each club in a country. Once you select a country from the drop-down list, you will show the badges of the clubs that play in that country. When you click a badge, the default logo in the site will be replaced with that badge.

Try It Out   Changing the Site Badge

1. First you need to change your current logo in the template. To be able to refer to the image in your code, it needs a name and ID attribute. Because the logo is placed inside the mainMenu.lbi library item, you should change the image there. If you have any pages open in Dreamweaver, close them before you change the library item. Open mainMenu.lbi from the Library folder and locate and select the logo in the top-left corner of the page in Design view. Type **imgDefaultBadge** as the name and **id** for the image below the thumbnail preview image on the Property inspector.

2. Remove the height and width attributes of the <img> tag. You can do that by clearing the height (H) and width (W) text boxes on the Property inspector. If you leave these attributes in place, the browser may incorrectly scale the proportions of the images if you use images with a different size than the default logo you are using. When you remove the attributes, each image takes up as much room as it needs. If all your images are of the same size, you can leave the height and width properties as they were. The HTML definition for the <img> tag now looks like this:

```
<tr>
  <td><img src="../Images/logo.gif" name="imgDefaultBadge"
      id="imgDefaultBadge"></td>
  <td><table border="0" align="right" cellpadding="0" cellspacing="0">
```

Save the library item. This updates the template and all other pages that use the library item and template as well. Close the library item; there are no other changes needed.

3. Create some images with the club badges on them. You can find 10 sample images in the code download but you can, of course, create your own. In that case, make sure you name them in

the correct format of badgeX.gif (where *X* is a number from 1 to 10), so your code can identify them. Make sure they are not too big; about 250 × 60 pixels is ideal.

In either case, place the 10 images in your Images folder in the local folder using Windows Explorer and use Dreamweaver's Put command to upload the images to your remote server. Right-click the Images folder on the Files panel and choose Put.

4. With the drop-down list and default badge in place, you'll need to write some ASP code that reacts to the country the user chooses. For each country in the list, display the badges for the clubs playing in that country. Open changeSiteBadge.asp, add an ASP code block right *before* the closing </form> tag, and add the following Select Case skeleton:

```
<%
Select Case Request.Form("lstCountry")
Case "" ' No country chosen yet
%>
 Please select a country from the list
<%
Case 1 ' England
%>


<%
Case 2 ' The Netherlands
%>


<%
Case 3 ' USA
%>


<%
End Select
%>
</form>
```

You may wonder why you added %> and <% ASP tags after each Case statement. Between the closing and opening ASP tags, you will place some HTML that displays the images for the country. Because you can't put plain HTML between ASP tags, you need to close and open each code block for every country.

The "Please select a country from the list" message is only shown the first time the page is requested.

5. Next, you are going to Insert the images that represent the badges for each club in a country. If you look at the Design view, you'll see four ASP blocks defined after the "Please select a country from the list" message. Each ASP code block is represented by a little icon with the letters "ASP" on it, as shown in Figure 10-25.

If you don't see the ASP code icons, turn on the option to show them. Open the Preferences dialog box (press Ctrl+U) and then make sure in the Invisible Elements category that Visual Server Markup Tags (ASP, CFML,...) is selected.

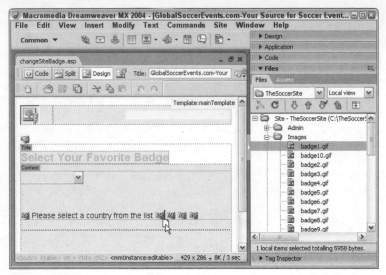

Figure 10-25

Drag the `badge1.gif` image from the `Images` folder and drop it between the first and second ASP icons to the right of the message in Design view, as shown in Figure 10-25. This inserts the image in the `Case` statement for England:

```
Case 1 ' England
%>
```

```
  <img src="Images/badge1.gif" width="257" height="58">
```

```
<%
Case 2 ' The Netherlands
```

You have quite a lot of different steps to perform on the images, so use the Dreamweaver IDE to apply all the necessary behaviors to one image and then copy and paste it to apply these behaviors to the other images. You will do this in the next Try It Out exercise.

6. Select the image you inserted in Step 5 in Design view and call it **badge1** using the Property inspector. Open the Behaviors panel on the Tag <img> panel group by pressing Shift+F3 and choose Swap Image from the plus (+) button menu. Dreamweaver notices the image you add to the template and lists it in the Swap Image dialog box, as shown in Figure 10-26.

Select the first image in the Images list (image "imgDefaultBadge") and then click Browse and browse to `badge1.gif` in the `Images` folder to set the Set Source To text box. Leave the two check boxes for preloading and restoring the image checked and click OK. Dreamweaver wraps the image in an `<a>` tag that looks like this:

```
<a href="javascript:;"
 onMouseOver="MM_swapImage('imgDefaultBadge','','Images/badge1.gif',1)"
 onMouseOut="MM_swapImgRestore()">
 <img src="Images/badge1.gif" name="badge1" width="257"
   height="58" border="0" id="badge1">
</a>
```

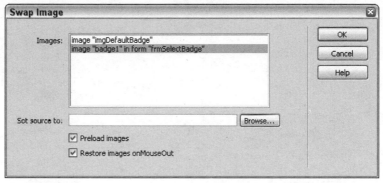

Figure 10-26

If you find that Dreamweaver doesn't add the <a> tag, you may have told Dreamweaver to create code for modern browsers only. If that's the case, click the plus (+) button on the Behaviors panel again, open Show Events For, and choose 3.0 and Later Browsers. This ensures the greatest browser compatibility. You'll need to redo the previous steps to get Dreamweaver to create the Swap Image behavior correctly.

Because you are creating an `onclick` handler for the `<img>` tag, you need to disable the click handler that Dreamweaver adds to the `<a>` tag for you. Otherwise, the `onclick` for your image won't fire. The easiest way to do that is to change this:

```
<a href="javascript:;"
```

to this:

```
<a href="#"
```

By changing `javascript:;` to #, you tell the browser that your link should not call JavaScript; you want it to be a normal HTML link. Linking to a # has no visual effect in the browser window but it allows the `onclick` event of the image nested in your `<a>` tag to fire.

7. Save and view the page, select England from the drop-down list, and hover your mouse pointer over the badge for the selected country. Once you do that, the default image at the top of your page changes to reflect the badge you are hovering over, as shown in Figure 10-27.

Figure 10-27

How It Works

You performed two important actions in this exercise. First, you added an ASP code block that displays badges of clubs for a specific country that has been chosen by the user. Right now, only one image is displayed, but you'll add more in the next Try It Out exercise.

```
Select Case Request.Form("lstCountry")
Case "" ' No country chosen yet
%>
 Please select a country from the list
<%
```

The same kind of check that determines which item should be selected in the list of countries is used to determine which badges to display for which country. If Request.Form("lstCountry") does not have a value because it equals an empty string (indicated by ""), a message instructs users to select a country from the list. Once the user makes a valid selection, some HTML code is generated, which contains the badges for the selected country.

Second, you applied a Swap Image behavior. You have seen in other chapters how this behavior works, so we won't go over the complete code that Dreamweaver creates for you. What's important is to see which image you need to swap when the user hovers over one of your badges:

```
<%
Case 1 ' England
%>
<a href="#"
 onMouseOver="MM_swapImage('imgDefaultBadge','','Images/badge1.gif',1)"
 onMouseOut="MM_swapImgRestore()">
```

```
<img src="Images/badge1.gif" name="badge1" width="257"
height="58" border="0" id="badge1">
</a>
```

You can see from this code that the image at the top of your page should be swapped by passing its name, `imgDefaultBadge`, to the `MM_swapImage` function. This causes the image to change when the user hovers over a badge. The `onMouseOut` event calls the `MM_swapImgRestore` function, which makes sure that the original image is restored when the user moves the mouse away from the image.

Now that you have your swap image behavior added to your badge, you'll need to make one more adjustment to the image. In the next Try It Out exercise, you'll create an `onclick` event handler that submits the form to the server when the user clicks an image. On the server, some ASP code finds out which image was clicked. This image is then placed as the site logo in the top left corner of the site. Once you have the `onclick` handler added to the image, you can copy the complete code for one image and paste it multiple times to create different badges for the various countries.

Try It Out   Finishing the Badge Chooser

1. You'll need to create a click handler that submits the form when you click one of the images with the badge on it. The click handler calls a custom JavaScript function that saves the name of the image in a hidden form field and then submits the form to the server.

In `changeSiteBadge.asp`, locate the image you have added for England in Design view, click it once to select it, and then press Ctrl+F5 to open the Tag Editor. Expand the Events list, click `onClick`, and then type **submitForm(this.name);** in the text box to the right. Click OK to close the Tag Editor dialog box.

2. Now that the first image is finished, copy the image code for each badge you create. Select the entire `<a>` tag using the tag selector at the bottom of the screen and press Ctrl+C to copy the code to the Clipboard. Deselect the code and click right after the closing `</a>`. Press Enter once and then press Ctrl+V to paste the code you copied in the page. Repeat this two more times so you end up with four images for England, each on its own line in Code view. Repeat this step but, this time, paste the code three times in the section for The Netherlands and three times for the USA.

3. Locate the second `<a>` tag, the one you created in Step 2, and replace all four occurrences of `badge1` with `badge2`. You'll find one in the `MM_swapImage` function, two in the `name` and `id` attributes of the image, and one in the `onclick` event handler of the image. Use Find and Replace (press Ctrl+F) to make it easier to replace the items. Repeat this step for the other two images for England, and name them **badge3** and **badge4**, respectively.

Your code for England should now look like this:

```
Case 1 ' England
%>
<a href="#"
 onMouseOver="MM_swapImage('imgDefaultBadge','','Images/badge1.gif',1)"
 onMouseOut="MM_swapImgRestore()">
 <img src="Images/badge1.gif" name="badge1" width="257"
    height="58" border="0" id="badge1" onClick="submitForm(this.name);">
</a>
```

```
<a href="#"
 onMouseOver="MM_swapImage('imgDefaultBadge','','Images/badge2.gif',1)"
 onMouseOut="MM_swapImgRestore()">
 <img src="Images/badge2.gif" name="badge2" width="257"
    height="58" border="0" id="badge2" onClick="submitForm(this.name);">
</a>
<a href="#"
 onMouseOver="MM_swapImage('imgDefaultBadge','','Images/badge3.gif',1)"
 onMouseOut="MM_swapImgRestore()">
 <img src="Images/badge3.gif" name="badge3" width="257"
    height="58" border="0" id="badge3" onClick="submitForm(this.name);">
</a>
<a href="#"
 onMouseOver="MM_swapImage('imgDefaultBadge','','Images/badge4.gif',1)"
 onMouseOut="MM_swapImgRestore()">
 <img src="Images/badge4.gif" name="badge4" width="257"
    height="58" border="0" id="badge4" onClick="submitForm(this.name);">
</a>
```

4. Repeat this step for the other six images you have on your page, numbering them from **badge5** to **badge10**. Save the page and view it in your browser. Choose a country from the list and hover your mouse over the images. Each image is shown at the top of the page when you hover over an image. If you get an incorrect image at the top, or a JavaScript error, you may have forgotten to change one of the names for the images, or misspelled it.

In Design view your page looks like Figure 10-28. Don't worry about all the teams' badges being displayed here; the ASP code ensures that only the correct badges appear in a visitor's Web browser.

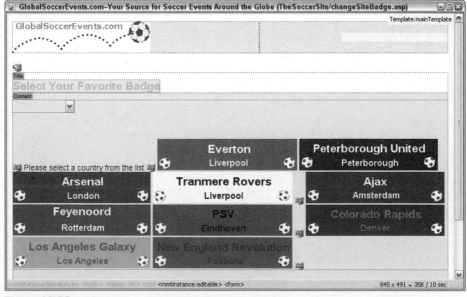

Figure 10-28

5. Return to `changeSiteBadge.asp` in Dreamweaver again and add a hidden text field at the top of the form, right after the opening `<form>` tag, by selecting Insert⇨Form⇨Hidden Field. Name it **txtSelectedBadge** and leave its value empty. This is how the hidden field looks after you click OK:

```
<form action="changeSiteBadge.asp" method="post" name="frmSelectBadge">

 <input name="txtSelectedBadge" type="hidden" value="">
 <select name="lstCountry" onChange="document.frmSelectBadge.submit();">
```

6. Add the following function to the JavaScript block at the top of the page right after the `MM_swapImage()` function that Dreamweaver creates, but before the closing `</script>` tag:

```
function submitForm(sSelectedBadge)
{
 document.frmSelectBadge.txtSelectedBadge.value = sSelectedBadge;
 document.frmSelectBadge.submit();
}
```

7. To give your visitors instructions on how to change the site logo, add the following code to the beginning of the ASP code block with the `Select Case` statement:

```
<br><br><br><br>
<%

If Request.Form ("lstCountry") <> "" Then %>
 Hover your mouse over an image to see how it looks in the upper
 left hand corner of the screen and then click it to make it stick.
 <br><br><br>
<%
End If
Select Case Request.Form("lstCountry")
Case "" ' No country chosen yet
```

This displays the instructive message only after the user chooses a country from the drop-down list.

8. As the last action in your page, add some server-side ASP code that saves the badge the user chooses in a cookie. Add an ASP code block to the top of the page, right after the line starting with `<%@LANGUAGE:`

```
<%@LANGUAGE="VBSCRIPT" CODEPAGE="1252"%>
<%

 If Request.Form("txtSelectedBadge") <> "" Then
  Response.Cookies("SelectedBadge") = Request.Form("txtSelectedBadge")
  Response.Cookies("SelectedBadge").Expires = Date() + 30
  Response.Redirect("mySite.asp")
 End If
%>
<!DOCTYPE HTML PUBLIC "-//W3C//DTD HTML 4.01 Transitional//EN"
 "http://www.w3.org/TR/html4/loose.dtd">
```

Save and close any page that's still open because the template is going to be updated again. To save all open files quickly, click the Save All button on the Standard toolbar (to the right of the Save button). Press Ctrl+Shift+W to close all open pages at once.

9. You need to make two small adjustments to your template and the library item. In the template, you'll need to retrieve the selected badge from the cookie and display the corresponding image. If there is no cookie present, the code falls back to the default badge for your site, called `logo.gif`. Open `mainTemplate.dwt.asp` from the `Templates` folder and type the following code right after the code block you created to retrieve the theme cookie:

```
iTheme = 1 ' Our default theme
End If
```

```
Dim sBadge
If Len(Request.Cookies("SelectedBadge")) > 0 Then
  sBadge = Request.Cookies("SelectedBadge")
Else
  sBadge = "logo" ' Our default logo
End If
%>
```

Make sure you *do not* save the template yet!

10. Open `mainMenu.lbi` from the `Library` folder. You need to change the `<img>` tag for the site badge in this file so its `src` attribute is based on the variable `sBadge`:

```
<tr>
```

```
<td><img src="../Images/<%=sBadge%>.gif" name="imgDefaultBadge"
    id="imgDefaultBadge"></td>
```

```
<td>
  <table border="0" align="right" cellpadding="0" cellspacing="0">
```

11. Save the library item by pressing Ctrl+S. Dreamweaver updates all the pages that are based on it, including your template. Next, switch back to `mainTemplate.dwt.asp` again and save it as well. Once again, Dreamweaver updates all pages based on this template. From now on, the site badge the user selects appears throughout the site.

The order in which you perform these steps is important. If you save the library item after you save the template, Dreamweaver doesn't correctly change the relative path to the image. Apparently, the library item engine gets confused by your dynamic image paths. This causes the image in pages in the root of your site to be referenced as follows:

```
<img src="../Images/<%=sBadge%>.gif" name="imgDefaultBadge"
    id="imgDefaultBadge">
```

As you can see, the leading two dots and the slash are now copied to pages in the root of your site as well. The template engine, however, correctly deals with this situation, updating the pages that use your template and correcting the problems. If you have already saved the template, make a minor change to it (add a space for instance), undo your change, and then resave the template. This causes the errors to be fixed as well. Alternatively, you can choose Modify⇨Templates⇨ Update Pages to reapply the template. After you update the pages based on the template, remove the DOCTYPE declaration again from the page `changeSiteBackground.asp` because it has been added back by the template updating.

There is one minor problem with this solution. Dreamweaver cannot resolve the value for `sBadge` at design-time, so it's unable to display your image in Design view. Fortunately, Dreamweaver displays a default "broken image" instead, so you can still see where the image is supposed to appear, as shown in Figure 10-29.

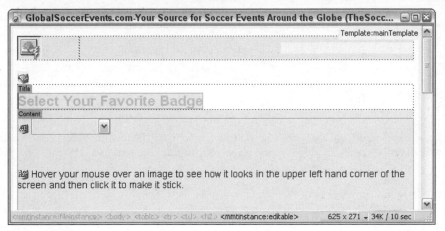

Figure 10-29

12. Upload any page that has changed to your remote server. Once again, the easiest way to do this is to right-click the site and choose Put. Open `mySite.asp` in your browser and then select the Change Site Badge menu item. Choose a country and hover over the images to change the badge in the upper-left corner of the page. Once you see a badge you like, click it. You will be redirected to `mySite.asp` again, where you'll see your new badge applied. From now on, all the pages in your site will show the user-selected badge instead of the default one.

How It Works

We have covered quite a lot of ground in this example, using a mix of client-side and server-side code and HTML. To see how it works, let's go over the steps you have taken, zooming in on the most important concepts.

When the user clicks an image, a custom JavaScript function called `submitForm` is called. You pass it a special value of `this.name`. In JavaScript `this` is a context-sensitive reference to the object that's currently using it. In this case, `this` is the image. Once you have the reference to the image, use its name property to retrieve its name. You could have passed 'badge1' instead, for example, but using `this.name` makes the code more flexible and easier to reuse because it changes dynamically for each image that uses it. If you had passed 'badge1' you would have needed to change the parameter for each image in your code.

The `submitForm` function does two simple things. It saves the name of the incoming image to a hidden form field and then it submits the form. Once the form is submitted, it gets processed on the server by the ASP code block you added to the top of your page. The first thing the code does is check whether the hidden form field has a value:

```
<%
  If Request.Form("txtSelectedBadge") <> "" Then
```

If it does, it means that the user has submitted the form by clicking an image, so the code can continue. Then the value from the hidden text field is retrieved and saved in a cookie. If you'd chosen image 7 for the Netherlands, the cookie would get the value `badge7`:

```
        Response.Cookies("SelectedBadge") = Request.Form("txtSelectedBadge")
        Response.Cookies("SelectedBadge").Expires = Date() + 30
```

Once the cookie is set, the user is redirected back to the page mySite.asp:

```
      Response.Redirect("mySite.asp")
    End If
  %>
```

Now that the badge the user selects is saved in a cookie, there is one more step you need to perform: You need to display the correct badge on each page. In the template, you used the following block of code:

```
    Dim sBadge
    If Len(Request.Cookies("SelectedBadge")) > 0 Then
      sBadge = Request.Cookies("SelectedBadge")
    Else
      sBadge = "logo" ' Our default logo
    End If
```

This is almost identical to the code you used to determine the background of your page.

At runtime, sBadge either contains the selected badge from the cookie or it contains the default logo. In both cases, the image is shown using the following code:

```
    <img src="../Images/<%=sBadge%>.gif" name="imgDefaultBadge" id="imgDefaultBadge">
```

This concludes the last example of how to create personalization features for your site. With the ability to change the logo, visitors can now fully change the appearance of the site and customize it to suit their favorite team's colors and badge, for example.

Summary

Personalization in a site can be very important if you want users to return to your site. If you give them the opportunity to change the site to suit their preferences, there is a greater chance they will come back. There are really many ways you can let users customize the site.

In this chapter we mainly looked at ways to change the visual appearance of the site. First we looked at how to apply a theme by letting users select one from a list. By supplying a preview image, users can easily decide what theme they like best. Once they select a theme, their decision is stored as a cookie, which in turn is used to dynamically hook up a style sheet to your site.

The predefined style sheets offered to your users in the form of a theme may be a bit limited. You can't possibly think of all combinations of background colors, text colors, and fonts that your users may come up with. That's why you created an HTML and JavaScript color picker to allow a user to select a custom color. In our example, you only used the color picker to influence the background of the site, but expanding this example for other site elements is easy. You could even generate a style sheet on the server using the FileSystemObject so users exercise full control over the look of your site.

The final example looked at ways to change the images used in the site. The example demonstrated some rollover effects in combination with server-side ASP script to save the name of the selected soccer club badge as a cookie. Because you used Dreamweaver's template feature, applying the club badge to all pages is simply a matter of changing one page.

There are many more features you could come up with to personalize the site. You are not limited to changing colors or images. Use the same principle demonstrated in this chapter to move the location of the menu and logo or you can even let the user decide which countries they want to display in the countries list.

However, storing each and every user preference in a cookie might become rather tedious if you have too many preferences the user can change. If you want to give your visitor fine-grained control over the site, it's better to use a database to store all the settings they have changed. In the next three chapters we will teach you how to work with databases with ASP in Dreamweaver. You won't use the database to expand these personalization features, but we will explain all the details so you can put a database into action for all your site-personalization tasks.

Why Not Try . . .

1. As you saw in the Try It Out exercise where you changed the background color of your site, only the border around the menu and content section of the page changed color. This is because the style definition for the `<td>` tag in your style sheet takes precedence over the style for the `<body>` tag defined in the template. One solution to this problem is to apply a style definition to each and every `<td>` in your site. This is not a very wise solution because there are lots of `<td>` tags in all your pages. Besides, this unnecessarily increases the page size, because for each page that gets requested, all those style definitions are transferred to the client browser. You also cannot use ASP in your CSS file, so you can't use the variable `sBackgroundColor` in that file to change the background color at runtime.

    Try to change the template page, `mainTemplate.dwt.asp`, so that it applies the background the user has chosen by formatting all your `<td>` tags. You'll need to "think outside the box" to solve this puzzle.

    Hint: Move the background definition for the `<td>` tag from the style sheet to the template page.

2. Changing colors through CSS definitions is not the only thing that you can customize in your site. You can also change the font size, font face, or even the location where your menu appears. Try to create another customization feature where a user can determine the location of the menu. You could offer the user a choice between a right-aligned menu (as it currently is) and a left-aligned menu (at the location where the logo is now). To do this, you need to add a page called `changeMenuLocation.asp`, for example, to your site. On that page, add a drop-down list containing two items, left-align and right-align, and make sure the page POSTs back to itself. When the user selects a new item from the list, save the selected preference in a cookie.

    Inside the library item for the menu, you need this cookie again to determine the location of the menu. Code something like this:

```
<% If Request.Cookies("MenuLocation") = "left-align" Then %>
  <!- HTML for Menu Here ->
  <!- HTML for Image Here ->
<% Else %>
  <!- HTML for Image Here ->
  <!- HTML for Menu Here ->
<% End If %>
```

Don't forget to add a link to this page on the My Site page.

3. Besides personalizing the visual appearance of the site, you can also customize its content. Say that a particular visitor is not interested in events in the UEFA Cup Category. Try to come up with a solution that meets the requirements from this demanding customer. Here are the steps to follow:

❑ Create a page called changeVisibleCategories.asp.

❑ Add a link to this page on mySite.asp.

❑ On changeVisibleCategories.asp, create check boxes for the categories that are available in the drop-down list on events.asp.

❑ Add a submit button so your visitors can submit their preference to the server.

❑ At the server, store the chosen categories in a cookie. The easiest way to do this is to use a cookie with keys, one for each category. Save True in the cookie if the category is chosen, otherwise save False:

```
Response.Cookies("Categories")("ChampionsLeague") = "True"
Response.Cookies("Categories")("UEFACup") = "False"
```

In events.asp, use this cookie again to determine which categories you need to add to the list. You only need to change the drop-down list; there is no need to make any modifications to the section that displays the information form the chosen category.

Hint: Working with check boxes is almost the same as working with text boxes. Here's a way to find out whether a check boxes is selected or not. Imagine you have the following check box:

```
<input name="chkUEFA" type="checkbox" value="UEFA">
```

To find out whether your user selected this check box or not, use the following code:

```
If Len(Request.Form("chkUEFA")) > 0 Then
  ' UEFA was selected
Else
  ' UEFA was not selected
End If
```

Make a backup copy of events.asp before you try any of this. You'll need a fresh version in the next chapter.

Getting Information from a Database

Imagine that you want to update a page on a site like GlobalSoccerEvents.com. You have to download the particular page from your Web server using FTP or some other network transportation method, edit the file, and then upload it again. This is fine for very small Web sites or for pages that don't change very often. However, you soon realize it's no fun editing a static, fixed Web site this way, especially if your data changes frequently. To avoid such tedious (and error-prone) editing you should consider applying a server-side technology such as ASP, just as you have been doing so far.

Technologies such as CGI powered the first interactive functions on sites—mostly search engines and feedback forms. Quite often, the results of a form were simply added to a text file stored on the server, and users were notified, with an unceremonious message, that their feedback was received. This was, however, the beginning of truly dynamic and interactive Web sites.

Nowadays, with the wide range of server-side technologies available (ASP, PHP, JSP, ASP.NET, ColdFusion, and so on), the amount of interactivity you can add to your Web site is limited only by your imagination, the time you have available, and the budget you or your client are willing to spend. Database-driven catalogs, online ordering systems, real-time parcel tracking, route planning, and discussion forums are just some of the possibilities that come to mind.

These interactive applications have one thing in common: They are *database-driven*. Imagine a route planner or a discussion forum without a database. The only way to offer such an application over the Internet without a database is to have a person on the other end (with a very good memory) who can process your information extremely quickly, update a page, and send it back to you. Not a likely scenario.

Databases are so important for functional Web sites that we will spend the next three chapters discussing them and putting them to use in the sample site. We start with an introduction in this chapter to databases and how to use them in Dreamweaver MX 2004. Chapters 12 and 13 deal with displaying data from a database and storing data in a database, respectively.

In this chapter you'll learn the following:

❑ What a database is

❑ What kinds of different databases exist

❑ How Dreamweaver MX 2004 uses databases

❑ How you can connect to a database at runtime

❑ How you can retrieve and use information from a database

What Is a Database?

If you spend any time around computers, you probably have a vague idea (at least) of what a database is. But what *exactly* is a database? In its simplest form, a definition of a database could be this: A collection of data arranged in such a way that it's easy to search through and retrieve data from.

This is both helpful and confusing to you. It's helpful because it explains at least that a database is about storing and retrieving data. It's confusing because it doesn't define the boundaries of a database. According to this definition, the huge pile of documents on your desk right now is a database as well. The search order you've defined may be a bit hard to explain to others, but for you the data has been arranged in such a way that you can easily and quickly (right?) find the document you need. Until one day when the pile becomes too big and collapses, of course.

A more accurate description of a database would be this: A collection of data that is arranged so that the data can easily be accessed, managed, and updated.

Under this definition, your pile of documents is no longer a database because it lacks the ability to be easily managed and updated: You just add new documents on top of the stack and hope for the best.

Note that this definition does not require the database to be electronic. However, for the purpose of this book, of course, we mean an electronic, computer-based database.

By far the most popular database today is the *relational database*. This kind of database is what you see quite often used with Web applications. There are other types of databases as well, like flat-file, object-relational, and object-oriented databases, but these are less common on the Internet.

A relational database is a *tabular database,* which means that data is stored in *tables* that are split up into *rows* and *columns*—rather like a spreadsheet. Each complete row contains all the information about a specific item, such as a user or product, and is commonly called a *record*. Each column, on the other hand, contains information about one specific property of all the items in the table. This can be clarified by an example. Figure 11-1 displays a table from a Microsoft Access database. This database is the one you are going to use throughout this and the next two chapters to expand the sample site, and it's available in the code you can download from www.wrox.com.

ID	Name	Password	AccessLevel
1	CharlesEBrown	VerySecret	Administrators
2	ToddMarks	EvenMoreSecret	Members
3	ImarSpaanjaars	TopSecret	Administrators
(AutoNumber)			

Figure 11-1

Don't worry if you don't have Microsoft Access installed on your system. You don't need it to use the sample database in the examples that are coming up. Microsoft Windows and Dreamweaver MX 2004 ship with everything you need to access .mdb database files from ASP pages.

As you can see, one row defines a person. Each person has a unique ID, a Name, a Password, and an AccessLevel. You'll use the information from this database in a later section, so we'll explain what those columns are used for then. The (AutoNumber) entry that you can see in the ID column means that the ID is automatically generated so that each record gets a different ID. Because this process is handled by the database, Access calls this ID column an AutoNumber column. Other terms for this technique you might encounter in other databases are *sequence* or *identity*. To make sure that each ID can only appear once in the entire ID column, you need to change the column into a *primary key*. By using a primary key in your database table, you uniquely identify each record in the table because the primary key has to be unique throughout the table. The database enforces this uniqueness: As soon as you try to add a record with an ID that already exists, the database throws an error and prevents the record from being inserted.

How you turn a column into a primary key depends on the database you use. In Access you do this by clicking the button with a yellow key on it in the table designer.

All the records of people together make up the table. You could call this table "People." In this case, however, the table stores a more specific type of person—the users of your Web site—so a better name for this table is "Users."

The term *relational* in the definition of a database refers to the relationship that exists between two or more tables in a database. Consider the list of soccer events you want to display on your Web site. You could create a table called Events to hold some information about the event, like its title, its starting date, and so on. Each event could also belong to a certain category, such as Champions League, UEFA Cup, and US Major League Soccer. You could take the easy way out and just create a text column called Category in the Events table. The data in the table would then be stored as shown in Figure 11-2.

ID	Title	StartDate	EndDate	Category
1	Olimpija - Shelbourne	8/14/2003	8/14/2003	UEFA Cup
2	Los Angeles Galaxy - New England	9/6/2003	9/6/2003	US Major League Soccer
3	D.C. United - Metrostars	9/25/2003	9/25/2003	US Major League Soccer

Figure 11-2

This is all nice and easy until you decide to change the description of the US Major League Soccer category to US Major League Soccer (MLS). In that case, you would have to update each individual event in the table and append *(MLS)* to the category. This is where *relationships* come in handy. Figure 11-3 shows another example, to clarify how relationships work.

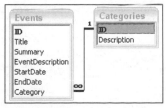

Figure 11-3

This figure shows the relationship between an event and a category. Instead of adding the category description to each individual event, you save all your categories in your Categories table once and give them a unique number (the primary key) that is stored in the ID column of the Categories table. Then, in the Events table, the Category column no longer holds the description for the category, but just the ID of the category from the Categories table. This way, you can use this ID to relate an event to a certain category. The infinity symbol and the number 1 on the relationship line indicate the type of relationship. In this case, it's a *one-to-many relationship*. This means that each event can only belong to one category, while a category can have many different events attached to it.

Suppose that you have defined the following categories in your database:

ID	Description
1	Champions League
2	UEFA Cup
3	National League
4	US Major League Soccer

To create a relationship between an event and a specific category, you can store the ID of the category you want in the Events table, instead of storing the complete name. The column Category is then said to contain a *foreign key*, where the foreign key points to a primary key in another table. Take a look at a simplified version of the Events table:

ID	Title	Category
1	Olimpija - Shelbourne	2
2	Los Angeles - D.C. United	4

The ID column for this table is also the primary key. This means that each ID can only appear once in the entire Events table, so you can uniquely identify an event from that table. The Title column holds a short description for the event and the Category column stores a foreign key; that is, it points to the primary key of the Categories table so you can find out to which category the event belongs.

In the Events table, you can see that the first event belongs to category 2, which is the UEFA Cup category. The second event belongs to US Major League Soccer. This technique, where possibly duplicated data is stored in its own table and then retrieved again using a foreign key, is called *normalization*. Not only does this save you from a lot of typing and from wasting space in the database (just a simple number is stored instead of text) it also gives you a flexible, powerful way to access and maintain your data. Now if you need to change one of your category descriptions, you only have to make the adjustment in one place, and all events related to this category will automatically benefit from this change.

In the design of the Users table, you can see a column called AccessLevel. This column is an ideal candidate for a foreign key as well. You could create a table called AccessLevels and only store the IDs from this table in the column AccessLevel in the Users table. In the sample site for this chapter we have chosen to put `AccessLevel` directly in the Users table. This allows you to focus on how to use data from a database and makes the code less complicated.

Over the course of this and the following two chapters, you'll learn how to retrieve data from the database, both from single and related tables. Although you have already seen some parts of it, we'll start by discussing the complete sample database that you are going to use in TheSoccerSite. We'll discuss the tables, their relationships, and the individual columns in the next section.

The Sample Database

A complete view of the design of a database and its relations is called a *database model*, or *database schema*. In this section you'll see a very simple version of a database model (see Figure 11-4). It's taken from the Microsoft Access Relationships view and it shows the tables and relationships in the sample database, which you'll use in the sample site.

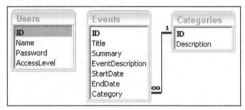

Figure 11-4

You can find the database in the code download for this book at www.wrox.com. *If you have Microsoft Access installed on your computer, you can open the database and play around with it a bit. Don't be afraid to mess things up because you can always revert to the downloaded version or download a fresh copy from your site.*

As you have seen, the Categories table is related to the Events table, while the Users table is unrelated. You could create a relationship between Users and Events by adding a `User` column to the Events table. This way, you could track which user creates or updates a certain event. For this sample site, we decided to leave out this relationship so things are easier to explain in the examples. But don't worry; there is still a link between the Events and Categories tables, so we'll be able to demonstrate how to use relations in a database.

The columns that you define in your tables can hold various types of information. For example, you may want to store a birthday as a date, while storing someone's name as text. These different types of information are called *data types*. In all database systems you see data types like Text, Date/Time, Number, Currency, and so on. Each column in your table must be of one of those types. By using a specific data type, the database makes sure that you don't accidentally insert the word *Soccer* in a column reserved for dates, for example.

Take a look at the columns that are defined in each table of the sample database so you can see what they are used for and what their data type is.

Users			
Column Name	**Data Type**	**Description**	
ID	AutoNumber	The unique ID of the user and the primary key of the Users table. The ID column can be used to track a certain user on your Web site, for example. Access will autogenerate this field.	
Name	Text	The name of the user. You use the Name field in this chapter to allow a user to log in to TheSoccerSite.	
Password	Text	The password that the user needs to access the site.	
AccessLevel	Text	The access level the user has when logging in. In the sample database, there are only two types: Members and Administrators. An Administrator can perform various maintenance functions on a site, while a Member can't.	

Events			
Column Name	**Data Type**	**Description**	
ID	AutoNumber	A unique ID of the event and the primary key for the Events table.	
Title	Text	A title, or description of the event.	
Summary	Text	A short version of what the event is about.	
Event Description	Memo. Memo is a specific kind of Text data type. The biggest difference is that it can hold large amounts of data, while a Text field is limited to 255 characters.	A detailed description of the event.	
StartDate	Date/Time	The start date of the event.	
EndDate	Date/Time	The end date of the event.	
Category	Number	The ID of the category the event belongs to. This is a foreign key and points to the ID column of the Categories table.	

Categories			
	Column Name	**Data Type**	**Description**
	ID	AutoNumber	A unique ID for the category and the primary key for the Categories table.
	Description	Text	The description, or name, of the category.

If you look closely at the table structure, you notice two things. First of all, each table in the database has an ID column. This isn't strictly necessary but it's often very useful because it allows you to identify each record in the table uniquely. If you don't have this primary key column, there is a chance that records may be duplicated. For example, for the Users table there may be two users with the same Name, Password, and AccessLevel. Although the Web site administrator should not allow this, it could be possible. By using an ID field, you can uniquely identify a record in your table, even if another record shares the same characteristics.

If you decide to add the ID column at a later stage in your development cycle, you may need to recode parts of your application so it can handle the new column correctly. That's why it's always good to add a unique ID column to every table you create right from the start.

The second thing to notice is that there are no spaces in column or table names. Although Access allows the use of spaces in column names, we strongly advise against using them. It will most likely cause all kinds of trouble later during development or while upsizing your database to another database system. To improve the readability of your column names, use an underscore to separate each word or start each word with a capital letter, like UserPreferences.

Different Kinds of Databases

For the sample site you'll build throughout this and the next two chapters, we have chosen to use a Microsoft Access database as the back-end system. The reason for an Access database is both its ease of use and the fact that it can be installed quite easily. The visual interface to create tables, relations, and other objects in the database, and the fact that it's relatively cheap, makes it an ideal tool for database design and prototyping. Also, because you can use Microsoft Access in your ASP pages on a Windows Web server without the need for additional software, Access is an ideal database.

However, while Access is a user-friendly database with which you can store and retrieve complex data quite easily, you need to be aware of its limitations. According to official Microsoft documents, the technical maximum number of concurrent, or simultaneous, users is 255. In practice, however, the limit of Access is reached sooner. Whenever you hit this limit depends on the structure of your Web site and database, whether you insert a lot of data or only read from the database, the productivity of your users, and other factors, but we have seen Web sites that were upgraded to a more powerful database when there were only 20 or 25 concurrent users. Note that 25 concurrent users is still quite a lot, though. It actually means 25 users requesting pages at the same time, which implies thousands and thousands of hits per day. You can find more information about Microsoft Access at www.microsoft.com/access.

Just so you know, there are alternatives that can do the same thing as Microsoft Access. Here's a list of a few of the most common and popular database systems available today:

❑ **Microsoft SQL Server:** Microsoft Access' big brother. It handles lots of users at the same time and has loads of features, which makes it a popular database system, supporting advanced database features like views, stored procedures, and transactions. Microsoft SQL Server can also be used in a Web farm environment, where many different Web servers and database servers handle requests as if they were one system. Microsoft SQL Server is a commercial product, which means it costs big bucks to use it on your Web site. If you are using an ISP (Internet Service Provider), there is a good chance they offer a package that includes SQL Server. You can find more information about SQL Server at www.microsoft.com/sql/, where you can also download a trial version of SQL Server.

❑ **Microsoft Desktop Engine (MSDE):** A "lite" version of SQL Server. It can be downloaded and used freely if you have a limited number of users (a maximum of five). MSDE uses the same technologies as the full version of SQL Server so it's easy to upgrade to SQL Server in case your site starts to grow and you need a bigger database. You can find more information about MSDE at www.microsoft.com/sql/msde/.

❑ **MySQL:** A very popular open-source database. It's more or less optimized for Web sites, as it's extremely fast at retrieving data. The latest release supports advanced features like transactions and stored procedures. MySQL is rather easy to install, runs on lots of different operating systems (including Windows, Linux, and Mac OS X), can be used from a wide variety of applications, and, best of all, it's free. You can find more information about MySQL at www.mysql.com.

❑ **PostgreSQL:** Another open-source database system. It supports most of the extended features that SQL Server and MySQL support, which makes it the "most advanced open source database available anywhere," according to the developers of the system. It's not as easy to install in Windows as either SQL Server or MySQL are, but there is a growing user community and commercial support available to help you get things running. Check www.postgresql.org for more information about PostgreSQL.

❑ **Oracle:** A commercial product that runs on a variety of platforms, including Unix, Linux, and Windows. It supports all the major features mentioned for the other databases and, according to Oracle Corporation, it is "the most scalable and full featured database available." You can find out more about Oracle Database at www.oracle.com, where you can also download a free developer's edition.

Securing a Database

Since Microsoft Access is a single file-based database, the location where you store the database is something you should consider carefully. If you store the database within the scope of your Web site, a malicious user can easily download it. Since sensitive information, such as usernames and passwords, is often stored in a database, you should take precautions to prevent this from happening.

Suppose your database is named TheSoccerSite.mdb and is located in a directory called Database under the root of the current site. Visitors can easily download the database by browsing to www.your domain.com/Database/TheSoccerSite.mdb. Obviously, this isn't something you would allow your users to do. There are two ways to overcome this problem:

❑ Place the database outside the scope of the Web site

❑ Restrict access to the database

On a Windows-based server, placing the database outside the scope of the Web site is as simple as moving it to any folder outside the directory structure of `C:\Inetpub\wwwroot`, which is usually the root folder of a Web site under IIS. Note that this location is only the default location; it's easy to set up other Web sites that use different folders. So if you create a folder called `C:\Databases` and place your `TheSoccerSite.mdb` file in that directory, the database can no longer be downloaded but you still can access it from your Web application. However, your site has now become a little more difficult to manage because you have files for your Web site in two different locations.

Alternatively, you can restrict access to the database so only authorized users are allowed to use or download the database. This method can only be used if your Web server and file system support this feature. On a Windows platform, this means you need IIS and have your file system formatted using NTFS (New Technology File System). You need to run Windows NT 4 Server, Windows 2000 Professional, Windows 2000 Server, Windows XP Professional, or an edition of Windows Server 2003.

If you're using Windows 2000 Professional Edition, your computer should be part of a Windows domain. Under Windows XP Professional you need to disable *simple sharing* to change security permissions. You can change this setting by opening Windows Explorer and choosing Folder Options from the Tools menu. You'll find the option at the end of the list on the View tab. Make sure that Use Simple File Sharing (Recommended) is not checked. Be sure to read the Windows documentation about this setting before you change it.

If you use Personal Web Server on Windows 98, for example, you're stuck with the first method.

This and the next two chapters assume you have placed the database in a folder called `Database` in your `TheSoccerSite` directory (`C:\Inetpub\wwwroot\TheSoccerSite\`) and that you have applied the right security restrictions to it. You will do this in the next Try It Out exercise. If you decide to store your database at a different location, be sure to change any path in the code that references the database.

Changing Access Permissions

Changing the permissions on a computer with IIS requires two steps: You'll need to restrict access to the database itself, and you'll need to change the security settings in IIS. In the following exercise, changes are made to the settings on your local computer, which should be your testing and remote server. If your remote server is a different computer, be sure to apply these changes there as well. If you have enough privileges on your own system, for example because you have administrative rights, you can perform the following steps yourself. Otherwise, you may need to get your system administrator or ISP to do this for you.

Try It Out   Restricting Access to the Database

1. First you need to change the security settings for the `TheSoccerSite.mdb` file on the file system. Instead of changing security settings for each individual file, change the settings on the parent folder. This way you can easily apply the same settings to each database you use in your site. You could, however, change the same settings on just the database file instead.

    Open Windows Explorer and browse to the directory where your site is located (`C:\Inetpub\wwwroot\TheSoccerSite`). Create a new folder inside it called **Database**. Copy the database file, `TheSoccerSite.mdb`, from the code download for this chapter to this new `Database` folder.

2. Right-click the new folder and choose Properties. Click the Security tab and you'll see a Database Properties dialog box similar to Figure 11-5.

Figure 11-5

If you don't see the Security tab, your disk drive may not support NTFS or you may have not disabled simple sharing for Windows XP. In the first case, use the first security option by moving the database folder outside the Web scope. In the second case, use the Options dialog box in Windows Explorer to disable simple sharing, as we described earlier.

In the Group or User Names section of the Database Properties dialog box you can see the users listed that currently have access to the folder. The names of the users and groups are shown in *MachineName\UserName* or *DomainName\UserName* format. You can see from Figure 11-5 that the machine is called TheSoccerServer and has a security group called Administrators.

3. If you are running Windows XP, click the Advanced button and then deselect the option Inherit from Parent the Permission Entries That Apply to Child Objects. Under Windows 2000, deselect the check box for Allow Inheritable Permissions from Parent to Propagate to This Object. In both cases, doing this allows you to set individual permissions on this folder instead of inheriting them from the parent folder.

You'll get a dialog box that allows you either to copy the permissions from the parent to this folder or remove them all. Click Copy and then click OK to close that dialog box. The settings from the parent will be copied to your Database folder.

Back in the Database Properties dialog box, if the Everyone group appears in the Group or User Names list, select it and click Remove. Repeat this step for the Users group on Windows XP. Removing permissions from the Everyone and Users groups by deleting their names from the list is generally a good idea because you don't want just anybody to be able to see and alter your files.

> Before you start changing permissions on every file on your system, we should warn you: Changing the wrong permissions for important files like system files can really mess up your system. Make sure you know what you are doing and take some time to read about file security in the Windows help system.

4. If names other than SYSTEM, Administrators, and CREATOR OWNER are listed, remove them too. Now the folder can't be accessed by anyone except the SYSTEM account, the creator of the database, and members from the Administrators group.

To allow the Web server to access the folder where the database resides, you need to give permissions to the account that IIS uses; on a standard Windows installation, the account is called IUSR_*MachineName,* where *MachineName* is the name of your computer. To add this account to the list of users, click the Add button. This brings up the Select Users or Groups dialog box, shown in Figure 11-6. The screen may look a bit different on Windows 2000.

Figure 11-6

5. Type **IUSR_***MachineName* in the text box at the bottom of the screen. Don't forget to replace *MachineName* with the name of your computer. Click OK to close the dialog box. Back in the Database Properties dialog box, you need to set the permissions for this newly added user.

6. Click the IUSR user in the Name box and select at least Modify, Read, and Write so the Web server allows this account both to read from and write to the database and save some temporary files that are created when the Web server accesses the database at runtime. If you have applied the security settings to just the database file instead of its parent folder, you still need to give the IUSR account Modify rights for the `Database` folder for these temporary files.

If you are not a member of the Administrators group, add your own account to the users that can access the database as well. In that case you need to repeat the steps you performed to add the IUSR account.

If your account has really limited permissions, you may need to contact your system administrator to change these settings for you.

When you are done, your Database Properties dialog box's Security tab should look similar to Figure 11-7.

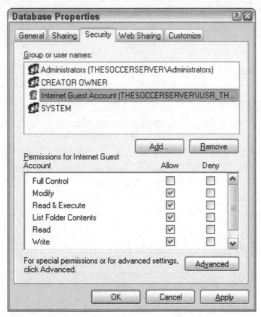

Figure 11-7

7. Click OK to close the dialog box.

8. Now it's time to change the settings in the Web server. Open the Internet Information Services management console, which can be found in Administrative Tools under Start⇨Programs or in the Control Panel. Open your Web site and locate the folder where the database resides, as shown in Figure 11-8.

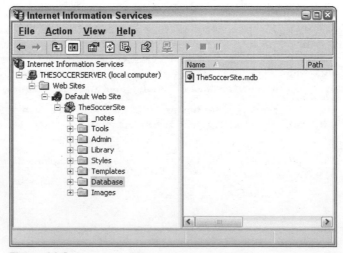

Figure 11-8

9.   Once you click the Database folder in the folder tree on the left, you'll see the database appear in the right pane. Right-click the Database folder in the tree and choose Properties. In the dialog box that appears, click the Directory Security tab and then click the Edit button under the Anonymous Access and Authentication Control section. Make sure the check box for Anonymous Access at the top is cleared and that Integrated Windows Authentication at the bottom is selected (see Figure 11-9).

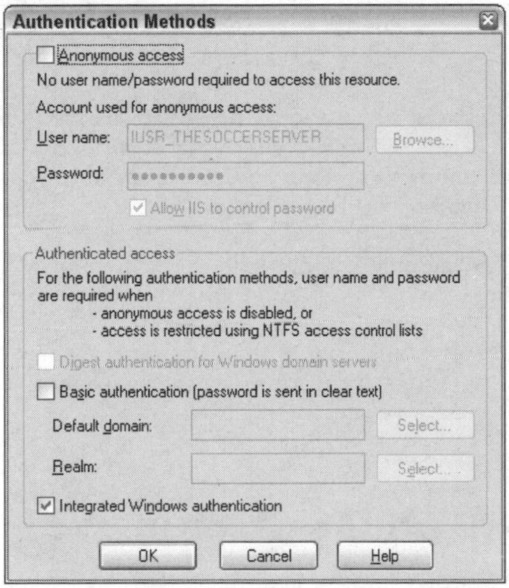

Figure 11-9

Disabling Anonymous Access prevents users from downloading the database without supplying a password, while Integrated Windows Authentication allows the Web server to use the database.

Click OK twice to accept these selections and close all open dialog boxes.

10. To test your new security settings, log off and log back in as a user with fewer privileges (the user shouldn't be listed in the Database Properties Security dialog box in Figure 11-7). If you are the only user on your system, you may need to create an additional user account. For Windows XP, find the User Accounts option in the Control Panel. For Windows 2000, right-click My Computer on the desktop, choose Manage, and then expand the Local Users and Groups item.

When you are logged in with the new user account, open your browser (you'll need to use Internet Explorer for this to work) and browse to http://localhost/TheSoccerSite/Database/TheSoccerSite.mdb. If everything works as expected, you'll be presented with a login dialog box where you can type the name and password of a user who is allowed to access the database to gain access to the file. Ordinary visitors don't have the required password, so your database is safe from prying eyes.

How It Works

Although you need to perform quite a lot of steps to protect your database, the principle behind it is quite simple. First the settings on the file system are changed, so only administrators, yourself, and the Web server are allowed to access the `Database` folder. Windows stores this information and won't allow access to any user who has not been assigned to the folder. Next you changed the settings on the `Database` folder in IIS by removing the Anonymous Access rights and setting the security mechanism to Integrated Windows Authentication instead. With Integrated Windows Authentication, the IUSR account is able to access your database. Because Internet Explorer supports Integrated Windows Authentication as well, you are able to download the database by supplying a valid username and password.

With Anonymous access enabled, requests to the file system are made under the context of the IUSR account. Since you gave this user the rights to access the database folder, it happily serves the database to anyone requesting it. By removing the Anonymous access, you force the user who wants to download your database to supply a valid username and password.

Notice that because the IUSR account is added to the list of accounts with access to the database, you can still use the database from within your Web application. It's just no longer possible to download the database without permission.

Now that you've finished with the security settings, it's time to take a look at some real work with databases.

Creating a Database-Driven Web Site

Before you can use a database in your Web site, you need to create a connection to that database in Dreamweaver MX 2004. This means you need to tell Dreamweaver what database you are using and where you store it. Dreamweaver then stores this information in a *connection string,* a file named after the connection, in the `Connections` folder.

As you can see, *connection* is the key word here. When you work with ASP pages in Dreamweaver, you have the choice of two connection methods: using a *DSN* (Data Source Name) or using a *custom connection string* (called DSN-less).

DSN Connection Strings

A DSN is a name that refers to either a file or registry setting that defines the options for a connection. The options can be quite diverse, as a DSN allows you to connect to a lot of different data sources.

You use a DSN-less connection in this and the next two chapters, but we'll walk you briefly through the process of creating your own DSN connection. Although a DSN-less connection is the preferred way to go, you may run into situations where a DSN is required, for instance when your ISP uses DSN connections.

Try It Out   **Creating a DSN**

   1.   To create a DSN, open the Data Sources (ODBC) control panel item, which you can find under Administrative Tools in the Start menu or in the Control Panel in Windows. Switch to the File DSN tab to see the dialog box shown in Figure 11-10.

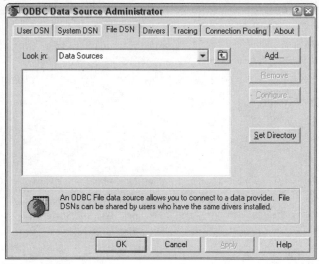

Figure 11-10

2. Click Add and you'll be presented with a wizard that takes you through the steps to create a DSN. In the first screen, select Microsoft Access Driver (*.mdb) from the list of drivers. Click Next.

3. On the second screen, type a name for the DSN, like **TheSoccerSite**. If you want to save your DSN in a different location than the default `C:\Program Files\Common Files\ODBC\Data Sources`, click Browse and select a new folder. When you're done, click Next and then click Finish.

4. In the ODBC Microsoft Access Setup dialog box (see Figure 11-11), click the Select button and then browse for your database in the `C:\Inetpub\wwwroot\TheSoccerSite\Database` folder. Select the database and then click OK.

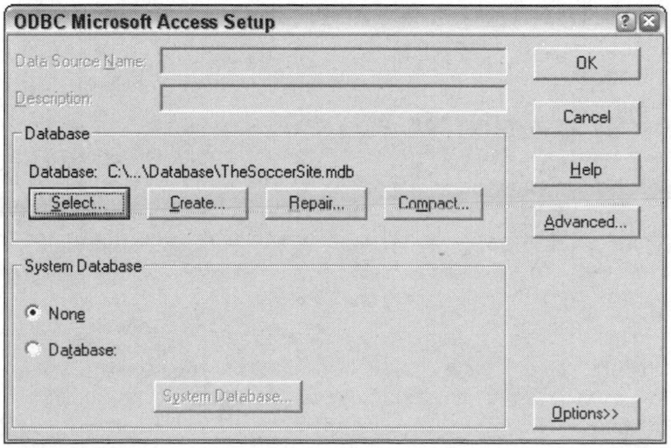

Figure 11-11

5. Click OK to close the ODBC Microsoft Access Setup dialog box and then click OK to close the ODBC Data Source Administrator dialog box as well.

6. Open the file you just created in Notepad (C:\Program Files\Common Files\ODBC\Data Sources\TheSoccerSite.dsn) and you'll see the following code:

```
[ODBC]
DRIVER=Microsoft Access Driver (*.mdb)
UID=admin
UserCommitSync=Yes
Threads=3
SafeTransactions=0
PageTimeout=5
MaxScanRows=8
MaxBufferSize=2048
FIL=MS Access
DriverId=25
DefaultDir=C:\Inetpub\wwwroot\TheSoccerSite\Database
DBQ=C:\Inetpub\wwwroot\TheSoccerSite\Database\TheSoccerSite.mdb
```

Instead of typing this information every time you need a connection, you can simply refer to the DSN by prefixing the DSN name with the keyword dsn=. Your complete connection string can look as simple as this:

```
dsn=TheSoccerSite;
```

How It Works

When you create the DSN, Windows creates a file named after your DSN, TheSoccerSite.dsn in your example. At runtime, when ASP needs to create a connection to your database, it looks at this file and sees where your database resides by looking at the DBQ variable, defined at the end of the DSN file. This database is then used in the connection to your site.

When you are working with a remote host, you will likely encounter a DSN because it allows your ISP to give you access to a database without the need to give you full access to the file system as well. In most cases, your ISP creates the DSN for you and gives you its name so you can simply refer to it in your code.

DSN-less Connection Strings

The other way to create a connection is to use a custom connection string. In fact, you should use a custom connection string wherever possible, although not all ISPs allow it. Not only will it perform faster because no file or registry lookup is necessary, but it's easier to maintain and transfer between two computers, such as your development and production servers. An example of a DSN-less connection could look like this:

```
Provider=Microsoft.Jet.OLEDB.4.0;Data Source=
  C:\Inetpub\wwwroot\TheSoccerSite\Database\TheSoccerSite.mdb;User
  Id=admin;Password=
```

This connection string defines a connection to a Microsoft Access database called TheSoccerSite.mdb located in C:\Inetpub\wwwroot\TheSoccerSite\Database and uses a username of admin and an empty password to connect to it because the Access database that is provided with this chapter is not protected with a password. If you want to connect to a protected database, you can pass in the username and password here. Notice the use of `Provider` to indicate the type of database that is going to be accessed. In the previous example, `Microsoft.Jet.OLEDB.4.0` is used to indicate that you want to use a Microsoft Access database.

A detailed discussion of all the different connection strings that are available is beyond the scope of this book, but you can find a comprehensive list of connection strings at www.able-consulting.com/ ADO_Conn.htm.

Before you create the connection in Dreamweaver, you need to make sure your Dreamweaver site meets all the requirements to work with dynamic data. Fortunately, Dreamweaver MX 2004 provides a simple three-step setup to help you prepare your site.

Try It Out   Creating a Connection in Dreamweaver MX 2004

1. Dreamweaver requires an open file in the current site before you can continue, so go ahead and open the file `login.asp` located in the root of your site TheSoccerSite.

2. Open the Databases panel in the Application panel group (press Ctrl+Shift+F10). The Databases panel informs you whether you are ready to create a connection or not, as shown in Figure 11-12.

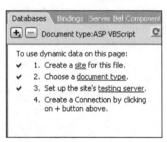

Figure 11-12

3. If there is no check mark before Item 2, click Document Type to bring up the Choose Document Type dialog box shown in Figure 11-13.

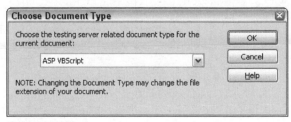

Figure 11-13

Make sure that ASP VBScript is selected in the list and click OK.

4.   If there is no check mark before Item 3, click Testing Server to bring up the Site Definition dialog box. Fill in the details required for a testing server. (If you are unsure what to fill in, refer to Chapter 7 where we showed you the settings for the remote server for the soccer site.)

5.   If all goes well, the first three items in the Databases panel now have a check mark in front of them and you are almost ready to create the actual connection to the database. If you haven't already done so, copy `TheSoccerSite.mdb` from the code download to the database folder at `C:\Inetpub\wwwroot\TheSoccerSite\Database`. On the Files panel in Dreamweaver, switch to Remote view, locate your database in the `Database` folder, right-click the file and then choose Get. This copies the database from the remote server to your local site.

6.   With the `login.asp` page open, click the plus (+) button on the Databases panel. This brings up a menu where you can choose between a Custom Connection String and a Data Source Name (DSN). A DSN-less connection is used in the sample site so go ahead and choose Custom Connection String. The Custom Connection String dialog box in Figure 11-14 appears.

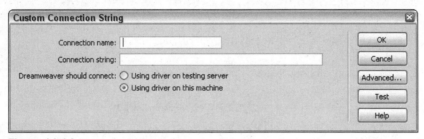

Figure 11-14

7.   Name the connection **connTheSoccerSite** in the Connection Name field. It's a good idea to pre-fix your variables in ASP with the type they are holding, so use *conn* to refer to *connection*.

8.   Type the following in the Connection String text field:

```
"Provider=Microsoft.Jet.OLEDB.4.0;Data Source=
  C:\Inetpub\wwwroot\TheSoccerSite\Database\TheSoccerSite.mdb;User
  Id=admin;Password="
```

9.   Click the Test button in the Custom Connection String dialog box. If all goes as planned, you'll be presented with a confirmation dialog box (see Figure 11-15).

Figure 11-15

If you get an error instead, make sure you have typed in the connection string exactly as we showed here. If it still doesn't work, make sure the path to the database matches the path you are using and you have the right permissions to access the database and the folder it resides in.

Most ISPs allow the use of custom connection strings. However, when you use an ISP, you often don't know the exact location of your database on the file system, so you can't refer to it directly in your connection string. When the database is stored in a folder within your Web root, you can use the `MapPath` method of the `Server` object to return the physical location of a file or folder on disk. If you use that method, change your connection string so it looks like this (although the complete connection string as shown here should be on one line):

```
"Provider=Microsoft.Jet.OLEDB.4.0;Data Source=" & Server.MapPath("Database") &
    "\TheSoccerSite.mdb;User Id=admin;Password="
```

The `Server.MapPath("Database")` command returns something like this:

```
C:\Inetpub\wwwroot\TheSoccerSite\Database
```

The complete path to the database in your connection string will therefore end up as this:

```
C:\Inetpub\wwwroot\TheSoccerSite\Database\TheSoccerSite.mdb
```

`Server.MapPath` returns a path that's relative to the current directory. If you use this method in a subfolder called `Admin`, for example, you need to pass `"../Database"` to this method to get the full location of the database folder in the root of your site. Because Dreamweaver can't resolve the value of the `Server.MapPath` statement at design-time, you can't use this connection string in Dreamweaver. To overcome this hurdle, use a local connection string when you are designing your pages and then change the connection string so it uses the `Server.MapPath` method when you upload your pages to your ISP.

10. If the test is successful, click OK to add the connection to your site. If it doesn't exist yet, Dreamweaver creates a directory called `Connections` in the root of your site and then saves an ASP file with the name of your connection in that directory. If you open that ASP file (it is called `connTheSoccerSite.asp`) in Dreamweaver, this is what you see:

```
<<%
' FileName="Connection_ado_conn_string.htm"
' Type="ADO"
' DesigntimeType="ADO"
' HTTP="false"
' Catalog=""
' Schema=""
Dim MM_connTheSoccerSite_STRING
MM_connTheSoccerSite_STRING = "Provider=Microsoft.Jet.OLEDB.4.0;Data Source=
    C:\Inetpub\wwwroot\TheSoccerSite\Database\TheSoccerSite.mdb;User
    Id=admin;Password="
%>
```

Dreamweaver creates a few comments describing the type of the connection, dimensions a variable called `MM_connTheSoccerSite_STRING`, and assigns your connection string to it. This file can later be included in other ASP files that need a connection so the connection string is available to all pages that require it.

How It Works

Adding a connection to a Dreamweaver site creates a file in the `Connections` folder. All the connections that are defined in that folder are available to you through the Databases panel of the Application panel group. Whenever you create code that depends on one of those connections, Dreamweaver MX 2004 adds an `Include` statement that refers to the ASP page with the connection. This way, you can manage your connection strings at one location, while you have access to them from any page in your site.

In the next example we show you what the `Include` statement looks like and how you can work with the connection you created.

Enhancing the Login Page

In Chapter 9 you created a rather simple login page. Usernames and passwords from a text file determined whom you wanted to grant access. Now that you know a little about how databases work, it's time to enhance the login page so it uses a database to validate users. This way, it's easier to maintain your user list. You can simply add or remove users in the `Users` table in the database instead of modifying the file `users.txt`.

To connect the database with the login form, Dreamweaver MX 2004 comes with a ready-made behavior that you can apply to a page containing a login form. It then creates the necessary code to connect to a database and validate a user.

The generated code uses *ADO* (ActiveX Data Objects) to perform the database actions. ADO is a Microsoft technology that enables you to connect to a wide variety of data sources using the same programming interface. You can connect to an Access, SQL Server, or Oracle database, or even text files and spreadsheets with pretty much the same code.

> *We cannot dive into every detail of ADO here but we encourage you to go to* `www.microsoft.com/data` *to find out more about ADO.*

With ADO, you can use T-SQL (usually abbreviated to just "SQL"), to retrieve, insert, update, and delete information in a database. T-SQL stands for *Transact-Structured Query Language* and is *the* language used with relational databases. SQL defines four main methods to retrieve and manipulate data: `SELECT`, `INSERT`, `UPDATE`, and `DELETE` (from their names, you can probably guess what they do). In this and the next chapter we'll use the `SELECT` statement to retrieve data from the database, while we focus on the other three in the following chapters in this section.

To see how SQL works, take a look at the following simple `SELECT` statement:

```
SELECT Name, Password FROM Users
```

This is a `SELECT` statement in its simplest form. All it does is select the Name and Password columns from the `Users` table. If there are multiple records in the table, all of them are returned. When you use ADO to retrieve information from a database, these records are returned as a *recordset*. You'll see more about this later.

To restrict the number of records, you can use a `WHERE` clause in your statement. The `WHERE` keyword should be followed by a column name and a criterion, for example:

```
SELECT Name, Password FROM Users
WHERE Name = 'DennisBergkamp'
```

This limits the number of records to those where the Name column contains `DennisBergkamp`. Using the WHERE clause like this is no guarantee that only one record is returned. If there is more than one record in the database with this name, all matching records are returned.

In the code above, the name `DennisBergkamp` is enclosed in apostrophes. This is a requirement by SQL for `text` data types. In Microsoft Access the # character is used to enclose data for a `date` field, whereas other databases use the apostrophe as well. *Numeric* values, on the other hand, are never enclosed.

Now that you have a basic understanding of how a SELECT statement works, it's time to try out an example that uses SELECT to check whether a user exists in your database or not. Don't worry if you don't understand all the details yet; Dreamweaver has a lot of functionality built in that makes using a database quite easy. In fact, most of the time Dreamweaver generates all the necessary code for you.

Try It Out   Making the Login Page Database-Driven

1. On the `login.asp` page, remove the code you added in Chapter 9 that validates the username and password. Remove the entire ASP code block at the top of the page that starts with this:

```
<%
Dim sErrorMessage
Dim sReferrer
If Request.Form("txtReferrer") = "" Then
 sReferrer = Request.QueryString("accessdenied")
```

and ends with this:

```
 "Login failed. Please type a valid username and password</span>"
 End If
End If
%>
```

   Since a database is used for the authentication process, you no longer need the file `users.txt` in your `Tools` folder. To increase the security of your site, delete the file or move it to a location outside your `Inetpub` folder.

2. Open the Server Behaviors panel (press Ctrl+F9), click the plus (+) button, and select User Authentication⇨Log In User. The Log In User dialog box appears.

   As you can see from the dialog box, Dreamweaver recognizes the login form you had on your page. It also sees that you have a connection defined so you can easily select that from the drop-down list. Once you select the connection, `connTheSoccerSite`, from the Validate Using Connection list, the list with table names changes so you can select the `Users` table as the one that contains information about your users. When you select that table, Dreamweaver shows a list with columns so you can point to a column that holds the username and password. Select Name and Password for the Username Column and Password Column drop-down lists, respectively.

3. Next you get the opportunity to select where you want to redirect your users after they log in. Select `Admin/admin.asp` for a successful login and `login.asp` for the redirect page when the login attempt fails. The Go to Previous URL (If It Exists) check box enables a nice feature. Imagine that a user requests a page that can only be accessed by authenticated users. If the user hasn't logged in yet, the login page will be displayed instead of the requested page. The name

of the page that was originally requested is passed to this login page and saved. After a success-ful login, the user is redirected back to the requested page. If the login page is requested directly, users are sent to the page specified in the If Login Succeeds Go To field. In Chapter 9, we demonstrated how you can create this mechanism yourself.

Leave the Restrict Access Based On method set to Username and Password for now. We'll demonstrate how to use the access level in the next section of this chapter. The Log In User dia-log box should look like Figure 11-16.

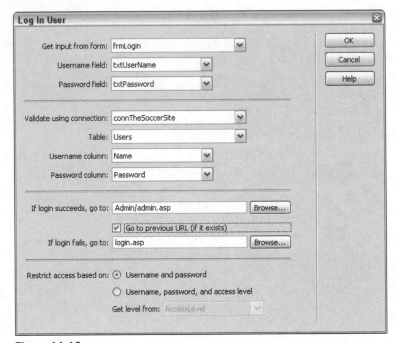

Figure 11-16

Click OK to apply the server behavior to your page and then save the page.

4. Before you can test your login page, add a few users to your database. If you have Microsoft Access installed, open the database `TheSoccerSite.mdb`. Make sure you open the database at your remote server (at `C:\Inetpub\wwwroot\TheSoccerSite\Database\`) and not the one at your local site. You'll see a screen similar to Figure 11-17.

Double-click the `Users` table and add two users, one with `AccessLevel` set to Administrators, the other with Members access. Remember the usernames and passwords for these users because you'll need them in Step 5.

Don't worry if you don't have Access installed. There are two sample users present in the database. There is an administrator with the username and password of "admin" and a member account that uses the username and password of "member."

You can close Access because there are no more changes to be made to the `Users` table.

Now that you have changed the database on the remote server, it's a good idea to use GET to have a copy of the database on your local site. To do this, locate the database in Remote view on the Files panel, right-click it, and choose GET.

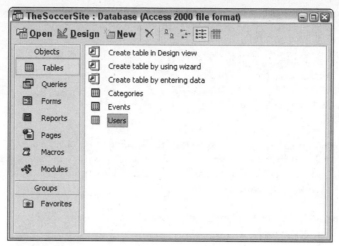

Figure 11-17

5. Open `login.asp` in your browser. Log in to the site as an administrator by using the username **admin** and the password **admin** or with the user you created in the previous step. If your login is successful, you'll see the `admin.asp` page appear. If login fails, you'll see the login page appear again. Close your browser, open the `login.asp` page again, and log in now with the member account using **member** as the username and password, or by using your own account. Even though you are not an administrator, you still gain access to `admin.asp`. We'll show you how to fix this after we explain how the login form works.

If you get an error indicating that the include file `connTheSoccerSite.asp` *is not found, locate the* `Connections` *folder in your Dreamweaver site in Local view, right-click it, and choose Put. This uploads the required connection file to your remote server.*

How It Works

When you add the Log In User behavior, Dreamweaver makes a modification to your login form and adds some ASP code to create the login functionality. In the form, only the `action` attribute is changed:

```
<form action="<%=MM_LoginAction%>" method ="post" name="frmLogin">
```

Instead of the hard-coded value of `login.asp`, Dreamweaver adds a variable called `MM_LoginAction`. You'll see in the discussion of the ASP code that in this case the effect is the same because `MM_LoginAction` contains `/TheSoccerSite/login.asp` when the page is requested.

The ASP code block that Dreamweaver inserts is quite large. To understand what happens here, let's break the code up and see what each section does:

```
<!--#include file="Connections/connTheSoccerSite.asp" -->
<%
' *** Validate request to log in to this site.
```

First, Dreamweaver adds an `#include` statement that refers to your connection. This way, the variable holding your connection string defined in that page is available to you, just as if you had declared it in this page. The benefit of the `Include` file is that you can easily change your connection string, without having to change each and every page that uses that connection by hand.

```
MM_LoginAction = Request.ServerVariables("URL")
If Request.QueryString<>"" Then _
      MM_LoginAction = MM_LoginAction + "?" + Request.QueryString
  MM_valUsername=CStr(Request.Form("txtUserName"))
  If MM_valUsername <> "" Then
```

Then the variable `MM_LoginAction` is assigned the value of the current page, `/TheSoccerSite/ login.asp`, by using `Request.ServerVariables("URL")`, which returns the complete name of the current page. If there is a QueryString passed to this page, Dreamweaver adds that to the `MM_Login Action` variable as well, so its value is preserved.

The username is retrieved from the form, converted to a string using the `CStr` function, and stored in a variable called `MM_valUsername`.

The `If` statement makes sure that the rest of the code is only executed when the user types a username in the login form.

```
MM_fldUserAuthorization=""
MM_redirectLoginSuccess="Admin/admin.asp"
MM_redirectLoginFailed="login.asp"
MM_flag="ADODB.Recordset"
```

The four variables are given a value:

❑   `MM_fldUserAuthorization` is not used in this example but it is used in the next section when we discuss access levels

❑   `MM_redirectLoginSuccess` and `MM_redirectLoginFailed` define the page that users are redirected to after they try to log in

❑   `MM_flag` contains the name of the ADO object that is used to connect to the database

```
  set MM_rsUser = Server.CreateObject(MM_flag)
```

Next, a recordset object is created by using the `Server.CreateObject` command you saw earlier in Chapter 9. A recordset represents all records that have been returned from the database by executing a query. Not only does it contain the requested records, it contains *metadata*, which gives information about the records in the recordset and is thus also known as "data about data." It describes the data type for each column in the recordset (Text, Memo, Date, Number, and so on), its name, and its length in the database, for example. At runtime, you can retrieve both the actual data and the metadata from the recordset.

```
MM_rsUser.ActiveConnection = MM_connTheSoccerSite_STRING
  MM_rsUser.Source = "SELECT Name, Password"
  If MM_fldUserAuthorization <> "" Then _
    MM_rsUser.Source = MM_rsUser.Source & "," & MM_fldUserAuthorization
    MM_rsUser.Source = MM_rsUser.Source & _
      " FROM Users WHERE Name='" & Replace(MM_valUsername,"'","''") & _
```

```
"' AND Password='" & _
Replace(Request.Form("txtPassword"),"'","''") & "'"
```

Once the recordset object is created, a connection is assigned by setting its `ActiveConnection` property. In this case `ActiveConnection` is set to the value `MM_connTheSoccerSite_STRING`, which holds your connection string. Remember that `MM_connTheSoccerSite_STRING` gets its value in your connection page, `connTheSoccerSite.asp`.

Then the `Source` property of the recordset is set. The `Source` property should contain the `SELECT` statement that is executed against your database. It selects the `Name` and `Password` from the `Users` table and, if `MM_fldUserAuthorization` has a value, it selects the column defined in that variable as well. Then the `SELECT` statement is restricted by adding a `WHERE` clause for the `Name` and `Password` columns. The values for the username and the password in the `WHERE` clause are retrieved from the variable `MM_valUsername` and the form variable `Request.Form("txtPassword")`, respectively.

After this bit of code has executed, the `Source` property contains a valid SQL `SELECT` statement, which could look like this:

```
SELECT Name, Password FROM Users WHERE Name='admin' AND Password='admin'
```

This looks remarkably similar to the SQL statement you saw earlier in this section.

The `CursorType` and `CursorLocation` determine whether a recordset is updatable and how you can navigate through the recordset:

```
MM_rsUser.CursorType = 0
MM_rsUser.CursorLocation = 2
MM_rsUser.LockType = 3
```

They also determine whether you can see changes to the database that have taken place since you executed your query. The more flexibility and functionality you add to the recordset, the slower it performs. Dreamweaver knows it only needs a lightweight version of the recordset, so it sets the options for optimal performance. The `LockType` defines the way records in the database are locked for other users while you are working with them.

> *It's beyond the scope of this book to give a detailed discussion about cursors and locks, but you can find comprehensive information about them in the ADO Programmer's Guide at* `msdn.microsoft.com/library/default.asp?url=/library/en-us/ado270/htm/pg_introduction.asp`*.*

Next, the recordset is opened by calling its `Open` method. At this point, a connection to your database is created and opened, the query gets sent to the database, and the records that are returned are stored in the recordset object:

```
MM_rsUser.Open
```

From the first line of the code block below, you can see that relational databases have been around for quite some time. In the old days, it was much more common to store database tables in single files. To find out if a table contained any more records, you could test whether you were at the "end of the file" (EOF).

ADO still uses the properties EOF and BOF ("beginning of the file") to see whether there are records in a recordset. The check for BOF that Dreamweaver inserts is not strictly necessary; if the recordset is empty (the username and password combination is not found in the Users table) then the EOF property is True:

```
If Not MM_rsUser.EOF Or Not MM_rsUser.BOF Then
 ' username and password match - this is a valid user
 Session("MM_Username") = MM_valUsername
 If (MM_fldUserAuthorization <> "") Then
  Session("MM_UserAuthorization") = _
    CStr(MM_rsUser.Fields.Item(MM_fldUserAuthorization).Value)
 Else
  Session("MM_UserAuthorization") = ""
 End If
 If CStr(Request.QueryString("accessdenied")) <> "" And true Then
    MM_redirectLoginSuccess = Request.QueryString("accessdenied")
 End If
 MM_rsUser.Close
 Response.Redirect(MM_redirectLoginSuccess)
End If
```

If the user is found, both EOF and BOF are False so the code in the If block executes. First the name of the user is stored in a session variable so it's available in all the pages in your Web site.

We'll defer the discussion about the MM_fldUserAuthorization variables to the next section of this chapter when we discuss access levels.

If the login page is called from a protected page, the name of that protected page is passed to the login page through the QueryString variable accessdenied. If this variable has a value, the user is redirected back to that page; otherwise, the default page you defined in the Log In User dialog box is shown. In both cases, the recordset is closed first to release the resources it uses.

```
 MM_rsUser.Close
 Response.Redirect(MM_redirectLoginFailed)
 End If
%>
```

Finally, if login fails, the recordset is closed and the user is redirected to the page defined in MM_redirectLoginFailed, which is the same login page again (login.asp).

Fine-Tuning Access to Your Site with Access Levels

The login page has really been improved by making it database-driven. Instead of using hard-coded values, you validate your users by querying a database. This makes it easier for you to manage your Web site. You can add and remove users in your database without modifying any pages. Now imagine that your site grows and more and more people visit your Web site on a regular basis. After a while you decide you want to provide extra service to regular visitors by offering them a better user experience in return for their loyal visits. At the same time, you want to provide the people working on your site, including yourself, access to specific areas of the site for maintenance purposes. Obviously, you don't want your regular visitors, or even your valued members, to access this part of the site, so now you need to distinguish between three groups: ordinary visitors, registered members, and administrators. In this section, you learn how to use the access-level feature in Dreamweaver to make this happen.

Access levels are a way to distinguish among different users on your site. They are simple text strings that you define yourself. The sample database from the chapter download shows an `AccessLevel` column in the `Users` table. In that column you store whatever permission you want to assign to a certain user. For example, a user who is allowed to maintain the Web site is granted administrator rights, while a regular visitor of your site is assigned the members' access level.

Once you assign users their access levels, you can restrict access to specific pages based on the user's level.

Although there is no real limitation to the number of access levels you can define, we recommend to keep this number low—three or four levels at the most. Once you establish too many levels, maintenance of your pages will become much harder because you need to remember who is allowed to do what on which page. Categorize your levels in logical groups, such as administrators, members, and candidate members.

To implement access levels in your Web site successfully, modify the login page so that the access level is retrieved from the database when the user logs in. That way you have the ability to limit access to individual pages so only users who have the correct access level are allowed to view the page. In the next section, you change the `login.asp` page again so it uses access levels. In a later Try It Out exercise we'll demonstrate how you can change the Admin page so that only members of the Administrators group can view it.

Try It Out 　 Applying Access Levels to the login.asp Page

1. Open the page `login.asp` in Dreamweaver and double-click Log In User in the Server Behaviors panel (press Ctrl+F9 to open the panel).

2. In the Restrict Access Based On section of the dialog box (see Figure 11-18), select Username, Password, and Access Level and make sure the database column AccessLevel is selected in the Get Level From drop-down list.

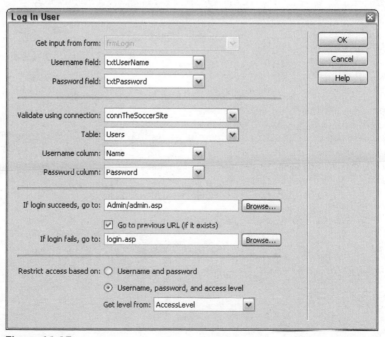

Figure 11-18

3. Click OK to apply the change and save the page.

That's all that is necessary to use access levels in your login page. If you run the page in the browser, you won't notice a difference. You can still log in with either the administrator or the member account and get access to admin.asp. This is because you also need to change the admin page so it uses access levels too. The next Try It Out exercise how to do this.

When you make changes by using Dreamweaver's server behaviors in ASP pages that are based on a template, you might get the error message shown in Figure 11-19 every now and then.

Figure 11-19

Unfortunately, this error message is wrong because all your modifications are made in regions of the template that you are allowed to edit. The best way to solve this problem is to click No, undo the changes you made in the page, save and close the page, and then reopen it. You are now able to add the server behavior correctly without getting this error. Hopefully this problem will be fixed in a future service release of Dreamweaver. To prevent the loss of work, save your page before you add a server behavior.

How It Works

When you select Username, Password, and Access Level as the restriction method, Dreamweaver takes the following one line of code:

```
MM_fldUserAuthorization=""
```

And changes it to this:

```
MM_fldUserAuthorization="AccessLevel"
```

This eventually changes the SELECT statement in the login procedure so that it queries the access level from the Users table too. AccessLevel refers to the column in your Users table where the access level for each user is stored.

Now when you look at the lines you skipped earlier on, you'll start to understand the principle of access levels:

```
If (MM_fldUserAuthorization <> "") Then
  Session("MM_UserAuthorization") = _
    CStr(MM_rsUser.Fields.Item(MM_fldUserAuthorization).Value)
Else
  Session("MM_UserAuthorization") = ""
End If
```

MM_fldUserAuthorization now has a value, so the code in the If block runs. The contents of the AccessLevel column from your database are stored as a session variable. This column is retrieved from the recordset with this statement:

```
CStr(MM_rsUser.Fields.Item(MM_fldUserAuthorization).Value)
```

The CStr call converts any value you pass to it to a string. The value that is passed to this method is retrieved from the recordset by using .Fields.Item(ColumnName). MM_fldUserAuthorization is passed in as the ColumnName, which, unsurprisingly, holds the AccessLevel column name. Finally, the results of the CStr method are stored in a session variable called MM_UserAuthorization. When an administrator logs in, the word *Administrators* is saved in the session variable. In other pages you can retrieve this variable again and find out what kind of user is requesting the page.

The changes you made to the login page go unnoticed until you modify a protected page to use the access levels. In Chapter 9 you created the admin.asp page, which used a simple form of access restriction. In the following Try It Out exercise, you'll modify that page so it uses access levels instead.

Try It Out   Changing the Admin Page So It Uses Access Levels

1. Open the admin.asp file from the Admin folder.

2. Open the Server Behaviors panel (press Ctrl+F9) and double-click the Restrict Access To Page() behavior.

3. Select the Username, Password, and Access Level option (see Figure 11-20).

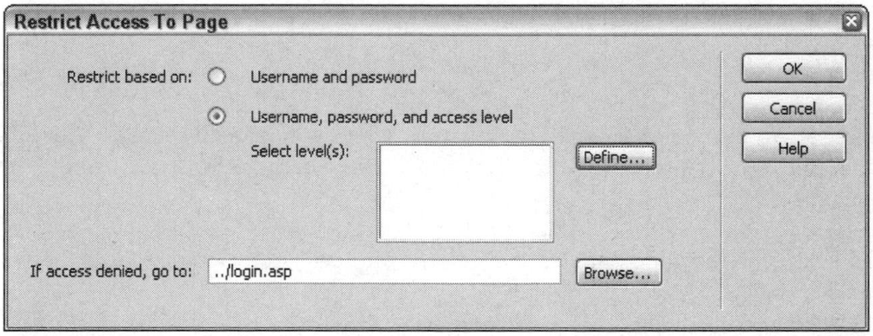

Figure 11-20

Click the Define button so you can create some access levels.

4. Click the plus (+) button and type **Administrators** in the Name field of the Define Access Levels dialog box. Press Tab.

5. Repeat Step 4 but type **Members** this time (see Figure 11-21).

   Click OK to close the dialog box.

6. Back in the Restrict Access To Page dialog box, select Administrators in the Select Level(s) list. It is possible to select multiple access levels in this dialog box but since you want to allow page access to just users at the Administrators level, make sure that Members is not selected. Click OK to apply the access level to the page. Dreamweaver saves the various access levels you defined in a note in your _notes folder so they can be used throughout the site.

Figure 11-21

7. Save the page, close any browser window you may have open, and then request `admin.asp` in your browser. Try to log in as a member, using **member** as the username and password. Because you are not an administrator, you won't get access to the page but you'll see the login page again.

8. Log in again but this time use **admin** as your username and password. Now you're granted access and you see the admin page.

How It Works

When you apply the access levels to the page, Dreamweaver makes two changes to the code. First, it changes this:

```
MM_authorizedUsers=""
```

to this:

```
MM_authorizedUsers="Administrators"
```

The variable `MM_authorizedUsers` holds a list of all levels that are allowed to view the page, separated by a comma. In this example, only Administrators is listed because only users at that level are allowed to view the page.

The second change in the code handles the way the authorization is applied:

```
If (true Or CStr(Session("MM_UserAuthorization"))="") Or _
  (InStr(1,MM_authorizedUsers,Session("MM_UserAuthorization"))>=1) Then
 MM_grantAccess = true
End If
```

That code is changed to this:

```
If (false Or CStr(Session("MM_UserAuthorization"))="") Or _
  (InStr(1,MM_authorizedUsers,Session("MM_UserAuthorization"))>=1) Then
 MM_grantAccess = true
End If
```

The old code block allows access to anyone. Because of the use of `If (true or...)`, which always evaluates to `True`, the code in the `If` block always executes, no matter whether the other checks return `True` or `False`. No matter what kind of user requests this page, if the session variable `MM_Username` contains a value, access to the page is granted.

The change from `true` to `false` in the `If` statement is necessary to disallow users access when both the other statements return `False` as well. If the session variable `MM_UserAuthorization` contains an empty string, the user has apparently no access level assigned and so cannot enter. If the session variable does exist, the following line determines whether the user has sufficient rights to view the page:

```
(InStr(1,MM_authorizedUsers,session("MM_UserAuthorization"))>=1)
```

The `InStr` function finds out if the value of one string is present in another. In this example, three arguments are passed to this function. The first argument indicates the starting position for the search. The entire string must be searched, so `1` is passed. The second argument is the string that is searched *in,* and the last argument is the string that is searched *for.* If the string that is searched for is not found within the other, `0` is returned. To clarify this, take a look at the same code but with the actual values filled in. Imagine the current user has an access level of Members and the page is protected so that only administrators are allowed to access it:

```
(InStr(1, "Administrators","Members")>=1)
```

Obviously, the string `Members` is not found in the string `Administrators`, so `0` is returned. Because 0 is not greater than or equal to 1, this block of code returns `False`.

Take a look at another example where there is still a user with an access level of Members, but this time the page can be viewed by both members and administrators:

```
(InStr(1, "Administrators,Members","Members")>=1)
```

The string `Members` is present in `Administrators,Members` so the `Instr` function returns a value greater than or equal to 1 (16 to be exact, the position of the `M` in the string).

Now imagine that an administrator is requesting the page. The original statement, where only an administrator has access to the page, now looks like this when the actual values are filled in:

```
If (false Or "Administrators"="") Or _
   (InStr(1,"Administrators","Administrators")>=1)
```

This time, the `InStr` function returns 1, so this code will result in the following:

```
If (false Or false) Or (true)
```

This equals `True` eventually, so the user is allowed access.

You may have noticed that, when you logged in as a member, you saw the `login.asp` page again, even though you are a valid user. You'll deal with this problem in the next Try It Out exercise.

This concludes our discussion on using access levels with the ready-made server behaviors that Dreamweaver provides. In the next section, we'll look at how you can extend and modify these behaviors to get finer-grained control of the authentication process.

Extending Access-Level Functionality

Using the standard access levels from Dreamweaver is a great and easy way to restrict access to certain pages in your Web site. But what if you want to restrict certain regions in your page instead of complete pages? You could, for example, show a list of navigation links in your menu and only display the link to the admin section when the current user is logged in and has administrator rights.

The current implementation of Dreamweaver does not provide this mechanism, so you have to do some coding yourself. Fortunately, you can reuse most of the code Dreamweaver generates in the Restrict Access behavior, so protecting regions in your page isn't too difficult.

In the next section, you'll modify your menu library item by creating a new menu item that links to the admin section. You'll use the access-level feature to hide the links to this admin section and the My Site page. After a successful login by an administrator or a member, one or both of the links are displayed in the menu, depending on the access level of the user. Because the library item is used in the template you have used for all your pages, the new menu is available throughout the site.

Try It Out **Protecting Page Regions**

1. Close any page you may have open in Dreamweaver and then open `mainMenu.lbi`, create some space between the My Site and Login menu items, and type a pair of opening and closing ASP tags (<% and %>) in the empty space:

```
<td>   </td>
<td><a href="../mySite.asp" id="mysite">My Site</a></td>
<td>   </td>

<%


%>
<td><a href="../login.asp" id="login">Login</a></td>
</tr>
```

2. Open the `admin.asp` page, locate the following block of code, and select it:

```
MM_authorizedUsers="Administrators"
MM_authFailedURL="../login.asp"
MM_grantAccess=false
If session("MM_Username") <> "" Then
 If (false Or CStr(session("MM_UserAuthorization"))="") Or _
  (InStr(1,MM_authorizedUsers,session("MM_UserAuthorization"))>=1) Then
   MM_grantAccess = true
 End If
End If
```

3. Copy the text to the Clipboard, close `admin.asp`, and then back in the library item paste the code between the ASP tags you entered in Step 1. The code in the menu should look like this:

```
<td><a href="../mySite.asp" id="mysite">My Site</a></td>
<td>   </td>

<%
 MM_authorizedUsers="Administrators"
 MM_authFailedURL="../login.asp"
 MM_grantAccess=false
```

```
    If Session("MM_Username") <> "" Then
     If (false Or CStr(Session("MM_UserAuthorization"))="") Or _
     (InStr(1,MM_authorizedUsers,Session("MM_UserAuthorization"))>=1) Then
      MM_grantAccess = true
     End If
    End If
    %>
    <td><a href="../login.asp" id="login">Login</a></td>
```

Don't worry if Dreamweaver applies incorrect color-coding to the rest of the page; the menu works just fine.

4. The `MM_authFailedURL` and `MM_grantAccess` variables are not used in this example, so you can remove the following two lines:

```
    MM_authFailedURL="../login.asp"
    MM_grantAccess=false
```

5. In earlier examples demonstrating the use of access levels, a user was redirected away from the page when they didn't have the necessary access levels. In this example, however, it works the other way around. An additional link is displayed when the user does have administrator rights.

Locate the line with `MM_grantAccess = true` inside the `If` block and delete it. On the line you just deleted, type a closing ASP script tag (%>), press Enter twice, and then type an opening ASP Code block (<%). Your code should now look like this:

```
    If (false Or CStr(Session("MM_UserAuthorization"))="") Or _
       (InStr(1,MM_authorizedUsers,Session("MM_UserAuthorization"))>=1) Then
     %>

     <%
    End If
```

6. Between the closing and opening ASP script tags, add a new menu item that links to the administrator's page. To do this, copy and paste one of the existing menu items and edit the details, changing the `href` and `id` values to **../Admin/admin.asp** and **admin**, respectively, and type **Admin** as the name of the menu.

Copy one of the empty `<td>` tags holding the three nonbreaking spaces and paste them after the Admin menu. This creates some room between this menu item and the Login menu item.

The complete code should now look like this:

```
<td>   </td>
<%
 MM_authorizedUsers="Administrators"
 If Session("MM_Username") <> "" Then
  If (false Or CStr(Session("MM_UserAuthorization"))="") Or _
    (InStr(1,MM_authorizedUsers,Session("MM_UserAuthorization"))>=1) Then
    %>
    <td><a href="../Admin/admin.asp" id="admin">Admin</a></td>
    <td>   </td>
    <%
  End If
 End If
%>
<td><a href="../login.asp" id="login">Login</a></td>
```

415

7. The link to My Site needs to be hidden as well, so only registered visitors can use this service. Copy the entire ASP code block that is used to show or hide the admin menu and paste it right before the `<td>` that contains the link to `mySite.asp`.

8. Cut the two lines that make up the menu item for My Site and paste them over the menu item for Admin inside the `If` statement of the code block you pasted in the previous step. Make sure you paste them in the copy of the code and not in the original admin menu item. Don't forget to include the line with the empty `<td>` element.

9. Since both members and administrators should be able to personalize their site, change the `MM_authorizedUsers` variable so it contains **Administrators,Members**. (Remember that access levels are separated with a comma and nothing else.) This is the code for the My Site menu item you should end up with:

```
<td><a href="../events.asp" id="events">Events</a></td>
<td>   </td>

<%
 MM_authorizedUsers="Administrators,Members"
 If Session("MM_Username") <> "" Then
  If (false Or CStr(Session("MM_UserAuthorization"))="") Or _
   (InStr(1,MM_authorizedUsers,Session("MM_UserAuthorization")))>=1) Then
  %>
   <td><a href="../mySite.asp" id="mysite">My Site</a></td>
   <td>   </td>
  <%
  End If
 End If
%>
<%
 MM_authorizedUsers="Administrators"
```

10. Save the library item and update all your pages that use the menu system. You may need to right-click your site in the Site panel and choose Put to save the pages to your remote server as well. If Dreamweaver asks you if you're sure you want to put the entire site, click OK.

11. Open `home.asp` in Dreamweaver and press F12 to view it in your browser. Notice that the links to the Admin page and My Site are not visible (see Figure 11-22).

If the logo on the top of your page ends up as broken image, Dreamweaver may have incorrectly changed the src attribute of the image in the template. To fix this, choose Modify⇨Templates⇨Update Pages and then click Start to let Dreamweaver update the pages. You need to upload the changed pages to your remote server again by using the Put command.

12. Click the Login link at the top-right corner of the screen and log in as administrator, using the username and password of **admin**. You'll be redirected to the admin section. Notice that both the Admin and the My Site menu items appear (see Figure 11-23). The menu items remain visible for the duration of your session.

Figure 11-22

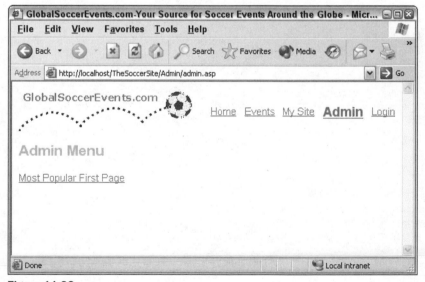

Figure 11-23

13. Close your browser, open `home.asp` in your browser again, and log in, but this time as a member. You'll see the My Site menu but, because of your limited set of permissions, the Admin menu is not displayed this time.

Notice that you are presented with the login page again. What went wrong? After all, you successfully logged in as a member, didn't you? The answer to this question can be found in your `login.asp` page. The login behavior in this page redirects a user to `Admin/admin.asp` after any successful login. However, this page is protected and only administrators can access it, so you're redirected to the login page and asked to log in again. This infinite loop can easily be fixed by changing the redirect page. Open `login.asp`, open the Server Behaviors panel by pressing Ctrl+F9 and double-click the Log In User behavior. Change `Admin/admin.asp` to `home.asp` in the If Login Succeeds Go To check box. Click OK and save the page.

14. If you still have your browser open, close it. This makes sure you get a new session and are forced to log in again. Open a new browser instance and browse to `home.asp`. Log in as a member. You'll be sent to the home page, with the My Site menu item visible (see Figure 11-24).

Figure 11-24

How It Works

You saw most of the code used in this example in the previous Try It Out exercise, so figuring out how it works shouldn't be too hard. The biggest change is the way the code checks the user levels:

```
MM_authorizedUsers="Administrators,Members"
If Session("MM_Username") <> "" Then
 If (false Or CStr(Session("MM_UserAuthorization"))="") Or _
```

```
    (InStr(1,MM_authorizedUsers,Session("MM_UserAuthorization"))>=1) Then
%>
    <td><a href="../mySite.asp" id="mysite">My Site</a></td>
    <td>   </td>
  End If
End If
```

Instead of setting the flag `MM_grantAccess` to `True` when the user has sufficient rights, the navigation links appear. No action is performed when the user is not part of the administrators or members level either (there is no `Else` clause for the `If` statement), so no link is displayed in that case.

Finally, the redirect page in `login.asp` is changed. Instead of being redirected to the admin section, a logged-in user is now always redirected back to the home page.

Summary

In this chapter we looked at the nature of databases and the way you can use them with Dreamweaver MX 2004. You saw what a database is, how tables are made up of columns and rows, and how you can relate those columns in different tables to each other. You also looked at a few different database systems and learned two ways to prevent your database from being downloaded by unauthorized users.

We demonstrated how to connect to a database from within Dreamweaver and from within your Web site. Using this knowledge you enhanced the login procedure and made it database-driven. This greatly improved the maintainability of the Web site because it's easier to add users to a database than to modify the login page every time a new administrator is assigned.

Next we introduced you to the concept of access levels: a means of fine-tuning the way users gain access to your site. We demonstrated a way to apply access levels to your admin page so only authorized users are allowed access to your admin pages.

Finally, we looked at a way to extend the access-level feature so you can use it to protect regions of your page, instead of blocking complete pages from being viewed.

In this chapter we mainly looked at how you can use data in a database to make decisions, such as whether a user is granted access to parts of your site or not. In the next chapter, you'll see how you can use a database to retrieve information and display it on pages in your site.

Why Not Try . . .

1.   Right now if login fails you just see the login page again. Try to add an error message to display when login fails.

   Hint: Create a variable called something like `sErrorMessage` *and display that using* `<%=sErrorMessage%>` *on your page somewhere, just as you did in Chapter 9.*

2.   At first you redirected visitors to `admin.asp` after they logged in because you only had administrators. Now that you also have a members group, you always redirect them to `home.asp`. Try

changing the login page so it redirects to `home.asp` when a member logs in and to `admin.asp` when an administrator logs in.

Hint: Change the variable `MM_redirectLoginSuccess` *right before it gets used in the* `Response.Redirect` *statement. Use* `Session("MM_UserAuthorization")` *and the* `InStr` *function to determine the type of user logging in.*

3. Right now, a user who requests `http://localhost/TheSoccerSite/mySite.asp` directly doesn't have to type a username and password because the page is not protected. Try adding the Restrict Access To Page behavior to this page. Don't forget to set the required user levels for this page.

Retrieving and Displaying Data from Databases

As you saw in Chapter 11, most Web sites on the Internet today use some kind of database to store information about customers, products, purchases, company info, and lots of other important data. In fact, it's hard to find an interactive Web site that does not use some kind of database. Business logic decisions that these applications need to make, like planning the shortest or cheapest route from one location to another, require a database to aid their complex decision-making processes.

Besides these business decisions, these applications make heavy use of databases to store data that needs to be displayed on the site. For example, route descriptions or real-time traffic information is stored in a database and then displayed on-screen when it's relevant and appropriate.

This chapter shows you how to display data from a database on a Web page. In particular, you will learn how to do the following:

❑   Display a list of soccer events that is retrieved from a database

❑   Create filters to influence the amount of data displayed on-screen

❑   Link lists of events to pages with more detail

❑   Present information in ready-to-eat chunks, in what we call *pageable lists*

As we have discussed before, events are an important element for any sports fan site. Most likely users come to your site to keep track of what is happening where and when in the world of sports, and which famous teams and soccer celebrities are going to be where. To keep your visitors happy, you have to keep your information about soccer events as up to date as possible. Not only does that mean you should add new events as soon as you get the information about them, but you should remove old and expired events as well. This ensures that your site is always up to date, which increases your credibility and the number of hits your site receives.

In Chapter 8, we showed you how to display static event information. You created a drop-down list with categories for your events, including UEFA Cup, National League, and so on. Once a user of your site chooses a category, the name of that category is displayed in an <h3> tag and a placeholder for the events from that category is shown as well. Inside the placeholder you could add a static list of your events, but it's obvious that this static list would be very difficult to maintain over time. As soon as the dates and descriptions of new events became available, you would have to update your page manually, and as soon as the event ended, you would have to update the page to remove the event from the listing.

Wouldn't it be nice if you could just add your events in advance and let the Web server decide when to show them? In this and subsequent sections, we'll show you how to do exactly that.

Displaying a List of Events

To display a dynamic list of events on your events page, you can use one of Dreamweaver's server behaviors, the *repeat region*. A repeat region does exactly what its name implies: It repeats a specific region that you define yourself. This region can contain both HTML (including images and links) and ASP, so you have a very flexible and powerful server behavior at your disposal. The nice thing about the repeat region is that you can hook it up to a recordset so that it repeats data from that recordset.

There is a little inconsistency in the way Dreamweaver MX 2004 names the repeat region. When you add it from the Server Behaviors panel, it's called a repeat region. When you add it from the Application Objects on the Insert menu or from the Application category of the Insert bar, it's called a repeated region. In both cases, we are talking about the same server behavior. We'll stick to the term repeat region in this chapter.

In the following exercise, you'll create a recordset to retrieve the events from your database. You'll need to modify the original page with events (events.asp) so it can display events from the database instead of the hard-coded text you added in Chapter 8. Notice that the functionality of the categories drop-down list will be temporarily broken. Don't worry; it will be restored in a later example in this chapter.

Try It Out   Making the Events List Database-Driven

1. Open the events.asp page in the root of your site and remove the following ASP Select Case code blocks that manage the visibility of the events:

```
</select>
</form>
```

```
<% Select Case iLastCategory
   Case 1 ' Champions League
   Response.Write("<h3>Champions League</h3>") %>
   — HTML Content for Champions League Events here —
<% Case 2 ' UEFA Cup
   Response.Write("<h3>UEFA Cup</h3>")  %>
   — HTML Content for UEFA Cup Events here —
<% Case 3 ' National League
   Response.Write("<h3>National League</h3>") %>
   — HTML Content for National League Events here —
<% Case 4 ' US Major League Soccer
   Response.Write("<h3>US Major League Soccer</h3>") %>
   — HTML Content for US Major League Soccer Events here —
<% Case Else ' No category chosen %>
   Please select a category from the drop-down list.
<% End Select %>
<!— InstanceEndEditable —></td>
```

Make sure you leave the form with the category drop-down list intact.

2. Position your cursor right *before* the closing `</form>` tag in Code view, choose Insert⇨Table, and enter the details shown in Figure 12-1 into the Table dialog box.

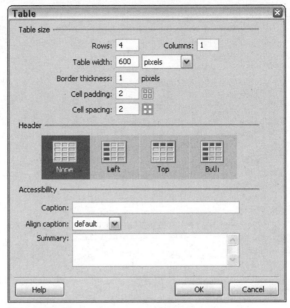

Figure 12-1

Setting the border to 1 makes it easier to see the table in Design view. After you apply a CSS class that changes the border of the table, you'll remove the `border` again by setting it to 0 in a later exercise.

Click OK to add the table to the page, and save the page.

3. Open the Server Behaviors panel by pressing Ctrl+F9, click the plus (+) button, and choose Recordset (Query) from the menu to open the Recordset dialog box. This dialog box provides two views: a Simple mode and an Advanced mode. Most examples in this and the next chapter require just the Simple mode because it's much easier to use and doesn't bother you with complicated details you don't need. If you see the Simple button in the dialog box, you are currently in Advanced mode, so click the Simple button to switch to Simple mode. You'll see the Recordset dialog box shown in Figure 12-2.

4. Name the recordset **rsEvents**. Notice that the name is prefixed with *rs* to indicate the data type of the variable in the code. Using the plural form of *Event* indicates that the recordset is meant to hold more than one event.

5. Choose your connection, **connTheSoccerSite**, which you created in Chapter 11, from the Connection drop-down list.

6. Choose Events from the Table drop-down list and then click the Selected radio button. Select the `EndDate`, `ID`, `StartDate`, `Summary`, and `Title` columns from the Columns list by holding down the Ctrl key while you click each name.

7. Select StartDate from the Sort drop-down list and make sure that Ascending is selected in the drop-down list next to it. The final Recordset dialog box should look like Figure 12-3.

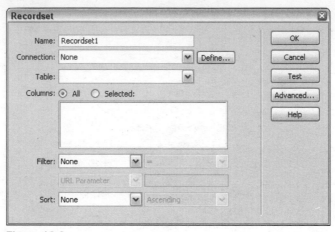

Figure 12-2

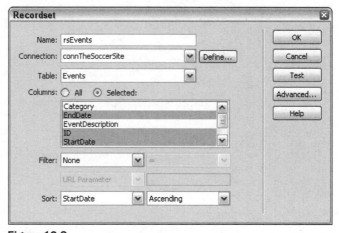

Figure 12-3

8. At this point, it's a good idea to test your SQL statement. Although you can be sure that the SQL that Dreamweaver creates is valid, you should test it to make sure you get the results from the database that you expect. Click the Test button to see a dialog box that lists all the records from the Events table in your database. Notice that you'll only see the columns that you selected in the Recordset dialog box. Close the Test SQL Statement dialog box by clicking OK.

9. Click OK to close the Recordset dialog box. Dreamweaver inserts some ASP code for the recordset into events.asp. Save the page.

How It Works

As soon as you click the OK button, Dreamweaver adds the following ASP code to the top of your page (we split the SQL statement over two lines to improve code readability):

```
<%@LANGUAGE="VBSCRIPT" CODEPAGE="1252"%>
<!-#include file="Connections/connTheSoccerSite.asp" ->
<%
Dim rsEvents
Dim rsEvents_numRows
Set rsEvents = Server.CreateObject("ADODB.Recordset")
rsEvents.ActiveConnection = MM_connTheSoccerSite_STRING
rsEvents.Source = "SELECT EndDate, ID, StartDate, Summary, Title " _
  & "FROM Events ORDER BY StartDate ASC"rsEvents.CursorType = 0
rsEvents.CursorLocation = 2
rsEvents.LockType = 1
rsEvents.Open()
rsEvents_numRows = 0
%>
<!-#include file="Tools/functions.asp"->
<% SetFirstVisitedPage() %>
```

If you think the code looks familiar, that's because you already saw most of it in Chapter 11. You saw the Include statement for your connection string and how an ADODB.Recordset was created and set up. The only thing new in this code is the rsEvents_numRows variable that keeps track of the total number of records available in the recordset.

With the recordset in place, you can now add columns from the recordset you just inserted to your HTML table. In this table, you display the title, summary, and start and end dates of each event.

Displaying the Events on events.asp

1. Open the Bindings panel in the Application panel group (press Ctrl+F10) and expand the rsEvents recordset. Switch to Design view and drag the Title column from the Bindings panel to the first row of the HTML table you created in the previous Try It Out exercise, as shown in Figure 12-4.

   This adds the text {rsEvents.Title} in the table cell. In Code view, you'll see
   <%=(rsEvents.Fields.Item("Title").Value)%>.

   Repeat this step for the Summary item by dragging it from the Bindings panel to the second row of the table.

2. In the third row, type **This event will last from StartDate until EndDate**. Double-click the word *StartDate* to select it and drag the column StartDate from the Bindings panel onto the selection in Design view. Dreamweaver replaces the selected text with a dynamic value for StartDate. Repeat this step for EndDate.

3. Now you'll need to format the way the date is displayed in the browser. By default, Dreamweaver does not interfere with the format, so the date appears the way the database passes it to the ASP page. In this example, the date should be presented a bit more nicely. Dreamweaver can apply various formatting functions to columns from a database. This way you can easily format special values like dates, currency, and numbers.

   Open the Server Behaviors panel again (press Ctrl+F9) and double-click the Dynamic Text (rsEvents.StartDate) entry to bring up the Dynamic Text dialog box. In the Format drop-down list in the lower part of the dialog box, choose the format Date/Time - Monday, January 17, 2000 (see Figure 12-5).

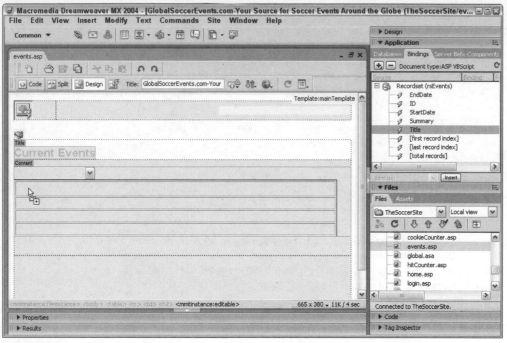

Figure 12-4

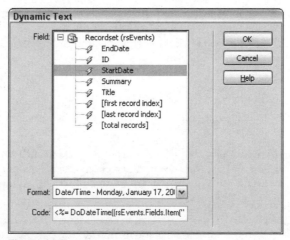

Figure 12-5

Click OK to close the dialog box. Repeat this step and apply the same formatting for EndDate. Your HTML table should now look like this in Code view:

```
<option value="4"<%=sSelected%>>US Major League Soccer</option>
</select>
```

```
<table width="600" border="1" cellspacing="2" cellpadding="2">
<tr>
 <td><%=(rsEvents.Fields.Item("Title").Value)%></td>
</tr>
<tr>
 <td><%=(rsEvents.Fields.Item("Summary").Value)%></td>
</tr>
<tr>
 <td>
  This event will last from
   <%= DoDateTime((rsEvents.Fields.Item("StartDate").Value), 1, 1033) %>
   until
   <%= DoDateTime((rsEvents.Fields.Item("EndDate").Value), 1, 1033) %>
 </td>
</tr>
<tr>
 <td> </td>
</tr>
</table>
</form>
```

Leave the fourth row of the table empty for now; it serves as a separator between the individual events in the list. Save the page again.

4. To improve the looks of the table, apply some CSS classes to the page. Open `mainStyles.css`, which you created in Chapter 9 from the `Styles` folder on the Files panel. Scroll to the end of the file and add the following custom CSS classes:

```
.clsSolidBlackBorder
{
 border: 1px solid black;
}
.clsHeading
{
 font-size: 14pt;
 font-weight: bold;
}
.clsSummary
{
 font-style: italic;
 font-weight: bold;
}
```

Remember that you can use the CSS Styles panel (press Shift+F11) to create these classes or you can type in the code directly. Copy and paste these classes into the three other style sheets that you created for the different themes in your site. Finally, save and close all four style sheet documents.

5. Back in `events.asp`, make sure you are in Code view and locate the opening `<table>` tag for the table that holds the list of events. Position your cursor right before the closing `>` of the tag and type **class="**. As soon as you type the quote character, Dreamweaver displays a list with classes from which you can select. Using your down-arrow, select clsSolidBlackBorder and then press Enter. Alternatively, select the entire table tag using the Tag selector, open the CSS Styles panel (press Shift+F11), right-click the class clsSolidBlackBorder, and choose Apply.

Your `<table>` tag should now look like this in Code view:

```
</select>
<table width="600" border="1" cellpadding="2" cellspacing="2"
    class="clsSolidBlackBorder">
<tr>
```

6. Click once inside the first row of the table in Design view and then, on the CSS Styles panel, right-click the class clsHeading and choose Apply. Dreamweaver is smart enough to figure out that the style should be applied to the complete `<td>` element. Repeat this step for the second row, but apply clsSummary to it. Finally, add an `<hr>` tag in the last row in Code view, replacing the ` ` it contains as a placeholder. On the Property inspector for the `<hr>` tag, set the height (H) to 1 pixel, deselect the Shading check box and set the Align attribute to Center. The code for the `<hr>` tag now looks like this:

```
<hr align="center" size="1" noshade>
```

This draws a line between each of the events displayed on your page.

7. To see how the page ends up in the browser, switch to Design view. Hide all visual aids by making sure there is a check mark before the menu item View➪Visual Aids➪Hide All (or press Ctrl+Shift+I). Doing this hides borders from tables, layers, frames, etc. so you can see a preview of how the final page looks. You should see something like Figure 12-6.

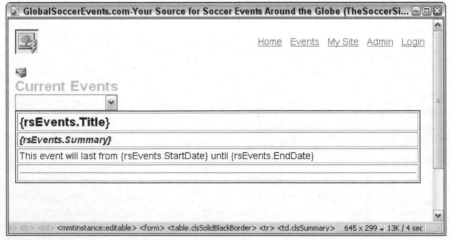

Figure 12-6

If you press Ctrl+Shift+I again, all visual aids will be turned back on.

8. Now that you have finished the design of one single table row, you can apply the repeat region behavior. A repeat region repeats a certain part of HTML and ASP code for each record it finds in the recordset used in the repeat region. In this example, all four `<tr>` elements that you created for each event in the `rsEvents` recordset need to be repeated. To apply the repeat behavior, first select all four `<tr>` elements in Code view:

```
</select>
<table width="600" border="1" cellpadding="2" cellspacing="2"
    class="clsSolidBlackBorder">
 <tr>
  <td class="clsHeading"><%=(rsEvents.Fields.Item("Title").Value)%></td>
 </tr>
 <tr>
  <td class="clsSummary"><%=(rsEvents.Fields.Item("Summary").Value)%></td>
 </tr>
 <tr>
  <td>
   This event will last from
   <%= DoDateTime((rsEvents.Fields.Item("StartDate").Value), 1, 1033) %>
   until
   <%= DoDateTime((rsEvents.Fields.Item("EndDate").Value), 1, 1033) %>
  </td>
 </tr>
 <tr>
  <td><hr align="center" size="1" noshade ></td>
 </tr>
</table>
</form>
```

Make sure you don't accidentally include the opening or closing tag of the table.

Open the Server Behaviors panel (press Ctrl+F9) and choose Repeat Region from the plus (+) button menu. In the Repeat Region dialog box that appears (see Figure 12-7), ensure that rsEvents is selected and click All Records in the Show section.

Figure 12-7

Click OK to apply the behavior. Dreamweaver adds some ASP code, both to the top of your page and inside the HTML table surrounding the region you selected to be repeated.

9. Remove the border from the table with events by changing the `border` attribute to **0** on the Property inspector. Save the page, open it in your browser, and you'll see the complete list of all events in your database, ordered by their start date (see Figure 12-8).

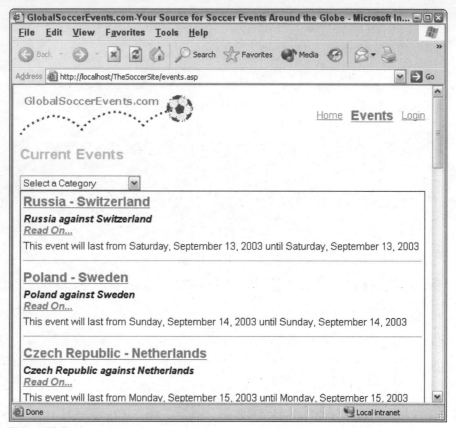

Figure 12-8

How It Works

A repeat region works by looping through a recordset and displaying a mix of static HTML and values retrieved from the recordset. It's also possible to use ASP code within the loop to display the results of built-in functions, format values from a recordset, or display variables. To get a better understanding of how this works, take at look at the code that Dreamweaver adds to your page when you add a recordset, when you transform your static HTML table in a repeat region, and when you dragged and dropped the column names on your table.

You already saw the code for the recordset in the previous Try It Out exercise. After the recordset code, Dreamweaver inserts code that creates two variables and assigns them a value:

```
rsEvents_numRows = 0
%>
```

```
<% Dim Repeat1__numRows
Dim Repeat1__index
Repeat1__numRows = -1
Repeat1__index = 0
rsEvents_numRows = rsEvents_numRows + Repeat1__numRows
%>
<!--#include file="Tools/functions.asp"-->
```

`Repeat1__numRows` determines the total number of rows displayed on one page and is often referred to as the *page size*. In this example, the number of events on the page is not limited, so Dreamweaver sets it to –1. `Repeat1__index` is used to count how many records have already been placed on the current page.

Next, take a look at the HTML table mixed with the ASP code so you understand how the table is created. We'll start with the table definition:

```
<table width="600" border="0" cellspacing="2" cellpadding="2"
   class="clsSolidBlackBorder" >

<%
 While ((Repeat1__numRows <> 0) AND (NOT rsEvents.EOF))
%>
<tr>
```

Only the rows inside the table need to be repeated, without repeating the actual table itself, so the `<table>` tag is placed outside the ASP code. The `While` statement then loops through each record in the recordset while `Repeat1__numRows` does not equal 0 and the recordset still contains records (`NOT rsEvents.EOF`).

`Repeat1__numRows` contains the hard-coded value of –1 in this example. This way, this condition always return `True`. You'll see this variable again when we discuss paging data later in the chapter.

We have already seen how the second condition works in the previous chapter where we touched briefly on the `EOF` and `BOF` properties of a recordset. The whole `While` statement can be simplified to something simpler to understand in pseudocode:

```
While (There are still Records in the Recordset)
```

> Pseudocode is often used to describe the logical flow of code without getting into many details of the code itself. It can help you in designing and explaining parts of your application. As you can see, this theory works well in this situation: The `While` statement is a lot easier to understand this way.

After the line with the `While` statement, the code repeats the HTML table rows. We'll look at two of them in more detail after we finish our discussion of the ASP code.

```
<%
 Repeat1__index=Repeat1__index+1
 Repeat1__numRows=Repeat1__numRows-1

 rsEvents.MoveNext()
Wend
%>
```

`Repeat1__index` and `Repeat1__numRows` aren't used until the navigational links are added to the page later in the chapter. The `MoveNext()` call moves to the next record in the recordset. If there are no more records left, a call to `MoveNext()` sets the `EOF` property to `True`. This causes the test in the `While` loop to return `False`, which ends the loop. The `Wend` statement finally closes the context for the `While` loop. Notice that the `While ... Wend` construct is a bit of old-fashioned code. You're more likely to encounter the `Do While ... Loop` constructs in hand-coded pages.

Now that you know how the looping code works to repeat an HTML region for every record in a record-set, take a look at the way the actual values from the columns in the recordset are displayed in the browser. Look carefully at the code for the `Title` column and the `StartDate` column but not at the others, because those are very similar to these two.

```
<tr>
 <td class="clsHeading"><%=(rsEvents.Fields.Item("Title").Value)%></td>
</tr>
```

First, a one-column table row with one cell is displayed. The cell contains the `Title` column from the recordset. As you have seen in Chapter 11, `rsEvents.Fields.Item("Title").Value` is used to retrieve the `Title` column from the recordset so it can be outputted to the browser. Since no special formatting to the actual data is required, the value of the Title column is send to the browser as-is by placing it between the familiar `<%=` and `%>` tags.

Both dates require some special formatting. The start date is formatted as follows:

```
This Event will last from <%=
  DoDateTime((rsEvents.Fields.Item("StartDate").Value), 1, 1033) %> until
```

It looks quite similar to the way the `Title` column is retrieved. What's different is the call to the `DoDateTime` function that has been added. The call to this function, which Dreamweaver has added to the page as well, requires three arguments: the date that needs to be converted, the date format to which the date should be converted, and the *locale*. The locale defines the way values like dates, currency, and numbers should be displayed on a Web page. Locales are based on a combination of language, country, and culture. For example, `1033` is the locale ID for English—United States.

You can find out more about locales in ASP by searching `msdn.microsoft.com` *for Session.LCID.*

Inside the `DoDateTime` function Dreamweaver temporarily switches the locale to one that uses a date format that matches the one you chose in the Dynamic Text dialog box. Then it calls `FormatDateTime`, a built-in ASP function, and passes it the date that needs to be converted. The `FormatDateTime` function then converts the date to the format specified by the locale.

Once the date has been formatted, the code restores the locale again so everything is back as it was. At the end, the results of the `FormatDateTime` function are returned so they can be displayed on the page.

You may have noticed that the `DoDateTime` function is placed inside a `<script>` block with the following opening tag:

```
<SCRIPT runat=SERVER language=VBSCRIPT>
```

Using `<script>` tags with a `runat=SERVER` attribute to denote an ASP code block is functionally equivalent to using `<%` and `%>`.

With relatively little effort you are now able to create a good-looking repeated table in Dreamweaver using a simple behavior. Of course the table uses some CSS to improve its visual appearance, but even without that, you can see the power of the behavior. There are, however, two limitations with the current implementation of this list of events:

❑   Events that have expired some time ago are still displayed

❑   The functionality of the category drop-down list that you created in Chapter 8 is broken

Besides these problems, imagine that you have lots of events. The list on the events page will be much too long to be presented at once. You need a way to break up the list into smaller pages so they are faster to download and easier to navigate. Also, there is no way to link to a page with more details about the event. If you followed the discussion on the data model in the previous chapter, you'll remember the Events table has an EventDescription column of type Memo. This column holds the details about your events. Wouldn't it be nice if you could link your list of events to a page where you can display all of the information you have available about an event?

In the next section, we demonstrate a solution to the first two problems, as they are closely related. We also build a solution to the other two problems towards the end of this chapter.

Extending the Repeat Region

The first two problems are related to each other. Both have to do with the amount of data pulled from the database. In the first case, the events should be filtered based on their end date. In the second case, the events must be filtered based on the category that has been assigned to the events. Both of these filters can be applied by adding a WHERE clause to the SELECT statement. In the next Try It Out exercise, you'll add this filter for the category. Because the date filter is a bit trickier, we'll discuss that separately.

Filtering Database Values Using a Drop-Down List

To filter the Events list so it shows only the events for a specific category, you need to pass the ID of the requested category to the database. The form with the lstCategory drop-down list (on the events page) submits to itself when the user chooses a new category from the list. The value for the chosen category is passed with the form's other contents, so it can be retrieved from the QueryString collection and passed to the WHERE clause of your SQL statement.

Try It Out   Filtering the Categories

1.   Open the rsEvents recordset on the events.asp page by double-clicking it in the Server Behaviors panel.

2.   Choose Category from the Filter list. Choose URL Parameter from the drop-down list below Category and then type **lstCategory** in the text field next to it. The Recordset dialog box should look like Figure 12-9.

Figure 12-9

Click OK so the changes are inserted in your page.

3. Save and run the page. Play around with the drop-down list on the page and notice that the category drop-down list works again, just as it did in Chapter 8.

4. When the page loads the first time, the drop down-list displays `Select a Category` and no events are displayed yet. This is, however, purely coincidence. The code that Dreamweaver inserts in your page tries to retrieve events from Category 1, even if the user hasn't made a choice from the drop-down list. If there were events in the Champions League category in the database, they would be displayed even if you hadn't made a selection yet. That's not very helpful for the user and might cause confusion. Instead, you might want to show all the records, without any filtering, if the user hasn't made a choice yet. To do this, change the default value for `rsEvents__MMColParam` from 1 to the word Category, like this:

```
Dim rsEvents__MMColParam
```
```
rsEvents__MMColParam = "Category"
If (Request.QueryString("lstCategory") <> "") Then
 rsEvents__MMColParam = Request.QueryString("lstCategory")
End If
```

The code now selects all events from all categories. Because the first option in the drop-down list now selects all records from the database, you should update the first option's name as well. A better description for the first item would be `All Events`:

```
<select name="lstCategory" onChange="document.frmSelectCategory.submit();">
  <option value="">All Events</option>
  <% If iLastCategory = 1 Then sSelected = " selected=""selected""" _
```

5. The drop-down list has still one little problem. As you'll recall from Chapter 8, the drop-down list is able to remember the category that's chosen last so it can be selected again when the user returns. The code that retrieves the cookie to preselect the item in the drop-down list is only executed when there is no value for the category drop-down list in the QueryString. The `<option>` element for `All Events` does not have a value so the previous cookie will be used to select an item in the list. For example, if you first select Champions League and then select All Events from the drop-down list, you'll notice that the list jumps back to Champions League. Fortunately, the fix is quite easy.

While still in `events.asp`, locate the code block that retrieves the value from the cookie (right after the call to `SetFirstVisitedPage()`) and add the following shaded lines:

```
Response.Cookies("LastCategory").Expires = Date() + 10
Else
  If Request.QueryString = "" Then
    ' Page is requested directly, so get the cookie
    If Len(Request.Cookies("LastCategory")) > 0 Then
     iLastCategory = CInt(Request.Cookies("LastCategory"))
    End If
  Else
    Response.Cookies("LastCategory") = ""
    Response.Cookies("LastCategory").Expires = Date() + 10
  End If
End If
```

6. Save and view the page. If you now choose UEFA Cup from the list, the item stays selected. If you navigate away from the page and return again, UEFA Cup is still shown in the drop-down list and the UEFA Cup events are listed. If you choose All Events from the drop-down, all the events are displayed on the page.

How It Works

Whenever the user selects a new item from the drop-down list, the form is submitted automatically. By using `Request.QueryString("lstCategory")` the value associated with the category the user chooses is retrieved and stored in `rsEvents__MMColParam`. This variable is then inserted into the SQL statement. In the end, the SQL statement looks as follows when you have chosen UEFA Cup from the drop-down list:

```
SELECT EndDate, ID, StartDate, Summary, Title FROM Events
   WHERE Category = 2 ORDER BY StartDate ASC
```

As you can see, the number 2 is passed as the category ID. The database determines which records match that category ID.

At first, when you load the page at Step 3, no records are returned. Dreamweaver has assigned a default value of 1 to the `rsEvents__MMColParam` parameter. There are currently no events in that category, so nothing is displayed. When you change the default value of 1 to the word *Category*, you get all events from all categories when you reload the page:

```
Dim rsEvents__MMColParam
rsEvents__MMColParam = "Category"
If (Request.QueryString("lstCategory") <> "") Then
```

There are also no records that have a category of type `Category`. This wouldn't even be possible because the `Category` column is a number and not text, so how are all the events retrieved from the database when the word `Category` is passed as the category? To understand this, take a look at the final SQL statement again:

```
SELECT EndDate, ID, StartDate, Summary, Title FROM Events
   WHERE Category = Category ORDER BY StartDate ASC
```

As you can see, the SQL statement is more or less the same. The number 2 is passed in the previous example and 2 is displayed in the SQL statement. This time the word Category is passed and the query displays Category as well. The reason that this works is that the database treats the second occurrence of Category as a column name and not as a value. So in pseudocode the database is asked to perform the following action:

```
SELECT All Records FROM Events
WHERE Column Category equals Column Category
```

By comparing two identical values, the contents of the column Category in this case, this statement always returns True and all records are selected.

The code that retrieves the value from the cookie for the selected drop-down list was expanded with the following additional lines of code:

```
If Request.QueryString = "" Then
 ' Page is requested directly, so get the cookie
 If Len(Request.Cookies("LastCategory")) > 0 Then
  iLastCategory = CInt(Request.Cookies("LastCategory"))
 End If

Else
 Response.Cookies("LastCategory") = ""
 Response.Cookies("LastCategory").Expires = Date() + 10
End If
```

A simple If statement checks if the entire QueryString equals an empty string. If it does, it means the page must have been requested directly. But if you choose All Events from the drop-down list, you can see from the Address bar of your browser that there *is* a QueryString (see Figure 12-10).

Figure 12-10

The QueryString does exist but its only element, lstCategory, does not have a value, so the code that saves the cookie doesn't run. But because there is a QueryString, the code in the second If block doesn't run either, so the cookie is no longer retrieved. Instead, the cookie is reset by setting its value to an empty string. This ensures that the next time the user requests the page, the All Events option is preselected again.

Filtering Values by Date

Now that you have the filter for the category drop-down list in place, the next step is to filter events based on their ending date. This ensures that the list of events is always up to date. Expired events are automatically hidden from the Events list.

Try It Out   A Date with the WHERE Clause

1. Open the page events.asp and locate Recordset (rsEvents) on the Server Behaviors panel. Double-click it to open the Recordset dialog box. If you are in Simple mode, click the Advanced button to switch to Advanced mode.

There are two ways to set up the date filter: Either let the database handle the filter or create it in ASP and pass it to the database. We'll start by discussing the first method, as that requires the least amount of code for your page.

Change the WHERE clause by changing the text in the SQL box so it now looks like this:

```
SELECT EndDate, ID, StartDate, Summary, Title
FROM Events
WHERE Category = MMColParam AND EndDate >= Date()
ORDER BY StartDate ASC
```

Click OK to apply the changes to your page.

2. Save the page and view it. The expired events have disappeared from the list. If you don't see any events at all, that may be because all the events in the database happened in the past.

A simple solution to this is to change the date of the events in the database (if you have Microsoft Access installed on your computer). Alternatively, you can run the file changeDatesOfEvents.asp in the code download for this chapter. To run the page, copy the page from the code download to your local site (C:\TheSoccerSite), open it in Dreamweaver, and press F12. The file changes the dates of the events in the database, so there will always be a few events with their end dates set in the past and a few events with a future date.

How It Works

The change to the code affects only one line:

```
rsEvents.Source = "SELECT EndDate, ID, StartDate, " & _
    " Summary, Title FROM Events WHERE Category = " + _
    Replace(rsEvents__MMColParam, "'", "''") + _
    " AND EndDate >= Date() ORDER BY StartDate ASC"
```

We added a few underscores again to break the code over four lines. As you can see, the WHERE clause is changed so it now also filters the EndDate column. By setting its criterion to >= Date(), only those records whose end date hasn't passed yet are selected. The ORDER BY clause sorts the records that are retrieved so that the oldest event is displayed first.

What's important about this change is that you understand *where* the WHERE clause is carried out. If you have your Web server running on a different computer from your database, their dates and times may differ because they are located in different time zones, for example. In the code example, the value of Date() is determined by the database because it is contained in the SQL string.

This code is more or less fixed to Microsoft Access. The Date() function in this case is a built-in function of that database. Microsoft SQL Server uses GetDate(), for example, so this code is likely to break when you try to connect to another kind of database. In the next section, we'll change the SQL statement so the date is generated by ASP and then passed to the database.

Try It Out   Your Second Date with the WHERE Clause

1. Open the recordset on events.asp and remove the part of the WHERE clause that filters the EndDate from the SQL text box in the Advanced mode of the Recordset dialog box. Your SQL statement should now look like this again:

```
SELECT EndDate, ID, StartDate, Summary, Title
FROM Events
WHERE Category = MMColParam
ORDER BY StartDate ASC
```

2. Click the plus (+) button on the Variables list. Type **Today** as the Name for the variable, **1/1/2100** for the Default Value, and **Date()** as the Run-time Value. Expand Tables in the Database items window and then expand the table Events. Click the column EndDate and then click the WHERE button. This adds EndDate to the WHERE clause of the SQL statement.

Next type >= #Today# as the criterion for EndDate in the SQL box. The # is a delimiter for a date in Access, just as the ' character is used in previous chapters to delimit text values. If all works out as expected, the Recordset dialog box looks like Figure 12-11.

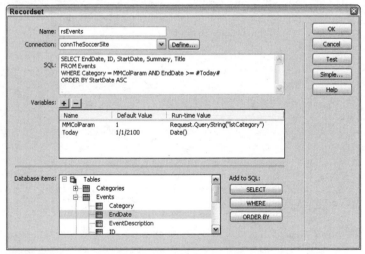

Figure 12-11

3. Save the page and view it in your browser. You'll see the same events as you saw at the end of the previous Try It Out exercise (see Figure 12-12).

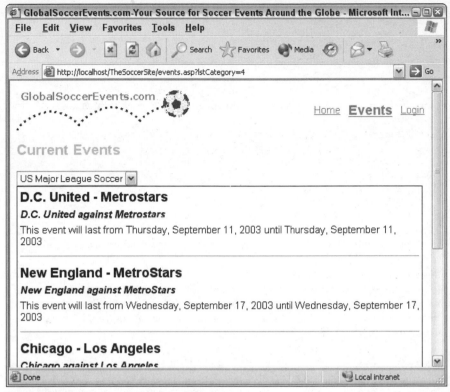

Figure 12-12

How It Works

This time, Dreamweaver added more code to accomplish the same thing. It inserted a code block to define the Today variable and it changed the SQL statement:

```
Dim rsEvents__Today
rsEvents__Today = "1/1/2100"
```

The variable rsEvents__Today is the same variable you created and called Today in the Recordset dialog box. Dreamweaver adds the prefix rsEvents__ to it to show which recordset the variable belongs to, and to enable you to have multiple recordsets with the same variable names. At runtime, this variable is filled with the value you assign to it before it is passed to the database. But first Dreamweaver assigns the hard-coded value of 1/1/2100 to your variable. This is the default value that's passed to the database if the ASP code is unable to create a valid value from the Date() statement. Dreamweaver also uses this default value when you click the Test button in the Recordset dialog box. The selected date is far away in the future, so you can be sure that no records will ever be selected accidentally. It's highly unlikely you'll create events that have an end date somewhere in the next century.

```
If (Date() <> "") Then
 rsEvents__Today = Date()
End If
```

Next, the value of Date() is assigned to variable rsEvents__Today, which is used in the SQL statement:

```
rsEvents.Source = "SELECT EndDate, ID, StartDate, Summary, " & _
   "Title FROM Events WHERE Category = " + _
   Replace(rsEvents__MMColParam, "'", "''") + _
   " AND EndDate >= #" + _
   Replace(rsEvents__Today, "'", "''") + _
   "# ORDER BY StartDate ASC"
```

Instead of passing the complete SQL statement to the database as is, this line of code inserts the value from rsEvents__Today in the SQL statement before it is passed to the database.

For this simple example, the outcome is the same for both ways to filter the events based on their end date. However, the second method is preferred to the first because it is easier to change the code later. Right now, you're just using a single date so there isn't much to change. But if you decide to add the time, or change the Today variable to select events from yesterday as well, it's easier to do this in the ASP code than directly in the SQL statement.

The Events list has now become a lot smarter: It's able to filter out expired events and you can let the user decide from which category to see events displayed. Now it's time to hook up your Events list to a details page so the user can see all the information you have available in your database about a specific event.

Viewing Details of an Event

Connecting your Events list to a details page is a simple two-step process. Dreamweaver MX 2004 comes with a ready-made server behavior to make this as easy as possible. First, you'll need to link each event in the list to a details page. In the second step, you'll create the details page where you show all information about a particular event.

Linking the Event List to the Details Page

On the events page you should create a hyperlink that takes your visitors to the details page. The title is an ideal candidate for this, so you can wrap it in an <a> element that sends the user to viewEventDetails.asp. You should also create a text link, like Read On..., which links to the same details page. This makes the list more intuitive for visitors who may not be aware that they can click the title.

Try It Out   Adding View Event Details Links

1. In Design view, click {rsEvents.Title} in the first row of the HTML table to select it.

2. Open the Server Behavior panel (press Ctrl+F9) and choose Go To Detail Page from the plus (+) menu.

In the Go To Detail Page dialog box, type **viewEventDetails.asp** as the Detail page and select ID for both the Pass URL Parameter and the Column lists. Make sure the dialog box looks the same as in Figure 12-13.

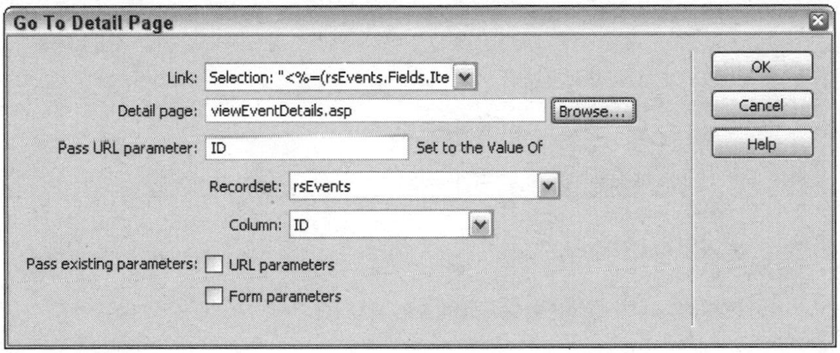

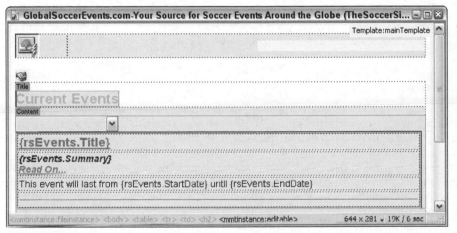

Figure 12-13

Click OK to add the behavior to your page. The text {rsEvents.Title} is now green and underlined in Design view to indicate that the hyperlink has been created.

3. Click once to the right of {rsEvents.Summary} in Design view so it's not selected but the cursor is immediately after the }. Press Shift+Enter to add a <br> tag and then type **Read On...** on the new line. Select the text Read On... and turn it into a link by applying the same server behavior as you did in Step 2. You page now looks like Figure 12-14 in Design view.

Figure 12-14

4. That's all you need to do to connect a list of records—your events in this example—to a page with more details. Save and run the page. You can see in Figure 12-15 that for each visible event, two links are added: The title and the words `Read On...` are now linked to the details page.

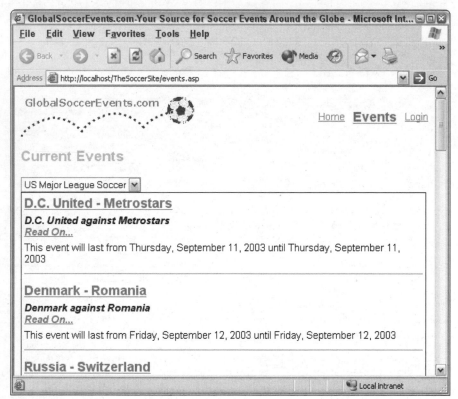

Figure 12-15

Don't worry about the error message you get stating that the details page isn't found when you click a link. After we explain how the Go To Detail Page server behavior works you get the opportunity to create the details page.

How It Works

Most of the code that Dreamweaver inserts is used to create a copy of the Form and QueryString values so they can be passed on to other pages. This way you could pass the Form and QueryString values from the current page to the next. If you do the same in the details page, you can pass those variables back again to the main events page through a Back button or link. This way you preserve the state of the category drop-down list, for example. This improves the usability of your site because a user stays in the category selected without having to select it again each time he returns from viewing the details of an event. It's best not to use this option to pass values from page to page because you can soon lose track of what you are sending where. If you only need to save the user's last selection, a cookie (as was used in Chapter 8) or a session variable would be much easier to implement.

Now look at the actual Go To Detail Page link:

```
<A href="viewEventDetails.asp?<%= MM_keepNone & MM_joinChar(MM_keepNone) & "ID=" &
rsEvents.Fields.Item("ID").Value %>"><%=(rsEvents.Fields.Item("Title").Value)%></A>
```

As you can see, it's quite simple. Dreamweaver wraps the title from the recordset in an <a> element. This link points to viewEventDetails.asp, the page where the details of your events are shown. Because the options to pass existing parameters to the next page is unselected in the Go To Detail Page dialog box, Dreamweaver inserts the variable MM_keepNone here, which means that no Form or QueryString values are sent to the receiving page. If you had checked URL parameters or Form parameters in the Go To Detail Page dialog box to preserve the values from QueryString or Form, you would have seen MM_keepURL, MM_keepForm, or MM_keepBoth appear here as well. Besides the preserved QueryString and Form variables, the ID of the current event record is appended to the link so you can use that ID in the details page you create next to retrieve your event.

Showing Details of an Event

On the details page you need to display just one event with the ID that is passed to this page through the QueryString. Passing the ID of the event through the QueryString makes it easier for your visitor to bookmark the page and come back later. When you add a bookmark in your browser, the complete address, including the QueryString, is saved so when you later revisit the page, you see the exact same event again. Notice, though, that this can generally create a problem as the browser can save a local copy of the page in its cache. If the page has changed since the user's last visit, they may end up with their local, outdated copy instead of the new one from the server. We'll show you how to solve this problem in the next Try It Out exercise.

On the details page, a recordset is used once again to retrieve the data. This time the recordset is filtered to just one record. The filter for the recordset retrieves the ID from the QueryString at runtime, just as you did with the category drop-down list earlier.

If the record is found, it can be displayed on the page. If it can't be found, a friendly error message appears explaining that the requested event could not be found. This is useful when the page is accidentally requested directly or when somebody tries to request an event that has been deleted in the meantime. This can happen when somebody opens your page from an old bookmark or through outdated information from a search engine, for example. In the next exercise you'll create and design the details page while you add the error message in a subsequent exercise.

Try It Out   **Displaying Details of a Requested Event**

1. Add a new page to the root of your site and call it **viewEventDetails.asp**. Make sure it is based on the main template for the site. Remove all three placeholders for the Title, Content, and Footer regions.

2. Add a new recordset by opening the Server Behaviors panel and choosing Recordset (Query) from the plus (+) button menu. Switch to Simple mode and name the recordset **rsEvent**. Since this recordset only contains one event, the singular form of *Event* is used to describe the recordset.

Your connection, `connTheSoccerSite`, should already be selected in the Connection list. Next, choose Events from the Table drop-down list and then click the radio button for the Selected item in the columns section. Select the columns that should be retrieved from the database. To do this, click the columns `EndDate`, `EventDescription`, `ID`, `StartDate`, `Summary`, and `Title` in the Columns list while holding down the Ctrl key.

3. Choose ID from the Filter list. Dreamweaver fills in the rest of the drop-down lists and text boxes. When you're done, the Recordset dialog box should look like Figure 12-16.

Figure 12-16

Click OK to insert the recordset to your page.

4. Now that you have the ASP code for the recordset in place, it's time to insert an HTML table that you can use to format your event record. In Design view, insert the table in the Content region of the page by selecting Insert⇨Table. Fill in the Table dialog box as shown in Figure 12-17.

Click OK to insert the table into the page.

5. Open the Bindings panel (press Ctrl+F10) and expand the item Recordset (rsEvent). Drag the Summary column from the panel and drop it in the first row of the table. Repeat this step by dragging EventDescription to the third row of the table.

6. In Design view, right-click the text `{rsEvent.Summary}` and choose clsSummary from the CSS Styles menu. The summary will now be displayed in a bold and italic font in Design view.

7. Inside the fourth cell, type **This event will last from StartDate until EndDate** and select `StartDate` by double-clicking it. From the Bindings panel, drag `StartDate` and drop it on the selected text. Repeat this for the `EndDate` text as well.

8. Next, you should format the dates again so the values appear a little more user-friendly on-screen. To do this, open the Server Behaviors panel by pressing Ctrl+F9 and then double-click the entry Dynamic Text (rsEvent.StartDate). Choose the **Date/Time - Monday, January 17, 2000** date and time format from the Format list again. Repeat this step for the `EndDate` column.

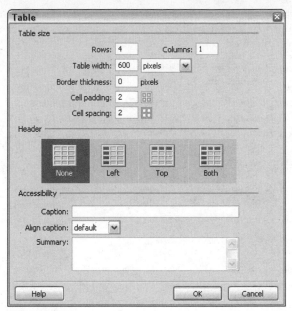

Figure 12-17

9. Switch back to the Bindings panel (press Ctrl+F10) and drag the column `Title` to the Title region of your template. Notice that Dreamweaver applies the CSS style for the `<h2>` tag to the text `{rsEvent.Title}` in Design view.

    Press Ctrl+Shift+I to hide the visual aids so you can see how your page appears in the browser (see Figure 12-18).

Figure 12-18

Press Ctrl+Shift+I again to turn the visual aids back on.

10. Previewing your page in Design view gives you a good idea how the page eventually looks in the browser, but wouldn't it be great if you could preview it with a real event from the database? Dreamweaver lets you do this with the Live Data view.

On the Document tool bar, next to the Design button is the Live Data View button with a lightning bolt on it. Go ahead and click it.

Dreamweaver updates the Design view so it shows the page with real data from the database (see Figure 12-19). Notice that the My Site and Admin menu items are hidden because you are not logged in. Dreamweaver even displays the site badge correctly because the Live Data view also executes the ASP script that assigns the default value of `logo` to the `sBadge` variable that is defined in the main template.

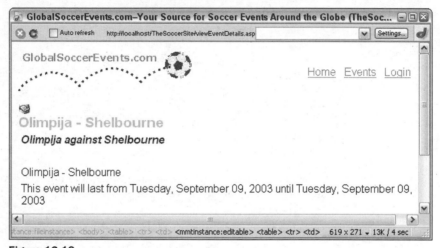

Figure 12-19

The cool thing about the Live Data view is that it's not a static view of the page like that which you get in your browser. You can use all the familiar Dreamweaver features to design your page. For example, you can resize your table so its contents fit nicely, move data-bound columns around (like `Title` or `Summary`) using drag and drop, or change them into a link. If you make a change, you need to refresh the Live Data view to see your changes. To do this, click the Refresh Live Data arrow on the toolbar that's been added below the Document toolbar (see Figure 12-20) or press Ctrl+R.

Figure 12-20

If you want to view a different event, type its ID in the text box after the page address on the tool bar, preceded by `ID=`. For example, type **ID=2** and press Enter to display the second event in the database. To have Dreamweaver accept the new ID when you press Enter, you must check Auto Refresh on the tool bar. Otherwise, you can just click the Refresh button when you add a new ID in the Address bar.

Click the Live Data View button again to return to the normal Design view.

11. The code that Dreamweaver inserts assigns a default value of 1 for the ID parameter in case it is not passed to the page through the QueryString. This can't really be used in this page because you could end up showing an event that was not requested by your user. By changing it to 0, you can be sure never to display an incorrect event because there is no event with an ID of 0 in the database. Locate the code block that sets the value at the very top of your page and then change it to this:

```
<!--#include file="Connections/connTheSoccerSite.asp" -->
<%
Dim rsEvent__MMColParam

rsEvent__MMColParam = "0"
If (Request.QueryString("ID") <> "") Then
 rsEvent__MMColParam = Request.QueryString("ID")
End If
%>
```

12. As the last step in this Try It Out exercise, you'll need to add some code that makes sure your `events.asp` page is not retrieved from the cache of the browser but requested from the server. This way, your visitors are always presented with the latest event information from the database. At the top of the page, add the following code block:

```
<%@LANGUAGE="VBSCRIPT" CODEPAGE="1252"%>

<%
 Response.ExpiresAbsolute = #1/1/1980#
 Response.AddHeader "cache-control", "private"
 Response.AddHeader "pragma", "no-cache"
%>
<!--#include file="Connections/connTheSoccerSite.asp" -->
```

How It Works

We have discussed all the techniques—the recordset, SQL statement, and variable for the WHERE clause—before. The only thing different from the `events.asp` page is that a dynamic column is added to the `Title` region of the template. There is nothing stopping you from dragging table columns from the Bindings panel to other locations in the page as well. If you want, you can even drag the `Title` column to the `<title></title>` section of the page in Code view. Since the recordset is declared and created at the top of the page, it is available throughout the entire page. By adding the event's title to the `<title>` section of the page, you cause the caption of the browser window to display the title of your event. Not only is this informative to the user requesting the details page, but it also helps search engines find the page. Most search engines treat text in the `<title>` section of a document with a higher priority than text in the body, so if you have some descriptive titles, the chance of someone finding your site through a search engine increases.

At the top of the page, the following code is added to prevent the page from being cached:

```
Response.ExpiresAbsolute = #1/1/1980#
Response.AddHeader "cache-control", "private"
Response.AddHeader "pragma", "no-cache"
```

This tells the browser and any caching servers, like proxy servers, that they can't cache the page and that they should consider it as expired immediately. This ensures that your visitors always get a fresh copy of the page.

Adding Error-Handling

Errors can occur whenever a requested event is not found in the database. The same error will occur at runtime if a user tries to request an event that is no longer available in the database. For example, if you request `viewEventDetails.asp` directly, there is no QueryString available, so the default value of 0 is passed to the database. Because there is no record with an ID of 0, the event can't be displayed. To prevent the error from occurring, you need to check whether the event is found in the database. If it can't be found, a friendly error message is displayed indicating what to do next.

Try It Out   Adding an Error Message

1. Dreamweaver comes with two handy behaviors that you can use to hide or show a page section when a record is not found in the database: Show Region If Recordset Is Empty and Show Region If Recordset Is Not Empty. Both behaviors can be found on the Show Region submenu of the plus (+) menu on the Server Behaviors panel.

In Code view locate the closing `</table>` tag of the HTML table that is used to display the event in `viewEventDetails.asp` and position your cursor right *behind* it. Press Shift+Enter twice to add two `<br>` tags.

Type the following text:

```
Unfortunately, the event you requested could not be found.<br>
Why don't you try your Main Event List instead?
```

Select the text `Main Event List` in the message in Code view and link it to `events.asp` by choosing Insert⇔Hyperlink. Browse to `events.asp` by clicking the folder icon. Back on the Hyperlink dialog box, click OK to insert the hyperlink in the page.

2. In Design view, select both lines of the error message. On the Property inspector, choose **clsErrorMessage** from the Style drop-down list. Dreamweaver puts the message between a pair of `<span>` tags and applies the CSS class to this span. In Design view, the error message turns red.

3. Select the `<span>` tag you just inserted using the Tag selector, open the Server Behaviors panel, click the plus (+) button, and select Show Region⇔Show Region If Recordset Is Empty. The Show Region If Recordset Is Empty dialog box opens, and since there is only one recordset in your page, rsEvent is already selected. Click OK to insert the behavior in your page. Your page should now look like Figure 12-21.

Notice the Show If label just above the error message to indicate that this section only appears when the recordset is empty.

4. Select the complete HTML table that displays your event using the Tag selector (you may need to click inside the table first to make `<table>` appear on the Tag selector bar). Click the plus (+) button and select Show Region⇔Show Region If Recordset Is Not Empty to apply this behavior to the selection. Once again, rsEvent is already selected for you.

5. Since the title of the page is also retrieved from the database, wrap it in a Show Region If Recordset Is Not Empty behavior as well. Select `{rsEvent.Title}` in the `Title` region of your template in Design view and apply the same server behavior as you did in the previous step.

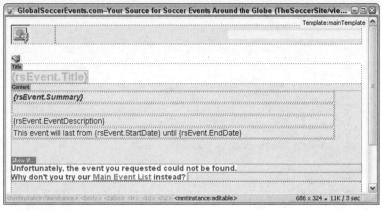

Figure 12-21

6. Save your page and then open it in your browser by pressing F12. The page will be displayed but you'll see the error message indicating that the event cannot be found (see Figure 12-22). This is expected because you are not passing an ID through the QueryString.

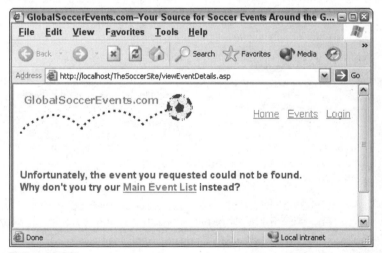

Figure 12-22

7. Click the Main Event List link to go to your events.asp page. Select a category from the drop-down list, click the title of an event, and you'll see the event appear while the error message is hidden (see Figure 12-23).

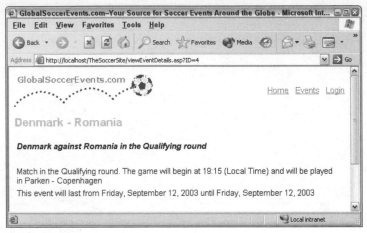

Figure 12-23

How It Works

In this exercise we have introduced a new concept: the server behaviors that hide or show a region of the page when a recordset is empty or not. The following code is responsible for displaying or hiding the error message:

```
<br>
<br>
<% If rsEvent.EOF And rsEvent.BOF Then %>
 <span class="clsErrorMessage"> Unfortunately, the event you requested
  could not be found.<br>
  Why don't you try your <a href="events.asp">Main Event List</a>
  instead?
 </span>
<% End If ' end rsEvent.EOF And rsEvent.BOF %>
<!- InstanceEndEditable -></td>
```

As you can see, the EOF and BOF properties of the recordset are used again. If both are True, there is no event in the recordset and the error message is displayed. The same principle is used for displaying the event; only this time both the EOF and the BOF properties must be False before the HTML table can be sent to the browser.

Your database-driven application is really starting to grow now. Your visitors can request a list of events, limit that list to events of a specific category they are interested in, and view the events' details. If all goes well, not only will the application grow, but your data will grow too. You are likely to add more and more events to the database. After a while, however, you may notice that the full list of events loads slowly because the list is much too long. In order not to appear as a slow site to your visitors, you need to think of a way to break up the page in smaller lists. The best way to do this is to present the data in "pages" with a limited number of events per page. By providing Next and Previous links, your visitors are able to navigate the entire list of events. This not only improves the download speed of the events page but also improves the usability of your pages. Ten pages with 10 events each are much easier to read and comprehend than one long list with 100 events.

The technique of showing data in manageable chunks is called, unsurprisingly, paging.

Paging Data

The concept behind *paging* is easy to understand: You just display a number of events until the page is full and then continue on the next page. In terms of books or printed sheets it's also very easy to apply; you'll be forced to continue on the next page after the current one is full.

Paging data from a recordset for Web page display is a whole different ball game. You need to take many issues into account, including the following:

❑ How many records do you want to show on a page?

❑ How many records do you have left in your recordset?

❑ How many pages are there in total?

❑ What page are you on currently?

If you're hand-coding this behavior, you have to keep track of these variables yourself. Happily, the Paging Behaviors that Dreamweaver supplies take care of all these issues for you. All you do is tell Dreamweaver that you want to enable paging and it generates the necessary code for you. The first step is to limit the number of records that are displayed in the HTML table. Then you'll add Next and Previous links so that users can navigate easily through the recordset.

Limiting the Events List

When you added the repeat region in the beginning of this chapter, Dreamweaver created most of the code required to limit the number of events on your events page, events.asp. You chose not to limit the number of records per page then, so Dreamweaver set Repeat1__numRows to –1.

In the next exercise you modify your repeat region behavior so that it displays only a defined number of records per page. You simply change the number of records that are displayed on each page in the Repeat Region server behavior. In a subsequent Try It Out exercise, you will add navigational links so that your visitors can request the entire list of events.

Try It Out   **Limiting the Number of Events**

1. In the events.asp page, locate Repeat Region (rsEvents) on the Server Behaviors panel and double-click it to open the Repeat Region dialog box.

Select the first radio button in the Show section and type in a number. For this example, type **5** as the number of records that should be displayed per page (see Figure 12-24).

Figure 12-24

Click OK to apply the change.

2.	Save the page and open it in your browser. Select the UEFA Cup category because it contains more than five events. If all works correctly, you only see the first five events displayed on the page.

How It Works

The code changes in just one place. At the top of the page Dreamweaver changes the value for `Repeat1__numRows` from –1 to 5:

```
Dim Repeat1__index
Repeat1__numRows = 5
Repeat1__index = 0
```

Look at the `While` loop for the repeat region again to understand how this affects the table:

```
While ((Repeat1__numRows <> 0) AND (NOT rsEvents.EOF))
%>
  ...
  HTML table here
  ...
<%
Repeat1__index=Repeat1__index+1
Repeat1__numRows=Repeat1__numRows-1
rsEvents.MoveNext()
Wend
%>
```

In the first example in an earlier Try It Out exercise, `Repeat1__numRows` starts at a value of –1. For each event in the recordset, 1 is subtracted from this value so the value is always smaller than 0. That way the loop continues until the end of the recordset (`EOF`) is reached.

Now consider the new value for `Repeat1__numRows`. It starts at 5. After the first loop, 1 is subtracted. This continues another four times until `Repeat1__numRows` is 0. Because the `While` loop is only allowed to continue when `Repeat1__numRows` is not equal to 0, the loop ends even if there are still records in the recordset. This way, only five records are displayed at the same time.

Navigating the Data

Right now, all that the repeat region behavior does is limit the number of records displayed on the page to five. To allow your users to see more than the first five records, provide them with navigational links. You can do that by adding a Previous and a Next link to the table with events. This way the user can navigate through the records by requesting either the next or previous page showing five events each.

Try It Out	**Creating Navigational Links**

1.	While still on `events.asp`, make sure you are in Code view and position your cursor between the closing tag of the ASP block of the repeat region and the closing table tag. Make sure it is outside the repeat region but still inside your HTML table. Type **\<tr\>\<td\>Previous\</td\>\</tr\>** to insert a new table row below the repeat region.

Switch to Design view and split the cell into two columns by right-clicking the table row you just inserted, and then choose Table⇨Split Cell. Set Split Cell Into to Columns and set Number of Columns to 2 (see Figure 12-25).

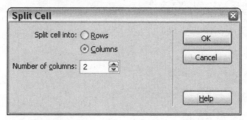

Figure 12-25

2. In the new cell you just added, type **Next** and then set the horizontal align attribute of the table cell to **Right** on the Property inspector. You should end up with this code:

```
Wend
%>

<tr>
 <td>Previous</td>
 <td align="right">Next</td>
</tr>
</table>
</form>
```

3. Highlight Next and open the Server Behaviors panel. Click the plus (+) button and choose Recordset Paging⇨Move to Next Record. You'll see the dialog box shown in Figure 12-26.

Figure 12-26

Click OK to add the code for the navigational link to the page.

4. Repeat Step 3 for the Previous link but select the Move to Previous Record instead.

5. Select the table row that contains the navigational links. The easiest way to do this is to click in the table row in Design view, next to Previous, for example, and click <tr> on the Tag selector. On the Server Behaviors panel, click the plus (+) button and choose Show Region⇨Show Region If Recordset Is Not Empty. This hides the navigation system when the user selects a category that does not contain any events.

6. Save the page and open it in your browser so it looks like Figure 12-27. Navigate to different pages using the two links. Notice that when you are at the last page, you can still click the Next button. We'll think of a solution to this problem after we explain how the navigation works.

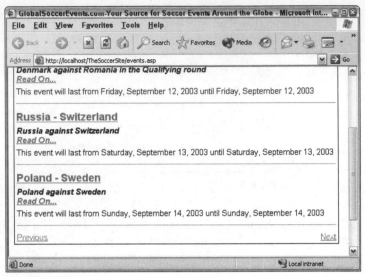

Figure 12-27

How It Works

The code that Dreamweaver adds tells the recordset to skip ahead the right number of records so that the page starts with the correct event. You want the first page to skip 0 records, the next page to skip 5 records, and so on.

The code that keeps track of which items should be placed on the next or previous page is placed inside the `<a>` tag of the Next and Previous links.

If you view the page in your browser, request the UEFA Cup category, click Next, and look at the HTML source, you'll see something like this:

```
<a href="/TheSoccerSite/events.asp?lstCategory=2&offset=5">Next</a>
```

The value for the drop-down list has been preserved in the URL that is linked to. This makes sure you stay in the same category when you click Next or Previous.

The `offset` parameter of the QueryString determines the first record of the next page. The number is zero-based, so an `offset` of 0 means that the first page with records 1 through 5 needs to be displayed. An `offset` of 5 defines the second page with records 6 through 10 on it, and so on.

The same principle is used for the Previous link. The code that Dreamweaver inserts contains a lot of comments that describe its inner workings, so if you are brave take a look at the nitty-gritty details of the navigation code.

Performance Considerations with Paging Data

The paging mechanism we demonstrate here is a lightweight way to present data to visitors. But even though only five records per page are sent to the browser, all records are retrieved from the database each time the page loads. The Dreamweaver code executes a SELECT statement against the database, retrieves all the records that match the criteria, and skips records until it hits the first record it needs to display. Then it outputs the required number of records to the page.

Imagine you have more than 700 events in your database and you want to view page 120, which contains records 596 through 600. You need to skip 595 records to get at the first record to display.

In fact, the situation is even worse. Quite often the Dreamweaver code loops through the recordset more than once. For example, when the code can't determine the number of records in the recordset, it loops through the entire recordset, counting each record. This looping causes your page to slow down considerably. With even larger recordsets containing thousands and thousands of records, your page may become so slow that its performance is no longer acceptable.

In a real-world scenario where you have a lot of data in your database, you need to look for other solutions. One solution to consider is a database server, like SQL Server, that supports a *server-side cursor*. With a server-side cursor, records you don't need are skipped at the database and only those you really need are put in the recordset. Another solution is to use a *stored procedure,* which is essentially a block of SQL statements that runs at the server. By using a stored procedure, you can limit the number of records that are retrieved from the database. A discussion of these solutions is beyond the scope of this book, however. For further information about them, get a copy of *Professional SQL Server 2000 Programming* by Robert Viera (Wrox, 2001).

Improving the Navigation System

As you may have noticed, the navigational links in the events.asp page are always visible, whether they can be used or not. Even when you are viewing the first page, the Previous link is displayed. Fortunately the code that handles the navigation uses some smart and defensive coding techniques. For example, the offset can never be smaller than 0 because it is impossible to have a negative page number. Using these techniques prevents you from getting an error when you accidentally request an incorrect page.

To avoid confusion for your visitors, you should hide the navigational links when there are no more records to show. Once again, the creators of Dreamweaver have thought about this too. They created four behaviors that can help you improve your navigation system. To display a region when you are at the first record in your recordset, you can use the Show Region If First Record behavior. To display a region when you are somewhere in the middle or towards the end of your recordset, you can use the Show Region If Not First Record behavior.

The other two behaviors—aptly called Show Region If Last Record and Show Region If Not Last Record—behave almost the same, only this time they check whether you are at the last record in your recordset or not. In the next section, you'll use them to display or hide your navigation system selectively. Note that although the name seems to imply that you can only use these behaviors on a page with a single record, you can also use these behaviors on a repeat region.

Try It Out   **Selectively Displaying the Navigational Links**

1. Select the Next navigational link by clicking it once in Design view and then select the `<a>` tag
in the Tag selector. You need to hide the complete link so it's important to select the complete
`<a>` element, as shown in Figure 12-28, and not just the word *Next*.

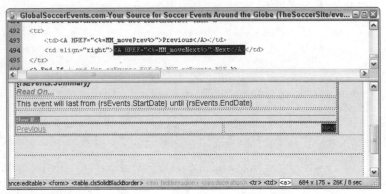

Figure 12-28

2. Open the Server Behaviors panel, click the plus (+) button, and select Show Region⇨Show
Region If Not Last Record. The `rsEvents` recordset is already selected in the list because it is
the only recordset defined in the page. Click OK to insert the behavior in the page.

3. Repeat Steps 1 and 2 for the Previous link but add the Show Region If Not First Record behavior.

4. Save and open the page in your browser. On the first page the Previous link has disappeared.
Once you click Next, the Previous link appears. Click Next a couple more times until you reach
the last page displaying the last few events for the category. The Next link disappears, as shown
in Figure 12-29. The number of times you have to click depends on the category you choose.

How It Works

To decide whether there are records left to display (display a Next link) or whether there are previous
records (display a Previous link), two variables are used for displaying and hiding the navigational
links: `MM_atTotal` and `MM_offset`.

The variable `MM_atTotal` is set to `True` when the recordset is at the last record. This variable is used to
determine whether the Next link should be displayed or not:

```
<td align="right">
<% If Not MM_atTotal Then %>
 <a href="<%=MM_moveNext%>">Next</a>
<% End If ' end Not MM_atTotal %> </td>
```

As you can see, the Next link is only displayed when `MM_atTotal` is not `True`.

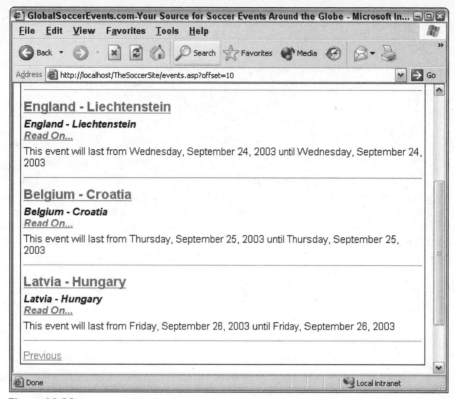

Figure 12-29

The same principle is used to hide or show the Previous link, but this time MM_offset is used to determine if the first page is displayed or not. If the offset is 0 the first page is displayed, so the Previous link is hidden.

Summary

In this chapter you have looked at ways to display data from your database on your Web page. You started off by simply displaying all events in the database on the page in a long list. You then enhanced the list by filtering the events based on their category and end date using variables in the SQL statement that is responsible for retrieving the events.

Next you hooked up each event in the list to a details page. This allows your visitors to request more information about a specific event. Displaying the details on a separate page avoids cluttering the Events list with too much data. It also allows visitors to bookmark the page so they can easily request the page in the future.

Finally, we introduced the concept of paging, a way to present data in manageable chunks. We showed you a way to break up the list of events into smaller pages that showed five events at a time. You added navigational links so visitors can navigate the complete list using the Previous and Next links.

Now that you know how to retrieve and display data from a database, it's time to look at ways to insert and update data in your database. After all, what good is a database if you have no way to insert data into it? The next chapter focuses on inserting, updating, and deleting data.

Why Not Try . . .

1. When visitors want to view the details of an event, they can click either the title of the event or the Read On link in the Events list. As soon as they open viewEventDetails.asp, however, there is no easy way to get back to the Events list page. Your visitors need to use the Back button of the browser to get back to events.asp. It would be much more user-friendly to add a Back button yourself, right below the event details. To successfully implement this functionality, you need an HTML button with its type set to button. In the onclick handler for the button, add the following JavaScript:

```
onClick="JavaScript:history.go(-1);"
```

To prevent the button from appearing when the error message is displayed, don't forget to wrap the button in a Show Region If Recordset Is Not Empty server behavior.

2. When visitors select the All Events item from the category drop-down list on events.asp, they see all events in categories. However, they can't see to which category the event belongs. Try to add the category name to the repeat region for each event. You need to use a Select Case statement to determine the name of the category from the category ID in the database. Your code should look similar to this:

```
<tr>
 <td colspan="2">
  This event belongs to the category:
  <%
  Select Case rsEvents.Fields.Item("Category").Value
   Case 1 ' Champions League
    Response.Write("Champions League")
   Case 2 ' UEFA Cup
    Response.Write("UEFA Cup")
   Case 3 ' National League
    Response.Write("National League")
   Case 4 ' US Major League Soccer
    Response.Write("US Major League Soccer")
  End Select
  %>
 </td>
</tr>
```

Because the Category column isn't currently selected in the SQL statement for the rsEvents recordset, you need to change the recordset so it selects that columns as well.

You'll see in the next chapter how to use SQL JOINS to retrieve the name of the category from the database as well, so you no longer need to use this hard-coded Select Case statement.

3.   We have used only Previous and Next in the navigation system to keep the concepts easy to explain. However, the page would be more user-friendly if you inserted First and Last links as well, so that users can skip directly to the beginning or end of the list. Add the First and Last links in the same table row that holds the Previous and Next links.

Hint: On the Server Behaviors panel there are two behaviors under the Recordset Paging menu item: Move to First Record and Move to Last Record. Use these to accomplish this task.

4.   Another improvement to the page would be to display the number of records in the recordset. For example, if you perform a search on msdn.microsoft.com you'll see something like this: "Record 1 to 20 of 217." Why not try to add a recordset navigation status to your page?

Hint: You'll find what you need under the Application Objects menu item of the Insert menu. Make sure you place the object in a region that gets hidden when the recordset is empty by clicking the plus (+) button and selecting Show Region⇨Show Region If Recordset Is Empty on the Server Behaviors panel.

Storing Information in a Database

In Chapter 12 we looked at *retrieving* data from a database and displaying it in an ASP page, but how does that data get into the database in the first place? When your database is sitting on the Web server, you usually don't have the luxury of simply opening the database with Microsoft Access directly and adding a few records or updating some details. You need a convenient way to update the database, which takes into account where it is. What you need is what you've provided your users so far: a Web interface. Through this Web interface, your administrators can easily create new events and update existing ones. Although expired events disappear automatically from your events list, you may also want to delete those old records every now and then to prevent the database from becoming too large and full of out-of-date data.

Currently, if you want to make a change to an event or create a new one, you have to download the database, make your changes using Microsoft Access on your local computer, and then upload the database again. While you are developing your Web site, this isn't a real problem. Often you need a copy of the database anyway to make changes to the tables and their structure.

In a real-world Web site, however, it's rather inconvenient to have to download the database every time you need to change some data. Besides the extra amount of work involved in downloading the database, you run the risk of ending up with a locked database just when you want to upload your database again. If the database is being used because someone is browsing the site, you won't be able to overwrite the database with your new version. Depending on how busy the site is, it may be impossible to overwrite the database without taking the site down first. When you upload the database again, you will obviously overwrite whatever data has been changed on the remote version since you first downloaded it. Besides these inconveniences, allowing your database to be downloaded isn't a good security practice because it might allow hackers to access your database as well. All in all, maintaining events through a Web interface is the way to go.

The solution to this problem is to create ASP pages that allow you to create, modify, and delete your events right in the database at the Web server. Fortunately, Dreamweaver MX 2004 makes this rather easy by supplying some ready-made objects, called *application objects*. There are nine application objects in total, of which we have already introduced a few, including the recordset and the repeat region. In this chapter you'll use four application objects—Record Insertion Form,

Record Update Form, Dynamic Table, and Recordset Navigation Bar—which make displaying, inserting, and updating data very easy indeed.

In this chapter you will learn how to do the following:

- ❑ Create a form that enables you to insert new events
- ❑ Create your own JavaScript validation function to check a form's contents before it is submitted
- ❑ Edit existing events in the database
- ❑ Delete events you no longer want

Maintaining Your Events

Although providing a Web interface to maintain events is very useful, obviously you don't want just anybody to fool around with your events. Only authorized administrators should be allowed to enter your maintenance section. In Chapter 11, you used access levels to control the links that appear to the Admin and My Site sections of your site and to control access to the individual pages in these sections. In this chapter, you build on that example by limiting access to those pages that allow you to create, change, and delete events that are stored in your database. Inside the admin section, you'll create a page that lists all events available in the database. The entrance page for all your maintenance tasks will look like Figure 13-1.

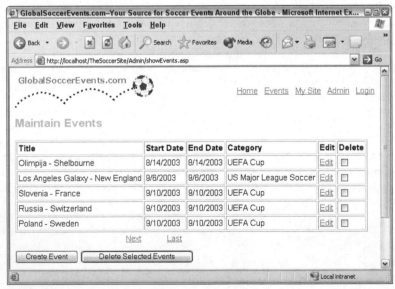

Figure 13-1

From this page, you or another administrator of your site can create a new event and update or delete existing events. The page that allows a user to update an event will look like Figure 13-2.

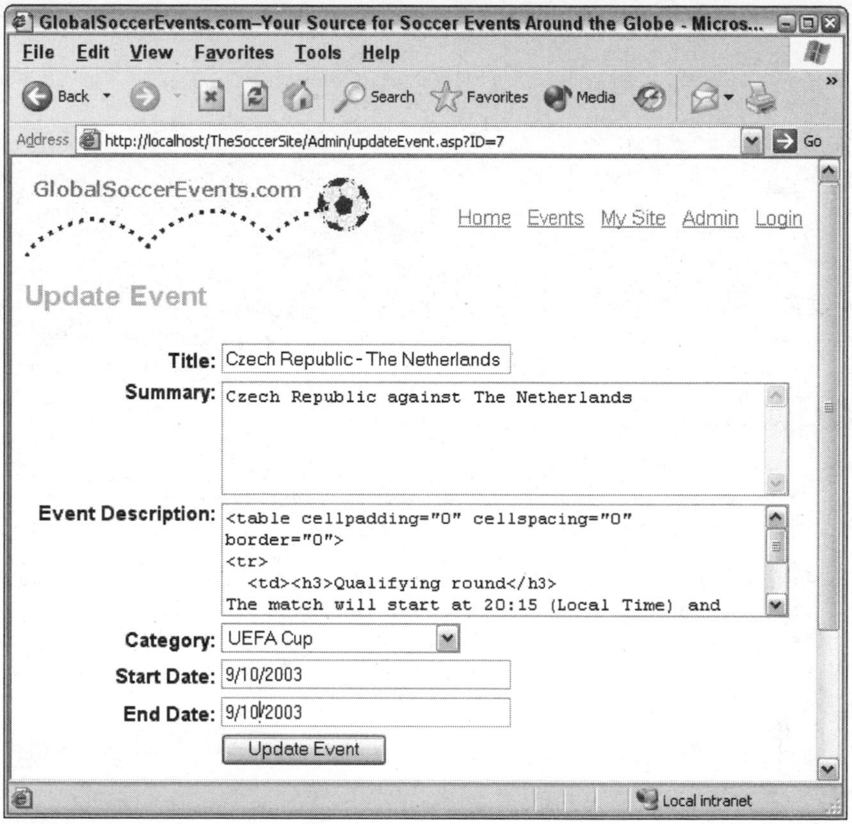

Figure 13-2

Introducing JOINs

In Chapter 11, we discussed ways to relate columns in a database table to each other. We described primary and foreign keys, and why it is useful to create a relationship between two tables. We also showed you that there is a relationship between the Events and the Categories table. This enables you to retrieve the description of the category for a specific event while only the ID of the category is stored in the Events table of the sample database. You'll use this relationship in this chapter because the list of events on the maintenance page will display the associated categories as well. Before we dive into the next Try It Out exercise, we need to discuss how database relationships are used in SQL statements.

To indicate to the database that you want to use this relationship, you use the keyword JOIN. There are various types of JOINs, such as the INNER JOIN and the OUTER JOIN. Essentially, an INNER JOIN is used to retrieve records from two tables, where the fields that the tables are joined on have an exact match. An OUTER JOIN returns all records from the first table, even if they don't match one in the second table. Take a look at the following example to see how this works.

Imagine you have the following events in your database:

Title	Category
Liverpool - Vitesse	2
Leeds - Málaga	4
New England - Columbus Crew	

As you can see, for the last event there is no category defined. Notice that we left out the other columns from the Events table to make it easier to explain how JOINs work. Imagine that you need to retrieve the events from the database, including the Description of the category for each event. If you only want to return an event when it has an associated category, you need to use an INNER JOIN in your query. The following SQL statement uses this kind of JOIN to return the records:

```
SELECT Events.Title, Categories.Description FROM Events INNER JOIN
    Categories ON Events.Category = Categories.ID
```

Notice that besides the keywords INNER JOIN you also need to indicate ON what columns you want to join. In this example, the category of the event (Events.Category) is related to the ID of the category (Categories.ID) so you can retrieve the Description column from the Categories table. As you'll recall from Chapter 11, Events.Category is a *foreign key* and it points to Categories.ID, the *primary key* of the Categories table.

Because an INNER JOIN is used, only the two records from the Events table that match a category in the Categories table are returned:

Liverpool - Vitesse	UEFA Cup
Leeds - Málaga	US Major League Soccer

Because the event New England - Columbus Crew has no category defined, it is not returned from the database with the query above. If, however, you are still interested in the event even if you don't know the category, change the JOIN type to an OUTER JOIN:

```
SELECT Events.Title, Categories.Description FROM Events LEFT OUTER JOIN
    Categories ON Events.Category = Categories.ID
```

Besides changing INNER to OUTER, the keyword LEFT is added to the JOIN statement. This is used to indicate from which table all records should be returned. Since the table Events is mentioned to the LEFT of the JOIN (it's mentioned first in the query), you get all results from the Events table, even if they don't have a matching category:

Liverpool - Vitesse	UEFA Cup
Leeds - Málaga	US Major League Soccer
New England - Columbus Crew	

If you change LEFT to RIGHT, you get all records from the Categories table instead.

As you can see in the SQL statements, we prefixed the column names with the name of the table they belong to. It's often necessary to prefix your column names with the table name if two tables have a column with the same name. In fact, we recommend you always prefix your column names because it makes your code easier to understand.

Now that you have a basic understanding of how you can use JOINs in your SQL statements, it's time to put that knowledge into practice.

Viewing Available Events

As you did when you created the events page in Chapter 12, you need to build a page that shows all events so you can select which ones to edit or delete. This time, you'll make use of some of the available application objects to make it even easier to display and navigate through the list of events. All existing event records are displayed—regardless of whether they have expired or not. Remember that you filtered out events from past dates in Chapter 12; this time, however, you need access to all records so you can edit or delete them if necessary.

Try It Out   **Showing a List with Available Events**

1. Add a new page based on the main template by opening the New Document dialog box (press Ctrl+N). On the Templates tab, select TheSoccerSite in the Templates For list and then double-click mainTemplate. Save it as **showEvents.asp** in the Admin folder you created in Chapter 8.

2. Give the page a title of **Maintain Events** in the Title region of the template. Remove the two placeholders for the Content and Footer regions of your template. Save the page and then choose Modify⇨Templates⇨Update Current Page from the menu bar to make Dreamweaver recalculate the links to the style sheets and the image for the logo.

3. Restrict access to the page so only administrators can access it. To do this, open the Server Behaviors panel (press Ctrl+F9), click the plus (+) button, and select Restrict Access to Page from the User Authentication menu. Set Restrict Based On to Username, Password, and Access Level by choosing the appropriate radio button and then choose Administrators in the Select level(s) list. If you accidentally removed one or more of the access levels earlier, click the Define button and create at least a new Administrators level, which you need for this chapter.

4. Select ../login.asp in the If Access Denied Go To text box. Instead of typing in the name directly, you can click Browse to select the file from the root of your site. Make sure that the Relative To drop-down list is set to Document. Save the page.

5. To access the maintenance page, you need to provide your users with a menu item that links to showEvents.asp on the main admin page. To do this, open admin.asp from the Admin folder and locate the link to popularFirstPage.asp.

6. In Design view, position your cursor right after this link and press Shift+Enter to insert a <br> tag. This makes sure the next link is on its own line. On this new line, type **Maintain Events**, highlight it, and then switch to Code view. Turn the selected text into a hyperlink by choosing Insert⇨Hyperlink from the menu bar.

7. Let the link point to the showEvents.asp page you just created by browsing to that file. Save the page and then close it (press Ctrl+F4 or Ctrl+W).

8. Add a recordset to showEvents.asp, which is used to retrieve the events from the Events table, so make sure you have the right page open. On the Server Behaviors panel, click the plus (+) button and choose Recordset (Query) from the resulting menu. The Recordset dialog box appears.

   The SQL statement you create requires more features than the Simple Recordset dialog box provides, so go into the Advanced view, shown in Figure 13-3, by clicking the Advanced button. (If you see the Simple button, you are already in Advanced mode).

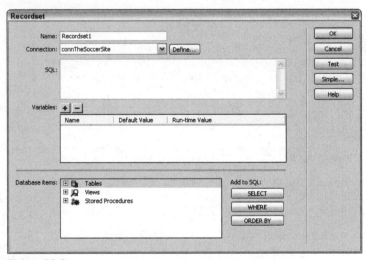

Figure 13-3

9. Name the recordset **rsEvents** and make sure connTheSoccerSite is selected in the Connection drop-down list.

10. In the Database items list, expand Tables and then Events. Select ID and then click the SELECT button to add the column ID to the SELECT list in the SQL box. Repeat this step for the columns Title, StartDate, and EndDate.

11. Add an ORDER BY clause to display the events in a specific order. In Chapter 12, the event list was ordered on the start date of the event, so the oldest event appeared at the top of the list. You need to do the same here, so select the column StartDate again in the Database Items list and click the Order By button. The Recordset dialog box should now look like Figure 13-4.

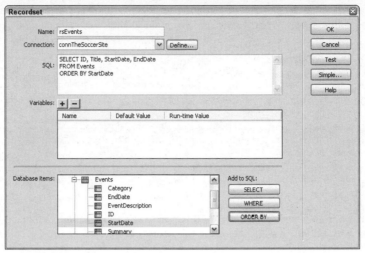

Figure 13-4

12. As a visual cue to the administrator, it is a good idea to show the category description of the event in the list as well. To do this, expand the Categories table in the Database items list. Select Description and click the SELECT button once more. Dreamweaver adds the `Description` column and the table name to the SQL statement. Unfortunately, Dreamweaver is unable to see the relation between the `Events` and `Categories` tables, so you need to modify the SQL statements to clarify this relation. In the SQL text box, find this code:

```
SELECT ID, Title, StartDate, EndDate, Description
FROM Events, Categories
ORDER BY StartDate
```

Change it to this:

```
SELECT ID, Title, StartDate, EndDate, Description
FROM Events INNER JOIN Categories ON Events.Category = Categories.ID
ORDER BY StartDate
```

This tells the database that the `Category` column from the event record is linked to an `ID` in the `Categories` table. This way, you can retrieve the `Description` of the `Category`, together with all the other event details.

13. Test if your SQL statement is valid by clicking the Test button. Instead of the expected records, Dreamweaver shows the message box shown in Figure 13-5.

Figure 13-5

You may recall from the discussion about JOINs earlier that sometimes you need to prefix column names with the name of the table to make it clear which table you are referring to. This is a situation where it is necessary to do so. The database is unable to see which table the ID is referring to in the SELECT statement because both the Events and Categories tables have an ID field. Dreamweaver is kind enough to warn you of this situation so you can correct it. The problem is easily solved by prefixing ID with the table name and a dot. This way, you are explicitly stating which table you are referring to. Change the SELECT statement to this:

```
SELECT Events.ID, Title, StartDate, EndDate, Description
FROM Events INNER JOIN Categories ON Events.Category = Categories.ID
ORDER BY StartDate
```

If you click the Test button again you'll see that the problem has gone away. You're presented with a list of your events together with a Description of the category.

Because it makes your SQL statement easier to read, add table prefixes to all your column names now, so you'll easily see table they come from. Your final SQL statement should now look like this:

```
SELECT Events.ID, Events.Title, Events.StartDate,
Events.EndDate, Categories.Description
FROM Events INNER JOIN Categories ON Events.Category = Categories.ID
ORDER BY Events.StartDate
```

14. Click OK to close the Recordset dialog box and insert the code for the recordset in the page.

15. With the recordset for your events in place, add an HTML table to the page that displays a list of all your events. In Chapter 12, you created the <table> skeleton yourself and used a repeat region to display the events. This time, you can let Dreamweaver do the hard work by adding a *dynamic table*. A dynamic table is a mix of HTML and ASP code that displays available records in a recordset. It also allows you to limit the number of rows displayed at the time, so you can easily add paging capabilities to your page.

In Design view, click inside the Content region of the template and select Insert⇨Application Objects⇨Dynamic Data⇨Dynamic Table from the menu bar. Alternatively, click the down arrow next to the Dynamic Data button on the Application category of the Insert bar and select Dynamic Table (see Figure 13-6).

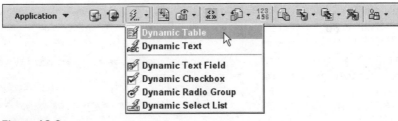

Figure 13-6

Whichever option you choose, you're presented with the Dynamic Table dialog box shown in Figure 13-7. Limit the number of records displayed at a time to **5** and set both Cell Padding and Cell Spacing to 2. Leave Border as 1 because it makes it easier to distinguish individual rows from each other.

Figure 13-7

16. Click OK. Dreamweaver inserts the table in your page, as shown in Figure 13-8.

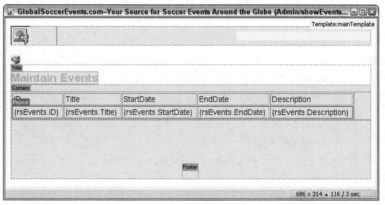

Figure 13-8

Dreamweaver also creates a table heading for you, so you can easily see what data is stored in each column.

17. Save the page and press F12 to view the page in your browser (see Figure 13-9). Because you need administrator's privileges to view the page, you're redirected to the login page instead. Type **admin** as the username and password (or use your own account if you created one in the database) and then click the Login button. You will see a list of your events. Its layout is far from perfect, and you can only see the first five events, but it's a good start.

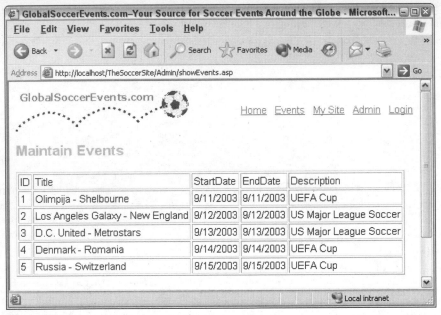

Figure 13-9

How It Works

You have already seen most of the techniques in this example used in the previous chapters, so we won't cover them here again. What's new to this example is that Dreamweaver inserted the whole table for you:

```
<td><!- InstanceBeginEditable name="Content" ->
 <table border="1" cellpadding="2" cellspacing="2">
  <tr>
   <td>ID</td>
   <td>Title</td>
   <td>StartDate</td>
   <td>EndDate</td>
  </tr>
<% While ((Repeat1__numRows <> 0) AND (NOT rsEvents.EOF)) %>
```

Dreamweaver inserts a `<td>` element for each column in the recordset. It uses the default column name as the header for the table.

Often this is exactly what you want, but in this case it isn't. Displaying the ID column doesn't make much sense because it's rather meaningless for an administrator. You only need the ID so you can use it to create a link to `updateEvent.asp` where you update the event. You'll create this page in a later exercise. In the next Try It Out exercise you'll remove this column from the dynamic table and change the headers of the other columns so they look better.

Try It Out   Enhancing Your Dynamic Table

1. Removing the ID column is easy. In Design View, right-click next to ID in the table cell for the header and choose Delete Column from the Table menu item. Notice that although you removed the ID column from the dynamic table, the ID is still retrieved from the database because you haven't modified the SQL statement. All you did was change the visual appearance of the table.

2. The database is quite happy with names like StartDate and EndDate but your users will expect the column names to look more friendly. Click StartDate in Design view and add a space between Start and Date. Repeat this for EndDate. Change Description in the last column to **Category**, as this better describes the contents of the column.

3. Select the entire first row of the table. The easiest way to do this is to click once in the Title cell and drag the mouse to the right. Release the mouse when it's over the cell for Category. Alternatively, click inside one of the cells of the first row and use the Tag selector to select the entire row. In both cases, you'll see a black border around the first row to indicate the selection. Press Ctrl+B to change the font of the heading to bold. Alternatively, press the Bold button (with a capital B on it) on the Property inspector. Dreamweaver wraps the text inside each table cell in <strong> tags in Code view.

4. In Code view, locate the </table> end tag of the dynamic table and place your cursor right *after* it:

```
%>
</table>
<!- InstanceEndEditable -></td>
```

Choose Insert⇨Application Objects⇨Recordset Paging⇨Recordset Navigation Bar. The Recordset Navigation Bar dialog box in Figure 13-10 appears.

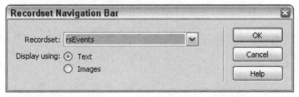

Figure 13-10

Select the recordset that the navigation bar should be attached to. Because there is only one recordset on the page, rsEvents is already selected for you. You can also choose between text links and image links. If you choose the latter, Dreamweaver inserts four default images (Next.gif, Previous.gif, First.gif, and Last.gif) in your current directory and uses them for navigation. You can, of course, change these images to something that fits your design more closely or change the code that Dreamweaver generates so the <img> tags point to an existing set of navigation images. This example uses text links because they look exactly like all your other navigation elements in your site, like the menu and navigational links on events.asp. This creates a more consistent look for the site.

5. Click OK. Dreamweaver inserts a new table with the navigational link directly after the dynamic table.

6. Select the entire table you just added using the Tag selector. You may need to click inside the `<table>` tag to have the table appear on the Tag selector. Change the horizontal alignment of the table from Center to Left. (The Align property is in the upper right corner of the Property inspector.)

7. Save the page and then view it in your browser. Log in again with **admin** as the username and password and you see the list of events, as shown in Figure 13-11. Some of the navigational links, such as First and Previous, are hidden when there are no records in the recordset to navigate to.

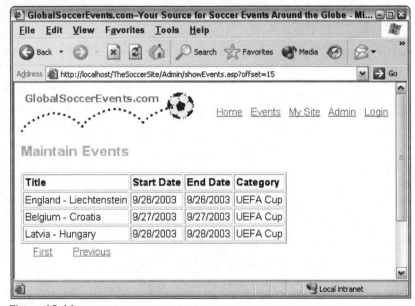

Figure 13-11

How It Works

When you inserted the recordset navigation bar, Dreamweaver added two blocks of code: an HTML table that selectively displays the navigational links and a lot of ASP code that runs when you click on a navigational link:

```
<table border="0" width="50%" align="center">
 <tr>
  <td width="23%" align="center">
  <% If MM_offset <> 0 Then %>
  <a href="<%=MM_moveFirst%>">First</a>
  <% End If ' end MM_offset <> 0 %>
  </td>
  <td width="31%" align="center"> <% If MM_offset <> 0 Then %>
```

```
      <a href="<%=MM_movePrev%>">Previous</a>
      <% End If ' end MM_offset <> 0 %>
    </td>
    <td width="23%" align="center"> <% If Not MM_atTotal Then %>
      <a href="<%=MM_moveNext%>">Next</a>
      <% End If ' end Not MM_atTotal %>
    </td>
    <td width="23%" align="center"> <% If Not MM_atTotal Then %>
      <a href="<%=MM_moveLast%>">Last</a>
      <% End If ' end Not MM_atTotal %>
    </td>
  </tr>
</table>
```

The HTML table is pretty straightforward and may look familiar to you. It's more or less the same as the Move to Next Record and Move to Previous Record server behaviors you used in the previous chapter. Based on a few variables like MM_atTotal and MM_offset this code determines whether some or all the navigational links need to be displayed.

The ASP code that gives these variables their value is also almost identical to the code in the previous chapter. Once again, it has lots of comments in it, so take a look at them if you want to find out all the details.

Now that you are able to display your list of events in manageable chunks, it's time to look at how you can create new events. In the next section we discuss how you can create ASP pages that allow you to insert new records in a database physically located on the Web server.

Creating New Events

Inserting data into a database with HTML and hand-coded ASP pages can be a difficult and cumbersome task. It requires a lot of knowledge about ASP and databases and you need to do a lot of coding yourself. However, Dreamweaver makes this task much easier with *application objects*. Without having to understand or type all the details that go on under the hood, you can easily create a Record Insertion Form application object and modify it to suit your needs. To create a form so that users can insert new records to the database, use the record insertion form and bind it to a specific table in your database.

A record insertion form consists of an HTML form with text boxes, other form elements for all the columns you select from a table, and a submit button. Once you fill in the fields and click that button, the page with the form submits to itself. At the server, the form's contents are retrieved and then used to create a SQL INSERT statement for all the fields on the form. This SQL statement is sent to the database to insert the record. Finally, when the record is inserted you redirect your user to a new page so they can view the new record.

Before you go ahead and create the record insertion form, you need to add a button on the showEvents.asp page that the user can click to go to the insert page. Use a button rather than a link because in a later Try It Out exercise an additional button is placed on the page that enables you to delete multiple events from your database. If you use a button to insert new events as well, your page will have a consistent look and feel.

Try It Out **Modifying the View Events Page**

1. Add a `<form>` element to the page. Open `showEvents.asp` from the `Admin` folder. Inside the Code view window locate the opening `<table>` tag of the dynamic table that displays the list of events. Position your cursor *before* the `<table>` tag.

2. Click Insert and choose Form⇨Form from the menu bar. Fill in the dialog box that appears so it looks like Figure 13-12.

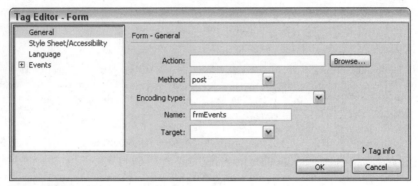

Figure 13-12

There is no need to fill in the Action attribute; the form is not used to submit to another page yet.

3. Click OK. Dreamweaver inserts a `<form>` tag:

```
<form action="" method="post" name="frmEvents"></form>
```

4. Cut the closing tag (`</form>`) and move it to the bottom of the page, right after the last `</table>` tag of the navigation table. This makes sure that the entire page is contained within the `<form>` element.

5. Position your cursor between the `</table>` tag and the `</form>` tag you just pasted. Press Shift+Enter twice to insert two `<br>` tags and then select the Forms category from the Insert panel. Click the Button icon to insert a new button on the page. Fill in the resulting dialog box as shown in Figure 13-13.

6. Before closing the dialog box, expand the Events category, locate the `onClick` event, and type the following code in the Input – onClick text box on the right:

```
document.location.href='createEvent.asp';
```

This bit of JavaScript requests the page `createEvent.asp` when the Create Event button is clicked.

7. Save the page, open it in your browser, and click the Create Event button. You'll get an error stating that `createEvent.asp` does not exist but at least you know the button works. In the next exercise you get the opportunity to create this page.

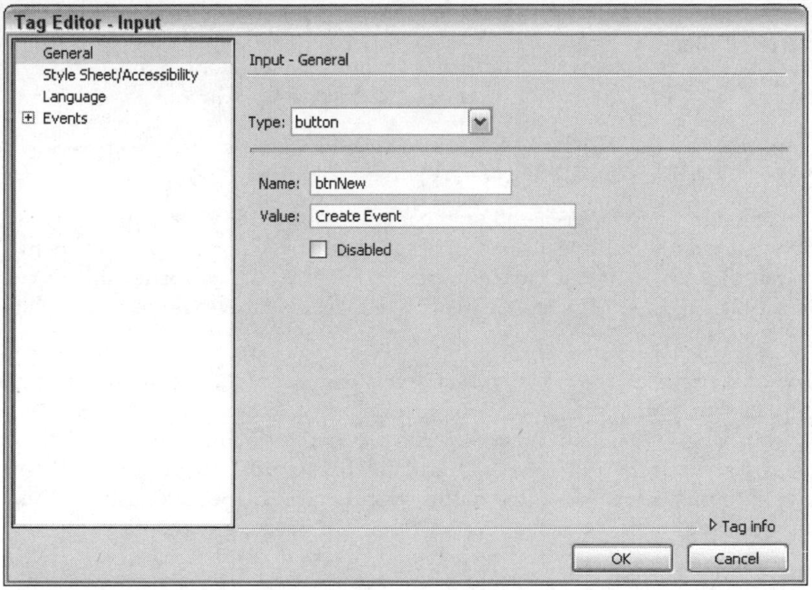

Figure 13-13

How It Works

The first thing you did was place the entire page within a <form> element. This form is necessary for older Netscape browsers because they won't display form controls like buttons when they are not placed inside a <form> container. In the next section of this chapter, information is posted from this page to another, so you need the form anyway. That is also the reason why the entire dynamic table is enclosed by the form and not just the button. The list of events will eventually hold check boxes that you can use to select events that you want to delete. These check boxes need to be inside a form as well if you want to submit them to another page, so the easiest thing to do is to wrap the entire content section of your page inside a <form> tag.

Next you added a Create Event button that takes the user to the createEvent.asp page. The code for the button looks like this:

```
<input name="btnNew" type="button"
    onClick="document.location.href='createEvent.asp';"
    value="Create Event">
```

When this button is clicked, the onClick event fires and transfers the user to createEvent.asp.

Adding a Simple Insert Form

In the following section you'll create a page that inserts a new event in the database. You'll add a Record Insertion Form application object to the page that takes care of all the form and database code. By adding a record insertion form you get a ready-made form with text boxes for all the fields you select from the Events table. The form also includes a button that allows users to submit the form. At the server, a SQL statement is created that contains all the values that have been sent with the form. This SQL statement is then passed to the database to insert the new event in the Events table. After the insertion takes place, you can redirect your user back to the page showEvents.asp.

Try It Out   Adding the Insert Form

1. Create a new page that is based on the main template for your site and save it as **createEvent.asp** in the Admin folder. Give the page a descriptive title, like **Create an Event**, in the Title region of the template. Remove the other two placeholders for the Content and Footer sections. Choose Modify⇨Templates⇨Update Current Page to let Dreamweaver recalculate the links in the page and then save the page.

2. To prevent regular visitors from seeing this page, apply a Restrict Access to Page behavior so only administrators are allowed to view it. Press Ctrl+F9 to open the Server Behaviors panel, click the plus (+) button, and choose Restrict Access to Page from the User Authentication menu. Set the restriction type to **Username, Password, and Access Level** and make sure that only Administrators is selected in the Select Levels list. Set the If Access Denied Go To box to **../login.asp** either by typing it in directly or by browsing to the file.

3. Before you can insert the form, you'll need to define a recordset that retrieves a list of categories from the database. The column Category of the Events table is numeric and linked to the Categories table. Because you don't want your users to type in a number for the category, you can offer them a friendly drop-down list with all the categories from the database. This way your users see the description of the categories while, under the hood, the ID is used. Because you need to point to this recordset on the record insertion form, it's necessary to create it first. On the Server Behaviors panel choose Recordset (Query) from the plus (+) button menu. Use the Simple view of this dialog box. Name the recordset **rsCategories** and select the table Categories in the Table list. Leave Columns set to All and choose Description from the Sort list. Leave Sort set to Ascending. Your final dialog box should look like Figure 13-14.

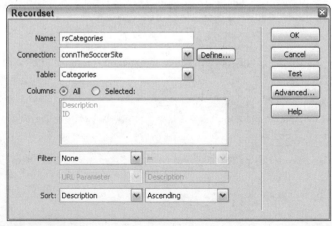

Figure 13-14

Click OK to insert the recordset in your page.

4. Position your cursor in the Content region of the template in Design view and then select Insert⇨Application Objects⇨Insert Record⇨Record Insertion Form Wizard.

5. On the Record Insertion Form dialog box, choose the connection connTheSoccerSite from the Connection list.

6. Once you choose the connection, the Insert Into Table list contains all the tables found in the database. Choose Events from this list. This is the table where the new event record is stored.

7. Click the Browse button and select showEvents.asp in the Admin folder as the page you want to redirect users to after the new event is inserted. Your dialog box should now look like Figure 13-15.

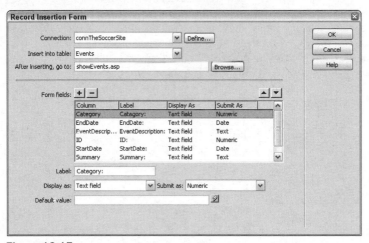

Figure 13-15

8. You may recall from Chapter 11 that the ID column is generated by the database automatically (its data type is AutoNumber), so there is no need to display it on the form. This means you need to remove it from the Form Fields list. Select ID in the Form Fields list and then click the minus (–) button.

9. Reorder the list so the items appear in a more natural way on the form. The dialog box includes two arrow buttons—up and down—which allow you to move the fields up and down the list to change their order. The order of the columns you define here is also used on the final insertion form. Select the Title column and click the up-arrow button repeatedly until Title is the first item in the list. Repeat this step for the other columns until the list looks like Figure 13-16.

Column	Label	Display As	Submit As	
Title	Title:	Text field	Text	
Summary	Summary:	Text field	Text	
EventDescription	EventDescription:	Text field	Text	
Category	Category:	Text field	Numeric	
StartDate	StartDate:	Text field	Date	
EndDate	EndDate:	Text field	Date	

Figure 13-16

10. Next, you'll need to change the form fields for some columns. For example, EventDescription is a Memo column in the database, which means it can hold literally thousands of characters. The standard text box that Dreamweaver adds for you is not very convenient because it has only a height of one line. Changing it to <textarea> allows your users to view and edit multiple lines at once. To change the type of the form control, click the EventDescription column and choose Text Area from the Display As drop-down list. Repeat this step for the Summary column too. Now users are presented with a text area 50 columns wide and 5 rows high. You can always change these sizes later using the Property inspector for the text area, or directly using Code view.

11. You'll also need to change the way the category is presented. Because it's not very convenient for users to type in a number, offer them a drop-down list with category descriptions instead. First click Category once in the Form Fields list and change the Display As drop-down list to **Menu**. The dialog box changes to show an extra button called Menu Properties. Click that button to open the Menu Properties dialog box where you can create the menu. Click the From Database option and fill in the fields as shown in Figure 13-17.

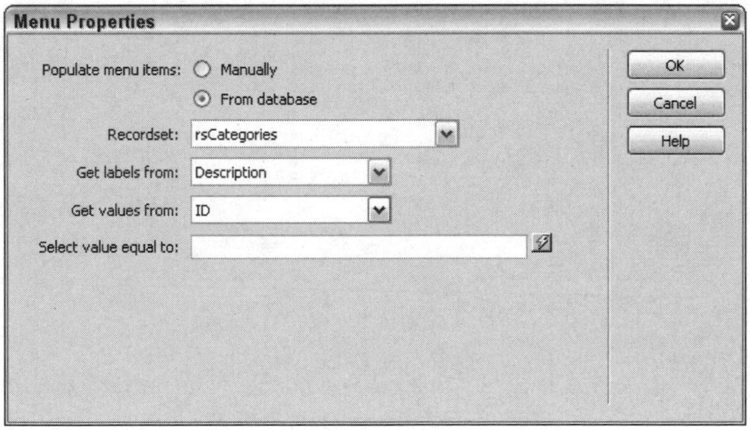

Figure 13-17

This creates a drop-down list showing descriptions of the categories so users can easily pick one. Under the hood, the ID of the category is used as the value for each <option> item. You can leave the Select Value Equal to Field empty. We'll explain what this field is used for when we discuss updating events later in this chapter.

Click OK to close the Menu Properties dialog box and then click OK again to insert the form in your page.

12. Right-click the Insert Record button at the end of the form in Design view and choose Label. Change the default text Insert Record to **Create Event** and click OK.

13. In Design view, add a space between the words `Event` and `Description` in the label for the text area `EventDescription`. This makes the label a little friendlier for users. Repeat this for the `StartDate` and `EndDate` labels, as well, so they read **Start Date** and **End Date**, respectively (see Figure 13-18).

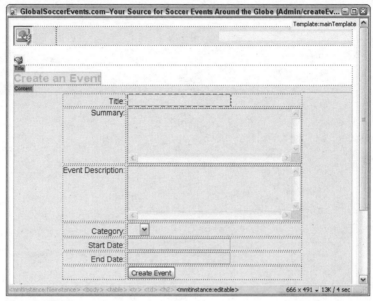

Figure 13-18

14. Select the entire first column of the table by dragging your mouse from the `Title` cell to the last cell at the bottom of the table. Press Ctrl+B to surround all captions with `<strong>` tags. This makes the captions stand out more so they're easier to distinguish from other page elements.

15. Save the page and open it in your browser (press F12). After you log in as administrator using **admin** as the username and password, you see the page where you can insert a new event, as shown in Figure 13-19.

Create a new event. Type the names of two clubs that you'd like to play against each other in the Title box. Type in a summary describing the event and then type in the full details for the event in the Event Description box. Select an appropriate category from the list and type in a date like **12/20/2003** in both the Start Date and the End Date text boxes. When you're done, click the Create Event button. You are redirected to `showEvents.asp` where your new event shows up in the list.

You get an error message when you try to insert invalid values. For example, you can't enter *Today* in the Start Date field. In the database this column has a data type of `date` so you can't put any text in it. In the next section we will change the form so it validates user input before submitting the form.

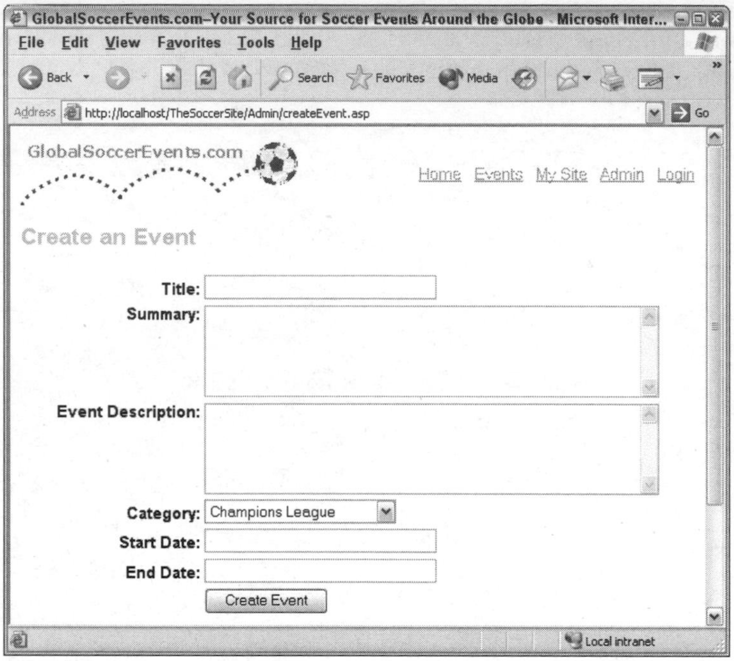

Figure 13-19

How It Works

When you add the Record Insertion Form application object, Dreamweaver adds two pieces of code. One block contains the HTML form and a table holding the text boxes, a drop-down list, and a button; the other contains ASP code that runs when you submit the form. It's quite a lot of code, so we won't show it all but we'll explain the general idea. To make it easier to follow along, open createEvent.asp in Dreamweaver and locate the following code for the HTML table in Code view:

```
<td><!- InstanceBeginEditable name="Content" ->
 <form method="post" action="<%=MM_editAction%>" name="form1">
  <table align="center">
   <tr valign="baseline">
    <td nowrap align="right"><strong>Title:</strong></td>
    <td> <input type="text" name="Title" value="" size="32"> </td>
   </tr>
   <tr>
    <td nowrap align="right" valign="top"><strong>Summary:</strong></td>
```

As you can see, the entire HTML table with the text fields and category drop-down list is wrapped inside a form. At runtime, the variable MM_editAction contains the name of the current page (createEvent.asp) so the page submits to itself.

Inside the table there is a row for each column of the Events table that you selected in the Record Insertion Form dialog box. For each column, a label and a form element are created. In this example, the label is `Title` and it has a corresponding form control named `Title` as well. The form control is a simple text input with a width of 32 characters. The name of the control is used in the ASP code at the server to retrieve the contents of the text box.

For the other columns in the table, the same kind of code is inserted. However, because you change the type of control for `Summary` and `EventDescription`, those fields now have a `<textarea>` instead of a simple text box.

The only part that's really different from the rest is the code for the category drop-down list:

```
<td nowrap align="right">Category:</td>
<td> <select name="Category">

<%
 While (NOT rsCategories.EOF)
%>
<option value="<%=(rsCategories.Fields.Item("ID").Value)%>">
 <%=(rsCategories.Fields.Item("Description").Value)%></option>
<%
 rsCategories.MoveNext()
Wend
If (rsCategories.CursorType > 0) Then
```

This code simply loops through the `rsCategories` recordset, writing out an `<option>` element for each category.

Now take a look at some of the ASP code that Dreamweaver created automatically at the top of the page, right after the code that takes care of the user authentication. There is quite a lot of code that we won't discuss in detail, but once again we'll explain the general concept.

```
<%
' *** Insert Record: set variables
If (CStr(Request("MM_insert")) = "form1") Then
  MM_editConnection = MM_connTheSoccerSite_STRING
```

When the form is submitted by clicking the Create Event button, the code in this `If` block runs. Inside this code block, Dreamweaver sets up the variables that are needed to insert a new event successfully, like the name of the connection and the page you want to redirect to after you create a new event. This block also defines two arrays that hold the column names and additional information, like whether a column is required or not. These arrays retrieve the contents from the form and build an SQL `INSERT` statement.

The SQL statement is build dynamically inside the second `If` block.

Before we discuss the code that creates this `INSERT` statement, let's step back for a while and take a look at how the database expects you to pass an `INSERT` statement. In its simplest form, an `INSERT` statement looks like this:

```
INSERT INTO TableName (Column1, Column2) VALUES('Value1', Value2)
```

The first statement, `INSERT INTO`, indicates that a new record should be inserted in the database. The second statement indicates which table (`TableName`) the new records should be inserted into. The comma-separated list of names between the parentheses refers to the columns (Column1 and Column2) into which the data should be inserted. Finally, the actual data values are passed. Notice that Value1 is enclosed in single-quotes. As we mentioned in Chapter 11, this is required for text data types.

Imagine the Events table only has one column, called Title. To insert a new record in that table, you have to create the following INSERT statement:

```
INSERT INTO Events (Title) VALUES('Peterborough United Vs Everton')
```

If you also want to include Category, your statement looks like this:

```
INSERT INTO Events (Title, Category)
  VALUES('Peterborough United Vs Everton', 3)
```

(We broke the code over two lines; in reality the code is passed to the database as one long line.) Now that you know how you need to pass an INSERT statement to the database, it's easier to understand the code that Dreamweaver creates:

```
<%
' *** Insert Record: construct a sql insert statement and execute it
Dim MM_tableValues
Dim MM_dbValues
If (CStr(Request("MM_insert")) <> "") Then
' create the sql insert statement
  MM_tableValues = ""
  MM_dbValues = ""
  For MM_i = LBound(MM_fields) To UBound(MM_fields) Step 2
  ...
  ...
    MM_tableValues = MM_tableValues & MM_columns(MM_i)
    MM_dbValues = MM_dbValues & MM_formVal
  Next
```

This code loops for each column in the array MM_fields to retrieve its name and value from the associated form control. The data type of each column is also examined, so the final SQL statement uses the correct delimiters for each value that is passed to the database.

Because the single-quote character has special meaning in SQL, Dreamweaver also makes sure that your data is sent to the database correctly by escaping all ' characters. This is necessary if you want to submit the literal value of a quote to the database, as in text strings such as "Event's Summary" or "O'Brien."

You saw before how to escape the double-quote (") in ASP by putting an additional double-quote before it. The same principle is used here again. If you pass two single-quotes ('') to the database, the database knows that you want to insert the literal value of just one single-quote. The code that Dreamweaver inserts simply uses the built-in ASP Replace function to replace each individual single-quote with two single-quotes.

At the end of the loop, you end up with two text strings containing a list with column names and a list with values that need to be inserted in the database.

```
MM_editQuery = "insert into " & MM_editTable & " (" & _
        MM_tableValues & ") values (" & MM_dbValues & ")"
```

The list of column names (MM_tableValues) and the list of values (MM_dbValues) are appended to the final SQL statement (MM_editQuery), together with the name of the table (MM_editTable) into which the record needs to be inserted.

At this point, your SQL INSERT statement could look like this:

```
insert into Events (Title,Summary,EventDescription,Category,StartDate,EndDate)
values ('Peterborough United Vs Everton','The Event''s Summary here',
'This is the Description of the Event',3,'10-23-2003','10-23-2003')
```

Notice that Dreamweaver has used single-quotes to enclose the date values. Although Access usually requires the # character, newer versions of the database support ' as well. Also notice that now two single-quotes in the event's Summary are passed to the database. As we explained earlier, this eventually results in one single-quote in the Summary column in the Events table.

With the complete SQL statement ready, it's time to send it to the database:

```
If (Not MM_abortEdit) Then
  ' execute the insert
  Set MM_editCmd = Server.CreateObject("ADODB.Command")
```

When there is no need to cancel the insertion (when MM_abortEdit is still False) the code goes ahead and creates an ADODB.Command object. A Command object is an object that is able to pass SQL statements through a Connection object to a database. The ADODB Command object is part of the ADO (ActiveX Data Objects) Object Model that is used to connect to a large number of data sources from ASP pages, Visual Basic, and many other programming languages. The Command object has many methods and properties and provides a flexible way to pass data to the database.

> *A detailed discussion of ADO and the Command object is beyond the scope of this book but if you are interested in learning more, check out the ADO reference section at* www.microsoft.com/data. *You can find the ADO Programmer's Guide and the ADO Programmer's Reference in the tree menu on the left.*

After the Command object has been created, it can be assigned a connection string and an SQL statement:

```
MM_editCmd.ActiveConnection = MM_editConnection
MM_editCmd.CommandText = MM_editQuery
```

The ActiveConnection property of the Command object indicates which connection you want to use. Behind the scenes, ADO creates a Connection object based on the connection string that is passed here. The CommandText property is set to MM_editQuery because this string contains the complete text for the SQL INSERT statement that needs to be sent to the database.

```
MM_editCmd.Execute
```

The Execute method of the Command object does all the real work. This method makes sure that an open connection to the database exists and that the SQL statement is passed to the database. This effectively inserts the event in the Events table.

```
    MM_editCmd.ActiveConnection.Close
```

Then the connection is closed again. This is good practice because leaving connections open longer than necessary decreases the performance of your Web site. A connection is a scarce resource and should be treated as such. In practice, this means you should open your connection as late as possible and close it again right after you're finished with it. (It's like the bank robber's "3G rule": *Go in, Get what you want, Get out.*)

Finally, if you have specified a redirect page, the user is sent to that page. In this example, this is showEvents.asp, where you can take a look at your newly added event in all its glory.

```
    If (MM_editRedirectUrl <> "") Then
      Response.Redirect(MM_editRedirectUrl)
    End If
  End If
End If
%>
```

Spicing Up the Form

The form that Dreamweaver generates works perfectly when you insert data because *you* know exactly what to insert and where. In the real world, however, it's good practice to make a page foolproof, especially when the data submitted is inserted into a live database. To make this happen, you need to add client-side JavaScript to validate the different HTML controls before they're submitted to the page. Adding a Cancel button to return to the previous page comes in handy when visitors accidentally navigate to this page and need a way out.

The Cancel button is rather simple to implement, so we discuss that first.

Try It Out   Adding the Cancel Button

1.   Open createEvent.asp and locate the Create Event button in Design view. Position the cursor to the right of the button in the blue area. Switch to Code view to place the cursor between value="Create Event"> and the closing </td> tag. This is where the Cancel button should appear. The switch to Code view is necessary because Dreamweaver adds a default button with type="submit" when you insert a button in Design view, and the button's type needs to be button in this example. Besides, you need to set some other properties for the button as well. By adding the button in Code view, Dreamweaver shows the Tag editor for the button, where you can set the necessary properties instead of just adding a default button.

2.   Click the Button icon on the Forms category of the Insert panel to open the Tag Editor dialog box for the input tag. Name the button **btnCancel** and set its value to Cancel. Expand Events on the left side of the dialog box and select the onClick item. Type the following JavaScript in the text box at the right:

```
if (confirm('Are you sure you want to cancel?'))
  document.location.href=' showEvents.asp';
```

3. Click the OK button to add the button to your page and then save the page.

4. Open the page in your browser, log in using the admin account again, and click the Cancel button on the Create an Event page. If you confirm by clicking OK, you'll be taken to the page that lists your events.

How It Works

This Cancel button looks pretty much the same as the one you created on showEvents.asp. However, this time the code that takes users to a new page is wrapped inside a confirm statement. This statement asks users if they are sure they want to cancel. If they confirm by clicking OK, they're taken to showEvents.asp again. If they click Cancel instead, they stay on createEvent.asp.

Checking User Input at the Client

Unfortunately, your users will undoubtedly type incorrect information into your form, either accidentally or on purpose. Catching most of the errors before users submit the page serves two purposes:

❑ The user gets a quick response stating that some of the data they entered is incorrect, without the need to submit the form to the server and wait for a response.

❑ There is less chance that you will end up with invalid or corrupt data in your database.

Even though you carry out client-side validation of form data, you still need to perform the same types of checks on the server because client-side validation can easily be circumvented by malicious users of your site.

To validate the data that is entered in the form, you need an opportunity to check the form data before the browser submits it. This is typically done using the onsubmit event of the form or the onclick event of a button that submits the form. In these events you call your validation routine, so if there is an error in the form you can cancel the action before the data is passed to the server.

To effectively add client-side validation, you need to make two modifications to your page. You need to add some code to the Submit button so that it calls a JavaScript function to validate the form. You also need to create a function that performs the validation and cancels the submit process if there is an error.

In Chapter 9 we discussed Dreamweaver's ready-made Validate Form behavior that allows you to check a few conditions, like required fields and data types of a field. However, the requirements for this page are not completely covered by what Dreamweaver offers. Instead of using the Dreamweaver behavior and then modifying it to suit your needs, we'll demonstrate how to create some custom validation from the ground up. In the next Try It Out exercise, you change the behavior of the Create Event button so that it calls a custom JavaScript function that performs the validation when it is clicked. In a later Try It Out exercise you add the code for the validation function.

Try It Out   Adding Validation

1. Open the page createEvent.asp, click the Create Event button in Design view, and then press Ctrl+F5 or right-click the button and choose Edit Tag <input>. Both methods open the Tag Editor dialog box

2. Expand the list of Events and then select onClick.

3. Add the following JavaScript to the input box in the right part of the dialog box:

```
return validateForm();
```

That's all you have to do for the button to call the `validateForm` function you are about to create.

How It Works

At first this code looks quite normal and similar to the code you added to the Cancel button. There is one big difference here and that's the `return` statement. By arranging the code so that the `validateForm` function returns either `true` or `false`, you can control whether or not the form is submitted: `false` stops the form from being submitted, while `true` allows it to proceed.

Now that you have changed your button so it calls the `validateForm` function when it gets clicked, it's time to create the actual function.

Try It Out   Creating a Form Validation Function

1. Before you create the validation function, it's a good idea to adjust the number of characters that your users are allowed to type in the text fields. The `Title` column in the database does not allow more than 75 characters so setting this value for the `maxlength` attribute of the text field prevents users from typing more characters than are allowed in the database. To limit the number of characters, click the text box for `Title` in Design view and set Max Chars on the Property inspector to **75**.

2. Switch to Code view and locate the closing `</title>` tag in the head section of the page. Two lines below it, find an editable region called `head`. Position your cursor right after the closing comment tag for this editable region and press Enter twice to create some room. You should end up with the following formatted code:

```
<!- InstanceEndEditable ->
<meta http-equiv="Content-Type" content="text/html; charset=iso-8859-1">

<!- InstanceBeginEditable name="head" ->
<!- InstanceEndEditable ->
<%
   Dim sBackgroundColor
```

The head section of the template is an ideal location to insert client-side JavaScript.

3. Choose Insert⇨HTML⇨Script Objects⇨Script to insert a `<script>` tag. Fill in the Script dialog box so it looks like Figure 13-20.

When you click OK, the skeleton for the JavaScript function is added to the page, surrounded by `<script>` tags.

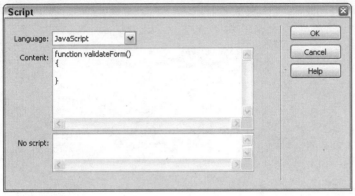

Figure 13-20

4. Type the following JavaScript code inside the body of the `validateForm` function, between the pair of curly brackets (and remember that this entire example is also available in the code download for Chapter 13, so you don't need to type all this yourself):

```
<script language="JavaScript" type="text/JavaScript">
function validateForm()
{
  // Create a reference to the Title textbox
  var formField = document.form1.Title;

  // See if the user typed anything in the textbox
  if (formField.value == '')
  {
    // If not, display error message and exit
    alert('Title cannot be empty');
    formField.focus();
    return false;
  }

  // Create a reference to the Summary text area
  formField = document.form1.Summary;

  // See if the user typed anything in the textbox
  if (formField.value == '')
  {
    // If not, display error message and exit
    alert('Summary cannot be empty');
    formField.focus();
    return false;
  }
  else
  {
```

```
    // Check summary field for its length. We accept 250 characters max.
    if (formField.value.length > 250)
    {
      // Text is too long, so display an error message
      alert('Summary cannot exceed 250 characters');
      formField.focus();
      return false;
    }
  }

  // Create a reference to the EventDescription text area
  formField = document.form1.EventDescription;
  // See if the user typed anything in the text area
  if (formField.value == '')
  {
    // If not, display error message and exit
    alert('The Event Description cannot be empty');
    formField.focus();
    return false;
  }

  // Create a reference to the start date textbox
  formField = document.form1.StartDate;

  // See if the user typed anything in the textbox
  if (formField.value == '')
  {
    // If not, display error message and exit
    alert('Start Date cannot be empty');
    formField.focus();
    return false;
  }

  // Check start date for a valid pattern, like 12/20/2003 or 12-20-2003
  var objRegExp = /^\d{1,2}(\-|\/|\.)\d{1,2}\1\d{4}$/
  if (!objRegExp.test(formField.value))
  {
    alert('This is not a valid date');
    formField.focus();
    return false;
  }

  // Create a reference to the end date textbox
  formField = document.form1.EndDate;

  // See if the user typed anything in the textbox
  if (formField.value == '')
  {
    // If not, display error message and exit
    alert('End Date cannot be empty');
    formField.focus();
    return false;
```

```
  }

  // Check end date for a valid pattern, like 12/20/2003 or 12-20.2003
  if (!objRegExp.test(formField.value))
  {
    alert('This is not a valid date');
    formField.focus();
    return false;
  }
  // If there are no errors, we can return true.
  return true;
}
</script>
```

5.   Save the page, open it in your browser (press F12), and then log in using the admin account. Leave all fields blank and then try to submit the form by clicking the Create Event button. It won't submit and you'll receive an error message indicating the problem (see Figure 13-21).

Figure 13-21

You'll need to complete all the required fields in a valid format before you can continue.

If you get a JavaScript error, or you don't see one of the error messages pop up when you try to submit the form with invalid data, make sure you have named all your fields correctly. JavaScript is case-sensitive so there is a big difference between a form field with a name of Title and one with the name of TITLE. If nothing seems to happen at all, check whether the Create Event button actually calls your validation function. The easiest way to check this is to add the following alert statement at the top of your function:

```
function validateForm()
{
  alert('Start of validation function');
  // Create a reference to the Title textbox
```

If you don't see the message indicating the start of the validation function, check the code in the onclick handler for the Create Event button. If it still doesn't work, make sure you typed in the code exactly as shown here or copy and paste it from the createEvents.asp page in the code download.

Don't forget to remove the line with the alert method once your form works correctly.

How It Works

The JavaScript code you added may look a little confusing at first but if we break it down, it's not as difficult as you might think.

```
var formField = document.form1.Title;
if (formField.value == '')
{
 alert('Title cannot be empty');
 formField.focus();
 return false;
}
```

In the first line of code, a variable called `formField` is created. It is assigned a reference to the `Title` text box on the `form1` form in your document using the general `document.FormName.ControlName` syntax. This is a shorthand trick that allows you to refer to the `Title` field by using `formField` instead of typing `document.form1.Title`. It works more or less the same as the `getDocumentById` method that is used in the menu code in that it creates a reference to an object in your page. However, using the `document.FormName.ControlName` syntax works only for forms. Almost all browsers understand this syntax, so you can be pretty sure that this solution is a cross-browser one.

The `formField` is asked for its value. If the field has been left empty by the user, the value will be an empty string (or `''`) and the code in the `If` block executes. The user is told what went wrong and the focus is set in the offending text box. This helps the user to pinpoint where the error occurred and makes it easier to type a new value. Finally, the function returns `false`. The moment you return `false` in a JavaScript function, execution stops so no other code in the same function is carried out.

This process is repeated for every text box on your form, reassigning the next text box to the variable `formField`.

There is an additional check that is performed with the `Summary` field. Because `Summary` is a text area, you can't restrict the number of characters that a user types in through an HTML attribute, as you did with the `Title` text box in Step 1. However, the database only allows 250 characters, so you need some JavaScript to check the length:

```
else
{
 if (formField.value.length > 250)
 {
  alert('Summary cannot exceed 250 characters');
  formField.focus();
  return false;
 }
}
```

To prevent users from submitting summaries that are too long (and boring to read!) you can check the length of the value of the text box. If it's longer than 250 characters, the code rejects the value and displays a message. This check is only performed in the `Else` clause because it doesn't make sense to check the length when you already know the field is empty.

To check the date, a *regular expression* is used, which is a very powerful technique to search for patterns of data.

```
var objRegExp = /^\d{1,2}(\-|\/|\.)\d{1,2}\1\d{4}$/
if (!objRegExp.test(formField.value))
{
 alert('This is not a valid date');
 formField.focus();
 return false;
}
```

Regular expressions are a very broad topic and there are lots of books devoted to just this subject. It's beyond the scope of this book to explain the concept in detail, but we'll give a short explanation of the code above. The regular expression used in this example checks if a value matches a specific pattern of nn-nn-nnnn, nn/nn/nnnn, or nn.nn.nnnn, where n is a number between 0 and 9. Use this pattern to validate a date, like "10/23/2003" or "10-23-2003."

The pattern that needs to be matched is built like this:

```
/^\d{1,2}(\-|\/|\.)\d{1,2}\1\d{4}$/
```

This looks extremely complicated, so let's break it down to see how it works.

The / at the beginning and at the end mark the start and the end of the expression. They are a bit like the " character that defines a string in ASP but this time it creates a regular expression instead of a string.

The ^ indicates that the string must begin with the pattern, so that "XX12-10-2003" is still an invalid value. The same is true for the $ symbol at the end: This does not allow for any further characters after the pattern.

The \d indicates a number and the {1, 2} behind it indicates that either one or two digits are allowed. The part between the parentheses indicates that a hyphen (–), a forward slash (/), or a dot (.) are allowed as the separator between the month, day, and year. These characters need to be escaped using a backslash (\) because they all have another special meaning in regular expressions. By escaping them with a backslash you indicate that you want the actual value of the character, not its special meaning. This is the same technique you used to escape the " and ' in ASP and SQL statements, respectively. You can see that the three escaped characters are separated by a | character (usually referred to as the *pipe* symbol). This character represents an *Or* condition. This means that either the hyphen *or* the forward slash *or* the dot are allowed as the separation character between the day, month, and year.

The pattern \d{1,2} is repeated to check for another one- or two-digit number. The same principle is used for the year, but this time only a four-digit year is accepted.

Do you notice the \1 right after the second \d{1, 2}? This is an advanced regular expression technique called *back referencing*. When the code checks for the separator character between the month and the day, the expression is enclosed in parentheses. The value from the expression is then stored in memory so it can be reused by using the \1 option. Effectively this says that if you used a dash (–) to separate the month from the day, you need to use a dash again to separate the day from the year.

Once the pattern is set up, it's time to test it against the value the user typed in the date box:

```
if (!objRegExp.test(formField.value))
```

The regular expression has a convenient method called `test` for this purpose. It expects a string that needs to be tested as a parameter. The method returns `true` if the string matches the pattern. However, in this case the code should only be executed if the pattern does not match. That's what the `!` symbol is used for: It reverses the outcome of the test method so the code in the `If` block executes only when the string does not match the pattern.

You may have noticed that this example of regular expressions has a limitation. For example, the date "33-14-0001" passes as a valid date, even though it is clearly invalid. However, with this implementation you can catch most errors in the format of the date that users make.

Don't worry if you don't fully understand how regular expressions work. What's important is that you know how to use them in your code. With the solution presented here, you can easily check for valid dates in your own projects and look real smart in the process.

Beginning JavaScript by Paul Wilton (Wrox, 2000) covers regular expressions in detail and is the next logical step to take if you want to learn more about programming in JavaScript.

Checking Data at the Client

It's possible to circumvent client-side validation by turning off JavaScript. This would allow users to send data to the database that they are not supposed to send. It's also quite easy for a determined individual to send incorrect data to your site simply by constructing their own form without any validation. In fact, that's a well-worn hacking technique.

In TheSoccerSite, the chance that somebody deliberately sends unexpected data is rather small because only trusted users are allowed to log in. If you're running a public Web site, however, where unauthorized users have the chance to submit data to your database (for example, on a registration form), it's important to check the data on the server before any changes are made to the database. This way you can be sure that only approved data is saved to the database. In Chapter 9 we touched on the subject of server-side validation briefly when we discussed how to check for empty values in the Username and Password text boxes.

Changing Existing Events

With the ability to create new events firmly established, the next logical step is to create a form that allows users to change existing events. Maybe somebody made a typo, the date of an event has changed, or you want to add some text to the description of the event. In all these cases you need to be able to change the data in the database.

On the page that shows a list with your events, `showEvents.asp`, add an Edit link next to each event. By clicking the Edit link, users are taken to the page where they can change the information for the event. To figure out which event needs to be retrieved from the database, the `ID` of the event is passed with the link in the QueryString.

To allow changing records in a database, Dreamweaver uses the Record Update Form application object. In many ways this form is similar to the record insertion form because it generates an HTML form field for each column in the table you want to update. It also generates the code that takes care of the actual update. The biggest difference is that the ASP code inserted in the page does not execute a SQL INSERT statement; it executes an UPDATE statement instead. In the following exercise you create the record update form and add an Edit link to your list of events on showEvents.asp to allow you to select an event you want to update.

Try It Out   The Record Update Form

1.   Create a new page based on the main template and save it as updateEvent.asp in the Admin folder (see Figure 13-22). Choose Modify⇨Templates⇨Update Current Page to have Dreamweaver recalculate the links to the style sheet and logo.

Figure 13-22

2.   In the Title region of the template, type **Update Event** and delete the other two placeholders for the Content and Footer sections.

3.   Restrict access to this page because only administrators should be allowed to update the events. To do this, open the Server Behaviors panel (press Ctrl+F9) and click the plus (+) button. Choose Restrict Access to Page from the User Authentication menu. Change Restrict Based On to Username, Password, and Access Level and select only Administrators in the Select Level(s) list. Finally, set If Access Denied Go To to **../login.asp**, your login page.

4.   Create a recordset that holds all rows from the Categories list in the database, just as you did for the record insertion form. On the Server Behaviors panel, click the plus (+) button and select Recordset (Query). If necessary, switch to Simple view by clicking the Simple button. Fill in the Recordset dialog box so it looks like Figure 13-23.

Figure 13-23

5. Click OK to close the Recordset dialog box and add the recordset to the page.

6. Add a second recordset by choosing Recordset (Query) from the plus (+) button on the Server Behaviors panel again. Name it **rsEvent** and select Events from the Table drop-down list. Leave the Columns option set to All and select **ID** from the Filter drop-down list. Your final Recordset dialog box now looks like Figure 13-24.

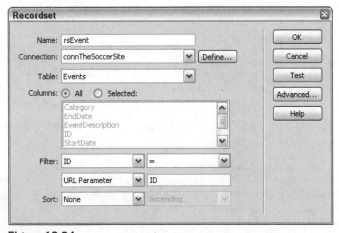

Figure 13-24

7. Click OK to insert the recordset in your page.

8. Back in the page, position your cursor in the content region of the template in Design view and select Insert⇨Application Objects⇨Update Record⇨Record Update Form Wizard. In this dialog box, be aware of the order of steps you are performing. If you first change Connection, then Table to Update, and then change Select Record From to rsEvent, Dreamweaver won't fill in the Default Value box at the end of the dialog box for each column. To make sure you get those values right, change Connection to connTheSoccerSite, change Select Record From to rsEvent, and then change Table to Update to Events. When you follow this order, everything will work as expected.

9. Select ID as the Unique Key column and remove the ID column from the Form Fields list by selecting it and then clicking the minus (–) button just above the dialog box. Click the Browse button and choose `showEvents.asp` in the `Admin` folder as the page you want to redirect to after you update the event.

10. For both the `Summary` and `EventDescription` columns click the column name in the Form Fields list and select Text Area from the drop-down list. Finally, reorder the columns in the Form Fields list by clicking the up- and down-arrow buttons at the top right of the list, so the Record Update Form dialog box looks like Figure 13-25.

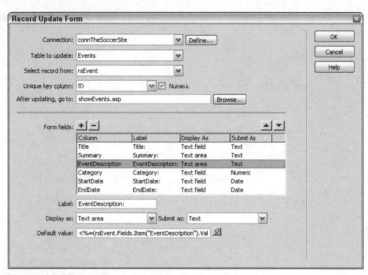

Figure 13-25

11. Change the way the category is displayed on the form. Just as with the record insertion form, the list with categories is presented as a drop-down list. While you're still in the Record Update Form dialog box, select the Category column in the Form Fields list and then select Menu from the Display As drop-down list. The dialog box changes and shows the Menu Properties button. Click it to open the Menu Properties dialog box where you can create the menu. Select the From Database option and fill in the fields as shown in Figure 13-26.

To preselect the right category for the event you want to update in the browser, make sure the value for Select Value Equal To is correct. To verify this, click the button with the little lightning bolt on it. This brings up the Dynamic Data dialog box shown in Figure 13-27.

The Category column from the `rsEvent` recordset should be preselected. Click OK to close this dialog box.

12. Click OK twice to accept your choices for both the Menu Properties and the Record Update Form dialog boxes. The record update form will be inserted in your document.

At times, Dreamweaver may present you with a message box that says you are making changes to the template that are not allowed. Unfortunately, this message is incorrect. If this happens, undo your changes, save and close the page, reopen it, and then insert the Record Update Form Wizard again.

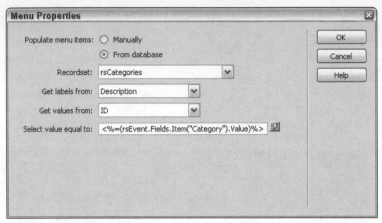

Figure 13-26

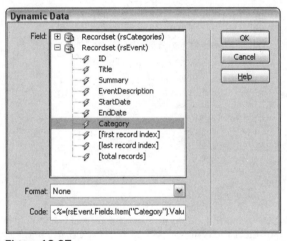

Figure 13-27

13. Just as you did with the record insertion form, you'll need to improve the labels that precede each form element. In Design view, add a space between the words Event and Description in the label for the text area EventDescription. Repeat this again for the StartDate and EndDate labels so they read Start Date and End Date, respectively. Select all the labels in the first column of the table in Design view and press Ctrl+B to make them bold. Finally, right-click the Update record button and choose Label. Change the label of the button to **Update Event**.

The record update form is now finished, so save the page and close it.

14. Next you need to modify the showEvents.asp page so you can choose an event you want to update. A common practice is to provide a hyperlink next to each record, which takes the user to the edit page in the same way as you did on your main events page. In the next four steps you are going to create an Edit link next to the Category column of the Dynamic Table application object. This link takes your users to `updateEvent.asp` for the selected event.

Open the `showEvents.asp` page in Design view, locate the dynamic table, and right-click in the cell with the word `Category`. Choose Table⇨Insert Rows or Columns to add a new column after the current column. Make sure you select Columns in the Insert option (see Figure 13-28).

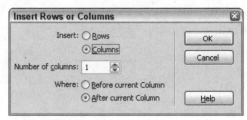

Figure 13-28

15. Type **Edit** in both cells that are created.

16. Select the text `Edit` in the first row by double-clicking it and press Ctrl+B to make the heading bold (see Figure 13-29).

Figure 13-29

17. Select the text `Edit` in the second row, open the Server Behaviors panel by pressing Ctrl+F9, click the plus (+) button, and add a Go to Detail Page behavior. Select `updateEvent.asp` from the `Admin` folder as the detail page. Make sure ID is chosen for both Pass URL Parameter and Column and that rsEvents is selected for Recordset (see Figure 13-30).

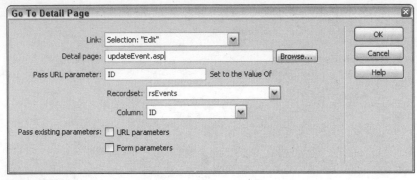

Figure 13-30

When you click OK, Dreamweaver turns the text Edit into a link that takes users to updateEvent.asp when they click it.

18. Save the page and open it in your browser (press F12). After you have logged in as an administrator, using **admin** for the username and password, you'll see a list of events with an Edit link in the last column, as shown in Figure 13-31.

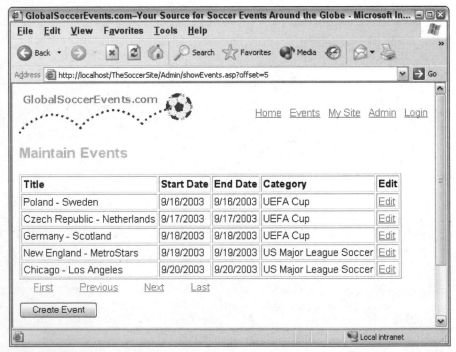

Figure 13-31

Scroll through the list using the Next and Last navigational links until you see an event you want to update. Click the Edit link for that event. You are taken to `updateEvent.asp`, where you can update the details of the event, as shown in Figure 13-32.

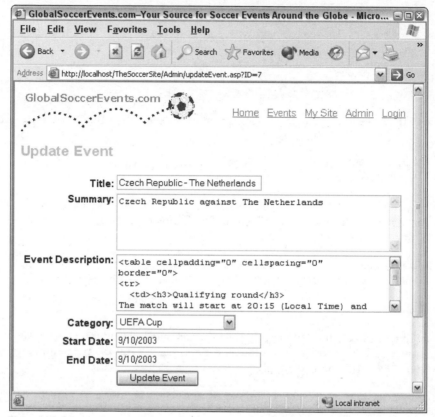

Figure 13-32

As you can see, the Event Description field contains HTML. Although this field is just a text column in the database, it's perfectly legal to insert HTML markup here. After all, HTML is stored as plain text. By adding HTML to the `Summary` and `EventDescription` fields, you have full control over the way this content appears in the browser. If you want, you can even add hyperlinks or references to images you have on your server.

You can also see that the Category drop-down list displays the correct category description for the event. To check that it really works, change the category, save your event, and edit the same event again. The category you chose is saved to the database and is now selected again.

How It Works

Most of the principles used in this example have been explained in the section where we discussed the record insertion form, so we won't cover them again. We will, however, look at the few differences between the Update form and the Insert form.

To find out which record needs to be updated, Dreamweaver adds a hidden form field that tracks the ID of the requested event:

```
<input type="hidden" name="MM_recordId"
    value="<%= rsEvents.Fields.Item("ID").Value %>">
```

Back at the server, this ID is used to identify the correct record to be updated in the WHERE clause of the UPDATE statement. When the page is submitted to update the record, the value holding the record ID is retrieved from the hidden form field and stored in the variable MM_RecordId:

```
MM_recordId = "" + Request.Form("MM_recordId") + ""
```

At the end of the code, just before the Execute method is called, the value of MM_recordId is appended to the SQL statement in the WHERE clause:

```
MM_editQuery = MM_editQuery & " WHERE " & MM_editColumn & " = " & _
        MM_recordId
```

The code that creates the SQL UPDATE statement follows the same pattern as for the INSERT statement. The code loops through the collection of fields in the Events table that need to be updated, and appends them to the final SQL statement.

Besides the WHERE clause, there are other differences between an INSERT statement and an UPDATE statement. Take a look at a simple UPDATE statement to see what those differences are:

```
UPDATE Events SET Title = 'My Title', Category = 4 WHERE ID = 3
```

The biggest differences are the SET keyword and the fact that each column name is directly followed by its value, instead of a separate list of column names and a list of values. Apart from that, most rules that apply to the INSERT statement also apply to UPDATE.

Now that you know how to display, create, and change events in your database, it's time to look at how you can delete events that you no longer need.

Deleting Events

Although you have already built in a feature that hides existing events after their end date passes, it might be convenient to be able to delete events as well. It is a good idea to clean up old and expired events once in a while to prevent your database from growing too large.

The way an administrator selects events for deletion is pretty much the same you select messages in a Web mail system like Yahoo Mail or Hotmail. Each event in the Events list has an associated check box in the last column of the table. To delete messages, click one or more check boxes and then click the Delete Selected Events button (see Figure 13-33).

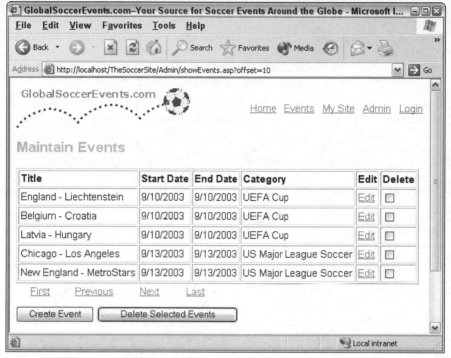

Figure 13-33

On showEvents.asp, you will add a check box at the end of each event's row. When an administrator chooses one or more events and then clicks the deletion button, the page is submitted to another page where the selected events are deleted. Right after the events are deleted from the database, the user is redirected back to showEvents.asp where the Event list is updated to reflect the changes.

Although Dreamweaver comes with some ready-made code to delete records from a database, its implementation is rather limited because it does not allow you to delete multiple records at once. The delete page you are going to create can handle deleting one or more events at the same time.

To accomplish all this, you need to perform two steps:

1. Modify the showEvents.asp page. Add a check box to each row for each event and a deletion button next to the Create Event button. If the check boxes for one or more events are selected when the deletion button is clicked, the associated events are deleted.

2. Create a delete page, which finds the ID values from the records that need to be deleted and creates a delete query that deletes the selected events.

The next exercise shows you how to add a column with check boxes to the events list. The delete page will be created in a later Try It Out exercise.

1. You changed the showEvents.asp page earlier in this chapter when you added the Create Event button. We said you could leave the action attribute empty because the form wasn't submitted to another page yet. This time, however, the deletion button needs to submit the form to the deleteEvents.asp page, so you need to modify the <form> tag.

Open showEvents.asp, locate the opening <form> tag in Code view, and click somewhere in the tag. On the Property inspector, type **deleteEvents.asp** in the Action text box. In Code view, the <form> tag should now look like this:

```
<form action="deleteEvents.asp" method="post" name="frmEvents">
```

2. The HTML table that holds the event details needs an additional column to hold the check boxes for each event. To insert that column, right-click inside the header cell for the Edit column in Design view and choose Insert Rows or Columns from the Table menu item. Choose Columns in the Insert section and make sure you insert it after the current column.

3. In the first row of the column you just added, type the word **Delete** and select it. Press Ctrl+B to make the heading bold, just as you did with the heading for the Edit column.

4. Next, you'll need to add a check box to the second row of the Delete column. Click inside that cell in Design view and then choose Check Box from the Form menu item on the Insert menu. On the Property inspector, change the default name that Dreamweaver inserts under the label Checkbox Name from checkbox to **chkDeleteEvent**.

5. To be able to find out to which event a check box belongs, give each check box a unique value. Open the Bindings panel by pressing Ctrl+F10 and expand Recordset (rsEvents). Click the ID column and drag it to the check box you just added in Design view. If you see a dashed border around the check box, release the mouse button. By dragging the ID column to the check box, Dreamweaver automatically binds the check box to the ID of the event. In Code view, your check box now looks like this:

```
<input name="chkDeleteEvent" type="checkbox" id="chkDeleteEvent"
    value="<%=(rsEvents.Fields.Item("ID").Value)%>">
```

Now you can identify each individual check box uniquely because the ID column is unique in the Events table. This identifier is used in the delete page, which you'll create in the next Try It Out exercise.

6. Add a submit button with the text **Delete Selected Events** to the form. Place this button right before the closing </form> tag so it's located next to the **Create Event** button. Make sure its type is set to **submit**, set its value to **Delete Selected Events**, and name the button **btnDelete**.

7. Right-click the button and choose Edit Tag <input>. Expand the Events list and then select the onClick item. In the text box at the right, add the following JavaScript:

```
return confirm('Are you sure you want to delete the selected events?');
```

This is how the code for the button should look:

```
<input name="btnDelete" type="submit" onClick="return confirm('Are you sure you
want to delete the selected events?');" value="Delete Selected Events">
```

Now when the user clicks the deletion button by accident, there's an option to cancel it.

8. Save the page and view the page in the browser. Log in and test the code by checking a few check boxes, and then click the Delete Selected Events button. The message shown in Figure 13-34 appears.

Figure 13-34

Click Cancel to test the functionality behind the Cancel button. You'll see that nothing happens to the list of events.

Click Delete Selected Events again but this time click OK. You now get an error message because the deleteEvents.asp pages cannot be found (yet).

How It Works

Each record in the recordset of events contains a unique ID in its ID field. This ID gives each check box in your events list a unique value as well:

```
<input name="chkDeleteEvent" type="checkbox" id="chkDeleteEvent"
    value="<%=(rsEvents.Fields.Item("ID").Value)%>">
```

When the code is executed, <%=(rsEvents.Fields.Item("ID").Value)%> is replaced with the actual value from the ID column. For example, when two events are displayed with ID values 7 and 8, this is how the check boxes end up in the HTML source:

```
<input name="chkDeleteEvent" type="checkbox" id="chkDeleteEvent" value="7">
<input name="chkDeleteEvent" type="checkbox" id="chkDeleteEvent" value="8">
```

Because all check boxes share the same name but have different values, you can iterate through all of the selected check boxes on the form and get their respective values to find out which event needs to be deleted.

The action attribute in the <form> tag dictates the page that the form is submitted to, which is deleteEvents.asp in this example. This page does all the magic by deleting the events from the database.

Now that you have a means to select specific events and submit their ID values to deleteEvents.asp, it's time to set up that page. The deleteEvents.asp page is a page that only performs a database DELETE query and does not contain any user interface. That is, the page isn't visible in the browser. The code for this page loops through all the check boxes that have been submitted with the form to retrieve their IDs. With them, a dynamic SQL DELETE statement is built. When the SQL statement is complete, it will be sent to the database, which takes care of deleting the requested events.

After the requested events are deleted, the user is redirected back to showEvents.asp.

Try It Out   **Adding the deleteEvents.asp Page**

1. Add a new ASP VB Script page to your site by choosing File⇨New. On the General tab, select Dynamic Page from the Category list and choose ASP VBScript from the Dynamic Page list. Save the page as **deleteEvents.asp** in the Admin folder.

2. Remove all content from the page by first pressing Ctrl+A and then pressing the Delete key in Code view. Because the deleteEvents.asp page doesn't have a user interface, there's no need to put any HTML in it. You still need to apply a Restrict Access to Page behavior because unauthorized users should not be able to delete events. To do this, open the Server Behaviors panel, click the plus (+) button, and choose Restrict Access to Page from the User Authentication menu. Set Restrict Based On to Username, Password, and Access Level and select only Administrators in the Select Level(s) list. Finally, fill in **../login.asp** in the If Access Denied Go To text box and click OK to apply the behavior.

3. Type the following code in the page, right after the closing %> tag that Dreamweaver adds for the Restrict Access to Page behavior. Notice that no other Dreamweaver behaviors or objects are used this time. It's time for some pure hand-coding!

```
Response.Redirect(MM_authFailedURL)
End If
%>
```

```
<!--#include file="../Connections/connTheSoccerSite.asp" -->
<%
Dim sEventIDList
' Build a comma separated list of Event IDs
For Each iRecordID In Request.Form("chkDeleteEvent")
  sEventIDList = sEventIDList & iRecordID & ","
Next

' This leaves a single comma at the end, so strip it off, but
' only if we have at least one event to delete
If Len(sEventIDList) > 0 Then
  sEventIDList = Left(sEventIDList, Len(sEventIDList)-1)

  ' Declare and create Connection Object
  Dim objConnection
  Set objConnection = Server.CreateObject("ADODB.Connection")
  objConnection.ConnectionString = MM_connTheSoccerSite_STRING

  ' Open the connection
  objConnection.Open

  ' Execute SQL statement against the database
  objConnection.Execute("DELETE FROM Events WHERE ID IN (" & _
    sEventIDList & ");")
  ' Close and clean up connection object
  objConnection.Close
  Set objConnection = Nothing
End If

' We're done, so redirect to showEvents.asp
Response.Redirect("showEvents.asp")
%>
```

4. Save the page and open `showEvents.asp` in your browser. If necessary, log in and select one or more events you want to delete by clicking their check boxes and then click the Delete Selected Events button. When you confirm the deletion, the events are removed from the list.

Notice that it looks as if the page just refreshes. In reality, two subsequent page calls are made: First the form on the `showEvents.asp` page is submitted to the `deleteEvents.asp` page. After the events have been deleted on this page, the browser is redirected back to the `showEvents.asp` page again. Because the events have been deleted from the database, they no longer show up in the list.

How It Works

In the previous Try It Out exercise we explained that each selected check box on the form gets submitted to the `deleteEvents.asp` page when the user clicks the Delete Selected Events button. In `deleteEvents.asp`, the code loops through the collection of all these check boxes and appends their value (which represents the ID of the event in the database) to a comma-separated list. This list is used in the final SQL DELETE statement, which is then passed to the database to delete the events. Right after that, the user is redirected back to `showEvents.asp`. Let's take a look at the code in more detail to see how it works.

The first line of code defines an `Include` file that you have seen in previous database examples:

```
<!--#include file="../Connections/connTheSoccerSite.asp" -->
```

Usually Dreamweaver adds this for you when you insert a recordset. However, it is perfectly legal to type the `Include` statement yourself so you get access to the connection string that is defined in it.

We have seen in other examples (in this and the previous two chapters) that you can use the WHERE clause to limit the number of records retrieved from the database. When you use a DELETE statement, the same rule applies. By adding a WHERE clause to your DELETE statement, you limit the number of records that are deleted. In this example, a special case of the WHERE clause is used. Instead of specifying the WHERE clause as this:

```
WHERE ColumnName = Value
```

The IN keyword is used to specify a list of records that need to be deleted:

```
WHERE ColumnName IN (Comma Separated List Of Values)
```

The IN keyword allows you easily to specify multiple IDs of events you want to delete by putting a comma-separated list of values between the parentheses. Without using IN, you would have to delete each event individually by executing the DELETE statement for each event. This is a lot slower than executing only one statement that deletes multiple events at once.

Alternatively, you could have changed your SQL statement to something like this:

```
DELETE FROM Events WHERE ID = 7 OR ID = 0 OR ID = 12
```

This is fine for only a few events, but with many ID values you want to delete, the string quickly becomes too big to see what's going on.

Take a look at how that string is built up:

```
Dim sEventIDList
' Build a comma separated list of Event IDs
For Each iRecordID In Request.Form("chkDeleteEvent")
  sEventIDList = sEventIDList & iRecordID & ","
Next
```

By looping through the Request.Form("chkDeleteEvent") collection, the value for each selected check box can be retrieved and then stored in iRecordID. This variable is appended to sEventIDList, separated by a comma. If you had chosen to delete three events with ID values of 7, 9, and 12, sEventIDList would now contain the following:

```
7,9,12,
```

You can't pass the last comma because that will confuse the database so you need to strip it from sEventIDList:

```
' This leaves a single comma at the end, so strip it off but
' only if we have at least one event to delete
If Len(sEventIDList) > 0 Then
  sEventIDList = Left(sEventIDList, Len(sEventIDList)-1)
```

Notice that the comma is only stripped if there is at least one event to delete. If there are no check boxes selected when the user clicks the Delete Selected Events button, sEventIDList will be an empty string with a length of 0.

Next, an instance of the ADODB.Connection object is declared and created. This connection object is used to send the DELETE statement to the database:

```
' Declare and create Connection Object
Dim objConnection
Set objConnection = Server.CreateObject("ADODB.Connection")
objConnection.ConnectionString = MM_connTheSoccerSite_STRING
' Open the connection
objConnection.Open
```

Just as before with the Command object, the Connection object is assigned a ConnectionString and then the connection is opened.

```
' Execute SQL statement against the database
objConnection.Execute("DELETE FROM Events WHERE ID IN (" & _
    sEventIDList & ");")
```

The value of sEventIDList is appended to the SQL statement, which then looks as follows if you consider the same three IDs used earlier:

```
DELETE FROM Events WHERE ID IN (7,9,12)
```

This statement is then sent to the database with the `Execute` method of the `Connection` object:

```
' Close and clean up connection object
objConnection.Close
Set objConnection = Nothing
End If
' We're done, so redirect to showEvents.asp
Response.Redirect("showEvents.asp")
```

Once the events have been deleted, the `Connection` object is closed and then cleaned up. When everything is done, the user is redirected back to the `showEvents.asp` page.

Because the delete page does not have a user interface—that is, no visible output is ever sent to the browser—it looks as though you never leave `showEvents.asp`. You now know that the delete page is visited before the updated list of events is displayed again.

Finishing GlobalSoccerEvents.com

Now that you have the ability to delete old or unwanted events from your database, you have come full circle. You can create new events, update them if necessary, and finally delete them when you no longer want them.

This page also finishes the site `www.GlobalSoccerEvents.com`. With the administration section finished, you have all the tools you need to offer users up-to-date information about soccer events around the world and provide them with a good browsing experience. If you look at the final product, you can see that you have accomplished quite a lot over the past seven chapters. Your site now offers the following features:

❑ Visitors to `www.GlobalSoccerEvents.com` can browse through your database of soccer events that take place around the world.

❑ Users can limit the list to the category of events they are interested in.

❑ You can offer loyal members an enhanced browsing experience by letting them change the appearance of the site on an individual basis. With this personalization feature, for which they need to log on, they can do the following:

    ❑ Choose a new theme for the site that changes colors, fonts, etc.

    ❑ Change the background color of the site to match their favorite color

    ❑ Choose their favorite club's badge as the logo for the site

❑ Only authorized administrators of your site can view statistics about the site's usage because you have restricted access to the admin section.

❑ Through your administrators menu, authorized administrators can maintain your event list by creating, changing, and deleting events in your database.

Although TheSoccerSite already has lots of functionality, a site like this is never finished. For inspiration, here's a list of possible additions to the site:

❑ Create a maintenance page so administrators can insert, update, and delete categories.

❑ Allow new users to sign up for the site as a member. This requires another Insert form where users can provide details about themselves, including their usernames and passwords. Look at the "Why Not Try" section at the end of this chapter for hints on how to do this.

❑ Provide an "I lost my password" service where you can display a user's password after they answer a secret question correctly.

❑ Accept user contributions. By allowing your visitors to contribute, you can increase the community feeling your site has. Depending on your audience, you may decide not to let visitors post information directly but keep their contributions hidden in the database until you approve it.

Of course, this site doesn't have to be limited to just soccer events. You could use all the tools and techniques you have learned in these chapters to create other sites as well, such as . . .

❑ **Your favorite actor site:** Start your own gossip magazine online.

❑ **Your favorite cat site:** Inform the world about your cat's continuous sleeping disease.

❑ **Your favorite hobby site:** Tell everyone you knitted a 20-foot sweater.

These examples are just for fun but, really, you are limited only by your own imagination and the time and budget you have available. Use this site's structure for a company intranet so you can inform people about upcoming meetings, the lunch menu, birthdays of colleagues, and so on. Use it to build a site where you and your friends share information about new or upcoming 3-D "shoot 'em ups," and where to play the best online games. Use it to create a traveler's site about your city or country so people can find out what's hot and what's not, what places to visit, and what neighborhoods to avoid.

As you can see, the list is virtually endless. We are sure that what you have learned while building the Soccer Site will definitely help in your own projects.

Summary

This has been quite an intensive chapter with a lot of examples and code. Fortunately, you can let Dreamweaver MX 2004 create and handle most of that code for you. By using some of the ready-made application objects you are able to create pages to insert, update, and delete records in your database. Only for the validation code and the page that deletes your events did you have to do some hand-coding.

You saw how you can easily create a list of events that you can browse by using the Dynamic Table application object together with the Recordset Navigation Bar application object.

We demonstrated how to create new events in your database using the Record Insertion Form application object. We looked at ways to validate data at the client before the information is stored in the database. We also saw how you can easily create a database-driven drop-down list with category descriptions so a user can pick an item from a list instead of typing in a number.

You then learned about the Record Update Form application object, which enables you to alter the events you have in your database. For this page you used the category drop-down list again so it's easy to move an event to a different category.

Finally, we looked at a way to delete events from the database. You saw how you can collect the ID values of events you want to delete and how to delete them from the database without using a Dreamweaver behavior.

With all this technical knowledge in your pocket, we think you're up to some larger-scale projects. In the next chapter, you learn about the architectural issues you need to consider when building scalable and easily manageable Web sites.

Why Not Try . . .

1. When there are no events in the database, the showEvents.asp page still shows the table row with all the column headers. Try to hide this row when there are no events to show and present a user-friendly message instead. You need to use the Show Region If Recordset Is Empty and the Show Region If Recordset Is Not Empty behaviors. You can find these behaviors on the Show Region menu item when you click the plus (+) button on the Server Behaviors panel.

2. Quite often, database records that are not in use currently are marked inactive in the database, rather than completely deleted. Why? Your events, for instance, might be of statistical use at some time down the road, even though you don't want them displayed on your Web site once they expire. Try adding a column called Active to your Events table and set its data type to yes/no. Then, modify your deleteEvents.asp file so that records marked for deletion by the user are modified so that the value of their Active column is no.

   Hint: You need to use an UPDATE SQL command to do this, not a DELETE command.

   Also, when the events recordset in events.asp is populated after a user has chosen a category from the drop-down list, modify the SELECT statement with a WHERE clause to hide the inactive events. You need something like the following SQL statement to accomplish this:

   ```
   SELECT Events.ID, Events.Title, Events.Summary, Events.Category, Events.StartDate,
   Events.EndDate FROM Events WHERE Events.Active = True)
   ```

3. Right now, when you create a new user account, you have to insert the user's record directly into the database. See if you can create a Record Insertion Form for a new user. You need to perform the following steps:

   a. Create a new page based on the main template and save it as **addUser.asp** in your Admin folder.

   b. If you don't want your visitors to create a new account themselves, you need to add a Restrict Access to Page behavior to the page so only administrators are allowed to access it.

   c. Insert a Record Insertion Form application object to the page using the Record Insertion Form Wizard. Make sure you create fields for just the username, password, and access level.

   d. Create a recordset called **rsUser** that selects all fields from the Users table.

   e. Apply a Check New User Name behavior to the page. You can find it in the User Authentication menu of the Server Behaviors panel. This behavior checks whether a specific username already exists in the database. If it does, it redirects the user to a page of your choosing. It also appends requsername=TheUserName to the QueryString so it's easy to display a message to the user that the account name has already been taken. You can use the following code to display that message:

```
<%
 If Len(Request.QueryString("requsername")) > 0 Then
   ' User name already exists
   Response.Write("<span class=""clsErrorMessage"">" & _
     "We're sorry, but the username " & Request.QueryString("requsername") & _
     " has already been taken.<br>Please select a new user name</span>")
 End If
%>
```

Put this message right after the opening <form> tag that Dreamweaver creates when you add the Record Insertion Form to the page. Now when a user tries to create an account that has already been taken, a warning message appears and the account is not be added to the database.

4. The page that allows an administrator to update an event does not have any validation code yet. Try to add the same validation function to the updateEvent.asp page. To make the code easy to maintain, move it to its own .js file. Here are the steps to make that happen:

   a. Add a JavaScript file to the site (you'll find it under the Other category of the New Document dialog box) and save it as **functions.js** in the Tools folder.

   b. Move the code for the function from createEvent.asp to the new functions.js file. Just copy the function; you can't use the <script> tags in the JavaScript file. Remove the empty <script> tags from createEvent.asp; they're no longer needed.

   c. Add a link to the JavaScript page you just created. To do this, right-click the script file in the Files panel and choose Add to Script Favorites. Open the Assets panel, open the Scripts category, and drag the file to the location where you just removed the old script tags.

   d. Repeat the last step for the updateEvent.asp.

   e. Add code to the onclick attribute for the Update Event button. Make sure it calls return validateForm();, just as in createEvent.asp.

   f. In case your visitor makes a mistake, or decides not to edit the event after all, a Cancel button would be useful on this page. Add the same Cancel button to updateEvent.asp as you did with createEvent.asp. Make sure it takes the user back to showEvents.asp.

5. When you open updateEvents.asp directly, you see a record update form that allows you to edit the first event in the database with ID of 1. This is because Dreamweaver adds this as the default ID in case no valid ID is passed to this page through the QueryString. If you delete this event from the database and then request the update page directly again, you get a runtime error because the requested event can't be found in the database.

To solve this problem, add the same kind of error message you created in the previous chapter for viewEventDetails.asp. You need to create an error message somewhere on your page and wrap it inside a Show Region If Recordset Is Empty server behavior. You should also wrap the entire record update form in a Show Region If Recordset Is Not Empty behavior, so you only see the update form when the record has been found in the database.

Part III: MediaEdge and Building Blocks

Designing an Effective Site with a Modular System

In this post dot-com boom time, customized site design and development has seen a need for a real change in the development cycle and in the process of creating digital content. No longer are the bulk of companies willing to pay for lengthy development time to build their sites, yet they still want all the bells and whistles that a fully dynamic site offers. As a result, there is a need now more than ever to work smarter, not harder.

One aspect of site design that is more prevalent now than in the past is the fact that site layout needs to focus the viewer's attention in one location. With thousands of sites created daily, visitors are spending less and less time viewing every site they encounter. When they can't find the pertinent information they seek quickly, they are apt to move on to the next site in their search.

In Chapters 14 through 18, you will develop the backbone of an actual site, namely MediaEdge's Web site, which can be found at www.media-edge.com. You'll create a central "building block" structure that allows you to use and reuse sections of code, not only dynamically generating every section of the company's corporate site but also helping to keep the viewer's focus in one central location.

The backbone that you create can be viewed in its raw state at www.media-edge.com/ BuildingBlockTechnology. This backbone will seem fairly basic to the end user, but behind the scenes you'll find an infinitely expandable, modular system built with an entirely reusable code-block and database structure. This will be apparent as you spend time creating the structure. Remember that you're only seeing the structure, not the finished site—which will come together when you add content to the central database that generates the pages based on your backbone structure.

In this chapter you will do the following:

- ❑ Start with an overview of Building Block Technology

- ❑ Look at the structure you create and compare it to more standard approaches to Web content layout

- ❑ Add a Flash search field

❑ Create the central structure for the site, `index.asp`

❑ Use a new server behavior to simplify the construction of this page

❑ Create a central Cascading Style Sheet

You're already familiar with some of the processes involved from your earlier travels through this book, but in this chapter you're aiming towards a somewhat different kind of site, using some common techniques and some less common ones. The first thing you should do is look into the structure of the site you're aiming at.

The MediaEdge Web Site

In Figure 14-1, which shows the MediaEdge Web site, each section is made from the same basic Building Block Technology, including the news in the upper left, the main viewing window, and the four navigation elements on the bottom. This technology was developed in the labs of MediaEdge to streamline the process of site development. You can use this technology to create a number of different content blocks including news "bloggers," e-commerce transactions, message boards, and media lists. Let's spend a little time looking into the architecture of this technology before moving on to see how you go about implementing it.

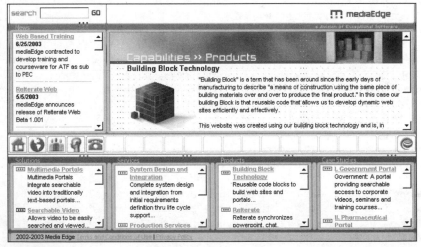

Figure 14-1

"Building block" is a term that has been used since the early days of manufacturing to describe a means of construction using the same unit of building materials over and over to produce the final product. For example, a brick house is built from lots of instances of the same single brick. Of course, house construction does not literally use the *same* brick over and over, but the process of creating multiple copies of the same brick and then joining them together is the basis for the process that you are going to use with this site. The difference is that you *will* be using the same brick over and over for each section of the site.

Overview of Building Block Technology

Building Block Technology (BBT), like most Web site architectures, consists of a series of files used in conjunction with each other. Unlike other architectures, though, which use a different page for each part of the site, BBT has just one file at its heart, `buildingBlock.asp`, which serves as the backbone for the presentation aspect of your site creation.

Figure 14-2 shows the concept of Building Block Technology. Within a central structure, there are a number of frames. In the case of the MediaEdge site, there are six frames: one central content frame and five subsidiary frames that you can use for subnavigation or any other kind of content desired. These frames never move or change; only the content within them changes.

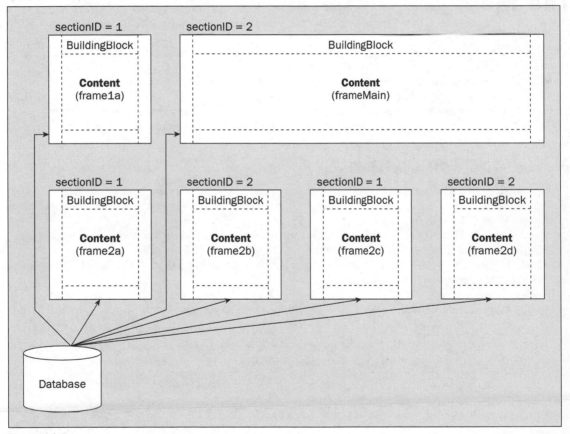

Figure 14-2

Each frame uses `buildingBlock.asp` within it. The `buildingBlock.asp` file outputs a 3 × 3 table, the central cell of which contains the content. The thin surrounding cells provide a border and can be dynamically filled with whatever border image is appropriate to the content.

Each instance of `buildingBlock.asp` pulls its dimensions, border graphics, and central content from a database. Thus, the same building block can be used to create any number of content elements, depending on what you put in the database. The whole structure is contained in a page called `index.asp`, which you will create in this chapter.

Each frame has a section ID that is related to the dynamic content displayed in the frame. Whereas other Web sites would use a different page for each block of content, BBT identifies *sections* of content, each of which has its own entry in the database. Whenever content needs to change—for example, when a user follows a link—each frame is informed what to display by the `sectionID` parameter, which is passed to it in the URL string. Each instance of `buildingBlock.asp` then pulls the correct content from the database. As the user navigates through the site, different sections are displayed by simply changing the `sectionID` variable on the URL string. Although the diagram in Figure 14-2 doesn't show it, there's a hidden navigation page present in another frame that looks after this whole side of things. You'll see this in just a moment when you look at the roles of this and the other files in the structure.

The basic concept is pretty simple. The implementation is a little more complicated but it will all drop into place as you create each of the component parts of the architecture. You'll see as you create your BBT backbone that this structure is especially useful for enabling people who aren't well versed in Web technologies to create and adapt content for their site without having to know how to create HTML or Active Server Pages (ASP) pages. To this end you'll be creating a content management system in Chapter 16 that allows you to maintain your site content without manually changing any HTML or ASP code.

Navigation and Content

Other files play a key role in assisting `buildingBlock.asp`. These files are `blockNav.asp`, `blockContent.asp`, `blockMain.asp`, and `blockStyles.css`. Let's see what each of these files does.

`blockNav.asp` is the first file we'll look at. It's the hidden navigation file we mentioned earlier. Essentially, any link in the site that opens new content within the BBT framework links to `blockNav.asp` which, in turn, checks the database to see what it needs to do, based on the `sectionID` that was passed to it. The three possibilities are as follows:

❑ Open up some local content (residing on the same server, part of your central content) in the main viewing window.

❑ Open up local content in the main viewing window plus related subsections in the subsidiary blocks (the four blocks on the bottom row of the site).

❑ Open up remote content (an external page) in your main viewing window.

Each of the blocks on the site then displays either the file `blockContent.asp` for each of the navigation frames, `blockMain.asp` for the main viewing window, or a file such as `intro.asp` for external content, which may or may not have dynamically generated content. Both `blockContent` and `blockMain` pull their content from the database, based on whatever the user just did. These pages are opened up within the respective instance of `buildingBlock.asp`. Figure 14-3 summarizes the process.

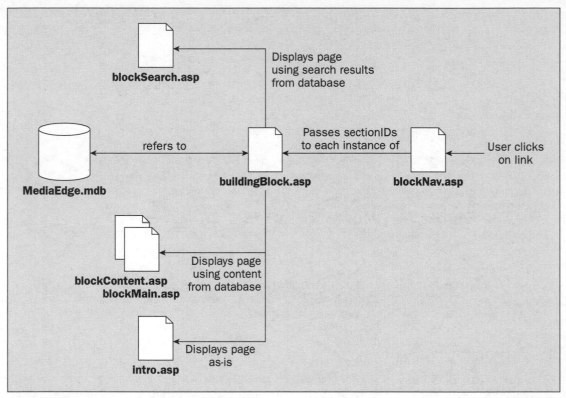

Figure 14-3

Now would be a good time to look at what the finished backbone looks like at www.media-edge.com/
BuildingBlockTechnology, shown in Figure 14-4. Click on the Building Block titles and the individual
items of content to see how they are all displayed in a central main frame, and see how the subnavigation
blocks load. You can, in addition, search under the terms *technology, building, block, item,* and the words *one*
through *five* to see how keywords are accessed from the database. Remember as you view this system that
this is the backbone—void of custom graphics, sound, or introduction—and has the bare minimum of
content possible in the database. Once you create this backbone, it is up to you to add your own graphics
and content and expand the system in any direction you choose. The sky's the limit. You can also compare
the bare bones structure to the live MediaEdge site at www.media-edge.com.

As you can see, we're using dummy content in each of the frames. In reality, you wouldn't display
exactly the same navigation in each of the frames. You might have different things going on in each one,
like news in one frame, weather in another, stock prices, sports results, or, as in the MediaEdge site, different groups of navigational links.

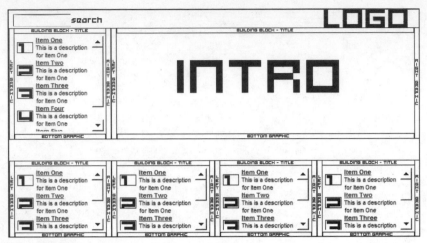

Figure 14-4

Hopefully this overview has given you a taste of what you are going to build and in some way demonstrates the reusable power of Building Block Technology. Let's look at current trends in Web page layout and how your system takes this layout to the next level.

The Layout

The recent trend in Web sites is to have content organized in such a way that individuals never feel they have left the current site by retaining as much of the surrounding structure as possible when loading additional content. Otherwise, for instance, if you have a list of links to external pages, every time you click a link, you almost get the feeling that you're traveling to a new location on the Web because you essentially abandon your old page with every click. We, on the other hand, are going to create a layout such that even if you want to link to external content, you can still remain on the same page and simply peer into the content of an additional site by loading it into the main viewing window of your framed structure. It's not necessarily an entirely new concept, granted, but its implementation certainly isn't commonplace either.

This aspect of your layout does, however, need to be used with discretion, as you can do an injustice to some sites by limiting their viewable area. A good example of a site that loads an entire new site into a frame layout is Ask Jeeves (www.ask.com). When you click on a link in Ask Jeeves, it pulls that content into a new frame and maintains the navigation bar of Ask Jeeves at the top. In this situation, though, the majority of the layout is dedicated towards the new page, with only a fraction of Ask Jeeves remaining.

Flash Web sites of late have done a good job of maintaining content on the screen, while still swapping out some of the content. Within a full Flash Web site you are restricted to one file throughout the experience. Some excellent examples include www.digitalorganism.com and www.egomedia.com. With HTML, however, the task of retaining familiar surroundings is quite a bit more difficult. HTML, by nature, needs to load a new page whenever the content on that page changes. With a site that has several links and no frames, the browser must essentially close the page and open a new one every time the user clicks on a link. With Flash sites it is possible to build entire interfaces that feel as though you are using an application. One drawback of this method is that it's not easy to build reusable code and there are far more people and companies currently supporting HTML than Flash development.

In the next few chapters you are going to create an HTML site, but one that maintains the design principles of a full Flash site. You are going to achieve this by making use of inline frames to keep as much of the content of the page fixed as possible while loading additional content. Inline frames, referred to as *iFrames*, can be placed anywhere on a Web page and can even scroll along with the rest of the contents of that page. Regular frames do not have this ability.

> *Before moving forward it is important to point out that iFrames are only supported in Internet Explorer 3.0 and later, Netscape 4.7 for Mac OS, Mozilla 1.2, and Netscape 6. The particular layout of iFrames in this section was designed for IE 5.5 and later (Windows) and IE 5.1 and later (Mac OS). The layout created in this chapter does not appear in Netscape.*

> *This site pushes the curve of Web development. If you want to appeal to the greatest number of users, then you should avoid iFrames and the use of Flash. More than 80 percent of current users' Web browsers can, however, properly view the layout and structure of the site you are about to create.*

The "typical" HTML site either has no frames or has two or more frames. In a Web site that has two frames, typically one frame is smaller and contains the navigational links and the other is quite large and shows the content. Even with this combination, the visitor still gets the feeling, unfortunately, of having to close the previous page completely and open an entirely new page, with only the navigation to keep them company in the new content. From the point of view of consistency, two frames are better than none (or one, depending on your point of view) because you can have one space on which users know to focus their attention for content, and another to hold the navigation.

You are going to take this concept of using frames to retain as much content on the page as possible to the next level. As you've seen, in MediaEdge's site, you will have six frames containing your Building Block Technology, and a seventh frame to hold your (hidden) block navigation file. Figure 14-5 shows a stripped-down representation of the frame layout. The gray cells represent iFrames and the white cells represent other table cells. The six content frames in the MediaEdge site are to hold the following:

❑ One frame contains your news content—frame1a in Figure 14-5.

❑ The next frame, frameMain, displays the bulk of your content.

❑ The bottom four frames, frame2a through frame2d, hold the navigation and quick description for each of the main sections of the site (Capabilities, Company, Support, and Contact).

In the end, the benefit of creating a site with this system is that you can make a custom Web site while only needing to create the following elements:

❑ An initial index page to hold the site's layout (yours will look as shown in Figure 14-4, but you could quite easily go for a different setup)

❑ The site's graphics

❑ Any additional content that you want displayed in the main frame

❑ A central Cascading Style Sheet

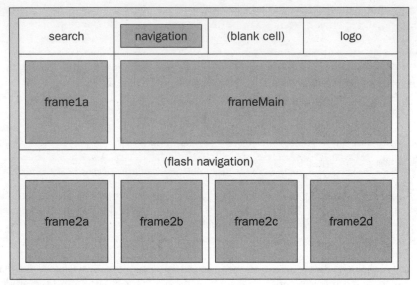

Figure 14-5

Every other aspect of site creation—including links, database table creation, connections to the database, code to display the bulk of the content from the database, positional elements of the content in each section, and cell widths and heights of the tables used—is dynamically generated using Building Block Technology or entered using content creation and management forms, so that development time is significantly reduced once the initial structure is set up.

Creating the MediaEdge Site

Figure 14-6 shows the simplified relationships between all the main files in the Building Block architecture. The content-management system will be created in Chapter 16; for now, all you need to know is that from there, content goes in the database.

In this chapter you are going to create the central resources (images folder and style sheet), the Flash search file search.swf, and index.asp, the structural page that defines the layout of your site. If you are unfamiliar with Macromedia Flash, it is a product similar to Dreamweaver MX 2004 in that it can be used to create Web sites, but it's also very different in that it creates vector-based animation and compiles a source file into a finalized .swf file.

When you start Dreamweaver MX 2004, you may be invited to create a site, choose an existing site to work on, or have a new untitled document opened for you. Either way, you begin here by defining a new site and creating your first file.

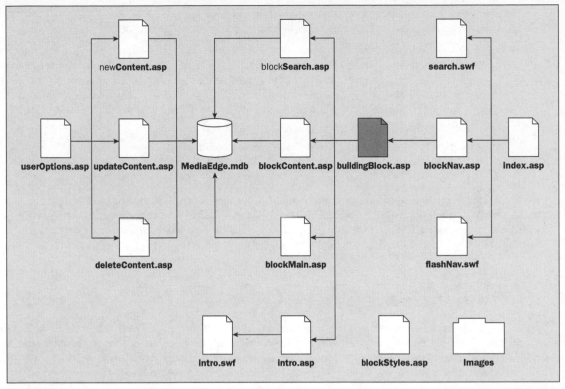

Figure 14-6

Try It Out   Creating the New Site

1. Start by creating a new site. Click on Create a Site for This File in the Server Behaviors panel, or Define a Site in the Sites panel. Make sure you're on the Basic tab of the dialog box that appears (unless you're comfortable with the Advanced tab). Name the site **MediaEdge** and click the Next button.

2. In the next field select Yes when asked if you want to use a server technology and choose ASP JavaScript. You'll be using JavaScript instead of VBScript in this section because that's what was actually used when we created the MediaEdge site.

3. When asked where you want to work with your files, you should choose whatever's appropriate. If you have a local server on your machine, like IIS, then choose to work locally. If you've been working with an external server throughout this book, then choose the relevant option. You will then be asked where to store your site. Again, this is up to you, but if you are developing locally then you should enter something like **c:\inetpub\wwwroot\mediaedge**.

4. Enter the URL to access the site through HTTP. If you are developing in the root Web folder on your own machine, simply use **localhost**. It is recommended, however, that you add a folder called **MediaEdge** to the folder on your machine and develop everything in that folder, in which case you should use this path. This keeps the site separate from any other sites you have developed or will develop in the future, including the other sites you created in this book.

5.   If you are working locally, you will be asked if you want to upload to a test server after working locally. Select accordingly. If you're not working locally, this step will not appear.

6.   After you're done with this dialog box, the next thing to do is create a new file. If you used the dialog box when launching Dreamweaver MX 2004 you will now select ASP JavaScript from the Create New menu. If you were using the Server Behaviors tab, Step 2 prompts you to choose a document type. If the Server Behaviors tab is grayed out, you'll want to add a new file to the site. (This window only appears active if you have an open file in the site.) Choose ASP JavaScript for the document type.

7.   Save the first untitled document in this Web site as `Index.asp`.

How It Works

When you create a new Site in Dreamweaver MX 2004, it saves several settings related to that site, which greatly reduces development time during future development. The biggest perks include saving the location of all site assets (both on the local system and a production server), the connection strings, location of databases, and any FTP information.

Creating Index.asp

`Index.asp` is the main layout page of your modular system and the only page that has static table definitions. `Index.asp` is also one of the few files you will need to edit to create additional custom sites using Building Block Technology after you've finished creating the framework, because it's this file that decides what shape your page will take—how many frames, what size and shape they are, and so on.

As we described in the "The Layout" section previously, for the MediaEdge site, `Index.asp` contains the main table layout with seven total iFrames. Six of the iFrames contain Building Blocks to display your news section, navigation elements, and your main content window. The seventh (hidden) frame contains a file called `blockNav.asp`, which controls all of the opening of additional files in each of the other six iFrames. These frames are named **navigation, frame1a, frameMain, frame2a, frame2b, frame2c,** and **frame2d**, respectively.

As you start you are simply going to create the table layout and position the iFrames. You will also add `blockNav.asp` to the navigation frame because it is the first file that needs to access the database and open the initial content on each of the other six iFrames. You will develop the database in Chapters 15, work with them further in Chapter 16, and create the navigation file itself in Chapter 17.

The loading of files in each of the six content frames goes through the file `blockNav.asp` for a specific reason. Every link in your site will always pass the `sectionID` to the navigation page, which will then perform a `location.replace` on each of the other iFrames to renew their content. `location.replace` is unique in that changing the contents of the iFrames will not cause the browser to add the page to the browser history. If it did, every click would leave a trace of up to six entries in the history. The `blockNav.asp` file will, however, be added to the history each time it is called—thus the back and forward buttons will work correctly to swap the content out in all six of the content frames at the same time.

Setting Up the Page Properties of Index.asp

You should always set up the page properties and add metadata for every Web page that you create. Web crawlers that index Web sites for search engines add the title of the Web site and metadata to the search engine's catalog. Without this information, your Web page could get filed in the junk drawer of "untitled documents" or not have sufficient descriptors to display your site accurately when a user searches for it or related sites. You'll do it here while you're busy setting up the page's properties, just so you don't have to remember to do it in a later chapter. By the time this chapter is done, Index.asp will be finished, along with some of the other files that Building Block Technology depends on.

> *We prefer to set the Left Margin, Top Margin, Margin Width, and Margin Height settings to 0 because we like it when Web pages abut the sides of the browser. This, of course, is certainly a personal preference.*

Try It Out   **Setting the Page Properties of Index.asp**

1.   Open Index.asp if it is not already open and select Modify⇨Page Properties to open the Page Properties dialog box for the Index.asp page, shown in Figure 14-7. Set the Title of the page to **mediaEdge**. Click the Appearance category and set the Background color to white (#FFFFFF). Also set the Left Margin, Top Margin, Margin Width, and Bottom Margin to 0.

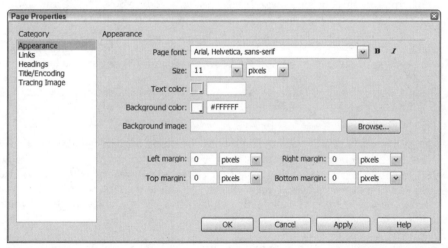

Figure 14-7

2.   Click OK, switch to the code window for Index.asp, and add the following meta tags. Add the tags within the header for the page, under the meta tag that's already there:

```
<meta http-equiv="Content-Type" content="text/html; charset=iso-8859-1">
```

```
<meta name="keywords"
    content="MediaEdge Block Technology Microsoft Visual Studio
            Government Plumtree robot portal learning HTML software Php
            ASP C++ JAVA XML XSLT VirageVideo Logger Flash Dreamweaver
            3D Final Cut Pro DVD">
```

```
<meta name="description"
      content="MediaEdge specializes in Multimedia Presentation
               and Information Display Solutions, from graphics
               creation to Indexable Video Solutions, Web Conferencing
               and Portal Development">
<meta name="robots" content="index nofollow">
```

Make sure to write your tags so that they pertain to the content on your page, and write all code without including the line breaks that are used for displaying the code in the chapter.

How It Works

Dreamweaver adds the basic meta information of `<meta http-equiv="Content-Type" content="text/html; charset=iso-8859-1">` to your page, which simply tells search engines what type of content can be found on the page. One of the best facilitators, however, to having your site get a good showing on most search engines is to add as many relevant keywords as possible to this `meta` tag. Be careful not to overdo it by adding irrelevant search terms, though—such behavior tends to get you kicked off of search listings.

The `keywords` metadata tag informs search engines to log your site in their various categories based on this `meta` information. In your own site, replace the words `MediaEdge`, `Block`, and so on with as many different descriptors about the content of your site as possible, up to a maximum of 200 characters.

You added two extra `meta` tags in Step 2, both of which play a key role in having your page indexed in the databases of search engines. These are the `description` and `robots` `meta` tags:

❑ The `description` `meta` tag acts as the main summary of your site when it is indexed by search engines. Some search engines, however, do not use the `description` metadata and instead rely on using the first piece of text they encounter as the summary.

❑ The `robots` metadata essentially tells *spiders* (the tools of search engines that travel through the Web and report back the contents of the various Web sites they encounter) whether or not to follow the links they encounter on a page. The site you are creating makes heavy use of iFrames, and you do not want your navigation elements within the iFrames to be displayed individually. Therefore, you want to add a note that your main page is an index page and you don't want the links on the page followed.

Each of the pages in your main viewing window, however, can be displayed individually, so you should add a similar `meta` tag for robots when you create the file `blockMain.asp` file in Chapter 17. These are the possible values for search engines to determine whether it should index the page and follow links:

❑ `index` tells the Web browser that the content on that page should be used as an initial page to display as a link in searches. `noindex` tells the Web browser that the page is not this kind of page.

❑ `follow` tells spiders to keep following links from the current page to index additional content within the site. `nofollow` tells spiders not to follow links.

Adding the Table Layout for the Building Block System

Now you are going to create the main table and layout for the site in Index.asp, which will hold all of your building blocks in its cells.

Try It Out   Creating the Table Layout for Index.asp

1. Start by inserting a new table into your file. At this point you do not have any visible content in the Design view of your file, so switch back to Design view and click on the screen to have your table line up on the top-left side of the page. Then select Insert⇨Table. Give the new table four rows, four columns, and a width of 760 pixels. Set the Border, Cell Padding, and Cell Spacing values to 0 (see Figure 14-8).

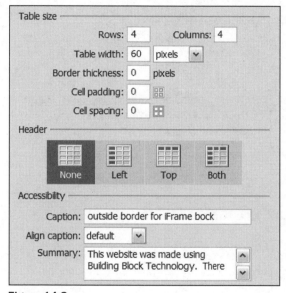

Figure 14-8

The standard that most individuals design for is still an 800 × 600 screen resolution. Soon the norm will be 1024 × 768 pixels since most users have moved away from archaic monitors, but you should still cater to those who have not. Keeping in mind that the browser has borders on the sides of the screen and has the toolbar and file options at the top of the screen, and that most PCs have a toolbar present on the bottom of the screen, it is currently best to design your sites to occupy about 760 × 420 pixels.

2. Set the dimension of each of the rows of this main layout table. Refer back to Figure 14-5 for a reminder of the layout you're trying to achieve:

❑ The first row is quite short and contains the search field, the hidden navigation frame, and the MediaEdge logo.

❑ The second row is taller, in order to contain your News section and the main viewing window.

❑ The third row is fairly short and holds a Flash navigation for Media-Edge's Web site, but it could hold a news ticker, additional contact information, or main button navigation if you desired. Since this is not a Flash book, you won't actually be building the Flash navigation. Just leave space for it in your page.

❑ The final row holds the remaining four building blocks with the bulk of the navigation for your site.

Set the height of each row by entering the values from the following table to the H field in the Property inspector for each corresponding row:

Row	Height
1	33 pixels
2	205 pixels
3	39 pixels
4	143 pixels

3. Join some of these cells together. Select all four cells of the third row by holding down Shift and clicking each cell in turn. Then select the Merges Selected Cells Using Spans button in the Property inspector (see Figure 14-9).

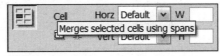

Figure 14-9

Select the last three cells of the second row and merge them in the same way. The resulting area will compose your main viewing window, and should look like a line drawing of the layout screenshots you've already seen.

4. For reasons that will become apparent later on, explicitly set the widths of the cells, even though they're already the right widths. If you don't, then later on those dynamic widths could resize themselves at will. Set the width of each of the bottom row of cells to 190 pixels. The rest of the table should then sort itself out.

How It Works

Just to recap, this table layout is the only static table in the entire site. Each of the cells created holds some content. The cells that play a key role are as follows:

❑ The first cell in the top row, which holds the search field

❑ The second cell of the top row, which holds your hidden navigation file

❑ The first cell of the second row, which holds your news section in a frame

- ❑ The largest cell you made by joining three cells in the second row, which acts as the main display window (also in a frame)

- ❑ The third row, which can hold a Flash navigation, news ticker, and so on—you'll just be leaving this space blank during your development, but see www.media-edge.com to see one example of this space in use

- ❑ The bottom four cells, which holds the main navigation content with links in four separate frames

Adding a Search Field Using Flash MX 2004

Since all of the content from your site is going to reside in a database, it benefits you to add search capabilities. You are going to simply add the search field here, and in Chapter 17 you'll explore the process of adding code that allows users to search the database. You could simply add a text field form object and create the form using HTML. But you want to make your form field match the appearance of the rest of the site, so you are going to add a Flash search field and button. The search field is created in Flash, so if you have that and are comfortable using it, you can look at the source code (search.fla) found in the download. If you don't have Flash MX 2004, don't worry. You're just going to add the "published" Flash file to your site anyway, for which you just need the finished file, search.swf, which is also in the download.

> If you do examine the source code, note the rectangle graphic behind the text. Without the graphic, the "hit state" or clickable area of the search text will be the actual pixels of the text itself. It is quite difficult to click the individual characters in the word search, so adding a background and making it clickable saves users from having to do so themselves.

When the user clicks the search button, Flash makes a getURL call and loads the page called blockSearch.asp. This is the page that instigates the search of the database. The Flash control is set to send variables via POST, so Flash automatically kicks the search criteria over to your search page. (You will create the blockSearch.asp file itself in Chapter 17.)

The published file is exported in Flash Player version 4 format because Flash Player is more than adequate to handle your getURL call. Ninety-four percent of all Web browsers have at least Flash Player 4 installed. With the Flash Player versions 5, 6, and now 7 having slightly less distribution, it is best when possible to fall back to an earlier version so as to function properly for the largest possible audience. The file also points to frameMain as the place to display the results.

Now you can add the Flash file to your site.

Try It Out   **Adding Macromedia Flash Objects in Dreamweaver**

Make sure the search.swf file (in the code download) is in your MediaEdge Web directory before continuing:

1. If it is not already open, open Index.asp and click on the top-left cell of your table layout in Design view and select Insert⇨Media⇨Flash (see Figure 14-10).

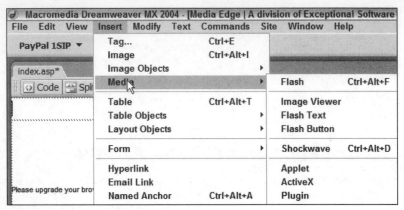

Figure 14-10

2. Select `search.swf`. Dreamweaver adds a placeholder with the same dimensions as your Flash object in the table cell, as shown in Figure 14-11.

Figure 14-11

A word of warning: This may shift your table widths. This should only happen if you didn't explicitly define the table's cell widths when you created the table.

3. Dreamweaver automatically adds the `object` and `embed` tags in your source code to display Flash content (see Figure 14-12). Since you published your Flash file as version 4, change the code in Code view so that this page will require only Flash Player 4 for this object. To do this, change the player version to 4 (`version = 4,0,0,0`) in the following line of code in Code view:

```
codebase="http://download.macromedia.com/pub/shockwave/cabs/flash/swflash.cab#
version=6,0,29,0"
```

Dreamweaver MX 2004 includes buttons in the Property inspector that allow you to launch both Flash MX and Fireworks MX to create .swf and image files. You can, in addition, click Play in the Property inspector to view the Flash object in action, without having to view your file in a Web browser.

How It Works

When a user types words to search for in the Flash text box, the Flash file makes a `getURL` call, which sends those variables to your search page. Flash files themselves require a plug-in known as the Flash Player, which has also recently been upgraded with Macromedia Flash MX 2004. The advantage of using Flash is that you can control the appearance of the text field and button.

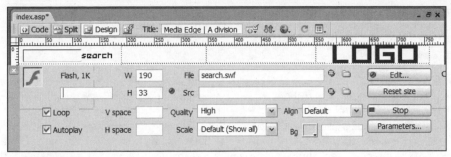

Figure 14-12

Creating a New Server Behavior

In the next chapter you are going to make some new server behaviors, including a dynamic image server behavior, and an iFrame server behavior for use inside the Building Block. Server behaviors are essentially reusable code stored within Dreamweaver that, when implemented, creates the HTML output dynamically. In this main layout file you want each Building Block to sit within a simple iFrame so you can target those frames and pass additional data to the Building Block to get it to show additional content depending on what section of the site the user navigates to.

The server behavior you are about to create will assist you in inserting seven similar iFrames into the table you created and prompt you for their names, which means that you don't have to go to the bother of creating the separate iFrames yourself.

Try It Out   Adding a New Server Behavior

1. Add a new server behavior to Dreamweaver (by clicking the + button in the top-left corner of the Server Behaviors tab in the applications panel and selecting New Server Behavior), and name it **blockSection** (see Figure 14-13).

Figure 14-13

2. Add a new code block by clicking the + button in the top-left corner of the Server Behavior Builder window. Go ahead and use the default block name, **blockSection_block1**, and click OK.

3. Include the following code in the Code Block field (make sure to replace the whole block, including the existing start and end ASP <% and %> tags):

```
<iFrame name="" width="100%" height="100%" scrolling="no"
        marginwidth="0" marginheight="0" frameborder="0">
  Please upgrade your browser
</iFrame>
```

We added the text "Please upgrade your browser because inline frames are only supported on certain browsers." For those browsers that cannot view inline frames, the user will see this alternative content.

4. You can provide a user-friendly interface to allow customization of key aspects of your server behavior when they are added to the code. There is one attribute in this code block whose value needs to change every time you implement this behavior, and that is the name of the iFrame.

Place your cursor between the quote marks following the name attribute of the iFrame tag. Then hit the Insert Parameter in Code Block button and give the parameter the name **blockName**.

When you are finished adding the variable your code block should look like this:

```
<iFrame name="@@blockName@@" width="100%" height="100%" scrolling="no"
        marginwidth="0" marginheight="0" frameborder="0">
  Please upgrade your browser
</iFrame>
```

Notice that you did not add a src=" . . ." attribute to your iFrame. Opening specific files for each iFrame is handled by blockNav.asp, which you will develop in Chapter 17.

5. Tell the server behavior where to place itself in your index page's code segments. Beneath the first block of code, set the Insert Code field to Relative to a Specific Tag, set the Tag field to td, and set the Relative Position field to After the Opening Tag, so the whole dialog box looks like Figure 14-14.

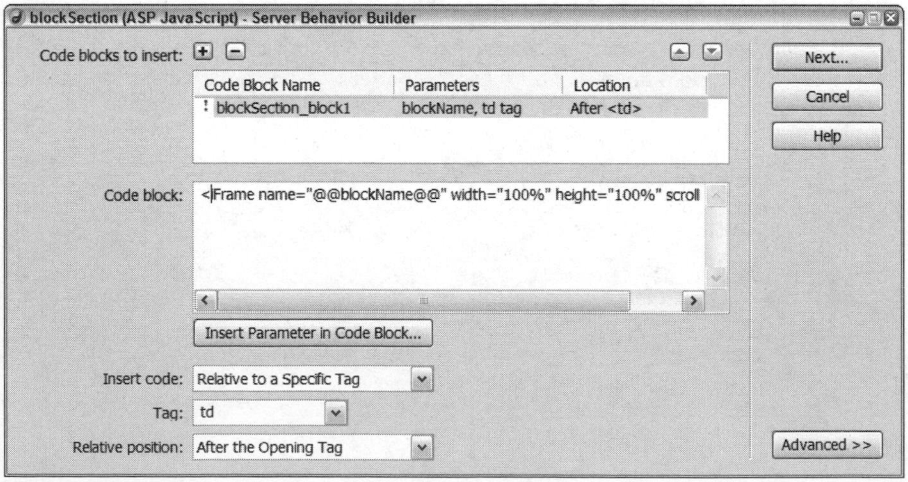

Figure 14-14

6. Click Next. You should see the Generate Behavior Dialog Box dialog box. You will not need to change any of the Display As values, so just click OK. Dreamweaver adds the appropriate code to your file.

How It Works

Server behaviors are great whenever you need to perform a repetitive action in Dreamweaver. In this case you needed to add the seven iFrames to your table layout, each with nearly identical attributes. The only differences between the iFrames are the name attribute (for all of the iFrames) and the src attribute (for the navigation iFrame only—which you will add later).

What you have done is make a behavior that adds the iFrames to the code and prompts you to add the value for the name attribute using a form field. That's why you added the @@blockName@@ parameter. You also told the behavior that it should add itself just after the <td> tag of the table cell you add it to.

In this fashion, Dreamweaver has cut out a large amount of the thinking and code writing for you. The next thing you have to do is to implement the behavior in your code.

Implementing the New Server Behavior

One of the great aspects of server behaviors is that when you opt for them to attach themselves to a particular tag in your document, Dreamweaver automatically lists all of the potential places to place the new behavior for you. In this case, you are going to add your new blockSection behavior to each of the seven cells of your table. You need to add iFrames to cells td[1], td[4], td[5], td[7], td[8], td[9], and td[10].

The enumeration of table cells (starting from td[0]) starts in the upper-left corner of the table and works left to right, top to bottom. If you select the cell where you want to add the server behavior, Dreamweaver automatically displays that table cell number as the td tag of the behavior for you when you come to the relevant dialog box.

Try It Out   Implementing a Server Behavior

1. Change to Design view. Click on cell td[4] (that's the first cell in the second row). Select blockSection from the Server Behavior + drop-down menu (see Figure 14-15).

In the resulting dialog box, enter the values shown in Figure 14-16 and click OK.

2. Repeat Step 1 for cells td[5], td[7], td[8], td[9], td[10], and lastly td[1]. Here's a complete list of the option values you should use for the seven cells to which you're adding this server behavior:

blockName	td tag
frame1a	td[4]
frameMain	td[5]
frame2a	td[7]
frame2b	td[8]
frame2c	td[9]
frame2d	td[10]
navigation	td[1]

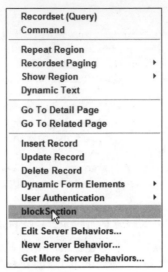

Figure 14-15

Figure 14-16

You should probably check that Dreamweaver has in fact added the iFrames between the `<td>` *and* `</td>` *tags because there have been occasions when it has placed them outside table cells despite being told to place them within. If you don't see the message "Please upgrade your browser" in each cell when you're done, it's messed up and you have to move the iFrames into the right place manually. They should go between the opening and closing* `td` *elements.*

Refer to the labeled image from earlier in the chapter to see where each of the iFrames ends up after adding all of them to the index page using the server behavior. Note that this is not what it should look like in Design view—it's just to show where everything goes.

3. Make one small tweak to the `<body>` element of `index.asp`. Add a call to open up the navigation file in the navigation frame once the page has fully loaded. To do so, switch to Code view, find the `<body>` tag, and change it to read as follows:

```
<body onLoad="this.open('blockNav.asp?sectionID=#', 'navigation')">
```

You should also remove the "Please upgrade your browser text from the content of the hidden navigation" iFrame.

How It Works

All you did here was add your server behavior to every cell that you want to contain an iFrame. The dialog box that popped up in Step 1 was directly due to the fact that you chose to supply the name of the iFrame as a parameter in the last exercise. If you'd added any other parameters to your code block then these would have appeared as well.

The navigation cell is a little bit different, as it contains the `blockNav.asp` file, which will be doing all of your navigation. It needed an `src` attribute to point to this page, so you added it. In the source attribute, you placed a # character, which you will need to swap out once you know the actual ID value of your intro section in the database. (Remember, we're using the term "section" to indicate a block of content of some kind.) Then the navigation page will initially point to your intro sequence, making sure that on first load you get the required introduction. Subsequently the navigation page will be tasked with other things, but we'll cover that when you code it in Chapter 17.

You create the database table that deals with the navigation in Chapter 16, and focus on building `blockNav.asp` in Chapter 17, where you will replace this # with the correct value from your database.

At this point, unfortunately, it is too early to see these iFrames in action. You first need to create the Building Block itself, add some content to the database, and, finally, create the navigation page that controls where each section appears. If you are dying to see a working example, visit www.media-edge.com for the completed site or www.media-edge.com/BuildingBlockTechnology to see just the backbone in action.

In the next chapter you will create the actual Building Block that goes inside your iFrames (see Figure 14-17) and pulls its content dynamically from the database. After completing the exercises in Chapter 17, the bigger picture will start to emerge.

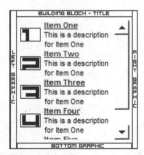

Figure 14-17

Using Images

Throughout Chapters 14 though 18, you will make use of several images for different aspects of the site creation. Default images have been created for you to work with (available in the code download) but you can create your own images if you'd like. The images in the download serve as a guide for your own images' dimensions. Create a folder called **images** in your site's root folder (for example `c:\inetpub\wwwroot\mediaedge`) and copy the default images into it. The first example of the default graphics is `logo.gif`; use this as a placeholder for your own site's logo in the upper-right cell of your table layout (see Figure 14-18).

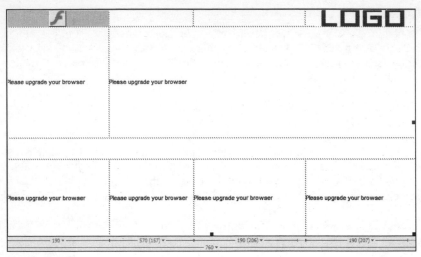

Figure 14-18

Using Cascading Style Sheets

The only other file that you are creating in this chapter is the file for your Cascading Style Sheet, which you will use in all the chapters to follow. The blockStyles.css file contains styles for the <p>, <td>, <h2>, and <body> tags. You also add your own class (.rfelement) to give padding to the iFrame that you create for your main Building Block in Chapter 15.

Try It Out   **Creating the CSS File**

1.   To add a stylesheet and styles, select Text⇨CSS Styles⇨New (see Figure 14-19). Note that you must have a page open in order to do this.

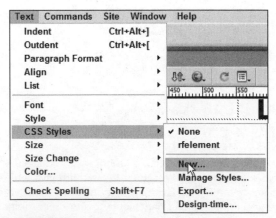

Figure 14-19

2. Add a style to the `<body>` attribute that makes the color of the scroll bars on the page match the color of your image viewer. This attribute, unfortunately, is not available in the Style Sheet window, so open `blockStyles.css` directly by clicking on the blckSyles tab to add the style.

    Once it's open, add the following code at the end of the file:

```
body
{
   scrollbar-base-color:#FFFFFF
}
```

3. Select the "Tag (redefines the look of a specific tag)" radio button in the CSS Style window and choose the paragraph tag (p) from the first drop-down menu. Leave the Define In attribute as (New Style Sheet File) and click OK (see Figure 14-20).

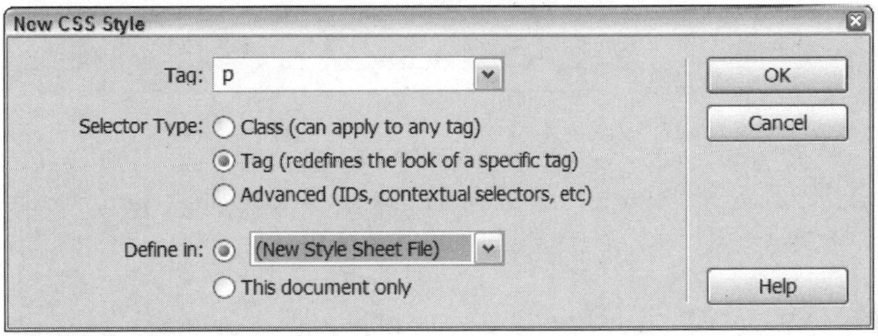

Figure 14-20

4. In the next dialog box, give the style sheet a name (**blockStyles.css**) and save it in your development folder. Save your `index.asp` file as well, and the `.css` file will appear in the list of files in the CSS Styles tab of the Design panel group.

    You may need to select View⇨Refresh to get blockStyles.css to appear in the design panel.

5. The next window is the CSS Style Definition window. Here you can specify details of the style that should be applied to anything within a `<p>` tag. Select the Type category, choose Arial, Helvetica, sans-serif for the Font field, and set the Size field to 11 pixels (you'll need to type this because it doesn't appear in the drop-down box), as shown in Figure 14-21.

6. Repeat Steps 2 through 5 to add two more style definitions—one each for the `<td>` and `<h2>` tags. This time, you should notice that the Define-In drop-down field is already pointing to your new file, `blockStyles.css`. Use the same settings for the `<td>` and `<h2>` tags that you did for the `<p>` tag but set the font size of the `<h2>` tag to 12 pixels.

    Dreamweaver gives you the capability to add many styles from menus in the New CSS Style window. However, we have found it easier to keep a long list of potential styles that we prefer using in a text document and then cut and paste the styles into our `.css` file as needed.

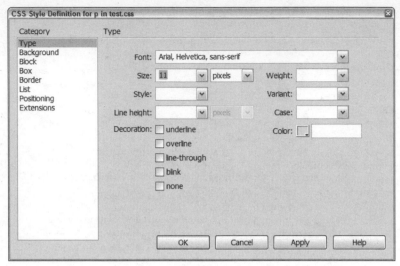

Figure 14-21

7. Add the custom style to the style sheet by adding the following code to `blockStyles.css`:

```
.rfelement
{
  clip: rect( );
  padding-top: 5px;
  padding-right: 0px;
  padding-bottom: 8px;
  padding-left: 8px
}
```

8. When you're finished, save the file. You'll add the `rfelement` style class to your `iFrame` tag in Chapter 15, which adds the padding around the iFrame based on the settings in the style sheet.

How It Works

You were introduced to Cascading Style Sheets (CSS) in Chapter 4, so we won't go into too much detail about how this works now.

The first important style that you define (after the font types and sizes) is the style for all of the scroll bars found on the site. Since you are making use of six iFrames that can potentially scroll, you want to add a style that changes the appearance of all of the scroll bars. You've set the base color to white (#FFFFFF):

```
body
{
    scrollbar-base-color:#FFFFFF
}
```

The final style (actually a style class) is for the iFrames within your building block in Chapter 15. Essentially, in those iFrames you add an additional attribute of class=".rfelement". This tells the browser it needs to consult blockStyles.css to find the additional attributes for the iFrame. In this style you set some padding for the top, bottom, and sides of the iFrame so the text within does not border the graphics on the outside of the iFrame.

Additionally you will see the line clip: rect(); which tells a browser that the shape with which to pad is a rectangle. Other shape options that can be used in style sheets include circles and polygons:

```
.rfelement
{
  clip: rect( );
  padding-top: 5px;
  padding-right: 0px;
  padding-bottom: 8px;
  padding-left: 8px
}
```

Summary

In this chapter we introduced the concept of Building Block Technology, where you create a single repeatable unit that gets all its content from a database. So far, you've created the layout page, index.asp, which sets the structure of the site. It's basically a table with a main content frame and five subframes (four of which act as dynamic navigation frames), as well as a Flash search field, space for additional Flash navigation, and the hidden navigation page. You also inserted the Flash search page and central style sheet for the site.

The six content iFrames (not including the navigation frame) each contain an instance of the Building Block page, which you will create in the next chapter. You also still need to create the database and navigation pages in the next few chapters.

The key thing to remember is that once you finish creating the entire Building Block structure in the following few chapters, the index.asp and blockStyles.css files created in this chapter are among the few files that you will ever be required to change to create another, completely custom Web site.

Why Not Try . . .

After you complete Chapters 14 through 18 and get a good understanding of how the Building Block structure fits together, definitely try creating some different layouts for a site. You can make a wide array of layouts and still use the same architecture and database to display all of your content. In this fashion you can swap appearances on the fly, or even have users select their own layouts from a list of possibilities.

15

Creating the Building Block

As we discussed in the previous chapter, HTML design and development has long suffered from a lack of means to create pages that truly maintain a consistent look and feel. This means that pages vary in length and organization of content. The unfortunate effect of HTML is that a new page needs to load every time a link is selected—leading to a sort of "blinking" effect as the old page disappears and the new page loads. Most people have become used to this aspect of HTML, but to put things into perspective, imagine that every time you clicked on an option in the File menu of a Windows application, the entire page went away and came back again.

The world is round! HTML development can still be improved and you shouldn't have to sit through a blank white screen as you wait for pages to load. There are no ship-consuming monsters ready to gobble you up if you do make use of frames. If we had never pushed the boundaries of accepted GUI development, we might all still be typing everything in DOS and sending mail via PINE. All that aside, we are proponents of usability. You should not be so radical as to exclude the majority of your users (particularly if you are creating a site designed to generate revenue, which is most sites' intention). However, with an enhanced user experience, you'll get a lot of your hits from word of mouth.

In most sites that have two frames—one for navigation and the other for the content—you still need to load a majority of the page each time a link is selected. Then, when new pages load, they tend to vary in size and make a viewer scroll down the entire page to read the content. Ideally, no scrolling would be necessary. Building Block Technology doesn't eliminate scrolling but it shows the initial content for more sections at once. Without having to scroll through the entire contents of one section to see if it has what you are looking for, you can scroll through a small amount of content of multiple sections before committing to one section to navigate further.

The structure you create in this section of the book is new and it makes heavy use of iFrames. However, it is necessary to create a page that maintains its organization of content and requires as little of that content as possible to swap out when a selection is made. This improves usability and also definitely advances beyond how sites have been constructed in the past. Our solution, at the same time, doubles as a tool that can significantly speed up development. Most sites that exemplify the characteristics you are striving for take significant time and energy to create. You, on the other hand, are creating this solution not just to take this one site to the next level but also to raise the bar for all other HTML sites you develop—without the extra development time.

In this chapter you will do the following:

- ❑ Define the Building Block's data source
- ❑ Incorporate Cascading Style Sheets, JavaScript, and ASP to build the block
- ❑ Connect the file buildingBlock.asp to a database
- ❑ Create the Building Block's recordsets
- ❑ Use iFrames within the Building Block
- ❑ Create server behaviors to assist in creating the Building Block

The Building Block

So far you've created only some of the supporting structures for the Building Block Technology. In this chapter you actually create the Building Block page itself. A Building Block is a reusable code block that allows you to develop Web sites and portals efficiently and effectively. In this chapter you create that reusable code block, buildingBlock.asp, as well as the database and a content file, blockContent.asp, which represents the heart of Building Block Technology, as shown in Figure 15-1.

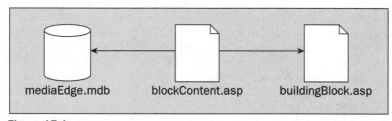

mediaEdge.mdb   blockContent.asp   buildingBlock.asp

Figure 15-1

In Chapter 14 you created the mortar that holds together the blocks using six iFrames and a seventh iFrame to hold the navigation file. The navigation file is triggered in the index page, or from a link, and loads the file buildingBlock.asp into each of the six iFrames. Each iFrame gets a different sectionID number that tells it what contents to display from the database. The buildingBlock.asp file really performs a similar role to index.asp, in that it provides the structure for content to take.

The buildingBlock.asp file is a 3 × 3 table that pulls its dimensions, border graphics, and central content from a database. It is essentially a completely dynamic information display container. Figure 15-2 shows the table layout with the larger central cell holding the content and the surrounding cells containing the dynamic border graphics. The blockContent.asp file is just one of the types of content file that can be inserted into the central content area of buildingBlock.asp:

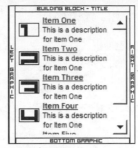

Figure 15-2

This Building Block can have any dimensions, from the full width of a page to the full height of a page, and any number of blocks can be present on one page at a time. Even the content displayed within the Building Block can have any dimensions because the central portion of the Building Block scrolls using an iFrame. In this case, you still make use of the scroll bar to display additional content. The content, however, is focused in particular areas and displays only items that are similar and should be grouped together—hopefully meaning you don't have to scroll around too much. Remember, in the MediaEdge site you have four navigation frames so you don't have to cram all your navigation into one of these. Scrolling shouldn't be a major problem.

Once you start using Building Block Technology, you will never have to type the same code twice. Simply change your values in the database and watch the Building Block do the work for you. So, without further ado, let's start by creating a base-level Building Block database.

The Building Block Database

The database and table relationships you are about to create are a key ingredient in the creation of this technology. The Building Block itself thrives on the information that it pulls from the database. Without a database to provide the information for the Building Block, it is impossible to have a dynamic solution. The information can ultimately reside in a flat-file database or an enterprise-level relational database, but it has to live independently of the Building Block itself. In your case you are going to create a Microsoft Access database that supports your Building Block, as it is an easy database to understand and add content to. At MediaEdge we use a Microsoft SQL Server 2000 database because it is robust and provides the ability to handle a large amount of traffic and access. The pros and cons of different database servers are covered in Chapter 11.

Creating the Database

The database that supports the Building Block itself has three tables: Sections, Section_Content, and Content, as shown in Figure 15-3. Although you're creating the basic structure now, you will add more fields to these tables and also add some more tables as you complete the site.

If necessary, before you create the database for this project, refer to Chapter 11 where you created the database for the previous site you built.

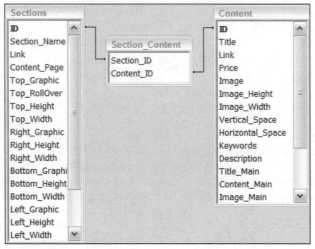

Figure 15-3

The two main tables are Sections and Content. Although it looks a little bit frightening, the Sections table simply holds all the data needed to create the borders and appearance of the Building Blocks, such as border widths and graphics to display. The Content table holds all the data needed to create each individual item of content (a single item consists of an image, title, and description). The final table, Section_Content, relates Content to Sections so that everything knows where it belongs.

Refer to the Building Block in Figure 15-2. This shows the Building Block with content within it. Each of the items (one to five) has its own entry in the Content table. It has its own graphic and link stored in the same record in this table. So the Content table is responsible for individual content *items*. Examples of items might include a single widget on an e-commerce site or a single news item in a blogger.

The content as a whole within this block is a *section*. Each section has a name and its own entry in the Sections table. This is also where the graphics and dimensions of the Building Block are set for that particular section. Each section also has a link, accessible by clicking the top graphic of the Building Block. Examples of sections might include "widgets for sale" in your e-commerce site, or "recent news" in your blogger.

This sample section has five items that are linked using the Section_Content table. Whenever you decide that a Building Block should contain a particular section of content, this table lets you link any number of items to a single section and display them all accordingly in the same block. You can have multiple items in a section, as you can see, but potentially you could also use the same content item in more than one section—for example, an individual widget item might additionally be found in the "hot new doomajiggies" section; or your news item may also be found in a section called "widget news" if you had more than one kind of news item.

This database structure, although small when compared to average database sizes, is a great representation of a solidly built larger relational database, having tables with unique IDs and additional tables that store those unique IDs relating items of content to one another. In Chapter 16 you delve into this concept further. For now, open Microsoft Access and get cracking.

Creating the Sections Table

As we've said, the Sections table has an individual entry for each block of content. Each content block, or section, defines its own Building Block dimensions and border graphics, the page to load in the center of the block, the link to attach to the title graphic, and the padding values for the iFrame contained within the block. The database stores these individual values for each content section.

Try It Out   Creating the Sections Table

1. Open Microsoft Access and create a new blank database (File⇨New), saving it as
    MediaEdge.mdb in the same directory as index.asp (which you created in Chapter 14).

    For convenience's sake, store the database in the same directory as the ASP files that access the database. When you expand this system and put it on a production server, you should place the database in a directory not accessible by HTTP. Read more about this in Chapter 11.

2. At this point you should see a selection window. Double-click the Create Table by Entering Data button to add content to the database

    You can see the fields in a column by looking at the table in Design view (View⇨Design View).

3. Enter the following values for field names in the database. You can add extra columns to the database by right-clicking and selecting Insert Column, and you can edit the name by double-clicking the column header. Add the corresponding first line of data to the table:

Field Name (column title)	Initial Data (in first row of cells)
Section_Name	Building_Block
Link	blockNav.asp?sectionID=1
Content_Page	blockContent.asp
Top_Graphic	images/title.gif
Top_RollOver	images/title_rollOver.gif
Top_Height	10
Top_Width	170
Right_Graphic	images/right.gif
Right_Height	143
Right_Width	10
Bottom_Graphic	images/bottom.gif
Bottom_Height	10

Table continued on following page

Field Name (column title)	Initial Data (in first row of cells)
Bottom_Width	170
Left_Graphic	images/left.gif
Left_Height	143
Left_Width	10
Padding_Top	5
Padding_Right	0
Padding_Bottom	5
Padding_Left	5

You are only entering the first row of data in this chapter, although you will be creating several more sections when you put the pieces together in Chapter 17.

4. Switch to Design view. You should be prompted to give your new table a name. Call the table **Sections** and, when asked if you want a primary key, choose Yes. Now make sure the data type of all of the numeric fields (Heights, Widths, and Padding) is Number. Access should have done this for you because you've already given it data to work from, but it's best to make sure it does what you want. When you're done, the results should look like Figure 15-4.

Field Name	Data Type
ID	AutoNumber
Section_Name	Text
Link	Text
Content_Page	Text
Top_Graphic	Text
Top_RollOver	Text
Top_Height	Number
Top_Width	Number
Right_Graphic	Text
Right_Height	Number
Right_Width	Number
Bottom_Graphic	Text
Bottom_Height	Number
Bottom_Width	Number
Left_Graphic	Text
Left_Height	Number
Left_Width	Number
Padding_Top	Number
Padding_Right	Number
Padding_Bottom	Number
Padding_Left	Number

Sections : Table

Figure 15-4

How It Works

This was pretty straightforward—all you did was create a database and table to contain the data you need to hold. As you finish the architecture in Chapter 17, you will see how this table plays a key role in the final site's functionality.

Each item in the Content table must have at least one corresponding entry in the Sections table. This entry is used to tell `frameMain` how that content should appear when that item is displayed in the main viewing window. If the content section itself contains subnavigation and needs to appear as a navigation frame in the bottom four iFrames created in the `index.asp` file, that item of content will have a second entry in the sections table. The first section entry is for the graphics for the block to display the item in the main viewing area (`frameMain`). The second entry holds the graphics for the Building Block found in the navigation blocks (`frame2a`, `frame2b`, `frame2c`, and `frame2d`)—similar to the sample block you are creating in this chapter. For instance, on MediaEdge's Web site (`www.media-edge.com`) notice that "Capabilities" is a navigation section at the bottom of the layout. If you click the title for that section, Capabilities content appears in the main viewing frame. This is because Capabilities has two sections in the database, one for the initial small section and another for the main viewing window.

Creating the Content Table

The Content table, as just described, contains all the content information for each item of content, including the Title, Link, Description, and Image to display for that item.

Try It Out   **Creating the Content Table**

1. Create a new table by entering data. Double-click the individual column headers, and enter the following data. Give the table the following column names and initial data:

   In the sample database for these chapters, the "Item One" section was entered into the Sections database as the second entry. Hence the "1" for the sectionID on the end of the `blockNav.asp` *URL for the Link field. The sectionID number needs to point to whatever the unique key is for that particular section item in the database.*

Field Name (column title)	Initial Data (in first row of cells)
Title	Item One
Link	blockNav.asp?sectionID=1
Description	This is a description for Item One
Image	images/item1.gif
Image_Height	20
Image_Width	30
Vertical_Space	2
Horizontal_Space	5

2. Add four more rows of data so you have some content to work with. For each new row enter the same data, replacing the word *One* with *Two,* and so on for *Three, Four,* and *Five* in the Title column, and item1.gif for item2.gif, and so on in the Image column. Make sure to increment the Link in the Link column as well

Check that these values match the sectionIDs of the Item One through Item Five content pages once you add them. Depending on what autonumbers Access assigns to things, you may have different numbers, especially if you end up deleting entries and adding them again.

3. Switch to Design view and save your new table. Save it as **Content** and choose Yes to add an ID column. Make sure the data types for the numeric columns are Number, as shown in Figure 15-5.

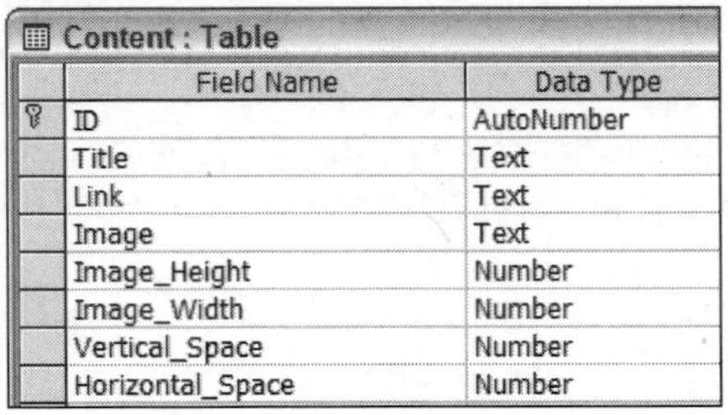

Content : Table	
Field Name	**Data Type**
ID	AutoNumber
Title	Text
Link	Text
Image	Text
Image_Height	Number
Image_Width	Number
Vertical_Space	Number
Horizontal_Space	Number

Figure 15-5

How It Works

The Content table, in addition to holding all the content for each content item, is also the table that is searched against by the search.asp file. This table holds all content information for the main information blocks in your site and can be customized as needed.

As you extend your own Building Blocks, you should add to this content table any information that you want displayed for each item of content. For instance, if you want to make an e-commerce site using this technology, you could add a Price field (column) to the table. In the file blockContent.asp, which you will create at the end of this chapter, or in any additional files that you develop, you could add a dynamic text entry that pulls that information from the Content table and displays it for that particular item.

In your case, you have two files that access the information in the content table, blockContent.asp and blockMain.asp. At the moment, for simplicity, only include the entries that drive blockContent.asp for the smaller frames. In Chapter 16 you will extend this table to include the information for each item relevant to displaying that item in the main viewing window (frameMain).

Creating the Section_Content Table

The Section_Content table is the smallest of all. It simply relates each item of content to the content section you want it to be displayed in. In this case, you are going to display each item of content you created for your test Building_Block section, described earlier in "Creating the Sections Table."

Try It Out   **Creating the Section_Content Table**

1. Close the Design view of your Content table and create the final new table. Create two fields called **Section_ID** and **Content_ID**.

2. Save the table as **Section_Content** but choose No when you're asked to add a unique key. Because this table relates the previous two tables, it does not need a unique ID for its items. Replace the first # with the ID for the Building_Block section you just made in the Sections table (most likely 1) and replace the second # with the ID number for Item One in the Content table. Switch to Design view and change both of these values to Number.

3. Add four more rows. Keep the Section_ID the same (whatever your Building_Block row in the Sections table is numbered) but change # to each of the additional ID values in the Content table. Those values in the Content table should have been autoincremented by Access when you created each new row.

How It Works

Remember, the Section_Content table records which content items should appear in each section. For instance, each item created in the Content table in the sample database, Item One through Item Five, needs to be displayed for the Building_Block section. All you do is link the single Section_ID to each Content_ID value in turn that you want to appear.

The Building_Block section, in the sample database, has a unique key of 1. The five items have unique keys of 1, 2, 3, 4, and 5. Therefore, the first five entries in the Section_Content table all have 1 for the value in the Section_ID column, and 1 through 5 for the values in the Content_ID column. Obviously, if your items have different values, you should use those.

The Section_Content table is a relational table that tells the Building Block which content items to display for which section. If you recall, the Building Block is passed an ID value for the section in the URL string. The Building Block uses that number in turn to pull information for the border graphics from the Sections table, and then matches that number with the corresponding content numbers in the Section_Content table. Finally, it dynamically loads each of the specified items of content into itself.

That is all there is to the database at this stage. You'll add more when you need it in the next chapter. Again, this is a bare-bones rendition of a database that supports Building Block Technology. The database can be expanded greatly to include all sorts of potential content; all you need to do is create new fields (columns) in the tables to hold any data you need and build in the functionality to your Building Block.

The next things you need to do are create the connection to your database and build the actual Building Block.

The Database Connection

After creating the database and placing it in the folder with the rest of your files, you need to tell Dreamweaver how to connect to your database. Again, as detailed in Chapter 11, it is a good idea to store your databases in a central location that is not accessible through HTTP. What that means is if you have all of your sites located, for instance, in the folder C:\Inetpub\wwwroot, then wwwroot is the root folder for your Web server. If you create a folder named databases and place it a level higher than content in the wwwroot folder (C:\Inetpub\databases), then it is still accessible to your ASP scripts, although nobody can access it directly through HTTP. Save the database in the same folder as your site as a convenience.

To gain access to your database, simply complete one step: Enter the custom connection string.

Try It Out — Connecting to the Database from Dreamweaver

1. Select Custom Connection String from the drop-down menu in the Databases tab of the Application panel, as shown in Figure 15-6.

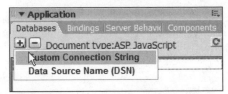

Figure 15-6

2. Name your connection **MediaEdge** and enter the following string in the Connection String field, as shown in Figure 15-7 (it's a single line, broken here because of space):

```
'Driver={Microsoft Access Driver (*.mdb)};DBQ=
C:\Inetpub\wwwroot\MediaEdge\MediaEdge.mdb;'
```

You may need to change the path `C:\Inetpub\wwwroot\MediaEdge\MediaEdge.mdb` *in the string above to match the location of your database, if yours is in a different location.*

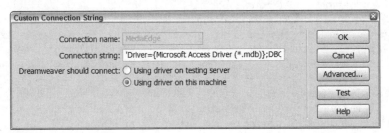

Figure 15-7

3. Select Using Driver on This Machine and click the Test button. You should get the response, "Connection was made successfully." If you get any errors, look for syntax errors in the connection string. Once you've connected successfully, click OK to close the window.

How It Works

The connection string tells your computer or the server (depending on your selection) which driver to use to communicate with the Access (.mdb) database.

Once you make a connection to the database, you should see the database tables appear in the Tree menu on the Databases tab of the Application panel. Just click the plus signs to expand the structure, as shown in Figure 15-8.

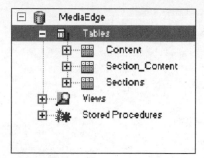

Figure 15-8

From this tree menu you can select any of the fields in your database and begin creating dynamic content—which, incidentally, is your next step.

Using the Database in buildingBlock.asp

As we mentioned previously, `buildingBlock.asp` is the main page of the Building Block Technology. This page grabs all your data from the Sections table and creates a rectangular content space on the page (within the iFrames in `index.asp`) based on the widths and heights of the graphics in the database that relate to the section number passed to the page.

You have five graphics for this initial Building Block: `title.gif`, `title_rollOver.gif`, `left.gif`, `right.gif`, and `bottom.gif` (all in the downloadable source files for this chapter). If you didn't create an images folder in the last chapter, then do so now in your main site directory and place those graphics in that folder. While you're doing that, there are also five graphics, labeled `item1` though `item5`, that also need to go in the images folder.

Obviously, before you can connect to the database from `buildingBlock.asp`, you need to create the page.

Try It Out   **Creating the buildingBlock.asp file**

1. Add a new ASP JavaScript page and save it as **buildingBlock.asp**.

2. Select Modify⇨Page Properties and type the following in the Title field, as shown in Figure 15-9:

```
<%=(Section.Fields.Item("Section_Name").Value)%>
```

3. Click the Appearance Category and set the background to white (#FFFFFF) or gray (#CCCCCC) if you want to view the padding around the iFrame. Also, set the Left Margin, Top Margin, Margin Width, and Margin Height all to 0. Click OK.

4. Attach the style sheet you made in Chapter 14 (`blockStyle.css`) by selecting Text⇨CSS Styles⇨Manage Styles, as shown in Figure 15-10. By default this attaches as a link, as opposed to importing all the styles into your file. It is important to keep it a link; that way, if you change the CSS file itself, all other files that link to it will reflect the changes made.

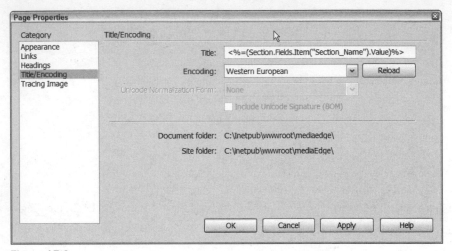

Figure 15-9

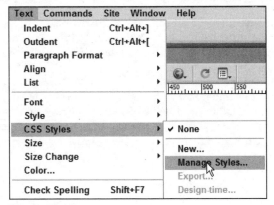

Figure 15-10

5. Add a new table to the workspace (Insert⇨Table) and give it 3 rows, 3 columns, 0 cell padding, and an initial width of 190.

6. Merge the three cells in the first column using the Merge Selected Cells Using Spans button in the Property inspector, as shown in Figure 15-11. Merge the three cells in the last column the same way.

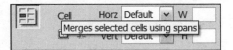

Figure 15-11

7. Give the left and right columns, which you merged in the previous step, a starting width of 10 pixels and a height of 190 pixels. Give the top and bottom cells of the middle column a width of 170 pixels and a height of 10 pixels. Compare the result of your table with Figure 15-12 for an idea of how this should look. You might need to add a height of 170 to the middle cell to make the outside cells accept a height of 190 pixels.

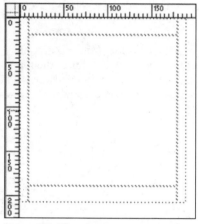

Figure 15-12

8. Switch to Code view to view the finished code for the table. It should look like this:

```
<table width="190" border="0" cellspacing="0" cellpadding="0">
  <tr>
    <td width="10" height="190" rowspan="3"> </td>
    <td width="170" height="10"> </td>
    <td width="10" height="190" rowspan="3"> </td>
  </tr>
  <tr>
    <td height="170"> </td>
  </tr>
  <tr>
    <td width="170" height="10"> </td>
  </tr>
</table>
```

How It Works

You set the title of the page to this:

```
<%=(Section.Fields.Item("Section_Name").Value)%>
```

This gives the Building Block a title equal to that of the section name for the current block (once you've created the recordset) pulled from the database. Section is the name of the recordset you create later on. Fields.Item("Section_Name").Value means that it takes the value of the field called Section_Name, which is appropriate since it holds the name of the section.

Later in the chapter, you will replace the static widths and heights of the table you just set with dynamically generated widths and heights calculated from the dimensions of the images stored in the database. This way, the table dimensions are solely dependent on the dynamic content inserted into the table. The width and height values are preserved throughout the bulk of the chapter; however, this is simply to allow you the ability to select any of the fields easily and see how it looks. If you do not put a placeholder image in a table cell that has no dimensions, the width and height reduces to a single pixel once you click outside the cell, unless there are adjacent cells with a fixed width or height. This can be fairly irritating when you're trying to select a particular cell and it all but disappears.

The center cell's width is set to equal the width of the top graphic, while the cell's height equals the height of the merged cells minus the combined heights of the top and bottom graphics. This way, when the content within the center cell is larger than the dimensions of the table, it will not expand to fit the content in view. Instead, the iFrame will scroll and your border graphics will remain, forming a joined rectangle, as shown in Figures 15-13 and 15-14.

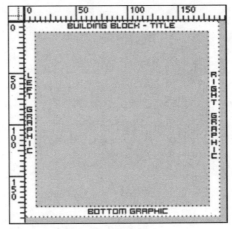

Figure 15-13

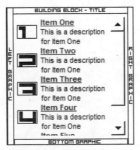

Figure 15-14

Adding a Rollover Image to the Building Block

You want to give your title graphic the ability to act as a button to display additional content for that section in your main viewing window (as described in Chapter 14). To do so, you need to make the title image a *rollover image* and pull the link dynamically from the database.

Try It Out   **Adding a Rollover Image to the Building Block**

1. Place the cursor in the top cell and click the Rollover Image button in the Common panel, as shown in Figure 15-15.

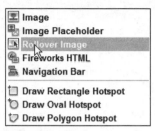

Figure 15-15

2. In the Insert Rollover Image dialog box, enter **Title** for Image Name. Enter the static links `/images/title.gif` and `/images/title_rollover.gif` in the Original Image and Rollover Image fields, respectively.

    Later on, you will convert all image links to dynamic links pulled from a database using a server behavior.

3. To generate the link dynamically, add the following line of code to the When Clicked, Go To URL field of the Insert Rollover Image dialog box:

```
<%=(Section.Fields.Item("Link").Value)%>
```

When you're done, the Insert Rollover Image dialog box should look like Figure 15-16.

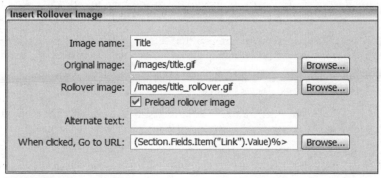

Figure 15-16

4. Go to where the rollover image was inserted in the code (hint: search for "Link" in Code view) and add `target="navigation"`. In this fashion, all clicks will make a change to the navigation frame, which you are going to develop in Chapters 16 and 17.

How It Works

Dreamweaver automatically adds two JavaScript functions to the current document that handle all the work for swapping out the image based on the values entered in the Insert Rollover Image dialog box.

The line of code in the When Clicked, Go To URL field looks like this:

```
<%=(Section.Fields.Item("Link").Value)%>
```

This line behaves in a similar way to the dynamic title you set for the page. It refers to a recordset that has yet to be created. Not to fear; that is your next order of business. You must add rollover images before including a recordset on your page because Dreamweaver attempts to add a second initialization tag when you do this the other way around.

There are a few combinations that might make a second tag appear at the top of the dynamic page you are working on. If this happens to you, simply eliminate the second tag, which will look similar to the following. This is one of the small bugs in Dreamweaver.

```
<%@LANGUAGE="JAVASCRIPT"%>
```

Creating the Building Block Recordset

Every static numeric value in your code will soon be swapped out with a dynamic value from your database. In doing so, your Building Block will be completely flexible: It can be drawn anywhere from one pixel wide to the width of a page, or from one pixel tall to the height of a page, or any value in between. The table's dimensions will depend solely on the widths and heights of your dynamically placed images. To accomplish this, you must start by creating a recordset from the values in the database.

Try It Out   Creating the Building Block Recordset

1. Select the Recordset (Query) option from the drop-down menu of the Server Behaviors tab, as shown in Figure 15-17.

2. Enter the value **Section** for the name of the Recordset. Choose the open database connection MediaEdge from the drop-down menu, and select Sections as the table from which to pull data.

3. Choose ID for the Filter field and place a URL parameter of **section** for the next two fields, as shown in Figure 15-18.

4. Test your recordset by clicking the Test button before closing it. Supply an ID that you know exists—for example, 1.

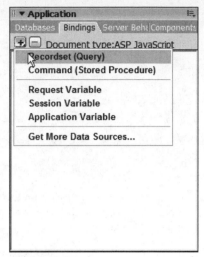

Figure 15-17

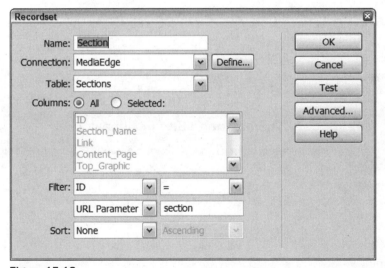

Figure 15-18

How It Works

The recordset that you created effectively grabs all the information in the Sections table of your database by selecting all columns in your recordset. Next you add a filter so that you only grab the one row of data that pertains to the section that this actual block should display—the one where the ID of the record is the same as the sectionID parameter on the URL string.

Dreamweaver automatically adds a default value of 1 for sectionID if no variable is received on the URL string. The default value can be seen in the first line of the following code block, which sets the parameter to the value of sectionID passed in on the URL string as long as it is neither undefined nor empty:

```
<%
  var Section__MMColParam = "1";
  if (String(Request.QueryString("sectionID")) != "undefined" &&
      String(Request.QueryString("sectionID")) != "")
  {
    Section__MMColParam = String(Request.QueryString("sectionID"));
  }
%>
```

When you test your recordset, if the test returns the values from the database for the record with the specified ID, then all is well and good. Otherwise, double-check your settings in the Recordset dialog box and make sure you are still connected to your database.

Now that you have finished creating the Section recordset that pulls all of your data from the database, it is time to create a dynamic image server behavior.

Creating a Dynamic Image Server Behavior

One of the biggest advances in Dreamweaver has been *server behaviors*. As you've seen in previous chapters, server behaviors allow you to create a reusable set of code that can be attached to any tag or location within your file. In this case, you are going to make a server behavior that swaps all your static image width and height values for those that are stored in the database.

Try It Out   **Creating a DynamicImage Server Behavior**

1. Select New Server Behavior from the drop-down menu of the Server Behaviors tab (see Figure 15-19).

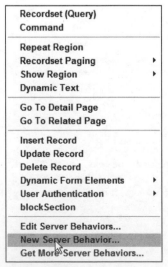

Figure 15-19

2. Select ASP JavaScript from the Document Type drop-down menu and name the behavior **DynamicImage**, as in Figure 15-20. Then click OK.

Figure 15-20

3. Click the + button to add a new code block. Use the default code block name, `DynamicImage_block1`. Paste the following code in the code block window:

```
<%=(@@Record_Set@@.Item("@@GraphicName@@").Value)%>
```

4. Select Relative to a Specific Tag in the Insert Code drop-down list, select the `img` tag in the Tag field, and select As the Value of an Attribute in the Relative Position field. Another drop-down menu appears in the Server Behavior Builder dialog box.

5. Select `src` in the Attribute field. When you're done, the dialog box will look like Figure 15-21.

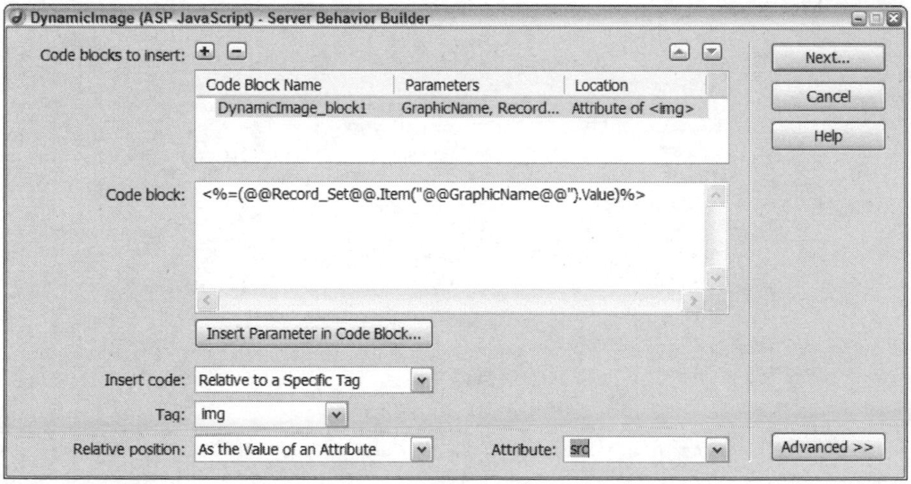

Figure 15-21

6. Keep the same window open and repeat Steps 3 through 5 to create two additional code blocks. This time, however, replace `@@GraphicName@@` with `@@GraphicWidth@@` for the second code block and replace `@@GraphicName@@` with `@@GraphicHeight@@` for the third code block. Also select width and height as the values of the Attribute field respectively, as opposed to `src`. When you create all three code blocks, the dialog box will look like Figure 15-22.

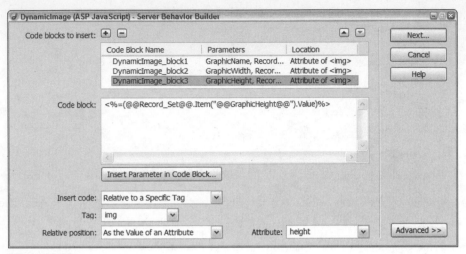

Figure 15-22

7. Click Next and then click the Display As column on a row with the Record_Set item. Select Recordset Menu. This allows you to choose from the current list of recordsets in the page in which you implement this DynamicImage server behavior (see Figure 15-23).

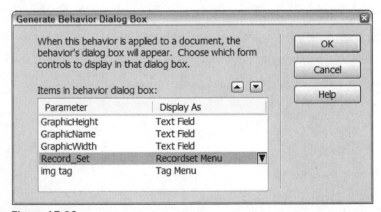

Figure 15-23

8. If you like, you can also reorder the fields to make a more intuitive input box later on. Click OK. Now you're finished creating the server behavior that allows you to make all width and height attributes dynamic.

How It Works

The three code blocks you added to the DynamicImage server behavior replace the static placeholders for the images with regard to width, height, and image source. Now instead of using the static placeholder images you had, the images and image properties are loaded into the block dynamically, based on the values for these properties found in the database for each block's particular section number.

Each code block you entered looks similar to the link code you entered for the rollover image. The difference, however, is that you now have parameters (which look like this: @@parameter@@) within the code block, which allows you to type in whatever values you need to vary each time you use the server behavior.

In the previous chapter you entered these parameters by placing the cursor within your code block and clicking the Insert Parameter in Code Block button. Here you simply typed them directly into the code field.

You are making the name of the recordset a user-input value so you can reuse your DynamicImage server behavior with other recordsets. You will need a DynamicImage in your `blockContent.asp` page, for instance, which will have a different recordset name. In this fashion you can have a dynamic image (an image whose file location is pulled dynamically from the database) pulled from any table in the database, not just the one you are currently using.

Dreamweaver, in addition, places the server behavior in the drop-down menu of the Server Behaviors tab on the Application panel (see Figure 15-24), which makes it particularly easy to reuse.

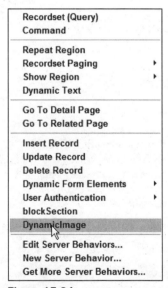

Figure 15-24

Making the Building Block's Images Dynamic

Because you made the DynamicImage server behavior attach itself to the img tag of an image, you need to give it somewhere to go by adding some images to the three remaining outside cells of your block. The simplest thing to do is insert an image placeholder for each of the remaining three outside cells of your table. Then attach the behavior to each of the images in the table.

Try it Out   Making the Building Block's Images Dynamic

1. Add placeholder images to the remaining three outside cells of your table by clicking on each cell and selecting Insert⇨Image Placeholder for each cell. You do not need to give the image a name or dimensions, just click OK. If dimensions are added by default, don't worry about them; you are going to delete them later.

2. Implement the server behavior for each of the four outside cells, along with the image that replaces the title when the user rolls the mouse over that graphic.

    Select the left placeholder image and select DynamicImage from the Server Behaviors + drop-down menu. A menu appears with fields for each of the parameters you entered in your code blocks.

    For the first image, enter the details as shown in Figure 15-25. Click OK.

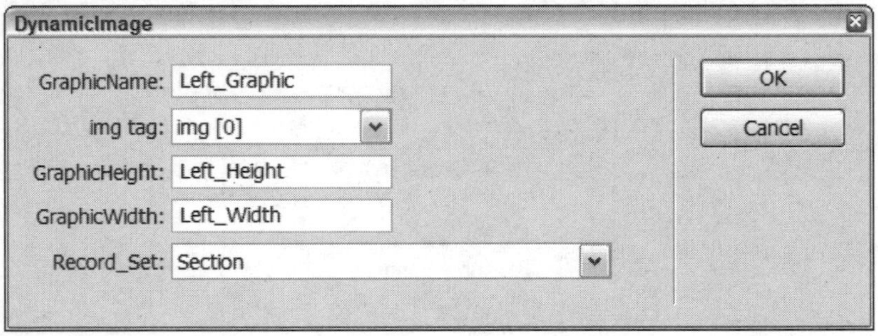

Figure 15-25

Remember that these fields can appear in any order, depending on the order of the fields you specified in the last dialog box when generating the server behavior. It's not actually that important, but if you prefer your fields to be in a certain order, you can make a habit of adjusting it in the final step when you're creating the behavior. If you want to go back and change it, select Server Behaviors⇨Edit Server Behaviors and select the behavior to edit.

3. After clicking the top image, select the DynamicImage again to create a second instance of the server behavior from the drop-down menu and enter the details shown in the following table:

Field	Value
GraphicName	Top_Graphic
img tag	Title
GraphicWidth	Top_Width
GraphicHeight	Top_Height
Record_Set	Section

4. Do the same again for a third and fourth DynamicImage.

Field	Value
GraphicName	Right_Graphic
img tag	Img[2]
GraphicWidth	Right_Width
GraphicHeight	Right_Height
Record_Set	Section
GraphicName	Bottom_Graphic
img tag	Img[3]
GraphicWidth	Bottom_Width
GraphicHeight	Bottom_Height
Record_Set	Section

5. Make sure the rollover graphic for the Building Block title is dynamic. This means that you need to replace the string /images/title_rollOver.gif with your dynamic line of code in two places:

   ❑ After the onMouseOver function call

   ❑ In the MM_preloadImages function call

The easiest thing to do is search and replace the string in the code window. Switch to Code view and find (Edit➪Find and Replace) the following string, which should occur twice in your code:

```
'images/title_rollover.gif'
```

Replace that string with this:

```
'<%=(Section.Fields.Item("Top_Rollover").Value)%>'
```

How It Works

You should now have five image placeholders (two for the title rollover and one for each border graphic) that pull their images from the images folder dynamically, depending on which record you've pulled out of your recordset (which is the same as the record used to supply the content to the block). Now you can use the buildingBlock.asp file over and over to display multiple sections of content, each with its own border graphics if desired. You never need to go back in to tweak the code for this file. That is a pretty cool thing.

Before moving on, you should note that you can check whether the correct dynamic content will display in your file by selecting the Live Data View icon from the Quick Actions panel, as shown in Figure 15-26.

Figure 15-26

If everything is okay, you should get results that look like Figure 15-27.

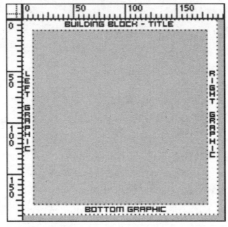

Figure 15-27

If not, the first thing you should check is whether Dreamweaver has correctly generated the image tag from your server behavior. The code should begin with:

```
<img name="" src="<%=(Section.Fields.Item("Bottom_Graphic").Value)%>"
```

Dreamweaver has been known to omit the word `Fields`, however. If this is the case, and you get an ASP error referencing these lines of code, just insert the word `Fields` (don't forget the extra dot).

Notice that the Server Behaviors tab now lists all of the items of dynamic content that you just added, as you can see in Figure 15-28. You can remove any one of the dynamic sections by simply deleting that section from this area. Dreamweaver does a pretty good job of knowing what code it should add and remove, and when to do it.

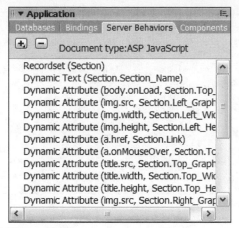

Figure 15-28

Inline Frames

An inline frame (iFrame) works much the same as a regular frame, letting you load additional HTML documents and refer to it by its NAME attribute, but it differs by being able to be positioned anywhere within a document, much like the OBJECT tag. In addition, iFrames can scroll along with text and objects within the body of another page.

> **iFrames are only supported on Windows in Internet Explorer 3.0 and above, Netscape 4.7 for Mac, Mozilla M12, and Netscape 6. This means that the comparatively small number of people with Netscape 4.7 on Windows, about five percent of all Internet users, are going to be out of luck.**

Just like your DynamicImage server behavior, you want to create an iFrame server behavior to help you implement an iFrame in your document.

Try It Out — Creating an iFrame Server Behavior for the Building Block

1. Add a new server behavior (see Figure 15-29). Name it **iFrame** and click OK.

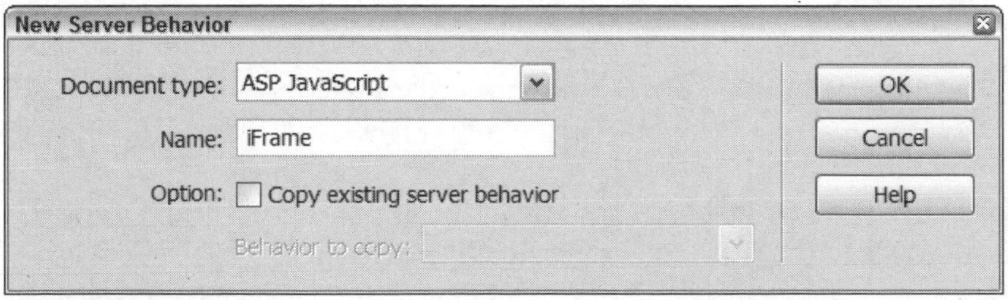

Figure 15-29

2. Add a new code block by clicking the + and leaving its default name. Include the following code in the Code Block field of the Server Behavior Builder dialog box:

```
<iFrame name="list" scrolling = "auto" marginwidth="0" marginheight="0"
src="<%=Section.Fields.Item("Content_Page").Value%>?section=<%=
(Section.Fields.Item("ID").Value)%>&list=true&width=<%=
(Section.Fields.Item("Top_Width").Value -
Section.Fields.Item("Padding_Left").Value -
Section.Fields.Item("Padding_Right").Value)%>" frameborder="0"
height="<%=(Section.Fields.Item("Left_Height").Value -
Section.Fields.Item("Top_Height").Value -
Section.Fields.Item("Bottom_Height").Value
-Section.Fields.Item("Padding_Top").Value -
Section.Fields.Item("Padding_Bottom").Value)%>" width="100%">
Please upgrade your browser</iFrame>
```

The code in the block above should appear as a single line, not with breaks in it as shown here. (One of the problems of a printed page's width!)

Still on the first block of code, make the Insert Code field equal to Relative to a Specific Tag, the Tag field equal to td, and the Relative Position field equal to After the Opening Tag.

3. Add a second code block by clicking the + and entering **rfelement** in the Code Block field. Set the remaining values shown in Figure 15-30.

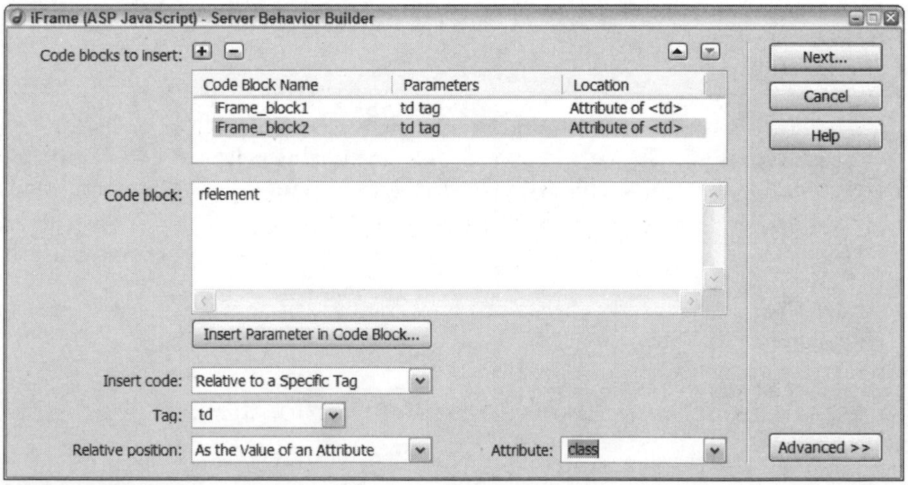

Figure 15-30

What this second block of code does is make the iFrame use the rfelement style class you created for iFrames in Chapter 14. This style adds padding to the sides of the content contained inside the iFrame.

4. After clicking Next in the Server Behavior Builder dialog box, simply click OK when you see the Generate Behavior dialog box. You will not need to adjust anything there.

5. Select your new iFrame server behavior from the drop-down menu of the Server Behaviors tab (see Figure 15-31) and attach it to the center cell of your table, td[3].

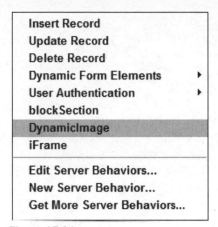

Figure 15-31

How It Works

Now to look at the code from the server behavior. Although it's really all one line, we'll break it down into pieces:

```
<iFrame name="list" scrolling = "auto" marginwidth="0" marginheight="0"
```

This is pretty uninteresting tag stuff. Let's look at the next part:

```
src="<%=Section.Fields.Item("Content_Page").Value%>
```

What this code does is create an iFrame containing your content file, whose name is dynamically pulled from the database. Content_Page holds the name of the page that loads into the Building Block, whether it's blockContent, blockMain, or another kind of page—say a Flash introduction or some other kind of content file you may have created to handle different kinds of presentation other than a simple list of links like blockContent. You then dynamically pass into this file the ID of the section content you want to display in it:

```
?sectionID=<%=(Section.Fields.Item("ID").Value)%>&list=true
```

The code also passes the maximum width to set the contents, so that the iFrame is not forced to scroll horizontally, only vertically:

```
&width=<%=(Section.Fields.Item("Top_Width").Value -
Section.Fields.Item("Padding_Left").Value -
Section.Fields.Item("Padding_Right").Value)%>"
frameborder="0"
```

Now you set the height and width of the *frame* (remember, what you just set was the maximum width of the *content*):

```
height="<%=(Section.Fields.Item("Left_Height").Value -
Section.Fields.Item("Top_Height").Value -
Section.Fields.Item("Bottom_Height").Value
-Section.Fields.Item("Padding_Top").Value -
Section.Fields.Item("Padding_Bottom").Value)%>"
width="100%">Please upgrade your browser</iFrame>
```

At this point you should see the alternative text in the center cell of your table. In this case, it reads "Please upgrade your browser." If not, check again that the server behavior really did put the iFrame inside the table tags and not after them. You can add any content that you want in the code block for users of non-compatible browsers but we're leaving it as this basic message for now, as you can see in Figure 15-32.

Figure 15-32

Dynamic Dimensions for the Center Cell

The final piece of business for buildingBlock.asp is to remove the last of the static heights and widths, as we mentioned when you created the initial table, and setting the width and height for the center cell. The center cell's width, for instance, needs to equal the width of the top graphic, minus the values set for the left_padding and right_padding of the iFrame.

The style sheet values for the padding of the iFrame have been included in the database so that you can accommodate those values when setting the width and height of the center cell. However, when you make your Building Block Technology more robust, it is a good idea to dynamically generate the blockStyles.css page based on input values in the database.

The easiest way to find the locations where you need to set the width and height of the center cell is to use a little search and replace trick.

Try It Out	Giving the Building Block's Center Cell Dynamic Dimensions

1. Click the center cell in Design view and enter two different arbitrary values for width and height in the Property inspector. For the sake of argument, use **111** and **222**.

2. Switch to Code view, select Edit⇨Find and Replace, and find the value. Make sure to change the drop-down menu to "source code" because the default is to search text only.

111

Replace this value with the following (make sure to enter this code as one line, with no breaks):

```
<%=(Section.Fields.Item("Top_Width").Value -
    Section.Fields.Item("Padding_Left").Value -
    Section.Fields.Item("Padding_Right").Value) %>
```

3. Do another string replace (Edit⇨Find and Replace) and find this value:

```
222
```

Replace it with the following code (again, enter the code as one line):

```
<%=(Section.Fields.Item("Left_Height").Value -
    Section.Fields.Item("Top_Height").Value -
    Section.Fields.Item("Bottom_Height").Value -
    Section.Fields.Item("Padding_Top").Value -
    Section.Fields.Item("Padding_Bottom").Value)%>
```

When you are finished making these changes, and you switch back over to Design view, your frame should look like Figure 15-33. Notice that the middle cell has pulled in tighter around the text. This is because the dimensions are now dynamic. When you view this block in a browser, or select Live Data view, it will again take shape closer to being square, getting its values from the surrounding graphics.

Figure 15-33

4. The very final piece of business, as mentioned at the start of this section, is to remove the static widths for the entire table. To do this, go to Code view and search for your start table tag (`<table`). Simply cut the `width` attribute out of the tag so that you are left with this:

```
<table border="0" cellspacing="0" cellpadding="0">
```

If you added widths and heights for each of the cells, and they still remain in the code, you can delete them as well. The table widths and heights will be determined by the dimensions of the graphics.

How It Works

This final addition to `buildingBlock.asp` cuts the last piece of static information about the block's center cell. Now the only information about the block that is not pulled directly from the database is the original layout of the cell, which is the 3×3 table. Everything else—the graphics, the dimensions, and the content to show within the table—is generated dynamically from your database.

That's all you need to do for `buildingBlock.asp`.

The last thing to look at in this chapter is creating a dynamic content page to populate your Building Block.

Creating Content

The sample content being placed in your Building Block is simple, to say the least, but the most important concept is that it is being written so that it is fully customizable—and completely dynamic, based on the values in the database. In this case you are writing a vertical list of items in your content database, but `blockContent.asp` could produce a pie chart, or a movie player, or even an interactive quiz. The important thing is to code each item the first time so that it is modular and can be used multiple times without having to go back and change the code. Later in the site, you'll create a second content page that will be set up differently to populate the main frame.

Start building your `blockContent.asp` page.

Try It Out   **Creating blockContent.asp**

1.   Create a new ASP page (File⇨New) and save it as `blockContent.asp`. Define the page properties (Modify⇨Page Properties) with a title **Building Block Technology**. Click Appearance and set the left margin, right margin, margin width, and margin height all to 0 and set the background color to white (#FFFFFF).

2.   Attach your style sheet to this page, `blockStyles.css` (Text⇨CSS Styles⇨Manage Styles).

3.   With Dreamweaver MX 2004 the line `<!DOCTYPE HTML PUBLIC "-//W3C//DTD HTML 4.01 Transitional//EN" http://www.w3.org/TR/html4/loose.dtd>` is added by default to every new page. This line, however, prevents any nonstandard style from appearing. To make sure your iFrame styles and scroll bar color appear, eliminate this line from the code.

4.   Insert a table (Insert⇨Table) and enter the values shown in Figure 15-34.

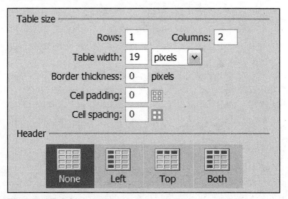

Figure 15-34

5.   Create a new recordset (Server Behaviors⇨+⇨New Recordset) and call it **Content**, but this time select the Advanced tab. You are going to add the SQL statement manually.

6.   In the Connection field, select your MediaEdge connection as before.

7. You need to get all of the content items in the Content table whose ID value corresponds to a Section_ID value of (sectionID), which is passed in the URL string from buildingBlock.asp. To do this, enter the following SQL statement in the SQL field of the dialog box:

```
SELECT ID, Title, Link, Image, Image_Height, Image_Width, Vertical_Space,
Horizontal_Space, Description FROM Content, Section_Content WHERE ID = Content_ID
AND Section_ID = MMColParam
```

8. Click the + next to Variables to add a new variable. Name it **MMColParam** and add a default value of 1 and runtime value of **Request.QueryString("section")**. Click OK.

9. Add an image placeholder in the left cell of the table. Don't worry about its name or dimensions.

10. Once again you need to make your image dynamic, so select your DynamicImage server behavior from the drop-down menu of the Server Behavior tab. This time, input the values shown in Figure 15-35.

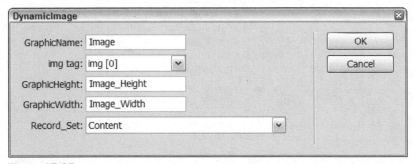

Figure 15-35

Here is another place where you have to make sure that Dreamweaver correctly inserted Content.Fields.Item rather than just Content.Item. It's probably easiest to do a search and replace. Note that when you do this, your page will work just fine but Dreamweaver will complain by putting an exclamation mark next to the server behavior and informing you that the Content.Fields recordset doesn't exist when you double-click the behavior to investigate. It will also try to regain control if you do this and may remove the Fields part again if you've added it.

11. Add horizontal and vertical padding for each image. Click on the image and, as you've done before, enter two arbitrary values for vertical space and horizontal space in the Property inspector, such as **111** and **222**. Switch to Code view, do a find and replace (Edit⇨Find and Replace), and remember to select "source code" from the drop down menu:

❑ Change vspace="111" to the following:

```
vspace="<%=(Content.Fields.Item("Vertical_Space").Value)%>"
```

❑ Change hspace="222" to the following:

```
hspace="<%=(Content.Fields.Item("Horizontal_Space").Value)%>"
```

12. Add your Title, Link, and Description from the database to the right cell of your table. Switch back to Design view and click the right cell of the table. Choose Dynamic Text from the drop-down menu in the Server Behaviors tab, as shown in Figure 15-36, and choose Title from the list of data in the Content recordset.

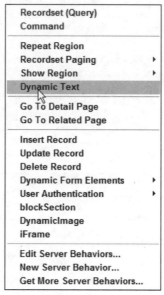

Figure 15-36

13. Click OK. Now highlight the dynamic title, enter the following code into the Link field of the Property inspector, and add a target of navigation in the target field (this will be explained in Chapters 16 and 17):

```
<%=(Content.Fields.Item("Link").Value)%>
```

When you are finished, your table should look like Figure 15-37.

Figure 15-37

Enter a soft return (Shift+Enter) after the closing link tag for the Title (</a>) and enter another dynamic text element, the Description.

14. Highlight the entire table and select Repeat Region from the Server Behaviors drop-down menu. This makes this one table duplicate every element vertically in the recordset for this particular section. Choose to display All Records, as shown in Figure 15-38.

Figure 15-38

After you click OK, Dreamweaver MX 2004 adds a Repeat tab to the section of code that repeats. Your table should now look like Figure 15-39.

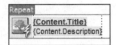

Figure 15-39

15. As a last order of business, make sure that the width of the entire table is locked in to the value of the width coming from `buildingBlock.asp` as the width in the URL string. This ensures that your table remains so narrow that it won't force the iFrame in `buildingBlock.asp` to have a horizontal scroll bar.

In Code view, find the following line:

```
table width="190"
```

Replace it with the following line:

```
table width="<%String(Request.QueryString("width"))%>"
```

16. When you are finished, go back and open `buildingBlock.asp` in a browser. You should see the final results of the combination of the two files, as shown in Figure 15-40.

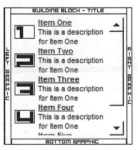

Figure 15-40

How It Works

The table you add is part of a repeating pattern of images on the left and title/link and description on the right. Your recordset is there to pull out just the relevant fields from the Content table where the ID is cross-referenced to the sectionID in the Section_Content table. The default ID passed in was set back when you created `buildingBlock.asp` and it corresponds to your first section, which consists of items 1 through 5:

```
SELECT ID, Title, Link, Image, Image_Height, Image_Width, Vertical_Space,
Horizontal_Space, Description FROM Content, Section_Content WHERE ID = Content_ID
AND Section_ID = MMColParam
```

`MMColParam` here takes its value from the Variable field you set in the recordset window:

```
<%Request.QueryString("sectionID"))%>
```

You will add several new fields to the Content database table in Chapter 16. You could have used `SELECT *` here, which would have pulled all fields from the Content table. That would be OK at the moment, but when you add the new fields (which are not relevant to you in this case) this would select them too. To avoid grabbing unneeded content from the database, it's a better idea to list only the tables and fields that are required.

You added an image placeholder and made it dynamic using your server behavior. You also made the image padding dynamic:

```
vspace="<%=(Content.Fields.Item("Vertical_Space").Value)%>"
hspace="<%=(Content.Fields.Item("Horizontal_Space").Value)%>"
```

In the table you added two lines of dynamic text, one for the title (including a dynamically generated link) and one for the description. You made the table a repeating unit, using a built-in server behavior, and finally made sure that the width of the table cell would not exceed the iFrame and cause it to scroll horizontally:

```
table width="<%String(Request.QueryString("width"))%>"
```

`blockContent.asp` is the main file you use in developing the navigation blocks of MediaEdge's Web site. `blockContent` is a nice, clean way to display dynamically generated lists of information with links from the data in the database. Of course, if you choose a different structure for `blockContent.asp`, you can display your information differently. The Content_Page field in the database specifies what page to display the content in, so you could have a `blockContent2.asp` that, for example, displays a single large image and title at a time, instead of all in a list. That way, anytime you want specific content to display in this manner, you could just point to `blockContent2.asp` in the database instead of `blockContent.asp`.

An infinite number of different display files can sit within the Building Block this way. The important thing is to keep them dynamic, so that the information they display remains completely independent of the page structure. Soon you will have a wide variety of information display files that can be swapped out at will.

Summary

In this chapter you built your fundamental Building Block, stemming from a simple 3 × 3 table. This block pulls the names and dimensions of its border graphics from a database, as well as the content it needs. The block can be made to contain your simple information list, `blockContent.asp`, or any number of different information display items, including charts, graphs, and various other media.

What you created is a basic code block that can be used, expanded upon, and exploited so that you won't ever have to touch this code again. More than that, you created a methodology for generating dynamic content so that the same code never has to be built more than once. The Building Block, by its very nature of being a self-contained dynamic information mechanism, helps revitalize HTML page layout and creation by keeping users' attention focused in well organized blocks—drastically cutting development time.

In the next chapter, you create a content management system that allows anyone to add content to the site whether or not they know how to code in HTML.

Why Not Try . . .

There were a few things we mentioned in this chapter that would be great ways of extending the Building Block. For instance, you could set the iFrame to scroll horizontally rather than vertically. You would need to include a height variable in the URL string, as opposed to a width variable. You would then need to set the maximum height of the contents within `blockContent.asp` to the height passed in the URL string, in a similar fashion to how you added a maximum width.

In Chapter 17 you will make a page very similar to `blockContent.asp`, called `blockMain.asp`, to show contents in the main viewing frame. These are simply two possibilities for displaying dynamically generated information. You could make an alternative `blockContent` to show the content in the database with an alternative layout—maybe you just want a table of thumbnail images with no text— or what about setting each image's `alt` text to the title of the item? You could call it `blockContentAlt.asp` and swap `blockContent.asp` for `blockContentAlt.asp` in the database.

If you think quite a bit ahead to the next big step in the evolution of this Building Block structure, you could detect the screen dimensions of the user's computer and have the block itself stretch or shrink to fit the available room on the user's monitor. You would simply have to use a nine-cell block and change your graphics to flat colors so that they could stretch or shrink and not distort. That way you would eliminate the need even to set table dimensions in the index file. The possibilities are endless; just attempt these modifications one at a time.

Creating a Content Management System

In this chapter you are going to create a content-management system (CMS) to manage content creation, updating, and deletion for the Content table of the database. As part of this, you'll also create an options page so the administrator can choose which of these actions to perform. The pages that you create only scratch the surface of the pages you can create as part of a CMS supporting your dynamic Web site, but will hopefully go a long way in opening up the possibilities to you. Before you contemplate creating any content-management system, though, you need to consider several factors that relate not just to the content creation pages but to content-management systems as a whole. These factors include the number of users, both those accessing the database overall and those who edit the data in the database; and also hosting, content storage, and publishing issues.

A content-management system makes it possible for users to edit a Web site even if they don't have HTML or Dreamweaver skills. Right now, there are tools on the market (such as Macromedia Contribute) that allow multiple individuals to edit the content of static Web sites without the need for a database, let alone a content-management system. So you should definitely weigh your options when thinking about creating content-management pages. If there is only one content administrator, and fairly static content, then it is definitely a time-saver (and cost-saver) to simply use static HTML. If, on the other hand, the site is changed almost daily and is created for a company with multiple contributors, then a content-management system is precisely what you need.

The areas covered in this chapter are the following:

- ❑ Adding new fields to your Content table
- ❑ Creating a new table to handle navigation in your database
- ❑ Overview of a content-management system
- ❑ Creating your content-management system, including pages for user options, content creation, content update, and content deletion

Updating the Database

Before we discuss your content-management system, there are a couple of things you need to do to your database. You need to add some fields to your Content table and you need to create a new table.

Adding Fields to the Content Table

In Chapter 15 you made a particularly generic and dynamic Building Block for displaying items of content. These items of content had simply a title, link, image, and description that were used to support showing the individual items of content in the news and navigation frames. You will now add fields for use with the main content frame because the dimensions of the border graphics obviously cannot be the same for the subsidiary frames as they are for the main frame.

Try It Out   Adding Fields to the Content Table

1.   Open your Access database and then opening the Content table.

2.   Add the following columns to the table: **Keywords, Title_Main, Content_Main, Image_Main, Image_Width_Main, Image_Height_Main, Vertical_Space_Main, Horizontal_Space_Main,** and **Background_Main.**

3.   Switch to Design view (View⇨Design View). Give Keywords, Title_Main, Image_Main, and Background_Main a data type of **Text**. Give Content_Main a data type of **Memo**, which will hold many more characters than the text data type, and make the remainder of the fields **Number**.

The database does not care about the order in which the different fields appear in the table. Organize the fields so that their placement makes sense to the people that have to access your database. Take time to order the fields of the Content table as shown in Figure 16-1. To do so, simply drag the rows around in Design view. Later in this chapter you will create a content creation page, and ordering the elements now will prevent you from having to order the form fields to add to the content creation page.

Field Name	Data Type
ID	AutoNumber
Title	Text
Link	Text
Price	Number
Image	Text
Image_Height	Number
Image_Width	Number
Vertical_Space	Number
Horizontal_Space	Number
Keywords	Text
Description	Text
Title_Main	Text
Content_Main	Memo
Image_Main	Text
Image_Width_Main	Number
Image_Height_Main	Number
Vertical_Space_Main	Number
Horizontal_Space_Main	Number
Background_Main	Text

Figure 16-1

How It Works

Let's just examine the purpose of the new fields you added. The Keywords column contains a list of keywords that are included with each item that are later going to be referenced by your search engine. The remainder of the fields added support displaying the content in your main frame, as described previously. Content_Main contains the content to be displayed when the content item is displayed in the main frame, as opposed to the alternative, which is to display the content in the navigation frames.

Creating a Subnavigation Table

Next you need to create one last table for use with your Building Block Technology: the Sections_Nav table. Similar to the Section_Content table, you need to create a table that manages the many-to-many relationships between the main navigation and the subnavigation. As we described previously, whenever you select a content item from a main navigation block, that content not only appears in the main viewing window but can trigger the opening of additional sections in the main navigation frames, for use as subsections. Figure 16-2 displays the MediaEdge Web site after a user has clicked on the title for the Capabilities section. The subnavigation windows now each show different links related to the area of content that interests you.

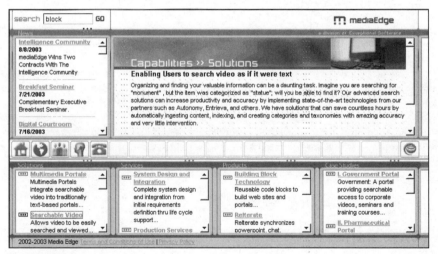

Figure 16-2

Try It Out   **Creating a Subnavigation Table**

1. Create a new table in your Access database and name it **Sections_Nav**.

2. Switch to Design view. When asked to add a primary key, select No. Add six fields and label them **Section_ID, frame1a, frame2a, frame2b, frame2c,** and **frame2d.** Set the data types to **Number**, as shown in Figure 16-3.

Field Name	Data Type
Section_ID	Number
frame1a	Number
frame2a	Number
frame2b	Number
frame2c	Number
frame2d	Number

Figure 16-3

Since the Sections_Nav table is used to show the relationship between parent sections and their subsections, it does not require its own primary key.

3. Save and close the Sections_Nav table.

How It Works

We'll wait until Chapter 17 to add data to this table because the numbers you enter depend entirely on the IDs all your other content takes in the other tables. The Sections_Nav table has six columns. The Section_ID of the Sections_Main section, whose title has been clicked, and the Section_IDs of the subsection sections should be opened in each of the frames, excluding the main frame.

To keep the database creation process brief, this same section is used in each of the navigation blocks. Ordinarily you wouldn't repeat the same navigational content in each of the blocks.

When any of the section titles are selected, the database is accessed and the relevant section is opened as a subnavigation block. In this case you'll simply reopen the Building_Block section in each of the navigation frames.

Now it's time to turn our attention to the content-management system. We'll start with an overview and discuss what content-management systems are and what they do, and then start to build one. You don't have time to build an entire content-management system but you can implement pages that add, delete, and modify content in the Content table, as well as create a User Options page.

Overview of a Content Management System

The principal functionality of a content-management system (CMS) is to separate presentation from content. Generally, content is stored in a database, added to and edited by the content-management system, and dished out to the presentation layer when requested. Figure 16-4 shows the process of entering data into the database via the admin page and having that data pull from the database and appear dynamically on the Web site.

In our case, a Microsoft Access database stores the information and Building Block Technology displays the information, so you are now going to look at adding and editing the content. Before you do so, however, here's an overview of the primary tasks of a CMS:

❑ Content creation

❑ Content storage

- ❑ Permissions storage
- ❑ Content publishing
- ❑ Content presentation

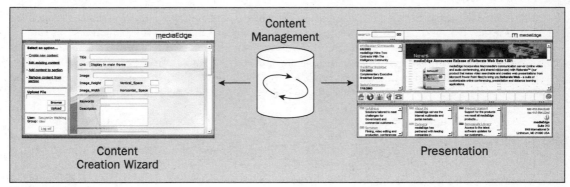

Figure 16-4

Content Creation

One of the most significant purposes of a CMS is to allow multiple, nontechnically savvy individuals to add content to a Web page. They should not have to know any HTML, for example. Therefore, most content creation pages are nothing more than forms prompting the user to enter pertinent information. Figure 16-5 displays a sample page from MediaEdge's content-management interface, which shows a content submission form and links to edit and remove existing content.

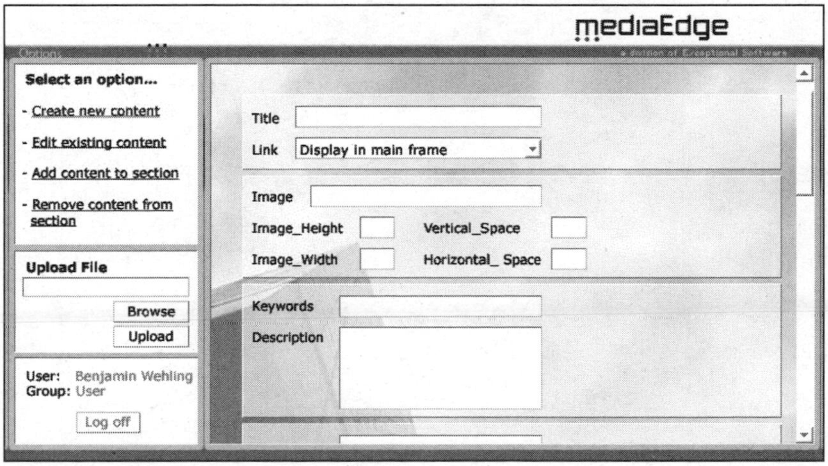

Figure 16-5

There are, of course, several other factors occurring behind the scenes that need to be addressed when creating the content submission forms, such as record locking, single-sourcing, metadata creation, linking, and ease of use.

Record Locking

To update information contained in a database, a content-management page must first access that information. If multiple individuals are trying to update the same information at the same time, this can cause a conflict in the database and inconsistent output data. Microsoft Access prevents this from occurring simply by allowing only one user to access one table, directly, at a time. If you open a table using Access, that table is locked to any other user. While this prevents conflict when accessing and updating data, this does not easily allow for multiple users to access the same table at the same time.

For this reason a content-manager is commonly relied upon so that multiple users can access and update the information in one table at the same time without having those changes conflict with each other. In a CMS information is grabbed from the database and typically shown on screen using HTML. The user edits the information without maintaining an active connection to the database. Record locking works so that users can access the same tables in the database, but when an individual accesses one particular item, that item is "locked" and additional users are prevented from accessing that information until the first user has finished.

Single-Sourcing

Another significant concept in CMSs is to have one single location for a specific item of content. That content, for instance, might need to show up in a variety of places on your site, but it should only have one home in the database. This ensures that you don't forget to make the same changes to all instances of, say, your contact details because the data lives only in one place. Figure 16-6 shows the tables you created in Chapter 15.

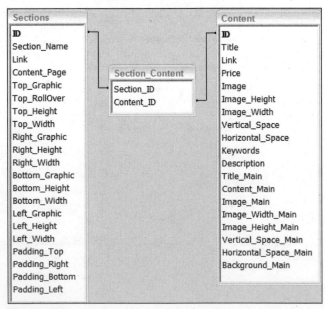

Figure 16-6

One of the three tables is the Section_Content table, which creates what is known as a "many-to-many" relationship (although you will use it only for the purpose of a "one-to-many" relationship). Let's take a moment to understand what these two types of relationship are.

Each item of content has only one location in the database—that is, one row of the Content table. Each item can, however, appear in several sections of your site. This is achieved by linking the unique keys of the Sections table with the unique keys of the Content table (using the Section_Content table).

Suppose you have an item of content titled "Plumtree Portal" with a unique key of 1. You might want to display this item in several locations (sections) on your site, such as Products, Services, and Support. Let's give these sections unique keys of 1, 2, and 3, respectively.

A unique key is such that no other row of content in the same table has the same value. Services and Plumtree can both have unique keys of 1 because they are located in separate tables. Services and Support, however, can never have the same unique key because they are located within the same table.

Thus in your Section_Content table you would have a "one-to-many" relationship like this:

Sections	Content
1 ("Products")	1 ("Plumtree Portal")
2 ("Services")	1 ("Plumtree Portal")
3 ("Support")	1 ("Plumtree Portal")

Notice that the data in the table consists only of numbers; we added captions to help you visualize what's going on.

There is a second option, in addition, such that you can use the Section_Content table to link multiple content items with each section. In the same way that you had five content items in your sample Building Block, you want to list multiple content items for each section. This is also a "one-to-many" relationship, since one section displays multiple items of content.

For example, keeping with Products as the section, let's now list all the content items in the Content table that are products—such as Virage Plug-in, Building Block Technology, Reiterate, and Plumtree Portal—with unique keys of 2, 3, 4, and 1, respectively. This would look as follows:

Sections	Content
1 ("Products")	1 ("Plumtree Portal")
1 ("Products")	2 ("Virage Plug-in")
1 ("Products")	3 ("Building Block Technology")
1 ("Products")	4 ("Reiterate")

Combining these two possibilities (having one content item appear in multiple sections, and having multiple items in one section) might seem somewhat convoluted, but this is called a "many-to-many" relationship. In fact, you need a many-to-many relationship between your content items and sections. You will have multiple items of content appear in the navigation sections of the site, but when sent to the main viewing frame, those same items appear in a second section. Therefore, the relationship is many items of content displayed in many different sections, or simply "many-to-many."

Metadata Creation

The Keywords field in your Content table stores the significant keywords for each item of content, which allow the search engine to find the best matches in your database for a particular search. Storing keywords in this fashion is one example of storing *metadata*.

> *Metadata specification makes the process of locating and categorizing resource information more efficient.*

Metadata is "data about data." In Chapter 14, for instance, you looked at adding metadata to the index page of your site to list keywords for that site, as well as a description for the site in general. In this fashion, metadata is used to give search engines, such as AltaVista, Google, and Yahoo!, information about your site so they can categorize it in their indexes.

> *For more information about best practices for metadata creation, check out the Dublin Core Metadata Initiative (www.dublincore.org), which promotes standards for metadata creation.*

Linking

In any Web site or portal there will be a number of links that need to be organized so that they are independent of the particular content they link to. That is, if they have titles, you run the risk of the title changing and making the link title obsolete or broken. When the content itself changes, it is important that the link to that content is either updated or is *independent* of the content in the first place.

In your Building Block structure, specifically in the Content and Sections tables, there are three fields that involve linking. The first link field, Link, in the Content table tells your system what section to open when selecting that item of content from the navigation frames. The links themselves actually all open the blockNav.asp file (which you'll create in Chapter 17) but pass it a unique ID. The blockNav.asp file then checks the Sections_Nav table (which you created in this chapter) to see if there are any subsections to open (if it finds the section ID in the Section_ID field), as well as opening the section with that ID in frameMain.

The links in the Sections table, however, are a little different. The Content_Page field determines which page will be used in the Building Block to display the content. You have already created one file in Chapter 15, blockContent.asp, which shows the descriptions for each item of content as a list. In Chapter 17 you will create a second file, blockMain.asp, to show the main content for each item in the main viewing frame, frameMain.

The last field in the database that relates to navigation is the Link field, which acts much in the same way as the Link field in the Content table. In the same fashion as the Content field, the Link field references the blockNav.asp file to open content in the main viewing window, as well as additional sections. The difference, however, is that this link also appears for the title of the main viewing frame.

In Chapter 17 you will look at adding those links to the database. The significant aspect of the links, however, is that they always pass the unique ID of the section or content, rather than the title or any of the other fields in the table. In passing the unique ID the links are such that they will never need to change, even if the title or other information for that section or content does change. The links, therefore, are independent of the section or content itself.

Ease of Use

Finally, and most importantly, any content creation page needs to be easy to use. As we mentioned in the beginning of the chapter, if content is fairly static there are resources available that make updates particularly easy. Even with a dynamic, database-driven site, however, the same ease of use needs to be present, or else all your work in creating the system will come to nothing.

Content Storage

The backbone of content-management is a central repository, in your case an Access database, plus the tools for adding, editing, and deleting that content. Most enterprise-level CMSs, in addition, include archiving and version control, integration with external systems, and security and reporting:

❑ **Archiving and version control.** Since there will be several people contributing and editing the content of the site, it is always a good idea to back up your database regularly—just in case you ever need to pull up old data. In your case this simply means saving your .mdb file elsewhere from time to time. Enterprise-level content-management systems, on the other hand, have entire scripts dedicated to performing this operation automatically. If for any reason data gets corrupted in the database, there are tools included to revert the database to the last archived version.

❑ **Integration with external systems.** As your content grows in size and you suddenly find you are a candidate for Fortune 500 status, you might need to integrate your content with that of another CMS. There are, in addition, entire companies focused on system integration, as there are many different content organization methods. Before developing a CMS, it would be a good idea to investigate the structure of other content-management systems with which you might need to integrate in the future. Following the architecture of preexisting systems that you might need to swap data with will make integration easier in the future.

❑ **Security and reporting.** There are three main areas that you will need to focus on to keep your site and management system secure: access to the directories that host the site, access to the database itself, and access to the CMS. In the Help menu of Microsoft Access there are instructions for adding a username and password to the database. Chapter 11 explains how to protect file directories and also add usernames and passwords to scripts.

Permissions Storage

In every content-management system, there tends to be a range of users who have different permissions to change and edit particular sections of content, and to perform certain tasks. With most systems, the very first thing you encounter before you can do anything is a login screen where you enter your username and password (see Figure 16-7).

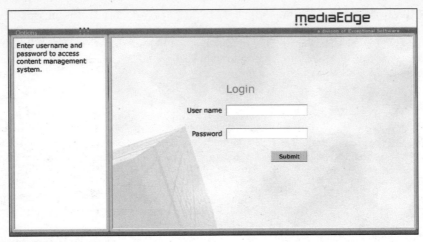

Figure 16-7

Much like a network environment, you need to have individuals with administrator privileges who can edit any aspect of the database, create new graphics for use on the pages, and approve other users' requests.

Take a look at Figure 16-8. It shows that user Todd Marks logged in as an administrator, which gives him the right to manage users, sections, and content.

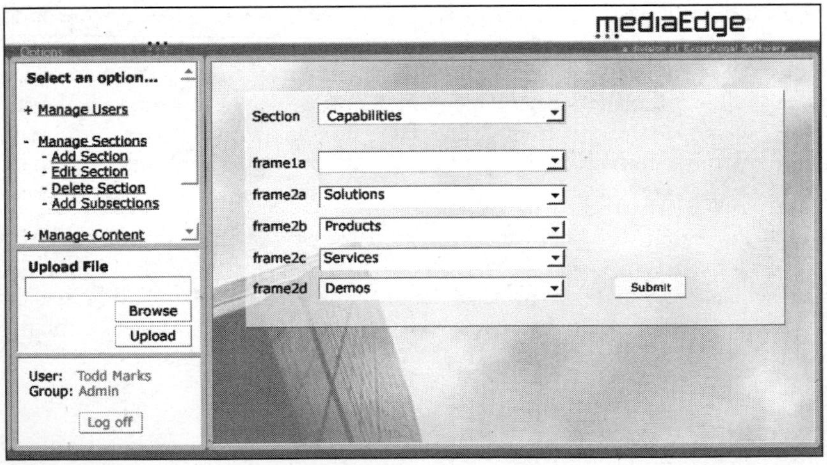

Figure 16-8

By contrast, Figure 16-5 showed user Benjamin Wehling logged on as a user, which gives him only the ability to manage content. Managing other users, as well as managing sections, is reserved only for individuals with administrator privileges.

Content Publishing

Publishing, in the sense we're interested in, is the process of getting information from the database to the presentation format. There are several aspects of publishing, similar to those of content creation, that need to be considered when investigating and building a content-management solution:

❑ **Customization.** Customization comes into play in several categories, from visual to functional. It is a good idea to define all visual customization with style sheets. As a rule of thumb, always attach a central style sheet, even if you don't think you are going to use it. Once the style sheet is in place, you can always add tag styles to this .css file and watch the other files assume those values.

As for functionality, the role of Building Blocks is fundamental to functional customization. The Building Block itself does not care what content it displays, as the links to the files are dynamically pulled from the database. In this fashion you can keep a large arsenal of pages that perform different tasks and swap them out at will. The Building Block, therefore, acts as a template allowing unlimited extensibility.

❑ **Support for multiple formats.** Most enterprise-level content-management systems export to multiple file formats, including HTML, Adobe Acrobat (PDF), Microsoft Word, and so on. In our case you are simply outputting to HTML, although when considering building a larger-scale CMS, consider a broader range of output options.

❑ **Usage statistics.** Several third-party tools, such as NetIQ WebTrends, show all of the statistical information for Web site visitation (www.netiq.com/Webtrends/). Similar tools are built into most enterprise-level content-management systems and should be used when large numbers of files are transferred and content changes daily.

Content Presentation

Several presentation factors are necessary with any Web site, not just when using CMSs. For the most part, all your presentation occurs in the functionality of your index page, Building Block, and block content pages.

In our case you are building a solution that is new and pushing the capabilities of HTML. Our solution does not conform to the normal standards of site creation, as it is cutting-edge development. Even so, the following should always be taken into consideration before creating any solution. Usability has a context; a site should be usable within the context of its purpose. (For instance, if you are designing a site for the Coca-Cola Company, you might want to color all the links red, as opposed to the standard blue.) It would be irresponsible not to take issues like these into account:

❑ **Usability and accessibility.** Any CMS, or any site for that matter, should not only conform to the W3C standards for usability and federal Section 508 standards for accessibility, but should also include basic strengths of easy navigation, clean page layout, and ease of finding pertinent information.

❑ **Cross-browser support.** Some companies desiring a CMS might only require that you cater to one browser. When this is not the case, however, you should at least consider Internet Explorer, Netscape, Mozilla, and Opera, as these are the browsers that get the most use.

❑ **Speed.** Any page, whether part of a normal site or a CMS, should be created and designed with download speed in mind. In our case your presentation only consists of four files, which are used over and over. You do, however, need to keep your database well organized and referenced easily, as the majority of your site's wait time will be caused by grabbing the data from your database.

❑ **Metadata.** As with the index page you created in Chapter 14, every page handled by a CMS should have its own metadata so that search engines and humans understand the basic content on that page. Later in this chapter, you will add fields to your content database for use in Chapter 17. One of those fields, Keywords, is a good example of storing metadata.

Building a Content Management System

The next section of this chapter looks at creating a few of the pages necessary to add content to your Content table. After covering the basics of a well-planned and structured CMS, it is now time to incorporate these methodologies into the content creation pages you use with the Building Block system.

There are several more pages you need to create to round out a complete CMS to use with the Building Block Technology, and we don't have the space to cover them all. These include creating, editing, and removing content from the Sections table, as well as setting up and editing the relationships in the Sections_Nav and Section_Content tables. After creating pages to work with your Content table, however, you should be able to make similar pages for the remainder of your pages. We get to this at the end in the "Why Not Try" section of the chapter.

Creating a User Options Page

In this chapter you will create three different pages to modify the data in the database: createContent.asp, updateContent.asp, and deleteContent.asp. Before you can create these pages, however, you must create one central page to access all your pages. This central page is your user options page.

When you round out your CMS, go back and limit access to the new admin folder that you are about to create and add a login to this page, which enables you to set permissions for different users. Taking such measures is described in the "Permissions Storage" section of this chapter, as well as in Chapter 9.

Try It Out   **Creating a User Options Page**

1. Create a new folder within your main site folder. Label it **admin**.

2. Create a new Dynamic ASP JavaScript page and save the new page as **userOptions.asp** in your new admin folder.

3. Modify the page properties (Modify⇨Page Properties) and give the new page a title of **User Options**. Change the Left Margin, Top Margin, Margin Width, and Margin Height values to 0.

4. Attach the central style sheet to the page (Text⇨CSS Styles⇨Attach Style Sheet). You will probably have to browse up one folder and select blockStyles.css.

5. Add the text **Select an Option...** to the top of the page. Change the text to a Heading 2 in the Property inspector, which will let your style sheet format it according to your standards.

6. Beneath the "Select an Option..." caption, add a form button (Insert⇨Form⇨Button). Click Yes when asked to add a form tag. Select the new button and add the text **Create New Content** as the button's label in the Property inspector. Also, select Submit Form for Action since you want the button to link to newContent.asp. Your page should look like Figure 16-9.

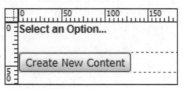

Figure 16-9

7. Click the red line defining the form and give the form an action of **newContent.asp** and a target of _self. Change the method to POST (see Figure 16-10).

Figure 16-10

How It Works

The Create New Content button and associated form is the simplest form element you are going to add to your userOptions page. By adding an action of newContent.asp and a target of _self, clicking on the Create New Content button simply opens the file newContent.asp in the current window.

Although it's not the most attractive form, with the help of the following pages you create, it will allow you to create, edit, and delete content from the Content table of your database.

Adding the Edit and Delete Buttons

Having added one button to the page, you're now going to add the other two. These are a little more complicated because in order to delete or edit content you have to supply some way of letting the user select what content will be affected. Do this with a simple combo box in each case. In Design view the form ends up looking like Figure 16-11, where the dashed red lines are Dreamweaver's indication that these are form elements.

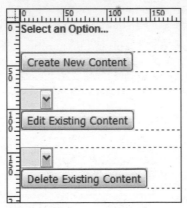

Figure 16-11

Of course, the combo boxes have to be populated with the titles of your current content items, so you'll need some way of doing this. Do this with a recordset.

Try It Out   **Building the Edit Content and Delete Content Functionality**

1. Create a new recordset on the page by selecting Recordset (Query) from the plus (+) menu in the Server Behaviors panel.

You created the last query of Chapter 15 in Advanced mode. If you are still in Advanced mode, switch to Simple mode now.

2. Name the new recordset currentContent, use the MediaEdge connection, select the Content table, and only select ID and Title from the Fields list by first clicking the Selected radio button. You do not need to add a filter, but sort by Title in Ascending order. When you're done the dialog box should look like Figure 16-12. Click OK.

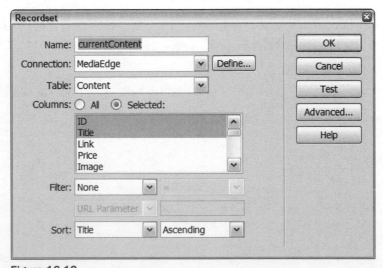

Figure 16-12

3. Add a drop-down list that users can select from to choose the title to edit or delete. To add a new form for the Edit Content option, place the cursor beneath the red line of the current form—the one consisting solely of the Create New Content button created in the previous section.

    You now need to add a new form to the page consisting of a drop-down list. Select List/Menu from the Form drop-down list (Insert⇨Form⇨List/Menu). When asked whether to add a form tag, select Yes.

4. Select the list box and check the List radio button in the Property inspector, and name the list **ID** (it will hold the IDs of your items of content), as shown in Figure 16-13.

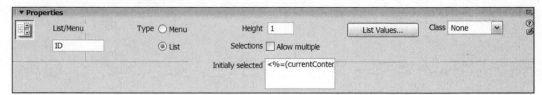

Figure 16-13

5. Select the Dynamic button from the Property inspector. In the Options From Recordset field, select currentContent from the list. Select a value of ID and a label of Title. The dialog box should look like Figure 16-14 at this point. Click OK to add the list.

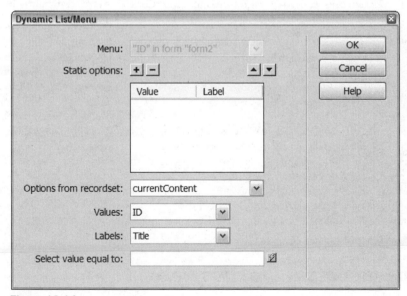

Figure 16-14

6. Add a button to submit this form to your `updateContent.asp` page, which pulls up the content information for this particular ID.

7. Click just to the right of the list box and press Shift+Enter to drop to the next line. Add a new form button, still within the second form (Insert⇨Form⇨Button).

8. Click the new button and label it **Edit Existing Content**.

9. Click the red line defining the form and give it an action of **updateContent.asp** in the Action field of the Property inspector. Change the method from POST to GET and select _self as the target (see Figure 16-15).

Figure 16-15

Now it's time to create the final form, the Delete Content list, and button.

10. Click the Edit Existing Content form (on the red line) and copy it (press Ctrl+C). Place the cursor below the form and paste it (press Ctrl+V).

11. Click the button in the new form and change its label to **Delete Existing Content**.

12. Click the form and change its action field to **deleteContent.asp** and its name to **form3**.

How It Works

What you created is really one form but is technically three separate forms because each of the options links to a separate page. The first option, to create new content, is different from the second two options in that it doesn't need to send any information to the newContent.asp page. You did not, therefore, need to change the method from POST to GET.

The main difference between POST and GET is that GET makes the sent variables visible on the URL string (which POST does not) and GET does not have the ability to hold as many variables and values as POST. In our case you are only sending one variable to each of the latter two pages to tell that page what content you need to update or delete. It is not necessary to make that variable invisible to the end user, so GET is more than sufficient. (For more information about POST and GET, refer back to Chapters 6 and 7.)

The next thing you need to do is create the rest of newContent.asp, updateContent.asp, and deleteContent.asp to finish this section of your content-management system.

Developing a Content Creation Page

As we mentioned earlier in the chapter, a content creation page is little more than a form field page to add content to the database. Figure 16-16 shows the form that you will end up with after completing the following exercise.

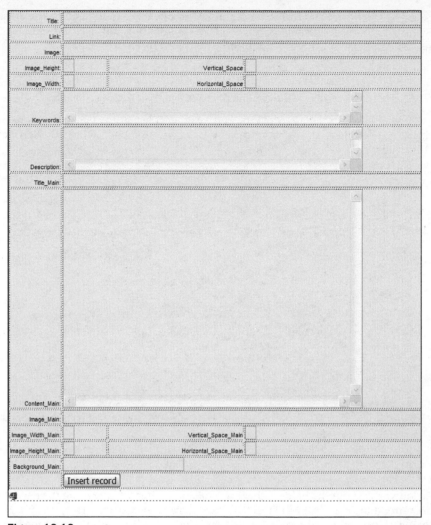

Figure 16-16

Try It Out   **Creating the Content Creation Page**

1. Create a new Dynamic ASP JavaScript page and save the new page as **newContent.asp** in the admin folder.

2. Modify the page properties (Modify⇨Page Properties) and give the new page a title of **Content Creation**. Set the Left Margin, Top Margin, Margin Width, and Margin Height values to 0.

3. Attach the central style sheet (Text⇨CSS Styles⇨Attach Style Sheet). You will have to browse up one folder and select `blockStyles.css`.

4. Create the recordset and form to add new content to the Content table of the database. The easiest way to do this in Dreamweaver MX 2004 is to use the built-in application objects. Select Insert➪Application Objects➪Insert Record➪Record Insertion Wizard.

5. Give the form the connection from the previous chapters, MediaEdge. Select Content as the table to insert the record into. In the After Inserting Go To field, browse to the current page, newContent.asp, which will make the page refresh itself after the insertion.

6. The ID field should not appear in the Form elements list as it was not included originally in form1 (see Figure 16-17), but if it does appear in your list, choose the value <ignore> from the Column drop down menu.

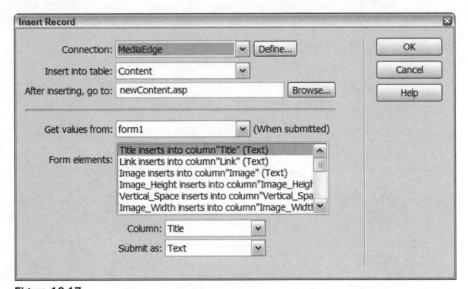

Figure 16-17

7. As long as you put the fields in the recommended order when adding the new elements to the Content table (as described in the "Adding Fields to the Content Table" section, earlier in this chapter), you can simply select OK and the form will automatically be added to your page. Figure 16-18 shows what the form looks like.

How It Works

What you would have had to type by hand in a text editor with painstaking detail now occurs behind the scenes using Dreamweaver. Dreamweaver inserted code to perform the following actions: connect to the database, create a SQL statement to add values to the database, add a form to solicit values to add to the database, add a function to grab the values from the form when the user clicks the Insert Record button, add a function to redirect the page after the values are added to the database, and finally close the database.

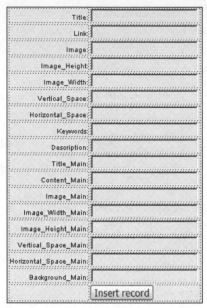

Figure 16-18

This form is more than sufficient to add new content to the database, and remarkably easy to add using Dreamweaver MX 2004. In its current state, however, there is very little room to add content to some of the fields, and too much in others. So go ahead and change some of the sizes and positions of the form fields to make it look like Figure 16-16, at the beginning of the section.

Try It Out   **Customizing the Form's Appearance**

1. Clicking each numeric field in turn, and set its Char Width and Max Chars values each to **3** in the Property inspector. The fields you need to do this for include Image_Height, Image_Width, Vertical_Space, Horizontal_Space, Image_Height_Main, Image_Width_Main, Vertical_Space_Main, and Horizontal_Space_Main.

2. To place the Vertical_Space and Horizontal_Space fields next to their corresponding Image_Height and Image_Width fields, so you are going to have to add two more columns to your table.

   Click on the outer border of the table, or select the table from the tags list on the bottom of the Design view, to get the table properties to show up. Change the value of Cols from 2 to 4, as shown in Figure 16-19.

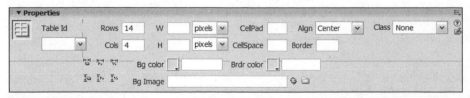

Figure 16-19

3. Highlight the Horizontal_Space and Vertical_Space elements and drag them to the table cells next to Image_Width and Image_Height. Do the same for the corresponding *xxx*_Main elements. When you're done, the form should look like Figure 16-20.

Drag the actual text and input box. You cannot drag the cells themselves, only their contents.

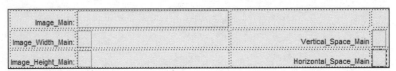

Figure 16-20

4. Highlight the cells in the unused rows (four in total) and press Delete, or else Control-click and cut them from the table.

5. What you want to do next is have the Vertical_Space and Horizontal_Space fields closer to those of Height and Width. To do this, merge the cells of the other rows.

Select the three rightmost cells of each row (one row at a time) that don't have Width, Height, Vertical_Space, or Horizontal_Space in it, and merge them (see Figure 16-21). This should account for ten rows total.

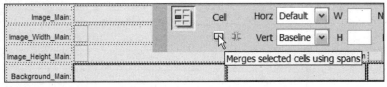

Figure 16-21

6. Drag the vertical dividers located between the height/width and vertical/horizontal fields. This allows the vertical and horizontal fields to draw closer to that of the image height and width fields. There are two vertical dividers that need to be dragged left. When you're done, the form should look like Figure 16-22.

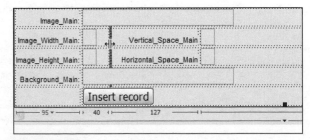

Figure 16-22

7. Select the two Vertical_Space and Horizontal_Space cells and align the text to the right.

8.   Give a lot more room to the Keywords, Description, and Content_Main fields. Click on each of the cells in turn, select the Multiline radio button for each field in the Property inspector, and give them 2, 4, and 20 lines, respectively.

    Give yourself some typing room to add new text for each of the form elements when users use this form, so click each of the cells in turn and give them a Char width of 100 (excluding your width, height, vertical space, and horizontal space text fields).

9.   Notice that the multiline tables have scroll bars added to the table, which makes them another 6 pixels wider and 6 pixels taller. If you are a compulsive type, you can play with the widths until all the right edges line up. In addition, give the total table a width smaller than the size of the contents (experiment with this); the table should pull nice and tight so that all the fields line up along the right edge. When you are finished, your table should finally look like Figure 16-16.

10.   Preview your table in the browser and make sure it looks the way you like.

If the text in your Vertical_Space or Horizontal_Space cells do not right-align correctly, make sure that Dreamweaver has not added static widths to these cells. You can determine this by clicking the individual cells and checking for widths in the Property inspector. If so, remove or alter those widths to fix the right-justification problems.

How It Works

In the pre-Dreamweaver days, typing all the code to set table and text box widths would have taken about three times as long. With Dreamweaver, everything is a lot easier. As you can see, it definitely makes the form much more usable to set dimensions for the text boxes. Now users have more room to type content into the content box and they can differentiate among image links, content, image dimensions, and so on.

Developing the Content Update Page

Creating a content update page is very similar to creating the content creation page. The difference is that you need to create a recordset of the existing data to update first. Then you can populate your form fields with this data. Start by creating the new page and recordset.

Try It Out   **Developing the Content Update Page**

1.   Create a new Dynamic ASP JavaScript page and save the new page as **updateContent.asp** in your admin folder.

2.   Select Modify⇨Page Properties and give the new page a title of **Content Update**. Set the Left Margin, Top Margin, Margin Width, and Margin Height values to 0.

3.   Attach your main style sheet as before (Text⇨CSS Styles⇨Attach Style Sheet). You might have to browse up one folder and select blockStyles.css.

4.   To add the recordset, click the plus (+) menu of the Server Behaviors panel and choose Recordset (Query). Name the recordset **updateContent**. Use the normal MediaEdge connection and select the Content table. Allow all columns to be selected and add a filter of ID = URL Parameter, with ID as the parameter. You do not need to sort any results, so the Recordset dialog box should look like Figure 16-23. Click OK to add the new recordset to your page.

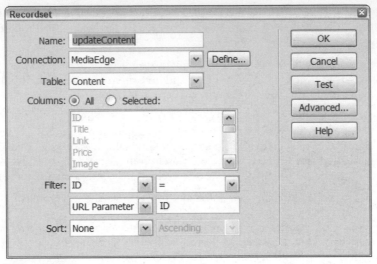

Figure 16-23

5. Select Insert⇨Application Objects⇨Update Record⇨Record Update Form Wizard.

6. Select the MediaEdge connection again, and Dreamweaver should automatically fill in most of the other settings (see Figure 16-24). The one setting that you need to add manually is the location of the page to go to after updating. In the After Updating Go To field, browse to the options file `userOptions.asp` and click OK.

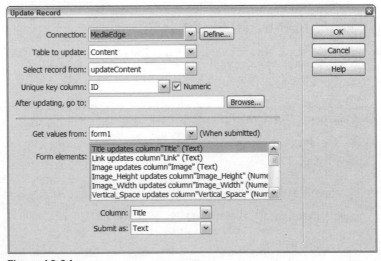

Figure 16-24

7. Click OK in this dialog box and watch Dreamweaver do its magic and create the update form shown in Figure 16-25.

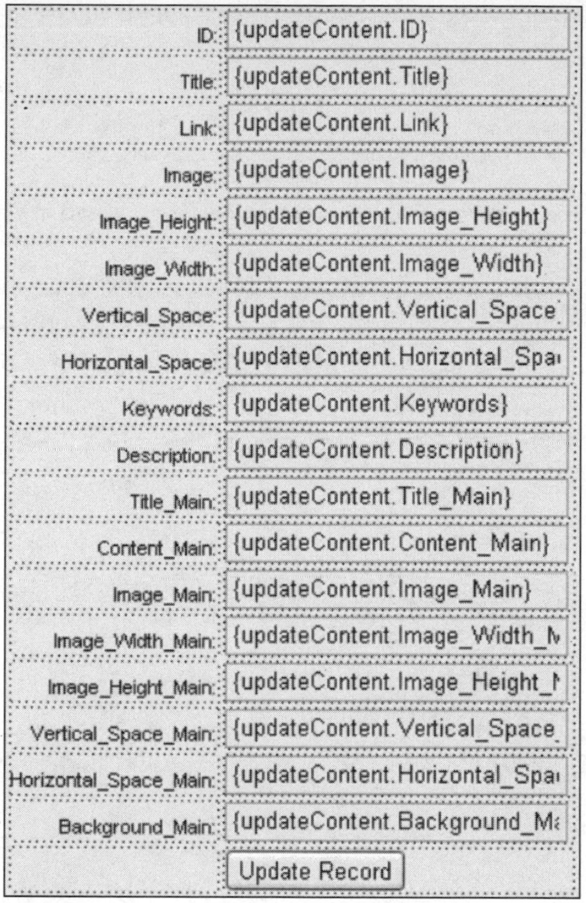

Figure 16-25

8. Make this form look identical to that of the contentCreation.asp page. To do this, simply repeat Steps 1 through 7 in the "Customizing the Form's Appearance" Try It Out exercise earlier in the chapter.

How It Works

This second page, unlike the first page, needs to grab data from the database before sending data back to the database. There are actually only two differences between the forms. First, contentUpdate.asp makes a query to the database based on the ID value passed into the page, and it displays the current values for that item of content in the form. Then, when you click Update Record on the contentUpdate.asp file, it writes back to the same row in the database from which it retrieved the information, as opposed to creating a new row in the database, which the newContent.asp page does.

Since your User Options page passes the ID of the content item to update to updateContent.asp, you need to include the ID in your recordset. Dreamweaver, however, automatically adds the ID field to your form—which you do not want. Dreamweaver itself can keep track of unique IDs for you; this is built into the Update Record window but it causes the following error if you try to pass that ID on to your Access database:

```
Microsoft OLE DB Provider for ODBC Drivers error '80040e14'
[Microsoft][ODBC Microsoft Access Driver] Cannot update 'ID';
field not updatable. /admin/updateContent.asp, line 81
```

Removing the ID from the form, and making sure that it is never passed to your Access database, is pretty simple, though, so let's take that approach.

Try It Out   **Removing the ID Field**

1. Click to the left of the row containing the ID field (it should show a right arrow) and hit Delete.

2. Switch to Code view. Locate the two variables MM_fieldsStr and MM_ColumnsStr towards the top of the page. Cut the initial part of each string, so that they both simply start with Title:

```
var MM_fieldsStr =
"Title|value|Link|value|Image|value|Image_Height|value|Vertical_Space|value|Image_W
idth|value|Horizontal_Space|value|keywords|value|Description|value|Title_Main|value
|Content_Main|value|Image_Main|value|Image_Width_Main|value|Vertical_Space_Main|val
ue|Image_Height_Main|value|Horizontal_Space_Main|value|Background_Main|value";
var MM_columnsStr =
"Title|',none,''|Link|',none,''|Image|',none,''|Image_Height|none,none,NULL|Vertica
l_Space|none,none,NULL|Image_Width|none,none,NULL|Horizontal_Space|none,none,NULL|k
eywords|',none,''|Description|',none,''|Title_Main|',none,''|Content_Main|',none,''
|Image_Main|',none,''|Image_Width_Main|none,none,NULL|Vertical_Space_Main|none,none
,NULL|Image_Height_Main|none,none,NULL|Horizontal_Space_Main|none,none,NULL|Backgro
und_Main|',none,''";
```

How It Works

The two strings tell Dreamweaver what to label the form fields so that it can go back and add the corresponding values back to the database when the form is submitted. Since you didn't want the ID value passed back to the database, and since you removed the row in the form that contained the ID value, you needed to delete the ID portion of these two strings to correspond to the fact that the ID row was no longer present.

Finally, create the last page to delete the content, deleteContent.asp.

Developing the Content Deletion Page

The last sample form in our group of three is the content deletion page. It is always a good idea to build in a system of checks so that users cannot haphazardly delete content. In our setup, the only check is that the Submit button in userOptions.asp sends them to deleteContent.asp where you will make sure they actually want to delete that item of content.

Try It Out   **Developing the Content Deletion Page**

1.   Create a new Dynamic ASP JavaScript page and save the new page as **deleteContent.asp** in your admin folder.

2.   Select Modify⇨Page Properties and give the new page a title of **Content Deletion**. Set the Left Margin, Top Margin, Margin Width, and Margin Height values to 0.

3.   Attach your central style sheet. You may have to browse up one folder and select `blockStyles.css`.

4.   To add the recordset, click the plus (+) menu of the Server Behaviors panel and choose Recordset (Query). Name the recordset **deleteContent**. Use the MediaEdge connection and select the Content table. Allow all columns to be selected and add a filter of ID = and a URL Parameter of ID. You do not need to sort any results. The Recordset dialog box should look like Figure 16-26.

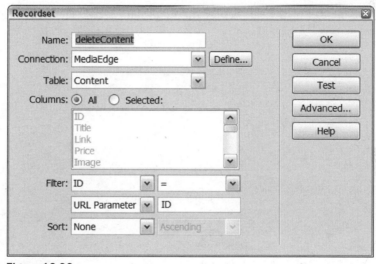

Figure 16-26

5.   In Design view add a form to the new page, which holds the Delete Record script. (Insert⇨Form⇨Form).

6.   Select Delete Record from the plus (+) menu of the Server Behaviors panel.

7.   Select the MediaEdge database connection. Most of the following will already be set, but you should make sure. Select Content in the Delete From Table field, deleteContent in the Select Record From field, ID for the Unique Key Column field, form1 for Delete By Submitting, and userOptions.asp for the After Deleting, Go To field. The Delete Record dialog box should look like Figure 16-27. Click OK.

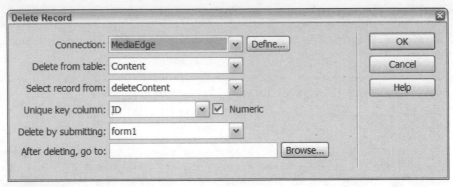

Figure 16-27

8. Add the text **Are you sure you want to delete** (include a space after *delete*) to the top of the page. Then select Dynamic Text from the drop-down menu of the Server Behaviors panel and select Title from your recordset (see Figure 16-28).

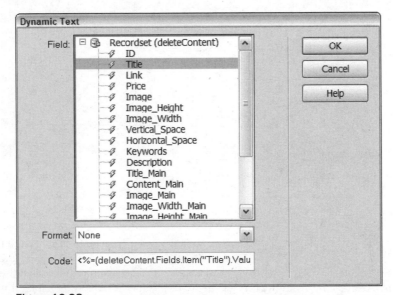

Figure 16-28

Lastly, add **from the Content table of the database?** (include a space before the word *from*).

9. Drop to the next line of the form (press Shift+Enter), add a form button (Insert⇨Form⇨Button), and change its label to Yes in the Property inspector.

How It Works

The `deleteContent.asp` page simply captures the ID value selected in `userOptions.asp` and deletes that item of content when the user clicks the Yes button in the form.

Dreamweaver, once again, does most of the hard work by adding the functions that access the database and delete the particular item of content using an SQL query.

Extending the Forms

These forms give the basic functionality you need to add, update, and delete information within a content-management system. From this point, however, there are an infinite number of ways of upgrading and customizing your CMS. Some of the recommended upgrades include the following:

❑ **Admin approval on all content changes.** As discussed from the outset, it's always good to establish different levels of access for content creation, updating, and deletion. Most enterprise-level content-management systems have an administrator that must give the OK to complete most tasks requested by users. For instance, if a user requests to delete an item of content, that request should send an e-mail to the CMS administrator who actually completes the deletion, or sends a response of "No way" to the renegade user. You are simply creating a check to ask whether the user truly wants to delete the page. You could make this same action send an e-mail instead.

❑ **Form validation.** No matter what the form, it is always a good idea to validate the content before allowing that form to be submitted. For instance, when field values are left blank, Microsoft Access gets unhappy and returns the following errors:

```
Microsoft OLE DB Provider for ODBC Drivers error '80004005'
[Microsoft][ODBC Microsoft Access Driver] Field 'Content.keywords'
cannot be a zero-length string. /admin/updateContent.asp, line 81
```

For this reason, it would be a good idea to make sure users enter compliant data, or you can add default values for blank fields in the database. You saw how to set up some simple form validation in Chapter 6.

❑ **List menu for the link options.** In Chapter 17 you put the Building Blocks to use and add not only content in the main viewing window, but subnavigation to the site as well. Essentially, there are three types of links that can be found in the database. Those links are to external content (links that go to a page not found in your directory system), to internal content (to blockMain.asp), or to open up subsections (blockNav.asp).

The references to blockMain.asp and blockNav.asp in the database require that the ID of the section they are either linking to, or displaying, is attached to the end of the URL string. For administrators to add this ID, they have to know it. This either requires that they have a very good memory, a list on hand of all the IDs of their content, or that they look it up in the database. None of these things should be necessary in a good, solid CMS. Ideally there should be a drop-down menu listing content names, for which the ID is passed when the form is submitted, just as you did above with the drop-down menus listing content to edit or delete.

What about links to new content not already in the database? The user form can be updated to simply prompt for what the user wishes to link to, such as a section or URL, and the CMS admin can then create the new section in the Sections table and add the link ID when he or she gets the e-mail message saying that a user creates or updates content that requires linking. In this fashion, the admin has the chance to create new graphics for the necessary sections and add the relevant navigational relationships in the Sections_Nav table.

❏ **HTML JavaScript editor.** There are several tools available on the Internet, such as JavaScript TTW ("through the Web") WYSIWYG ("what you see is what you get") HTML editors, that you can add to your content creation page. These enable users to add not just text, but HTML content as well so that even novices can add font styles, alignment, and links to a Web page without needing third-party software. This functionality is a great means of allowing anybody to add inline links to page's content.

For a great list of TTW WYSIWYG editors, check out the University of Bristol's IS site (www.bris.ac.uk/is/projects/cms/ttw/ttw.html).

❏ **FTP capabilities.** Another key ingredient to making an easy-to-use content creation page is to add a file upload script on the same page as the content creation form fields. To do this you need to start the FTP server on your computer (for IIS users), give users permission to upload files, and install or write some code allowing you to upload documents and images using your browser. An example of this is AspUpload by Persits Software (www.aspupload.com).

Summary

In this chapter you adjusted your database by adding fields to your Content table and adding a Sections_Nav table that looks after your navigation. The full implications of these changes will become clear in the next chapter when you create the navigation page and add enough test content to your system to see it in action.

You also created part of a content-management system, specifically the central options page and the content creation, modification, and deletion pages. As you begin to expand your CMS, begin by extending these forms, but keep in mind the full range of possibilities described in the CMS overview. Remember too that there is a fair amount of data about your Building Block structure that you don't have access to in your existing CMS pages—in fact, everything but the content table is unreachable. However, using these techniques you should be able to create at least basic pages for each of the other tables in the database.

In the next chapter you will create the navigation file (blockNav.asp) and a second content file (blockMain.asp) and add some test content to the database so you can get everything running.

Why Not Try . . .

1. Finish the content-management userOptions page by adding form elements to add, edit, and remove sections in the Sections table. Then add options to add, edit, and remove subsection relationships in the Sections_Nav table, and the Section_Content table (you may wish to wait until you finish the rest of the chapters in Section 2 so that you are more fully aware of how these tables work). To create the pages, simply follow the steps earlier but access the respective table instead of Content. Since these tables are quite a bit smaller than the Content table, you should have an easier time making these pages.

2. Another change you can make to your system would be to add the pages themselves to the Building Block system so that you can keep the same look and feel in the administration pages as you do for the rest of the site.

Completing the Building Block Structure

Up to this point you've built most of the Building Block structure, but you still have a few files to create. You first made the index page to lay out the frames in which you load your Building Blocks, then the actual Building Block file, and you then rounded out your database and created a few sample pages to add data to your database. The last piece of the puzzle is to actually put the block to use.

You will now finish the last few support files, including blockNav.asp, blockMain.asp, and blockSearch.asp. After completing these files you will add test data to the database and watch as your site takes form. Lastly, you will look at incorporating different components and gadgets into your Building Block Technology and discuss other extensions of the Building Block—which we will expand upon in the final chapter of this book.

In this chapter you will do the following:

❑   Develop the blockNav.asp, blockMain.asp, and blockSearch.asp files

❑   Add values to the database and bring the block to life

First, you revisit the Building Block architecture diagram we laid out in Chapter 14 (see Figure 17-1). Notice that you have created most of the files you need, but there are a few pieces still to put in place.

In Chapter 14 we took the time to discuss the top-level significance of each of the files that support buildingBlock.asp but deferred the deep discussion of these files to this chapter. Now is the time to finish the conversation and build the files. Let's start by solidifying your understanding of how the files fit together. Then you will actually build the navigation file and build and explore the other files in the associations chart above: blockMain.asp, blockSearch.asp, and intro.asp.

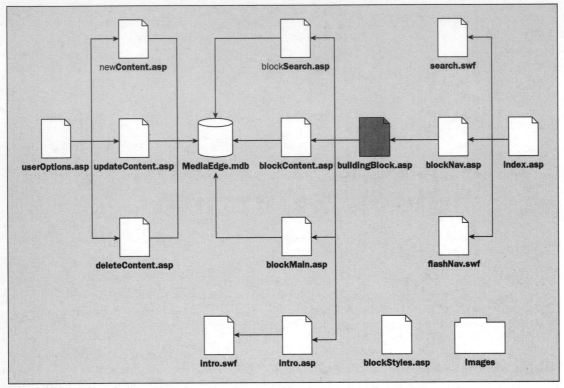

newContent.asp

blockSearch.asp

search.swf

userOptions.asp updateContent.asp MediaEdge.mdb blockContent.asp buildingBlock.asp blockNav.asp index.asp

deleteContent.asp

blockMain.asp

flashNav.swf

intro.swf intro.asp blockStyles.asp Images

Figure 17-1

Block Navigation

The one file we've discussed the most besides buildingBlock.asp is its kissing cousin, blockNav.asp. This file is the hub for all the linking and loading of Building Blocks that takes place in this system. In Chapter 16, where you created the content-management system, you created the Sections_Nav table that holds the ID values of the sections to load, based on the sectionID value you pass to blockNav.asp when you call it. Shortly, we'll look more at how this table fits into the picture.

It might help to conceptualize the navigation structure if you look at blockNav.asp alongside more familiar navigation systems shown in Figure 17-2, like tree menus (left) or JavaScript drop-down menus (right).

In each of these, you have top-level navigation items that expand into further subnavigation. The same way that a tree menu displays additional content when you click on one of the elements of the menu, or a JavaScript drop-down menu displays additional items when you roll over one of the items in the top row, the six frames from your initial layout are used to display main navigation blocks and their subnavigation blocks. The difference between Building Blocks and traditional navigation elements, however, is that the Building Blocks themselves are both the navigation and the content at the same time.

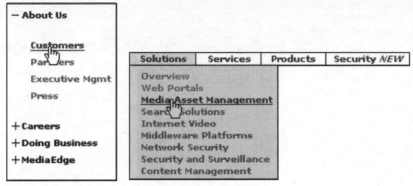

Figure 17-2

Remember, there are really only three "types" of links in the Building Block structure. If you recall, the three types of internal links do one of the following:

❑ Open internal content in the main viewing window

❑ Open internal content in the main viewing window, plus subsections in your main navigation blocks

❑ Open external content in the main viewing window

The only link that requires an entry in the Sections_Nav table is the second one: when a link requires subsections to appear in any of the frames besides frameMain. If there *is* an entry in the Sections_Nav table, then the file buildingBlock.asp is loaded into each of the frames that have an entry in the Sections_Nav table, and this copy of buildingBlock.asp is passed the value for the section to open. If there is no entry in the database, then no subnavigation blocks are opened. Now to see this at work:

1. Any link on the site points to blockNav.asp and sends a unique section ID that is stored in the database for that particular link (Step 1 in Figure 17-3).

2. The blockNav.asp file checks the Sections_Nav table to see if there are entries in the Section_ID field. If there are, it grabs the section numbers for each of the other five fields, frame1a through frame2d, if they are present (Step 2).

3. The file buildingBlock.asp is once again opened in each of the navigation frames but this time each copy is sent the ID of its sections from the Sections_Nav table (Step 3).

We've simplified Figure 17-3 to show only the lower frames but of course the same principle applies to the other frames as well. In the source files for this chapter, the same section (Building Block, ID=1) is used repeatedly as both sections and subsections. When you add sections to your database for your site, you will need to change these values to the unique IDs of the sections and subsections you want to display. You'll add new sections to the database at the end of this chapter.

Once you understand how the navigation works, the other concepts fall right into place. As this is a new architecture, it's understandable that it might take a few tries to get used to how it works.

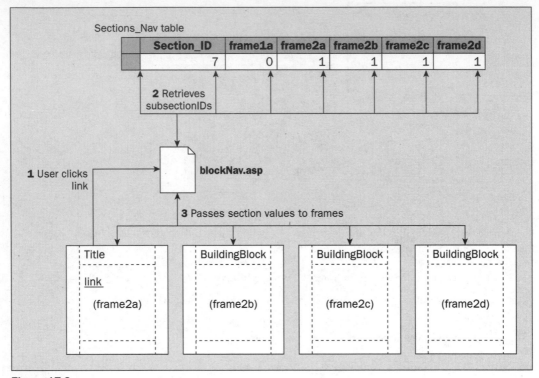

Figure 17-3

Creating the New Files

The next thing you need to do is to create the blockNav.asp file itself. Remember that this page is hidden in a frame on your index.asp page, so it doesn't need to contain any visible elements. On the other hand, it has to deal with all the facets of navigation, including providing a meaningful browser history. Refer to Chapter 14 for an overview of the navigational structure.

Try It Out   **Creating the blockNav.asp File**

1. Create a new Dynamic ASP JavaScript page (File⇨New) and save the new page as **blockNav.asp** in your site folder.

2. Edit the page properties as usual. This time, however, you want to dynamically title the navigation page. Modify the page properties (Modify⇨Page Properties) and give the new page Left Margin, Top Margin, Margin Width, and Margin Height values of 0. Give the page this title:

```
<%=(Title.Fields.Item("Section_Name").Value)%>
```

3. On this page, you'll need two recordsets. The first recordset accesses the Sections table to determine the title of the section based on the SectionID, so you can add the dynamic name to the file using the code above. The second recordset is responsible for accessing the Sections_Nav table of the database to determine what subsections, if any, need to appear in the navigation blocks.

Add the first new recordset by selecting Recordset (Query) from the plus (+) menu of the Server Behaviors panel. Name the recordset **Title** and use the MediaEdge connection. Select the Sections table, choose just the ID and Section_Name columns, and filter based on ID equal to the URL Parameter of sectionID. When you're done, the Recordset dialog box should look like Figure 17-4.

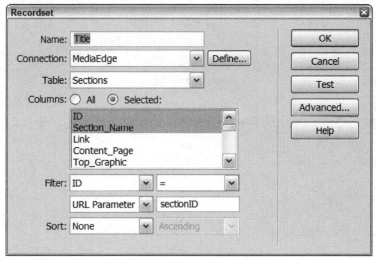

Figure 17-4

4. Add a second new recordset and name it **Navigation**. Select the Sections_Nav table, leaving all columns selected, and filter based on Section_ID equal to the URL Parameter of SectionID (see Figure 17-5).

Recordset

Name: Navigation

Connection: MediaEdge Define...

Table: Sections_Nav

Columns: ● All ○ Selected:

Section_ID
frame1a
frame2a
frame2b
frame2c

Filter: Section_ID =

URL Parameter SectionID

Sort: None Ascending

OK
Cancel
Test
Advanced...
Help

Figure 17-5

607

5. Add some code after the second block of code Dreamweaver inserted, setting defaults for the values of frameMain, frame1a, frame2a, frame2b, frame2c, and frame2d. Add the following (shaded) lines of code:

```
var Navigation_numRows = 0;

if (Navigation.BOF && Navigation.EOF) {
  var frameMain = Navigation__MMColParam.replace(/'/g, "'\'") + "";
  var frame1a = 0;
  var frame2a = 0;
  var frame2b = 0;
  var frame2c = 0;
  var frame2d = 0;
} else {
  var frameMain = Navigation.Fields.Item("Section_ID").Value;
  var frame1a = Navigation.Fields.Item("frame1a").Value;
  var frame2a = Navigation.Fields.Item("frame2a").Value;
  var frame2b = Navigation.Fields.Item("frame2b").Value;
  var frame2c = Navigation.Fields.Item("frame2c").Value;
  var frame2d = Navigation.Fields.Item("frame2d").Value;
}
%>
```

This code needs to go before the ending ASP tag (%>) of the second block of code that Dreamweaver adds to the `blockNav.asp` *file*

6. Set up and adjust the code to handle the links. To open up the subelements in the navigation frames, you will be using `location.replace`. Luckily for you, Dreamweaver MX 2004 has a built-in behavior for redirecting the page. You'll need to alter the code a bit to accommodate your iFrames, as well as add a conditional statement to make sure that each frame requires redirecting, but all in all this behavior saves you some work. Switch back to Design view and click on the desktop.

7. Select Go to URL from the plus (+) menu of the Behaviors tab of the Tag <form> panel group. When the Go to URL window appears onscreen, add the following code to the URL field of the window:

```
<%=(Navigation.Fields.Item("frame1a").Value)%>
```

Click OK.

8. Alter the code that Dreamweaver adds just a bit. First, find this portion of code in the function `MM_goToURL()`:

```
eval(args[i]+".location='"+args[i+1]+"'");
```

Since you are making a link from within an iFrame, you need the link to surface back to the topmost level, and you need to add the static portion of the URL pointing to `buildingBlock.asp`. To do so, simply change the line of code above to the following (type it all on one line):

```
eval("parent."+args[i]+".location.replace
('buildingBlock.asp?section="+args[i+1]+"')");
```

9. Alter the call to the function `MM_goToURL` in the body tag. At this point you are only making the call one time, but you actually want to make the call five times, once for each of the blocks `frame1a`, `frame2a`, `frame2b`, `frame2c`, and `frame2d` to load the subnavigation. You also need to open the new blocks in their respective iFrames.

Find the following call in the body tag of your code:

```
onLoad="MM_goToURL('parent','<%=(Navigation.Fields.Item("frame1a"Value)%>');return
document.MM_returnValue"
```

Change it to this:

```
onLoad="
  MM_goToURL('frameMain','<%=frameMain%>');
  MM_goToURL('frame1a','<%=frame1a%>');
  MM_goToURL('frame2a','<%=frame2a%>');
  MM_goToURL('frame2b','<%=frame2b%>');
  MM_goToURL('frame2c','<%=frame2c%>');
  MM_goToURL('frame2d','<%=frame2d%>');
  return document.MM_returnValue"
```

10. Make sure that a subnavigation block is only opened if there is a value for that block in the Sections_Nav table. Since you entered a value of zero as the default value, you can simply check to make sure the value for that cell in the table is not equal to zero using a conditional statement. If it is not equal to zero, then you make the call to open the new block, otherwise you make no such call.

Find the `eval` statement in the function `MM_goToURL`. Change the surrounding code as follows (don't forget the closing brace, }). When you are finished, your `MM_goToURL()` function should appear as follows (without the line breaks):

```
function MM_goToURL() { //v3.0
 var i, args=MM_goToURL.arguments; document.MM_returnValue = false;
 for (i=0; i<(args.length-1); i+=2) {
   if (args[i+1] != 0) {
     eval("parent."+args[i]+".location.replace('buildingBlock.asp
       ?section="+args[i+1]+"')");
   }
 }
}
```

How It Works

You set the page properties as usual, except for the dynamic title. This allows you to record relevant titles in the browser history. We'll discuss this in more detail shortly when you look at the `location.replace` function.

You then create two recordsets, one to supply the title for the page and the other to check for the presence of subsections for the section loaded into the page. In the first, only the ID and title are required, so that's all you select. The ID is matched to the ID on the URL string and the corresponding title is used in the title of the page.

The next thing you do is set default values for a set of variables that will store the IDs of the sections to display in each subframe. If the main section you're displaying does not have any subsections, then you don't want to have to structure your database so that you still have to create an entry in the Sections_Nav table in the database with values all equal to zero. Instead, check to see if any values were returned from the database, and if not, you will set the values equal to zero:

```
if (Navigation.BOF && Navigation.EOF) {
  var frameMain = Navigation__MMColParam.replace(/'/g, "'\'") + "";
  var frame1a = 0;
  var frame2a = 0;
  var frame2b = 0;
  var frame2c = 0;
  var frame2d = 0;
```

On the other hand, if values are returned then you want to store them:

```
} else {
  var frameMain = Navigation.Fields.Item("Section_ID").Value;
  var frame1a = Navigation.Fields.Item("frame1a").Value;
  var frame2a = Navigation.Fields.Item("frame2a").Value;
  var frame2b = Navigation.Fields.Item("frame2b").Value;
  var frame2c = Navigation.Fields.Item("frame2c").Value;
  var frame2d = Navigation.Fields.Item("frame2d").Value;
```

Now you set up a dynamic URL to go to from `frame1a`. Actually, you later change this when you expand the code to accommodate your many frames and the variables you set in the previous step, but on its own this would have the desired effect for `frame1a`—pulling in the URL that's contained in the database for this particular record:

```
<%=(Navigation.Fields.Item("frame1a").Value)%>
```

Then you make sure that the link can point to the correct level in your structure. Since it's calling from within an iFrame inside a table, you need to use `parent` twice to get to the top of the hierarchy. The other part you add is the pointer to `buildingBlock.asp`. The whole statement substitutes the correct frame and section number for the new content:

```
eval("parent."+args[i]+".location.replace('buildingBlock.asp
?sectionID="+args[i+1]+"')");
```

The arguments in the above statement are set in the next code you alter, which makes sure each frame receives the correct section:

```
onLoad="
  MM_goToURL('frameMain','<%=frameMain%>');
  MM_goToURL('frame1a','<%=frame1a%>');
  MM_goToURL('frame2a','<%=frame2a%>');
  MM_goToURL('frame2b','<%=frame2b%>');
  MM_goToURL('frame2c','<%=frame2c%>');
  MM_goToURL('frame2d','<%=frame2d%>');
  return document.MM_returnValue"
```

Finally, you set an `if` statement to check whether the recordset contains any data or not. If not, then BOF and EOF will both be `true`. That means that the frame does not contain any subnavigation and so should not be evaluated.

Let's take a closer look at the `location.replace` action you use to load the content for your frames.

Using location.replace

The first step you took in creating `blockNav.asp` is to give the page title a dynamic name. Since `blockNav.asp` is the only file linked to in a normal fashion (all the other frames' content is loaded using `location.replace`) it is the only file that appears in the browser history. By giving `blockNav.asp` a dynamically generated name based on the `sectionID` passed to the file, the name of the content that appears with that `sectionID` ends up showing in the browser history. If, for instance, you open your browser (with the default page set to `wrox.com`), go to the Building Block site, click on a section title (which opens up Building Block Technology in the main frame), and then select Item One, Item Two, and Item Three, in that order, your browser's history will look like Figure 17-6.

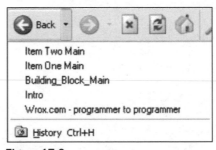

Figure 17-6

This is the history that you would instinctively expect to appear. But if you had used `location.href` to load the content into each frame, every frame would have added its own entry to the browser's history—which is not desirable since you want the subsections to appear together.

If you switch location.replace to location.href in the source files and click a link in your site, you should see the undesirable results we're talking about. Every frame is handled individually when clicking the Back button, thus requiring up to six Back button clicks to get to where you started from.

There are two remaining pieces of the puzzle that need to be added to `blockNav.asp`, namely the addition of a session variable and the confirmation that the navigation page does not cache.

Session Variables

If a user enters search terms in the Flash search field, those terms are sent along with the `sectionID` for the search section to the `blockNav.asp` file. For example:

```
blockNav.asp?sectionID=10&keywords=building+block+technology
```

The value of sectionID *here may be different in your own case depending on what the value of Section_ID your Search section ends up having in the database.*

Those search terms need to make their way to the blockSearch.asp page (although blockNav.asp actually opens up the buildingBlock.asp file and not blockSearch.asp directly). Those terms could be passed to the Building Block page and, from there, passed on to the search page. This is only ever a consideration when the Building Block page opens the search page so, instead, this situation can be resolved by using a session variable.

Session variables are variables that are stored on the server (such as strings or integers, and even objects like recordsets) and can be referenced by any of the pages that the server is processing within the context of an active user's session. Essentially, the first time a user comes to your site, the server starts a session for that user. In this fashion session variables can be very powerful for storing user information or other such variables or, in this case, search terms. But be warned—using too many session variables can greatly reduce the processing speed of a Web site.

By the way, you can also turn off this feature in your IIS settings if you are not going to need sessions.

Once the session has started, session objects and variables can be stored on the server. For more information about the objects you can use and variables you can create, check out the Session Object entry in the Reference section of the Code panel (see Figure 17-7). Dreamweaver provides a pretty good description of all of the possibilities of working with sessions.

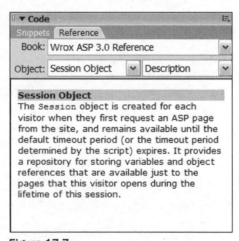

Figure 17-7

Try It Out   Adding a Session Variable

Try adding the session variable that stores the keywords for later access by blockSearch.asp.

If you do not still have blockNav.asp open, open the file and add this code directly after the first block of code that sets the value of Navigation__MMColParam):

```
 Navigation__MMColParam = String(Request.QueryString("sectionID"));
 }
 Session("keywords")=String(Request.QueryString("keywords"));
 %>
```

Actually, this line of code can go anywhere as long as it's within a block of ASP, but we prefer to put it here.

How It Works

Your line of code simply defines a session variable and fills it with the keywords part of the query string. Later on, the session variable is going to be retrieved by blockSearch.asp so it can use the terms to search the database.

Preventing Page Caching

The last order of business for blockNav.asp is to add code to prevent the page from caching. When the Flash search field passes the keywords to the blockNav.asp page, those keywords are sent to the blockSearch.asp page using the URL string. The navigation page is then responsible for creating the session variable for the keywords. If, however, a cached version of the page is in use when the call to the page has been made, then the session variable is not recreated and could potentially be set to the wrong search terms. For this reason it is essential to prevent the page from caching.

Try It Out   Preventing a Page from Caching

In ASP the best way to prevent a page from caching is to do so before the rest of the page is processed by the browser.

Add the following shaded code to the top of the page:

```
<%@language script (%@LANGUAGE="JAVASCRIPT" CODEPAGE="1252"%>
<% Response.CacheControl = "no-cache" %>
<% Response.AddHeader ("Pragma", "no-cache") %>
<% Response.Expires = -1 %>
```

How It Works

The code is the most thorough for preventing the page from caching. The first line with the no-cache setting for CacheControl works with HTTP 1.1 servers to prevent the page from caching. "Pragma", "no-cache" is for legacy HTTP 1.0 servers and the last line, Expires = -1, tells the browser that the page expires immediately (making it always request the page from the server, as opposed to the browser's cache).

Now to move on to create another central Building Block file, blockMain.asp, which works similarly to blockContent.asp but is used for displaying content in frameMain.

Creating blockMain.asp

One of the last files you need to create in this chapter is blockMain.asp (see Figure 17-8). Fortunately, blockMain.asp functions similarly to the blockContent.asp file that you created in Chapter 15, so the steps and methodology should be familiar.

Figure 17-8

Try It Out — Creating the blockMain.asp File

Once again, the content for blockMain.asp is built dynamically from the database and consists simply of a graphic, title, content, and background. Whereas blockContent was designed for the smaller frames and provides a list of links to the main content, blockMain displays content in the main frame and includes the full content from the database rather than just the summary description:

1. Create a new Dynamic ASP JavaScript page, save it as **blockMain.asp**, and modify the page properties (Modify⇨Page Properties), naming the page **Building Block Technology**. Set the Left Margin, Right Margin, Margin Width, and Margin Height values all to 0 and set a Background Color value of white (#FFFFFF). Don't close this dialog box yet.

2. Add a background image to the page. Enter this code into the Background Image field:

```
<%=(Content.Fields.Item("Background_Main").Value)%>
```

3. Once again attach the style sheet to this page, blockStyles.css (Text⇨CSS Styles⇨Attach Style Sheet).

4. Define a table to hold the content on the page. Set the width of the table equal to the width passed in from buildingBlock.asp so that your content does not require the iFrame that contains it to scroll horizontally.

Insert a table (Insert⇨Table) and enter the values shown in Figure 17-9. Width is set to `<%String (Request.QueryString("width"))%>`.

5. In the top table cell add an image placeholder (Insert⇨Image Placeholder) and click OK

6. Create a new recordset and call it **Content**. This time select the Advanced tab.

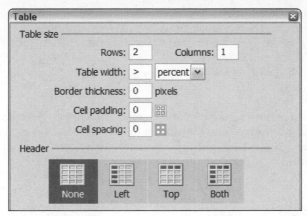

Figure 17-9

7. You only need the values in the database that pertain to the main content frame. Plus, you need to get all of the content items in the Content table whose ID value corresponds to a Section_ID value of Section, which is passed on the URL string from `buildingBlock.asp`.

Start by naming your recordset **Content** and use the connection MediaEdge. Enter the following SQL statement in the SQL field of the recordset window:

```
SELECT ID, Title_Main, Content_Main, Image_Main, Image_Width_Main,
Image_Height_Main,
 Vertical_Space_Main, Horizontal_Space_Main, Background_Main
FROM Content, Section_Content
WHERE ID = Content_ID AND Section_ID = MMColParam
```

8. Click the plus (+) next to Variables to add a new variable. Name it **MMColParam** and add a default value of 1 and runtime value of Request.QueryString("section"). Click OK.

9. As in previous chapters, you need to make your image dynamic, so select your DynamicImage Server Behavior from the drop-down menu of the Server Behaviors panel. This time, input the values shown in Figure 17-10.

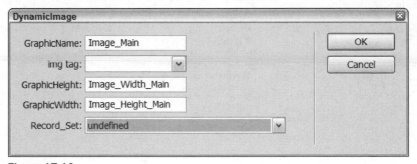

Figure 17-10

615

Here is another place where you have to make sure Dreamweaver correctly inserted
`Content.Fields.Item` *rather than just* `Content.Item`*. It's probably fastest just to do a search and replace. Note that when you do this, your page will work just fine, but Dreamweaver will complain by putting an exclamation mark next to the server behavior and informing you that the recordset* `Content.Fields` *doesn't exist when you double-click the behavior to investigate. It will also try to regain control if you do this and may remove the Fields part again if you added it.*

10. Add padding for the image, as you did when creating the `blockContent` page. Click the image and enter two arbitrary values for H Space and V Space in the Property inspector for the image, such as 111 and 222. Switch over to Code view and perform a find and replace (Edit⇨Find and Replace). Change `hspace="111"` to the following:

```
hspace="<%=(Content.Fields.Item("Horizontal_Space_Main").Value)%>"
```

Also change `vspace="222"` to this:

```
vspace="<%=(Content.Fields.Item("Vertical_Space_Main").Value)%>"
```

11. Add your Title_Main and Content_Main content from the database to the bottom cell of your table. Click the bottom cell of the table and choose Dynamic Text from the drop-down menu in the Server Behaviors panel (see Figure 17-11). Then choose Title_Main from the list of data in the `Content` recordset.

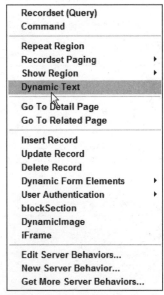

Figure 17-11

Enter a soft return (press Shift+Enter) after Title_Main and enter another dynamic text element, **Content_Main**.

Finally, highlight the entire table and select Repeat Region from the Server Behaviors drop-down menu. This makes this one table duplicate vertically for every element in the recordset for this particular section. Choose to display All Records, as shown in Figure 17-12.

Figure 17-12

The repeat region will look like Figure 17-13 when you're done.

Figure 17-13

How It Works

The `blockMain.asp` file works very similarly to `blockContent.asp`. The only difference is that different information is pulled from the database and displayed as two rows as opposed to two columns. You could, in addition, make a version of `blockMain` that could be used as an alternative to `blockContent`, and vice versa. Every time you make an additional content file, remember to keep it completely dynamic and only include elements of structure, not content.

Search Capabilities

Since you have all of your content stored in a database, it would be really handy to create a search engine so that users can type in keywords and search for that information in the database. In Chapter 16 you extended the Content table of the database not only to contain additional information for the main frame but also keywords to search against with `blockSearch.asp`. After finding a match in the database, the image, title, and description are displayed in the main frame, just as in `blockContent.asp` (see Figure 17-14).

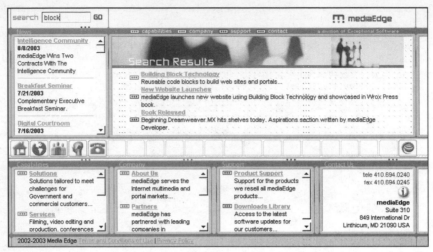

Figure 17-14

Try It Out   Creating the blockSearch.asp File

1. Create a new Dynamic ASP JavaScript page and save the new page as **blockSearch.asp** in your site folder.

2. Modify the page properties and give the new page a Left Margin, Top Margin, Margin Width, and Margin Height value of 0. Name the page **Building Block Technology**.

3. Attach your central style sheet, blockStyles.css, to this page (Text⇨CSS Styles⇨Attach Style Sheet).

4. Once again prevent this page from caching in the browser, since you want to ensure that the most recent results are accessed based on the content retrieved from the database.

You are going to use the same technique that you explored in the "Block Navigation" section earlier in this chapter. Add the following shaded lines of code directly beneath the @Language declaration at the top of the page:

```
<%@LANGUAGE="JAVASCRIPT" CODEPAGE="1252"%>

<% Response.CacheControl = "no-cache" %>
<% Response.AddHeader ("Pragma", "no-cache") %>
<% Response.Expires = -1 %>
```

5. As with the majority of the files you have created for this block solution, you are going to want to add a recordset to grab the keywords out of the database to search against. The difference here, however, is that you are going to dynamically build the SQL statement based on the search terms stored as a session variable.

To start, add a new recordset, giving it the name **Search**. If you are still in Advanced mode from the previous section, switch back over to Simple mode.

Access the Content table and select all of the columns from ID to Description. Filter based on keywords equal to the session variable Keywords, and sort by ID and Ascending. The Recordset dialog box should look like Figure 17-15. Click OK.

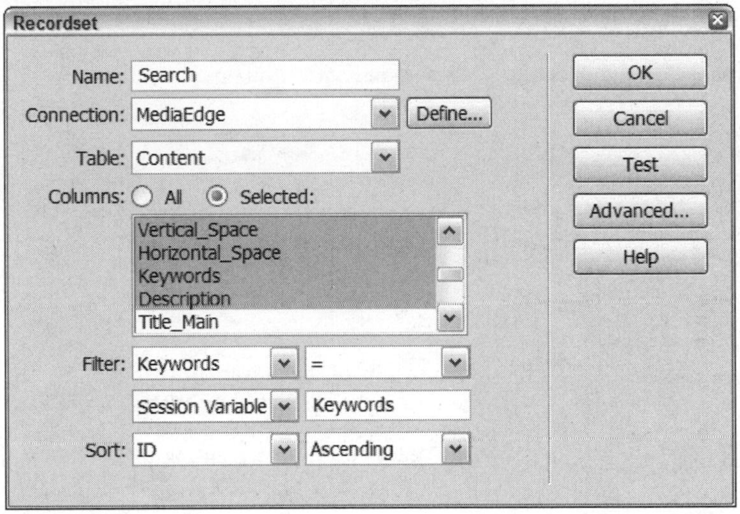

Figure 17-15

6.   Add the shaded code block after the first section of code Dreamweaver automatically inserted after creating the Search recordset:

```
<%
var Search__MMColParam = "Building Block Technology";
if (String(Session("keywords")) != "undefined" &&
  String(Session("keywords")) != "") {
    Search__MMColParam = String(Session("keywords"));
}
%>
```

```
<%
// build a loop to search against all terms
var keywords = Search__MMColParam.split(' ');
var query = "("
for (var x=0; x<keywords.length; x++) {
  query+= "(LCASE(keywords) LIKE LCASE('%" + keywords[x] + "%')";
  if (x != (keywords.length - 1)) { query += ") OR "; }
}
query += "))";
%>
```

7.   Now that you have added the code to create a query based on all the search terms entered in the search field, change your SQL statement to include the new query. Change the portion of the main SQL query where it reads as follows:

```
WHERE keywords = '"+ Search__MMColParam.replace(/'/g, "''") + "' ORDER BY ID ASC";
```

619

Replace that code with the following:

```
WHERE " + query + " ORDER BY ID ASC";
```

8. Add code to inform users if their search produces zero results, and then add code to output the search results themselves if there are results to display.

Add the following code block immediately after the opening `<body>` tag:

```
<% if(Search.EOF){
   Response.Write("<p>You found 0 Results<br><ul>" +
   "<li>Check your spelling.</li><br> " +
   "<li>Try different or fewer keywords.</li><br> " +
   "<li>Remove quotation marks.</li><br> " +
   "<li>Exclude words like AND, OR, and NOT<br></li></ul></p>");
   }
%>
```

9. Add the code to display the actual results of the search. Luckily you can reuse the same code block you created for `blockContent.asp`. Either follow Steps 3 and 8–14 from the "Creating blockContent.asp" Try It Out exercise in Chapter 15 (but use the name Search for the recordset, instead of Content) or simply copy and paste (or type) the following code blocks from `blockContent.asp` after the previous code you placed in the body. Just be sure to change all of the Content references to Search:

```
<% while ((Repeat1__numRows- != 0) && (!Search.EOF)) { %>
<table width="<%String(Request.QueryString("width"))%>" border="0" cellspacing="0"
cellpadding="0">
 <tr>
  <td><img src="<%=(Search.Fields.Item("Image").Value)%>" alt=""
width="<%=(Search.Fields.Item("Image_Width").Value)%>"
height="<%=(Search.Fields.Item("Image_Height").Value)%>"
hspace="<%=(Search.Fields.Item("Horizontal_Space").Value)%>"
vspace="<%=(Search.Fields.Item("Vertical_Space").Value)%>" align="top"></td>
  <td><b><a href="<%=(Search.Fields.Item("Link").Value)%>"
target="navigation"><%=(Search.Fields.Item("Title").Value)%></a><br></b>
<%=(Search.Fields.Item("Description").Value)%> </td>
 </tr>
</table>
<%
 Repeat1__index++;
 Search.MoveNext();
}
%>
```

Also add this code just before the opening `<html>` tag:

```
<%
var Repeat1__numRows = -1;
var Repeat1__index = 0;
Search_numRows += Repeat1__numRows;
%>
```

How It Works

The first thing that occurs in the process of searching against the database is that the search terms are sent to `blockNav.asp` on the URL string, where they are saved as a session variable:

```
blockNav.asp?sectionID=20&keywords=building+block+technology
```

After `blockNav.asp` opens `buildingBlock.asp`, which in turn opens `blockSearch.asp`, those keywords are retrieved and stored as the variable `Search__MMColParam` in a block of code created by Dreamweaver when you created your recordset.

After grabbing the session variable that holds the search string, you added the following code block, which dynamically builds the query string:

```
<%
// build a loop to search against all terms
var keywords = Search__MMColParam.split(' ');
var query = "("
for (var x=0; x<keywords.length; x++) {
    query+= "(LCASE(keywords) LIKE LCASE('%" + keywords[x] + "%')";
    if (x != (keywords.length - 1)) { query += ") OR "; }
}
query += "))";
    %>
```

The first thing this code does is take the `Search__MMColParam` variable and convert it into an array using the `split` function. The `split` function then looks for all occurrences of the character passed into the function, in this case a space, and uses that as the delimiter to create the array containing the original strings. After that, you loop through the array and dynamically build the WHERE clause of your larger SQL query. If someone searches for "Sadie Willow," that portion of the query ends up looking like this:

```
((LCASE(keywords) LIKE LCASE('%Sadie%')) OR (LCASE(keywords) LIKE
LCASE('%Willow%')))
```

The first part of the query, `LCASE(keywords)`, converts the string found in the Keywords column of the Content table to all lowercase characters. Then `LIKE LCASE("%Sadie%")` checks that string to see if there are any matches with the lowercase string "sadie". If there is a match, that row is added to your search recordset. Notice, in addition, the use of the `%` character. This character acts as a wildcard in the search. Say, for instance, an individual searched for the string "will". If this were the case, then they would still get any entries with a keyword of `willow`, since portions of words are accepted with the wildcard representing the rest of the word.

Next, you added your dynamically built query to the SQL query as a whole after the WHERE clause and before the clause ORDER BY ID ASC. The ORDER BY keyword arranges the results according to a particular column in the database, in this case the ID column, and ASC arranges the results in ascending order:

```
WHERE " + query + " ORDER BY ID ASC;
```

One of the last bits of code you added tells users when they enter a string that produces no results. If the search recordset is empty after completing the SQL query against the database (`Search.EOF` stands for the *end of file*) then you write out a few tips to help the reader with their searching:

```
<% if(Search.EOF){
    Response.Write("<p>You found 0 Results<br><ul>" +
    "<li>Check your spelling.</li><br> " +
    "<li>Try different or fewer keywords.</li><br> " +
    "<li>Remove quotation marks.</li><br> " +
    "<li>Exclude words like AND, OR, and NOT<br></li></ul></p>");
    }
%>
```

Adding Content Data

At this point you are done creating all the files that make up your system. Now that they exist, you shouldn't have to go back and rebuild any of these files, as they are completely dynamic and can adjust for any content you throw at them. All you need to do is keep the original version of the files and then work off that copy for each additional site you create. If you make any improvement to the files as you create a new site, add that feature to the original core files and be sure to make it dynamic.

The last piece of the puzzle that you need to complete is to add some data to the database so that you can see all your files work in conjunction with each other. Let's start with a quick overview of adding content before you move into actually adding data to get your files moving.

One of the most important things to remember about adding content to the database is to keep track of the section IDs for the various sections, as you must enter the section ID on the end of the URL string for the Link field in both the Sections table and the Content table. In our source files there is a sample database that you can use to test your files, but which will almost certainly end up being different from the database you create. If any entries are added and removed, the autonumbering will no longer be sequential and you may have section IDs that the sample database does not, and vice versa. This is typical for a table with unique keys, so you just have to remember to keep track of the sections you need to link to.

> *Your content management system can be created to display a list of the section IDs to choose from. This way, you don't need to have the world's greatest memory.*

Adding Content to the Sections Table

Up to this point you have created all four necessary tables in the database: Sections_Nav, Sections, Section_Content, and Content (see Figure 17-16). You have entered enough data to display the smaller Building Block navigation frames. Now you must round out the data to demonstrate the complete application framework, including adding content to display the items in the main viewing frame, data to associate sections with subsections, and entering additional content files such as index.asp.

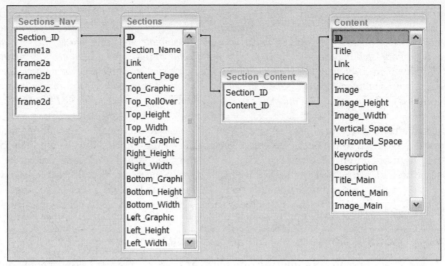

Figure 17-16

Remember that the Sections table holds, for each Building Block, all the border graphics, positional values for those graphics, and which content template file to display in the center. This includes the four navigation blocks in the bottom of your site, the news block in the left of your first row, and the main viewing frame on the right of your first row. Each entry in the Sections table deals with one block of content, which may or may not use all the different frames on the page.

Notice in Figure 17-17 (showing the Sections table after some more data has been added to it, which you'll do later on) that the Building_Block section's Link includes the variable and value `sectionID=7`. Now that you have an understanding of how `blockNav.asp` works, you can see how the associations between sections and their main content section are made through linking. In Chapter 15 you included this link (though with `sectionID=1`) but that is where you stopped.

		ID	Section_Name	Content_Page	Link
	+	1	Building_Block	blockContent.asp	blockNav.asp?sectionID=2
	+	2	Building_Block_Main	blockMain.asp	blockMain.asp
	+	3	Item One Main	blockMain.asp	// new window
	+	4	Item Two Main	blockMain.asp	// new window
	+	5	Item Three Main	blockMain.asp	// new window
	+	6	Item Four Main	blockMain.asp	// new window
Ø	+	7	Item Five Main	blockMain.asp	// new window
	+	8	Intro	intro.asp	// new window
	+	9	Top Left Block	blockContent.asp	blockNav.asp?sectionID=7
	+	10	Search	blockSearch.asp	blockSearch.asp
*		(AutoNumber)			

Figure 17-17

Whenever you want to link to the main content of a section, do so by creating and linking to a section of the same name, followed by "_Main." As we mentioned previously, all items of content have either one _Main section in the section database or two sections, with the second section in place to act as a navigation block.

You might wonder why you created the system so that you have to create a separate _Main section for everything you want to display in the main window. If you look again at the Sections table, you'll see that each section deals with its own graphics and content template page, so if you try to combine both sections into one, you have to create a whole new set of fields in the table to deal with the "main" version of the content. In many cases there isn't even a main version so all these fields are there for nothing, which takes up a bit of space and also involves passing many extraneous fields around your recordsets. The way it is at the moment, you only have to store _Main data if you actually need it.

To get the system working, the first thing you need to do is add sections to the Sections table. The only section you have added to the Sections table thus far is Building_Block. Now, as we mentioned previously, every item of content requires a main section for use with the main frame since it's the section ID you pass on the URL string and not the content ID. So far in the Content table you only have Items 1–5 and you have yet to create main sections for them. You also need to add a section for the Building_Block_Main, Intro, the Top Left block, and a section for use with displaying the search results.

Try It Out   Adding Content to the Sections Table

1. Make sure all the images from the download are in your images folder. There are a few new ones, for use as border graphics around the main frame and top left frame, which are taller than the others.

2. Open your Access database, MediaEdge.mdb. Add nine new rows to the Sections table: **Building_Block_Main, Item One Main to Item Five Main, Intro, Top Left Block,** and **Search.**

3. If you haven't downloaded the sample database for this chapter, do so at this point. You can find the file at www.wrox.com. Once you have the files downloaded, open up the MediaEdge.mdb file for Chapter 17 and copy the data for the nine newly added rows into your database.

4. Make sure the links for Building_Block and Top Left Block have a sectionID value equal to the ID of the Building_Block_Main section.

Your ID values might have ended up differently if you added or removed any rows from the database as you completed Chapters 15 and 16. If you haven't added and removed any rows in the database, your IDs should go in ascending order from 1 to 10. If that is the case, then you will have blockNav.asp?sectionID=2.

How It Works

As you know, the sectionID value on the end of the URL string tells the buildingBlock.asp file what sectionID to pass to the blockNav.asp file when the link is clicked. The Content_Page field tells the buildingBlock.asp file what file to display in the inside iFrame in the Building Block. For example, you created blockContent.asp to contain a list of items and their images and links.

Notice, in addition, that the sections that appear in the main content frame have blockMain.asp in the Content_Page field. Also notice that no link has been included for these rows, but the comment //new window has (remember that the link field holds the link *from* this section and would be accessible by clicking on the title bar of the main frame in this case). A great add-on feature to this overall functionality would be to give users the ability to open the current main content in a new browser window when they click that section's corresponding title graphic. You would then simply need to create a new file to handle this and add the name of that file in the link column for each section.

The Intro section opens the file `Intro.asp`, the Search section uses the file `blockSearch.asp`, and the Top Left Block uses the same display as the other navigation blocks, namely `blockContent.asp`.

The Intro and Search blocks are two examples of files other than your generic `blockContent` or `blockMain` files that can be opened up within the Building Blocks. There are always occasions where you need to create some one-off functionality, but you will find that the Building Block system fully supports this eventuality—just create the page you want and reference it in the correct field in the database. At the end of this chapter we will take a deeper look into the large variety of files that could be created.

`Intro.asp` is a bit of an exception for the Building Block structure, as it does not contain dynamic content. It's simply a Flash introduction that is used just once. For that matter, it's a good example of how to incorporate additional files and code other than Building Block files within the structure.

Many sites have implemented Flash animations within the context of their HTML sites. The source files include a basic Flash introduction if you want to implement it (the same way as you did for the search file), but leave the creation of the introduction up to you. If you would like to learn more about Flash, check out some of these books:

❑   *Flash MX 3D Graphics Bible* by Matthew David (Wiley, 2003)

❑   *Macromedia Flash MX 2004 ActionScript Bible* by Robert Reinhardt and Joey Lott (Wiley, 2004)

❑   *50 Fast Macromedia Flash MX Techniques* by Ellen Finkelstein and Gurdy Leete (Wiley, 2002)

Adding Content to the Content Table

The next table, the Content table, is nearly complete in regard to entries, but take a moment to add content to the additional sections you added to this table in Chapter 15: Keywords, Title_Main, Content_Main, Image_Main, Image_Width_Main, Image_Height_Main, Vertical_Space_Main, and Background_Main. There is also one item of content, keeping with the sections you have included in the Sections table, that you need to add.

Try It Out   **Adding Content to the Content Table**

1.   While still in your Access database, start by adding one new row to the Content table for your Building Block Technology item.

2.   Once again, open the `MediaEdge.mdb` file you downloaded from `www.wrox.com`. This time, open the Content table and copy the values into your newly added row for the new item.

3.   Additionally, in Chapter 15 you added the fields for ID through Description. Now fill in the Title_Main through Background_Main fields.

4.   Make sure the `sectionIDs` in the Link field match up with the respective values in the Sections table. The Building Block link should point to the Building Block_Main section.

How It Works

The Content table holds all the data necessary for each individual item of content, including descriptive data to use when it is included in a list in the navigation blocks, keywords for use with the `blockSearch.asp` page, and _Main content for use when that particular item is displayed in the main viewing frame.

As you add new functionality for particular items of content you can add new fields to this content table and create your recordsets using those fields, omitting fields that you do not need. You could change the database structure and add new tables for content if you need to. You could then add lookup tables so that you can always reference the section and content ID, rather than rely on using section or content names, which might be subject to change.

File Associations

Associations between the Sections and Content items tell the Building Blocks what items of content they need to display in each section, and section-to-section relationships in the Sections_Nav table let the blockNav.asp file know what subsections to open for each section.

Try It Out   Adding Associations in the Section_Content Table

So far, you need about 16 different associations (rows in the Section_Content table) to get your system rolling. You should already have five rows set up to get items 1–5 to appear in the list as part of the Building_Block section. You added these rows in Chapter 15. Add the remaining 11 now.

Add an entry for each remaining section in the Sections table to link them to their main frame content. Use the Sections table to look up the IDs for the Building_Block_Main and Item One Main through Item Five Main sections, and place them in the Section_ID column of the Section_Content table. Now find the corresponding content IDs in the Content table and add it in the Content_ID column here. The following table details the numbers you need to match up:

Section_ID	Content_ID
Building Block	Item One
Building Block	Item Two
Building Block	Item Three
Building Block	Item Four
Building Block	Item Five
Building Block Main	Building Block Technology
ItemOne_Main	Item One
ItemTwo_Main	Item Two
ItemThree_Main	Item Three
ItemFour_Main	Item Four
ItemFive_Main	Item Five
Top Left Block	Item One
Top Left Block	Item Two
Top Left Block	Item Three
Top Left Block	Item Four
Top Left Block	Item Five

Earlier, you created a new Top Left Block section, in which you want the same items 1–5 to appear. For our demo, you're using these same items everywhere. At the moment the Top Left Block and Building Block sections are identical in content; later, you'll create file associations in the Sections_Nav table that only open the content in the top-left block.

How It Works

As described in Chapter 15, `blockContent.asp` looks to this table to see what content items are supposed to appear on the page. It pulls out all the ID values of the Content items that are matched up with the `sectionID` it's been passed on the URL string.

In the same fashion, `blockMain.asp` looks to this table to see what items it should display. In this table, lone numbers on the left are most likely main sections, since only one item of content is ever displayed at a time in the main frame. At least, that's the way you have set it up. With a little work you could have lists of content items appearing in the main frame if you wanted to.

Try It Out   Adding Associations in the Sections_Nav Table

The last order of business to get your site rolling is to add some section and subsection IDs to the Sections_Nav table. You must make two associations, one for the subsections when the title of a Building_Block section has been selected, and a second to open the initial frames when the page first loads:

1.   Add the `sectionID` of the Building Block_Main section to the Section_ID column of the first row (instead of 2 in Figure 17-18). Then add 0 to the `frame1a` field. For this example you don't want to replace the top-left block when you select the link on the title of the Building Block. Finally, add 1 for each of the remaining four columns as you are simply going to open up the Building_Block section in each of these frames.

Section_ID	frame1a	frame2a	frame2b	frame2c	frame2d
2	0	1	1	1	1
8	9	1	1	1	1
0	0	0	0	0	0

Figure 17-18

If the ID of the first Building_Block section you created is not 1, substitute your value here.

2.   Add a section and subsection for use when the page first loads. Start by adding the ID for the Intro section in the Sections table to the Section_ID field (where the 8 is in Figure 17-18). Then add the ID for the Top Left Block section to the `frame1a` column (in place of 9), and the ID for the Building_Block section in each of the remaining columns of the Sections_Nav table.

3.   There's just one more thing that you need to do to get everything working. Change a value in the `index.asp` page where you had previously left a placeholder. It doesn't really have anything to do with the Sections_Nav table, but without it you won't load any initial content into the page.

Open `index.asp` in Dreamweaver and find your placeholder, `sectionID=#`. Replace that # with the ID value of your Intro section in the Sections table. That's it—you're done!

If you haven't had to add and remove rows to the Sections table, that ID will be 8.

How It Works

As we've said, the Sections_Nav table simply tells `blockNav.asp` what subsections it should open for each section. It's quite simple and probably doesn't need any further explanation. You also went back and changed the very first thing to appear on the page when it is first loaded, by pointing `blockNav.asp` to the Intro section in `index.asp`.

That was the last change you needed to enter in the database to get your system working in its entirety. When you are finished, the site should resemble Figure 17-19.

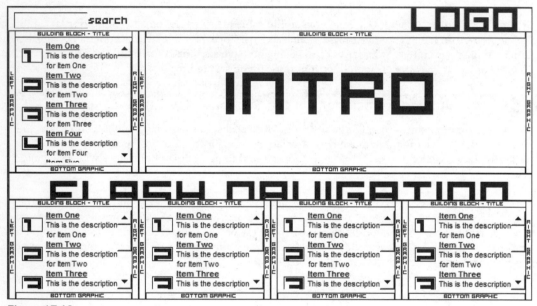

Figure 17-19

> You can see a working demo of this content if you visit `www.media-edge.com/`
> `BuildingBlockTechnology`.

You've now completed the basic Building Block site. Using just this framework, you can create your own dynamic site, even without changing any of the ASP pages. Of course, the time will most likely come when you want to display content in a different way and you'll have to create new content template pages in addition to `blockContent` and `blockMain`, or perhaps even add fields to the database. The most important thing is that you understand how all of the data relates to each other, so you can add your own data and round out your own content management solution to access and edit that data.

Loading Different Types of Content

You can extend the framework using various other components that are on the market. Some of those component "add-ons" include stock tickers, world news bloggers, horoscopes, movie listings, and weather conditions. Ordinarily these components are included within the confines of an entire page, or navigation frame, and sometimes seem a little out of place. Using the Building Block system, however, you can now add these separate components or gadgets to a block by itself and make it truly an integrated part of your site's system.

You can now create border graphics for each of these add-ons and easily make them appear as part of your main page or have them appear as subsections through navigating your site. The options are endless once you start thinking in terms of block structure and reusability. The following image displays an array of different gadgets that add some neat functionality to a site. (The particular gadgets in Figure 17-20 are available at www.plumtree.com.)

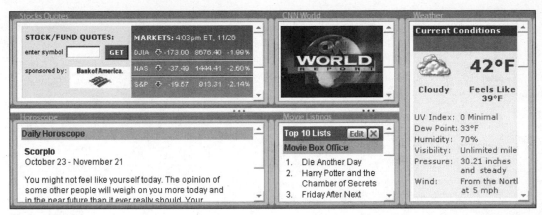

Figure 17-20

In the next chapter we will look at a hot spot for downloading custom components from Macromedia: namely, the Macromedia Exchange.

Summary

In this chapter you created the final files that complete and round out your Building Block structure. These files were the blockNav.asp file, the blockMain.asp file, and finally the blockSearch.asp file. After completing each of these files and filling in data for your database you were able to view the complete functionality of your Building Block system.

MediaEdge's Web site, displayed throughout this book, is a great example of adding custom graphics and content to the Building Block technology to create a site in its entirety using this system. MediaEdge's site uses the Building Block structure and adds some unique features including Flash navigation, Flash intro, and sound. To see MediaEdge's site in action, check out www.media-edge.com and compare it to the backbone structure you created (also visible at www.media-edge.com/BuildingBlockTechnology).

Why Not Try . . .

Now that you have finished the entire architecture for this project, the next step is definitely changing it. As we mentioned, you can switch the graphics and change the arrangement of any frame in the initial index file. In doing so, you can give your site a whole new look. Also try a different number of frames or different dimensions of frames. The architecture stays the same but you just need to alter the database, index, and blockNav files. If you do make changes, send an e-mail to Todd.Marks@exceptionalsoftware.com.

Going Beyond with Dreamweaver MX 2004 Extensions

In Chapters 14 through 17, you created a great reusable structure that allows you to easily swap various pages of functionality in and out as desired. Towards the end of Chapter 17 we discussed how easy it would be to add a component or gadget to an existing page. Now you are going to take measures that will give you a great number of these components at your fingertips, as well as make them available as drag-and-drop elements within Dreamweaver MX 2004. This is possible through the use of Macromedia extensions and the Extension Manager.

An extension allows users to add new features to an application. In the case of Dreamweaver, you can literally build onto the application by creating extensions and sharing them with others. You can also capitalize on extensions built by others, which allows you to add functionality and capabilities not only to Dreamweaver but to your pages and sites as well.

In this chapter you will do the following:

❑   Install the Extension Manager

❑   Explore the Macromedia Exchange

❑   Add an e-commerce extension to the Building Block Framework

Dreamweaver Extensions

In Chapter 17 we looked at how the organization of your Building Block Technology allows you to add additional content pages in the database, and how those pages appear within the block of one of your sections. Dreamweaver extensions are built around the same concept, such that additional functionality can be included in the Configuration folder of the application and appear within the application itself.

Fortunately, you don't need to know very much about extensions in order to begin to use them. The extensions themselves are made simply with HTML and JavaScript (and, for more robust extensions, C++). They are packaged using XML (Extensible Markup Language) and a handy tool called the *Extension Manager*. This tool is also what enables you to install and package extensions, and keep them organized.

Installing the Extension Manager

Before you can do anything with extensions, you must first install the Extension Manager. You can download the Extension Manager for free from the Macromedia Web site.

If you have installed the Extension Manager in the past with Dreamweaver 4, you can always upgrade it by simply downloading and installing the latest version. Find out what version you have by opening the Extension Manager and selecting Help⇨About Macromedia Extension Manager. As of the release of this book, the most current version of the Extension Manager is 1.6.062.

Try It Out   **Installing the Extension Manager**

1. To download the Extension Manager, go directly to the download page www.macromedia.com/exchange/em_download (see Figure 18-1).

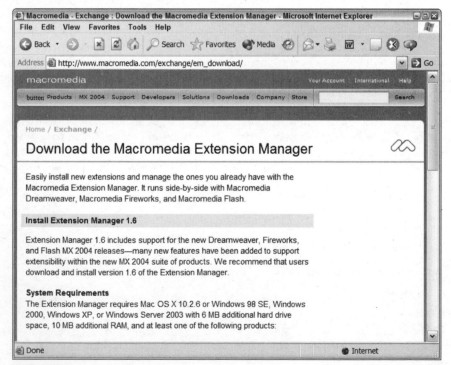

Figure 18-1

2. Download the Extension Manager installation file by clicking on the link for either Mac OS or Windows. (The latest release may be more recent than those shown in Figure 18-2.)

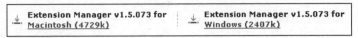

Figure 18-2

3. Once the install file (`em_install.hqx` or `em_install.exe`) has fully downloaded, double-click the file to begin the installation process. Note that you'll need to close down any Macromedia products that use the Extension Manager before installation. These include:

- ❏ Dreamweaver MX 2004, Dreamweaver MX, and Dreamweaver 4
- ❏ Dreamweaver UltraDev 4
- ❏ Flash MX 2004, Flash MX, and Flash 5
- ❏ Fireworks MX

4. After you install the Extension Manager, you can run it by selecting Commands⇨Manage Extensions in any of the aforementioned Macromedia applications (see Figure 18-3).

Figure 18-3

How It Works

What you did here was fairly simple. After downloading the Extension Manager, it's now available to all your Macromedia products. The extensions you install will appear in the corresponding list for each relevant application.

Next we look at using the Extension Manager and installing extensions.

Using the Extension Manager

The Extension Manager has essentially four main functions: Install Extension, Package Extension, Submit Extension, and Remove Extension. All of these options can be found in the File menu of the Extension Manager. In the center of the Extension Manager you see a drop-down list all of the applications you have installed on your machine that support the Extension Manager. In Figure 18-4, you can see that Dreamweaver MX 2004, Fireworks MX 2004, Flash MX, and Flash MX 2004 are installed.

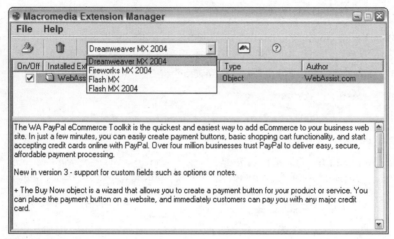

Figure 18-4

Whenever you install an extension, it appears in a list of extensions grouped by application. In Figure 18-4, you can see that the last extension selected was the WebAssist PayPal eCommerce extension you will install later in this chapter. When you install the Extension Manager for the first time, you have no extensions listed and so you must build your collection.

In addition to the name of the extension and the extension author's name, there is a host of information for each extension that you can find in the scrolling window beneath the list of extensions for that application. This information typically includes how to implement the extension and where to seek additional help or future versions of it.

Most extensions can be found in one location, the Macromedia Exchange. At the time this book went to press, there were more than 860 extensions available for Dreamweaver and more than 5,425 extensions total. There are, in addition, a number of Web sites available that provide Dreamweaver extensions, which are listed at the end of this chapter.

Extension Format

Extensions come in the form of an .mxp file, which works similarly to a .zip file in that it is a package containing several other files. These files include graphics to add to the Insert bar, the JavaScript and

HTML files that form the code blocks for the extension, and an .mxi (XML) file that tells the Extension Manager where to place everything.

All files for Dreamweaver Extensions are placed in the Configuration folder (C:\Program Files\ Macromedia\Dreamweaver MX 2004\Configuration), as long as you let Dreamweaver install it in the default folder. If you browse that folder, you will notice that most of the code blocks and behaviors that are already part of Dreamweaver actually reside within Dreamweaver in the same way as the extensions you install yourself, as shown in Figure 18-5. If you open any of the folders, you will see that most of the features of the application that you use every day are nothing more than HTML and JavaScript files. By designing the architecture of Dreamweaver in this fashion, Macromedia has made the product one of the most easily extensible applications there is.

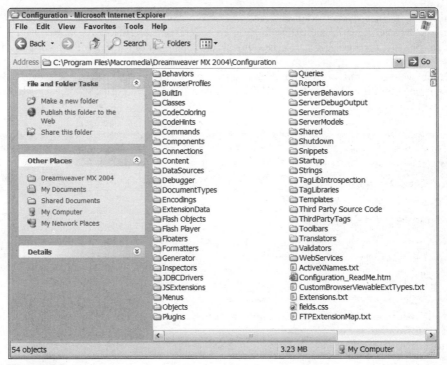

Figure 18-5

As we mentioned, most of the extensions—even the built-in objects and behaviors—add an icon and tab to the Insert bar. Depending on how the .mxi file is written, people can add extensions to any of the preexisting folders, create a new folder (adding a new tab in the Insert bar), and even add multiple extensions to the same new tab on the Insert bar. Each of the following tabs and icons on the Insert bar is contained in the Configuration folder in the same fashion as any of the objects or behaviors (see Figure 18-6).

Figure 18-6

When you drag the icon onto the page to implement any of the extensions, you will see a form field window open, which allows you to enter data to customize the extension, as you do for every other object you implement in Dreamweaver.

Macromedia Exchange for Dreamweaver

The main page of the Dreamweaver Exchange, shown in Figure 18-7, has a few items of interest that you should consider visiting first, including the Dreamweaver Exchange Top 10, located in the right column of the main page. It is a good idea to keep abreast of the new extensions, as more are added daily.

In the Dreamweaver Exchange section of the page, the Our Picks drop-down list shows many categories to choose from, including Accessibility, DHTML/Layers, Learning, Navigation, Rich Media, Scripting, Security, and Commerce.

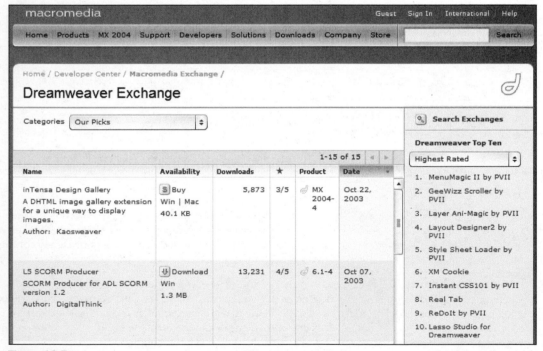

Figure 18-7

The following list describes some of the types of extensions at the Macromedia Dreamweaver Exchange, as well as a description of some of the extensions currently available for download:

- ❑ **Accessibility:** Extensions that make pages more accessible to individuals with disabilities. Among the extensions listed in this category are testing scripts to determine the usability of your site to see if it meets 508 and W3C standards (by UsableNet Inc.), and an extension that overrides the Dreamweaver Image Object to allow for alt text and a longdesc URL within the form field (by LMH).

- ❑ **App Servers:** Extensions that help connect to databases or work with middleware scripts such as ColdFusion, PHP, ASP, and JSP. Among these are an extension to incorporate an Atomz Search (by Atomz) and a Context Help Toolbar Extension (by Tom Muck).

- ❑ **Browsers:** Extensions that help with browser detection and redirection, including extensions to set a default browser home page (by Victor Hugo Chalian) and a WinTimer Extension to close pop-up windows after a preset time (by Al Sparber).

- ❑ **DHTML/Layers:** Extensions that allow Dynamic HTML objects on your page, including draggable layers, drop-down menus, scrollers, and page transitions.

- ❑ **Navigation:** Extensions to aid in creating, including, and maintaining Web site navigation. These extensions include an Anchors Extension to list and allow for linking to any anchors in a given page (by Scott Richards), close a browser window, and add a collapsible menu.

- ❑ **Security:** Extensions that add security features such as ignoring right mouse clicks and making sure your site is opened in its designated frameset, even when the page is opened directly.

- ❑ **Text:** Extensions that allow for text editing within a page in Dreamweaver and within a browser page. Examples include tools to change the case of text on a page or add particular math symbols and special characters.

- ❑ **Commerce:** Extensions that assist in developing e-commerce sites including a JUST ADDCommerce Shopping Cart Extension (by Rich Media Technologies, Inc.) and a PayPal Shopping Cart Extension (by Paul Davis).

Ratings

After you select one of these categories you will see a list of returned results. If you select any of these results, you are taken to the download page for that extension. You can also select More, which takes you to a list of all extensions in that category. In that list, shown in Figure 18-8, you will notice a few columns of interest. The first thing you should pay close attention to is the star rating. This score is based directly on the average of all votes of individuals who have left comments in the past and rated the component.

The comments and ratings are a good testament to the usefulness of the component. There are, unfortunately, a few dud components in the list, so before you take the time to download, install, and attempt to implement any component, save yourself a lot of time by checking up first on others' experiences with the component.

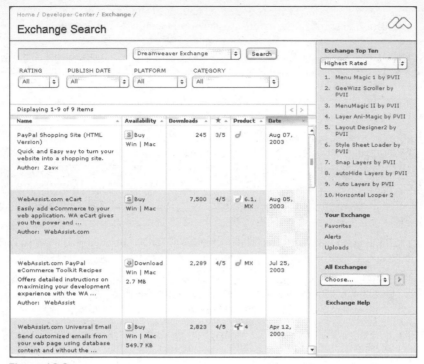

Figure 18-8

Adding the PayPal Shopping Cart Extension

Once you find an extension that meets your needs, you need to add it to your Web page. In the rest of this chapter, you're going to download an e-commerce extension and add it to the MediaEdge site. Specifically, this extension lets you accept payments from users through the PayPal online service.

There are actually quite a few PayPal extensions in the Dreamweaver Exchange. The extension that you are going to use, `PayPal304.mxp` written by WebAssist.com, was created for Dreamweaver MX and uses Dreamweaver MX's Document Object Model to add itself to the Insert menu of the application. This extension has been incorporated into a more robust WebAssist.com eCart extension that is currently available on the Macromedia Exchange for $129.99, but you are going to simply download the free extension from WebAssist's Web site instead.

Try It Out   Incorporating E-commerce Functionality in the Building Block Structure

1. Go to the Macromedia Exchange (`www.macromedia.com/exchange`). If you haven't created an account here before, do so now (it's free).

2. Select the Commerce category in the Dreamweaver drop-down list on the main page of the Exchange. Select the WebAssist.com eCart extension (see Figure 18-9).

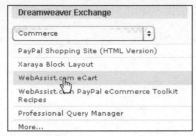

Figure 18-9

After the information page loads, click the Buy button under the extension's title, as shown in Figure 18-10.

Figure 18-10

3. Alternatively, you could select More from the extension's drop-down list on the main page of the Exchange, which returns a list of all Dreamweaver extensions. You can then refine the list by entering **PayPal** in the Search field and browse to the WebAssist.com eCart extension and click Buy.

4. After clicking the Buy button, your browser opens to the URL: www.Webassist.com/Products/ProductDetails.asp?PID=19&RID=71. Note that this is the more robust $129.99 extension. To get the free component that we are going to use, change the Product ID (PID) in the URL from 19 to **18**. When you are done, hit Enter and you will now see the free PayPal extension available for download. Notice that, after you have changed the variable value in the URL, the version of the Toolkit should say version 3.0.4 (see Figure 18-11)

5. Click the Get Now button for the WA PayPal eCommerce Toolkit.

Figure 18-11

You are directed to a user agreement; click Accept. Next, enter your name and e-mail address and click on the Get Software Now button. Last, you will be directed to a secure checkout page where you can download the extension. Click `PayPal304.mxp` and download the extension to your default Downloaded Extensions folder (see Figure 18-12.)

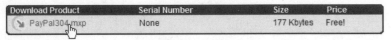

Download Product	Serial Number	Size	Price
PayPal304.mxp	None	177 Kbytes	Free!

Figure 18-12

6. Open the `blockMain.asp` page from your root folder in Dreamweaver. You are going to use the same functionality as you added before, but you are now going to add a Buy option beneath each item title that links to PayPal. Save this file as **blockMainPayPal.asp**.

7. Open the Macromedia Extension Manager (Commands⇨Manage Extensions) or open the Extension Manager directly from the Programs folder. Make sure the drop-down list is set to Dreamweaver MX 2004 and click the Install New Extension button. Browse to the `PayPal304.mxp` file.

Accept the license agreement and click OK. You should now see the extension appear in your list of Dreamweaver MX 2004 extensions, as shown in Figure 18-13.

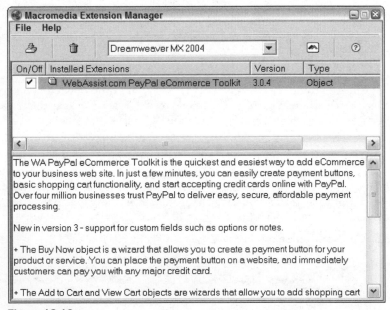

Figure 18-13

8. You will next be instructed to close and restart Dreamweaver. This is so the extension can be included in the Insert bar within Dreamweaver. When you reopen Dreamweaver, you should now see a PayPal 1SIP option in the Insert menu drop-down list (see Figure 18-14). Select that option and you will see four e-commerce icons appear in the insert menu.

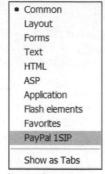

Figure 18-14

How It Works

Now that you have installed the PayPal extension, it resides in the Dreamweaver MX 2004 Programs folder and appears in the Insert menu of Dreamweaver until you remove it. After you install several extensions and have gained an understanding of how to use them, you will find that they speed up development time tremendously. You will also find that you can add a new tier of functionality to your work, which would have seemed arduous or impossible in the past.

The next thing you need to do is to add a column to your Content table to hold the prices for each item.

Try It Out   **Adding Values to the Database Content Table**

1. Open the `MediaEdge.mdb` database in Microsoft Access and open the Content table.

2. Right-click the Image column and choose Insert Column from the drop-down menu. Double-click the title for the newly added field and change the name to **Price**.

3. For each of the Items One through Five, add the value **5** in the Price column. Save and close the Content table.

4. Add the page to the Sections table so the prices show up next to the descriptions of the items. Open the Sections table and change each of the items' Content_Page entries from `blockMain.asp` to **blockMainPayPal.asp**, as shown in Figure 18-15. (You will create the `blockMainPayPal.asp` page next.) Save and close the Sections table.

	ID	Section_Name	Content_Page
+	1	Building_Block	blockContent.asp
+	2	Building_Block_Main	blockMainPayPal.asp
+	3	Item One Main	blockMainPayPal.asp
+	4	Item Two Main	blockMainPayPal.asp
+	5	Item Three Main	blockMainPayPal.asp
+	6	Item Four Main	blockMainPayPal.asp
+	7	Item Five Main	blockMainPayPal.asp
+	8	Intro	intro.asp
+	9	Top Left Block	blockContent.asp
+	10	Search	blockSearch.asp

Figure 18-15

How It Works

By adding a Price column to the database you will be able to assign dollar figures to your items of content. In this case you assigned your fictitious items, Item One through Item Five, the value of $5. You also changed the page that references these items from `blockMain.asp` to `blockMainPayPal.asp`.

Now that you've made your changes to the database, you need to sign up for a PayPal business account. After that, you will create the `blockMainPayPal.asp` page, which pulls not just the items, but now the dollar figures from the database and passes those values to PayPal when a user selects one of your items to buy.

Try It Out   **Sign Up for a PayPal Business Account**

Before you can use the WebAssist extension you have to sign up for a PayPal business account to sell items on your site through PayPal. You can do this fairly easily on PayPal's Web site.

If you don't want to sign up for a PayPal account, then just follow along with these steps to see how easy it is to implement the functionality. If you already have a PayPal account, you can skip this step.

1. Open your browser to PayPal's Web site, `www.paypal.com`. Click the Sign Up button in the top right corner of the page, click the Business Account option, and select your country from the drop-down list. Click Continue.

2. Enter your information in the form to sign up. There should be three steps to complete in process (see Figure 18-16).

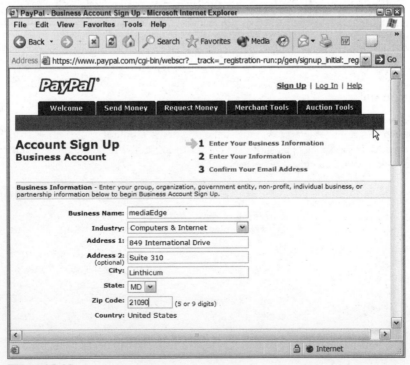

Figure 18-16

How It Works

By signing up for a PayPal business account you will be able to accept money over the Web. PayPal has a secure service that handles the transactions and then e-mails you when an item has been purchased. PayPal also has shopping cart functionality, which allows users to select multiple items to purchase and then pay for them all at the same time.

After you sign up for a PayPal business account you will be sent a confirmation e-mail that you must respond to and type in your password to verify your account. After you have done that you are ready to start accepting money online and can complete the next exercise.

Try It Out **Adding the E-commerce Functionality**

Now you will need to switch back over to Dreamweaver, where you will add a button to the item to allow a user to purchase it using PayPal. Start by allowing the user to purchase one item and then see how you would go about allowing the user to purchase multiple items with a shopping cart.

1. Switch to Design view. Add a soft return after the dynamic title you previously created (press Shift+Enter) and select the PayPal 1SIP option in the Insert bar's drop-down menu, if you have not already done so.

2. Click the Single Item Purchase (PayPal 1SIP) button, as shown in Figure 18-17, and the WebAssist eCommerce wizard will pop up on-screen. Complete Steps 1–6 in the wizard to add the e-commerce button beneath the title, as follows:

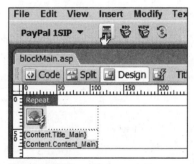

Figure 18-17

Step 1 Enter the e-mail address that you used to set up your PayPal account.

Step 2 Select the appearance of the button that you want for your site. For now, just click Next and use the initially selected button.

Step 3 Enter **111** for the name of the item, enter **222** for the ID/number, and enter **333** for the price of the item. You are going to make these numbers dynamic in Code view, so you are adding arbitrary strings now that you can later search for. Select your currency type and leave the multiple item selection unselected. When you're done, the dialog box should look like Figure 18-18.

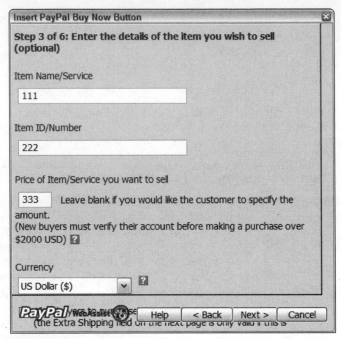

Figure 18-18

Step 4 Enter in **4.95** for the dollar amount of each of the base shipping, extra shipping, and handling for the item. In the future, you will have to change these values depending on what item you're selling.

Step 5 If you have a secure portion of your server, `https:`, and you want to add a logo to the payment page, add that logo here.

Step 6 If you want to redirect customers to specific pages for successful completion or cancellation, create them and point to them here.

3. Review the information and click the Finish button. When you are done, you should see the PayPal button appear beneath the title on the page, as shown in Figure 18-19.

Figure 18-19

How It Works

At this point you have finished the steps necessary to add a Buy Now button to the page. The form that contains the button has all the information to pass the item name, ID, and price to the PayPal account that you set up. If you were to run and test this page now for Item One, for instance, clicking the Buy Now button would pass values to PayPal and you could pay for the item. The only problem is that you would be buying an item named 111 for $333. You had to enter generic numbers such as 111, 222, and 333 because the wizard would not have allowed you to enter the ASP strings to make these values dynamic. You can now replace those values in the code to include your dynamic content. You are going to add a dynamic name, ID, and price.

Try It Out   **Adding Dynamic Values**

1. Switch to Code view and perform a find and replace on the following:

Replace 111 with this:

```
<%=(Content.Fields.Item("Title_Main").Value)%>
```

Replace 222 with this:

```
<%=(Content.Fields.Item("ID").Value)%>
```

Replace 333 with this:

```
<%=(Content.Fields.Item("Price").Value)%>
```

2. Since you recently added Price to the database, you are going to need to make sure you add it to the query of the database so that you have that information along with the title and ID for this item.

While still in Code view, find the SQL query in the document and add Price to the list. When you are finished, the query should look like this:

```
Content.Source = "SELECT ID, Price, Title_Main, Content_Main, Image_Main,
Image_Width_Main, Image_Height_Main, Vertical_Space_Main, Horizontal_Space_Main,
Background_Main FROM Content, Section_Content WHERE ID = Content_ID AND Section_ID
= "+ Section__MMColParam.replace(/'/g, "\'") + "";
```

When you are finished you should be able to test your page, click on any of the items, and have the payment button appear beneath the title for that item, as shown in Figure 18-20.

Figure 18-20

How It Works

Now that you have switched the values of 111, 222, and 333 with dynamic values from the database, and changed your SQL statement, it makes a little more sense to test the page and click the Buy Now button. At this point, for instance, if you select Item One and click the Buy Now button, you would be purchasing Item One for $5. This is definitely a better deal then 111 for $333, but go ahead and create some items of your own to sell after you complete this chapter.

By default the form that appears in the main viewing frame of your site when a user clicks the Buy Now button replaces the current page's content. If your Building Block structure has a larger main frame than the sample files, this might be absolutely ideal for you. The user can purchase the item without leaving your frame structure. You might feel that opening the form in the frame is a bit restricting, in which case you can always choose to open the form in a new browser window.

Try It Out   Opening PayPal in a New Browser Window

It is actually quite simple to get the form to appear in a new window. You simply need to add the line in the `form` field in `blockMainPayPal.asp` to open in a new window as opposed to the current window.

Add `target="_blank"` to the starting `<form>` tag. When you are finished it should look like this:

```
<form action="https://www.paypal.com/cgi-bin/Webscr" target="_blank"
    method="post">
```

Now when you click the Buy Now button, a new browser window is launched which can be expanded to fill the screen, as shown in Figure 18-21. Our usual policy is not to open new windows, if possible, in an effort to keep the user's focus in one place. In this case, however, it would be much more troublesome to fill out the form in the small space of the main viewing area. It makes more sense to open the new window so the user has plenty of room to see the entire PayPal screen.

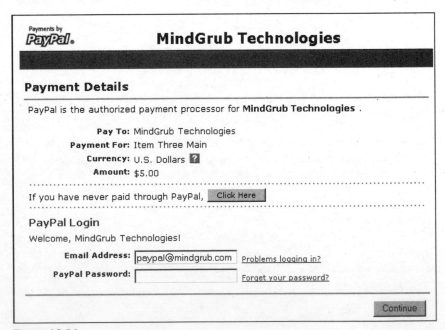

Figure 18-21

How It Works

You added a Price field in the Content table to store your prices. The more types of data you store in the Content table, the more you should redesign your database to contain the different types. Otherwise, you will have a lot of content data for which price is meaningless, such as news items. To do this you could create a ContentSaleItems table, or a ContentNews table, and so on. In the additional content files you create, such as blockMainPayPal, you would create the recordset from the ContentSaleItems table as opposed to the Content table.

When adding PayPal functionality to your page, you used the single item purchase button. In fact, all of the buttons in the Insert menu for the PayPal extension more or less perform the same task. The slight difference is that they send slightly different values to the WebAssist wizard. If, for instance, you had selected the button to add an item to the cart as opposed to a single item purchase, the user would be shown a shopping cart before checking out, as shown in Figure 18-22. This way they can purchase multiple items from your site at the same time.

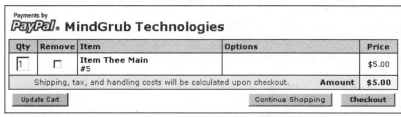

Figure 18-22

PayPal, on its end, creates an acceptance page that knows what information to display based on particular variables that are passed to that page. In the case of the WebAssist wizard, it takes care of all the variables that need to be sent; you simply fill out the form.

When the user clicks on the button to submit the form, those variables are sent to PayPal's Web site to an HTTPS server. An HTTPS server is different from a typical HTTP server in that all information passed is encrypted. In this fashion, PayPal can accept a user's credit card details and not worry much about hackers trying to view the credit card numbers as they are passed from the Web page to the server. When you open PayPal's Web site to pay for an item, the browser should show you a security alert to let you know you are entering a secure site.

PayPal provides a great way for developers to add e-commerce functionality to their sites without having to contract with a local bank and monitor all of the online banking transactions. PayPal makes it really easy because they send you an e-mail when the user has paid, so you can ship good ol' Item Three out the door with confidence.

Summary

In this chapter you learned how to find and implement an e-commerce extension in Dreamweaver. Of course, each extension is different. Anybody can take these tools and create a highly dynamic Web site for any purpose.

Building Block Technology provides the means to develop something once and simply reuse it for additional projects. As you create new pages in the future, such as the `blockMainpayPal.asp` page you created in this chapter, you can store those pages in a central folder and reuse them as needed in your future work. This eliminates the need to reinvent the wheel with every project and save yourself a lot of time and money in the process.

Why Not Try . . .

Come up with some things to sell and replace those with Items One through Five. As lucrative as those items seem, not one person bought any of them when the first edition of this book came out.

Go through the Macromedia Exchange and find five other extensions that you think would be useful. Install those extensions as you installed the PayPal extension. Create a page to utilize those extensions. From there, incorporate this new page into your Building Block structure.

After using others' components for some time and honing your HTML, JavaScript, and maybe even XML abilities, create some of your own extensions. If they are useful, then share and share alike and post those gems on the Macromedia Exchange.

Dreamweaver MX 2004 has made great strides to allow users to create their own extensions for use with Dreamweaver. As long as you understand HTML, JavaScript, and XML, you can begin customizing and extending Dreamweaver. Add your own custom icons to the Insert tab, add new items to the navigation menus, as well as create new forms to prompt for links, content, color selections, or any additional customization options you can think of.

Dreamweaver MX 2004 is extensible largely because it was created using a solid Document Object Model (DOM). This simply means there is a standardized means of adding to the application or accessing the information within the application. The bulk of the instructions for adding particular items, as we mentioned previously, are found within the `.mxi` files that ship with each component.

When an extension is added to Dreamweaver, it is placed within the Configuration folder (`C:\Program Files\Macromedia\Dreamweaver MX\Configuration`). Before you create the elements of your own extension, read through a few of the `.mxi` files used in conjunction with these extensions, found within the Extensions folder in this directory.

In the `.mxi` files you will find XML information that instructs the Extension Manager where to place all of the files included with the extension, as well as information to display within the Extension Manager and Dreamweaver itself. There are folders designated for Commands, Inspectors, Objects, and Shared Items, and you should dig around to see how previously installed extensions have made use of each.

Additional Resources

Here are a few good places to look for extensions:

❑ Macromedia Exchange (`www.macromedia.com/exchange`)

❑ The Dreamweaver Team Extensions (`www.dwteam.com/extensions`)

❑   Rabi's Dreamweaver Extensions (`www.dreamweaver-extensions.com`)

❑   Joseph Lowery's Dreamweaver Extensions Database (`www.idest.com/cgi-bin/database.cgi`)

You can, in addition, read up on creating your own extensions in a number of resources, including the PDF version of Macromedia's `mxi_file_format` file, available at `http://download.macromedia.com/pub/dw_exchange/mxi_file_format.pdf`.

There are also several sites and groups dedicated to extending not just Dreamweaver but applications in general. A good starting place is to join the Macromedia Dreamweaver Extensibility newsgroup (`www.macromedia.com/support/dreamweaver/extend/form`) and venture out from there.

Have fun!

Part IV: Appendixes

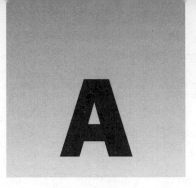

Using ASP.NET with Dreamweaver MX 2004

ASP.NET combines the Microsoft .NET development environment with traditional Active Server Pages (ASP) technology. You can use ASP.NET to build much more powerful Web applications with greater functionality, with greater ease, and in less time than ASP. What makes ASP.NET different from ASP is that you can program it with a variety of powerful programming languages such as Visual Basic .NET, C# .NET, and C++ .NET. This gives you greater flexibility and, because these are object-oriented languages, yields quicker development time.

A full discussion of ASP.NET is well beyond the scope of this appendix. We will take just a brief look at how Dreamweaver MX 2004 assists in developing ASP.NET pages. You will discover that, by knowing just a few simple concepts, you can build ASP.NET pages with little or no involvement with code.

What You Need

To use ASP.NET, you must have IIS (Internet Information Services) and the .NET Framework installed. We discussed the installation of IIS in Chapter 1. The .NET Framework is available, free of charge, from www.microsoft.com/net/basics/framework.asp.

The .NET Framework installation program analyzes your operating system and prompts you for any additional files that might be needed from your operating system CD.

> *Currently, ASP.NET only runs on Windows and IIS. However, there are open source projects developing versions of ASP.NET to run on Linux and other operating systems. If you're interested, you can find details about the Mono project at* www.go-mono.com.

As you progress through this appendix, we assume that you have worked through the book and therefore understand the general concepts and principles of dynamic Web sites. This allows us to concentrate on getting your ASP.NET pages up and running quickly.

Setting Up the Site

Like the ASP sites you created in the book, your ASP.NET site needs to run from the IIS server root directory. To set up an ASP.NET version of The Cooking Place Web site you created in Section 1, follow these steps:

1. Unzip the files for this tutorial underneath the folder `C:\intepup\wwwroot`. This creates the structure `C:\inetpub\wwwroot\thecookingplaceaspnet`. The files contain an Access database called Recipes, the `images` folder, and a template (in the `template` folder) called `myLook`.

2. Launch Dreamweaver MX 2004 and close the empty Open Document dialog box if necessary. Start a new site as discussed in Chapter 2. Your first screen should look like Figure A-1.

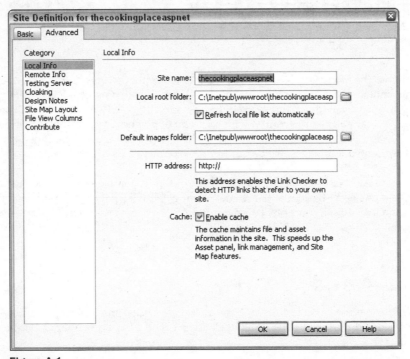

Figure A-1

3. Click the Advanced tab. In the Local Info category, fill in the fields as shown in Figure A-1. For purposes of this tutorial, you do not need a default images folder.

4. Switch to the Remote Info category and fill in the fields as shown in Figure A-2.

    You won't need to set the upload and refresh options because you are already using the root folder and there is nothing to Put.

5. Switch to the Testing Server category and fill in the fields as shown in Figure A-3.

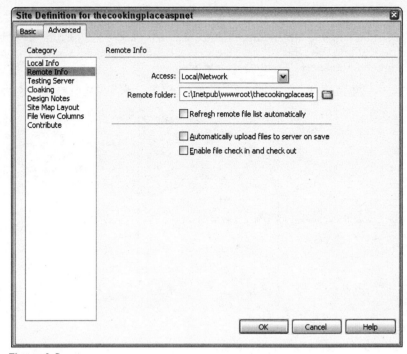

Figure A-2

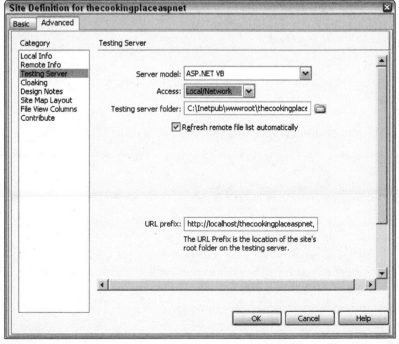

Figure A-3

Select ASP.NET VB as the server model. The .NET environment can work with two main languages: Visual Basic .NET (VB.NET) and C#. Microsoft created multiple languages to accommodate programmers from different backgrounds. The syntax of VB.NET is very close to that of Visual Basic 6, and the syntax of C# is very close to that of Java and C++. If you are more comfortable with Java, select C# as the server model.

6. Once all the fields are filled in, click OK. The Files panel should now resemble Figure A-4.

Figure A-4

Your site is now defined and ready to start working.

Setting Up an ASP.NET Page

You are now ready to set up your first .NET page. This example is a simple one to illustrate fundamental concepts:

1. Select File⇨New to see the New Document dialog box shown in Figure A-5.

2. Select the Dynamic page category and choose ASP.NET VB as the dynamic page type.

3. If you switch to Code view, you'll see this first line of code:

```
<%@ Page Language="VB" ContentType="text/html" ResponseEncoding="iso-8859-1" %>
```

This line defines the page as containing VB.NET code. If you selected ASP.NET C# as your dynamic file type, this line would show Language="C#" instead.

4. Switch back to Design view. Using the Assets panel, select the myLook template from the Templates category and apply it to this page. The page should now look like Figure A-6.

This page, with the template, is based on The Cooking Place site you created earlier in the book. The template contains a two-column table in an editable region. You will place data from a database into this area.

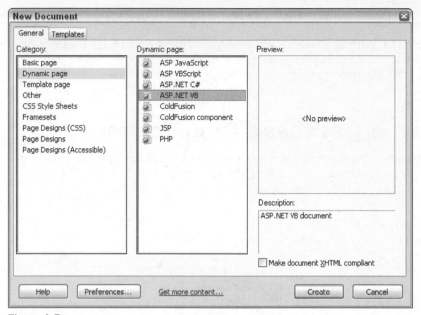

Figure A-5

Figure A-6

For the purposes of this exercise, the buttons are not functional.

5. Save this file as **recipes.aspx**.

When you created ASP pages earlier in the book you saved them with the file extension .asp so that the Web server would recognize dynamic pages in your site. Similarly, ASP.NET pages use the file extension .aspx so that the Web server recognizes such pages and performs the necessary processing.

Creating a Database Connection

Now you're ready to connect to a database so that you can fill your ASP.NET page with some interesting data. At this point, things start to get a little different from what you did in ASP, but if you follow these steps, you won't have any problem:

1. Open the Application panel group and select the Bindings panel.

2. Steps 1, 2, and 3 of the check list should be completed, as shown in Figure A-7.

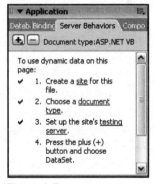

Figure A-7

3. Click Deploy, located toward the bottom of the Bindings panel, to open the Deploy Supporting Files to Testing Server dialog box shown in Figure A-8.

Figure A-8

This establishes a connection between Dreamweaver and the .NET Framework. You only need to do this once. Don't change any settings; simply click Deploy.

4. After clicking Deploy, you will see a dialog box confirming whether or not the file is deployed. (It doesn't hurt to check the deployment every once in a while just in case a file has been corrupted or deleted.)

5. Click the plus (+) button located in the upper-left corner of the Bindings panel and select Dataset (Query). You'll see the DataSet dialog box shown in Figure A-9.

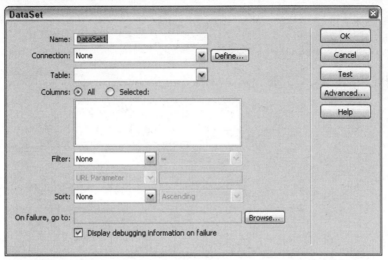

Figure A-9

6. Name the dataset **recipeList**.

7. Click the Define button next to the Connection field, and you'll see the Connections for Site dialog box shown in Figure A-10.

Figure A-10

8. Click New and then select OLE DB Connection. The dialog box in Figure A-11 appears.

OLE DB Connection
Connection name: recipes
Connection string:
Build...
Templates...
OK
Cancel
Advanced...
Test
Help
Connection information is saved in the web.config file in the site's local root folder. If the testing server is not this computer and it has a version of web.config, you may wish to copy it to this computer before proceeding. After creating a connection, copy the local version of web.config back to the testing server.

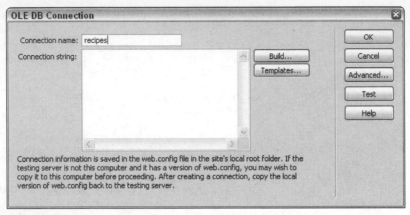

Figure A-11

9. Name the connection **recipes** and then click the Templates button. The Connection String Template dialog box shown in Figure A-12 appears. Select Microsoft Access 2000 (Microsoft Jet 4.0 Provider) from the list.

Connection String Template
Select template:
Oracle (Microsoft Provider)
Oracle (Oracle Provider)
Microsoft SQL Server
Microsoft Access 97 (Microsoft Jet 3.5 Provider)
Microsoft Access 2000 (Microsoft Jet 4.0 Provider)
UDL file
OK
Cancel
Help

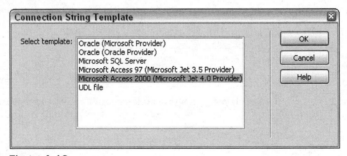

Figure A-12

10. After you click OK, your OLE DB Connection dialog box looks like Figure A-13.

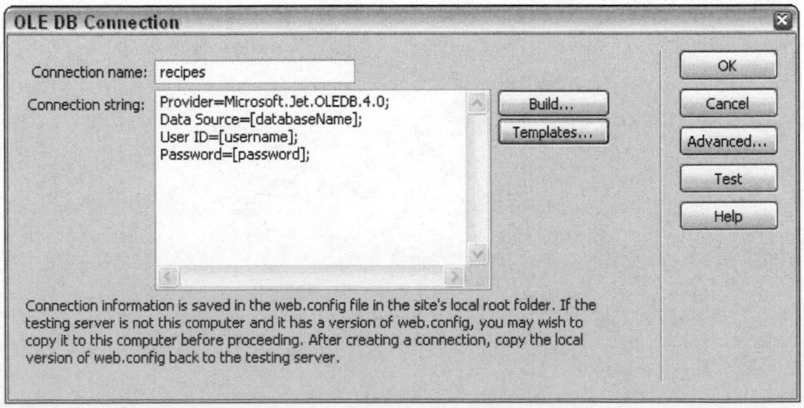

OLE DB Connection
Connection name: recipes
Connection string:
Provider=Microsoft.Jet.OLEDB.4.0;
Data Source=[databaseName];
User ID=[username];
Password=[password];
Build...
Templates...
OK
Cancel
Advanced...
Test
Help
Connection information is saved in the web.config file in the site's local root folder. If the testing server is not this computer and it has a version of web.config, you may wish to copy it to this computer before proceeding. After creating a connection, copy the local version of web.config back to the testing server.

Figure A-13

11. This is where things start to get a little tricky. Delete everything in the connection string after the phrase `Data Source=`. You can do this because you do not need a user ID or password for this database. The connection string should now look like Figure A-14.

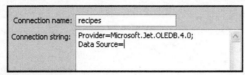

Figure A-14

12. After `Data Source=`, type the path to the database file: **C:\inetpub\wwwroot\thecooking-placeaspnet\recipe.mdb**

13. After you type this string, test your connection by clicking Test. If the connection is made successfully, you'll see the dialog box shown in Figure A-15.

Figure A-15

If the connection is not successful, you should double-check that you entered the correct path to the database in Step 12.

14. Click OK to close the dialog box informing you of the successful connection.

15. Click OK to close the OLE DB Connection dialog box, and then click Done to close the remaining connections box. In the resulting DataSet dialog box (see Figure A-16), select the **recipes** connection you just created for the Connection.

The database for this example is quite small. It has only one table (recipes) and two columns (Recipe and region).

Select the recipes table and All the columns. If you want, you can set a Sort on Region for Ascending but it isn't necessary to use any of the SQL filters discussed earlier in the book.

16. Click OK. From this point on, things will be pretty similar to how you did them earlier in ASP.

17. Click the plus (+) to expand the dataset. You'll see two fields in the Bindings panel, as shown in Figure A-17.

18. Drag the region field into the first cell of the table and the Recipe field into the second cell, as shown in Figure A-18.

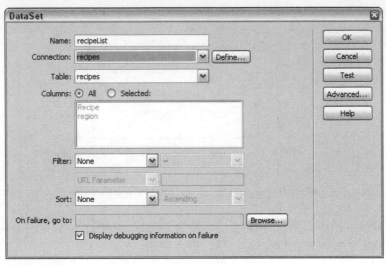

Figure A-16

Figure A-17

Figure A-18

19. Preview the data by clicking the Live Data view button (see Figure A-19).

Figure A-19

At this point, you only see one row of data. You can easily remedy that, if you recall, by controlling the server behaviors.

20. Shut off the Live Data view and highlight the data row, but do *not* highlight the header row because you do not want the headings to repeat.

21. Select the Server Behaviors panel and then click the plus (+) in the upper-left corner. Select Repeat Region. The Repeat Region dialog box in Figure A-20 appears.

Figure A-20

22. Click OK and then select Live Data view again. Your table should now resemble Figure A-21. Just as in ASP, you can add server behaviors to move around multiple pages of data.

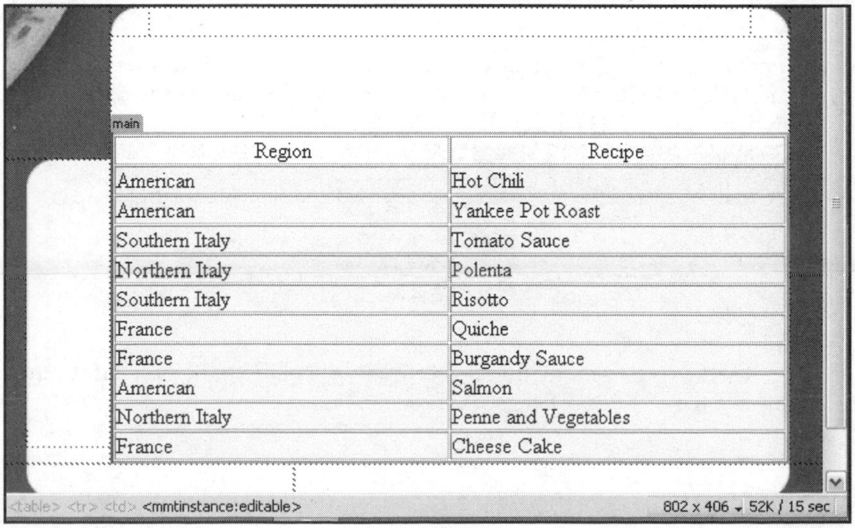

Region	Recipe
American	Hot Chili
American	Yankee Pot Roast
Southern Italy	Tomato Sauce
Northern Italy	Polenta
Southern Italy	Risotto
France	Quiche
France	Burgandy Sauce
American	Salmon
Northern Italy	Penne and Vegetables
France	Cheese Cake

Figure A-21

23.   Save the page and then preview it in your browser.

> You just developed an ASP.NET page and ran it. The great thing was that you did
> not need to touch the code at all. Dreamweaver handled it automatically.

If Something Goes Wrong

If, for some reason, things do not go as planned, if may be because the .NET Framework was not
installed properly. Your first step is to double-check your installation procedure. It is beyond the scope of
this book to examine all the possible things that could go wrong. However, a common problem occurs
when you install the .NET Framework while an anti-virus program is running. This could lead to
improper installation into the Windows Registry. Microsoft has developed a fix for this, the details of
which you can find in a Microsoft Knowledge Base article called "HOWTO: Repair IIS Mapping After
You Remove and Reinstall IIS" at `http://support.microsoft.com/?id=306005`. This procedure can
fix a whole range of problems.

Finding .NET Tools

You may not have noticed this but when Dreamweaver saw you were defining an ASP NET VB page, it
placed another panel, called ASP.NET, in the Insert panel group (see Figure A-22).

Figure A-22

This new panel contains most of the tools you need to build an ASP.NET form. For the most part, these
form controls are identical to what you used in ASP, although here each of the controls is prefaced by the
letters *asp,* as shown in Figure A-23 for Button.

Figure A-23

Dreamweaver handles the coding for all these controls. By clicking on the very last button on the panel
you will see a complete list of ASP.NET tags, as shown in Figure A-24.

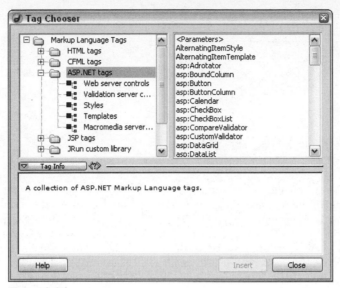

Figure A-24

The complete list of .NET tags appear in the Tag Chooser, divided into categories based on their function.

Further Reading

We hope this short tutorial shows you that moving to ASP.NET is not as intimidating as it may first seem. The process is not hugely different from working with ASP, and Dreamweaver makes the process flow effortlessly.

If you're interested in learning more about ASP.NET, these books provide you with introductory tutorials:

❑   *Beginning ASP.NET 1.0 with C#* by Chris Goode et al. (Wrox, 2002)

❑   *Beginning ASP.NET 1.0 with Visual Basic .NET* by Chris Goode et al. (Wrox, 2002)

You can also find out more about ASP.NET at these Web sites:

❑   www.asp.net

❑   http://msdn.microsoft.com/net

Using PHP and MySQL with Dreamweaver MX 2004

PHP is a scripting language for building interactive and dynamic Web sites. Like ASP, PHP instructions are embedded within the HTML code. Unlike ASP, it is supported on just about any Web server and platform you can think of—and usually doesn't require high system specifications. Because of its flexibility and ease of use, PHP has become the workhorse of the Internet. Because PHP is free and can run on fairly low-end Linux boxes, many Web hosting companies support PHP for much less cost than they do ASP—making it ideal for budget-conscious Webmasters.

What You Need

PHP installs easily in either Windows or UNIX environments. However, you do need a Web server to run it. If you are running Windows NT, Windows 2000, or Windows XP Professional, you can use IIS (Internet Information Services) to run it. If you do not want to use IIS, or you are a UNIX user, you can use the Apache server, which is available from www.apache.org. (Detailed instructions for installing this server can be found in Appendix C.)

You will also need PHP itself, which consists of a language interpreter and code library. This is available from www.php.net. There are many different installations available, some of which include the full source code. Choose the one that best suits your computer and personal preferences. If you are a beginner, install the binary version with the installer.

The MySQL database server goes with PHP like eggs and ham. Both are free, run on a variety of platforms, and are quick and easy to learn. You can pick up MySQL from www.mysql.com. You need to install it according to the instructions on the site. Again, if you are a beginner, install the binary version with the installer.

For this tutorial, you will need to create a recipes database with a table called Recipes. That table contains two text fields: Region and Recipe. Once you have the table set up, you can either make up some data to practice with or import the data from the recipes.txt file found in the downloaded files for this book.

Dreamweaver MX 2004 and PHP

You may be wondering why we are putting you through all the trouble of learning MySQL. Why not just connect to an Access database like the rest of this book does?

As we said from the outset, PHP and MySQL are very closely linked. Because of this, Dreamweaver MX 2004 supports only a MySQL database connection when developing a PHP site. Other connections are possible but Dreamweaver does not support them and they are beyond the scope of this book. We strongly suggest that you refer to the PHP site referenced above for instructions on how to make alternative database connection.

Preparing the Database

Unlike programs such as Microsoft Access, MySQL does not install itself in the operating system's environment. For that reason, you need to do a bit of work to create and populate your database. Since our real focus is Dreamweaver, this will just be a quick tutorial and not an extensive discussion of MySQL's intricacies.

Assuming you have MySQL and PHP installed properly, begin by starting MySQL. For this exercise, we assume that you installed MySQL under `c:\mysql`.

1. Open Windows Explorer and navigate to `c:\mysql\bin`. Your screen should contain something like the icon shown in Figure B-1.

2. Double-click on the Administrator tool. While starting the server up, you will see the administrator appear briefly on your screen and then create a traffic light icon in your system tray. That icon indicates that it is running. If you click the traffic light and select Show Me, you should see the Administration window shown in Figure B-2.

3. You don't need to do anything with the administrator for this exercise. Instead, you will be working from the command prompt. Open your command prompt and maneuver to the `C:\mysql\bin` directory (or whatever directory MySQL is installed in on your computer). To test if the server is working properly, type the following:

mysqlshow -u <your user name> -p <your password>

Use the user name and password particular to your setup and machine. Your screen command prompt should look something like Figure B-3.

4. To access the commands of MySQL, start the MySQL client by typing the following:

mysql -u <your user name> -p <your password> -h <your host name>

In many cases, you can use `localhost` as the host name. After the opening Welcome message, your prompt should change to `mysql>`, as shown in Figure B-4.

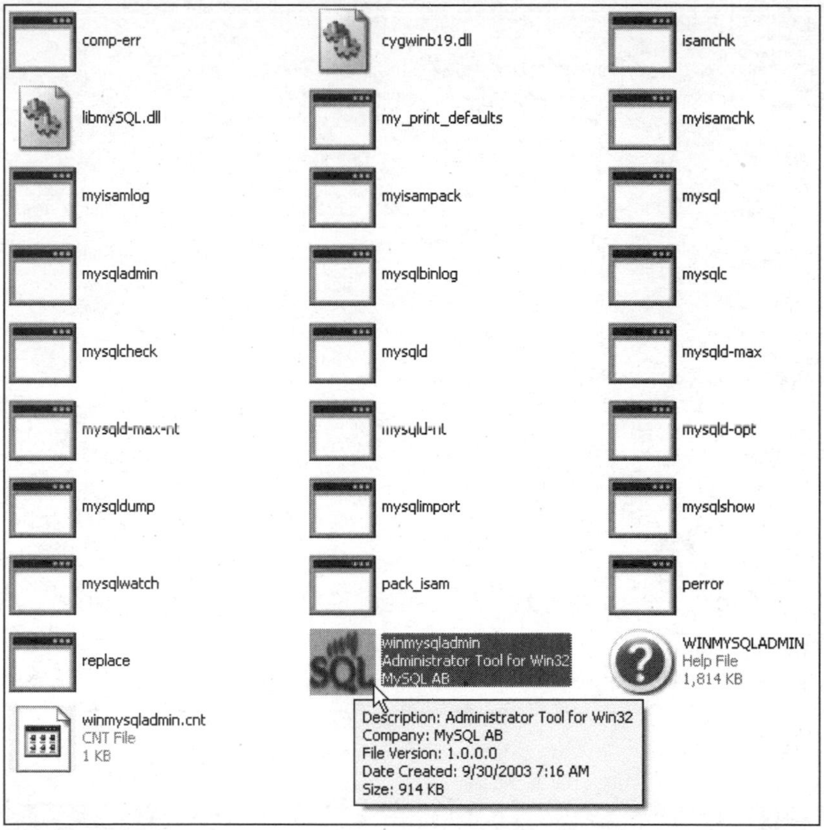

Figure B-1

5. You are now ready to create your database. At the mysql prompt, type the following:

CREATE DATABASE recipes;

Note the semicolon at the end of the CREATE command. Capitalization is not required; it is just accepted convention. You should receive a confirmation message that the database has been created.

6. Activate the database by typing the following:

USE recipes;

You should now receive a prompt saying the database was changed.

7. Place a table in the database to hold your data. This table is a simple one with only two fields: Region and Recipe. They are both text fields: Region is 15 characters in length and Recipe is 25 characters in length. Name the table **tblRecipes**. Create it by typing the following at the mysql prompt:

CREATE TABLE tblRecipes (region CHAR(15), recipe CHAR(25));

You should receive a confirmation message.

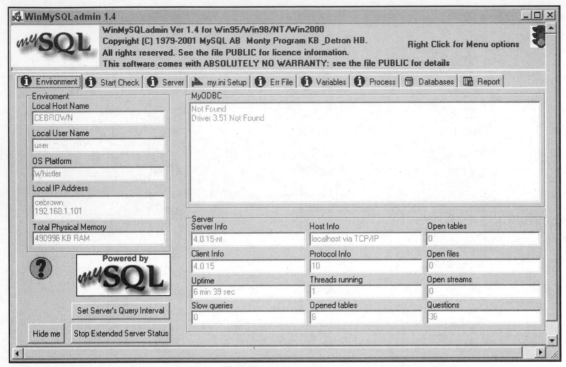

Figure B-2

Figure B-3

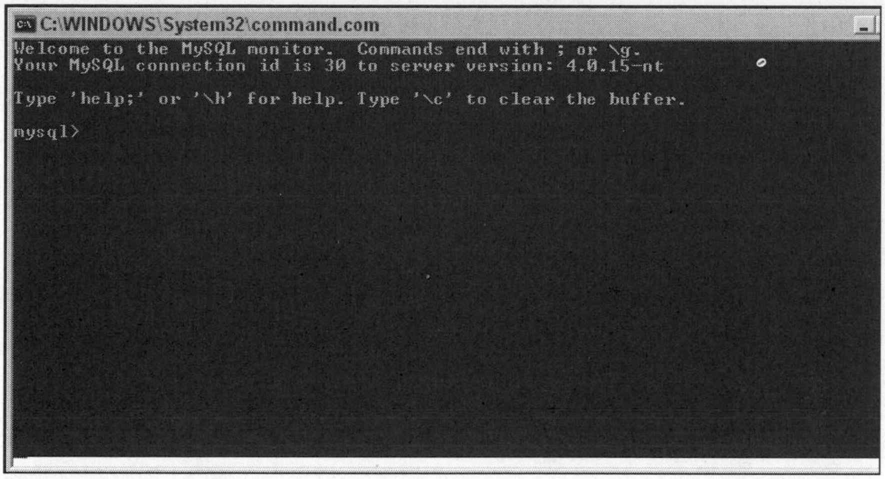

Figure B-4

8. Insert some data into your database. At the prompt, type the following:

INSERT INTO tblRecipes VALUES ('American', 'Hot Chili');

After pressing Enter, you should receive a confirmation that the row was added.

9. To repeat the process, press the up arrow key to return to the previous command and change the values to insert each of the following pairs of values into the table:

- ❑ 'American', 'Yankee Pot Roast'
- ❑ 'Southern Italy', 'Tomato Sauce'
- ❑ 'Northern Italy', 'Polenta'
- ❑ 'Southern Italy', 'Risotto'
- ❑ 'France', 'Quiche'
- ❑ 'France', 'Burgundy Sauce'
- ❑ 'American', 'Salmon'
- ❑ 'Northern Italy', 'Penne and Vegetables'
- ❑ 'France', Cheese Cake'
- ❑ 'American', 'Pumpkin Muffins'
- ❑ 'France', 'Bouillabaisse'

10. Once you're done, type **quit** to leave the client and close the command prompt window.

Setting Up the Site

Like many of the other sites in this book, a PHP site needs to run from the IIS server root directory:

1. Unzip the files for this tutorial underneath the folder `C:\inetpub\wwwroot`. This creates the structure `C:\inetpub\wwwroot\thecookingplacephp`.

2. Launch Dreamweaver MX 2004 and close the empty document if necessary. Using the menu bar, define a new site as described in Chapter 1.

3. On the Advanced tab, in the Local Info category, fill in the fields as shown in Figure B-5.

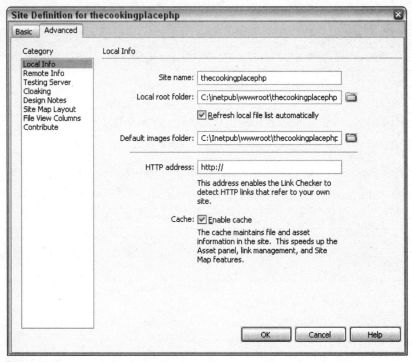

Figure B-5

4. Switch to the Remote Info category and fill in the fields as shown in the Figure B-6. Since you are using the IIS root as the local directory, it is not necessary to select the Automatically Upload Files to Server on Save option. Also, you can leave the Check In Check Out option unchecked.

5. Switch to the Testing Server category and fill in the fields as shown in Figure B-7.

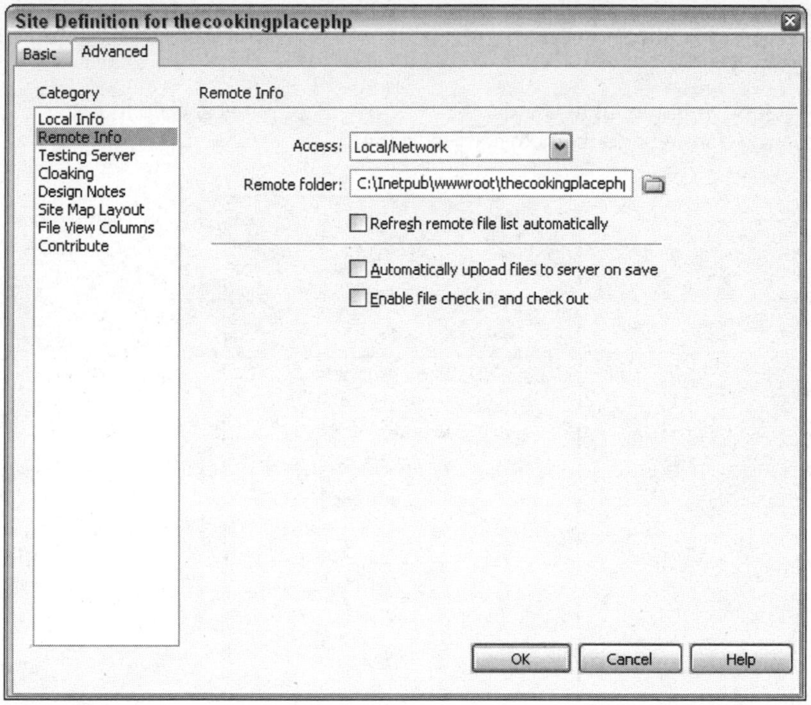

Site Definition for thecookingplacephp

Basic | Advanced

Category

- Local Info
- Remote Info
- Testing Server
- Cloaking
- Design Notes
- Site Map Layout
- File View Columns
- Contribute

Remote Info

Access: Local/Network

Remote folder: C:\Inetpub\wwwroot\thecookingplacephp

☐ Refresh remote file list automatically

☐ Automatically upload files to server on save
☐ Enable file check in and check out

OK | Cancel | Help

Figure B-6

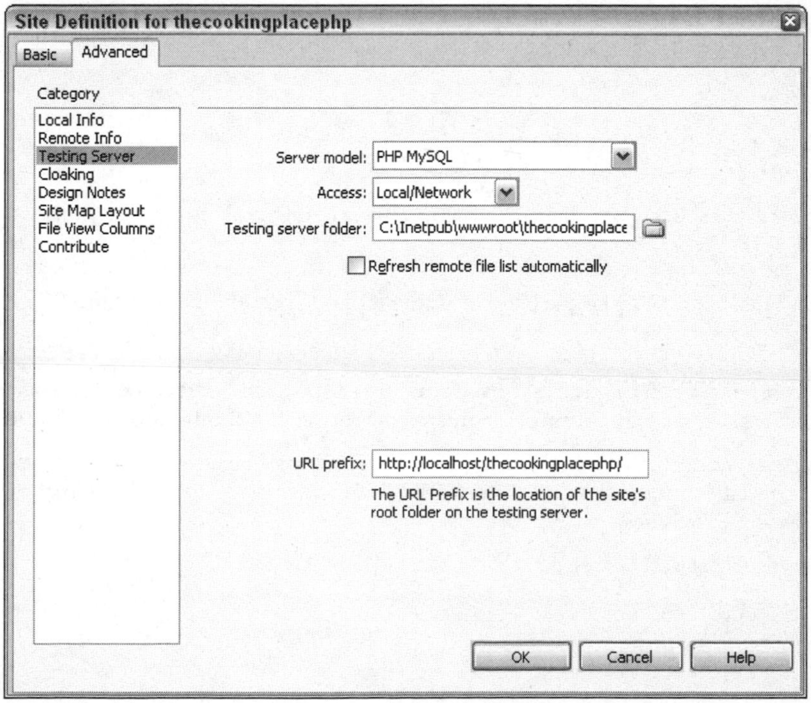

Site Definition for thecookingplacephp

Basic | Advanced

Category

- Local Info
- Remote Info
- Testing Server
- Cloaking
- Design Notes
- Site Map Layout
- File View Columns
- Contribute

Server model: PHP MySQL

Access: Local/Network

Testing server folder: C:\Inetpub\wwwroot\thecookingplace

☐ Refresh remote file list automatically

URL prefix: http://localhost/thecookingplacephp/

The URL Prefix is the location of the site's
root folder on the testing server.

OK | Cancel | Help

Figure B-7

Like many of the other examples in the book, your site runs under the URL http://localhost. Just fill in **thecookingplacephp/** after it. (Note that in basic setup, you can test this prefix.)

6. Once you've filled in all the fields, click OK. The Files panel should look like Figure B-8. Your site is now defined and ready to start working.

Figure B-8

Setting Up a PHP Page

You are now ready to set up your first PHP page. This example is a simple one to illustrate fundamental concepts:

1. Select File⇨New to open the New Document dialog box shown in Figure B-9.

2. Select the Dynamic Page category and select PHP as the dynamic page type.

3. If necessary, switch to Design view. Using the Assets panel, select the myLook template from the Templates category and apply it to this page. The results should look like Figure B-10.

   This page, with the template, is based on The Cooking Place site you created earlier in the book. The template contains a two-column table in an editable region. You can place data from a database into this area.

4. Save this file as **recipes.php**.

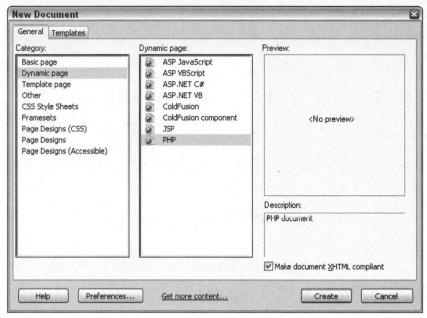

Figure B-9

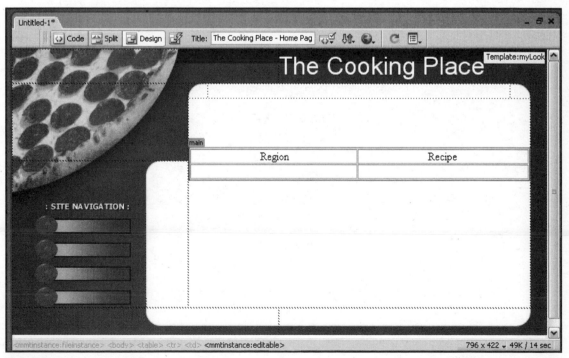

Figure B-10

When you created ASP pages earlier in the book you saved them with the file extension .asp so that the Web server would recognize dynamic pages in your site. Similarly, PHP pages use the file extension .php so that the Web server recognizes such pages and performs the necessary processing.

Creating a Database Connection

PHP is compatible with the MySQL database server and Dreamweaver recognizes that compatibility in making the database connection. This connection is very easy to make:

1. Return to the Dreamweaver PHP page you created earlier. Open the Database panel in the Application panel group, as shown in Figure B-11.

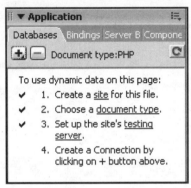

Figure B-11

2. Click the plus (+) located in the upper-left corner (see Figure B-12).

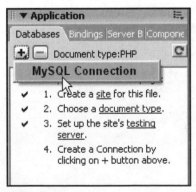

Figure B-12

3. Notice that the only choice is MySQL Connection. Select it and then see the MySQL Connection dialog box.

4. As shown in Figure B-13, name the connection **connRecipes**. For most MySQL Server connections used as a testing server, the MySQL server name is **localhost**. (Note that this won't work unless the PHP server is running also.) Enter the user name and password you selected when setting up MySQL.

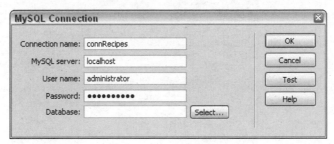

Figure B-13

5. For the Database field, either enter the name or click the Select button. You should see something like Figure B-14.

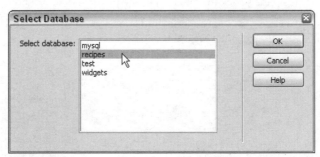

Figure B-14

6. Select recipes and click OK. You will be returned to the Connection panel.

7. Test your connection by using the Test button. If all is successful, you should get the message shown in Figure B-15.

Figure B-15

8. Click OK twice. Your Databases panel should now reflect the Recipes database structure as shown in Figure B-16.

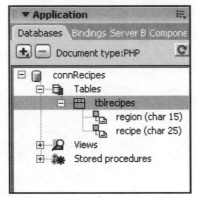

Figure B-16

9. Select the Bindings panel, click the plus (+) in the upper left, and then select Recordset (Query).

10. Name the recordset **recipes** (or any name you choose) and select **connRecipes** as the connection. The screen should look like Figure B-17.

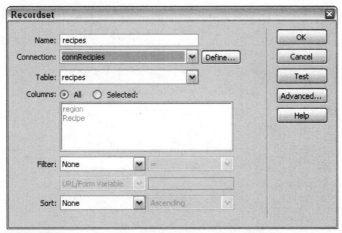

Figure B-17

The database is really small for this example. It just has one table (Recipes) with two columns (Recipe and Region).

11. Select the table and all the columns. If you want, set a Sort on Region for Ascending. It is not necessary to use any of the SQL filters discussed earlier in the book. Click OK.

From this point on, things are pretty much the same as you learned in ASP. The Bindings panel should now look like Figure B-18.

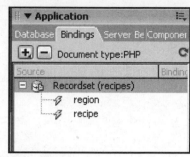

Figure B-18

12. Drag the Region field into the first cell of the table and the Recipe field into the second cell. Your finished result should look like Figure B-19.

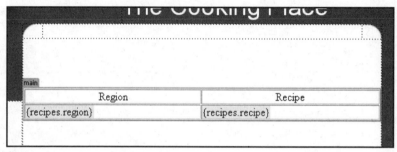

Figure B-19

13. Preview your data by using the Live Data view button, shown in Figure B-20. You are only seeing one row of your data. You can easily remedy that by controlling the server behaviors.

Figure B-20

14. Shut off the Live Data view and highlight the data row, but do *not* highlight the header row because you do not want the data to repeat.

15. Click plus (+) in the upper left of the Behaviors panel and then select Repeat Region. Set the dialog box that appears as shown in Figure B-21. Click OK.

Figure B-21

16. Select Live Data view again. Your page should look like Figure B-22. As in ASP, you can add server behaviors to navigate around multiple pages of data.

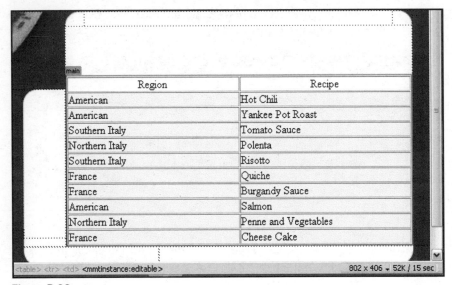

Figure B-22

17. Save the page and preview it in your browser.

> You just developed your first PHP page and ran it. The nice part is that you did not need to touch the code. Dreamweaver handled it automatically.

Finding PHP Tools

You may not have noticed this but when Dreamweaver saw that you were working in PHP, it placed an additional panel in the Insert panel group (see Figure B-23).

Figure B-23

The last button gives you only a couple of additional tags, as shown in Figure B-24.

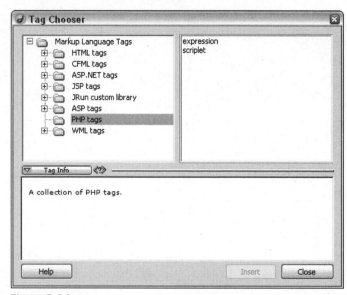

Figure B-24

Further Reading

You can learn more about PHP and MySQL from the following books:

- ❑ *Beginning PHP4* by Wankyu Choi et al. (Wrox, 2000)

- ❑ *Dreamweaver MX: PHP Web Development* by Gareth Downes-Powell (Wrox, 2002)

- ❑ *PHP and MySQL For Dummies, Second Edition* by Janet Valade (Wiley, 2004)

- ❑ *Making Use of PHP* by Ashok Appu (Wiley, 2002)

- ❑ *PHP Bible, Second Edition* by Tom Converse and Joyce Park (Wiley, 2002)

- ❑ *MySQL/PHP Database Applications, Second Edition* by Brad Bulger, Jay Greenspan, and David Wall (Wiley, 2003)

Using JavaServer Pages with Dreamweaver MX 2004

One of the most popular programming languages today is Java. This language is platform-independent and used in a variety of programming situations.

JavaServer Pages (JSP) is the ASP of the Java world. Java connects to the database through the use of the *Java Database Connection* drivers (JDBC). Of all the technologies to use, this is the most difficult to set up. However, because it's Java, it is also the most platform-independent.

In this appendix we'll have a look at how to get JSP working with Dreamweaver, using one specific setup.

What You Need

To use this technology, you need to do a bit of setting up. At the very minimum, you need to begin by installing the Java Software Developer Kit (SDK). This can be downloaded from `http://java.sun.com`.

There are three editions of the Java SDK: Java 2 Standard Edition (J2SE), Java 2 Enterprise Edition (J2EE), and the Java 2 Micro Edition (J2ME). In most situations, the Standard Edition is adequate for JSP development. In addition, you need the Standard Edition in order to install the Enterprise Edition, which extends its functionality. Once you have it installed (make note of the directory it's installed in), you need to refer to the documentation to set up the proper *environment variables* and paths based upon your operating system. If you work with either Windows 2000 or Windows XP Professional, you would:

1. Select Start⇨Control Panel.
2. Once in the Control Panel, select the System icon, go to the Advanced tab, and select Environment Variables to open the dialog box shown in Figure C-1.

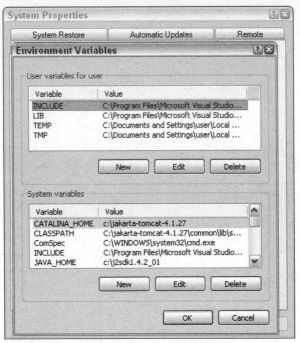

Figure C-1

3. From the lower window, scroll down and select Path. Click Edit.

4. Click in the Variable Value field and press the End key on your keyboard to get to the end of the value.

5. Type a semicolon (;) and the path of your Java directory followed by **\bin**. For example, **c:\j2skd1.4.2_01\bin**.

6. Click OK to select the change.

7. Click the New button and, for the new system variable's name, type **JAVA_HOME**. For the value, just use the top directory. For example, **c:\j2skd1.4.2_01**.

8. Click OK to select and then OK again to leave the Environment Variables screen. Finally click OK to leave the system properties. Leave the Control Panel open for now.

9. To test your Java settings, go to the command prompt and type (in all lowercase) **java -version**. If you get a prompt telling you the version of Java you have, it is working fine.

10. Once the Java environment is set up, you need to install a Java Enterprise Server for JSP to function. This serves the same function as ColdFusion, ASP Server, .NET Framework, and so on. There are several servers available that are either free or low cost. Although Macromedia has its own server, JRun, the industry standard (and a little easier for the beginner) is the Apache-Tomcat server, which you can download at http://jakarta.apache.org/tomcat.

It unzips, depending on the version you download, to a directory such as "jakarta-tomcat-4.1.27." Make note of the directory. Return to the Environment Variables panel you used for Java:

1. Create a new system variable called **CATALINA_HOME** and give as its value the directory the server is installed in. For example, **c:\jakarta-tomcat-4.1.27**.

2. After accepting that variable, create another system variable called **CLASSPATH**. Using the above example, enter it using your directory name as the following (note the semicolon at the end):

   c:\jakarta-tomcat-4.1.27\common\lib\servlet.jar;

3. Click OK until you're back at the Control Panel and then close it.

Now test your settings by going to Windows Explorer and looking for the `bin` directory under the `tomcat` directory you just created. Look for the file `startup.bat`. This opens a command window showing a number of commands occurring. Leave this window open and minimized as long as the server is running.

To test the server, go to your Web browser and give it the URL **http://localhost:8080**. You should see something like Figure C-2.

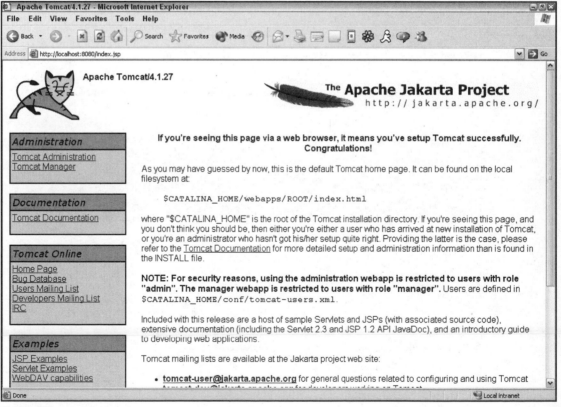

Figure C-2

If you see this, you are all set to program in JSP.

For the time being, shut down the server by either returning to the `bin` directory and selecting `shutdown.bat`, or close the command window. You can also close the preceding screen in your browser.

Setting Up the Site

Unlike your other setups in this book, this one is a little tricky. In most of your examples, you have set up your files under `c:\inetpub\wwwroot` to accommodate IIS. Since you are using the Tomcat server, you will be setting up your files under the `Webapps` directory. For example, `c:\jakarta-tomcat-4.1.27\Webapps`.

Normally this requires you to write an XML file to map the server to the correct URL. That is usually beyond the scope of most beginning users. So, instead, do a little beginner's trick of putting your files under the `Webapps\examples` directory, which has the proper XML file there ready to go. For purposes of this exercise, use the directory name of `c:\jakarta-tomcat-4.1.27\Webapps\examples` for your examples. If your directory name is different, adjust accordingly.

1. Unzip the files for this example, found at www.wrox.com to `c:\jakarta-tomcat-4.1.27\Webapps\examples`. You should now have a directory called `c:\jakarta-tomcat-4.1.27\Webapps\examples\thecookingplace`. This contains all of your image files, a database called `recipes.mdb`, and the template folder containing `myLook.dwt`.

2. Launch Dreamweaver MX 2004 and close the empty Open Document dialog box if necessary. Choose Site⇨Manage Sites⇨New⇨Site and fill in the fields as shown in Figure C-3 (assuming you use the Basic tab).

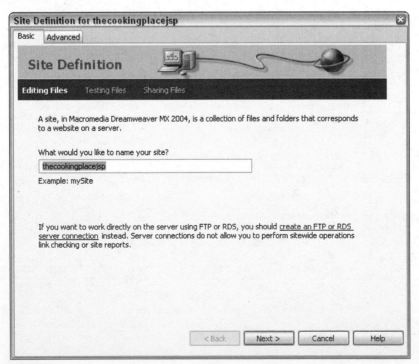

Figure C-3

3. Click Next and fill in the fields as shown in Figure C-4. This tells Dreamweaver that your choice of server technology uses the JSP model.

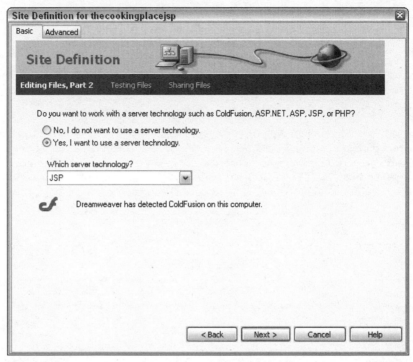

Figure C-4

4. Click Next. Here you tell Dreamweaver you will be editing the files on this machine. Select the directory you created under the Tomcat Webapps as the working directory, as shown in Figure C-5.

5. Click Next and enter the URL exactly as shown in Figure C-6:

http://localhost:8080/examples/thecookingplace/

6. Test the URL setting now. Click the Test URL button. If all is set up properly, you will get the message shown in Figure C-7. Click OK to close the message box.

Don't forget to start up the server again before testing or you will get an error message. As before, go to the server's bin *directory and run* startup.bat.

7. Click Next. Now you come to the screen shown in Figure C-8. Select Yes to choose using the remote server.

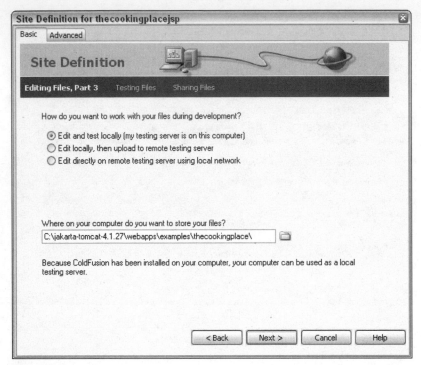

Figure C-5

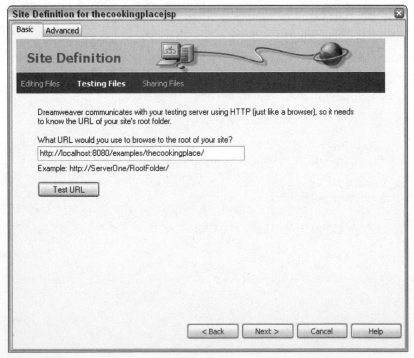

Figure C-6

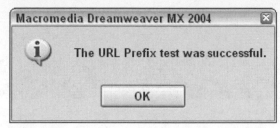

Figure C-7

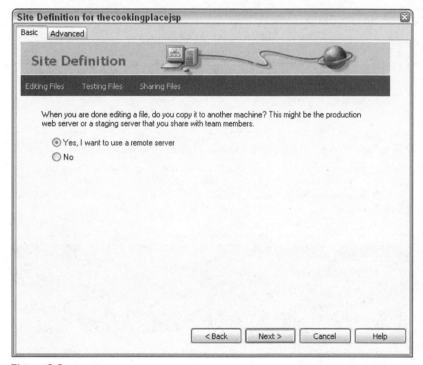

Figure C-8

8. Click Next. For this example you want to use the same directory as the remote server. Use the settings shown in Figure C-9.

9. After you click Next, select No so you don't enable Check In and Check Out, as shown in Figure C-10.

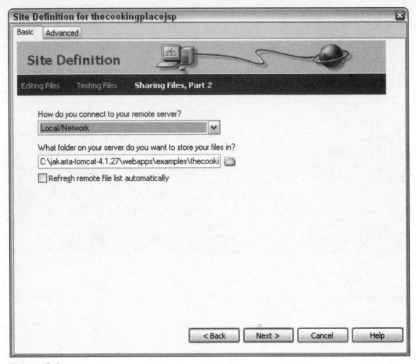

Figure C-9

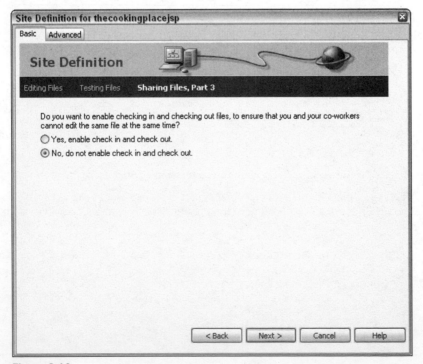

Figure C-10

10. Click Next to review your settings as shown in Figure C-11. If all is well, click Done and then click Done again to leave the Manage Site panel. Your site is now defined and ready to start working.

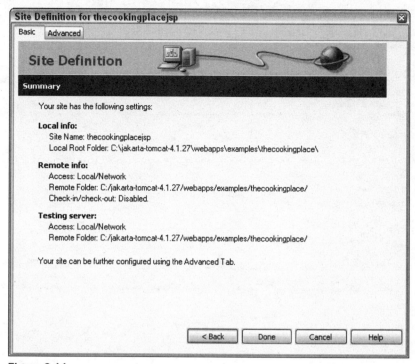

Figure C-11

Setting Up a JSP Page

You are now ready to set up your first JSP page. This example is a simple one to illustrate fundamental concepts:

1. Select File⇨New.

2. Select the Dynamic Page category and choose JSP as the dynamic page type.

3. Make sure you are in Design view. Using the Assets panel select the myLook template from the Templates category and apply it to this page. The results should look like Figure C-12.

   This page, with the template, is based on The Cooking Place site you created earlier in the book. The template contains a two-column table in an editable region. You will place data from a database into this area.

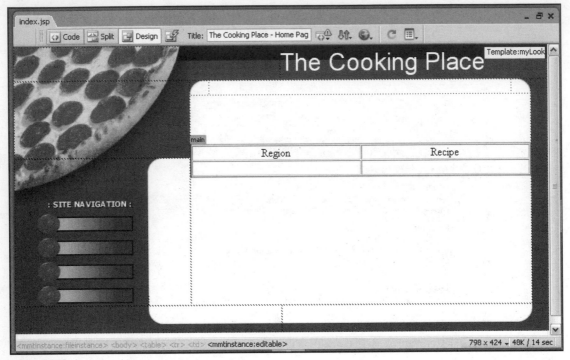

Figure C-12

4. Save the page as **index.jsp**.

When you created ASP pages earlier in the book you saved them with the file extension .asp so that the Web server would recognize dynamic pages in your site. Similarly, JSP pages use the file extension .jsp so that the Web server recognizes such pages and performs the necessary processing.

Creating a Database Connection

There are several ways you can set up your database connection. For this exercise, you will use the ODBC bridge in Windows:

1. Select Start⇨Control Panel⇨Administrative Tools⇨Data Sources (ODBC). This opens the ODBC Data Source Administrator dialog box, shown in Figure C-13.

2. Select MS Access Database / Microsoft Access Driver (*.mdb) and click Finish.

3. As shown in Figure C-14, name your Data Source Name (DSN) as **recipeData**. Click Select after you've named it.

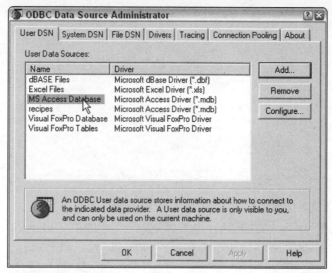

Figure C-13

Figure C-14

4. As shown in Figure C-15, navigate to the working folder in the Tomcat directory and select the file recipes.mdb. Click OK.

5. Keep clicking OK till you return to the ODBC Data Source Administrator dialog box. Close it and return to Dreamweaver. You are now all set to connect to the database. From this point on, things are pretty much the same as you learned in ASP, with one small exception.

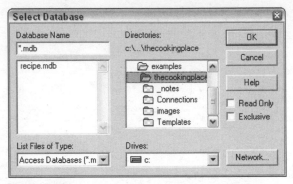

Figure C-15

6. Click on plus (+) in the Databases panel. It opens a list of the Java database connectors available in Dreamweaver MX 2004 (shown in Figure C-16).

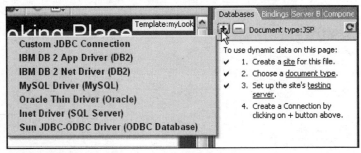

Figure C-16

7. Since you are using the ODBC bridge, select Sun JDBC-ODBC Driver (ODBC Database). Enter the settings shown in Figure C-17. Call the connection **connRecipes** (short for connection) and for the URL substitute the database name `recipes` for the OBBC name. Select the Using Driver On This Machine option.

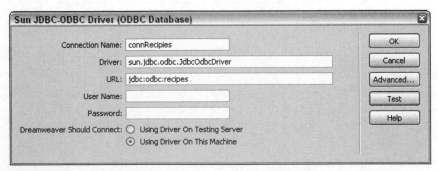

Figure C-17

8. To check the connection, click the Test button. You should get the prompt shown in Figure C-18.

Figure C-18

9. After clicking OK to close the prompt and then OK again to close the ODBC Database dialog box, the Databases panel should look like Figure C-19.

Figure C-19

10. Select the Bindings panel and click plus (+). Select Recordset (Query) to see the Recordset dialog box shown in Figure C-20.

11. Enter the settings shown in Figure C-20. For this example use the `recipes` table with all columns selected. After clicking OK, the Bindings panel should look like Figure C-21.

12. Drag the Region field into the first cell of your table and drag Recipe field into the second cell, as shown in Figure C-22.

    Before you can preview your data with the Live Data view button, use the techniques you learned at the beginning of this appendix and start the Tomcat server. If you don't, you will not be able to view your live data. Once it is started, click the Live Data view button shown in Figure C-23.

695

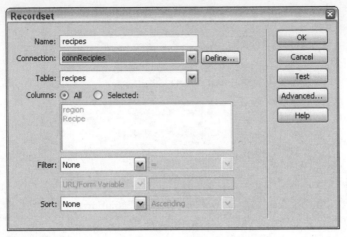

Figure C-20

Figure C-21

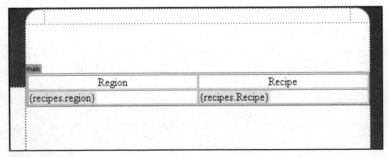

Region	Recipe
{recipes.region}	{recipes.Recipe}

Figure C-22

Figure C-23

As shown in Figure C-24, you are seeing only one row of your data. You can easily remedy that by controlling the server behaviors.

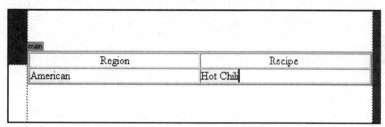

Figure C-24

13. Shut off the Live Data view and highlight the data row, but do *not* highlight the header row because you do not want the headings to repeat.

14. Select the Server Behaviors panel.

15. Click the plus (+) in the upper-left corner.

16. Select Repeat Region to open the Repeat Region dialog box shown in Figure C-25.

Figure C-25

17. Click OK. Go to Live Data view again. It should look like Figure C-26. As in ASP, you can also add server behaviors to move around multiple pages of data.

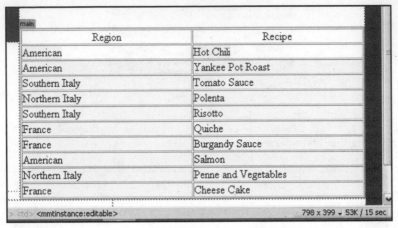

Figure C-26

18. Save the page and preview it in your browser.

> You just developed your first JSP page and ran it. The nice part is that you did not
> need to touch the code. Dreamweaver handled it automatically.

JSP Tools

When you declare the page as using JSP technology, Dreamweaver helps you out by adding a JSP panel
to the Insert panel group (shown in Figure C-27).

Figure C-27

The last button takes you to a more complete list of JSP controls, as seen in Figure C-28.

As you can see, this Tag Chooser dialog box provides a complete list of JSP tags divided into categories.

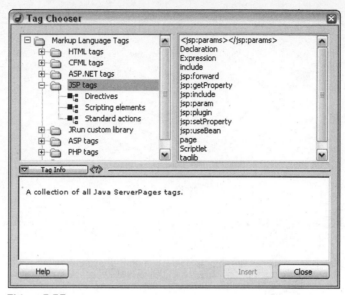

Figure C-28

Further Reading

The following books are available from Wiley publications:

- ❑ *JSP Weekend Crash Course* by Geremy Kawaller and William Massie (Wiley, 2001)

- ❑ *Mastering JSP Custom Tags and Tag Libraries* by James Goodwill (Wiley, 2002)

- ❑ *Making Use of JSP* by Madhushree Ganguli (Wiley, 2002)

- ❑ *JavaServer Pages: Your Visual Blueprint for Designing Dynamic Content with JSP* by Paul Whitehead (Wiley, 2001)

- ❑ *JSP, Servlets, and MySQL* by David Harms (Wiley, 2001)

Using ColdFusion MX with Dreamweaver MX 2004

ColdFusion MX is a server-side platform developed by Macromedia for the Macromedia Studio MX environment. ColdFusion MX connects seamlessly with the other MX products, including Dreamweaver MX 2004 and Flash MX. This close relationship opens up a number of new possibilities for Web design and development.

A full discussion of ColdFusion MX is well beyond the scope of this appendix. We will take just a brief look at how Dreamweaver assists in developing ColdFusion pages. You will discover that by knowing just a few simple concepts, you can build ColdFusion pages with little or no involvement with code.

What You Need

In order to use ColdFusion, you must have a ColdFusion server installed. This is available free of charge from Macromedia at www.macromedia.com/software/trial_download/. The trial download is for the Enterprise Edition. After 30 days it becomes a fully functioning Developer Edition with a limited development license (local development purposes only).

There are two ways to install the server: as part of IIS or in standalone mode. Refer to the documentation from Macromedia to understand the differences fully.

As you progress through this appendix, we assume that the ColdFusion server is installed as part of IIS. However, we'll give you some things to watch out for in standalone mode.

Setting Up the Site

Like the ASP sites you created in the book, your site needs to run from the IIS server root directory. To set up a ColdFusion MX version of The Cooking Place Web site you created in Section 1:

1. Create the following directory on your local machine: C:\thecookingplacecf.

2. Unzip the tutorial files found at www.wrox.com and place them under the c:\inetpub\www root folder. This should create the structure c:\inetpub\wwwroot\thecookingplacecf. The code contains an Access database called Recipes, the images folder, and a template (in the template folder) called myLook.

There are two ways to install the ColdFusion server: either as part of IIS or as a standalone server. For this exercise, we assume it's installed as part of IIS. If it's not, however, install the files under the ColdFusion server's root folder (which is also wwwroot). If you are working in standalone mode, just adjust the file locations accordingly in this exercise.

3. Launch Dreamweaver MX 2004 and close the empty Open Document dialog box if necessary. Start a new site.

4. Click the Advanced tab and choose the Local Info category. Fill in the fields as shown in Figure D-1.

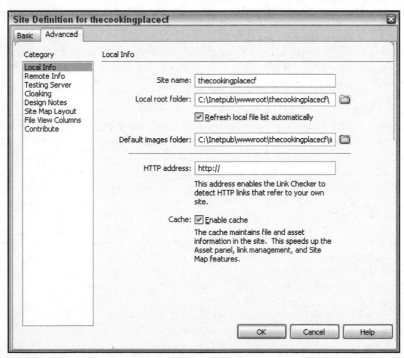

Figure D-1

If you install ColdFusion as a standalone server, the `http://` *address is probably* `http://local host:8500/thecookingplacecf.`

5.   Switch to the Remote Info category and fill in the fields as shown in Figure D-2.

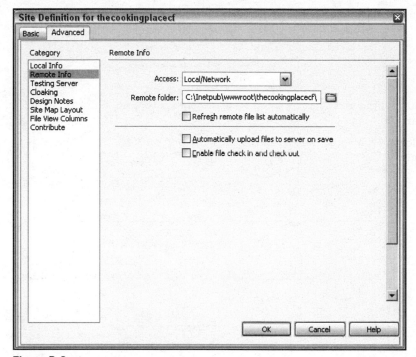

Figure D-2

If you install the standalone version of ColdFusion, don't install the server root directory below IIS. Instead, install it below `C:\coldfusionmx\wwwroot.` *It is also not necessary to update the server for this simple example because you are already working in the root folder.*

6.   Switch to the Testing Server category and fill in the fields as shown in Figure D-3. Select ColdFusion as the server model.

7.   Once all the fields are filled in, click OK. The Site panel should look like Figure D-4.

Your site is now defined and ready to start working.

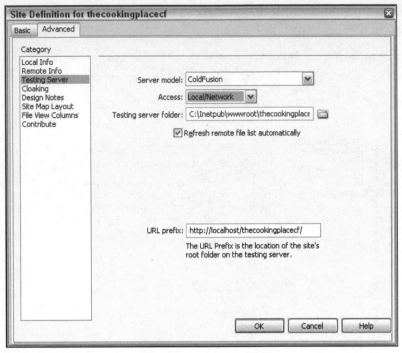

Figure D-3

Figure D-4

Setting Up a ColdFusion Page

You are now ready to set up your first ColdFusion page. This example is a simple one to illustrate fundamental concepts:

1.   Select File⇨New.

2. Select the Dynamic Page category and choose ColdFusion as the dynamic page type, as shown in Figure D-5.

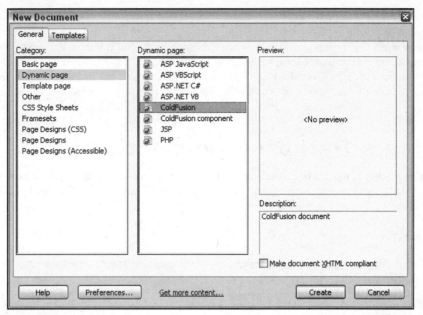

Figure D-5

3. Make sure you are in Design view. Using the Assets panel, select the myLook template from the Templates category and apply it to this page. The page should now look like Figure D-6.

Figure D-6

This page, with the template, is based on The Cooking Place site you created earlier in the book. The template contains a two-column table in an editable region. You will place data from a database into this area.

4. Save this file as **recipes.cfm**.

When you created ASP pages earlier in the book you saved them with the file extension .asp so that the Web server would recognize dynamic pages in your site. Similarly, the ColdFusion MX environment uses the file extension .cfm to tell it to do its job. This is true whether you are installed in IIS or standalone mode. In IIS mode, the document is sent over to ColdFusion as soon as the `.cfm` extension is seen.

Creating a Database Connection

Now you're ready to connect to a database so that you can fill your ColdFusion page with some interesting data. At this point, things start to get different from what you did in ASP, but if you follow these steps, you won't have any problem:

1. Select Start⇨ColdFusion MX⇨Administrator. You'll see the login screen shown in Figure D-7.

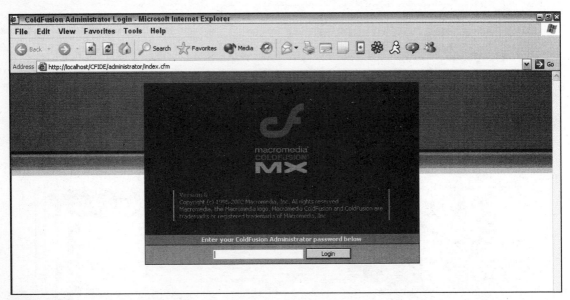

Figure D-7

2. Enter the password you selected during installation and click Login. You'll now see the screen shown in Figure D-8.

3. Click Data Sources under the Data & Services category in the left navigation bar. This displays the screen shown in Figure D-9.

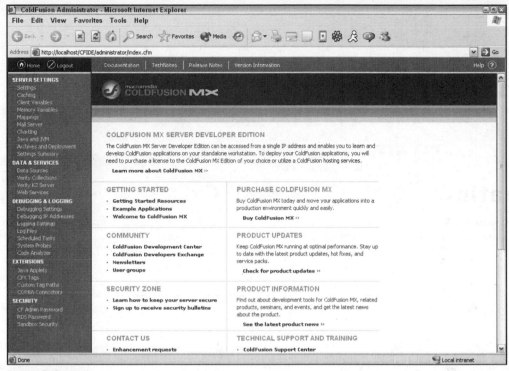

Figure D-8

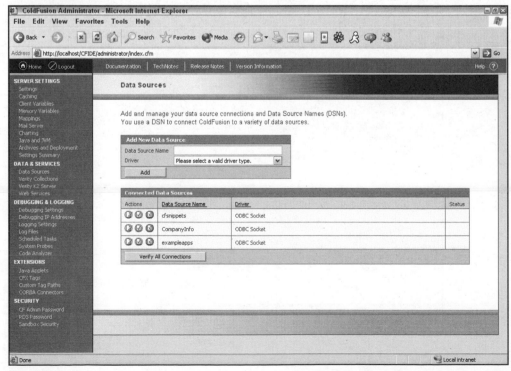

Figure D-9

4. For Data Source Name type **recipes**.

5. Select Microsoft Access as the Driver type and click the Add button. You'll see the Microsoft Access Data Source dialog box shown in Figure D-10.

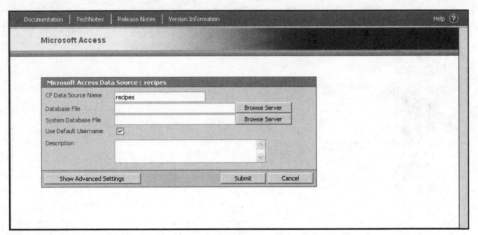

Figure D-10

6. To select the database file, click the Browse Server button next to the Database File field. This opens the Browser Server dialog box shown in Figure D-11.

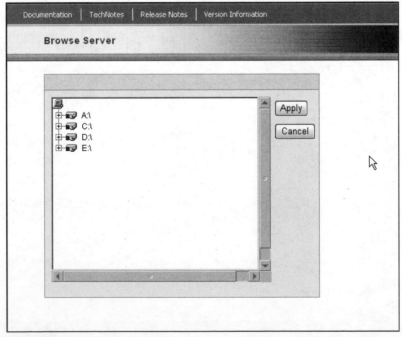

Figure D-11

7. Navigate to the `C:inetpub\wwwroot\thecookingplacecf\` folder in which you should have placed the database file after downloading it.

8. Select `recipe.mdb` and then click Apply. The Microsoft Access Data Source dialog box should now look like Figure D-12.

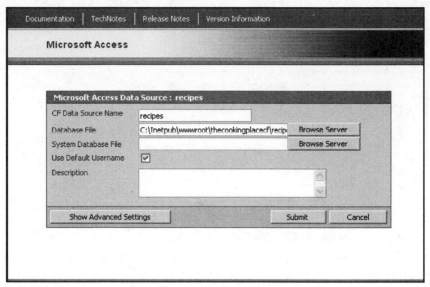

Figure D-12

9. Click Submit. You'll be returned to the Data Sources screen shown in Figure D-13.

You should see the recipes database in the list, along with ok in the Status column. Verify your database connection anytime by clicking the Verify All Connections button.

After the database connection has been made, close the ColdFusion Administrator by simply closing the browser window.

10. Return to the ColdFusion page you created earlier and open the Databases panel in the Application panel group (see Figure D-14).

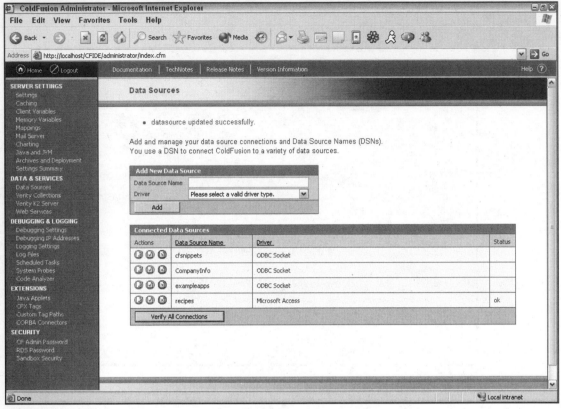

Figure D-13

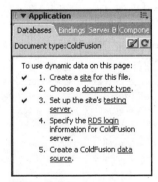

Figure D-14

11. Click the RDS login link to connect your site with the ColdFusion database connections, as shown in Figure D-15.

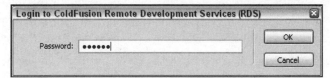

Figure D-15

The password you need to enter is the same as the Administrator password.

12. After clicking OK, you should see the same list of databases in the Databases panel that you saw earlier (see Figure D-16).

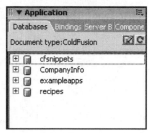

Figure D-16

13. Click the plus (+) button located in the upper-left corner of the Bindings panel and select Recordset (Query). This opens the Recordset dialog box shown in Figure D-17.

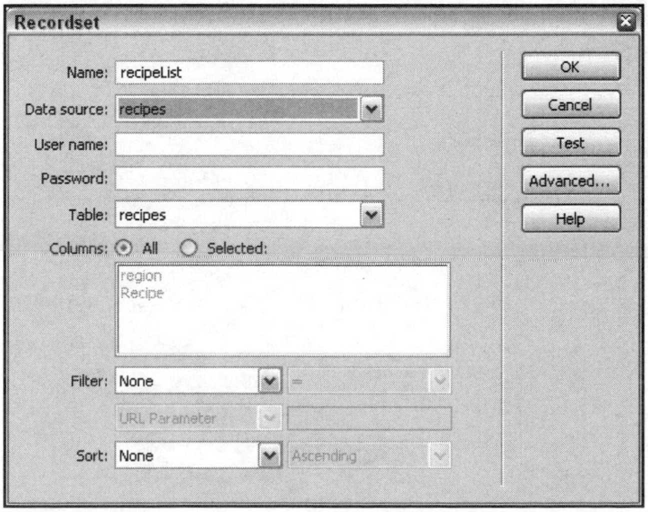

Figure D-17

14. Name the recordset **recipeList** and select `recipes` as the data source.

15. Select the recipes connection you just created for the connection. The database is really small for this example. It just has one table (Recipes) with two columns (Recipe and Region).

16. Select the table and all the columns. If you want, you can set a Sort on Region for Ascending. It is not necessary to use any of the SQL filters discussed earlier in the book.

17. Click OK. From this point on, things will be pretty much the same as you learned in ASP earlier in the book.

18. Click plus (+) to expand the recordset and you'll see two fields in the Bindings panel, as shown in Figure D-18.

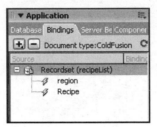

Figure D-18

19. Drag the Region field into the first cell of the table and drag the Recipe field into the second cell, as shown in Figure D-19.

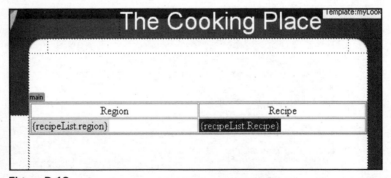

Figure D-19

20. Preview the data by clicking the Live Data view button (see Figure D-20).

Figure D-20

At this point, you only see one row of data. You can easily remedy that, if you recall, by controlling the server behaviors.

21. Shut off the Live Data view and highlight the data row, but do *not* highlight the header row because you do not want the headings to repeat.

22. Select the Server Behaviors panel and then click the plus (+) in the upper-left corner. Select Repeat Region. The Repeat Region dialog box in Figure D-21 appears.

Figure D-21

23. Click OK and then select Live Data view again. Your table should now look like Figure D-22. Just as in ASP, you can add server behaviors to move around multiple pages of data.

The Cooking Place Template:myLook

main

Region	Recipe
American	Hot Chili
American	Yankee Pot Roast
Southern Italy	Tomato Sauce
Northern Italy	Polenta
Southern Italy	Risotto
France	Quiche
France	Burgandy Sauce
American	Salmon
Northern Italy	Penne and Vegetables
France	Cheese Cake

‹tr› ‹td› <mmtinstance:editable>   802 x 406 ▾ 51K / 15 sec

Figure D-22

24. Save the page and then preview it in your browser.

> **You just developed a ColdFusion page and ran it. The great thing was that you did not need to touch the code at all. Dreamweaver handled it automatically.**

ColdFusion Tools

When Dreamweaver saw you were defining a ColdFusion page, it placed a new panel in the Insert panel group (see Figure D-23).

Figure D-23

The Advanced button has a drop-down arrow just to the right of it. If you click it, the menu opens up. The last selection, More Tags, gives you a more complete list of CFML tags (see Figure D-24).

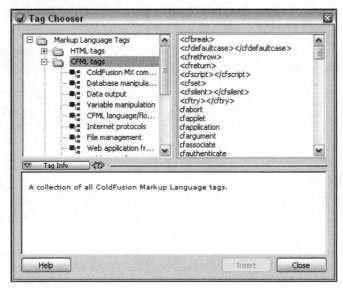

Figure D-24

As you can see, the Tag Chooser provides a complete list of ColdFusion tags divided into categories.

Further Reading

We hope this short tutorial shows you that moving to ColdFusion MX is not as intimidating as it may first seem. The process is not very different from working with ASP, and Dreamweaver makes the process flow effortlessly.

If you're interested in learning more about ColdFusion, you can find out more at the official Macromedia ColdFusion Web site: www.macromedia.com/software/coldfusion/.

Using a Remote Server

Throughout this book we've been using an installation of Microsoft Internet Information Services (IIS) that we've referred to as the *local server* or *testing server* on which to run your ASP Web sites. IIS is only available for Microsoft Windows 2000 and Windows XP Professional. If you're running Dreamweaver MX 2004 on Microsoft Windows XP Home Edition or on Mac OS and you want to build the dynamic Web sites described in this book, you'll need to use a *remote server*.

A remote server is a Web server that runs on another computer. That computer could be part of a network in your company or at home. It could be provided by a third party such as a commercial Web hosting company. This means that you can develop and edit a Web site on your machine using Dreamweaver MX 2004 and run the site on another computer—across the room from you as part of a local network or on the other side of the world where your Web site is one of hundreds running on the same machine as part of a Web farm.

In this chapter we'll run through the steps you need to take in order to use a remote server to test your dynamic Web site. We'll be concentrating on ASP-based Web sites (as we do throughout the book) but the concepts we cover also apply to ASP.NET, JSP, and PHP Web sites.

> *You can also find information on using a remote server in the Dreamweaver MX 2004 Help system. It is located at Preparing to Build Dynamic Sites⇨What you need to build Web applications.*

You do the following:

❑   Work through the options to use a remote server

❑   Discuss ASP hosting solutions that are available to you

Setting Up a Site to Use a Remote Server

The steps for setting up a Web site to run on a remote server are similar to those for running a site on a local server:

1.   Define a new site. Call it **myRemoteSite**, as shown in Figure E-1.

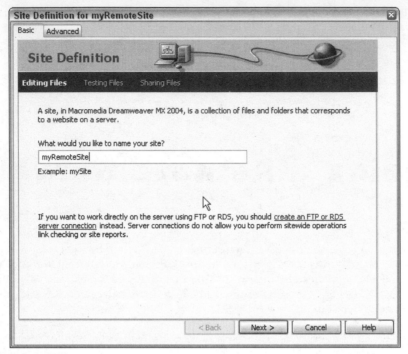

Figure E-1

2. Click Next. Set the server technology for the Web site to be ASP VBScript, as shown in Figure E-2.

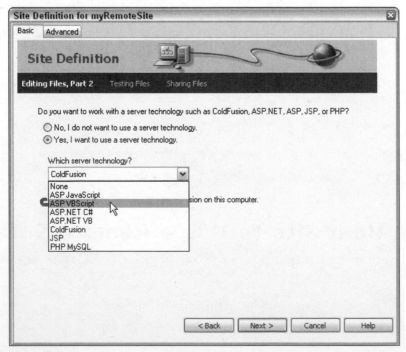

Figure E-2

3. Click Next. On the next screen, you're presented with four options for how to work with the files that make up your Web site. You can do the following:

❑ Edit the files locally and run them on your local machine. This is the option you used earlier in the book. If you have an ASP Web server on your computer, use this option to run the Web site with it.

❑ Edit the files locally and then upload the files so that the Web site runs on a remote server.

❑ Run the Web site on a remote server (on a local network) and edit the files directly on the server as well.

❑ Run the Web site on a remote server (that you communicate with using FTP or RDS network protocols) and edit the files directly on the server as well.

Select the second option (Edit Locally, Then Upload to Remote Testing Server) and store the files that make up the Web site in a convenient location. In Figure E-3, we chose `C:\myRemoteSite\`.

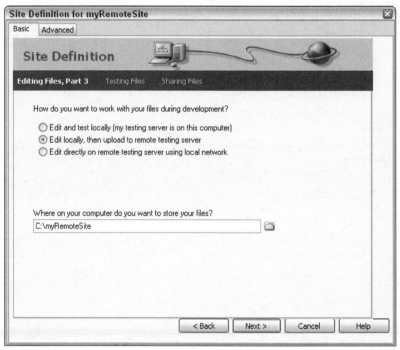

Figure E-3

4. Click Next. Select how you will connect to the remote server (called a *testing server* here). There are four options, as shown in Figure E-4:

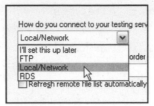

Figure E-4

❑ **I'll set this up later:** This is just as it says. It means you are going to set up the remote server at some future point in time.

❑ **Local/Network:** You should select this option if you are going to run the site on a network or from your local machine. If you select this option, specify the location that the files should be stored on the network or local machine so that the server can access them (see Figure E-5).

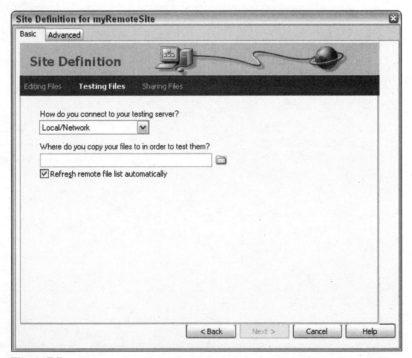

Figure E-5

❑ **FTP:** This stands for *File Transfer Protocol*. Use this option to connect to a remote server either on a local network or on a remote Web host. If you select this option, you need to specify a number of options: the address of the FTP server, the folder to store the files on the FTP server, your login to the server, and your password, as shown in Figure E-6.

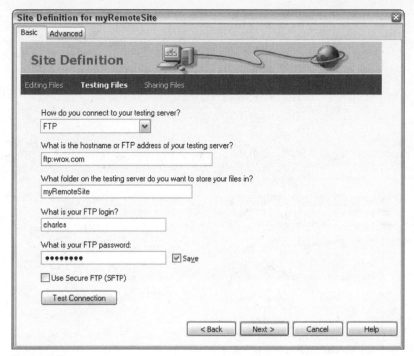

Figure E-6

Once you fill in the details, check that the connection works by clicking the Test Connection button. If everything works OK, you'll see the confirmation dialog box shown in Figure E-7.

Figure E-7

If there is a problem connecting to the FTP server, Dreamweaver provides you with an error message that hopefully helps you track down the source of the problem. For example, in Figure E-8, we attempted to store our files in a folder on the FTP server that doesn't exist.

❑ **RDS:** This stands for *Remote Development Services*. You can only use this option if you connect to a server running ColdFusion. Because we're concerned with ASP development for now, we won't cover the options for RDS here.

Figure E-8

5. If you select FTP and fill in the details of your Web server, you'll next be prompted for the URL for your site. In Figure E-9, we've specified that it will be www.wrox.com/remoteWebSite.

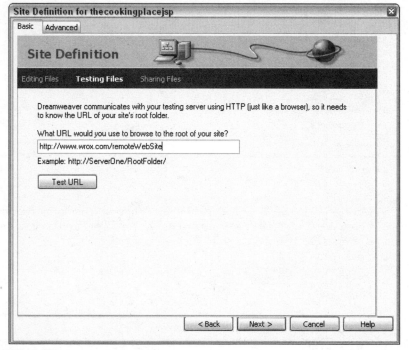

Figure E-9

Test that the URL works by clicking the Test URL button. If there are no problems you'll see the dialog box shown in Figure E-10. Click OK to close the confirmation dialog box.

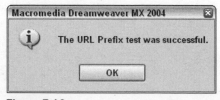

Figure E-10

6. The next screen has you decide how you want sharing files to be handled. This is beyond the scope of this appendix, so accept the default setting of No, Do Not Enable Check In and Check Out.

7. On the final screen, shown in Figure E-11, you see a summary of the settings for your site.

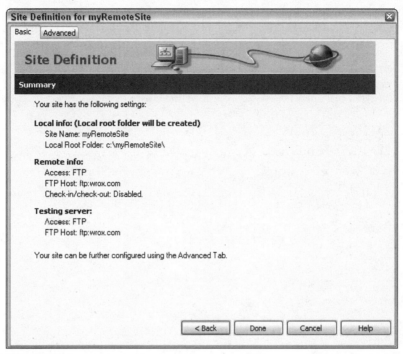

Figure E-11

If you need to change any of the settings for your site at this stage, you can access the settings using the Advanced tab.

ASP Web Hosts

There are dozens of different quality *Web hosts* that can run your ASP Web sites. The services they provide, and the cost of those services, vary enormously from provider to provider.

If you're just looking for a server to test your site as you develop it, you'll probably be happy with the level of service that a host provides for free. But free hosting normally lacks sophisticated management tools and usually limits the size of your Web site and amount of data that can be downloaded from it in a given period of time (your "bandwidth allowance"). In addition, the host may require your site to carry advertising banners. By paying a small fee per month or per year, you can access better Web hosting solutions that often include direct FTP access to your site and a far greater bandwidth allowance.

Integrating Dreamweaver MX 2004 with Fireworks MX 2004 and Flash MX 2004

Beginning with Macromedia Studio MX, Macromedia tightly integrated its family of programs. The Studio MX 2004 environment builds on that philosophy and creates even more seamless integration than previously. Dreamweaver MX 2004 serves as the focal, or coordinating, point for all the other programs.

This appendix looks at integrating Dreamweaver MX 2004 with Fireworks MX 2004 and Flash MX 2004. These packages help you add impressive graphics and animation to your site.

Integrating with Fireworks MX 2004

Fireworks MX 2004 is the graphics editor of the MX 2004 environment. With it you can manipulate images, create sophisticated menu bars, and optimize graphics so that you balance smaller file size with better image quality. In addition, you can create GIF animations and very sophisticated rollover and visual effects for your Web site.

An extensive discussion of the capabilities of Fireworks MX 2004 could occupy an entire book. However, this relatively simple exercise (a static site) demonstrates how to integrate it with Dreamweaver MX 2004.

> *We assume that you have Fireworks and Flash already loaded on your computer. If you don't, you can download free 30-day evaluation copies to try it out at* www.macromedia.com.

1. Download the files for Appendix F from www.wrox.com and install them in the location of your choice. They unzip in the folder thecookingplaceappendf.

2. Launch Dreamweaver MX 2004 and go to the Site menu option.

3. Select Site⇨Manage Sites⇨New⇨Site.

4. Click the Advanced tab. In the Local Info category fill in the fields as shown in Figure F-1. Because you are not using any server technology for this site, you can ignore the options in the Remote Info category.

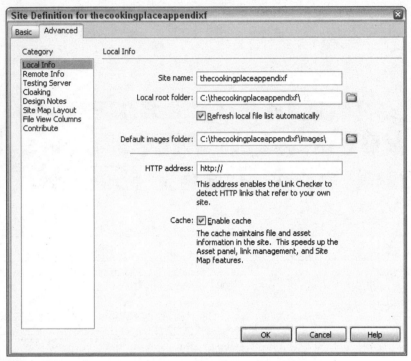

Figure F-1

5. Click OK. The Files panel should now look like Figure F-2.

Figure F-2

6. Create a new HTML page and apply the myLook template to it. The site should now look like Figure F-3.

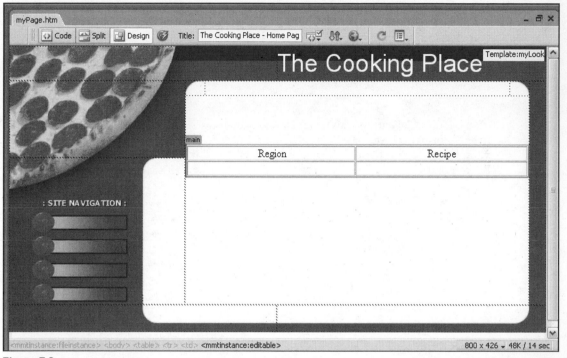

Figure F-3

7. Save the file and call it **myPage.htm**.

When you first created The Cooking Place site in Section 1, you created rollover effects for the buttons. We are going to do something a little different here and just use Fireworks MX 2004 to create some simple labels for your buttons. However, because you are using a template, you must edit from that template.

8. Open the myLook template file and click the first button image located on the left side (see Figure F-4).

Figure F-4

9. If you look in the Edit section of the Property inspector, you will see a button with the Fireworks logo on it (see Figure F-5).

Figure F-5

10. Click the Fireworks button. This should launch you into Fireworks MX 2004. Firworks uses a native file format called PNG (*Portable Network Graphics*) as its file format. Because you are using the graphic image `buttonblank.gif`, you will be asked if you want to convert the image to PNG format (see Figure F-6). Click the Use This File button.

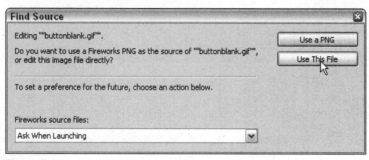

Figure F-6

11. You will be taken to the main Fireworks screen, shown in Figure F-7. You should find the basic layout similar to that in Dreamweaver.

12. If you find the size a little small to work with, enlarge it by clicking the zoom tool located in the lower right corner of the canvas (see Figure F-8). This zooming does not affect the image file at all.

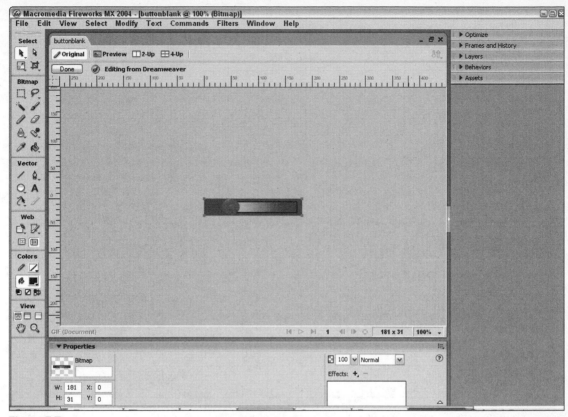

Figure F-7

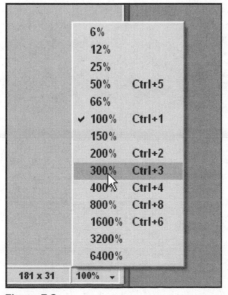

Figure F-8

13. Located along the left side of the interface is the Tools panel, shown in Figure F-9. This contains most of the drawing tools you use in Fireworks. Click the Text tool in the Vector section.

Figure F-9

14. Notice that the context-sensitive Property inspector changes as it does in Dreamweaver. Set the font size to 10, color to White, Bold, Italic, and the Horizontal Scale to 150%. Your panel should look like Figure F-10.

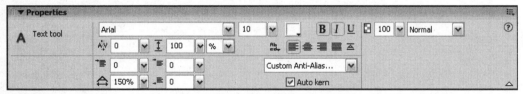

Figure F-10

15. Click in the text area of the button and type **Home** (see Figure F-11).

Figure F-11

16. If the text's position is off a bit and you want to correct it, click the Select tool in the Tools panel (see Figure F-12) and move the text box to the desired position.

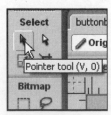

Figure F-12

17. Once the text is just the way you want it, click the Done button located at the top left of the canvas (see Figure F-13).

Figure F-13

You are now back in Dreamweaver and the new text appears on the button, as shown in Figure F-14.

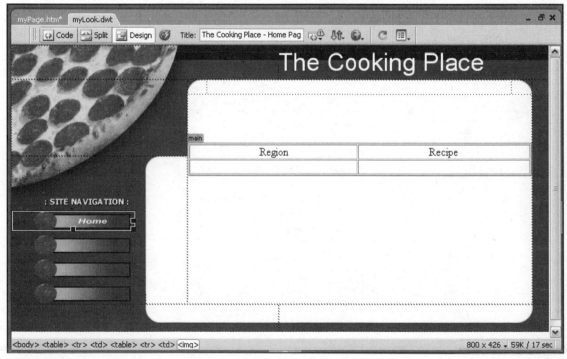

Figure F-14

18. When you save the template, it updates any pages linked to it.

19. Add text to the other buttons and save the template.

That's all there is to editing Dreamweaver images within Fireworks. As you can see, it is a seamless and quick process. A good knowledge of Fireworks MX 2004 will greatly extend the capabilities of working in Dreamweaver MX 2004.

Integrating with Flash MX 2004

Flash plays an increasingly important role in Web design. Because it uses relatively few resources and is browser-independent, for instance, it is the ideal medium for Web sites that want to position themselves for the wireless market.

We will not explain how to develop Flash movies. That is beyond the scope of this appendix. However, we have provided a completed Flash file among the download files for this appendix (in the Flash folder). Flash uses the file extension .swf (pronounced "swiff").

As you will see, Dreamweaver MX 2004 makes it easy to incorporate a Flash file into a Web site. It even provides a menu for entering special parameters in the HTML tags that call it.

In the following exercise, you replace The Cooking Place logo with an animated Flash banner:

1. If it is not already open from the previous Fireworks exercise, open the myLook.dwt template.

2. Select the text *The Cooking Place* and delete it.

3. Locate the Flash file cookingplacelogo.swf in the Flash folder on the Files panel (see Figure F-15).

Figure F-15

Because the file is an external element to the page, it is also an asset. As such, you can drag it directly from the Assets panel.

4. Select the Assets panel and then click the Flash logo button on the left side (see Figure F-16).

5. There is a preview button located in the upper-right corner of the preview window. By clicking it, you can preview the Flash movie. Give it a try.

Figure F-16

6. Drag the file `cookingplacelogo.swf` to the same location where you deleted *The Cooking Place* in Step 2 (see Figure F-17).

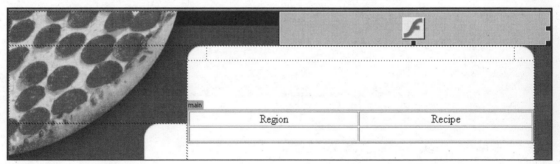

Figure F-17

7. Notice the Property inspector. It now contains buttons for controlling the Flash movie, as shown in Figure F-18.

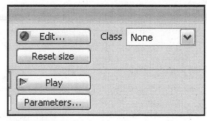

Figure F-18

8. In order to edit the Flash movie from Dreamweaver, you must have the movie's source file. A source file is a Flash file with the extension `.fla`. Click the Play button to preview the movie in the location.

9. Save the template and update the `myPage.htm` file.

10. If it is not open, bring up the `myPage.htm` file and preview it in the browser. You should see a nice animated banner where *The Cooking Place* formerly appeared.

As you can see, this is easy. However, there is one small problem: The Flash movie cuts off part of the background of the cell.

You can easily fix this problem. All you need to do is add a parameter to the calling HTML code that instructs the Flash file to make the background transparent.

This feature may not work in some versions of Netscape and earlier versions of Internet Explorer.

11. Close the Web browser, open the template if necessary, and click the Flash file placeholder.

12. Click the Parameters button in the Property inspector. This opens the Parameters dialog box shown in Figure F-19.

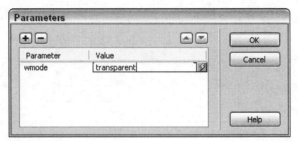

Figure F-19

13. In the Parameter column, type **wmode**.

14. In the Value column, type **transparent**.

15. Click OK.

16. Save the template and update `myPage.htm`.

17. Preview `myPage.htm` in the browser. If all works properly, the Flash animation should look as though it's floating freely over the Web page.

That's all there is to incorporating media files, such as Flash, into Web pages. Dreamweaver MX 2004 handles all the mechanics and coding. If you look at the code, you should see something like this:

```
<object classid="clsid:D27CDB6E-AE6D-11cf-96B8-444553540000"
codebase="http://download.macromedia.com/pub/shockwave/cabs/flash/swflash.cab#versi
on=6,0,29,0" width="390" height="50">
    <param name="movie" value="../Flash/cookingplacelogo.swf">
    <param name="quality" value="high">
```

```
            <param name="wmode" value="transparent">
            <embed src="../Flash/cookingplacelogo.swf" width="390" height="50"
    quality="high" pluginspage="http://www.macromedia.com/go/getflashplayer"
    type="application/x-shockwave-flash" wmode="transparent"></embed>
        </object>
```

Inserting files from other multimedia sources, such as sound files, involves similar procedures.

While this was just a brief tour, you can see the power behind these Macromedia programs. Fireworks MX 2004 helps you create dynamic graphics, and Fireworks MX 2004 helps you create exciting animations that will grab and keep your site visitors' attention.

Index